A PRACTICAL APPROACH TO

CIVIL PROCEDURE

A PRACTICAL APPROACH TO

CIVIL PROCEDURE

THIRTEENTH EDITION

Stuart Sime, Barrister

BPTC Course Director, The City Law School

City University, London

OXFORD
UNIVERSITY PRESS

OXFORD
UNIVERSITY PRESS

Great Clarendon Street, Oxford OX2 6DP

Oxford University Press is a department of the University of Oxford.
It furthers the University's objective of excellence in research, scholarship,
and education by publishing worldwide in

Oxford New York

Auckland Cape Town Dar es Salaam Hong Kong Karachi
Kuala Lumpur Madrid Melbourne Mexico City Nairobi
New Delhi Shanghai Taipei Toronto

With offices in

Argentina Austria Brazil Chile Czech Republic France Greece
Guatemala Hungary Italy Japan Poland Portugal Singapore
South Korea Switzerland Thailand Turkey Ukraine Vietnam

Published in the United States
by Oxford University Press Inc., New York

Tenth edition 2007
Eleventh edition 2008
Twelfth edition 2009

British Library Cataloguing in Publication Data
Data available

Typeset by Newgen Imaging Systems (P) Ltd, Chennai, India
Printed in Great Britain
on acid-free paper by
CPI Antony Rowe, Chippenham, Wiltshire

ISBN 978–0–19–958973–9

1 3 5 7 9 10 8 6 4 2

CONTENTS SUMMARY

CONTENTS

PREFACE

Any lawyer practising in the civil courts needs a thorough grasp of practice and procedure. Indeed, knowledge of procedure is probably as important as knowledge of the substantive law. It is not sufficient to have a strong case on the law and facts. It is also important to be able to advance a claim effectively and efficiently from its early stages through to trial (if needs be) in order to ensure the client attains the best result possible given the strengths and weaknesses of the case. Every year a great many cases are won and lost on purely procedural grounds. Further, good use of court procedure can result in a case being materially strengthened. The converse is that poor use of procedure can cause avoidable harm to the client's prospects of success.

Civil procedure can be a very daunting subject. First, there are a number of statutes dealing with the jurisdiction of the civil courts. Secondly, there is a substantial rule book comprising detailed rules of court (the Civil Procedure Rules 1998, SI 1998/3132) supplemented by numerous practice directions. The Rules and practice directions are available from the Stationery Office in a three-volume loose-leaf publication and are available at <**http://www.justice.gov.uk**>, and are printed in full in practitioners' books, such as *Blackstone's Civil Practice* and the White Book. There are also official court guides which deal with the practice, sometimes in considerable detail, in the Queen's Bench and Chancery Divisions of the High Court and also the specialist courts, such as the Commercial Court. Statutory provisions, rules, and practice directions can only deal with what should happen in the general run of cases. The courts are, on a day-to-day basis, faced with claims which are unusual, with cases where exceptions should be made to rules worded in a general way or where a more sophisticated approach may be required, and with cases that have not been conducted fully in accordance with the rules. There is therefore a substantial body of relevant case law dealing with procedural issues. Furthermore, there are some areas where procedural and substantive law issues converge.

What the student and newly qualified litigator needs is an accessible introduction to the subject. I hope this new edition of this book will continue to perform this function. It seeks to explain the various procedures that either may or must be followed as a claim progresses from its early stages through its interim stages and on to trial, enforcement, and any possible appeal in a straightforward way, but with sufficient detail for the new practitioner to be able to cope with most problems that commonly arise. A number of forms and precedents are included in this book to bring to life the procedures that are discussed. Often they are far shorter than ones that would be met in practice in order to concentrate on what the documents look like, and it should also be borne in mind that there are usually several different approaches used by different lawyers in drafting court documents.

Over the years I have received considerable guidance regarding the practical workings of the civil courts from numerous colleagues at the Treasury Solicitor's Office, chambers, and the City Law School. I would particularly like to record my debt to John Haynes and Frank O'Connell from my time at the Treasury Solicitor's Office, and Robert Deacon, my pupil master at 11 Stone Buildings, Lincoln's Inn, for all the practical experience and know-how they freely shared with me. I wish to thank Mr Roger Winter-Smith of Messrs Windsors, London N17, and Mr Evan Ashfield of 169 Temple Chambers, London EC4Y 0DA. The staff of Oxford University Press have done an excellent job in the preparation of the new edition. I am especially grateful to my wife Wendy for her encouragement and support during the period when the book was being written.

The text covers changes in the CPR and practice directions, including those taking effect in 2010, and case law developments to April 2010. Perhaps the most noticeable change is the new Supreme Court which replaced the House of Lords in October 2009. There are also new procedures on low value (up to £10,000) road traffic personal injuries claims, which are considered in the new Chapter 6, and the coverage of insolvency proceedings takes into account the modernization programme implemented by the Insolvency (Amendment) Rules 2010 (SI 2010/686). Of great importance for the future development of civil procedure is Sir Rupert Jackson's Review of Civil Litigation Costs (December 2009, Ministry of Justice). This makes detailed recommendations covering most aspects of the litigation process from the pre-action protocols through to the detailed assessment of costs, and will result in wide-ranging future amendments to both the rules and the funding of litigation.

Stuart Sime
London
April 2010

ABBREVIATIONS

ADR	alternative dispute resolution
AJA 1999	Access to Justice Act 1999
app	appendix
AQ	allocation questionnaire
art	article
A/S	acknowledgment of service
ATE	after the event litigation insurance
BCP	*Blackstone's Civil Practice* (Oxford University Press)
Brussels Convention	Convention on jurisdiction and the enforcement of judgments in civil and commercial matters signed at Brussels on 27 September 1968
BTE	before the event litigation insurance (legal expenses insurance)
CA	Court of Appeal
CCA 1984	County Courts Act 1984
CCR	County Court Rules 1981
Central Office	Administrative offices of the QBD in the RCJ in London
CEA 1968	Civil Evidence Act 1968
CEA 1972	Civil Evidence Act 1972
CEA 1995	Civil Evidence Act 1995
CFA	conditional fee agreement
ChD	Chancery Division
CJJA 1982	Civil Jurisdiction and Judgments Act 1982
CJJA 1991	Civil Jurisdiction and Judgments Act 1991
cl	clause
CLS	Community Legal Service
CLSA 1990	Courts and Legal Services Act 1990
CNF	claims notification form (used in the RTA protocol)
Commercial Court Guide	Admiralty and Commercial Courts Guide
CPFO	Civil Proceedings Fees Order 2008 (SI 2008/1053) as amended
CPR	Civil Procedure Rules 1998 (SI 1998/3132) as amended
CRU	Compensation Recovery Unit, part of the Department for Social Development, and provides certificates of State benefits paid to personal injuries claimants
DX	document exchange
ECHR	European Court of Human Rights
ECJ	European Court of Justice
EC Treaty	Treaty Establishing the European Community
EEO Regulation	Council Regulation (EC) No 805/2004
EFTA	European Free Trade Association
EOP (Regulation)	European order for payment; Regulation (EC) No 1896/2006 of 12 December 2006

EU	European Union
FamD	Family Division
fi. fa.	*fieri facias*
GLO	group litigation order
Hague Convention	Hague Convention on the Service Abroad of Judicial and Extra-judicial Documents in Civil or Commercial Matters (1965)
HL	House of Lords (replaced by the Supreme Court: October 2009)
IA 1986	Insolvency Act 1986
IR 1986	Insolvency Rules 1986 (SI 1986/1925) as amended
Jurisdiction Order 1991	High Court and County Courts Jurisdiction Order 1991 (SI 1991/724)
Judgments Regulation	Council Regulation (EC) No 44/2001 on jurisdiction and the recognition and enforcement of judgments in civil and commercial matters
LA 1980	Limitation Act 1980
Lugano Convention	Convention on jurisdiction and the enforcement of judgments in civil and commercial matters, 16 September 1988
Member States	Member States of the Jurisdiction Regulation
MF	Mckenzie friend
MIB	Motor Insurers' Bureau
MRO	medical reporting organization
ord	order
para	paragraph
PC	Privy Council
PD	practice direction
PI protocol	Pre-action Protocol for Personal Injury Claims
QBD	Queen's Bench Division
r	rule
RCJ	Royal Courts of Justice, Strand, London
reg	regulation
RSC	Rules of the Supreme Court 1965
RTA	road traffic accident
s	section
SC	Supreme Court
SCA 1981	Senior Courts Act 1981
Sch	Schedule
SCR	Supreme Court Rules 2009 (SI 2009/1604)
Service Regulation	Council Regulation (EC) No 1348/2000, reproduced as the annex to PD 6B
SoGA 1979	Sale of Goods Act 1979
SI	statutory instrument
TCC	Technology and Construction Court
White Book	*Civil Practice* (Sweet and Maxwell)

TABLE OF CASES

TABLE OF STATUTES

TABLE OF SECONDARY LEGISLATION

Other rules

Codes

Agreements

TABLE OF EC AND INTERNATIONAL LEGISLATION

1

INTRODUCTION

This book deals with the mechanics of how legal and equitable rights are asserted, determined, and enforced through the civil courts. The civil courts perform the important function of resolving disputes that cannot be resolved by agreement between the parties. **1.01**

It is axiomatic that the courts exist to do justice between the parties who come to them. Justice is not simply a matter of achieving the right result. It has long been recognized that where justice is delayed justice may be denied. However, the law is often far from straightforward, and frequently the factual background to a dispute needs considerable investigation before it is ready to go to trial. **1.02**

Litigants are often unable to cope with the complexities of the law on their own, and have to seek assistance from the legal profession. Litigation can be very expensive, and the important topic of funding will be considered further in Chapter 4. **1.03**

The cost and delays inherent in litigation, together with the stress and management of time often involved, mean that it is invariably best if matters can be resolved amicably without resorting to court proceedings. Pre-action protocols on reasonable conduct to resolve matters before starting proceedings are discussed in Chapter 5, and alternative dispute resolution (ADR) procedures are discussed in Chapter 6. However, some people simply refuse to negotiate, or ignore correspondence, or make unrealistic offers, or insist on continuing with **1.04** conduct infringing another's rights. In such cases the injured party may have little option but to commence proceedings.

1.05 Court proceedings fall into two categories. Proceedings are most frequently used for resolving civil disputes. For example, it may be necessary to go to court to enforce payment under a contract, or to seek compensation for personal injuries where a reasonable offer is not forthcoming, or to seek an injunction to restrain tortious conduct which the defendant threatens to continue. In the second category, it is necessary to apply to the court for an order before certain conduct can be safely undertaken. For example, executors may seek the court's directions if the terms of a testator's will are unclear, or the court's approval may be sought where parties have agreed a settlement of a dispute where the claimant is a child.

A THE LEGAL PROFESSION

1.06 In England and Wales there is a split legal profession, with solicitors and barristers (the latter are also known as counsel). In general, solicitors provide the direct point of contact with clients, and provide from within their firms most legal services for clients. Barristers provide a referral service of specialist advisory, drafting, and advocacy services as and when instructed by solicitors. A solicitor will, therefore, have general day-to-day management of a case, conducting the correspondence and negotiations, and gathering the evidence, but may instruct a barrister for specific tasks in the course of the litigation, such as drafting the statements of case and representing the client at hearings.

1.07 Solicitors may be in practice on their own (sole practitioners), but it is rather more common for solicitors to work in partnerships. A solicitors' firm will typically have a number of fully qualified solicitors as partners, and other fully qualified solicitors as employed assistant solicitors. The firm may have non-solicitor fee earners, such as legal executives (who have qualifications granted by the Institute of Legal Executives), and non-qualified fee earners, such as litigation managers and clerks. The firm may also have some trainees and para-legals (who assist the lawyers, but are not themselves legally qualified), and will have a number of administrative employees.

1.08 Barristers are sole practitioners, but are usually tenants in sets of chambers having a number of members. At the top of the profession are Queen's Counsel ('silks'), with the bulk of the profession made up of 'juniors'. Barristers completing their training are called pupils. The point of contact between solicitors and barristers is the barristers' clerk.

B LAWYERS' DUTIES

1.09 Solicitors are officers of the court (Solicitors Act 1974, s 50(1)), and consequently have duties not only to do their best for their clients, but also never to deceive or mislead the court (see the Solicitors' Code of Conduct 2007, r 11.01(1) (see <**http://www.sra.org.uk/solicitors/**

code-of-conduct.page>)). Counsel are under similar obligations (see the Code of Conduct of the Bar of England and Wales, para 302 (see <**http://www.barstandardsboard.org.uk/standardsandguidance/codeofconduct/**>)), providing that barristers must assist the court in the administration of justice, and must not deceive or knowingly or recklessly mislead the court.

C INITIAL INSTRUCTIONS

The first interview with the client

When a member of the public goes to a solicitor's office for the first time, the solicitor will ask about the nature of the problem and what it is that the potential client is seeking to achieve. Where the matter involves a transaction or linked transactions with €15,000 or more being paid to or by the client, the solicitor must be shown and keep a record of identification evidence, such as a passport, or photo-card driving licence, or birth certificate, proving the identity of the client (Money Laundering Regulations 2003 (SI 2003/3075), reg 4). Most statutory instruments can be found at <**http://www.opsi.gov.uk**>. So far as possible, clients are encouraged to relate the facts of the case in their own words, so that the true problem can be identified. This will enable the solicitor to decide whether to accept instructions from the client. It will also form the basis of the client's written statement that will be used if proceedings are issued, which will usually be drawn up by the solicitor and signed by the client. **1.10**

If the solicitor decides to take the case, a plan of action should be agreed with the client in relation to any further inquiries that need to be made. The client will usually be asked to provide details of any witnesses to the events in question, and the solicitor will arrange for signed statements to be taken from them. The solicitor will advise whether it will be necessary to obtain expert advice on any aspects of the case, and must advise the client on the duty to the court to preserve all relevant documents (including documents adverse to the client's case). The solicitor will usually ask to be provided with copies of all relevant documents at an early stage. The client will be advised to keep a continuing note of all relevant developments if the dispute is of a continuing nature, such as a nuisance. Where the client is suffering continuing losses, the client will be advised to keep a record of those losses. This arises, eg, if a commercial client has an ongoing loss of profits, and in many personal injuries claims, where the claimant may need continuing medical treatment and might incur expenditure on prescriptions, medical appliances, and travel, etc. Where the client is seeking to bring a claim, it is common for inquiries to be made about the financial standing of the proposed defendants to ensure that they are worth suing. During the early stages of preparation, the parties' investigations and correspondence for the purposes of litigation are protected from disclosure by legal professional privilege. **1.11**

The question of payment for the solicitor's services should be discussed at the first interview. If the solicitor is prepared to conduct the case on a publicly funded basis and if the client qualifies, initial advice may be given as legal help under the Community Legal Service (see 4.22). In all cases where it appears that a client may be eligible for public funding the solicitor is under a duty to advise that it is available. Where public funding is to be applied for, the client must be advised about the payment of contributions and, most importantly, the effect of the statutory charge (see 4.42ff). **1.12**

1.13 In privately funded cases, the solicitor should consider whether the case should be taken on a conditional fee basis (see 4.15ff) or on a traditional retainer with the client being liable for his or her own solicitor's costs regardless of the result. The client will need to be given an estimate of the likely costs. The client may be asked for a payment on account, and should be advised about the billing arrangements. The client should also be advised about the possible costs orders at trial. The general rule is that the loser will be ordered to pay the winner's costs, but as costs between parties are assessed on a different basis from the costs payable by a client to its solicitor, even the victorious party will usually have a net liability for costs to its solicitor (see Chapter 43). In other cases, the client may be able to rely on an insurance company or trade union to meet costs.

1.14 The solicitor may be able to advise the client about the merits of the case and its financial and other implications at the first interview. If it is not possible to give full advice at that stage, advice will be given when the necessary inquiries have been completed. In many cases solicitors will instruct counsel (barristers) to give specialist advice on the merits and remedies available, such advice being given either orally in conference or in writing in the form of counsel's opinion. The initial advice on costs and other matters, such as the identity of the fee earner conducting the case and information about complaints procedures, must be confirmed in a client care letter (see figure 4.1).

1.15 The solicitor should also agree with the client the scope of the solicitor's authority in relation to the dispute. In particular, it should be agreed whether the solicitor should correspond with the other side, and whether proceedings should be instituted. The solicitor should keep the client informed of developments and of any changes in the risks of litigation.

1.16 A solicitor retained by a defendant has similar duties regarding preserving and preparing evidence, and advising on costs, funding, and the merits. It is of particular importance to advise a defendant of the possibilities of settling on reasonable terms, and of making a Part 36 offer to protect the defendant's position on costs. A Part 36 offer is a formal offer to settle the dispute on stated terms. These offers provide for an acceptance period of at least 21 days. If they are not accepted, the usual position is that, if the claimant wins the case but fails to do better than the offer, the claimant will be awarded costs only up to the 21st day after the offer was made, but will be ordered to pay the defendant's costs thereafter. Making a shrewd Part 36 offer very soon after being notified of a dispute is an extremely effective way of disposing of many claims. If the offer is not accepted, the claimant is left with double the usual pressure: not only must they win, but they must also obtain a judgment which is more advantageous than the offer if they are to recover all their costs. Pre-action offers under Part 36 are considered at 5.30ff, with the main discussion in Chapter 42.

Written instructions

1.17 Solicitors receive instructions by letter most frequently from established clients. Such clients may well be very familiar with the litigation process, as where a hire-purchase company has a large number of customers who fall into arrears on their instalments. In an ideal world all the necessary information and documentary evidence for the solicitor to conduct the case through its initial stages will be enclosed with the written instructions. However, written instructions are not always complete, and the solicitor may need to clarify certain matters, ensure there are no further relevant documents in the client's possession, take statements from witnesses, ensure evidence is preserved, etc.

D CONFIDENTIALITY AND CONFLICT OF INTEREST

A solicitor or barrister owes a duty of confidentiality to his or her clients. Consequently a solicitor or barrister must not disclose documents or talk about a client's case with anyone not connected with the case without the client's instructions. This duty is buttressed by the fact that documents and information in the hands of the solicitor or barrister are protected by legal professional privilege. It sometimes happens that a solicitor is approached by a prospective client in relation to a dispute with someone who is an existing client of the solicitor's firm. Where this happens, or where it subsequently appears that joint clients in fact have conflicting interests, the solicitor will, in general, have to refuse to act for one or both parties. It may be that, after receiving full advice on the potential conflict, both parties agree to the solicitor acting for them both. **1.18**

A solicitor who is possessed of relevant confidential information will be restrained from acting against the former client (*Re a Firm of Solicitors* [1992] QB 959). In the case of a firm previously retained by a client, the partners and employees who are in possession of confidential information may be restrained from acting against the former client, and this extends to them if they change firms. Members and employees of the firm who never had possession of relevant confidential information are in a rather more complex position. While they remain with the firm they will, generally, be precluded from acting against the former client of the firm, but it is possible they may be allowed to act if there is no real (as opposed to fanciful) risk that relevant confidential information might have been communicated to them (*Re a Firm of Solicitors* [1992] QB 959). **1.19**

In *Bolkiah v KPMG* [1999] 2 AC 222 the claimant had retained the defendant firm of accountants in his private capacity to provide extensive litigation support services of a kind commonly provided by solicitors in relation to proceedings he was involved in. In the course of this retainer the defendants became privy to detailed information relating to the claimant's financial affairs, and no less than 168 of the defendants' employees were involved. Some months after the conclusion of the claimant's action, the defendants were retained by the claimant's former employer (the Brunei Investment Agency, BIA) to investigate the location of substantial funds that had been transferred during his period of employment. Aware of a possible conflict of interest, the defendants erected an information barrier (also known as a 'Chinese wall') around the department conducting the BIA investigation. The defendants did not, however, ask for the claimant's consent to them acting for the BIA. It was held that the claimant was entitled to an injunction restraining the defendants from continuing to act in the BIA investigation. Such injunctions will be granted unless the firm produces clear and convincing evidence that effective measures have been taken to ensure that no disclosure of the former client's affairs will be made to the department acting for the new client, and that there is no risk of the former client's information reaching the department acting for the new client. Although, in some cases, Chinese walls may be sufficient protection, there is a very **1.20** heavy burden on the firm to prove this, and it will be very difficult for the firm to do so unless those measures were an established part of the firm's organizational structure.

E PRE-ACTION CORRESPONDENCE

1.21 After taking instructions from a client, a solicitor will usually enter into correspondence with the other side to the dispute. It is usual in most cases to have a period of negotiations before court proceedings are commenced. Sometimes receipt of a solicitor's letter by the other side will indicate that the client is taking the dispute seriously and will encourage them to make a reasonable offer in settlement of the matter without the need to resort to proceedings. There is detailed guidance on the content of pre-action correspondence: see Chapter 5. This includes providing full details of the claim and giving the other side a reasonable opportunity, perhaps through the use of alternative dispute resolution, to come to terms before issuing proceedings.

F ADR OR COURT PROCEEDINGS

1.22 Where negotiations fail, the claimant must either drop the case, consider using an alternative dispute resolution ('ADR') procedure, or commence proceedings.

Advantages and disadvantages of ADR and litigation

1.23 Advantages claimed for ADR include:

(a) ADR procedures are more flexible than litigation;
(b) ADR procedures are usually simpler than litigation, with less demanding preparation required, and the strict rules of evidence not applying;
(c) ADR procedures can be arranged to suit the convenience of the parties, in a suitable location, resulting in a minimum of disruption to their businesses;
(d) ADR is often speedier than litigation;
(e) trials in litigation are generally in public, whereas ADR takes place in private;
(f) ADR is usually less stressful than litigation;
(g) ADR can produce solutions going beyond the strict parameters of the original dispute. A court only has jurisdiction to make orders within the confines of the issues raised by the statements of case;
(h) ADR is less confrontational, which means it provides a better prospect of enabling parties to maintain long-term relationships (eg, between businesses or neighbours. There are situations, eg, where there is a distribution contract, or a commercial lease, where the parties are tied into a long-term relationship in any event);
(i) ADR is felt to be less expensive than litigation;
(j) arbitration awards are generally final, so usually avoid the risk of the parties facing an appeal; and

(k) arbitration works well in international disputes, where arbitration awards can be easily enforced across different jurisdictions, provided the country in question is one of the more than 140 countries that are signatories to the New York Convention 1958 (see <**http://www.uncitral.org**>).

Disadvantages involved in ADR procedures can include the following: **1.24**

(a) ADR procedures agreed before a dispute arose may be inappropriate for resolving the actual dispute that has arisen;
(b) where parties agree to ADR after a dispute has arisen, the parties may find it difficult to agree the details of the procedure to be followed (such as the identity of the arbitrator or mediator, payment of fees, rules to govern the ADR);
(c) in ADR procedures where the parties have to pay fees to the arbitrator or mediator, the fees may make the process more expensive than litigation;
(d) ADR can on occasion be an expensive, time-consuming diversion, particularly if one of the parties is not genuine about their participation in the procedure;
(e) a party with a strong case on the law and evidence may have to abandon their actual rights if the ADR procedure is to achieve anything;
(f) litigation may become inevitable if an arbitrator makes an error of law or jurisdiction, thereby substantially increasing the costs and delay;
(g) ADR procedures sometimes become unworkable if there are multiple parties; and
(h) enforcement of the amount determined (by agreement or by the tribunal) is easier in litigation, particularly when compared to non-arbitration ADR procedures.

Where the balance lies in any individual case depends on the circumstances. If a party needs a remedy that only a court can provide, there is no real option. If both sides to a dispute realize that each has strengths and weaknesses, mediation or conciliation can save them both from becoming embroiled in protracted litigation. Parties faced with a two-week trial may well find a day spent in mediation will save them a great deal of time and costs. Parties with a sensitive business dispute may prefer to arbitrate in order to ensure there is no public trial. Sometimes a party with a very strong case (but not sufficiently strong to seek summary judgment) will achieve a great deal by using ADR. For example, the services of a mediator might make it plain to the other side that there are substantial problems with their case, and they should be more realistic about settling the claim. **1.25**

The choice between using ADR or going to court may also turn on what the client is seeking to achieve. It may be that one mode of dispute resolution is better at delivering the required result than the other. By using ADR, any of the following may be achieved: **1.26**

(a) a change in the way the other party behaves, or measures to prevent a similar problem arising again;
(b) putting right a mistake;
(c) a promise that the other party will not do something;
(d) the repair or replacement of an item purchased;
(e) an apology, or an explanation; or
(f) compensation.

Court proceedings may result in: **1.27**

(a) a prohibitory injunction (eg, to stop tortious conduct);

(b) specific performance of a contractual obligation;
(c) rectification of a document, or rescission of a contract;
(d) the return of property (land or goods);
(e) compensation; or
(f) a declaration from the court about the respective rights of the parties.

1.28 A client whose main interest is to obtain compensation may achieve that goal by using mediation or resorting to litigation. On the other hand, a client who is more interested in preventing the same thing happening to other people, or in getting an apology, may be best advised to use a complaints procedure followed up by a reference to the relevant ombudsman. Some matters are very urgent and important, and going to court may be the only way to safeguard the client's interests. Examples are where there is an imminent threat to the client's property, or where publication of a libel is likely to happen in the next edition of a newspaper. Further, there are some cases where court approval is essential, eg, cases involving unclear provisions in wills, and approval of compromises for clients who lack legal capacity. If limitation is about to expire, it may be necessary to issue court proceedings in order to preserve the client's rights.

1.29 A related problem is in deciding the best time to attempt some form of ADR. Premature attempts at mediation can waste costs. Delaying making a reference to ADR can mean that a case passes the point where costs already expended by both sides make a negotiated settlement almost impossible. See *Nigel Witham Ltd v Smith* [2008] CILL 2557.

Range of ADR procedures

1.30 ADR takes many forms (see table 1.1). The various commercial dispute resolution services have put together various different dispute resolution models, together with published rules. The result is that parties have access to a range of different ADR procedures, and can choose the one which is best suited for resolving their dispute. Arbitration is intended to be a direct replacement for litigation, with an arbitrator making a decision which is binding on the

Table 1.1 ADR procedures

Type	Main features	Suitable cases
Commercial arbitration	Determination by professional arbitrator. Complex and potentially expensive procedure. Avoids court and avoids appeals.	Commercial cases Building disputes Contracts with arbitration clauses
Adjudication in construction disputes	Speedy independent adjudication of disputes involving builders. Enables contractors to get paid without delay. Not final.	Non-payment for building work
Mediation (formal)	Mediator facilitates negotiation, but does not make decisions. Aims at negotiated settlement or narrowing of issues. Mediator often a senior professional.	Personal injuries Clinical disputes Professional negligence General litigation
Community mediation	Mediator acts as a facilitator. Usually adopts a more informal approach than in formal mediation. Mediator often respected member of the community.	Neighbour disputes Antisocial behaviour

Table 1.1 *continued*

Type	Main features	Suitable cases
Neutral evaluation	Expert in field considers evidence and expresses a view. Not binding, but may assist parties in assessing strengths and weaknesses and hence making informed decisions on offers to settle.	Usually where there is a complex or key expert issue
Grievance and complaints procedures	Various professional bodies and trade associations have codes of conduct with grievance or complaints procedures. Can be swift, cost may be borne by the organization. Remedies may be limited.	Dispute with body which is a member of an organization with such a procedure
Ombudsman	Consider where there has been maladministration (public services) or service not provided in accordance with good practice (business sector).	Dispute with body with ombudsman scheme
Councillor/Member of Parliament	Letter to politician or visit to politician's surgery. Politician raises matter with responsible body. Depends on political weight of the politician consulted.	Usually where a public authority is responsible for the problem
Negotiation	Party and party correspondence or round table negotiation. Can be inexpensive and quick. Can be totally ineffective.	All types of dispute

parties. Other ADR procedures provide a means of finding a solution, but leave litigation open if the parties do not reach a compromise. For example, mediation can assist the parties in focusing on the issues that are causing the problem, which in turn can help them in reaching an agreement either of the whole dispute, or in relation to aspects of the dispute. If they do not reach an overall compromise, litigation is available to decide the unresolved matters.

The cost of ADR

While ADR is generally regarded as being cheaper than litigation, it can still be expensive. **1.31**
Much depends on the type of ADR used, and the value and complexity of the dispute. For example:

(a) community mediation is usually free. Parties may incur travel and other expenses;
(b) ombudsman schemes are free to the person complaining;
(c) family mediation services often charge an hourly rate. Some have a scale of fees, based on the financial circumstances of the client. Family mediation may be funded through the Community Legal Service;
(d) commercial mediation service providers charge according to the complexity and value of the claim. Mediation fees are calculated on the basis of an instruction fee per party (typically in the region of £250) plus an hourly mediation rate ranging from £200 per hour for junior mediators to £600 per hour for senior mediators. There may also be room hire costs and fees for other services. It is possible that the Community Legal Service fund will pay the cost of mediation for a party who is financially eligible;

(e) consumer arbitration schemes typically cost between £10 and £100, but some are free; and
(f) commercial arbitration providers may charge a Registration Fee, and/or a deposit (both of which could be up to about £2,500), and/or daily or hourly fees for the arbitrator or arbitrators. Some arbitrations use panels of three arbitrators. Fees and room charges are usually similar to the amounts payable for commercial mediation.

G REFERENCE TO ADR

1.32 Use of ADR is almost always voluntary, so usually rests on an agreement between the parties. Either party (or the court itself if proceedings are issued) can suggest using an ADR scheme in an attempt to find common ground. Likewise, the procedural rules governing most tribunals (eg, the Tribunal Procedure (Upper Tribunal) Rules 2008 (SI 2008/2698)) say the tribunal should bring to the attention of the parties the availability of ADR, and should facilitate the use of ADR. The standard ADR order used in the Commercial Court is shown in figure 1.1.

Figure 1.1 Commercial Court ADR Order

1. On or before [date] the parties shall exchange lists of three neutral individuals who are available to conduct ADR procedures in this case prior to [date]. Each party may [in addition] [in the alternative] provide a list identifying the constitution of one or more panels of neutral individuals who are available to conduct ADR procedures in this case prior to [date].
2. On or before [date] the parties shall in good faith endeavour to agree a neutral individual or panel from the lists so exchanged and provided.
3. Failing such agreement by [date] the Case Management Conference will be restored to enable the Court to facilitate agreement on a neutral individual or panel.
4. The parties shall take such serious steps as they may be advised to resolve their disputes by ADR procedures before the neutral individual or panel so chosen by no later than [date].
5. If the case is not finally settled, the parties shall inform the Court by letter prior to [disclosure of documents/exchange of witness statements/exchange of experts' reports] what steps towards ADR have been taken and (without prejudice to matters of privilege) why such steps have failed. If the parties have failed to initiate ADR procedures the Case Management Conference is to be restored for further consideration of the case.
6. [Costs].

Note: The term 'ADR procedures' is deliberately used in the draft ADR order. This is in order to emphasize that (save where otherwise provided) the parties are free to use the ADR procedure that they regard as most suitable, be it mediation, early neutral evaluation, non-binding arbitration, etc.

1.33 The parties can agree to use ADR either before or after a dispute arises. Contracting parties who anticipate possible problems ahead may insert an ADR clause into their contract, sometimes as part of the contract's standard terms and conditions. See table 1.2 for typical clauses. Such a clause has to be adhered to. If legal proceedings are commenced in breach of an agreement to use ADR, particularly arbitration (for which, see the Arbitration Act 1996, s 9), the court is likely to grant a stay of the proceedings or even an anti-suit injunction, and award costs on the indemnity basis (see 22.52 and 35.82).

Table 1.2 ADR Contract Clauses

Type of clause	Wording
Reference to arbitration	Any dispute or difference arising out of or in connection with this contract shall be determined by the appointment of a single arbitrator to be agreed between the parties, or failing agreement within 14 days after either party has given to the other a written request to concur in the appointment of an arbitrator, by an arbitrator to be appointed by the President or a Vice President of the Chartered Institute of Arbitrators. The seat of the arbitration shall be England and Wales.
Rules for the arbitration	The arbitration shall be governed by both the Arbitration Act 1996 and the Controlled Cost Rules of the Chartered Institute of Arbitrators (2000 Edition) ('the Rules'), or any amendments to those provisions. The Rules are deemed to be incorporated by reference into this clause.
Reference to construction adjudication	A party to this contract ('the referring party') may at any time give notice ('the notice') in writing to the other party of its intention to refer a dispute arising under the contract to adjudication.
Rules for construction adjudication	The parties may agree the identity of the adjudicator. Where an adjudicator is not agreed within two days of the notice being given, the referring party shall immediately apply to [name of adjudication provider] for the nomination of an adjudicator, which nomination shall be communicated to the parties within five days of receipt of the application. Within seven days of the notice the referring party shall refer the dispute to the adjudicator. The adjudicator shall reach a decision within 28 days of referral or such longer period as is agreed by the parties after the dispute has been referred. The adjudicator may extend the period of 28 days by up to 14 days, with the consent of the party by whom the dispute was referred.
Mediation	Any dispute arising out of or in connection with this contract shall, at first instance, be referred to a mediator for resolution. The parties shall attempt to agree upon the appointment of a mediator, upon receipt, by either of them, of a written notice to concur in such appointment. Should the parties fail to agree within 14 days, either party, upon giving written notice, may apply to the President or the Deputy President, for the time being, of the Chartered Institute of Arbitrators, for the appointment of a mediator.

H MAIN STAGES IN COURT PROCEEDINGS

When commencing proceedings, decisions have to be made about the appropriate court and type of proceedings to use. Generally, as discussed at 2.18ff and especially 2.22, the claimant has a complete choice between commencing proceedings in either the High Court or a county court. Broadly, however, the High Court should be used only for the most important cases (see 2.32) and those worth more than £25,000. Personal injuries cases must be commenced in a county court unless the amount claimed exceeds £50,000 (see 2.29). As a guide, the main stages in a common law claim, whether it is proceeding in a county court or the High Court, are shown in figure 1.2. 1.34

Figure 1.2 General sequence of events in claims under the CPR

Pre-action Protocol

↓

Issue claim form

↓

Service of claim form and Particulars of claim

↓

Acknowledgment of service (optional)

↓

Defence

↓

Reply (optional)

↓

Allocation questionnaires

↓

Track allocation and directions

↓

Case management conference (if ordered by the court)

↓

Lists of documents

↓

Inspection of documents

↓

Witness statements

↓

Experts' reports

↓

Without prejudice meeting of experts

↓

Pre-trial checklists

↓

Listing for trial

↓

Pre-trial review (if ordered by the court)

Issue of a claim form

1.35 Court proceedings are commenced by issuing a claim form. This involves drawing up the document on the appropriate form (usually form N1), taking (or sending by post) copies of it to the court office, paying a fee, and having the claim form stamped with the court's official seal. There are specialist claim forms for use in certain types of proceedings (eg, the Admiralty and Commercial Courts), and an alternative 'Part 8' claim form for proceedings pursuant to statute and for questions of construction (see Chapter 19).

Time stops running for limitation purposes on the date proceedings are brought. Generally, a defendant has a complete defence if the relevant limitation period has expired before proceedings are brought, although in some cases the court has a discretion to allow proceedings to continue despite the expiry of the primary limitation period. Limitation is discussed in some detail in Chapter 7. 1.36

Service of process

As a general rule, the defendant must be served with the claim form together with a 'response pack' within four months after issue. In non-specialist cases service may be by the claimant or the court. Usually, the court will serve by first-class post. Where service is effected by the claimant, a number of methods of service are permitted, but the most common are by first-class post, insertion through the letterbox at the defendant's address, and delivery to the defendant in person. In general litigation a defendant is required to respond to service within 14 days after service of the particulars of claim. In the Commercial Court the defendant must respond within 14 days of service of the claim form. This is done by returning a form of acknowledgment of service (which should have been part of the response pack) to the court office, by using the forms of admission and defence and counterclaim enclosed with the response pack, or by filing a formal defence. 1.37

Statements of case

In common law claims, the factual contentions advanced by both parties must be reduced into writing in formal documents known as statements of case. These are discussed further in Chapter 13. The claimant's case is contained in the particulars of claim. This sets out the facts in a structured way, and is designed to show how the legal requirements of the claimant's causes of action against the defendant are satisfied. Particulars of claim are sometimes incorporated in the claim form, and sometimes kept separate. If separate, they should be served on the defendant no later than 14 days after service of the claim form. 1.38

The next statement of case is the defence, which is drawn up by the defendant. It responds to the allegations made in the particulars of claim, and sets up any specific defences available to the defendant. A defendant with a cross-claim against the claimant may add a counterclaim to the defence. Often, the only statements of case are the claim and defence. However, it is not uncommon for the claimant to respond with a reply, and, if the defendant has counterclaimed, with a defence to counterclaim (a claimant doing both will serve a reply and defence to counterclaim). 1.39

Track allocation

In general litigation, the court will send allocation questionnaires to the parties in cases where defences have been filed. These must be completed and returned within a short period of time (stated on the form), and should provide the court with information to enable it to assess how complicated and important the claim is likely to be. On the basis of this information the procedural judge will allocate the claim to one of three case management tracks. The small claims track aims to provide a swift and inexpensive procedure for simple claims worth no more than £5,000. The fast track provides a fuller, but still streamlined, procedure for somewhat more important cases, typically with a value between £5,000 and £25,000. The multi-track is 1.40

used for cases worth typically in excess of £25,000. At the same time as allocating the case to a track, the procedural judge will give directions for the further steps required to prepare the claim for final determination, with the level of preparation laid down being proportionate to the value and complexity of the case. Commercial Court claims are automatically treated as allocated to the multi-track.

Disclosure

1.41 After track allocation, in cases proceeding on the fast track or multi-track, the parties are required to serve on each other lists of documents. These list all the documents material to the case which are or have been in their possession, custody, or power. The documents are divided into those which it is accepted can be seen by the other side, those which are protected by privilege, and those no longer with the party making the list. Documents must be disclosed whether they support or undermine the case of the party holding them. After lists have been exchanged, the parties are entitled to inspect each other's documents, other than those covered by privilege. Usually this is done by providing photocopies. Disclosure is discussed further in Chapter 29.

Exchange of evidence

1.42 The parties must give full disclosure to each other of all relevant material in advance of trial. Advance disclosure is intended to serve several purposes:

(a) to allow the parties to assess the true strengths of their cases in advance of trial;
(b) to promote settlements;
(c) to prevent the parties being taken by surprise at trial; and
(d) to prevent unnecessary adjournments.

1.43 Thus, in addition to disclosing material documents, directions invariably require the parties to exchange the written reports of experts and the statements of factual witnesses they intend to call at trial. Where a party intends to adduce hearsay evidence at trial, adequate notice identifying the hearsay evidence must be served on the other side usually at the same time as witness statements are exchanged. These matters are discussed in Chapters 31 to 33.

Listing for trial

1.44 The courts try to list cases for final determination as soon as possible. In small claims track cases this is done at track allocation. In fast track cases the trial should be no later than 30 weeks after allocation. There is no set time limit for multi-track cases. In fast track and multi-track cases the court may give a fixed hearing date (a 'fixture'), or a 'trial window'. Most Commercial Court cases are given fixed trial dates. To assist the listing process, and to ensure the claim is in fact ready for trial, the court may send pre-trial checklists to the parties, and may hold listing hearings and pre-trial reviews.

Trial

At trial, witnesses will be called to give oral testimony on the facts left in contention by the statements of case, and the court will consider the contemporaneous documentation and any other relevant and admissible evidence adduced by either side. Trials are normally conducted by a judge sitting alone. After hearing the evidence and submissions by counsel, the judge will give final judgment on the issues between the parties: see Chapter 39. **1.45**

Assessment of costs

After giving judgment, the judge will hear submissions on the question of costs. Normally costs follow the event, which means that the party winning at trial recovers its costs from the other side: see Chapter 43. The party awarded its costs then needs to have them quantified into a sum of money. In the absence of agreement, this is done through the process of assessment, described at 43.08. **1.46**

2

THE CIVIL COURTS

2.01 Civil proceedings in England and Wales may be conducted in magistrates' courts, county courts, and the High Court. Magistrates' courts have a relatively limited jurisdiction over civil matters, and will be considered only in outline in this book. Appeals are usually taken to the next more senior tier of the judicial system (for example, an appeal from a district judge is taken to the circuit judge), with further appeals to the Court of Appeal and the Supreme Court. Appeals are considered in Chapter 46. This chapter deals first with the composition and administration of the civil courts, and then with matters relating to jurisdiction and the allocation of business.

2.02 In addition, a wide range of civil disputes are determined in various tribunals, including employment tribunals and social security tribunals. The composition of and procedure followed by tribunals are regulated by the Tribunals, Courts and Enforcement Act 2007 and by rules laid down by statutory instruments, particularly various First-Tier Tribunal Rules (such as the Tribunal Procedure (First-Tier Tribunal) (Health, Education and Social Care Chamber) Rules 2008 (SI 2008/2699) and the Tribunal Procedure (Upper Tribunal) Rules 2008 (SI 2008/2698)). Certain old-form tribunal rules have been adopted into the present system as if they are Tribunal Procedure Rules, such as the Lands Tribunal Rules 1996 (see the Transfer of Tribunal Functions (Lands Tribunal and Miscellaneous Amendments) Order 2009, art 4). Tribunals will only be considered further in this book where their procedures impact on the traditional courts system.

A COMPOSITION AND ADMINISTRATION

Magistrates' courts

2.03 England and Wales are divided into commission areas, with each commission area covering one county, apart from London, which is divided into six commission areas. The commission areas are divided into petty sessional divisions, each served by a magistrates' court. Magistrates are appointed to act for their commission area, and can theoretically sit in any court in that area, but in practice they normally sit only in the division to which they are assigned. There are about 300 district judges and deputy district judges sitting in the magistrates' courts, and approximately 30,000 lay magistrates in England and Wales, of whom about 55 per cent are men. About 2,000 appointments are made each year. Appointments are made by the Lord Chancellor, who acts on the recommendation of local advisory committees. Some people, such as undischarged bankrupts and those convicted of corrupt practices at elections, are disqualified from appointment. Otherwise, appointments are made on the basis of suitability for the work by reason of character and ability. The intention is that magistrates should represent as wide a cross-section of the community as is possible.

There is no requirement for lay magistrates to have any legal qualifications. However, they **2.04** do receive a course of basic training when they are appointed, and further training thereafter. They are also required to sit at least 20 times each year, so over a period of time acquire a fair amount of practical experience.

The administration of each magistrates' court is run by a magistrates' clerk, who may be **2.05** assisted by a number of assistants. Assistants must be legally qualified, and clerks must be barristers, solicitors, or assistants of at least five years' standing.

Cases are usually heard by benches of three magistrates. If the chairman of the petty sessional **2.06** division or one of the deputy chairmen elected under the Justices of the Peace Act 1979, s 17, is present he or she will preside over the proceedings. Otherwise, the most senior magistrate presides. The chairman is addressed as 'Sir' or 'Madam'. Courts hearing family proceedings are known as family proceedings courts, and must not comprise more than three justices, all of whom must be members of a family panel. A family proceedings court must, so far as practicable, include both a man and a woman. Appointment to a family panel depends on the magistrate's suitability for deciding family proceedings (see Magistrates' Courts Act 1980, ss 66 and 67).

In all cases, the clerk or one of the assistants will be present throughout the hearing to advise **2.07** the bench on questions of law and procedure. However, decisions are made by the magistrates alone. Each member has a single vote, and decisions, whether unanimous or by a majority, are pronounced by the chairman.

County courts

There are about 220 county courts in England and Wales, each one serving its surrounding **2.08** district (CCA 1984, s 1). Most civil claims can be commenced in any county court, but defended claims may be transferred either automatically or in the court's discretion (see 11.19).

Each court is presided over by a circuit judge, who is a professional lawyer with a seven-year **2.09** judicial appointment qualification (Tribunals, Courts and Enforcement Act 2007, Sch 10). Circuit judges sit in the Crown Court as well as the county courts, the intention being to give them a broad spectrum of judicial experience. County court trials are mainly conducted by circuit judges and by recorders sitting alone. Recorders are part-time judges. They are barristers or solicitors who are still in private practice and who are appointed to sit in the

Crown Court and county courts for a number of weeks each year. If through pressure of work it becomes expedient to do so, it is possible to appoint deputy circuit judges and assistant recorders as a temporary measure under the Courts Act 1971, s 24. The correct mode of address for circuit judges, recorders, and their deputies is 'Your Honour'.

2.10 Each district also has one or more district judges, who must have a five-year general qualification. District judges conduct most of the interim proceedings in the county courts. They also conduct most small-claims hearings (see Chapter 25) and possession claims, and have power to conduct trials where the amount claimed does not exceed £25,000. District judges are addressed as 'Sir' or 'Madam'.

2.11 The administrative staff of the courts are civil servants employed by the Ministry of Justice. They are headed by the court manager, and most correspondence with the court should be addressed to that official. Some quasi-judicial functions connected with enforcing judgments are fulfilled by the administrative staff, but they are mainly involved in drawing up, issuing, and serving court documents and maintaining court records. Bailiffs, whose responsibilities include physically enforcing judgments and serving documents, are also employed by the Ministry of Justice. Most of the administration work connected with the courts is done locally, but to cater for bulk users of the courts, such as hire-purchase, mail order, and public utility companies, proceedings in debt recovery claims may be issued by the Production Centre in Northampton. Claimants using the Production Centre deliver their draft claim forms in computer-readable form, and the Centre produces computer-printed claim forms which are dispatched using automatic mailing equipment. A claimant may choose whether to have a Production Centre claim treated as issued in any county court.

High Court

2.12 The High Court, Crown Court, and Court of Appeal together comprise the Senior Courts of England and Wales (Constitutional Reform Act 2005, s 59(1)). The main administrative offices and court facilities of the High Court are located at the Royal Courts of Justice ('RCJ'), Strand, London. In addition, there are 137 district registries, which are established by the Senior Courts Act 1981, ss 99 to 103. Each registry serves the districts of the county courts listed in the Civil Courts Order 1983. All claims involving disputes in London must be commenced in the RCJ. Claims based on disputes outside London may be commenced either in the RCJ or the appropriate district registry at the claimant's choice. Generally, the practice in the district registries must follow that in London, but there are some small differences.

2.13 The High Court consists of three Divisions, namely the Queen's Bench Division ('QBD'), Chancery Division ('ChD'), and Family Division ('FamD'). Each Division has its own judiciary and its own administrative offices for issuing process, arranging interim hearings and trials, and for enforcement, etc. Further, specialist courts exist within the QBD and ChD to deal with particular classes of cases. These include the Commercial Court, the Admiralty Court, the Technology and Construction Court, and the Companies Court. Each of these also has its own judges and administrative offices. In addition, public law matters, particularly applications for judicial review, are dealt with separately in the Crown Office.

2.14 Trials in the High Court are conducted by the justices of the High Court, also known as 'puisne judges', and by deputy judges. Interim applications in the QBD and ChD of the High

Court in London are dealt with by judicial officers known as masters. Interim applications in the Commercial Court are dealt with by a Commercial Court judge. In the district registries, interim applications are dealt with by district judges. Unless they have trial jurisdiction over the claim, and with some other exceptions, masters and district judges cannot grant interim injunctions. Deputy High Court judges, masters, and district judges can never try claims under the Human Rights Act 1998, s 7(1)(a) in respect of a judicial act, nor claims for declarations of incompatibility under s 4 (PD 2B, para 7A). High Court district judges often also hold the office of district judge for the local county court. The correct mode of address for the justices of the High Court and for deputy judges sitting as High Court judges is 'My Lord' or 'My Lady', and 'Your Lordship' or 'Your Ladyship'. Masters are addressed 'Master', and district judges are addressed 'Sir' or 'Madam'.

As in the county court, the administrative work of the High Court is performed by civil servants employed by the Ministry of Justice. However, enforcement is conducted by enforcement officers, who, unlike bailiffs, their county court equivalents, are not civil servants. **2.15**

B JURISDICTION

Magistrates' courts

Obviously, most of the work conducted in the magistrates' courts relates to criminal prosecutions. However, they also have jurisdiction over a number of civil matters. Civil jurisdiction is given by various statutes. Often, magistrates are given the task of dealing with cases in the grey area between the civil and criminal law. It is sometimes difficult to determine whether an application under a particular statute is civil or criminal, but, generally, if liability under a statute results in the possible imposition of a penalty, it probably creates a criminal offence. Procedurally, the distinction is whether the applicant needs to request the issue of a summons by complaint or by information. Civil matters are commenced by filing complaints, criminal matters by filing informations. **2.16**

Magistrates' jurisdiction includes family law matters, and making orders against those defaulting in the payment of their local government taxes. Many statutes allow civil applications to be made to the magistrates, mostly on technical regulatory matters. **2.17**

Division of business between the county courts and High Court

The county courts and the High Court have concurrent jurisdiction over most categories of cases: see CLSA 1990, s 1, and the High Court and County Courts Jurisdiction Order 1991 (SI 1991/724) ('Jurisdiction Order 1991'). Although the general rule is that the claimant is free to choose whether to issue proceedings in a county court or the High Court, special provision is made for a number of categories of cases, and the rules relating to these categories will be considered below. Also, even where the claimant has a choice between the county court and the High Court, there are further rules on trial venue which should **2.18** be taken into account, as the future need to transfer the claim may result in delay and wasted costs.

Cases allocated exclusively to the county court

2.19 County courts have exclusive jurisdiction over a small number of cases. Two examples are:

(a) claims to enforce regulated agreements and linked transactions under the Consumer Credit Act 1974 where the upper credit limit is £25,000 (Consumer Credit Act, s 141; SI 1998/996);
(b) claims to redress unlawful sexual discrimination under the Sex Discrimination Act 1975, s 66.

Claims which should be brought in a county court

2.20 There are a number of statutes which, while not precluding applications pursuant to their provisions being brought in the High Court, provide that if the proceedings are brought in the High Court the applicant will not be entitled to recover any costs. The effect is to channel almost all applications under such statutes into the county courts. Examples are:

(a) applications under the right-to-buy legislation in Part V of the Housing Act 1985 (see s 181);
(b) applications in respect of secure tenancies in Part IV of the Housing Act 1985 (see s 110);
(c) applications by tenants and landlords under the Rent Act 1977 (see s 141);
(d) applications under the Rent (Agriculture) Act 1976 (see s 26).

2.21 Another device to encourage use of the county courts is adopted by the Housing Act 1988, Part I, which deals with assured tenancies and assured shorthold tenancies. Section 40(4) of the Act provides that, if an application under Part I is made to the High Court rather than a county court, the applicant will not be entitled to recover more in the way of costs than if the application had been taken in a county court. Note that under CPR, r 55.3, proceedings for the recovery of land must be commenced in the court for the district in which the land is situated.

Concurrent jurisdiction

2.22 The bulk of civil proceedings can be brought either in the High Court or a county court at the claimant's option. These include:

(a) claims in contract and in tort (CCA 1984, s 15);
(b) claims for the recovery of land (CCA 1984, s 21);
(c) applications for orders under the Inheritance (Provision for Family and Dependants) Act 1975, s 2 (CCA 1984, s 25);
(d) applications for relief from forfeiture (CCA 1984, s 139);
(e) applications under the Landlord and Tenant Act 1954, Part II, in relation to the security of tenure of business tenants (Landlord and Tenant Act 1954, s 63).

Cases where there is limited county court jurisdiction

2.23 In a number of classes of cases the High Court and county courts have concurrent jurisdiction if the value of the case falls below a statutory limit, but if its value exceeds that limit, the case can only be brought in the High Court. There are two main types of limit. The first is a limitation of £5,000 on the amount claimed in the action. The other is a limitation on the value of the estate, trust, or property subject to the proceedings of £30,000.

Cases subject to a £5,000 limit for county court proceedings are unusual, but include applications for compensation for defective search certificates under the Local Land Charges Act 1975. **2.24**

Instances of cases where county court jurisdiction is subject to the £30,000 limit are: **2.25**

(a) proceedings under various provisions of the Law of Property Act 1925, such as applying for requisitions in conveyancing under s 49;
(b) contentious probate proceedings (CCA 1984, s 32);
(c) proceedings to vacate land charges under the Land Charges Act 1976, s 1(6);
(d) general equitable jurisdiction, eg, administration of estates, execution of trusts, and proceedings for specific performance (CCA 1984, s 23).

There are also a number of other limitations on the jurisdiction of the county courts. For example, admiralty claims in the nature of salvage can be brought in a county court if the value of the property saved does not exceed £15,000, and proceedings relating to companies can be brought in a county court only if the company's paid-up share capital does not exceed £120,000. **2.26**

Cases allocated exclusively to the High Court

The following categories of cases can only be brought in the High Court: **2.27**

(a) applications for judicial review (CCA 1984, s 38(3));
(b) actions for libel or slander (CCA 1984, s 15(2)(b));
(c) actions in which the title to any toll, fair, market, or franchise is in question (CCA 1984, s 15(2)(a));
(d) applications concerning decisions of local authority auditors (Jurisdiction Order 1991, art 6);
(e) claims under the Human Rights Act 1998, s 7(1)(a) in respect of a judicial act.

Questions involving the validity of patents fall within the meaning of 'franchise' in (c) above, but provision has been made for a special patents county court: see 2.43. **2.28**

Personal injuries cases

Special provision is made for personal injuries cases by the Jurisdiction Order 1991, art 5, which provides that, where the claimant does not reasonably expect to recover more than £50,000, the claim must be commenced in a county court. The term 'personal injuries' includes disease, impairment of physical or mental condition, and death. The value of the claim is determined as at the date the claim is commenced, and is calculated by adding together: **2.29**

(a) general damages for pain, suffering, and loss of amenity relating to the injury itself;
(b) special damages for actual financial losses incurred to date; and

(c) future losses, such as loss of earnings and the cost of future medical care. Future losses are calculated by finding the claimant's annual loss and multiplying it by a number of years' purchase, and applying a modifier based on the claimant's educational background and any disability. The multiplier is dependent on factors such as the claimant's age and likely retirement age, and takes into account the benefit to the claimant of getting the money in advance. The modifier reflects factors, other than death, which affect the claimant's future income-earning capacity (claimants with better educational qualifications tend to have greater job security, and those who are more disabled less job security). Details can be found in the Ogden tables.

2.30 In making this calculation the following rules are applied:

(a) any sums which are required to be paid to the Secretary of State by virtue of the recoupment of benefits provisions under the Social Security (Recovery of Benefits) Act 1997 are taken to be part of the claim;
(b) claims for interest and costs are disregarded;
(c) no account is taken of a possible finding of contributory negligence; and
(d) if provisional damages are claimed, no account is taken of the possibility of a future application for further damages.

2.31 The great majority of personal injuries claims are for less than £50,000, and so will usually be commenced in a county court. It is very rare for general damages alone to exceed £50,000, but where the claimant has suffered a significant permanent injury which has resulted in ongoing loss of earnings or a permanent need for medical care, future losses can far exceed £50,000. If High Court proceedings are justified, the claimant must endorse the claim form with a statement that the value of the claim exceeds £50,000 (PD 7A, para 3.6).

Trial allocation

2.32 One of the factors which should influence the decision about where to commence proceedings if the claimant has a choice is the likely venue of any trial. The policy is to reserve High Court trials for the cases which genuinely need to be tried by a High Court judge. To this end, the courts may, either of their own initiative or on the application of either party, transfer proceedings either up to the High Court or down to an appropriate county court (see CCA 1984, ss 40 and 42). Chancery Division cases, if transferred, normally go to the Central London County Court. The main rules for determining trial allocation are contained in the Jurisdiction Order 1991, art 7.

2.33 First, equity and contentious probate proceedings involving no more than £30,000 which are commenced in a county court will also be tried there. For other types of proceedings, art 7 lays down a number of *prima facie* rules which are subject to the court deciding otherwise in the light of four statutory criteria. The *prima facie* rules are that:

(a) claims valued at less than £25,000 on the date that transfer is considered should be tried in a county court;
(b) claims between £25,000 and £50,000 are flexibly allocated between the High Court and the county courts; and
(c) claims over £50,000 should be tried in the High Court.

Proceedings including at least one claim seeking relief having no quantifiable value (such as many injunctions) are not subject to any *prima facie* rule, and are simply allocated by applying the statutory criteria. The criteria are: **2.34**

(a) the financial substance of the claim, including the value of any counterclaim;
(b) whether the claim is otherwise important and, in particular, whether it raises questions of importance to persons who are not parties or questions of general public interest;
(c) the complexity of the facts, legal issues, remedies, or procedures involved; and
(d) (although not sufficient on its own) whether a transfer is likely to result in a more speedy trial of the claim.

Commencing in the wrong court

Generally, when proceedings are commenced in the wrong court they will be transferred to the correct court, and the claimant will usually be penalized by being made to pay the costs of the application to transfer the claim and, if ultimately successful, may have any award of costs reduced by up to 25 per cent (SCA 1981, s 51(8) and (9)). However, if the court is satisfied that the claimant knew or ought to have known that the proceedings were being commenced in the wrong court, the court has a discretion whether to order a transfer or to strike out the proceedings (CCA 1984, ss 40(1)(b) and 42(1)(b)). According to *Restick v Crickmore* [1994] 1 WLR 420, striking out is inappropriate for bona fide mistakes, but would be a proper response to instances where starting in the wrong court was a deliberate attempt to harass a defendant, or a deliberate attempt to run up unnecessary costs, or was done in defiance of a warning from the defendant about the proper venue for the proceedings. **2.35**

C HIGH COURT DIVISIONS

Business is allocated between the three High Court Divisions in accordance with the SCA 1981, s 61 and Sch 1. The broad effect is that: **2.36**

(a) the QBD deals with all judicial review, admiralty, and commercial matters. In addition, it is usually the most appropriate division for dealing with claims seeking common law remedies (debt, damages, recovery of land, recovery of goods), which includes most claims in contract and tort;
(b) the ChD has been assigned all cases involving the sale, exchange, or partition of land; mortgages; execution of trusts; administration of estates; bankruptcy; taking of partnership accounts; rectification, etc. of deeds; probate; intellectual property; and company matters. It can also deal with other areas, such as claims in contract and tort, which are not assigned specifically to either of the other divisions; and
(c) the FamD has been assigned all matrimonial and related matters.

It is possible to transfer claims between Divisions under CPR, r 30.5, and this will be appropriate where a claim is proceeding in one Division but raises specialist points which would be within the expertise and knowledge of judges in another Division. However, a case will not usually be transferred merely because it would be dealt with more speedily or efficiently **2.37** elsewhere: see *Barclays Bank plc v Bemister* [1989] 1 WLR 128. If a case is assigned by the SCA 1981 to one Division but is inadvertently commenced in the wrong Division, it will usually be transferred with very little argument, as there is a danger that judges dealing with unfamiliar cases may make mistakes, as happened in *Apac Rowena Ltd v Norpol Packaging Ltd* [1991] 4 All ER 516.

D SPECIALIST COURTS

Technology and Construction Court

2.38 Cases in the QBD, ChD, or county courts may be dealt with in the Technology and Construction Court ('TCC') if they involve prolonged examination of documents or accounts, or technical, scientific, or local investigations. Typically, the TCC deals with civil engineering and building disputes, professional negligence cases involving architects, surveyors, and accountants, and information technology cases. Cases may be commenced in the TCC, or may be transferred there at a later stage. Once in the TCC all statements of case are marked 'Technology and Construction Court' in the top right corner below the entry for the parent court classified as either 'HCJ' (the most heavy and complex cases, which will be tried by a High Court judge) or 'SCJ' (all other TCC claims, which will be tried by a senior circuit judge, who is addressed as 'Your Honour'). The case is then allocated to a named TCC judge. The TCC judges keep close control over the cases assigned to them, dealing with all interim applications as well as the trial. All TCC cases are allocated to the multi-track (CPR, r 60.6). It is common for Scott schedules to be ordered as part of the trial preparations. A Scott schedule is usually drawn up by the claimant, and sets out the detailed allegations against the defendant in tabular form. Commonly, there will be columns setting out the alleged defects, their cause, any remedial works, and the sum claimed, with further columns for the defendant's answers and the court's award. Trials before TCC judges are conducted as nearly as possible in the same way as other High Court trials.

Commercial Court

2.39 Claims of a commercial nature in the QBD of the High Court may be commenced in or transferred to the Commercial Court. Statements of case are marked 'Commercial Court' after the entry relating to the division. Similar claims in Bristol, Birmingham, Cardiff, Chester, Mold, Leeds, Newcastle upon Tyne, Manchester, and Liverpool are entered in the 'mercantile court'. The cases covered include those involving shipping, international carriage of goods, insurance, banking, international credit, mercantile contractual disputes, and commercial arbitrations. Commercial cases are often very weighty pieces of litigation, and despite the requirement that commercial statements of case must be in point form and must be as brief as possible, statements of case in the Commercial Court are often characterized by length and complexity.

2.40 Similar provision has been made for county court claims, where the Central London County Court has a Mercantile List for claims relating to commercial and business transactions. The intention is that cases will be entered on this list only where the value of the claim exceeds £25,000. For trial allocation purposes (see 2.32–2.34), the presumption that claims will be tried in the High Court applies only to Mercantile List cases in the county court where the value of the claim exceeds £200,000, rather than the usual £50,000.

Admiralty Court

Admiralty jurisdiction is exercised by the QBD of the High Court (see SCA 1981, ss 20 to 24). **2.41**
Admiralty cases include claims to the possession or ownership of ships, for damage received or done by a ship, for personal injuries involving ships, for damage to goods carried by ship, and for salvage or towage. Admiralty claims may be either *in rem* or *in personam*. A claim *in rem* is usually against a ship, although it may be against cargo or freight. It allows the claimant to arrest the *res*, which provides security for the claimant and is obviously useful if the true defendant is resident abroad. A claim *in personam* is similar to general actions against named defendants. The Admiralty Court largely follows the practice in the Commercial Court.

Companies Court

The Companies Court is a part of the ChD and deals with applications under the Companies **2.42**
Act 2006, the Insurance Companies Act 1982, the Insolvency Act 1986, and the Company Directors Disqualification Act 1986. It has its own special practice direction, PD 49A, and, in relation to insolvency matters, PD Insolvency Proceedings.

Patents Court

All High Court proceedings involving the validity, revocation, amendment, and alleged **2.43**
infringement of patents and registered designs are brought in the Patents Court of the ChD. There are also designated Patents County Courts (Copyright, Designs and Patents Act 1988, s 287(1)), where patent matters are dealt with by the patents judge (CPR, r 63.4A). The Patents Court has its own practice direction (PD 63), and its own court guide.

KEY POINTS SUMMARY

- For most civil claims the claimant has a free choice between the High Court and the county **2.44**
  courts.
- Broadly, the High Court should be used for the more important and complex claims.
- Broadly, common law claims are suitable for the QBD, whereas equity claims are more suitable for the ChD.
- The Commercial Court deals with QBD claims involving international and domestic trade, banking, and insurance. There are Mercantile Courts in certain District Registries and a Mercantile List in the Central London County Court for similar cases.

- Masters deal with interim applications in the QBD and ChD. In the Commercial Court they are dealt with by Commercial Court judges. In the county courts and District Registries of the High Court they are dealt with by district judges.
- Trials are generally dealt with by judges in the High Court, and circuit judges in the county courts.

3

OVERRIDING OBJECTIVE AND HUMAN RIGHTS

One of the fundamental concepts of the CPR is that they contain, as the very first rule, a statement of the overall purpose behind the civil justice system. This is known as the 'overriding objective', which is to deal with cases justly. By CPR, r 1.2, the court has to give effect to the overriding objective when making decisions and when interpreting the rules. The parties are, by r 1.3, required to help the court to further the overriding objective. By r 1.4 the court must further the overriding objective by actively managing cases. It is therefore a pervading concept that must always be kept in mind at all stages in civil proceedings. **3.01**

Of similar importance is the Human Rights Act 1998. By s 3(1), so far as it is possible to do so, primary legislation and subordinate legislation (which includes the CPR) must be read and given effect to in a way which is compatible with the rights set out in the European Convention on Human Rights. Section 2(1) provides that a court determining a question which arises in connection with a Convention right must take into account any judgment, decision, declaration, or advisory opinion of the European Court of Human Rights. Although lawyers have to take a responsible attitude in raising human rights points (*Daniels v Walker* [2000] 1 WLR 1382), such points do arise on occasion when courts are considering procedural **3.02** applications, and the CPR and practice directions have been drafted with a view to being compatible with the Convention.

3.03 This chapter will consider the sources of procedural law, the general principles relevant to civil procedure established by the overriding objective, and the European Convention on Human Rights, and also some rules on how the courts approach construing the CPR. Where human rights points arise in relation to specific areas of civil procedure, they will also be discussed in the relevant chapters of this book.

A SOURCES OF PROCEDURAL LAW

Statutory sources

3.04 The primary source of law governing procedure in the High Court and Court of Appeal is the Senior Courts Act 1981 ('SCA 1981'). The SCA 1981 used to be known as the Supreme Court Act 1981, but had to be re-named when the Supreme Court replaced the House of Lords in October 2009. The equivalent source for the county courts is the County Courts Act 1984 ('CCA 1984'). Both statutes are often expressed in very wide terms, leaving the detailed mechanics of many of the procedures used in the courts to be set out in rules of court. By the Civil Procedure Act 1997, s 2, a body known as the Civil Procedure Rule Committee is empowered to make rules governing the practice and procedure to be followed in the civil courts. By s 1(3) the rules must be both simple and simply expressed. The principal rules made by the Committee are the Civil Procedure Rules 1998 (SI 1998/3132) ('CPR'). The CPR are divided into Parts, each divided into a number of rules. Various provisions from the previous rules of court have been preserved for the time being in Schs 1 and 2 to the CPR. Preserved rules from the former High Court rules (the Rules of the Supreme Court 1965 (SI 1965/1776), or 'RSC') are to be found in CPR, Sch 1, and preserved rules from the former county court rules (the County Court Rules 1981 (SI 1981/1687), or 'CCR') are to be found in CPR, Sch 2.

Practice Directions

3.05 Most of the Parts of the CPR, and several of the provisions found in the schedules to the CPR, are supplemented by one or more detailed practice directions ('PD'). Thus, PD 39A and PD 39B supplement CPR, Part 39. Practice directions may be made by the Lord Chief Justice, or his nominee, with the agreement of the Lord Chancellor (Civil Procedure Act 1997, s 5(1) as amended), or with the approval of the Lord Chancellor and Lord Chief Justice (s 5(2)). 'Practice directions' for this purpose covers both practice directions expressly supplementing the CPR and general practice directions which in the past were made by the courts from time to time (s 9(1)). A purported practice direction that did not comply with the procedures in s 5 will be ultra vires (*Bovale Ltd v Secretary of State for Communities and Local Government* [2009] 1 WLR 2274). In contrast, a judge is permitted to lay down guidance suggesting procedures that should be followed without infringing s 5, provided the guidance is consistent with the CPR and main practice directions (*Bovale Ltd v Secretary of State for Communities and Local Government*).

The rules and practice directions are amended from time to time to take account of legislative changes and changes in practice. The CPR, PDs, and preserved provisions from the RSC and CCR can be found in BCP, app 1. Electronic versions can be found: 3.06

(a) for statutes, at **<http://www.opsi.gov.uk/acts.htm>**;
(b) for the CPR, PDs, court forms, etc., at **<http://www.justice.gov.uk>**.

Judicial sources

Although the CPR and practice directions are of quite considerable length, very often they state the principles to be applied on the various procedures available in general terms, leaving details to be worked out by the courts on a case-by-case basis. 3.07

Lacunae in the County Court Rules

It is provided by the CCA 1984, s 76, that: 3.08

> In any case not expressly provided for by or in pursuance of this Act, the general principles of practice in the High Court may be adopted and applied to proceedings in a county court.

While s 76 continues in force, the need to fall back on the section has been drastically reduced by the introduction of the CPR with its unified system of rules covering the High Court and county courts. 3.09

Inherent jurisdiction

Inherent jurisdiction of the High Court

Being the successor to the old common law courts, the High Court has inherent jurisdiction to control its procedure to ensure its proceedings are not used to achieve injustice. Perhaps the most important statement on this subject is that of Lord Diplock in *Bremer Vulkan Schiffbau und Maschinenfabrik v South India Shipping Corporation Ltd* [1981] AC 909 at 977, where his lordship said the High Court has: 3.10

> ...a general power to control its own procedure so as to prevent its being used to achieve injustice. Such a power is inherent in its constitutional function as a court of justice. Every civilised system of government requires that the State should make available to all its citizens a means for the just and peaceful settlement of disputes between them as to their respective legal rights. The means provided are courts of justice to which every citizen has a constitutional right of access in the role of plaintiff to obtain the remedy to which he claims to be entitled in consequence of an alleged breach of his legal or equitable rights by some other citizen, the defendant. Whether or not to avail himself of this right of access to the court lies exclusively within the plaintiff's choice; if he chooses to do so, the defendant has no option in the matter; his subjection to the jurisdiction of the court is compulsory. So, it would stultify the constitutional role of the High Court as a court of justice if it were not armed with power to prevent its process being misused in such a way as to diminish its capability of arriving at a just decision of the dispute.

Thus, where a party in a High Court claim makes an application for an order which is not contemplated by the SCA 1981 or the CPR or seeks an order in circumstances not envisaged 3.11

by those provisions, it is always possible for the court to grant relief by resorting to its inherent jurisdiction. Procedures such as freezing injunctions (see Chapter 36) and search orders (Chapter 37) were initially developed by means of the exercise of the High Court's inherent jurisdiction. As an area develops there comes a point when it might be codified by statutory provisions (for example by the Civil Procedure Act 1997 and CPR Part 25 for freezing injunctions and search orders). At that stage the better view is that the inherent jurisdiction no longer applies as the source of the jurisdiction, having been replaced in that area by the provisions in the statute or CPR (*Harrison v Tew* [1990] 2 AC 523; *Raja v Van Hoogstraten (No 9)* [2009] 1 WLR 1143).

Inherent jurisdiction of the county courts

3.12 Being a creature of statute, it was always thought that the county courts had no inherent jurisdiction. Following the rather surprising decision of *Langley v North West Water Authority* [1991] 1 WLR 697, this is possibly no longer the case. Allowing county courts the same scope to act in their inherent jurisdiction is certainly consistent with the principle that under the CPR the High Court and county courts (subject to express restrictions in the CCA 1984, SCA 1981 and Jurisdiction Order 1991) have co-extensive jurisdiction. On the other hand, the Court of Appeal in *Devon County Council v B* (1997) *The Times*, 1 January 1997, following *D v D (County Court Jurisdiction: Injunctions)* [1993] 2 FLR 802, held that county courts have no inherent jurisdiction in relation to the exercise of their powers in children's cases. It is possible that these decisions turn on the Children Act 1989, s 100(3), which provides that applications for the exercise of the court's inherent jurisdiction relating to children by local authorities can only be made with the permission of the High Court, rather than on a general lack of inherent jurisdiction.

B THE OVERRIDING OBJECTIVE

3.13 Rule 1.1 of the CPR provides:

(1) These rules are a new procedural code with the overriding objective of enabling the court to deal with cases justly.
(2) Dealing with a case justly includes, so far as is practicable—

(a) ensuring that the parties are on an equal footing;
(b) saving expense;
(c) dealing with the case in ways which are proportionate—
  (i) to the amount of money involved;
  (ii) to the importance of the case;
  (iii) to the complexity of the issues; and
  (iv) to the financial position of each party;
(d) ensuring that it is dealt with expeditiously and fairly; and
(e) allotting to it an appropriate share of the court's resources, while taking into account the need to allot resources to other cases.

C ACTIVE CASE MANAGEMENT

Rule 1.4(1) of the CPR provides that the court must further the overriding objective by actively managing cases. By r 1.4(2), active case management includes: **3.14**

(a) encouraging the parties to cooperate with each other in the conduct of the proceedings;
(b) identifying the issues at an early stage;
(c) deciding promptly which issues need full investigation and trial and accordingly disposing summarily of the others;
(d) deciding the order in which issues are to be resolved;
(e) encouraging the parties to use an alternative dispute resolution procedure if the court considers that appropriate and facilitating the use of such procedure;
(f) helping the parties to settle the whole or part of the case;
(g) fixing timetables or otherwise controlling the progress of the case;
(h) considering whether the likely benefits of taking a particular step justify the cost of taking it;
(i) dealing with as many aspects of the case as it can on the same occasion;
(j) dealing with the case without the parties needing to attend at court;
(k) making use of technology; and
(l) giving directions to ensure that the trial of a case proceeds quickly and efficiently.

General case management

In the general run of cases there will be active judicial case management at the following stages: **3.15**

(a) At the allocation stage, where not only will the court allocate the case to one of the case management tracks, but it will also give directions setting a timetable for the future steps to be taken in the case. Judges take a particularly active part in case management conferences and other procedural hearings, where they seek to identify and limit the issues between the parties, and ensure the necessary preparatory work for the trial is done within the shortest reasonable time. See Chapter 14.
(b) When the court gives directions on the evidence it will permit to be adduced at trial. This particularly applies to expert evidence, which the court may say is totally unnecessary; or it may say that there should be a single, jointly instructed, expert; or that expert evidence will be restricted to written reports. See Chapter 31.
(c) Regarding listing for trial. The court will be concerned to ensure the trial takes place with as little delay as possible, will make such orders as may be necessary to ensure avoidable delays do not occur, and will make directions to ensure the parties realize they are working towards a trial date or trial window which will only be moved as a last resort. Parties guilty of delay will be penalized by the imposition of sanctions. See Chapters 28 and 38.
(d) At the trial itself, where the court has wide powers to control the sequence of events and to impose time limits on the presentation of evidence and on speeches. See Chapter 39.

(e) Regarding costs, where the proportionality concept may be applied to reduce costs which are out of proportion to the value and complexity of the case, and where parties who have not abided by the ethos encapsulated by the overriding objective may find that they are penalized in costs. See Chapter 43.

Specific instances of active case management

3.16 Active case management can arise in other circumstances as well. For example, the court can take the initiative by staying proceedings which appear to disclose no reasonable cause of action (see Chapter 22), or by listing a summary judgment hearing where it appears a claim or defence has no real prospect of success (see Chapter 21). The court has a general power to make orders and directions of its own initiative (see Chapter 20), and may require a party to provide further information about the issues or evidence in the case, or about the progress made in the case (see Chapter 16). The result is that although litigation is conducted in an adversarial manner, the parties are not at liberty to do as they wish, but must conduct their cases within a framework controlled by the court.

Making use of technology

3.17 The courts are increasingly aware of the savings that can be made by the use of developing technology. Judges may contact solicitors by telephone on small procedural points rather than requiring them to attend court. There is provision in the rules for holding interim hearings by telephone (see Chapter 20). Some documents, particularly draft orders (which are often revised before being approved by the judge), must be submitted to the court by e-mail or on a digital storage device to facilitate production of the formal order. PD 5C provides a scheme, operating in the Admiralty, Commercial and London Mercantile Courts, and the Technology and Construction Courts and the Chancery Division of the High Court at the Royal Courts of Justice, for the electronic issuing of claim forms and electronic filing of documents. On occasion, the court will go even further, such as by allowing evidence to be given by video conferencing, or by ordering that substantial parts of the documentation be provided in electronic form, supported by hypertext or other links to enable the judge to move rapidly from one document to another. Use of technology to this extent is far more likely in particularly heavy litigation. In *Morris v Bank of America National Trust* [2000] 1 All ER 954, the Court of Appeal stressed that use of technology is acceptable only if it will save time or money, and if it will not unfairly prejudice any of the parties.

D INTERPRETING THE CIVIL PROCEDURE RULES

Purposive interpretation

3.18 Courts apply a purposive approach to the interpretation of the CPR, not a restrictive or technical approach (*YD (Turkey) v Secretary of State for the Home Department* [2006] 1 WLR 1646, *R (Corner House Research) v Director of the Serious Fraud Office* [2008] EWHC 246 (Admin)).

New procedural code

By virtue of r 1.1(1), the CPR are declared to be 'a new procedural code'. Making the CPR a new procedural code means that a new start was made (*Re a Debtor (No 1 of 1987)* [1989] 1 WLR 271, a case under the Insolvency Rules 1986, SI 1986/1925, where the same approach is taken). The CPR are not merely a more modern restatement of the old rules (the RSC and CCR), but a complete replacement of those rules. Leading cases adopting this approach include *Biguzzi v Rank Leisure plc* [1999] 1 WLR 1926 on sanctions (see 28.17) and *Nasser v United Bank of Kuwait* [2002] 1 WLR 1868 on security for costs (see 24.20). **3.19**

The courts have found it increasingly difficult to maintain this approach, and there are many examples where old cases (and sometimes the wording of the old rules) have been applied as a guide to the interpretation or application of the CPR. Where the CPR completely fail to deal with a matter, the court can adopt provisions from the pre-CPR rules or practice (*Carnegie v Giessen* [2005] 1 WLR 2510). Examples where the courts have resorted to pre-CPR cases as a guide to current practice include: *Nomura International plc v Grenada Group Ltd* [2007] 2 All ER (Comm) 878 on a technical point in relation to striking out; *Adelson v Associated Newspapers Ltd* [2008] 1 WLR 585 on substituting parties after limitation (see 15.32); *City and Country Properties Ltd v Kamali* [2007] 1 WLR 1219 in relation to the address for service of a defendant while temporarily out of the jurisdiction (see 8.19); and *Vedatech Corporation v Seagate Software Information* (2001) LTL 29/11/01 on security for costs (see 24.21). *Dubai Bank Ltd v Galadari (No 3)* [1990] 1 WLR 731 was applied by *Rubin v Expandable Ltd* [2008] 1 WLR 1099, in interpreting the meaning of 'mentioned' in CPR, r 31.14, and *MA Holdings Ltd v R (George Wimpey UK Ltd)* [2008] NPC 6 applied *Warren v Uttlesford District Council* (1996) COD 262 on non-parties seeking permission to appeal. It could be objected that all these cases are unsound as they fail to apply the principle that the CPR is a new procedural code. They are probably better considered as practical law-making in circumstances where the courts are faced with situations not expressly covered by the CPR. **3.20**

Overriding objective as a guide to interpretation

Where there are no express words in the CPR dealing with a situation, the court is bound to consider which interpretation best reflects the overriding objective when construing the rules (CPR, r 1.2(b); *Totty v Snowden* [2002] 1 WLR 1384 at [34]). Use of the overriding objective is considered more fully at 3.28ff. **3.21**

Natural meaning when interpreting the CPR

The CPR have been deliberately drafted in a plain English style in order to make them intelligible to lay people using the courts. When construing the rules the courts primarily seek to find the natural meaning of the words used. Although CPR, r 1.2(b), says that the court must seek to give effect to the overriding objective when it interprets any rule, the Court of Appeal has said this does not apply when the words of a rule are clear. In *Vinos v Marks & Spencer plc* [2001] 3 All ER 784 (approved in *Godwin v Swindon Borough Council* [2002] 1 WLR 997), May LJ said that interpretation to achieve the overriding objective does not enable the court to say that provisions which are quite plain mean what they do not mean, nor that the plain meaning of the rules should be ignored. The court cannot, therefore, assume a **3.22** discretion in order to assist a deserving case where there is no jurisdiction to make an order, even by resorting to the overriding objective (*Godwin v Swindon Borough Council* [2002] 1 WLR 997 at [45]).

Human rights as a guide to interpretation

3.23 *Goode v Martin* [2002] 1 WLR 1828 held that what would have been the plain meaning of a provision of the CPR applying traditional rules of construction could be avoided in a case where that meaning would have infringed a party's rights under the European Convention on Human Rights. The Human Rights Act 1998, s 3(1), provides that 'so far as it is possible to do so, primary legislation and subordinate legislation must be read and given effect in a way which is compatible with the Convention rights'. To do this, the court was prepared to read additional words into a rule. Further discussion of the impact of the Human Rights Act 1998 on civil procedure can be found at 3.34ff.

Rules of precedent

3.24 Where a provision of the CPR has been construed by a previous decision of a higher court, subsequent cases have to apply the provision in the same way as the previous, binding, decision. The basic rules of precedent are that, although the Supreme Court (until October 2009, the House of Lords) can sometimes depart from its previous rulings, decisions (as opposed to *obiter dicta*) of the Supreme Court, House of Lords, and Court of Appeal are binding on the Court of Appeal and all lower courts. Previous decisions from the county courts and of High Court judges are no more than persuasive. Exceptions to the rules of precedent are applied with great care. Where the point in the previous authority was assumed without argument, even where the point was essential to the earlier decision, a later court can depart from that assumption after hearing full argument (*Kadhim v Brent London Borough Council* (2001) *The Times*, 27 March 2001).

Citing authorities

3.25 *Practice Direction (Citation of Authorities)* [2001] 1 WLR 1001 provides that the following types of authorities should not be cited unless they establish a new principle or extend the law:

(a) law reports of applications attended by one party only;
(b) applications for permission to appeal;
(c) applications that only decide the application is arguable; and
(d) county court cases (other than to illustrate damages in personal injuries claims or to illustrate current authority where no higher authorities are available).

3.26 The same *Practice Direction* says that skeleton arguments will have to justify reliance on decisions that merely apply decided law to the facts, and also decisions from other jurisdictions. Decisions of the ECJ and organs of the European Convention on Human Rights are treated as domestic authorities for this purpose. For each authority cited, the skeleton must state the proposition of law the case demonstrates, and refer to the passages in support. Any bundle or list of authorities must contain a certificate by the advocate that these requirements have been complied with.

Practice Direction (Judgments: Form and Citation) [2001] 1 WLR 194 and *Practice Direction* [2002] 1 All ER 351 introduced a neutral citation method for higher court judgments. A judgment may be cited in the format *Smith v Jones* [2002] EWCA Civ 10 at [30]; [2002] QB 124. 'EWCA' stands for England and Wales, Court of Appeal. 'Civ 10' stands for Civil Division, 10th case of 2002. 'At [30]' stands for paragraph 30 of the judgment (with the paragraph numbering continuing into the second and subsequent judgments). This is designed to assist publication of judgments on the worldwide web. Reports cited in court should be taken from the official Law Reports, and from other series only if unavailable from the Law Reports. Lawyers were criticized in *Bank of Scotland v Henry Butcher* (2003) *The Times*, 20 February 2003 for using the All England Reports and All England Reports Reprint rather than the Weekly Law Reports and English Reports. *Practice Direction (Judgments: Form and Citation)* [2001] 1 WLR 194 also provides that it is permissible to cite judgments by means of copies reproduced from electronic sources. Such copies should preferably be in 12-point font (although 10- or 11-point fonts are acceptable), and the advocate presenting the report must be satisfied that it has not been reproduced in a garbled form. **3.27**

E APPLICATION OF THE OVERRIDING OBJECTIVE

Dealing with cases justly

The main concept in CPR, r 1.1, means that the primary concern of the court is doing justice. Shutting a litigant out through a technical breach of the rules will not often be consistent with this, because the primary purpose of the civil courts is to decide cases on their merits, not to reject them through procedural default. An example of this is *Chilton v Surrey County Council* (1999) LTL 24/6/99, where the Court of Appeal indicated that dealing with a claim justly involved dealing with the real claim, and allowed the claimant to rely on a revised statement of past and future loss and expense quantifying the claim at about £400,000 rather than the original statement, which indicated a claim value of about £5,000. Conversely, standing witnesses down in advance of an application to adjourn a trial was regarded as failing to act justly in *Albon v Naza Motor Trading Sdn Bhd* (2007) LTL 19/11/07, because it prevented the court from determining the application on its merits. **3.28**

Equal footing

In *Maltez v Lewis* (1999) *The Times*, 4 May 1999, the concept of dealing with the parties on an equal footing was held not to extend to the court being able to prevent a party from instructing the lawyers of its choice, even if one side could not afford lawyers as expensive as those being used by the other. In *McPhilemy v Times Newspapers Ltd* [1999] 3 All ER 775, the Master of the Rolls said that, if a party wanted the court to restrain the activities of another party with the object of achieving greater equality, the party making the application had to demonstrate it was itself conducting the proceedings with a desire to limit expense so far as practical. However, the powers of the court to restrain excess did not extend to preventing a party from putting forward allegations which were central to its case. That said, it was open to the court to attempt to control how those allegations were litigated with a view to limiting costs. **3.29**

Proportionality

3.30 Proportionality lies at the heart of much of the CPR. The existence of the three case management tracks (Chapters 25 to 27) is designed to ensure that procedures for preparing cases for trial are in line with the importance and value of each case. Controlling costs is reflected in requirements such as providing costs estimates to the court (see 43.04) and restricting the numbers of experts parties can use (Chapter 31). Proportionality is also important in relation to the imposition of sanctions (Chapter 28) (eg, *Lambeth LBC v Onayomake* (2007) *The Times*, 2 November 2007, where a striking-out order was regarded as disproportionate for relatively minor defaults) and in relation to the extent of searches that may be needed when giving disclosure of documents (Chapter 29). Applications, even if they have some merit, but are on minor matters which the court might regard as tactical posturing, may be dismissed on grounds of proportionality (*TIP Communications LLC v Motorola Ltd* [2009] EWHC 212 (Pat)). Taking a point that particulars of claim were served one minute late was regarded as unmeritorious in the absence of prejudice in *Rogers v East Kent Hospitals NHS Trust* [2009] LS Law Med 153.

Dealing with cases expeditiously and fairly, and saving expense

3.31 In *Adan v Securicor Custodial Services Ltd* [2005] PIQR P79 the claimant asked the court to use CPR, r 3.1(2)(i), which gives the court a power to order separate trials, so that his claim for damages could be decided when he was discharged from long-term hospitalization. The application was refused as contrary to the overriding objective. It would have exposed the defendant's insurers to an uncertain liability for an indefinite period, which was oppressive and undesirable. In *Re Hoicrest Ltd* [2000] 1 WLR 414 it was held that, on the facts, the case was not an appropriate one for using the Part 8 procedure (see Chapter 19). Instead of striking out the proceedings (see Chapter 22), the Court of Appeal allowed the claim to continue as an ordinary Chancery claim, as that was more cost-effective than forcing the claimant to start again by issuing fresh proceedings. This approach was overlooked in *Re Osea Road Camp Sites Ltd* [2005] 1 WLR 760, where a claim was struck out on the ground that the proceedings in question had to be commenced by petition.

Allotting an appropriate share of the court's resources

3.32 In *Stephenson (SBJ) Ltd v Mandy* (1999) *The Times*, 21 July 1999, the Court of Appeal refused to consider the merits of an interim appeal because there was only a short time to trial so the appeal was not a good use of the court's resources. An appeal was also dismissed in *Adoko v Jemal* (1999) *The Times*, 8 July 1999, on the ground of allotting to it no more than an appropriate share of the court's resources. In this case the appellant had failed to correct the notice of appeal despite a warning from the respondent that it was seriously defective, and had failed to comply with the directions relating to appeal bundles. The Court of Appeal spent over an hour trying to sort out the papers, and then decided it was inappropriate that any further share of the court's resources should be allocated to the appeal.

Cooperating

3.33 In *Chilton v Surrey County Council* (1999) LTL 24/6/99, the Court of Appeal decided against the defendant partly because it seemed that the defendant was attempting to take tactical advantage of a mistake by the claimant's solicitors in forgetting to serve the revised statement of past and future loss and expense rather than cooperating with the claimant's solicitors to put matters right. Solicitors were criticized in *King v Telegraph Group Ltd* [2005] 1 WLR 2282, for sending a letter of claim in vituperative language which the court felt was designed to raise hostility and increase costs. There was a breach of the duty to cooperate in *Hertsmere Primary Care Trust v Administrators of Balasubramanium's Estate* [2005] 3 All ER 274, where a party refused to tell the other side the nature of a technical error in a Part 36 offer.

F HUMAN RIGHTS

The European Convention on Human Rights was brought into effect in the United Kingdom by the Human Rights Act 1998. The text of the Act and the Convention can be found in *Blackstone's Civil Practice* (BCP), app 6. In so far as it is possible to do so, primary and subordinate legislation must be read and given effect in a way which is compatible with the rights set out in the Convention (Human Rights Act 1998, s 3(1)). A court finding a statute conflicting with the Convention may make a declaration of incompatibility under s 4, though such a declaration should only be granted to a claimant who is or could be personally adversely affected by the impugned legislation (*Lancashire County Council v Taylor* [2005] 1 WLR 2668). It is unlawful for a public authority to act in a way which is incompatible with a Convention right (s 6(1)). A person who is a victim of any such unlawful act may rely on their Convention rights in any court proceedings, and may bring proceedings under the Act against the public authority (s 7). If the court finds that the public authority has acted unlawfully (or proposes to do so), it may grant such relief or remedy as it considers appropriate (s 8(1)). Damages, however, can only be granted if the court is satisfied that such an award is necessary to afford just satisfaction to the claimant (s 8(3), and see 3.65). The Convention generally only applies to breaches occurring within the territory of a contracting State, and it is only in cases of extreme unfairness that the court will give indirect effect to the Convention (*Barnette v Government of the United States of America* [2004] 1 WLR 2241). However, the actions of British consular officials abroad can be subject to the Convention (*R (B) v Secretary of State for Foreign and Commonwealth Affairs* [2005] QB 643). **3.34**

Where a party seeks to rely in civil proceedings on any provision or right, or seeks a remedy available, under the Human Rights Act 1998, this must be stated in their statement of case with precise details of the rights relied upon and remedies sought (PD 16, para 15.1). This is why claim forms ask the question (under the heading) whether the claim raises any issues under the Act (see figure 8.1). Giving notice to the Crown, and intervention by the appropriate minister, are considered at 3.59–3.60. **3.35**

A court or tribunal determining a question which has arisen in connection with a Convention right must take into account judgments, etc., of the European Court of Human Rights ('ECHR') (Human Rights Act 1998, s 2). One consequence of this has been a move away from a literalistic approach to interpretation towards a purposive approach concentrating on achieving the aims of the Convention right under consideration (*Godin-Mendoza v Ghaidan* [2004] 2 AC 557). The wording of s 2 means that decisions of the ECHR are not binding, but provide authoritative guidance in domestic courts (*R (S) v Chief Constable of South Yorkshire* [2004] 1 WLR 2196). Where there is clear and consistent ECHR case law on a point, a domestic court will need a strong reason before departing from it (*R (Ullah) v Special Adjudicator* [2004] 2 AC **3.36**

323). However, where there is a House of Lords decision on a point, a domestic court below the House of Lords must follow the House of Lords decision even if there is a subsequent conflicting ECHR decision (*Leeds City Council v Price* [2005] 1 WLR 1825).

3.37 The main provisions from the Convention having a direct impact on civil procedure are arts 6, 8, and 10. These provide protection for fair hearings in court proceedings, a right to respect for private and family life, and a right of freedom of expression. The concept of proportionality is considered in the chapter on judicial review at 45.28–45.30.

Right to a fair hearing

Principles relating to a fair hearing

3.38 Article 6(1) of the European Convention on Human Rights provides:

> In the determination of his civil rights and obligations or of any criminal charge against him, everyone is entitled to a fair and public hearing within a reasonable time by an independent and impartial tribunal established by law. Judgment shall be pronounced publicly but the press and public may be excluded from all or part of the trial in the interest of morals, public order or national security in a democratic society, where the interests of juveniles or the protection of the private life of the parties so require, or to the extent strictly necessary in the opinion of the court in special circumstances where publicity would prejudice the interests of justice.

3.39 The basic principle underlying art 6(1) is that civil claims must be capable of being submitted to a judge for adjudication (*Fayed v United Kingdom* (Case No 18/1993/423/502) (1994) 18 EHRR 383). It typically applies where the only forum for deciding a dispute is not an independent and impartial tribunal, or where there are procedural bars on bringing a claim, or where procedural bars prevent a claim being decided on its merits. Article 6(1) is not engaged where the complaint is about how the law is framed, and it cannot be used as a means of creating a substantive right having no basis in national law (*Wilson v First County Trust (No 2)* [2004] 1 AC 816).

3.40 Where it is alleged that art 6 is infringed by a statute which replaces a right to litigate with an administrative system (such as the Child Support Act 1991), or by a tribunal system with limited rights of recourse to the courts, *R (Kehoe) v Secretary of State for Work and Pensions* [2004] 1 WLR 2757 shows there are three questions to be answered:

(a) whether the case involved a determination of the claimant's 'civil rights and obligations'. These are not limited to rights protected by private as opposed to public law. A public law decision can come within the meaning of the expression in art 6 if it has an effect on the claimant's private law rights (*Ringeisen v Austria (No 1)* (1971) 1 EHRR 455; *R (Alconbury Developments Ltd) v Secretary of State for the Environment, Transport and the Regions* [2003] 2 AC 295);
(b) whether the administrative determination of the claimant's rights was subject to control by a court having full jurisdiction to deal with the case as the nature of the case required (*R (Alconbury Developments Ltd) v Secretary of State for the Environment, Transport and the Regions*). The right to resort to judicial review of administrative decisions should satisfy art 6 provided there is no substantial factual investigation required: see *Tower Hamlets London Borough Council v Begum* [2003] 2 AC 430; and
(c) where the claimant's right of access to a court is restricted, whether the restrictions satisfied the test of proportionality. This requires a balance between the legitimate objectives

of the administrative scheme and the means used to achieve them (*R (Kehoe) v Secretary of State for Work and Pensions*).

Rights established by art 6

Under art 6(1) litigants are entitled to a fair hearing before an impartial tribunal. It is for this reason that most, but not all, hearings in civil cases, whether they be trials or interim applications, are in public (CPR, r 39.2; *Werner v Austria* (1997) 26 EHRR 310, and *Clibbery v Allan* [2002] Fam 261). CPR, r 39.2 was challenged as ultra vires in *R (Pelling) v Bow County Court* [2001] UKHRR 165 on the ground that it allows some hearings to be conducted in private, but the challenge was unsuccessful. By way of exception to the general rule, the denial of a hearing and pronouncement of judgment in public in child custody proceedings under the Family Proceedings Rules 1991 (SI 1991/1247), r 4.16(7), is justifiable under art 6(1) of the Convention (*B v United Kingdom* [2001] 2 FCR 221). Although generally art 6(1) requires hearings to be conducted in the presence of the parties, this is only necessary in civil cases where the court has to make a decision relating to a party's personal character (*Muyldermans v Belgium* (1991) 15 EHRR 204). **3.41**

In order to be fair the parties should be afforded equality of arms. While this means that parties should be given adequate time and facilities to pursue their case (*R v Secretary of State for the Home Department, ex p Quaquah* [2000] HRLR 325), it does not mean that a party should be prevented from being represented by a Queen's Counsel on the ground that the other side cannot afford to pay the fees commanded by a QC (*Maltez v Lewis* (1999) *The Times*, 4 May 1999). **3.42**

All the circumstances of the case will be considered in deciding whether a hearing is held within a reasonable time, including the importance and difficulties of the case and the conduct of the parties (*EDC v United Kingdom* [1998] BCC 370). A stay pending payment of the costs of an earlier claim does not conflict with the European Convention on Human Rights, art 6(1). Such a stay can be imposed even where the parties were not entirely the same, provided the second claim arose out of substantially the same facts as the previous claim (*Stevens v School of Oriental and African Studies* (2000) *The Times*, 2 February 2001). **3.43**

Compliance with art 6 requires reasons to be given for a court's decisions. The detail required by art 6 does not exceed that required by domestic law (*English v Emery Reimbold and Strick Ltd* [2002] 1 WLR 2409), but must be sufficient for an appeal court to understand the basis for the decision should there be an appeal. Reasons, even if short and even if for costs orders, must be clear, and cannot be left to inference (*Lavelle v Lavelle* (2004) *The Times*, 9 March 2004). **3.44**

Application of art 6 to civil litigation

Before implementation of the Convention, the House of Lords held that a judge should not sit at a hearing if there was a real danger of bias (*R v Gough* [1993] AC 646). European Convention jurisprudence has established that there will be a breach of art 6 if there is an objectively justified reason or fear of a lack of impartiality on the part of the judge dealing with a case. Accordingly, English judges should now excuse themselves from sitting, not where there is a real danger of bias, but where a fair-minded and informed observer would conclude there was a real possibility of bias (*Porter v Magill* [2002] 2 AC 357). Under art 6(1) judgments must be supported by sufficient reasoning for the parties to be able to understand **3.45** in broad terms why the decision was reached (*Stefan v General Medical Council* [1999] 1 WLR 1293). The level of detail required depends on the nature of the decision. Short reasons are usually all that is given on a refusal of permission to appeal. Just because reasons are short does not mean they infringe art 6(1) (*Hyams v Plender* [2001] 1 WLR 32 at [17]).

3.46 Time limits and limitation periods may infringe art 6(1) if they are disproportionately short (*Perez de Rada Cavanilles v Spain* (1998) 29 EHRR 109, where a three-day time limit was held to infringe art 6(1)). The periods laid down by the Limitation Act 1980 are unlikely to be seen as infringing art 6(1) (see *Stubbings v United Kingdom* (1997) 23 EHRR 213). In *Goode v Martin* [2002] 1 WLR 1828, art 6(1) was used by the court as a basis for reading additional words into CPR, r 17.4, which otherwise would have prevented the claimant from bringing her real claim to trial.

3.47 Applications for summary judgment have been said to be consistent with the need to have a fair trial under art 6(1) (*Three Rivers District Council v Bank of England (No 3)* [2003] 2 AC 1). Likewise, an order for security for costs does not infringe art 6(1), although the right of access to the courts has to be taken into account (*Nasser v United Bank of Kuwait* [2002] 1 WLR 1868). The essential policy when considering matters such as security for costs, CFAs, and costs orders against non-parties, is that the need to protect the successful party by granting an effective costs order has to yield to the right of access to the courts to litigate the dispute in the first place (*Hamilton v Al Fayed (No 2)* [2003] QB 1175 applying art 6(1)).

Right to respect for private and family life

3.48 Article 8 of the European Convention on Human Rights provides:

1. Everyone has the right to respect for his private and family life, his home and his correspondence.
2. There shall be no interference by a public authority with the exercise of this right except such as is in accordance with the law and is necessary in a democratic society in the interests of national security, public safety or the economic well being of the country, for the prevention of disorder or crime, for the protection of health or morals, or for the protection of the rights and freedoms of others.

3.49 Article 8 provides a qualified (see art 8(2)) protection for private and family life. Family life includes the relationships between spouses, parents and children, unmarried couples and their children, and also grandparents and grandchildren (*Marckx v Belgium* (1979) 2 EHRR 330), but not relationships between same-sex couples (*M v Secretary of State for Work and Pensions* [2006] 2 AC 91). The article probably does not protect corporations (*R v Broadcasting Standards Commission, ex p British Broadcasting Corporation* [2001] QB 885). Substantive rules, such as the immunity from suit in respect of out-of-court statements relating to the investigation of crime, often need to be re-assessed to determine whether they comply with Convention rights (*Weston v Weston* [2009] 2 WLR 838, where the established law was held to comply with art 8(2)).

3.50 Article 8(1) may be invoked to protect personal and private details about individuals, information about children, private correspondence, and telephone conversations (see *Halford v United Kingdom* (1997) 24 EHRR 523, which involved telephone conversations from a private office at work). A balance sometimes has to be struck between the protection in art 8(1) and the need for a fair trial in art 6(1). In *Clibbery v Allan* [2002] Fam 261 at [82], it was held that this balance is usually struck in favour of confidentiality where a family law hearing involves children, but is more tilted towards disclosure and open justice when the information involves adults.

Article 8 may have an impact on the use of videos in civil proceedings. They are sometimes used by defendants in personal injuries claims in cross-examining the claimant by playing certain parts of a covertly shot video of the claimant going to the shops, hospital, at work, or in the garden in order to undermine the claimant. Such use will usually be legitimate, but a direction is likely to be made limiting the footage to be shown (in *Rall v Hume* [2001] 3 All ER 248 a direction was made limited to 20 minutes). Although the court will wish to uphold art 8, a video shot inside the claimant's home in clear breach of art 8 was allowed in evidence in *Jones v University of Warwick* [2003] 1 WLR 954. **3.51**

There are limits on the effect of art 8. Since the House of Lords decision in *Wainwright v Home Office* [2004] 2 AC 406 it has been clear there is no tort of invasion of privacy, either at common law or as a result of art 8. Further, it was held in *Marcic v Thames Water Utilities Ltd* [2004] 2 AC 42 that a failure to provide adequate sewerage facilities did not give householders affected by flooding any rights against the water company, whether at common law or under art 8, going beyond the scheme set out in the Water Industry Act 1991. The right of a public authority landlord to enforce a claim for possession under domestic law will, in most cases, provide the justification required by art 8(2) for an interference with an occupier's right to respect of his home under art 8(1) (*Kay v Lambeth London Borough Council* [2006] 2 AC 465). **3.52**

Freedom of expression

Article 10 of the European Convention on Human Rights provides: **3.53**

1. Everyone has the right to freedom of expression. This right shall include freedom to hold opinions and to receive and impart information and ideas without interference by public authority and regardless of frontiers. This article shall not prevent States from requiring the licensing of broadcasting, television or cinema enterprises.
2. The exercise of these freedoms, since it carries with it duties and responsibilities, may be subject to such formalities, conditions, restrictions or penalties as are prescribed by law and are necessary in a democratic society, in the interests of national security, territorial integrity or public safety, for the prevention of disorder or crime, for the protection of health or morals, for the protection of the reputation or rights of others, for preventing the disclosure of information received in confidence, or for maintaining the authority and impartiality of the judiciary.

Article 10(1) provides that everyone has the right to freedom of expression. This right is subject to safeguards in art 10(2), which include restrictions for the protection of the reputation or rights of others. The Human Rights Act 1998, s 12(3), provides that no relief to restrain publication before trial which might affect the art 10(1) right is to be allowed 'unless the court is satisfied that the applicant is likely to establish that the publication should not be allowed'. This has altered the common law test (as set out in *American Cyanamid Co v Ethicon Ltd* [1975] AC 396: see 35.63) in applications for interim injunctions where art 10 rights are in **3.54** issue. While s 12(3) has an important impact in breach of confidence claims, it does not affect the common law position in defamation claims where the defendant relies on the defence of justification (*Greene v Associated Newspapers Ltd* [2005] QB 972).

3.55 Interim injunctions in claims for breach of confidence should normally be governed by *American Cyanamid*, as adapted by the Human Rights Act 1998, s 12(3). Instead of merely showing a serious issue to be tried, in most cases the applicant must establish a case which will probably ('more likely than not') succeed at trial. The court will then exercise its discretion, taking into account the jurisprudence on art 10 and any other relevant matters. In *Cream Holdings v Banerjee* [2005] 1 AC 253, the House of Lords said the court must adopt a flexible approach to s 12(3). If demanding a case that will probably succeed does not achieve the legislative intention behind s 12(3), or fails to give effect to countervailing Convention rights, a lesser degree of likelihood will suffice to satisfy the test. A balance has to be struck between the competing interests in protecting private and family life under art 8(1), freedom of expression under art 10(1), and the protection of the reputation and rights of others under art 10(2): see *Campbell v Mirror Group Newspapers plc* [2004] 2 AC 457. For more detailed discussion see 35.65.

G PROCEDURAL ASPECTS ON RAISING HUMAN RIGHTS POINTS

Jurisdiction

3.56 Claims under the Human Rights Act 1998, s 7(1)(a) in respect of a judicial act must be brought in the High Court (CPR, r 7.11) and within a year of the act complained of (s 7(5)). Other civil claims under the Human Rights Act 1998 can be brought in a county court or the High Court. Deputy High Court judges, masters, and district judges cannot try claims under the Human Rights Act 1998, s 7(1)(a), in respect of a judicial act, nor claims for declarations of incompatibility under s 4 (PD 2B, para 7A).

Statement of case

3.57 Claim forms and appeal notices have boxes on the printed forms for indicating whether the case or appeal raises any point under the Human Rights Act 1998. In addition, the statement of case or appeal notice must set out full details of the human rights point, including the Convention right relied upon, the alleged infringement, and the relief sought (PD 16, para 15.1 and PD 52, para 5.1A).

3.58 In claims for damages in respect of a judicial act the claim must be stated in the statement of case, notice given to the Crown (usually the Lord Chancellor), and the appropriate minister may be joined either on application by the minister or by direction of the court (r 19.4A(3), (4)).

Intervention in human rights claims

3.59 The court may not make a declaration of incompatibility under the Human Rights Act 1998, s 4 (for which see 3.64–3.65), unless 21 days' notice has been given to the Crown (Human Rights Act 1998, s 5 and CPR, r 19.4A(1)). Directions requiring notice to be given will usually be made at a case management conference (PD 19A, para 6.2). In these cases a minister, or other person permitted by the Human Rights Act 1998, is entitled to be joined as a party on giving notice to the court (r 19.4A(2)).

Where claims are made for damages under the Human Rights Act 1998, ss 7(1) or 9(3), in respect of a judicial act, notice must be given to the Crown (r 19.4A(3)). Where the appropriate person (defined in s 9(5) as the minister responsible for the relevant court) does not apply to be joined to such a claim within 21 days or such other period as the court directs, the court may itself join the appropriate minister as a party (r 19.4A(4)). **3.60**

Transfer

If there is a real prospect of the court making a declaration of incompatibility under the Human Rights Act 1998, s 4, that is a factor to be taken into account in considering whether to transfer the claim to the High Court (CPR, r 30.3(2)(g)). **3.61**

Previous findings

In claims for remedies under the Human Rights Act 1998, s 7, in respect of judicial acts alleged to have infringed rights under art 5 of the European Convention (to liberty and security of person), the court hearing the claim may, but is not required to, proceed on the basis of the finding of another court or tribunal that the claimant's rights have been infringed (CPR, r 33.9). **3.62**

Authorities

Lists of authorities relied upon for interpretation under the Human Rights Act 1998, s 2, must be given to the court and the other parties not less than three days before the hearing (PD 39A, para 8.1). **3.63**

Remedies under the Human Rights Act 1998

Under the Human Rights Act 1998, s 8(1), the court may grant such relief or remedy, or make such order, within its powers as it considers just and appropriate. The restriction to granting relief within its powers means that quashing orders, mandatory orders, and prohibitory orders cannot be granted in county court proceedings (because of CCA 1984, s 38(3)). Where the court is satisfied that a legislative provision is incompatible with a Convention right it has a discretion to make a declaration of incompatibility under the Human Rights Act 1998, s 4. Declarations of incompatibility cannot be made by a county court (s 4(5)), and there are restrictions on the making of such declarations in respect of secondary legislation (s 4(4)). Declarations of incompatibility cannot be made where statutes simply fail to protect Convention rights: they are restricted to situations where actual provisions are incompatible (*Re S (Minors) (Care Order: Implementation of Care Plan)* [2002] 2 AC 291 at 322). A declaration of incompatibility does not annul the infringing statutory provision, and is not even binding on the parties to the proceedings in which it is made (s 4(6)). Its main purpose is to alert the legislature to the problem, and enable amending legislation to be passed through a fast track procedure. **3.64**

3.65 Damages for breach of Convention rights should be awarded only where this is 'necessary' to afford just satisfaction to the victim: Human Rights Act 1998, s 8(3). Where a breach has clearly caused significant pecuniary loss, damages may be awarded to place the claimant in the position they would have been in without the breach (*Anufrijeva v Southwark London Borough Council* [2004] QB 1124 at [59]). In other cases, where a breach may result in distress, anxiety, and possibly psychiatric trauma, the primary remedy is to grant a declaration, with damages seen as a last resort. The seriousness of the breach, and resource implications, are important factors (*Anufrijeva v Southwark London Borough Council* [2004] QB 1124). Where damages are appropriate, they should be no lower than in comparable torts, and should so far as possible reflect the English level of damages (*R (KB) v South London and West Region Mental Health Tribunal* [2004] QB 936).

Determining claims for damages for breach of human rights

3.66 There is concern that the costs of bringing claims for compensation for breach of human rights can be disproportionate to the amount of compensation awarded. Normally, these claims must be brought by judicial review, but if damages is the only remedy sought they have to be brought by ordinary claim. Such claims are brought in the Administrative Court (*Anufrijeva v Southwark London Borough Council* [2004] QB 1124). This case made the point that alternatives to litigation, such as making a complaint to an ombudsman, should be considered, and that damages claims should be determined in a summary manner, with no more than three cases being cited, and hearings lasting no more than half a day.

KEY POINTS SUMMARY

3.67
- The CPR and PDs are the procedural rules governing civil proceedings. They are a 'new procedural code', so for most purposes pre-1999 cases are redundant.
- Gaps in the CPR may be filled by resorting to the court's inherent jurisdiction or, very exceptionally, old procedural rules.
- The most important rule is the 'overriding objective' of dealing with claims justly.
- The courts seek to give effect to the overriding objective by active case management.
- It is unlawful for a public authority to act in a way which is incompatible with an ECHR right.
- In civil litigation, the most important Convention rights are the right to a fair trial (art 6), the right to respect for private and family life (art 8), and the right to freedom of expression (art 10).
- Where the court is invited to make a declaration of incompatibility, the relevant minister has to be notified and may intervene.

4

FUNDING LITIGATION

It is a practical fact that litigation can be expensive, and often takes a considerable time to bring to a conclusion. Solicitors acting for a potential litigant are under a professional duty to advise the client on the likely cost of bringing the matter to court, and also to advise on the possible costs liability to the other side. This is important, because the usual rule is that an unsuccessful party will be ordered to pay the costs of the successful party. People contemplating going to law therefore have to take into account the fact that if the claim is unsuccessful they will potentially have to pay not only their own lawyers' fees and expenses, but also those of the other side. If a claim is successful, the other side will normally be ordered to pay costs, but (even if they have the financial means to pay) there is often a difference between what must be paid to one's own solicitors (because these costs are assessed on the indemnity basis: see 43.09), and what is recoverable from the other side, which is usually assessed on the less generous standard basis. **4.01**

Lawyers acting for a party are entitled to seek payment on account as the claim progresses, and are not always expected to wait until the conclusion of the case before asking for payment. A client making payments on account is also not so likely to be taken by surprise by a very large bill. An important consideration for many clients is whether their lawyers will take a case through to trial, if needs be, without demanding any money, or no more than relatively small amounts of money, on account of costs until after the case is completed. If their lawyers are unwilling to act on this basis, clients who are unable to afford to pay either have to abandon their claims, or seek funding from an outside source for their claims. **4.02**

A DUTY TO ADVISE CLIENTS ON FUNDING

4.03 Solicitors are under a professional duty to ensure their clients know the options on funding, and understand their main features. The Solicitors' Code of Conduct 2007 provides that solicitors must discuss with their clients how, when, and by whom any costs are to be met. A breach of the costs provisions of the Solicitors' Code of Conduct does not render the retainer illegal, but can be taken into account in assessing the amount of costs payable (*Garbutt v Edwards* [2006] 1 WLR 2907). The options that should be considered include:

(a) whether the client may be eligible for help under the Community Legal Service (which superseded legal aid from 1 April 2000);
(b) whether the client should be offered the option of funding the claim under a conditional fee agreement ('CFA');
(c) whether the client's liability for own costs may already be covered by insurance;
(d) whether the client's liability for own costs may be met by an employer or trade union or other organization of which the client is a member; and
(e) whether the client's liability for another party's costs may be covered by prepurchased insurance (often called before the event or 'BTE' insurance) and, if not, whether it would be advisable for another party's costs to be covered by after the event ('ATE') insurance.

B TRADITIONAL RETAINER

4.04 The traditional method is for the client to pay the solicitor's costs of conducting a case at an agreed hourly rate. Until relatively recent times, arrangements between solicitors and clients were often very lax, with little or nothing said about charging rates or the incidence of billing for the solicitor's charges. Solicitors often simply relied on being able to charge at reasonable rates for the work they did. If they delayed in billing their clients, the first bill could come as a big shock to the client. Rule 2.02 of the Solicitors' Code of Conduct 2007 requires a solicitor to provide a client with a detailed client care letter at the outset of a retainer which should give the name and status of the person with day-to-day conduct of the case, and whom that person reports to. The letter must give the best information possible about the likely overall cost of the matter, contain details of charging rates, and say when bills are likely to be sent. An example is shown in figure 4.1.

Figure 4.1 Client care letter

Smallwood & Co., Solicitors
Mrs Jane Goddard
Europa Games Importers (Morton) Ltd
Snow Hill Industrial Estate
Morton
Gloucestershire

Figure 4.1 *continued*

Dear Mrs Goddard

Claim against Commodities & Freight Carriers Ltd

I am writing to confirm our discussion in which you confirmed the board of Europa Games Importers (Morton) Ltd wish to instruct this firm to pursue a claim for damages for breach of contract against Commodities & Freight Carriers Ltd. I am Paul Grainer, and I will be dealing with the company's claim. I am an assistant solicitor in this firm.

Board Resolution

At our meeting you agreed to provide me with a copy of the relevant board resolution resolving to pursue this claim and instruct this firm. You also agreed to provide me with copies of the company's last two sets of filed accounts.

Estimated Costs

At this stage I can give no more than a general estimate of the cost of this claim, as one of the most important factors in determining the legal costs in pursuing a claim is the extent to which the defendant will oppose the claim. In some cases a satisfactory settlement can be negotiated without the need for proceedings, but in others proceedings have to be issued in order to focus the defendant's mind on the claim and to convince him that he must treat the claim seriously. In other cases proceedings have to be taken to trial in order to get the court's ruling on the claim. I ought to mention that the majority of claims are settled without a trial taking place.

Although it is impossible to give a precise estimate for the overall costs, the rate charged by this firm for my work is based on an hourly expense rate with an element of profit. The hourly rate for your claim will be £152.00. As a general guide, most letters and telephone conversations are charged on a unit basis, with each unit being 6 minutes or 1/10 of an hour. Meetings with you and witnesses, preparing documents and long letters, and attending court will be charged based on the time spent, or, if estimated, at the rate of 10 minutes per page. My estimate is that this claim will involve approximately 50 hours of time, but it could be more if the claim is heavily defended, or rather less if the defendant is willing to negotiate an early settlement. You will be informed if there is any alteration in this estimate as the claim develops.

Steps in the Claim

I expect that the following steps will be necessary for the purposes of your claim: preparation of your written statement; detailed letter of claim to the defendant; correspondence with the defendant's insurers and solicitors throughout the claim; obtaining an expert's report; obtaining details of your financial losses; issuing court proceedings; preparing statements of case; considering documents served by the defendant's solicitors in the proceedings; disclosing all relevant documentation to the defendant; completing various court documents; tracing and taking statements from other witnesses; possible attendance at court for a case management conference; arranging for a barrister to represent your company at trial; preparing papers for trial; attending trial; dealing with recovery of damages and costs, which may include preparation of a detailed bill.

Responsibility for Disbursements

Court fees, expert's reports, experts attending trial, and barristers' fees are known as 'disbursements', and have to be paid in addition to this firm's expense rate costs. Disbursements are likely to be in the region of £3,500.

In this case I expect to recover damages from the defendant and a contribution towards your company's costs. Regardless of the outcome of the case, you will be fully liable for this

Figure 4.1 *continued*

firm's costs and disbursements. If costs are recovered from the defendant these are likely to cover the bulk of the costs incurred by this firm, but I have to warn you that it is not uncommon for there to be a shortfall between the costs recovered from the other side and the costs of this firm, which the company will remain liable to pay.

Other Methods of Funding

I must advise you that if you bring proceedings and the claim fails, it is most likely that the court will order you to pay the defendant's costs. There are legal expenses insurance policies which may be taken out to cover both your legal costs and those of your opponent, which we discussed when we met. At this stage you do not wish to take this further, but as the claim progresses this may need to be reconsidered. We also discussed conditional fee, or 'no win, no fee', arrangements, which you also decided against at this stage. Again, this may need to be reconsidered, particularly if proceedings are to be issued. We discussed help under the Community Legal Service, but, as I advised, this is not available for claims brought by companies.

Next Steps

Every effort will be made to deal with your claim efficiently and quickly. However, if any problems arise which we cannot resolve between ourselves, there is a complaints procedure in operation in this firm. The initial point of contact is Miss Rosemary Williams, who is a partner in the firm, and you should contact her in the event of a complaint. Mr Smallwood, the senior partner, has final responsibility for all complaints. I can provide a copy of our complaints procedure on request.

When you have had a chance to consider this letter, please sign one of the copies provided and return it to me. The other copy is for your records. If there is anything in this letter or about your claim that you wish to discuss, please feel free to telephone or arrange an appointment.

Yours sincerely

4.05 Charge-out rates are based on the salaries of the staff and fee earners working at the solicitor's office together with an element representing the firm's profits. The modern approach is to fix a single hourly rate for each fee earner in the firm (or grade of fee earner) taking these factors into account. A variation on this approach is to adopt regional rates for different grades of fee earner based on guideline rates published by the Supreme Court Costs Office. These can be seen in BCP, Chapter 68, tables 68.3 to 68.5. Grade A covers solicitors with over eight years' post-qualification experience in litigation. Grade B covers more junior solicitors and senior legal executives with over four years' litigation experience. Grade C covers legal executives and fee earners of equivalent experience. Grade D covers trainees and para-legals. An alternative method has been to quote a lower hourly rate, but to add a mark-up of a variable percentage (say 50 per cent for ordinary litigation). Clients tend to find being quoted a simple hourly rate easier to understand.

4.06 In addition, the client will be expected to pay for disbursements. These are sums paid by the firm during the course of litigation in respect of experts' and counsel's fees, the cost of making copies of photographs, and similar expenditure. It is normal for solicitors to ask for sums on account of costs when they are first retained, and periodically during the course of litigation.

C LEGAL EXPENSES INSURANCE

Some clients have the benefit of legal expenses insurance, often as part of their motor or home insurance policies (BTE insurance). In these cases the costs incurred on behalf of the client will be met by the legal expenses insurer. Often these insurers require the client's lawyers to provide advice on the merits of the claim from time to time so they can assess whether continuing the litigation can be justified under the terms of the insurance. **4.07**

D AFTER THE EVENT INSURANCE

A client will often be justifiably concerned about meeting the potential liability for the other side's costs if the case is unsuccessful. The usual rule is that the unsuccessful party in proceedings is ordered to pay the successful party's costs (CPR, r 44.3(2)). The other side's costs generally have to be paid out of the losing party's personal resources. It may be possible for the client to arrange ATE insurance to cover the other side's costs. Unless the prospects of success are very high, such insurance is quite expensive, with the premium being related to the likely level of the other side's costs and the risk of losing. The premium is potentially recoverable against the unsuccessful party (r 44.3A). **4.08**

Callery v Gray [2001] 1 WLR 2112 and *Callery v Gray (No 2)* [2001] 1 WLR 2142 considered arguments on whether the insurance premium for ATE insurance covering the claimant's liability for the defendant's costs could be recovered from the defendant in a case which was settled before substantive proceedings were issued. It was held that this could be recovered in costs-only proceedings under CPR, r 44.12A, as 'insurance against the risk of . . . liability' within the Access to Justice Act 1999 (AJA 1999), s 29. Further, provided the premium is reasonable, it will usually be recoverable against an unsuccessful defendant even if it is taken out soon after the solicitors are retained, and before the defendant's response to the claim is known. The premium in the claim was £350. On the facts this was not manifestly disproportionate to the risk, and could be recovered against the defendant. These two cases were left undisturbed by the House of Lords (*Callery v Gray (Nos 1 and 2)* [2002] 1 WLR 2000) on the basis that guidance in this area is best provided by the Court of Appeal. **4.09**

A number of companies offer claimants comprehensive packages which include ATE insurance in return for a single 'premium'. In *Re Claims Direct Test Cases* [2003] 4 All ER 508 the court investigated the insurance element of the Claims Direct scheme, which charged customers a premium of £1,250. It was held that the insurance element of the premium recoverable under the AJA 1999, s 29, was £621.13. Any work done by a claims manager which would otherwise have had to be done by the solicitor was held to be properly recoverable as part of the solicitor's bill. **4.10**

Where a claimant has BTE insurance, perhaps as an adjunct to a motor insurance policy, then in the ordinary course of events the BTE insurer should be used, and it would be unreasonable for the claimant to enter into an ATE policy in conjunction with a CFA (*Sarwar v Alam* [2002] 1 WLR 125). Checking whether there is BTE cover, or funding from a trade union or employer, **4.11** should be one of the first tasks of a solicitor taking on new instructions. Where BTE insurance will cover the claim, it is likely to be unreasonable to allow the premium for ATE cover under the AJA 1999, s 29. However, where the BTE cover under the driver's policy is available to a claimant who was a passenger claiming against that driver, it may well be reasonable to enter into an ATE policy (with the premium being recoverable against the driver), particularly where the driver refuses consent or where the policy allows the driver's BTE insurer full conduct and control of the claim against the driver (*Sarwar v Alam*).

E MAINTENANCE AND CHAMPERTY

4.12 A solicitor wishing to assist a client who cannot afford the costs of litigation may be prepared to take up the case on terms that payment for the work done on the client's behalf will be sought only if the claim is successful. Agreements of this sort have traditionally been regarded as illegal and unenforceable, because they savour of champerty and maintenance. 'Maintenance' describes supporting or intermeddling in litigation without just cause. 'Champerty' is an aggravated form of maintenance under which the person intermeddling with the litigation seeks to obtain a share in the proceeds of the suit (see *Giles v Thompson* [1994] 1 AC 142). Despite the fact that maintenance and champerty are no longer crimes or torts (since the Criminal Law Act 1967), contracts savouring of maintenance or champerty remain contrary to public policy and are, in contract terms, illegal (see s 14(2)). The illegality in the funding arrangement also meant that a successful party with an illegal funding arrangement could not recover costs from the losing party, by reason of the so-called 'indemnity principle'.

4.13 The law in this area has been developing. With effect from 1 April 2000 legal aid was replaced by the Community Legal Service. One of the effects of this reform was that far less public money was available for funding civil proceedings than had been available under the legal aid scheme. To compensate for this, and to preserve meaningful rights to access to justice for those who were no longer entitled to legal aid (and also to assist middle-income members of the public), the CLSA 1990 and the Access to Justice Act 1999 were passed to encourage the use of one particular form of contingency fee arrangement, known as conditional fee agreements (CFA) (see 4.15). Since 2 June 2003, it has been possible to enter into a special type of CFA under which the client is liable to pay his legal representative's costs only to the extent that they are recovered from the other side (Conditional Fee Agreements (Miscellaneous Amendments) Regulations 2003 (SI 2003/1240)), abrogating the indemnity principle for this type of CFA.

4.14 Further development is proposed in the *Jackson Review of Civil Litigation Costs* (2009, Ministry of Justice). Among the proposals are the abolition of the indemnity principle, abolishing the recoverability of success fees from unsuccessful parties, and the legalization of contingency fees. In a successful contingency fee case the legal representatives receive a percentage of the damages recovered by their client, whereas in a CFA case the success fee element is simply a percentage uplift of the normal costs that are payable by the unsuccessful party.

F CONDITIONAL FEE AGREEMENTS

Nature of CFAs

Under a CFA a solicitor may agree that the client will be liable to pay his or her costs only if the claim is successful, but if it is successful, the solicitor will be entitled to charge at his or her usual rate (the 'base costs') plus a 'success fee' calculated as a percentage uplift on those usual costs. The success fee will be a percentage of the costs otherwise chargeable to the client, and should be related to the risks involved in the litigation. It cannot be more than 100 per cent of the solicitor's usual fees. Subject to insurance, the costs of the other side may still be payable by the client. **4.15**

Statutory authorization for CFAs was conferred by the CLSA 1990, s 58. Since 1998 it has been possible to enter into CFAs in all types of civil litigation other than family work (Conditional Fee Agreements Order 1998 (SI 1998/1860)). Any concern that a CFA complying with the statutory requirements might be attacked by the opposite side as savouring of maintenance or champerty was removed by *Hodgson v Imperial Tobacco Ltd* [1998] 1 WLR 1056. Most of the technical rules on the format of CFAs were revoked with effect from 1 November 2005 (Conditional Fee Agreements (Revocation) Regulations 2005 (SI 2005/2305)). The only continuing requirements are that a CFA must: **4.16**

(a) be in writing;
(b) relate to a type of case where CFAs are permitted (all civil proceedings other than family cases); and
(c) specify the success fee, if any, which must not exceed 100 per cent.

In cases where counsel is instructed there will be a CFA between the client and the solicitor and a second CFA between the solicitor and counsel. Model forms of CFAs have been drafted in consultation between the Law Society and the Bar Council. **4.17**

Although entering into a CFA with one's solicitor means not being liable to pay for that solicitor's work if the case is lost, a major concern for most clients is whether they will then be liable to pay the other side's costs. The answer is that, in accordance with the rule that costs normally follow the event, they usually will. However, there are several insurance companies that provide ATE policies designed precisely to cover this situation at a reasonably modest cost. A further question is whether the client or the solicitor should meet the disbursements payable (such as court and experts' fees). This will be dealt with in the CFA between the client and the solicitor. The result is that most clients entering into CFAs will have to pay a modest premium for insurance against the risk of paying the costs of the other side, and may (depending on the agreement with the solicitor) have to pay the disbursements. **4.18**

Notice to the other side

So that opponents know what they are up against, the lawyers acting under a CFA are required to disclose to the other side (as part of the pre-action protocol, and when they take the first step in litigation) that they are acting under a CFA (PD Costs, para 19.2). This is done using form N251. It must state the date of the CFA, identify the claims to which the CFA relates, **4.19** indicate whether ATE insurance has been taken out, and, if so, the date of the policy, the name of the insurer, and the claims to which it relates (para 19.4). There is no obligation to give details of the success fee.

Costs against non-funded party

4.20 A party who is successful will usually be awarded costs against the unsuccessful party. If the successful party has the benefit of a CFA, the usual costs order includes not only the lawyers' base costs, but also most of the success fee and any ATE or BTE insurance premium (CPR, r 44.3A). The part of the success fee that can be recovered against the unsuccessful party is the uplift relating to the risks of the litigation. The unsuccessful party cannot be ordered to pay any part of the success fee relating to the cost to the legal representatives of delayed receipt of their fees and expenses (r 44.3B(1)(a)). The recoverable uplift applies to the costs of the proceedings including the costs of any assessment of costs (see *Crane v Canons Leisure Centre* [2008] 2 All ER 931 and 43.05 to 43.12).

Level of the success fee

4.21 The maximum success fee is 100 per cent of the legal representatives' base costs. Theoretically, a 100 per cent success fee is appropriate for a claim with a 50:50 chance of success. This is because, if the lawyers have two such cases, they will get double their fees on the successful claim, and nothing for the unsuccessful claim. At the other end of the scale, in *Callery v Gray* [2001] 1 WLR 2112 (confirmed by the House of Lords [2002] 1 WLR 2000), Lord Woolf LCJ made the point that it could not be said that any case was without risk. A standard 12.5 per cent success fee is provided by CPR, r 45.11(2), for simple road traffic claims worth up to £10,000 which are settled without issuing proceedings. For road traffic claims exceeding the small claims track threshold, r 45.16 provides for a 12.5 per cent success fee if a claim concludes before trial, and a 100 per cent success fee if a claim concludes at trial. For employers' liability personal injury claims the usual success fees are 25 per cent if the claim is settled before trial, and 100 per cent if the claim reaches trial (r 45.21). If there are special features impacting on prospects then of course some other level of uplift may be appropriate.

G COMMUNITY LEGAL SERVICE

4.22 Public funding of litigation is administered by the Legal Services Commission, with funding in civil cases being provided by help under the Community Legal Service ('CLS'). The CLS fund is used to provide appropriate legal services that effectively meet the needs of individuals (AJA 1999, s 4). Restrictions mentioned in s 4 include the need to have regard to the nature and importance of the legal problem, the priorities set by the government, and the resources made available to the fund. The courts have no power to provide litigants with such funding (*Perotti v Collyer-Bristow* [2004] 2 All ER 189). The scheme encompasses advice, assistance and representation by lawyers, and also other types of services including those provided by the not-for-profit sector. The CLS may use the fund by making contracts with, or grants to, service providers. It may itself provide services to the public, and it may make loans and grants to individuals so they can purchase services themselves (s 6).

Levels of service

There are various 'levels of service' under the Community Legal Service. The idea is that the amount of public funding given to a case should be commensurate with its needs, so that limited funding will be given if that is all that is needed, but that full public funding will be given to the most deserving cases. **4.23**

Legal help

This is the lowest level of service, and includes providing advice and legal assistance on things like how the law applies to a particular case. It is intended for people on low incomes who need initial advice and to assist with the early investigation of claims, and is intended to provide a limited amount of legal help at a modest cost to the taxpayer. **4.24**

Help at court

This authorizes legal representation for the purposes of a particular hearing, without the lawyer becoming the client's legal representative in the proceedings. Again, the intention is that limited legal assistance will be given, covering no more than is necessary, so as to keep the cost to the taxpayer to the minimum. **4.25**

Legal representation

This covers individuals contemplating legal proceedings or who are parties to proceedings, and will fund 'litigation services', 'advocacy services', and all the legal assistance usually given before and during proceedings, and in achieving or giving effect to any compromise. Legal representation is not a level of service in itself, but encompasses the following levels: **4.26**

(a) 'investigative help', which is aimed at cases which require substantial investigation before an assessment can be made whether legal proceedings are justified;
(b) 'full representation', which, subject to any restrictions imposed on an individual case, can provide full public funding for bringing or defending a claim; and
(c) 'controlled legal representation'. This covers work involving cases before a mental health review tribunal and asylum and immigration tribunals.

Family help

Family help may be provided in relation to family disputes, and may include assistance in resolving a dispute through negotiation or otherwise. It does not cover representation at a contested final hearing or appeal. It encompasses two levels of service. Family help (lower) is limited to all steps up to issue of proceedings. It is controlled work, which means it can only be provided by firms with a family category specialist quality mark. Family help (higher) can be used to issue proceedings and for representation in such proceedings other than at a contested final hearing. It is licensed work, which can only be provided by contracting organizations with a family category specialist quality mark. **4.27**

Specific directions

Other services are not strictly levels of service covered by the main Community Legal Service scheme, but there is some public funding of other cases if a specific order or **4.28** direction is made. This may happen in important test cases and possibly also in group litigation.

Excluded categories

4.29 Public funding under the Community Legal Service is not available in claims for damages for personal injuries or death (except that clinical disputes are within the scheme). Also excluded are:

(a) negligent damage to property;
(b) conveyancing;
(c) boundary disputes;
(d) the making of wills;
(e) matters relating to trust law (except applications in relation to ownership or possession of the applicant's home);
(f) defamation and malicious falsehood (although in *Steel v United Kingdom* (Application No 6841/01) (2005) *The Times*, 16 February 2005, the denial of public funding for a complex libel case was found to be a breach of the European Convention on Human Rights, art 6(1));
(g) matters relating to company or partnership law;
(h) matters relating to the carrying on of a business; and
(i) attending asylum interviews.

CLS Contracting

4.30 Only organizations who have entered into the Unified Contract (2007) with the CLS are able to commence controlled work and licensed work in civil categories of law or the residual list. All the phrases in the previous sentence have special meanings. Broadly they mean that a provider has to have a standard contract with the CLS if it is to provide:

(a) initial advice or representation in controlled work, which comprises:
- legal help
- help at court
- controlled legal representation before the Mental Health Review Tribunal, Immigration Appeal Tribunal, and immigration adjudicators
- family help (lower)

(b) licensed work, which covers:
- all legal representation in civil matters not falling into any other category
- family help (higher).

Financial eligibility

4.31 Help under the Community Legal Service is available to clients who are unable to afford to litigate. The financial limits are set at very low levels, although they are subject to annual uprating (Community Legal Service (Financial) Regulations 2000 (SI 2000/516) as amended). Some Children Act 1989 and related cases do not have any financial eligibility requirement (reg 3). For other types of case, generally, applicants in receipt of certain means-tested State benefits, such as income support and income-based jobseeker's allowance, are eligible (reg 4). Other applicants have to satisfy the eligibility requirements in reg 5, which prescribes different financial limits for different types of levels of help under the Community Legal Service scheme. There are detailed rules on what is included, and on matters to be deducted and disregarded.

Those who satisfy the eligibility rules fall into two categories. Those who are least well off **4.32**
receive funding entirely financed by the State. Those over certain stated limits have to pay contributions towards the cost of the legal services provided (reg 38), which are payable by one-off payments or by instalments, to the assessing authority. This will be the Legal Services Commission in relation to legal representation, otherwise the supplier of the legal services (regs 2 and 38(5)).

Individual

Public funding under the Community Legal Service is available only to individuals (AJA 1999, **4.33**
s 4). Consequently, help is not available to limited liability companies, although it may be available to partnerships, though not on matters of partnership law or relating to the carrying-on of the firm's business (see 4.29).

Criteria for funding

There are detailed rules setting out the criteria for granting the different levels of help under **4.34**
the Community Legal Service laid down by the Funding Code produced by the Legal Services Commission under the AJA 1999, s 8. These are intended to reflect the requirements of the different levels of service, and also to ensure that public money is targeted at the cases that deserve or need it. For example, there are nine criteria for granting full representation:

(a) Funding may be refused if there is alternative funding (other than by way of CFAs, but see (g) below) available.
(b) Funding may be refused if there is a complaint system or ombudsman which should be tried first.
(c) Funding may be refused if the application is premature.
(d) Funding may be refused if another level of service is more appropriate.
(e) Funding may be refused if it is unreasonable, eg, in the light of other proceedings.
(f) Funding will be refused if the claim is likely to be allocated to the small claims track.
(g) Funding will be refused in cases where funding under a CFA is suitable and if the client is likely to be able to enter into such an arrangement.
(h) Funding will be refused if the prospects are unclear (for which investigative help may be appropriate); or the prospects are borderline (unless funding should be given because of public interest reasons or the overwhelming importance of the claim to the client); or if the prospects are poor.
(i) Funding will or may be refused on cost–benefit grounds.

There are further criteria for funding set out in the Funding Code which are applied in very **4.35**
expensive claims (Funding Code, section 6); judicial review cases (section 7); claims against public authorities (section 8); clinical negligence claims (section 9); housing cases (section

10); family matters (section 11); mental health matters (section 12); and immigration cases (section 13).

Merits of the case

4.36 The Funding Code divides cases into six categories regarding the prospects of success on the substantive dispute:

(a) 'very good', meaning 80 per cent or more;
(b) 'good', meaning 60 per cent to 80 per cent;
(c) 'moderate', meaning 50 per cent to 60 per cent;
(d) 'borderline', meaning that because of difficult disputes of fact, law, or expert evidence it is not possible to say that the prospects of success are better than 50 per cent, but not being so weak as to fall into the 'poor' category;
(e) 'poor', meaning clearly less than 50 per cent, so the claim is likely to fail; and
(f) 'unclear', meaning that the case does not fall into any of the other categories because further investigation is needed.

Cost–benefit criteria

4.37 Funding will be refused if the benefit to be gained does not justify the level of costs likely to be incurred.

4.38 In money claims, help under the Community Legal Service may, in general, be granted only if:

(a) the prospects are very good (80 per cent plus), and the value of the claim exceeds the likely level of the costs;
(b) the prospects are good (60–80 per cent), and the value of the claim is at least twice the likely level of costs; or
(c) the prospects are moderate (50–60 per cent, category (c)), and the value of the claim is at least four times the likely level of costs.

4.39 In non-money claims the test is whether the likely benefits justify the likely costs, such that a reasonable private paying client would be prepared to litigate.

4.40 Funding may be allowed despite costs outstripping the benefits, given the risks, if there is a wider public interest or if the claim is of overwhelming importance to the client, such as where the claim concerns the life, liberty, physical safety, or housing of the applicant or his family.

Counsel advising in publicly funded cases

4.41 Counsel are frequently instructed to advise on the merits of cases for the purpose of obtaining or continuing public funding. Guidelines for this purpose have been drafted by the Legal Services Commission, and appear as Annex E of the Code of Conduct of the Bar of England and Wales. Counsel instructed for this purpose should consider whether it is necessary to have a conference in order to assess the reliability of the evidence where it is likely to be contested.

In making this decision counsel should take into account whether such a conference is likely to be cost-effective. The written opinion produced should state the level of service for which it is being written, and the category of case involved. Any relevant excluded work should be identified. It should then address the issues so as to provide the information and counsel's opinion on the law that the Commission will require in making its decision whether to grant public funding. It should be written in sufficient detail to enable the Commission to assess the relative strength of opposing cases, and to form a view on the likely outcome of legal points, without having to go outside the opinion. It should also draw attention to any lack of material which might bear on the outcome. It should address the relevant criteria for the funding decision (this does not mean that every criterion needs to be mentioned), and also any relevant wider public interest. An important issue, of course, is counsel's view on the merits for the purposes of cost–benefit assessment. The likely level of costs is usually a matter dealt with by the solicitors in the case.

Statutory charge

By virtue of the AJA 1999, s 10(7), the sums expended by the Legal Services Commission in funding the case and any other sums (such as interest on late payments of contributions) constitute a first charge on any property recovered or preserved in the proceedings or by any settlement or compromise of the dispute. This means that any money (or other property) recovered in a publicly funded claim automatically becomes the subject of an unwanted charge in favour of the State, which can use the damages recovered to reimburse itself for the costs incurred on behalf of the publicly funded client. **4.42**

The underlying principle is to place a publicly funded party in a similar position to a party privately funding litigation, whose primary responsibility at the end of proceedings is to pay the costs incurred by his or her own solicitors in bringing or defending the claim. **4.43**

The charge applies only if there is a net liability to the Legal Services Commission. This means that it is first necessary to calculate the total costs incurred on behalf of the publicly funded client, then deduct any contributions paid by the publicly funded client, and also deduct any costs paid by the other side. The statutory charge will be for the amount, if any, of the balance. The charge attaches to any property recovered or preserved in the claim. This includes, in the case of proceedings concluded by a court order, any property or money which was the subject matter of the proceedings, and in the case of proceedings concluded by a settlement, any property or money received under the settlement, even if it was not claimed in the proceedings (*Van Hoorn v Law Society* [1985] QB 106). Property is 'recovered' if the publicly funded client gains ownership or possession of it through the proceedings. It is 'preserved' if another's claim to ownership or possession is defeated. **4.44**

A number of exemptions to the statutory charge are laid down by the Community Legal Service (Financial) Regulations 2000 (SI 2000/516), reg 44. **4.45**

Whenever property is recovered or preserved for a publicly funded person, it is the duty of that person's solicitor to inform the Commission immediately so that the charge can be registered and enforced. It can be enforced in the same way as other charges (Community Legal **4.46**

Service (Financial) Regulations 2000 (SI 2000/516), reg 51). Enforcement can be postponed if immediate repayment would be unreasonable and if the charge relates to property to be used as a home for the client or his dependants, or, where the relevant proceedings are family proceedings, it relates to money to pay for such a home (reg 52). Simple interest, at 5 per cent per annum until 30 September 2005, and then at 8 per cent per annum, is payable on the amount used for this purpose (reg 53).

4.47 Solicitors have professional duties to advise clients who apply for public funding of the effects of the statutory charge. This should be done both personally and in writing.

Payment to Commission of sums received

4.48 By reason of the fact that costs and damages recovered by a publicly funded party are subject to the first charge in favour of the Legal Services Commission, only the publicly funded party's solicitor or the Commission can give a valid discharge for the amount paid (Community Legal Service (Costs) Regulations 2000 (SI 2000/441), reg 18). In no circumstances should damages or costs be paid to the publicly funded party directly. Money paid to the client's solicitor must be paid forthwith to the Commission (reg 20). It is then applied, after assessment or agreement of the publicly funded party's costs, in discharging the costs protected by the Commission's statutory charge, and the balance (if any) is then paid to the client (reg 22). Publicly funded clients need to be aware that there is an additional delay in actually receiving any money from a successful claim caused by this requirement to pay sums recovered to the Commission pending assessment of the publicly funded costs.

Revocation and discharge

4.49 Public funding may be revoked or discharged on a number of grounds. Decisions to revoke are made on the ground of misconduct by the publicly funded client, whereas discharge may occur for perfectly innocent reasons, such as the death of the client, completion of the work, or where the client's circumstances change so he or she is no longer eligible. The solicitor's retainer terminates immediately (subject to any review) on the withdrawal of public funding by revocation or discharge (Community Legal Service (Costs) Regulations 2000 (SI 2000/441), reg 4). Revocation of public funding means that the client is treated as never having been publicly funded. In such a case the client is required to pay to the Commission all costs paid or payable under the certificate, and is liable to pay the solicitor the difference between the full indemnity-basis costs incurred by the solicitor and the lower public funding rates payable to the solicitor from the Commission (Community Legal Service (Financial) Regulations 2000 (SI 2000/516), reg 41). Discharge of a certificate operates only in the future, so the client remains treated as covered by the certificate until the date it is discharged.

Duties to the Commission

4.50 Publicly funded clients and their legal representatives are under continuing duties to comply with the provisions of the AJA 1999 and the regulations and Funding Code made under the Act. These duties are directed at ensuring that public funding is granted and continued only in justifiable cases. Legal representatives owe a duty to bring to the attention of the Legal

Services Commission any matter which might affect the client's entitlement to funding or the terms of the certificate. Where counsel are under an obligation to draw matters to the attention of the Commission, this is usually done by drawing it to the attention of the solicitors and asking them to pass it on to the Commission. Solicitors must draw matters relevant to this duty directly to the attention of the Commission.

Protection against costs and costs against the Legal Services Commission

Publicly funded litigants are generally protected against having to pay the costs of the other side if they are unsuccessful, by virtue of the AJA 1999, s 11(1), and the Community Legal Service (Costs Protection) Regulations 2000 (SI 2000/824). This is considered further at 43.68ff, together with the related topic of obtaining costs orders against the Legal Services Commission where an unsuccessful claimant has the benefit of costs protection under s 11(1). **4.51**

KEY POINTS SUMMARY

- Solicitors are under a professional duty to advise clients on the options for funding litigation. **4.52**
- The advice, and agreed funding method, should be confirmed in writing in a 'client care letter'.
- Most commercial clients simply pay their lawyers under the traditional retainer, normally with an agreed hourly rate.
- CFAs, or 'no win, no fee' agreements, are increasingly common. They allow a lawyer to agree not to charge the client if the proceedings are unsuccessful, but to charge an uplift or 'success fee' of up to 100 per cent over the solicitor's usual costs if the proceedings are successful.
- Public funding is administered by the Legal Services Commission under the Community Legal Service.
- Public funding is rarely met in commercial litigation. It is restricted to individuals with modest income and capital, and there are wide exclusions from the scheme. Even where the scheme applies, there are exacting requirements to be met before public funding becomes available.

5

PRE-ACTION PROTOCOLS

5.01 In almost every case, before proceedings are issued, it is expected that the claimant will enter into correspondence to give the intended defendant a chance to negotiate a compromise to the dispute. If this is successful, both sides will save a great deal in legal costs and the effort required in conducting litigation. There are exceptions. Where a limitation period is about to expire, or if the claimant needs to apply for a freezing or search order, pre-action correspondence may be extremely unwise (see, eg, 36.04). For most cases, however, the courts expect the parties to make clear to each other their allegations and answers on the main issues in the dispute, and to cooperate with each other in making pre-action investigations into the evidence (particularly investigations involving experts). Doing so will put the parties in a position where they can make offers to settle on an informed basis at an early stage without needing to have recourse to proceedings.

A PRE-ACTION PROTOCOLS

To promote consistency in the approach to pre-action correspondence and investigations the Ministry of Justice has published eleven pre-action protocols, covering personal injury, low value road traffic accidents ('RTA'), clinical negligence, disease and illness, rent arrears, housing disrepair, mortgage possession, construction and engineering, professional negligence, defamation, and judicial review cases. Compliance with an applicable protocol is regarded as the normal, reasonable approach to pre-action conduct, and any departure may have to be explained to a court if litigation ensues, and may be met with sanctions imposed by the court (see 5.23). They apply to third party proceedings (Chapter 18) as well as to normal proceedings between claimants and defendants (*Daejan Investments Ltd v Park West Club Ltd* [2004] BLR 223). **5.02**

The published protocols do not cover commercial and contractual claims, or many other types of litigation. Such cases are governed by general pre-action guidance set out in PD Pre-action conduct, described at 5.04–5.05. This chapter will then describe the important features of the professional negligence and personal injuries protocols. It then discusses pre-action notification of defendants in road traffic cases and claims against the Motor Insurers' Bureau. It ends by considering pre-action offers to settle. The RTA protocol, which has detailed related rules within the CPR, is described in Chapter 6. **5.03**

B CASES NOT COVERED BY PRE-ACTION PROTOCOLS

In cases not covered by an approved protocol, the court will expect the parties, in accordance with the overriding objective, to act reasonably in exchanging information and documents relevant to the claim and generally in trying to avoid the necessity for the start of proceedings. This means that the parties should follow a reasonable procedure, suitable to the particular circumstances. Normally this will involve the claimant writing a detailed letter of claim complying with the requirements of PD Pre-action conduct, Annex A, para 2. These include setting out the facts and the basis of the claim, what the claimant wants from the defendant, and a list of the essential documents relied upon in support of the claim. The letter should include the principal matters relied upon, rather than needing to set out every detail (*TJ Brent Ltd v Black and Veatch Consulting Ltd* [2008] EWHC 1497 (TCC)). A party who has entered into a CFA or taken out ATE insurance should notify the other side immediately, which often means with the letter before claim (this applies to all cases, including those covered by specific protocols: see PD Pre-action conduct, para 9.3). If a claimant brings and loses a claim not governed by any pre-action protocol without having sent a letter before claim, the court may make an order for indemnity basis costs (*Phoenix Finance Ltd v Fédération Internationale de l'Automobile* (2002) *The Times*, 27 June 2002 and see 43.27). **5.04**

The defendant should be given a reasonable time to reply, based on the nature of the case. In simple debt cases this may be 14 days, rising to 90 days in complex matters (PD Pre-action conduct, para 7.2). A full response should say whether liability is accepted in full, or in part, or denied (Annex A, para 4.1). If liability is denied the response must give detailed reasons **5.05** and list the essential documents relied upon (Annex A, para 4.2). Both parties are entitled to ask for copies of documents in the possession of the other side, which must not be used by the recipient for purposes other than resolving the dispute (para 9.2). Both parties should consider whether the claim could be settled by using mediation or some other form of alternative dispute resolution ('ADR') (see 1.03). Although parties are never obliged to use ADR, the courts increasingly see litigation as the last resort, and parties may be required to provide evidence that they considered ADR before issuing proceedings (para 8.1). Both sides should attempt to resolve the dispute by making realistic Part 36 offers (see 5.30–5.36) before proceedings are commenced. If expert evidence is required, the parties should consider how best to minimize expense, such as through instructing a single joint expert (para 9.4, and see 5.16).

C PROFESSIONAL NEGLIGENCE PRE-ACTION PROTOCOL

5.06 The professional negligence protocol applies to claims against professionals in tort and for breach of the contractual duty to act with reasonable skill and care, and also to claims for breach of fiduciary duty. It does not govern claims against architects, engineers, and quantity surveyors (which are governed by the construction and engineering dispute protocol) or claims in medical negligence (which are governed by the clinical disputes protocol) (para C2.2).

5.07 Under the protocol, as soon as the claimant decides there is a reasonable chance he will be suing, he is encouraged to notify the professional by sending a preliminary notice (para B1.1). This should give a brief outline of the grievance, and if possible, an indication of the value of the claim (para B1.2). The professional should acknowledge this notice within 21 days (para B1.4). The parties are required to consider whether some form of ADR would be more suitable than litigation (para B6.1). Both sides may be required to provide the court with evidence that ADR was considered. Proceedings should not be issued while settlement is being actively explored. While the parties cannot be forced to mediate or enter into any form of ADR (para B6.4), a failure to even consider ADR may be taken into account on costs. If they do attempt ADR, the steps required by the protocol may need to be adjusted (para C3.3).

5.08 When the claimant decides he has grounds for a claim, he should write a detailed letter before claim to the professional (paras B2.1 and 2.2, and see figure 5.1). Letters before claim do not have the same formal status as statements of case (see Chapter 13), and can be departed from as investigations produce a fuller picture of the circumstances (para B2.3). The professional should acknowledge receipt of the letter of claim within 21 days (para B3.1), and has three months from the date of the acknowledgment to investigate the case (para B4.1). During this stage the parties should supply promptly whatever information or documentation is reasonably requested from the other side and which will assist in clarifying or resolving the issues in the dispute (paras B4.3 and C5.1). The protocol encourages the use of joint experts (para B7.2), but recognizes it may be appropriate for each side to instruct their own experts (paras B7.1, B7.3, and C6.1 to C6.4).

Figure 5.1 Letter before claim

Smallwood & Co., Solicitors
4 Market Place, Corby, Northamptonshire NN17 6AL
Messrs Clifford & Stephens
38 High Street
Corby
Northants

Dear Sir

Valuation of Shares in Wilson Joinery Company Limited
We are instructed by Mr Graham Johnson to claim damages for breach of contract and negligence in respect of your valuation dated 19 May 2009 of the 20,000 ordinary shares ('the shares') in Wilson Joinery Company Limited ('the Company') purchased by our client in June 2009.

We have also written to Mrs Elizabeth Crouch, the vendor of the shares, in a related dispute concerning alleged misrepresentations and breach of contract in relation to the sale of the shares. A copy of that letter is enclosed.

Background Facts
As you are aware, your firm was retained by our client to value the shares in March 2009 following the procedure set out in the Articles of Association of the Company for the purchase of shares at a fair valuation. Copies of the Articles, the letter of instruction, your letter confirming your appointment, and your letter setting out your valuation of the shares, are enclosed. You valued the shares at £240,000, and our client bought the shares for that sum (copy letters and transfer enclosed).

Recent management accounts (copies of which are also enclosed) that have come into our client's possession show that the Company is and has throughout been insolvent.

Legal Basis of Claim
Our client alleges you are in breach of contract and negligent in that your firm:

(a) failed to conduct the valuation exercise competently or with reasonable skill and care;
(b) used historic cost valuations for assets which were no longer owned by the Company or which had suffered serious depreciation at the time of your valuation;
(c) failed to take into account prospective liabilities adequately or at all;
(d) failed to make proper provision for bad debts.

Consequences of Breach
As a result of these breaches, you valued the shares in the Company at £240,000, whereas in fact the Company was insolvent at that time and the shares were worthless. At that time the Company was likely to be wound up or struck off the register in the near future, and there was no prospect of a legal distribution to the shareholders. Acting on your firm's advice, and as a result of your failure to exercise reasonable skill and care and other breaches, our client paid £240,000 for the shares. If our client had been given correct advice by your firm he would have been advised against buying the shares, he would not have bought them, and he would not have lost the purchase price he in fact paid.

Figure 5.1 *continued*

Our client holds your firm responsible for this loss, and seeks damages in the sum of £240,000 together with interest at the rate of 8 per cent per annum from the date of the share purchase.

Experts

No expert has been appointed at this stage. Our view is that a valuation expert will be needed to report on the approach to valuing the shares adopted by your firm, and on the financial position of the Company and the value of the shares at the time your firm advised our client. Please let us know in your response to this letter whether you agree to the joint instruction of an expert for these purposes. If you agree, we will provide you with a list of names from which we hope we can select an agreed jointly instructed expert.

Response

The Professional Negligence Pre-action protocol applies to this matter. Please forward a copy of this letter to your insurers immediately. Under the Protocol you are required to acknowledge this letter within 21 days of receiving it. The Protocol allows you three months from the date of acknowledgment to investigate this claim and send a letter of response or letter of settlement.

Yours faithfully,

Smallwood & Co.

5.09 When his investigations are completed the professional should send the claimant a letter of response and/or a letter of settlement. A letter of response should be an open letter (which the claimant can disclose to the court) giving a reasoned response to the letter before claim. It must make clear what, if anything, is admitted, and give specific comments on the allegations made by the claimant if liability is denied (para B5.2). If professional fees are outstanding this must be made clear (para C2.5). A letter of settlement is usually written without prejudice (and so is privileged), may give the professional's views on the issues (if there is no letter of response), and makes a settlement proposal or asks for further information to enable the professional to formulate settlement proposals (para B5.4). If liability is denied without any proposals for settlement, the claimant is free to issue proceedings (para B5.5). Otherwise, the parties should enter into negotiations, aiming to conclude matters within six months of the date of the acknowledgment to the letter of claim (para B5.6). Before commencing proceedings the claimant should give the professional 14 days' notice (para B8.2), and the parties should attempt to identify the issues still in dispute (para B5.7(b)).

D PERSONAL INJURY PROTOCOL

5.10 The Pre-action Protocol for Personal Injury Claims ('PI protocol') is designed primarily for personal injuries claims worth up to £25,000 or, in other words, cases likely to be allocated to the fast track if proceedings are commenced. The spirit of the protocol should be followed in larger cases. Low value (between £1,000 and £10,000) RTA claims are covered by the RTA protocol, which is discussed in Chapter 6. The parties can depart from the detail in the PI protocol, but the court will want an explanation of the reasons for departing from it if proceedings are subsequently issued. The protocol lays down a number of steps that should be taken before proceedings are issued, and also provides templates for the more important letters that ought to be written.

In the early stages, the claimant may choose to send an informal letter to the defendant or the defendant's insurer intimating the claim. Doing so will not start the protocol timetable, but provides an informal means of opening the channels of communication. It also provides a fair warning to the defendant that a claim is going to be made, and enables the defendant's insurer to contact and interview witnesses at an early stage and while the events should be reasonably fresh in their memories. **5.11**

The formal protocol procedure is commenced by sending two copies of a letter before claim to the defendant. If a case ceases to be covered by the RTA protocol (see Chapter 6), the claims notification form (CNF) (see 6.10) may be used as the letter before claim (PI protocol, para 2.10A). One copy is for the defendant and the other for his insurer. If the insurer is known, the letters should be sent separately. The letter should contain a clear summary of the facts, the nature of the injuries, and details of the financial losses claimed. If possible the letter before claim should indicate which documents should be disclosed by the defendant at this stage. Detailed lists of the types of documents that should be disclosed for different types of personal injuries cases are set out in annexes to the protocol. By way of example, the list for road traffic accident cases is set out as figure 5.2. There are even more detailed lists for accidents at work, especially in cases where specific statutory provisions apply. **5.12**

The defendant must reply in 21 days naming any insurer. A failure to reply within this time justifies the issue of proceedings without further compliance with the protocol. The defendant, or the defendant's insurer, has a maximum of three months from acknowledging the letter before claim to investigate the claim and state whether liability is denied, and, if so, on what grounds. Both parties are required to consider whether early rehabilitative treatment will be of benefit to the claimant (para 4.1 and Annex D). Both parties are also obliged to consider whether mediation or other ADR procedures should be used, and may be penalized in costs if this is ignored (paras 2.16 to 2.19). **5.13**

In cases where the defendant disputes liability there is a requirement that the defendant must disclose documents relevant to liability (these should be in the categories identified by the claimant in the letter before claim), which must be enclosed with the denial letter. If contributory negligence is alleged, the claimant should respond to the allegations raised within a reasonable time (say a month). The claimant is obliged to send a schedule of special damages (see figure 13.2), together with supporting documents, to the defendant as soon as possible thereafter. The next step will be to obtain medical evidence dealing with the client's injuries. The protocol encourages the use of a jointly selected medical expert, which is discussed more fully at 5.16ff. **5.14**

Figure 5.2 Standard disclosure list for road traffic accident cases

SECTION A

In all cases where liability is at issue:

(i) Documents identifying the nature, extent and location of damage to defendant's vehicle where there is any dispute about point of impact.

Figure 5.2 *continued*

(ii) MOT certificate where relevant.

(iii) Maintenance records where vehicle defect is alleged or it is alleged by defendant that there was an unforeseen defect which caused or contributed to the accident.

SECTION B

Accident involving commercial vehicle as potential defendant:

(i) Tachograph charts or entry from individual control book.

(ii) Maintenance and repair records required for operators' licence where vehicle defect is alleged or it is alleged by defendants that there was an unforeseen defect which caused or contributed to the accident.

SECTION C

Cases against local authorities where highway design defect is alleged:

(i) Documents produced to comply with section 39 of the Road Traffic Act 1988 in respect of the duty designed to promote road safety to include studies into road accidents in the relevant area and documents relating to measures recommended to prevent accidents in the relevant area.

5.15 Once these steps have been taken the parties are encouraged to consider negotiating and using ADR procedures before starting proceedings. At this stage the parties should have reasonable evidence on both liability and quantum, and should be able to make informed Part 36 offers (see 5.30ff) in an attempt to settle without the need for proceedings. Before issuing proceedings it might be sensible for the parties jointly to review the issues in dispute and the evidence likely to be required. If proceedings are imminent, any insurer acting for the defendant should be invited to nominate solicitors within 7–14 days of the intended date of issue.

E INSTRUCTION OF EXPERTS

5.16 Different protocols have different approaches to the appointment of experts. Complex disputes often justify each side instructing their own experts. In such cases each side chooses who they will instruct, based largely on who their lawyers think will be most convincing in court. Several of the protocols encourage joint instruction of experts. This involves the parties agreeing on an expert, and both parties giving instructions to the expert (ideally by an agreed letter of instruction, but otherwise by separate letters of instruction). A variation is the joint selection of experts, a procedure encouraged by the PI protocol. Under joint selection, the claimant (or any other party) should give the other party a list of the name(s) of one or more experts in the relevant specialty who are considered to be suitable to instruct. Within 14 days the defendant may indicate an objection to one or more of the listed experts. Provided the defendant does not object to all the proposed experts, the claimant should then instruct a mutually acceptable expert from those remaining from the original list.

5.17 If the defendant objects to all the listed experts, the parties may instruct experts of their own choice. It would be for the court to decide subsequently, if proceedings are issued, whether either party had acted unreasonably.

Some solicitors choose to obtain medical reports through medical agencies, rather than directly from a specific doctor or hospital. The defendant's prior consent to this being done should be sought, and if the defendant so requests, the agency should be asked to provide in advance the names of the doctor(s) whom they are considering instructing. **5.18**

A model form of letter of instruction can be seen in figure 5.3. This is adapted slightly from the model letter contained in the personal injury pre-action protocol. **5.19**

Figure 5.3 Model letter of instruction to medical expert

Dear Sir or Madam
Our client: Phillippa May Myers
Our client's address: 47 Forest Road, Corby, Northants
Our client's DoB: 14 July 1972
Telephone No: 01536 764 9933
Date of accident: 17 July 2008
We are acting for Phillippa Myers in connection with injuries received in a road traffic accident on 17 July 2008. The main injuries appear to have been fractures to her right leg, a whiplash injury to her cervical spine, and a nervous reaction involving disturbance of sleep, flashbacks, and panic attacks, particularly when travelling by car.

Examination and Report
We should be obliged if you would examine our client and let us have a full and detailed report dealing with any relevant pre-accident medical history, the injuries sustained, treatment received and present condition, dealing in particular with the capacity for work and giving a prognosis.

It is central to our assessment of the extent of our client's injuries to establish the extent and duration of any continuing disability. Accordingly, in the prognosis section we would ask you specifically to comment on any areas of continuing complaint or disability or impact on daily living. If there is such continuing disability you should comment upon the level of suffering or inconvenience caused and, if you are able, give your view as to when or if the complaint or disability is likely to resolve.

Appointment with Client and Fees
Please send our client an appointment direct for this purpose. Should you be able to offer a cancellation appointment please contact our client direct. We confirm we will be responsible for your reasonable fees.

We are obtaining the notes and records from our client's GP and hospitals attended, and will forward them to you when they are to hand.

Format of Report
In order to comply with Court Rules we would be grateful if you would address your report to 'The Court'. The report must refer to this letter and to any other written or oral instructions given, it must give details of your qualifications and of any literature or other materials used in compiling the report, and where there is a range of opinion it must summarize the range of opinion and give reasons for your opinion. At the end of the report you will need to include a statement that you understand your duty to the Court and have complied with it. Above your signature please include a statement in the following terms: 'I confirm that insofar as the facts stated in my report are within my own knowledge I have made clear which they are

Figure 5.3 *continued*

and I believe them to be true, and that the opinions I have expressed represent my true and complete professional opinion.'

In order to avoid further correspondence we can confirm that on the evidence we have there is no reason to suspect we may be pursuing a claim against the hospital or its staff.

Time for Report

We look forward to receiving your report within six weeks. If you will not be able to prepare your report within this period please telephone us upon receipt of these instructions.

When acknowledging these instructions it would assist if you could give an estimate as to the likely timescale for the provision of your report and also an indication as to your fee.

Yours faithfully

Smallwood & Co.

F LIMITATION DIFFICULTIES

5.20 If the claimant consults a solicitor close to the end of the limitation period, the solicitor should give as much notice to the defendant of the intention to commence proceedings as is practicable. The parties may invite the court to extend the time for service of supporting documents and/or service of the Defence, alternatively, for a stay of proceedings pending completion of the steps required by any applicable protocol.

G FAILURE TO COMPLY

5.21 Obviously, there will be cases where either or both parties fail to comply with the requirements of a protocol. There may be a rational justification for doing so, and if this is accepted by the court there will be no adverse consequences. Where a failure to comply arises through slackness or deliberate flouting, a claimant may be justified in commencing proceedings without going through the rest of the procedures laid down in the protocol, and either party may find they are penalized by the court at a later stage.

5.22 *Charles Church Developments Ltd v Stent Foundations Ltd* [2007] CILL 2477 expressed the view that the court should consider any costs penalty for non-compliance with a pre-action protocol at an early stage. In practice, this is often left until the end of the case. Sanctions should not be imposed if there has been substantial compliance with the relevant protocol (*TJ Brent Ltd v Black and Veatch Consulting Ltd* [2008] EWHC 1497 (TCC)) and the court will not be concerned with minor or technical shortcomings (PD Pre-action conduct, para 4.3). Parties are required to plead whether they have complied with the protocol in their statement of case (para 9.7).

5.23 If, taking into account the overall effect of any non-compliance, the court decides to impose a sanction, it may by PD Pre-action conduct, para 4.6:

(a) order a stay of the proceedings to allow compliance with the protocol;
(b) order the party at fault to pay all or part of the costs of the proceedings. The order should be proportionate to the breach. A failure to negotiate was reflected by a 10–15 per cent reduction in costs in *Straker v Tudor Rose* [2007] EWCA Civ 368;

(c) order the party at fault to pay those costs on an indemnity basis;
(d) if the party at fault is a claimant in whose favour an order for the payment of damages or some specified sum is subsequently made, deprive that party of interest on such sum and in respect of such period as may be specified, and/or award interest at a lower rate than that at which interest would otherwise have been awarded;
(e) if the party at fault is a defendant and an order for the payment of damages or some specified sum is subsequently made in favour of the claimant, award interest on such sum and in respect of such period as may be specified at a higher rate, not exceeding 10 per cent above base rate, rather than the rate at which interest would otherwise have been awarded.

Further, the court may make an order that the defaulting party should pay a sum of money into court if the default was without good reason (CPR, r 3.1(5)). **5.24**

H ROAD TRAFFIC ACT 1988

The Road Traffic Act 1988 provides for the compulsory insurance of drivers of road vehicles against liability in respect of death or bodily injury of any person, or in respect of damage to property caused by the use of a vehicle on a road (s 145). Provided the claimant gives the defendant's insurer notice of the proceedings before or within seven days after they are commenced, the insurer is obliged to satisfy any judgment that may be obtained. **5.25**

I MOTOR INSURERS' BUREAU

Compulsory insurance will not provide an insurer who will pay an injured claimant's damages if the motorist responsible for the injury fails to stop at the scene of the accident, or if the motorist was uninsured. To cover these situations the Secretary of State has entered into two agreements with the Motor Insurers' Bureau providing for compensation to be payable in these circumstances. The Motor Insurers' Bureau ('MIB') is a company registered under the Companies Acts, and effectively represents the motor insurance companies. **5.26**

One of the agreements is the Motor Insurers' Bureau (Compensation of Victims of Untraced Drivers) Agreement 2003. It applies to cases where someone is killed or injured by an untraced motorist and where, on the balance of probabilities, the untraced driver would have been liable to the victim. The accident has to be reported to the police within 14 days, or as soon as is reasonable, and the applicant must have cooperated with the police. An application for compensation must be made to the MIB within three years of the accident. Time does not run against a child until they reach 18 (*Byrne v Motor Insurers' Bureau* [2009] QB 66). The application is then investigated by the MIB, which may reject the application, or make an award in a similar manner to that used by the court. The agreement also contains detailed provisions for appeals. **5.27**

The other agreement is the Motor Insurers' Bureau (Compensation of Victims of Uninsured Drivers) Agreement 1999. By cl 7 of the agreement, the MIB will incur no liability unless an application is made in the prescribed form, and unless certain information and documents **5.28** are provided to the MIB relating to the proceedings against the uninsured driver and other matters. Proper notice of the bringing of proceedings must be given within 14 days of commencement (cl 9(1)). 'Proper notice' means notice that proceedings have been commenced, provision of the sealed claim form or another official document evidencing issue of the proceedings, and copies of:

(a) any insurance policy providing benefits in the event of the victim's death or injury;
(b) all relevant correspondence;
(c) the particulars of claim; and
(d) documents served with the particulars of claim (ie, medical report and schedule of special damages).

5.29 The particulars of claim, medical report, and schedule of special damages may be served on the MIB no later than seven days after service on the defendant. Provided these, and certain other, requirements are satisfied, the MIB will pay the amount of any unsatisfied judgment to the claimant (cl 5(1)).

J PRE-ACTION PART 36 OFFERS

5.30 As mentioned in the introduction to Chapter 4, the usual rule in litigation is that the winner will recover its costs from the losing party. A person receiving a pre-action letter before claim may, on investigating the matter, come to the view there is some merit in the claim. Possibilities are:

(a) that the claim is bound to succeed for the full amount claimed. In this type of case there may be little alternative but to pay in full, or make proposals to pay by instalments;
(b) that the claim is bound to succeed, but the sum claimed is excessive, unclear, or arguably more than might be awarded by the court;
(c) that the claim has some prospects of success on the merits, with quantum accepted in full subject to liability; or
(d) that the claim has some prospects of success, and quantum is disputed.

5.31 In each of these situations the proposed defendant is likely to be best advised to make an offer to settle. The terms offered will depend on the legal advice given on the prospects of success on liability and the range of likely awards on quantum. An offer to settle may take one of several forms. It may be made in a face-to-face meeting, by telephone, electronically, or by letter, and can be made:

(a) in an 'open' communication. This has the disadvantage that, if the offer is not accepted, it may be used by the other side as an admission on liability and quantum. If the offer is refused, it can be used on the question of costs. Open offers tend to be used by parties who are confident of their position;
(b) in a 'without prejudice' communication (see 29.47–29.51). This has the advantage that the offer cannot be referred to in court for any purpose, but the disadvantage is that it also cannot be used on the question of costs; or

(c) in a communication (usually a letter) treated as 'without prejudice save as to costs'. This is also known as a Part 36 offer, or Calderbank offer. It cannot be used by either side on the questions of liability and quantum, but can be referred to on the question of costs.

A Part 36 offer must be in writing, either in a letter or by using form N242A (PD 36A, para 1.1), state on its face that it is intended to have the consequences of Part 36 (CPR, r 36.2(2)(b)), and specify a period of not less than 21 days within which the defendant will be liable for the claimant's costs if the offer is accepted (rr 36.2(2)(c) and 36.2(3)). This 21-day period is called the 'relevant period'. The offer must be clear on whether it relates to the whole or part of the claim or to an issue (r 36.2(2)(d)), and whether it takes into account any counterclaim (r 36.2(2)(e)). In money claims a single sum of money must be offered (r 36.4(1)), which is treated as inclusive of interest to the end of the relevant period (r 36.3(3)). There are further required formalities in personal injury claims regarding the deduction of state benefits, claims for future pecuniary loss, and provisional damages claims (see 42.06–42.11). **5.32**

If the Part 36 offer is accepted, it takes effect in accordance with its terms. **5.33**

The practical reason for making a Part 36 offer is that, if it is not accepted, the issue regarding costs in the proceedings is whether the judgment in the proceedings is for a sum exceeding the amount of the offer (taking interest into account). If the judgment does not exceed the amount of the offer, the theory is that the claimant should have accepted the offer, so that the claimant is responsible for both sides' costs from the expiry of the relevant period. In such a case, at trial the judge will usually, unless it is thought unjust to do so: **5.34**

(a) award the claimant its costs up to the expiry of the relevant period; and
(b) award the defendant its costs thereafter (r 36.14).

A proposed defendant who makes a Part 36 offer shortly after receiving a letter of claim can potentially throw the entire costs risk of the litigation onto the proposed claimant, even if the claimant wins on liability, provided the offer is at least as good as the final award. Proposed claimants therefore have to be very cautious about ignoring or rejecting these offers. **5.35**

Proposed claimants can also make Part 36 offers. Such an offer from a claimant is a proposal to accept a specified sum (or other terms) in settlement of the claim. If a claimant's Part 36 offer is not accepted, and if the claimant does at least as well as the offer when the claim is finally disposed of, the court may award indemnity basis costs (see 43.09–43.11) and enhanced rates of interest (r 36.14). **5.36**

KEY POINTS SUMMARY

- Pre-action protocols give guidance on the exchange of information and evidence before proceedings are commenced. **5.37**
- Litigation is seen as a last resort. Parties are expected to have at least considered ADR before issuing proceedings.
- There are eleven published protocols.
- In cases not covered by a published protocol, parties must comply with the ethos of the protocols and the guidance given in PD Pre-action conduct.

6

LOW VALUE ROAD TRAFFIC ACCIDENT CLAIMS

6.01 There are approximately 750,000 road traffic accidents ('RTAs') involving personal injuries each year. Of these, about 500,000 are cases where the value of the personal injuries claim is below £10,000 (*Jackson Review of Civil Litigation Costs* (2009, Ministry of Justice, para 22.2.5). Claimant solicitors and defendant insurers and solicitors increasingly deal with these cases on a commoditized basis, a process which is encouraged by the reforms introduced by the Legal Services Act 2007. 'Commoditization' is not an exact term, but describes the move away from each client having a personal relationship with their solicitor and receiving a personalized service, to clients being introduced to solicitors through referral agencies with legal services being conducted in a cost-efficient way, often for a fixed fee.

6.02 Referrals to solicitors are regulated by the Solicitors Code of Conduct 2007, r 9. This places duties on the solicitor not to allow payment of a referral fee to compromise their independence or ability to provide advice in the best interests of the client, and to provide written information of the financial arrangement to the client. Referral agencies include BTE insurers, claims management companies (who often advertise for customers on television etc.) and trade unions. In 2009 referral fees ranged from £250 to £900. Solicitors taking on referred clients obviously have to make sufficient money on the claim to cover this fee, together with the expense to the firm in processing the claim and an element of profit. The referral fee is not itself recoverable from the other side if the claim is successful, so there is pressure on solicitors who pay referral fees to either do as little work as possible on a case if their costs are fixed, or to engage in costs building (a disreputable practice of doing barely necessary work to inflate their costs) if their costs are not fixed. Most solicitors do not give in to these pressures, but they were recognized as real problems in the *Jackson Review of Civil Litigation Costs*.

Two particular features of the commoditized approach to RTA personal injury claims are the use of medical reporting organizations ('MROs') and computerized systems for assessing damages for pain, suffering, and loss of amenity. MROs are medical agencies that provide medical experts who write reports and appear as expert witnesses in personal injuries claims. A MRO will charge fees for its services, which are recoverable from the unsuccessful party as disbursements when costs are assessed (Chapter 43 and *Woollard v Fowler* (24 May 2006, unreported). There are complaints that commonly only 35 to 50 per cent of the fees charged by MROs are paid to the medical experts providing the expert evidence (*Jackson Review of Civil Litigation Costs*, para 22.3.21). There are two main software systems which are used primarily by defendants' insurers in quantifying damages for pain, suffering, and loss of amenity. Problems discussed in the *Jackson Review of Civil Litigation Costs*, chapter 21, included unthinking settlement of cases on the figure provided by the computer, evidence that in all cases that went to a hearing (literally 100 per cent of such cases) awards by the courts exceeded the figure provided by the software, and limited authority given by insurance companies to claims negotiators to exceed the computer-based figure. **6.03**

It is in this context that the Ministry of Justice has promulgated the RTA protocol and a number of related provisions in the CPR. They are designed to provide a streamlined and swift process for settling by agreement road traffic personal injuries claims where liability is admitted and damages are in the range of £1,000 to £10,000. It provides a highly regulated system for dealing with these claims, with short, fixed periods for most of the necessary steps, prescribed interim payments, and a regime of fixed costs. It received lukewarm approval in the *Jackson Review of Civil Litigation Costs*, primarily because the level of detail in its provisions runs counter to one of the principal recommendations of the *Review*, that higher priority should be given to simplicity in the drafting of the rules, practice directions, and court guides governing civil procedure (recommendation 2). **6.04**

The process under the RTA protocol is divided into three stages, which are shown in general terms in figure 6.1. **6.05**

A CASES COVERED BY THE RTA PROTOCOL

A claim will be covered by the RTA protocol if: **6.06**

(a) the claim is for damages arising from a road traffic accident (RTA protocol, para 4.1(1));
(b) the accident was on or after 30 April 2010 (para 4.1(1));
(c) the defendant was a road user (para 4.4(1));
(d) the claim includes damages in respect of personal injury (para 4.1(2));

(e) the claimant values the claim between £1,000 and £10,000 on a full liability basis (para 4.1(3), (4)); and
(f) the claim does not fall into any of the excluded categories (para 4.4) (see 6.08).

Figure 6.1 RTA protocol: the three stages

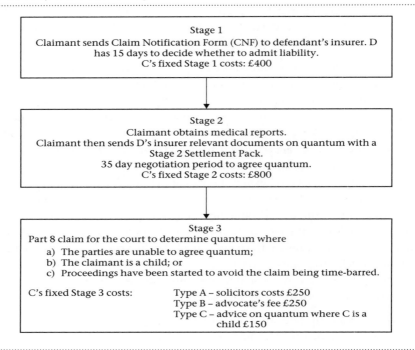

Stage 1
Claimant sends Claim Notification Form (CNF) to defendant's insurer. D has 15 days to decide whether to admit liability.
C's fixed Stage 1 costs: £400

↓

Stage 2
Claimant obtains medical reports.
Claimant then sends D's insurer relevant documents on quantum with a Stage 2 Settlement Pack.
35 day negotiation period to agree quantum.
C's fixed Stage 2 costs: £800

↓

Stage 3
Part 8 claim for the court to determine quantum where
a) The parties are unable to agree quantum;
b) The claimant is a child; or
c) Proceedings have been started to avoid the claim being time-barred.

C's fixed Stage 3 costs:
Type A – solicitors costs £250
Type B – advocate's fee £250
Type C – advice on quantum where C is a child £150

Valuing the claim

6.07 The £1,000 lower limit is calculated applying the small claims threshold (see 14.22–14.25), which is why primarily this means damages for pain, suffering, and loss of amenity must be less than £1,000. These claims are excluded from the RTA protocol because there is a no-costs rule in small claims track cases (see 25.14), which is inconsistent with the fixed costs regime under the RTA protocol. In deciding whether the claim exceeds £10,000 the claimant should:

(a) include pecuniary losses;
(b) exclude the value of vehicle related damage (para 4.3); and
(c) exclude interest (para 4.1(3)).

Excluded cases

6.08 The following situations are outside the RTA protocol (para 4.4), namely cases:

(1) made to the MIB pursuant to the Untraced Drivers' Agreement 2003 (see 5.27);
(2) where the claimant or defendant is deceased;

(3) where the claimant or defendant is a protected party (see 17.07);
(4) where the claimant is bankrupt; or
(5) where the defendant's vehicle is registered outside the United Kingdom.

B STAGE 1: CLAIM NOTIFICATION

Figure 6.2 is a flow diagram showing the steps that have to be followed in Stages 1 and 2 of **6.09** the RTA protocol.

Starting the RTA protocol process

The RTA protocol procedure is commenced by the claimant completing a claim notifica- **6.10** tion form ('CNF', which is available on the HM Court Service website at <**http://www.hmcourts-service.gov.uk**> as form RTA 1). All boxes in the CNF that are marked as mandatory must be completed before it is sent. The claimant must make a reasonable attempt to complete those boxes that are not marked as mandatory (RTA protocol, para 6.3). Details of rehabilitation, following the principles in the Rehabilitation Code in the PI protocol (see 5.13), must be included in the CNF (para 6.7). There is an obligation to state whether any vehicle damage claim is being dealt with separately by third parties, or, if not, to include details of the vehicle damage claim together with relevant invoices and receipts (para 6.4). The CNF must be verified by a statement of truth. On the electronically completed form, this requirement is satisfied by entering the name of the person verifying the form in the signature box (para 6.6).

The CNF must be sent electronically to the defendant's insurer. The relevant address should **6.11** be available on the RTA PI Claims Process website at <**http://www.rtapiclaimsprocess.org.uk**>. To make use of this website it is necessary to register online. At the same time as the CNF is sent to the insurer, or as soon as practicable thereafter, a 'Defendant Only CNF' (form RTA 2) must be sent to the defendant by first-class post (para 6.2).

Apart from this defendant only CNF, all communications under the RTA protocol must be **6.12** sent electronically (para 5.1). There is an obligation on the claimant to include electronic contact details on the CNF. The obligation to use electronic communications presumably means that supporting documents need to be scanned before being sent (although this is not spelt out in the RTA protocol).

Response by defendant's insurer

An electronic acknowledgment must be sent by the defendant's insurer on the next business **6.13** day after receipt of the CNF (RTA protocol, para 6.10). The insurer has 15 days to investigate liability, and must complete the 'Insurer Response' section of the CNF ('the CNF response') and send it to the claimant within 15 business days of receipt of the CNF. The principal question for the insurer is whether liability will be admitted, with a secondary question of whether there will be an allegation of contributory negligence. If liability is denied, brief reasons for

Figure 6.2 Flow diagram of Stages 1 and 2 under the RTA protocol

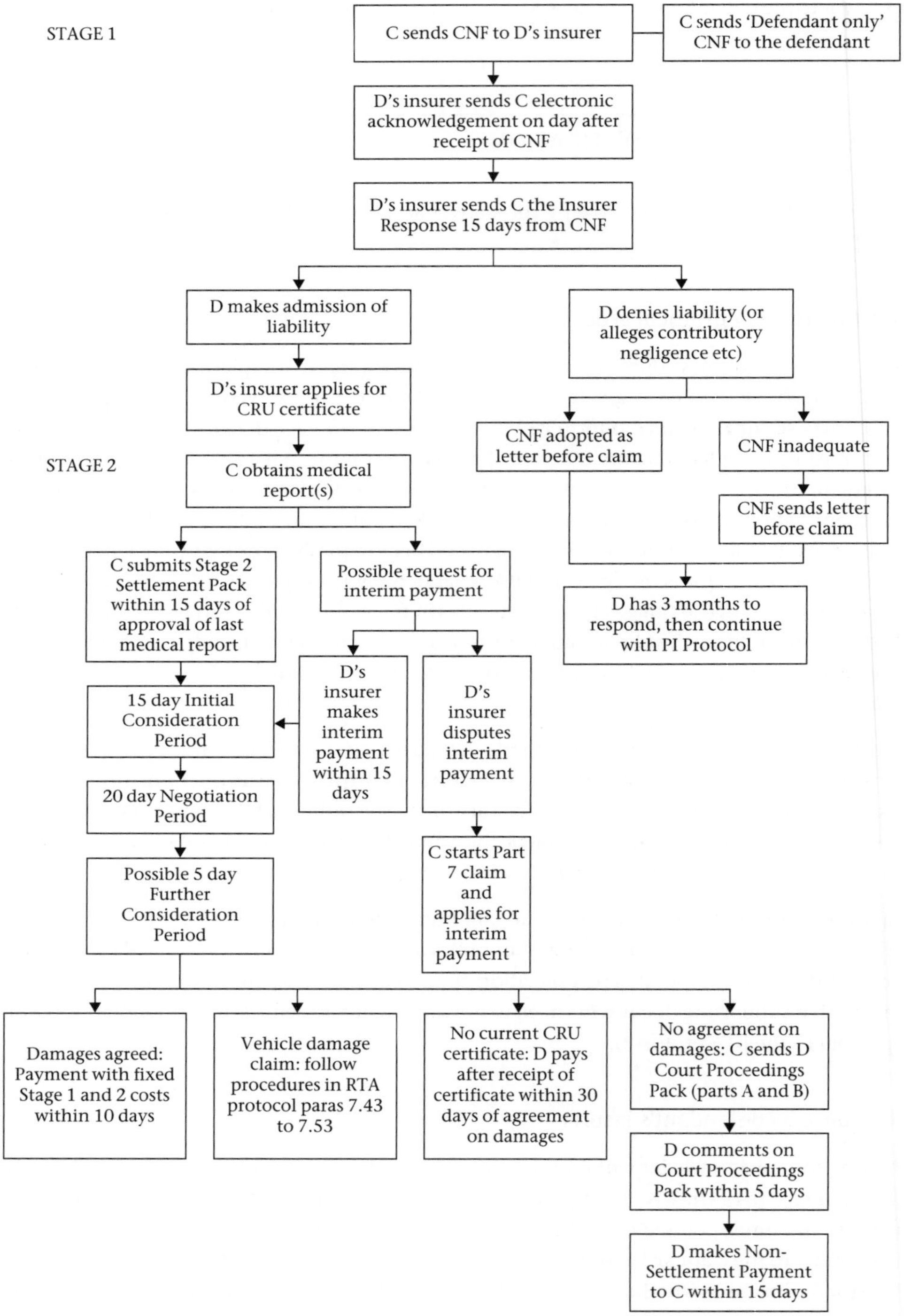

that denial must be set out in the CNF response (para 6.16). An admission of liability for the purposes of the RTA protocol is by para 1.1(14) an admission that:

(a) the accident occurred;
(b) the accident was caused by the defendant's breach of duty; and
(c) the defendant caused some loss to the claimant, the nature and extent of which is not admitted.

CRU certificate

The defendant must, before the end of Stage 1, apply to the Compensation Recovery Unit ('CRU') for a certificate of recoverable benefits (RTA protocol, para 6.12). This is needed for negotiation purposes, and sets out the amount that the defendant has to pay to the government in reimbursement of state benefits paid to the claimant as a result of the relevant injury. **6.14**

Stage 1 fixed costs

Except where the claimant is a child, the defendant must pay the Stage 1 fixed costs in cases where liability is admitted or liability is admitted with an allegation of contributory negligence restricted to the claimant's admitted failure to wear a seat belt (RTA protocol, para 6.18). These costs must be paid within 10 days after sending the CNF response to the claimant. **6.15**

Unrepresented claimants

Claimants who act in person have to comply with the RTA protocol. There is a decided measure of unreality about how litigants in person are expected to find out all that is needed, from identifying the various sources (the protocol, various provisions within the CPR, and PD 8B), to registering online with RTA PI Claims Process, submitting an electronic CNF to the appropriate insurer, and attaching scanned supporting documents. The only concession is that after such a claimant has sent the CNF the defendant's insurer is required to explain the period within which a response must be sent and that the claimant may obtain independent legal advice, for example from a legal representative, a Citizens Advice Bureau, a local law centre, or a trade union (RTA protocol, para 5.10). The fixed costs in RTA protocol cases only apply where a claimant has a legal representative (para 4.5), so litigants in person are entitled to normal costs at litigant in person rates. **6.16**

C STAGE 2: MEDICAL EVIDENCE AND NEGOTIATION

Medical evidence

On completion of Stage 1, the claimant should obtain a medical report, if one has not already been obtained (RTA protocol, para 7.1). Medical experts may, but do not have to, use the medical report standard form (RTA 3). It is expected that most claimants will obtain a medical report from one expert (para 7.4). Where it is clear that one expert cannot deal with all elements of the **6.17** injury, the claimant may obtain a report from a second medical expert in a different discipline. Those two medical experts may each separately recommend that the claimant obtain a further initial medical report from a medical expert in a different discipline, thus leading to a theoretical maximum of four claimant experts (para 7.5). Updating reports may also be obtained (para 7.6). The claimant must check the factual accuracy of any medical report before it is sent to the defendant. There will be no further opportunity for the claimant to challenge the factual accuracy of a medical report after it has been sent to the defendant (para 7.2).

Stay for updating reports

6.18 Where subsequent medical reports need to be obtained the parties should agree to stay the process in the protocol for a suitable period (RTA protocol, para 7.7).

Interim payment

6.19 Where there is a stay for updating reports, the claimant can request an interim payment of £1,000, which generally the defendant's insurer must pay within 10 days (RTA protocol, paras 7.7–7.10). A claimant may make a request for an interim payment exceeding £1,000, in which case the defendant's insurer has 15 days to consider the matter. If the defendant fails to make the interim payment, or if the claimant is not satisfied with the defendant's response to the request, the claimant has 10 days to give notice that the claim will no longer be governed by the RTA protocol.

Stage 2 settlement pack

6.20 After obtaining the necessary medical reports, the claimant must send the defendant's insurers a Stage 2 settlement pack within 15 days of the claimant approving the final medical report and agreeing to rely on the prognosis in that report (RTA protocol, para 7.26). This pack consists of:

(a) the Stage 2 settlement pack form (form RTA 5). This includes space for the claimant to make an offer of what they will accept in settlement of the claim. Where the defendant alleges contributory negligence because of the claimant's failure to wear a seat belt, the form must give the claimant's suggested percentage reduction (which may be 0 per cent);
(b) a medical report or reports;
(c) evidence of pecuniary losses; and
(d) evidence of disbursements (for example the cost of any medical report).

Consideration of claim and negotiation

6.21 There is a 35-day period (which can be extended by agreement) for consideration of the Stage 2 settlement pack by the defendant ('the total consideration period', RTA protocol, para 7.29). This includes an initial period of up to 15 days for the defendant to consider the documents and make an offer. Within this period the defendant must either accept the offer made by the claimant on the Stage 2 settlement pack form or make a counter-offer using that form (para

7.31). When making a counter-offer the defendant must propose an amount for each head of damage. Where the defendant has obtained a CRU certificate the counter-offer must state the name and amount of any deductible amount (para 7.35). If there is no current CRU certificate, a fresh certificate will be needed (paras 7.41, 7.42, 7.54, and 7.65). The defendant must also explain in the counter-offer why a particular head of damage is less than the amount claimed by the claimant. The explanation will assist the claimant when negotiating a settlement and will allow both parties to focus on those areas of the claim that remain in dispute (para 7.34).

Once the initial consideration period has elapsed, the defendant can only withdraw the admission of liability with the claimant's consent (CPR, r 14.1B(2)(a)). **6.22**

The remaining 20 days is for any further negotiation between the parties ('the negotiation period'). If there is an offer within five days of the end of the 35-day period, there is an automatic five-day extension to give time for the other side to consider whether to accept the offer (para 5.30). **6.23**

Terms of offers

Any offer to settle made at any stage by either party will automatically include, and cannot exclude (RTA protocol, para 7.37): **6.24**

(a) the Stage 2 fixed costs in CPR, r 45.29;
(b) an agreement in principle to pay disbursements;
(c) a success fee in accordance with r 45.31(1).

Payment after acceptance of offer

Where the claimant is an adult and the claim is settled during Stage 2, the defendant must pay: **6.25**

(a) the agreed damages less any deductible amount which is payable to the CRU and any interim payment;
(b) any unpaid Stage 1 fixed costs;
(c) the Stage 2 fixed costs;
(d) the disbursements allowed in accordance with CPR, r 45.30; and
(e) a success fee in accordance with r 45.31 for Stage 1 and Stage 2 fixed costs.

These sums must be paid within 10 days of the end of the initial consideration period or negotiation period during which the parties agreed the settlement (RTA protocol, para 7.40). **6.26**

Failure to compromise

If the parties do not reach agreement in the total consideration period, the claimant is required by RTA protocol, para 7.55, to send the defendant's insurer the court proceedings pack (parts A and B) (forms RTA 6 and RTA 7), which must contain: **6.27**

(a) the final offer and counter-offer from the Stage 2 settlement pack form;
(b) supporting comments from both parties on disputed heads of damages; and
(c) the claimant's offer, and any counter-offer from the defendant.

6.28 The court proceedings pack (part A) must not raise anything that has not been raised in the Stage 2 settlement pack form (para 7.57). The defendant has five days to make any comments on this pack (paras 5.58 and 5.60), and can nominate a solicitor to accept service of court proceedings (para 5.59).

Stage 2 payment

6.29 Where the claimant is an adult, the defendant must within 15 days of receipt of the court proceedings pack make a payment to the claimant of:

(a) the final offer of damages made by the defendant in the court proceedings pack, less any deductible amount which is payable to the CRU and any interim payment;
(b) any unpaid Stage 1 fixed costs;
(c) the Stage 2 fixed costs; and
(d) any agreed disbursements.

D STAGE 3: PART 8 CLAIM TO DETERMINE QUANTUM

6.30 Figure 6.3 is a flow diagram showing the steps that have to be followed in Stage 3 in cases governed by the RTA protocol. Stage 3 involves a Part 8 claim to assess damages where the claim has not been settled in Stages 1 or 2. The procedure followed under PD 8B is a substantially modified version of the normal Part 8 procedure described in Chapter 19. Most of the provisions of CPR, Part 8 are disapplied (para 2.2), except for rr 8.2 (the Part 8 claim form), 8.4 (consequences of not acknowledging service), and 8.9(a) and (b) (CPR provisions on statements of case and entering judgments on admissions do not apply).

Filing and service

6.31 By PD 8B, para 6.1, the claimant must file with the claim form and serve on the defendant:

(a) the court proceedings pack (part A);
(b) the court proceedings pack (part B) (the claimant and defendant's final offers) in a sealed envelope. These are treated as modified Part 36 offers (a subject dealt with in Chapter 42), and must not be communicated to the court until the claim is determined (CPR, r 36.20(1));
(c) copies of medical reports;
(d) evidence of special damages;
(e) evidence of disbursements; and
(f) any notice of funding.

6.32 The claimant can only use documents that have already been sent to the defendant under the RTA protocol (para 6.3).

Acknowledgment of service

The defendant must file and serve an acknowledgment of service in Form N210B not more than 14 days after service of the claim form (PD 8B, para 8.1). At the same time the defendant must file any notice of funding and a current CRU certificate (para 8.2). **6.33**

Where the defendant opposes the claim because the claimant has either not followed the RTA protocol or has filed and served additional or new evidence with the claim form that had not been provided under the RTA protocol, the court will dismiss the claim and the claimant may start proceedings under Part 7 (para 9.1). **6.34**

Figure 6.3 Flow diagram of Stage 3 under the RTA protocol

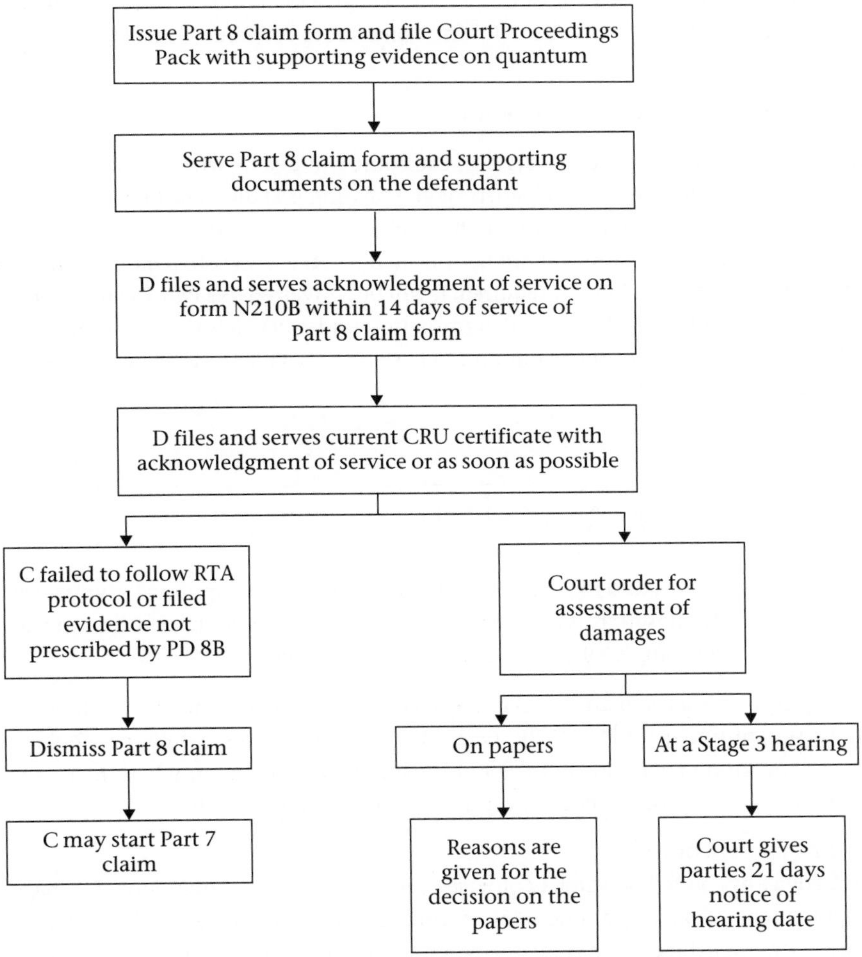

Changing to or from the PD 8B procedure

6.35 The court can order a Part 7 claim to proceed as if it was governed by the Stage 3 procedure in PD 8B (PD 8B, para 4.1). It may also order a PD 8B claim which is unsuitable for the PD 8B procedure to continue as if it were a Part 7 claim (para 7.2(2)).

Withdrawal of RTA protocol admissions and offers

6.36 Once the Part 8 claim under PD 8B has been issued, the defendant can only withdraw an admission made under the RTA protocol with the consent of all the other parties or with the court's permission (CPR, r 14.1B(2)(b)). An application for permission is made using the Part 23 procedure described in Chapter 20.

6.37 A party may only withdraw a RTA protocol offer after proceedings have started with the court's permission (PD 8B, para 10.1). Where the court gives permission the claim will no longer continue under the Stage 3 procedure and the court will give directions. The court will only give permission where there is good reason for the claim not to continue under Stage 3.

Directions for determination of quantum

6.38 After the defendant acknowledges service, the court will decide whether the assessment of damages will be conducted on the papers or at a hearing (PD 8B, para 11.1). There will be a hearing if it is requested by the claimant on the claim form or the defendant on the acknowledgment of service. The claim will not be allocated to a track (PD 8B, para 17.1). If the court concludes that further evidence is required, it will be converted to a Part 7 claim and will not proceed under PD 8B (para 7.2(1)). A determination under PD 8B is therefore a matter of the court assessing the value of the claim on the basis of the evidence gathered under Stages 1 and 2 of the RTA protocol.

E CHILD SETTLEMENT APPLICATIONS

6.39 Where the claimant is a child the prudent course is to obtain court approval of any settlement (see CPR, r 21.10(2)). It is for this reason that the automatic payment provisions in Stage 2 of the RTA protocol only apply where the claimant is not a child.

6.40 Court approval of a settlement in a claim by a child which is governed by the RTA protocol has to be sought under PD 8B (PD 8B, para 1.1(2)). In these cases, PD 8B, para 6.5 provides that the claimant must provide to the court the following documents when the Part 8 claim is issued in addition to the standard documents required under PD 8B:

(a) a draft consent order;
(b) the advice by counsel, solicitor, or other legal representative on the amount of damages; and
(c) a statement verified by a statement of truth signed by the litigation friend which confirms whether the child has recovered in accordance with the prognosis and whether there are any continuing symptoms.

This statement at sub-para (c) above enables the court to decide whether to order the child to attend the settlement hearing. At the hearing the court will decide whether the proposed settlement terms are fair compensation for the benefit of the child. Where the settlement is not approved the claim will no longer continue under the Stage 3 Procedure and the court will give directions (para 12.5). **6.41**

F LIMITATION

Where compliance with the RTA protocol is not possible before the expiry of the limitation period, the claimant may start proceedings and apply to the court for an order to stay (ie, suspend) the proceedings while the parties take steps to follow the protocol (RTA protocol, para 5.7 and see 22.50). Such proceedings should be commenced under Part 8 and follow the procedure in PD 8B. If the parties are unable to reach a settlement while the claim is stayed by the end of Stage 2 of the protocol, the claimant must, in order to proceed to Stage 3, apply to lift the stay and request directions in the existing proceedings (para 5.8). **6.42**

G FIXED COSTS UNDER THE RTA PROTOCOL

There is a detailed system of fixed costs in RTA protocol claims. The basic amounts are included in figure 6.1. The detailed rules are in CPR, rr 45.27–45.39, and the effect of the parties' final offers (which are revealed to the judge once the claim is determined) is as set out in r 36.21. **6.43**

H CASES WHERE PARTIES CAN DISCONTINUE FOLLOWING THE RTA PROTOCOL

The RTA protocol ceases to apply in the following situations: **6.44**

(a) where, at any stage, the claimant notifies the defendant that the claim has now been revalued at more than £10,000 (RTA protocol, para 4.2);
(b) where the defendant notifies the claimant that it considers that inadequate mandatory information has been provided in the CNF (paras 6.8 and 6.15(4)(a));
(c) where the defendant alleges contributory negligence (other than in relation to the claimant's admitted failure to wear a seat belt) (para 6.15(1));
(d) where the defendant does not admit liability within the 15 days allowed for sending the CNF response (para 6.15(3));
(e) where the defendant does not complete and send the CNF response within the 15 days allowed (para 6.15(2));

(f) where the defendant notifies the claimant that the defendant considers that if proceedings were issued the small claims track would be the normal track for that claim (para 6.15 (4)(b));
(g) where the defendant fails to pay the Stage 1 fixed costs within the 10-day period specified in para 6.18, and the claimant gives written notice that the claim will no longer continue under the protocol to the defendant within 10 days thereafter (para 6.19);
(h) where the claimant is not satisfied with the defendant's response to a request for an interim payment in Stage 2 (paras 7.21 and 7.22);
(i) where the defendant gives notice to the claimant within the initial 15-day consideration period after receiving the Stage 2 settlement pack that the defendant considers that the small claims track would be the normal track for the claim (para 7.32(a)); or
(j) where the defendant gives notice to the claimant within the initial 15-day consideration period after receiving the Stage 2 settlement pack withdrawing the admission of causation claim (para 7.32(b));
(k) where the defendant does not respond within the initial 15-day consideration period (para 7.33);
(l) where a party withdraws an offer made in the Stage 2 settlement pack form after the total consideration period (para 7.39);
(m) where the defendant fails to make the Stage 2 payment (para 7.66); and
(n) where the claimant gives notice to the defendant that the claim is unsuitable for the protocol (eg, because there are complex issues of fact or law in relation to the vehicle-related damages) (para 7.67).

6.45 Where a claim drops out of the RTA protocol in Stage 1, pre-action conduct should continue under the PI protocol where appropriate (para 6.17). Generally, the CNF will stand as the letter before claim for the purposes of the PI protocol, unless the CNF is regarded as inadequate. Where a case drops out of the RTA protocol in Stage 2, further progress is often through starting a Part 7 claim (paras 7.21, 7.22, 7.32, 7.39, and 7.66). Claims which are discontinued under the protocol cannot subsequently re-enter the process (para 5.11).

KEY POINTS SUMMARY

6.46
- The RTA protocol is for road traffic accident personal injury claims between £1,000 and £10,000 where the defendant admits liability.
- Stage 1 covers the commencement of the protocol by sending the CNF, with a response by the defendant's insurer.
- Stage 2 covers obtaining medical reports followed by a 35-day period of consideration and negotiation.
- The expectation is that many cases will be settled at Stage 2, together with fixed costs.
- If the case is not settled, Stage 2 ends with the claimant sending the defendant's insurer a court proceedings pack (parts A and B), and the defendant making a part payment consisting of the minimum amounts that will become payable after Stage 3.
- Stage 3 is a Part 8 claim leading to an assessment of damages by the court.

7

LIMITATION

Expiry of a limitation period provides a defendant with a complete defence to a claim. Lord Griffiths in *Donovan v Gwentoys Ltd* [1990] 1 WLR 472 said, 'the primary purpose of the limitation period is to protect a defendant from the injustice of having to face a stale claim, that is a claim with which he never expected to have to deal'. If a claim is brought a long time after the events in question, the likelihood is that evidence which may have been available earlier may have been lost, and the memories of witnesses who may still be available will inevitably have faded or become confused. Further, it is contrary to general policy to keep people perpetually at risk. **7.01**

Limitation is a procedural defence. It will not be taken by the court of its own motion, but must be specifically set out in the defence (PD 16, para 13.1). Time-barred cases rarely go to trial. If the claimant is unwilling to discontinue the claim, it is usually possible for the defendant to apply successfully for the claim to be struck out (see Chapter 22) as an abuse of the court's process. **7.02**

Normally, the only consequence of the expiry of a limitation period is that the defendant acquires a technical defence to the claim. The claimant still has a cause of action, but one that cannot be enforced. In cases of adverse possession of land and conversion, expiry of the limitation period has the additional consequence of extinguishing the party's title to the land or goods. Extinguishing title does not infringe art 1 of the First Protocol of the European Convention on Human Rights (*J A Pye (Oxford) Ltd v United Kingdom* (Application No 44302.02) (2007) 23 BHRC 405). **7.03**

A LIMITATION PERIODS

7.04 Most limitation periods are laid down in the Limitation Act 1980 ('LA 1980') as amended. Several other statutes lay down limitation periods, and some procedural rules impose time limits which act rather like limitation periods. There has been a move in recent legislation towards flexible limitation periods for some types of cases, which will be considered at 7.52ff. However, the usual rule is that no objection can be taken to a claim started on the last day of the limitation period, but there is a complete defence if proceedings are issued one day late. Table 7.1 sets out the limitation periods for the most important classes of cases.

Table 7.1 Limitation periods

Class of claim		Limitation period
1	Fraudulent breach of trust	None (LA 1980, s 21(1)(a))
2	Recovery of land	12 years (LA 1980, s 15(1))
3	Recovery of money secured by mortgage	12 years (LA 1980, s 20(1))
4	Specialty	12 years (LA 1980, s 8(1))
5	Recovery of a sum due under statute	6 years (LA 1980, s 9(1))
6	Enforcement of a judgment	6 years (LA 1980, s 24(1))
7	Contract	6 years (LA 1980, s 5)
8	Recovery of trust property and breach of trust	6 years (LA 1980, s 21(3))
9	Recovery of arrears of rent	6 years (LA 1980, s 19)
10	Tort (except those listed below)	6 years (LA 1980, s 2)
11	Defective Premises Act 1972 claims	Defective Premises Act 1972, s 1(5))
12	Personal injuries claims	3 years (LA 1980, s 11(4))
13	Fatal Accidents Act 1976 claims	3 years (LA 1980, s 12(2))
14	Personal injuries or damage to property claims under the Consumer Protection Act 1987	3 years (LA 1980, s 11A)
15	Carriage by Air Act 1961 claims	2 years (Carriage by Air Act 1961, Sch 1)
16	Claims for personal injuries or damage to vessel, cargo, or property, or personal injuries to passengers at sea	2 years (Merchant Shipping Act 1995, s 190(3) and Sch 6, Part I, art 16)
17	Contribution under the Civil Liability (Contribution) Act 1978	2 years (LA 1980, s 10(1))
18	Contribution under the Maritime Conventions Act 1911	1 year (Merchant Shipping Act 1995, s 190(4))
19	Defamation and malicious falsehood	1 year (LA 1980, s 4A)
20	Claims under the Human Rights Act 1998, s 7(1)(a)	1 year (Human Rights Act 1998, s 7(5))
21	Applications for judicial review	3 months (CPR, r 54.5)
22	Unfair dismissal under the Employment Rights Act 1996	3 months (Employment Rights Act 1996, s 111(2))

Table 7.1 *continued*

Class of claim		Limitation period
23	Applications for new business tenancies under the Landlord and Tenant Act 1954, Part II	If made by the tenant, not before 2 months after the tenant's request for a new tenancy under s 26 (s 29A(3)), and whether by the tenant or landlord, not after the date specified in any s 25 notice or the day before the date specified in any s 26 request (s 29A(2))
24	Claims for an account	Period applicable to claim on which account is based (LA 1980, s 23)

Category of action

It is sometimes difficult to determine which category a particular case falls into. A claim which is outside the provisions of the LA 1980 is not subject to a strict period of limitation (*Nelson v Rye* [1996] 1 WLR 1378). It may, however, be subject to a time limit by analogy to the LA 1980 (see LA 1980, s 36 and *Coulthard v Disco Mix Club Ltd* [1999] 2 All ER 457), or it may be subject to the defences of laches and acquiescence (as in *Nelson v Rye*, but see the discussion at 7.07). Further, if there is no limitation period, the court may still strike out the proceedings as an abuse of process. In *Taylor v Ribby Hall Leisure Ltd* [1998] 1 WLR 400 an application to commit was delayed by about five years. It was struck out, the court taking into account factors such as the prospects of the court exercising its supervisory powers at the hearing, and the public interest in the efficient administration of justice and the compliance with court orders and undertakings. **7.05**

Categorization problems in trusts and equity claims

The main rules are the six-year limitation period in claims for breach of trust and to recover trust property (LA 1980, s 21(3)), and the unlimited period for bringing claims in respect of any fraud or fraudulent breach of trust to which the trustee was party or privy (s 21(1)(a)) and for claims to recover from a trustee trust property in the possession of the trustee or which was previously received by the trustee and converted to the trustee's use (s 21(1)(b)). A trustee who had negligently left trust money with a solicitor who then embezzled it, but who was not a party to nor privy to the solicitor's fraud was held in *Thorne v Heard* [1894] 1 Ch 599 to be entitled to rely on a limitation defence after six years (class 8 in table 7.1). On the other hand, a claim for an account of profits against a director following a deliberate non-disclosure of an interest was held in *Gwembe Valley Development Co Ltd v Koshy* (2003) LTL 28/7/03 to be a fraudulent breach of trust within s 21(1)(a), with the result that there was no period of limitation. It was held that a breach of trust was fraudulent if it was dishonest. In *Re Pantone 485 Ltd, Miller v Bain* [2002] 1 BCLC 266 it was held that use of a beneficiary's money for the benefit of the fiduciary amounts to a conversion for the use of the fiduciary, and thereby brings the claim within s 21(1)(b) (so there is no limitation period). In *Clarke (executor of the Will of Francis Bacon, deceased) v Marlborough Fine Art (London) Ltd* (2001) *The Times*, 5 July 2001, it was said that it is probable that in undue influence claims the only time-related defences available were laches and acquiescence (and presumably, affirmation). **7.06**

7.07 In *Nelson v Rye* [1996] 1 WLR 1378 it was held that a claim for breach of fiduciary duty *simpliciter* is outside the provisions of the LA 1980, and so is not subject to any limitation period. This case has been called into question by subsequent decisions, particularly *Paragon Finance plc v D B Thakerer and Co* [1999] 1 All ER 400. In *Nelson v Rye* the claimant was a musician and sought accounts from his former manager stretching back 11 years before proceedings were issued. Millett LJ in *Paragon Finance plc v D B Thakerer and Co* pointed out that every agent owes fiduciary duties to his principal, and without something more the claim would have been subject to the usual six-year limitation period. The defendant in *Nelson v Rye* was no more than an accounting party who had failed to account. To have been entitled to a longer limitation period, the claimant would have had to show, among other things, that the defendant owed fiduciary duties in relation to the money.

7.08 Millett LJ in *Paragon Finance plc v D B Thakerer and Co* (and followed in *Coulthard v Disco Mix Club Ltd* [1999] 2 All ER 457) further pointed out that there is a distinction between two categories of constructive trust claim:

(a) Where the constructive trustee, although not expressly appointed as a trustee, has assumed the duties of a trustee before the events which are alleged to constitute the breach of trust. In this category the defendant is a real trustee, and the provisions of the LA 1980, s 21(1), may apply if the other conditions of the subsection are satisfied, with the result that there may be an unlimited period for bringing proceedings. An example is *James v Williams* [2000] Ch 1.

(b) Where the constructive trust is merely the creation of the court as a remedy to meet the alleged wrongdoing. This includes claims of knowing and dishonest assistance in the fraudulent breach of trust of another (*Cattley v Pollard* [2007] Ch 353). In this category there is no real trust, and usually no prospect of a proprietary remedy. The defendant is merely said to be liable to account as a constructive trustee. In this category the other provisions of the LA 1980 apply, with the result that the period will usually be six years from accrual.

Categorization problems in personal injuries claims

7.09 Claims for personal injuries (class 12 in table 7.1) comprise all claims in negligence, nuisance, and breach of duty (including contractual and statutory duties) where the claim to relief consists of or includes damages in respect of personal injuries to the claimant or any other person (LA 1980, s 11(1)). Under LA 1980, s 11(4), the basic limitation period for such claims is three years. An attempt was made to avoid this limitation period in *Letang v Cooper* [1965] 1 QB 232. The claimant was injured when the defendant drove his car over her legs while she was sunbathing on the grass in the car park of a hotel. Proceedings were issued four years afterwards, but the cause of action was pleaded both in negligence and in trespass to the person. The Court of Appeal overruled the trial judge and held the claim was time-barred. Two reasons were advanced. One was that where an injury is inflicted negligently rather than intentionally, the only cause of action is in negligence, so the claimant is unable to rely on the six-year limitation period in trespass (class 10). The second reason was that the phrase 'breach of duty' in what is now LA 1980, s 11(1), covered a breach of any duty under the law of tort. Between 1993 and 2008 (see *Stubbings v Webb* [1993] 2 AC 498 and *A v Hoare* [2008] 1 AC 844), the courts applied a false distinction between intentional and unintentional trespasses to the person. Intentional cases were said to be governed by the six-year limitation period for general tort claims in LA 1980, s 2. However, this meant that the date of knowledge (LA 1980, s 14) and discretion (LA 1980, s 33) provisions did not apply, generating unjust results. For example, the perpetrator of child abuse had a cast iron limitation defence six years after limitation started to run, whereas a secondary party (such as the child's mother, or the proprietors of a care home) could be perpetually at risk of being sued because of the effect of ss 14 and 33. *A v Hoare* departed from *Stubbings v Webb*, applying *Practice Statement (House of Lords: Judicial Precedent)* [1966] 1 WLR 1234, with the result that all personal injury claims are governed by the three-year limitation period and ss 14 and 33.

A negligent failure by an education authority to improve the consequences of the claimant's dyslexia by appropriate teaching, or a negligent failure to treat a physical injury, are both claims for personal injuries (*Adams v Bracknell Forest Borough Council* [2005] 1 AC 76), and are governed by the usual three-year limitation period. Further, a claim in professional negligence against a solicitor arising out of the firm's handling of a divorce ancillary relief claim, which included a claim for anxiety and stress arising out of the firm's alleged mishandling of her claim, became, for that reason, a claim in respect of personal injuries and subject to a three-year limitation period rather than the usual six-year period for claims in tort and breach of contract (*Oates v Harte Reade and Co* [1999] PIQR P120). **7.10**

Other categories

Claims to recover the principal due under a mortgage, even after the mortgaged property is sold, are governed by the 12-year limitation period in class 3, whereas claims for interest are limited to six years by s 20(5) (*Bristol and West plc v Bartlett* [2003] 1 WLR 284). A claim to recover rent due under a lease under seal is governed by the six-year limitation period in class 9, not the 12 years in class 4 (*Romain v Scuba TV Ltd* [1997] QB 887). Although statutes are specialties, money claims pursuant to statute are governed by the six-year period in s 9 (class 5) (see *Central Electricity Board v Halifax Corporation* [1963] AC 785 and *Re Farmizer (Products) Ltd* [1997] 1 BCLC 589), whereas claims for other remedies pursuant to statute will be governed by the 12-year period in s 8 (class 4). A claim for damages for infringement of a right conferred by Community law amounts to a breach of statutory duty, and so is subject to a six-year limitation period in tort (class 10) (*R v Secretary of State for Transport, ex p Factortame Ltd (No 7)* [2001] 1 WLR 942). **7.11**

Foreign limitation periods

Where, in accordance with the rules of private international law, the law of any other country is to be taken into account in any claim in England and Wales, the law of that other country relating to limitation must be applied (Foreign Limitation Periods Act 1984). **7.12**

B ACCRUAL OF CAUSE OF ACTION

The rules on accrual fix the date from which time begins to run for limitation purposes. Lindley LJ in *Reeves v Butcher* [1891] 2 QB 509 stated the general rule which is '. . . that the statute runs from the earliest time at which an action could be brought'. 'Cause of action' was **7.13** defined by Lord Esher MR in *Read v Brown* (1888) 22 QBD 128 as encompassing 'every fact which it would be necessary for the [claimant] to prove, if traversed, in order to support his right to the judgment of the court'. In other words, time runs from the point when facts exist establishing all the essential elements of the cause of action. A distinction is drawn between the substantive elements and mere procedural requirements. Thus, a solicitor can commence a claim to recover costs from a client only if at least a month has elapsed since a bill for those costs has been delivered to the client (Solicitors Act 1974, s 69(1)). In *Coburn v Colledge* [1897] 1 QB 702 it was held that the requirement to furnish a bill was only a procedural matter, and time ran from completion of the work as opposed to delivery of the bill. Sometimes this can be a difficult distinction to draw. *Sevcon Ltd v Lucas CAV Ltd* [1986] 1 WLR 462 concerned the Patents Act 1949, s 13(4), which contained a proviso: 'Provided that an applicant shall not be entitled to institute any proceedings for infringement until the patent has been sealed'. It was held that the cause of action accrued on the date of the infringement, but could not be enforced until the procedural requirement of sealing was met. *Sevcon Ltd v Lucas CAV Ltd* was applied to claims to the personal estate of a deceased person by *Re Loftus* [2005] 1 WLR 1890 which held that time runs under the LA 1980, s 22(a) from the end of the executor's year.

7.14 In addition to the elements of the cause of action being present, there must be a party capable of suing and a party liable to be sued. So, if goods are converted after the owner has died intestate, time runs only from the date letters of administration are taken out (*Thomson v Lord Clanmorris* [1900] 1 Ch 718 *per* Vaughan Williams LJ). On the other hand, time continues running during a period in which the defendant is an undischarged bankrupt (*Anglo Manx Group Ltd v Aitken* [2002] BPIR 215). If it is necessary to restore a company against which a claim is to be made to the register, the date of accrual remains based on the date of the breach (or other element of the cause of action), not on the date of restoration (*Smith v White Knight Laundry Ltd* [2001] 1 WLR 616). Although the court has power under the Companies Act 2006, s 1030(3), to direct that the period between dissolution and restoration shall not count for the purposes of limitation, a direction under this provision should not normally be made unless notice of the application had been served on all parties who could be expected to oppose it.

Accrual in claims for the recovery of land

7.15 Detailed rules dealing with accrual in recovery of land cases are set out in LA 1980, Sch 1. Broadly, time runs from the taking of adverse possession where the person bringing the claim has a present interest in the land but will be delayed until the determination of the preceding interest in the case of future interests. The rules on 'adverse possession' were restated in *J A Pye (Oxford) Ltd v Graham* [2003] 1 AC 419, and apply in all claims for the recovery of land (*Ashe v National Westminster Bank plc* [2008] 1 WLR 710). The question is whether the defendant squatter had dispossessed the paper owner by going into ordinary possession of the land for the requisite 12 years without the consent of the owner. There are two elements, factual possession, which requires an appropriate degree of physical control, and an intention to possess, which is an intention to exclude the world at large, including the paper owner, so far as that is reasonably practicable and so far as the processes of the law will allow.

7.16 The provisions of the LA 1980 as regards registered land were replaced as from 13 October 2003 by the Land Registration Act 2002, Schs 6 and 12. These support the principle under the 2002 Act that the register is to be a complete and accurate record of the state of the title to registered land at any given time, so that it is possible to investigate title to land online, and with the absolute minimum of additional inquiries and inspections. Under the 2002 Act a person claiming adverse possession of registered land for at least 10 years is allowed to apply for registration. The usual evidence of adverse possession is required. The registered owner and any chargees and other interested persons are then served with notice of the application, and they may serve counter-notice. If they fail to do so, the applicant will be registered as the registered proprietor in place of the former proprietor, and free from former charges. If counter-notice is served the application is dismissed unless one of three grounds is established. These are that it would be unfair to dispossess the applicant because of an equity by estoppel; that the applicant has an independent right that suggests he ought to be registered as the owner; or that there has been a reasonable mistake as to boundaries. If an exception applies the applicant will be registered in place of the registered proprietor, and this happens notwithstanding objections from registered chargees. However, charges will continue to apply unless as a matter of general law the applicant's rights have priority over the charge. Where prior charges continue to apply the applicant can apply for an apportionment of the charges between the land acquired by adverse possession and the remainder of the original title.

If an application under the 2002 Act is dismissed the registered owner then has two years in **7.17** which to take action to evict the person claiming adverse possession or otherwise regularize the position. If they fail to do so, once the two years have elapsed the person claiming adverse possession may re-apply for registration, and, if still in possession, will be automatically registered in place of the existing registered owner. If this happens, the applicant is registered with a new, separate title, and takes free of any former registered charge.

Beneficiaries with future interests

A right of action for non-fraudulent breach of trust does not accrue until a future interest falls **7.18** into possession (LA 1980, s 21(3)).

Shortfall on mortgage

A claim to recover the shortfall of money advanced by a building society secured by a **7.19** traditionally worded mortgage accrues when the principal money becomes payable. This will usually be the date of first default (*West Bromwich Building Society v Wilkinson* [2005] 1 WLR 2303).

Money due under statute

In *Swansea City Council v Glass* [1992] QB 844 the council brought a claim to recover the cost **7.20** of repairing a house owned by the defendant and let to a tenant where the defendant had failed to effect necessary repairs. The claim was brought under the Housing Act 1957, s 10(3), and was commenced over six years after the work was done, but less than six years after a demand for payment. It was held that time ran from completion of the work, so the claim was statute-barred.

Contract

7.21 Time runs from the breach of contract. When this is depends on the nature of the obligation sued on and the terms of the contract, and also on whether a repudiatory breach is accepted by the claimant. Applying the general rule, causes of action in breach of contract will accrue as follows:

(a) In claims for breach of the implied terms as to satisfactory quality, etc., in the Sale of Goods Act 1979 ('SoGA 1979'), time normally starts running on delivery of the goods (*Battley v Faulkner* (1820) 3 B & Ald 288).
(b) In claims for late delivery of goods, time runs from the contractual date for delivery.
(c) In claims based on the implied term as to title to goods sold, time runs from the date of the contract, or, in the case of an agreement to sell, from the date title was to pass (see SoGA 1979, s 12(1)).
(d) Claims for the price of goods sold accrue on the contractual date for payment (SoGA 1979, s 49(2)), failing which on the date property in the goods passes to the buyer (s 49(1)) or the date the buyer is informed that the seller is ready and willing to deliver (s 28).
(e) In claims based on defective building work, time usually starts running on practical or substantial completion.
(f) Claims for the price of entire contracts for work and services accrue on completion of the work (*Emery v Day* (1834) 1 Cr M & R 245).
(g) In a construction contract where the price is payable by instalments due on stated dates, time runs in respect of each instalment from the due date (*Henry Boot Construction Ltd v Alstom Combined Cycles Ltd* [2005] 1 WLR 3850).
(h) Claims by banks to recover overdrafts from customers normally accrue on service of a demand in writing (LA 1980, s 6). There is an exception in s 6 relating to loans where the debtor also enters into a collateral obligation to pay, such as by delivering a promissory note, but most bank overdrafts fall into the main category.
(i) Claims against sureties and guarantors usually accrue on default by the principal debtor (*Parr's Banking Co v Yates* [1898] 2 QB 460).
(j) Accrual in the case of negotiable instruments is somewhat complicated. Claims against acceptors and makers based on non-payment accrue on the maturity of the instrument, unless it is a bill of exchange which is accepted after maturity, in which case time runs from the date of acceptance (Bills of Exchange Act 1882, s 10(2)). Bills of exchange often mature on fixed dates, but if they mature (say) a fixed period of time after sight, time starts running on the expiry of that fixed period after acceptance (or after noting or protesting if it is not accepted) (s 14(3)). A claim against a drawer or endorser after dishonour by non-payment accrues when the bill is duly presented for payment and payment is refused or cannot be obtained, or, if presentment is excused, when the bill is overdue and unpaid (s 47(2)).
(k) Accrual in claims against insurers depends on the terms of the policy. The general rule is that time starts running at the date of the loss. For example, claims for constructive total loss accrue on the date of the casualty (*Bank of America National Trust v Chrismas* [1994] 1 All ER 401). However, it is open to the parties to displace the general rule by creating conditions precedent to the insured's right to payment. For example, in *Virk v Gan Life Holdings plc* (1999) 52 BMLR 207 critical illness benefit became payable under a policy if

the insured survived 30 days after suffering a stroke. It was held that time started running 30 days after the stroke.

In cases where the claimant has accepted an anticipatory breach as a repudiation, time starts running from the date of acceptance rather than the contractual date for performance of the obligation in question (*Reeves v Butcher* [1891] 2 QB 509). Claims for consequential losses, such as salvage charges arising out of a claim based on the loss of a ship, against an insurer are not separate causes of action, so accrual turns on the date of the underlying cause of action (the casualty), not on the date the consequential loss was incurred (*Bank of America National Trust v Chrismas* [1994] 1 All ER 401). There are several types of contractual obligation that give rise to continuing or repeated breaches. An example of a continuing breach is a failure to comply with a covenant to keep in repair (*Spoor v Green* (1874) LR 9 Ex 99 at 111), and an example of a repeated breach is a failure to pay rent (*Archbold v Scully* (1861) 9 HL Cas 360). In these cases the claimant will be able to succeed in respect of the consequences of breach over the six-year period (twelve years for claims on a specialty) before the claim form is issued. **7.22**

General claims in tort

The general rule is that, in addition to proving that the defendant is guilty of some wrongful conduct, liability in tort can only be established on proof of damage. Usually, damage is the final matter to come into existence, so the usual rule is that time runs in tort from the date when damage is sustained. The important date is the date damage was sustained, not the date on which the claimant discovered the damage (*Cartledge v E Jopling and Sons Ltd* [1963] AC 758). In a claim against a solicitor for negligent advice, actual damage is suffered when the advice is acted upon, such as by executing a document (*Forster v Outred and Co* [1982] 1 WLR 86). In *Watkins v Jones Maidment Wilson* [2008] PNLR 23, negligent advice resulted in an immediate measurable loss because the claimant lost the chance of negotiating a better agreement. In *Pirelli General Cable Works Ltd v Oscar Faber and Partners* [1983] 2 AC 1 it was held that a cause of action for negligent design of a chimney arose when cracking in the structure first developed, and not when the damage could have been or was in fact discovered. Where a claimant seeks to sue a solicitor for negligently allowing a claim to be struck out (as a sanction for breach of directions or the requirements of the CPR), time runs from the date when the claimant had no arguable basis for avoiding the claim being struck out, not from the date on which it was actually struck out (*Khan v R M Falvey & Co* [2002] PNLR 28; but see also *Cohen v Kingsley Napley* [2006] PNLR 22). Where the claim is in respect of a transaction entered into through a breach of duty owed by the defendant to the claimant (such as a loan agreement entered into in reliance on a negligent property valuation), time will run from the date the transaction was entered into if the claimant suffered a loss there and then. If there was no immediate loss, such as where the security for a loan was worth more than the loan when it was first advanced (albeit not as much as the defendant's valuation), time will start running only when the value of the security falls below the amount of the loan (see the discussion in *First National Commercial Bank plc v Humberts* [1995] 2 All ER 673). **7.23**

If a person injured in an accident later dies as a result of those injuries, the cause of action vesting in the injured person's estate under the Law Reform (Miscellaneous Provisions) Act **7.24**

1934 accrued at the date of the accident. However, the related cause of action for the benefit of the injured person's dependants under the Fatal Accidents Act 1976, s 1, accrues on the date of death, with the result there are two limitation periods (*Reader v Molesworths Bright Clegg* [2007] 1 WLR 1082).

7.25 The decision in *Darley Main Colliery v Mitchell* (1886) 11 App Cas 127 on continuing torts giving a fresh cause of action each time damage is suffered applies to subsidence claims and trespass claims based on leaving things on the claimant's land. The same principle was applied in *Phonographic Performance Ltd v Department of Trade and Industry* [2004] 1 WLR 2893, a claim for breach of statutory duty against the Crown for failing to implement an EC Directive.

Trespass and libel

7.26 These are actionable per se, so time runs from the wrongful act since there is no requirement to prove damage.

Conversion

7.27 Time runs from the date the goods were converted. A number of special rules apply:

(a) where goods are converted more than once, the original six-year period continues to run and is not renewed (LA 1980, s 3(1));
(b) at the end of the original six-year period the true owner's title is extinguished (LA 1980, s 3(2));
(c) subject to (d) below, there is no time limit where goods are stolen (LA 1980, s 4);
(d) where goods are converted (but not stolen) and are then stolen at a later date, proceedings in respect of the theft are barred once the true owner's title is extinguished under s 3(2) by virtue of the original conversion (LA 1980, s 4(1)).

Personal injuries claims: date of knowledge

7.28 Time runs in personal injuries claims from the date the cause of action accrued or, if later, the date of the claimant's date of knowledge (LA 1980, s 11(4)). Date of knowledge is defined by s 14(1) as:

> ...the date on which [the claimant] first had knowledge of the following facts—
>
> (a) that the injury in question was significant; and
> (b) that the injury was attributable in whole or in part to the act or omission which is alleged to constitute negligence, nuisance or breach of duty; and
> (c) the identity of the defendant; and
> (d) if it is alleged that the act or omission was that of a person other than the defendant, the identity of that person and the additional facts supporting the bringing of an action against the defendant.

7.29 The subsection concludes by providing that knowledge that any acts or omissions did or did not, as a matter of law, involve negligence, nuisance, or breach of duty is irrelevant.

7.30 The claimant is taken to know facts observable or ascertainable by him or her, and also facts ascertainable with the help of expert advice which it would have been reasonable to obtain (LA 1980, s 14(3)). A substantially objective test has to be applied to s 14(3) (*Adams v Bracknell*

Forest Borough Council [2005] 1 AC 76). It is to be expected that claimants who have suffered significant injuries will seek professional advice on the cause of their problems, even if they have serious difficulties with reading and writing as a result of unaddressed dyslexia (*Adams v Bracknell Forest Borough Council*). A claimant who eventually makes a claim against a drug company in respect of the effects of an allegedly defective drug may well have consulted a doctor at an early stage when possibly drug-related symptoms first became apparent. A doctor is likely to concentrate on a solution to the patient's problems rather than give advice on attributing blame. Therefore, whether the doctor's knowledge about the cause of the claimant's symptoms should be attributed to the claimant depends on whether in the circumstances it would have been reasonable to expect the claimant to have asked the doctor about cause as well as cure (*Nash v Eli Lilly and Co* [1993] 1 WLR 782).

In *Ali v Courtaulds Textiles Ltd* (1999) *The Times*, 28 May 1999, the Court of Appeal held that the claimant in an industrial deafness case could not be said to know his deafness was attributable to his working conditions, as opposed to being age-induced, until after he had been advised by his doctors. In *Copeland v Smith* [2000] 1 WLR 1371, the claimant's solicitor was dilatory in obtaining a police road accident report, which would have included the details of the defendant's identity. It was held that the proviso to s 14(3) was not intended to give an extended period to a person whose solicitor acted in a dilatory manner in obtaining information which is obtainable without particular expertise, and the claimant was fixed with constructive knowledge which the claimant's solicitors ought to have acquired. **7.31**

It was held in *H v N* (2004) LTL 29/4/04 to be legitimate for a claimant to restrict a claim to post-traumatic stress disorder which arose in a delayed form, and not to include a claim for alleged underlying (and earlier) physical abuse. In such a case the 'injury in question' for the purposes of s 14(1)(a) is the subsequent post-traumatic stress disorder. An injury is 'significant' for the purposes of LA 1980, s 14(1)(a), if the claimant would reasonably have considered it sufficiently serious to justify proceedings against a defendant who does not dispute liability and is able to satisfy any judgment. The court has to find what the claimant knew (and should have known under s 14(3)) about his injuries, and then decide whether a reasonable person with that knowledge would have considered the injuries sufficiently serious to justify commencing proceedings (*A v Hoare* [2008] 1 AC 844). The burden of proof on whether the claimant knew an injury was significant is on the defendant (*Furniss v Firth Brown Tools Ltd* [2008] EWCA Civ 182). It was held in *Stephen v Riverside Health Authority* (1989) *The Times*, 29 November 1989, that the early symptoms of cancer arising from excessive radiation received from a medical X-ray did not amount to a significant injury. The presence of pleural plaques as a result of exposure to asbestos was held to be no injury at all in *Rothwell v Chemical and Insulating Co Ltd* [2008] 1 AC 28, because the evidence was that pleural plaques cause no symptoms and do not increase susceptibility to asbestos-related diseases. **7.32**

As to s 14(1)(b), it is clear that knowledge detailed enough to enable the claimant's advisers to draft particulars of claim is not required before time starts to run, and there is no requirement that the claimant must be aware that the defendant's conduct is actionable. To hold that this is the case would be contrary to the final words of s 14(1) that knowledge that any acts or omissions do or do not constitute negligence as a matter of law is irrelevant. Time runs under this element when the claimant (or the claimant's doctor) concluded there was a real possibility that the defendant's activities caused the claimant's injury, such that a reasonable person would then investigate the link further (*Kew v* **7.33**

Bettamix Ltd [2007] PIQR P210). In *Broadley v Guy Clapham and Co* [1994] 4 All ER 439 the claimant had gone into hospital for a knee operation, and left suffering from a condition known as foot drop. It was held that time started to run when the claimant had both a 'broad knowledge' that the operation had caused an injury to her foot, and specific knowledge that the operation had been carried out in such a way as to damage a nerve in her leg (the cause of her foot-drop condition). She had the requisite broad knowledge shortly after the operation, and should have had the specific knowledge within a few months after the operation if she had taken the appropriate expert advice. Whether the relevant facts could be known only after obtaining an expert's report depends on the complexity of the case (*Hendy v Milton Keynes Health Authority* (1991) 3 Med LR 114). Thus, in *Forbes v Wandsworth Health Authority* [1997] QB 402 the claimant was admitted to hospital for an operation to cure circulation problems in his leg. The operation was not a success, and a fortnight later his leg was amputated. He did not obtain actual knowledge of the default of the hospital that he later relied on in proceedings for medical negligence until he received advice from a consultant 10 years later. It was held that, where an operation was expected to be successful, but ended up with disappointing results, the patient had to be allowed a reasonable time in which to get over the shock and to take stock of the situation before being expected to seek advice for the purpose of bringing a claim. Where the results were serious, as in this case, the taking-stock period would be in the region of 12 to 18 months. From that point the patient would be fixed with constructive knowledge, and time would start running for limitation purposes.

7.34 Time was postponed in *Cressey v E Timm and Son Ltd* [2005] 1 WLR 3926 on the ground that the claimant did not know the precise legal identity of his employer, because his pay slips were issued by one company, but he was employed by a different, but related, company.

Fatal accidents and death: date of knowledge

7.35 Time runs in claims brought by dependants under the Fatal Accidents Act 1976 from the date of death or the 'date of knowledge' (as set out in 7.28) of the person for whose benefit the proceedings are brought (LA 1980, s 12). In proceedings brought for the benefit of the deceased's estate under the Law Reform (Miscellaneous Provisions) Act 1934 time runs from the date of death or the personal representative's 'date of knowledge' (LA 1980, s 11(5)).

Defective products

7.36 Claims under the Consumer Protection Act 1987 in respect of personal injuries or damage to property accrue on the date of damage or the 'date of knowledge' (LA 1980, s 11A(4)).

Accrual in contribution claims

7.37 Contribution claims accrue on the date the amount of the underlying liability is fixed, disregarding any possible appeal. If determined by the court, time runs from judgment; if fixed by agreement, time runs from the date of settlement (LA 1980, s 10(3) and (4)). In the case of split trials, time runs from the judgment on liability (*Aer Lingus v Gildacroft Ltd* [2006] 1 WLR

1173). Where a firm agreement to settle the primary claim is made, time starts running immediately under s 10(4), and does not start again if the agreement is subsequently recorded in a consent order. However, if the agreement contains a term requiring a consent order before it takes effect, time will run from the order not the agreement. See *Knight v Rochdale Healthcare NHS Trust* [2004] 1 WLR 371.

C CALCULATING THE LIMITATION PERIOD

Time runs from the day following the day on which the cause of action arose, as parts of a day are ignored (*Marren v Dawson Bentley and Co Ltd* [1961] 2 QB 135). It runs until the claim is brought, as opposed to issued (*Barnes v St Helens Metropolitan Borough Council (Practice Note)* [2007] 1 WLR 879) or served (*per* Lord Diplock in *Thompson v Brown* [1981] 1 WLR 744). As claim forms are date-stamped when they are issued, the date of issue is often the best evidence of when the claim is brought. A claimant may send a claim form to the court office for issue. Letters requesting the issue of claim forms will be date-stamped on receipt, and the date of receipt will stop time running for limitation purposes if the court does not issue the claim form on the same day (PD 7A, paras 5.1 and 5.2). An inquiry as to the date on which a claim form was received by the court should be directed to a court officer (para 5.3). Ultimately, however, a claim is brought when the claimant delivers all the relevant documents to the court office for issue (even if the office is closed at that time: see *Barnes v St Helens Metropolitan Borough Council (Practice Note)*). If the court office is closed on the final day of the limitation period, proceedings are deemed to be in time if they are issued on the next day the court office is open (*Pritam Kaur v S Russell and Sons Ltd* [1973] QB 337). Paragraph 5.4 goes on to say that parties should recognize the importance of establishing the date of receipt if a limitation period is approaching, and should take steps to record the date of receipt. In cases where limitation might be a problem, it is usually best to make a personal attendance at court to issue the proceedings. **7.38**

Additional claims under Part 20 are commenced for limitation purposes on the date the claim form under Part 20 is issued (LA 1980, s 35(1)(a)). This is because s 35(1)(a) uses the word 'commenced' rather than 'brought', a point confirmed in relation to third-party proceedings by CPR, r 20.7(2). **7.39**

Disability

There are two categories of persons under disability: children and persons of unsound mind. By virtue of LA 1980, s 28, time does not run against a child until that person's 18th birthday. Also by virtue of s 28, time does not run against a person of unsound mind if that person was under disability at the date the cause of action accrued. Thus, an adult who is immediately rendered of unsound mind by an accident is not subject to limitation until he or she recovers. The same applies to a child who has a cause of action while of sound mind, but who becomes of unsound mind before reaching the age of majority. However, time will continue to run during a period of mental disorder where a cause of action accrues to an adult who was of sound mind at the date of accrual. **7.40**

Fraud

7.41 In claims based on fraud, the limitation period does not begin to run until the claimant discovers the fraud or could with reasonable diligence have discovered it (LA 1980, s 32(1)(a)). Time does not run while the claimant merely suspects dishonesty (*Barnstaple Boat Co Ltd v Jones* [2008] 1 All ER 1124). This provision applies only where fraud is the essence of the claim. A claim in conversion where the defendant has incidentally been guilty of fraud or dishonesty does not bring the provision into effect (*Beaman v ARTS Ltd* [1949] 1 KB 550).

Concealment

7.42 Time does not run where any fact relevant to the claim has been deliberately concealed by the defendant until the concealment is discovered or with reasonable diligence could have been discovered (LA 1980, s 32(1)(b)). In *Cave v Robinson Jarvis & Rolf* [2003] 1 AC 384 the House of Lords overruled previous Court of Appeal authorities, including *Brocklesbury v Armitage & Guest* [2002] 1 WLR 598 (which had given an unduly wide interpretation of s 32(1)(b)), and held that s 32(1)(b) deprives a defendant of a limitation defence:

(a) where the defendant has taken active steps to conceal his breach of duty after he has become aware of it; and
(b) where the defendant is guilty of deliberate wrongdoing and conceals or fails to disclose it in circumstances where the wrongdoing is unlikely to be discovered for some time.

7.43 However, the mere fact that the defendant intended to do the act complained of does not mean that s 32(1)(b) applies to prevent time running. If the defendant is unaware of his alleged error or that he may have failed to take proper care, there is nothing for the defendant to disclose, and time is not prevented from running by s 32(1)(b). Consequently, time will run where a surgeon negligently leaves a swab inside a patient; and where an anaesthetist negligently administers the wrong drug; and where a solicitor gives a client negligent advice. Time will not run if the surgeon deliberately left the swab inside the patient, or if the lawyer after giving negligent advice fails to disclose other facts which he is under a duty to disclose to the client which would have alerted the client to the negligent nature of the advice.

Mistake

7.44 Where the claim is for relief from the consequences of a mistake, time does not run until the mistake is, or could with reasonable diligence have been, discovered (LA 1980, s 32(1)(c)). What amounts to 'reasonable diligence' is a question of fact. In *Peco Arts Inc v Hazlitt Gallery Ltd* [1983] 1 WLR 1315, a case involving an alleged mistake over whether a nineteenth-century drawing was an original signed by the artist, it was held that the term meant doing what an ordinary prudent buyer of a valuable work of art would do. In *Kleinwort Benson Ltd v Lincoln City Council* [1999] 2 AC 349, the House of Lords held that the LA 1980, s 32(1)(c) applies to all mistakes, whether of fact or of law, so that it could apply where the claimant had paid money to the defendant under a mistake of law.

7.45 There are difficult cases on this topic, as shown by *Deutsche Morgan Grenfell Group plc v Inland Revenue Commissioners* [2007] 1 AC 558, HL. The taxpayer brought a claim in restitution based on the disadvantage it suffered through paying tax early as a result of a mistake of law. The point of tax law was settled by a decision of the European Court of Justice ('ECJ'). It was held by the House of Lords that s 32(1)(c) applied, and time ran against the taxpayer from the date it discovered the mistake, which on the facts was the date of the decision of the ECJ. Lord Hoffmann considered the distinction between a mistake about the law, which comes within s 32(1)(c), and merely having a doubt as to the legal position, which does not. On the facts the taxpayer was labouring under a mistake of law, even after the taxpayer became aware that another taxpayer was taking the tax point to the ECJ. This was because the taxpayer took the view that the existing tax statute had to be complied with despite the challenge.

Latent damage

It follows from the decision in *Pirelli General Cable Works Ltd v Oscar Faber and Partners* [1983] 2 AC 1, noted at 7.23, that it is possible for a claim in tort to be statute-barred before the claimant knows that damage has been sustained, because time runs from the date of damage rather than discovery. To mitigate this position the Latent Damage Act 1986 inserted ss 14A and 14B into the LA 1980. These provisions apply to actions for negligence other than for personal injuries (s 14A(1)). They are restricted to claims in tort, and do not extend to claims for 'contractual negligence' (*Société Commerciale de Réassurance v ERAS (International) Ltd* [1992] 2 All ER 82). **7.46**

Two alternative periods of limitation are provided by LA 1980, s 14A(4), namely, six years from accrual and three years from the 'starting date'. The first of these periods is simply the usual period for actions in tort. The 'starting date' is the earliest date the claimant knew: **7.47**

(a) that the relevant damage was sufficiently serious to justify proceedings; and
(b) that the damage was attributable to the alleged negligence; and
(c) the defendant's identity.

A claimant is also fixed with constructive knowledge from facts observable or ascertainable by himself or with the help of an appropriate expert (s 14A(10)). This is a reference to advice from an independent expert rather than the potential defendant (*Williams v Lishman, Sidwell, Campbell and Price Ltd* [2009] PNLR 34).

These concepts are very similar to those in s 14 (see 7.28) and it was accepted in *Hallam-Eames v Merrett* (1995) *The Times*, 25 January 1995 that the authorities on s 14 apply to applications under s 14A. 'Knowledge' in s 14A means knowing with sufficient confidence to justify embarking on the preliminaries to issuing proceedings. Under condition (b), it is clear the claimant does not need to know that the defendant's conduct could be characterized as negligent. Instead, it is enough for the claimant to have broad knowledge of the facts on which the complaint is based, combined with knowing as a real possibility that the alleged acts or omissions caused the damage under condition (a) (*Haward v Fawcetts* [2006] 1 WLR 682). **7.48**

In order to give some protection to defendants who might otherwise be perpetually at risk, s 14B provides a longstop or overriding time limit for bringing proceedings of 15 years from the act or omission alleged to constitute the negligence causing the claimant's damage. **7.49**

Judgments

By the LA 1980, s 24(1), an action may not be brought upon any judgment after the expiry of six years from the date on which the judgment became enforceable. In *Re a Debtor (No 50A–SD–95)* [1997] Ch 310 a judgment creditor served a statutory demand based on a judgment **7.50** entered eight years previously. It was held that bankruptcy proceedings based on the statutory demand constituted an 'action' on the judgment, and would be time-barred under s 24. However, bringing an 'action' on a judgment is limited to a fresh action, and does not include proceedings by way of execution (*Lowsley v Forbes* [1999] 1 AC 329). If enforcement proceedings are brought more than six years after judgment, the LA 1980, s 24(2), will limit the interest that can be claimed on the judgment debt to that accrued over six years.

Acknowledgments and part-payments

7.51 Under the LA 1980, s 29, acknowledging title to land, acknowledging a debt, and making part payments have the effect of renewing the limitation period from the date of acknowledgment or payment. Under s 30 any acknowledgment must be in writing and signed by the person liable or his agent. A typed signature on a telex is enough (*Good Challenger Navengante SA v Metalexportimport SA* [2004] 1 Lloyd's Rep 67). An acknowledgment in a pleading takes effect on its date, and is not a continuing acknowledgment (*Ofulue v Bossert* [2009] 1 AC 990). However, an acknowledgment in a privileged communication cannot be used under s 29 (*Ofulue v Bossert*). The part-payment of rent or interest due at any time does not extend the time for claiming the balance (s 29(6)), but a payment made outside a repayment schedule has the effect of renewing the limitation period (*International Finance Corporation v Utexafrica Sprl* (2001) LTL 9/5/01).

D DISCRETION

Judicial review

7.52 The three-month time limit for bringing judicial review proceedings can be extended if good reasons are shown: see 45.49–45.50.

Defamation

7.53 Where defamation or malicious falsehood proceedings are not commenced within the one-year time limit, the court may direct that the limitation period shall not apply if it appears equitable to allow the action to proceed, having regard to the balance of prejudice between the claimant and the defendant (LA 1980, s 32A, as substituted by the Defamation Act 1996, s 5). This section has been modelled on the existing s 33, which provides a similar discretion in personal injuries cases, and which is considered in some detail in 7.54ff. Permission was granted in *Wood v Chief Constable of West Midlands Police* (2004) *The Times*, 13 December 2004, to add an alternative claim for slander four years after the event by way of an amendment at the close of evidence in a libel trial.

Personal injuries claims

7.54 A wide discretion is given to override the usual three-year limitation period in personal injuries claims by LA 1980, s 33, which in part provides:

(1) If it appears to the court that it would be equitable to allow an action to proceed having regard to the degree to which—

(a) the provisions of section 11 or 11A or 12 of this Act prejudice the plaintiff or any person whom he represents; and
(b) any decision of the court under this subsection would prejudice the defendant or any person whom he represents; the court may direct that those provisions shall not apply to the action, or shall not apply to any specified cause of action to which the action relates.

...

(2) In acting under this section the court shall have regard to all the circumstances of the case and in particular to—
(a) the length of, and the reasons for, the delay on the part of the plaintiff;
(b) the extent to which, having regard to the delay, the evidence adduced or likely to be adduced by the plaintiff or the defendant is or is likely to be less cogent than if the action had been brought within the time allowed by section 11, by section 11A or (as the case may be) by section 12;
(c) the conduct of the defendant after the cause of action arose, including the extent (if any) to which he responded to requests reasonably made by the plaintiff for information or inspection for the purpose of ascertaining facts which were or might be relevant to the plaintiff's cause of action against the defendant;
(d) the duration of any disability of the plaintiff arising after the date of the accrual of the cause of action;
(e) the extent to which the plaintiff acted promptly and reasonably once he knew whether or not the act or omission of the defendant, to which the injury was attributable, might be capable at that time of giving rise to an action for damages;
(f) the steps, if any, taken by the plaintiff to obtain medical, legal, or other expert advice and the nature of any such advice he may have received.

The factors set out in s 33(3) are those which experience had indicated were of real importance in considering where the balance of prejudice was likely to lie. The delay referred to in para (a) is the same as that referred to in para (b), namely, the delay after the expiry of the primary limitation period as extended, if appropriate, by the claimant's date of knowledge under s 14 (*Long v Tolchard and Sons Ltd* (1999) *The Times*, 5 January 2000), although only limited weight will be given to reasons for delay after the date of knowledge in cases where s 14 extends the normal limitation period (*KR v Bryn Alyn Community (Holdings) Ltd* [2003] QB 1441). The reasons for the delay to be considered are those of the claimant: it is a subjective test (*Coad v Cornwall and Isles of Scilly Health Authority* [1997] 1 WLR 189). Having found what the reason is for the delay, the court must then decide whether the reason is good or bad. The question of cogency in para (b) is concerned only with the loss or adverse effect on evidence through the passage of time. A court is not entitled in an application under s 33 to find prejudice to the defendant by assuming that omissions or contradictions in the claimant's evidence may be excused by the trial judge (*Nash v Eli Lilly and Co* [1993] 1 WLR 782). **7.55**

The period of disability referred to in para (d) is one of mental disability arising after the accrual of the cause of action, and hence one which does not prevent time running (see 7.40). **7.56**

The leading authority on s 33 is *Thompson v Brown* [1981] 1 WLR 744, in which the House of Lords held that the court has a discretion unfettered by any rules of practice, that the **7.57** court must consider all the circumstances of the case, and is not restricted to the matters specifically set out in s 33(3). Lord Diplock said in that case that a direction under s 33 is always prejudicial to the defendant, but the extent of the prejudice is related to the strength or otherwise of the claim or defence. One factor not mentioned in s 33(3), but of considerable importance, is whether the claimant has an alternative claim in negligence against his or her solicitor for failing to issue proceedings in time. This factor can be discounted if there is real doubt about the strength of the claim against the solicitor, and in any event the claimant will suffer some prejudice through further delay, instructing unknown solicitors to pursue the new claim, the old solicitors knowing the weaknesses of the original claim, and possible restrictions in obtaining disclosure against the original defendants.

7.58 A second factor not mentioned in s 33(3) which is always regarded as being of considerable importance is the delay between the accident and the defendant being informed of the claim. The reason is that a defendant who is informed of the potential claim at an early stage has the opportunity to investigate the facts while the events are still fresh in witnesses' memories, even if proceedings are issued rather late, and hence cannot complain of significant prejudice under s 33(3)(b). This seems to have been a significant factor in *Thompson v Brown* and also in *Hartley v Birmingham City District Council* [1992] 1 WLR 968. In *Cain v Francis* [2009] QB 754 it was held that in early notification cases, financial prejudice to the defendant should not be taken into account. Conversely, in *Donovan v Gwentoys Ltd* [1990] 1 WLR 472 there was a delay in excess of six years before the defendants were given full details of the claim. In fact proceedings were issued only six months late, as the claimant was a child at the date of the accident. She instructed solicitors 19 days before her 18th birthday, so she had an alternative claim against her solicitors. It was held that the delay in notifying the defendants was an extremely important consideration, that it would be inequitable to require the defendants to meet such a stale claim, and the claimant would suffer only the slightest prejudice in being required to sue her solicitors. Permission was refused. The different results in the cases in this paragraph turn on whether there is forensic prejudice as a result of the delay (*McDonnell v Walker* [2010] PIQR P5).

7.59 Parker LJ in *Hartley v Birmingham City District Council* [1992] 1 WLR 968 expressed the view that the merits of the claimant's case are of little importance, on the ground that the stronger the merits the greater the prejudice to both the claimant and the defendant of the decision under s 33 going against them. This is contrary to Lord Diplock's judgment in *Thompson v Brown*, and contrary to subsequent cases. These include *Nash v Eli Lilly and Co* [1993] 1 WLR 782, where a finding that the claims were weak was regarded as an important factor in refusing to make orders under s 33, and *Long v Tolchard and Sons Ltd* (1999) *The Times*, 5 January 2000, where it was said that, if the claimant has a strong, or even a cast-iron, case against the original tortfeasor, that is an important factor to place into the balance that has to be struck. Of course, like all the other factors, the strength of the case is not determinative of the application.

7.60 Many reasons for not bringing a claim, such as a reluctance to sue one's present employer, can be important factors under s 33. So, in *McCafferty v Metropolitan Police District Receiver* [1977] 1 WLR 1073 Lawton LJ said, '. . . the court should be understanding of men who, after taking an overall view of their situation, come to the conclusion that they would prefer to go on working rather than become involved in litigation'. Likewise, deciding not to sue a defendant at a time when the defendant had no money to pay any judgment may justify a period of delay (*A v Hoare* [2008] 1 AC 844).

Discretionary extension of the limitation period under s 33 has no application in cases governed by the two-year limitation period under the Convention relating to the Carriage of Passengers and their Luggage by Sea (as enacted by the Merchant Shipping Act 1995; class 16 in table 7.1): see *Higham v Stena Sealink Ltd* [1996] 1 WLR 1107. **7.61**

Applications under s 33 should generally be made to a judge, although in the county courts they can be made to a district judge if the value of the claim does not exceed £25,000 (the trial jurisdiction for district judges): *Hughes v Jones* [1996] PIQR P380. It is incumbent on the claimant to disclose all relevant circumstances at the hearing of the application and, if this is breached, the decision may be set aside (*Long v Tolchard and Sons Ltd* (1999) *The Times*, 5 January 2000). **7.62**

Issuing a second claim

At one time it was held that the LA 1980, s 33, could only be used to disapply limitation if the claimant had not previously brought proceedings in respect of the accident in question (*Walkley v Precision Forgings Ltd* [1979] 1 WLR 606). This meant that s 33 could not be used if proceedings had been brought within limitation, but did not proceed to trial for any reason, and a second claim was then issued outside the limitation period. This restriction was removed by *Horton v Sadler* [2007] 1 AC 307. **7.63**

E EQUITABLE REMEDIES, LACHES, AND ACQUIESCENCE

By LA 1980, s 36(1), the usual time limits in the Act do 'not apply to any claim for specific performance of a contract or for an injunction or for other equitable relief, except in so far as any such time limit may be applied by the court by analogy'. The court refused to apply any limitation period (other than laches and acquiescence) to a claim for specific performance in *P&O Nedlloyd BV v Arab Metals Co (No 2)* [2007] 1 WLR 2288. **7.64**

The defences of laches and acquiescence are preserved by s 36(2). Laches operates to bar equitable relief (only), and applies where the defendant has detrimentally relied on delay in bringing a claim (*Fisher v Brooker* [2009] 1 WLR 1764, HL). The period of delay, the events during that period, and the balance of justice are taken into account in deciding whether a claim is barred by laches. The defence of acquiescence applies where there has been an encouragement or allowance of a party to believe something to his detriment (*Jones v Stones* [1999] 1 WLR 1739). There is probably no difference between these formulations of laches and acquiescence, a point noted in *Fisher v Brooker*. The first question is whether one party, by its action or inaction, has encouraged the other party to believe a certain state of affairs. The second question is whether there was reliance on that encouragement. Thirdly, whether in all the circumstances of the case it would be unconscionable for the first party to then insist on its legal rights. It is incorrect to concentrate on the period of delay as being enough of itself. **7.65**

7.66 The period of delay likely to give rise to these equitable defences depends on the nature of the relief claimed and the facts of the case. Delay in the context of interim injunctions is considered in 35.86. In the case of actions to redeem mortgages, a period of 20 years was said to be a convenient guide in *Weld v Petre* [1929] 1 Ch 33. Laches was held to be a defence where a shareholder failed to assert his rights for 24 years in *Lynch v James Lynch and Sons (Transport) Ltd* (2000) LTL 8/3/00.

KEY POINTS SUMMARY

7.67
- Limitation runs from accrual, which is when all the necessary elements for the cause of action are in existence.
- Technically, time runs from the day after the accident or breach (parts of days are disregarded), and stops running when the claim is brought. This is when the claimant has done everything they can to issue the claim form.
- Time does not run if the claimant is under disability, and in cases of fraud, mistake, and concealment.
- In personal injury and latent damage claims time will not start running until the claimant has the requisite 'knowledge'.
- In personal injury and defamation claims the court has a discretion to 'disapply' the primary limitation period.
- If a claim is time-barred, the defendant should plead limitation in the defence, and should consider applying to strike out the claim as an abuse of process (Chapter 22).

8

ISSUING AND SERVING

The usual way to commence civil proceedings is by issuing a claim form. There is a prescribed form for the claim form, N1. There are some other methods of commencing proceedings, and they will be considered in Chapter 19. Issuing a claim involves the court sealing the claim form with its official seal. This is not quite the same thing as 'bringing' a claim for the purposes of stopping time running for limitation purposes (see 7.38), although often the two events will happen on the same day. Generally, a claim form must be served within four months of being issued. In certain circumstances the four-month period may be extended, which is a subject considered in Chapter 9. The main topics that will be considered in this chapter will be issuing **8.01** and serving proceedings. There are slightly different rules governing service of documents other than the claim form, and these will be considered towards the end of the chapter.

A CLAIM FORM

8.02 It is the responsibility of the claimant's solicitors to prepare the claim form before issue. For most proceedings there is a general-purpose claim form (form N1: see figure 8.1) that can be used. There are certain specialized claim forms, such as the N1(CC) (see figure 8.2) used in the Commercial Court and forms N5, N5A, and N5B used in possession claims. A completed claim form will:

(a) set out the names and addresses of the respective parties;
(b) give a concise statement of the nature of the claim;
(c) state the remedy sought; and
(d) contain a statement of value where the claim is for money.

Figure 8.1 Form N1 Claim form

Royal Arms	Claim Form	In the High Court of Justice Queen's Bench Division Claim No HQ10 87105	
Claimant Stephenson Hyperlinks Plc			
	SEAL		
Defendant Lomax Fishing Equipment Limited			
Brief details of claim	Sums due for breach of contract		
Value	£63,372.50 plus accrued interest of £7,861.66		
Defendant's name and address			£
Lomax Fishing Equipment Limited		Amount claimed	71,234.16
20 Morton Street		Court fee	630.00
Nottingham		Solicitor's costs	To be assessed
NG3 4TF		Issue date	22.9.2010

Does, or will, your claim include issues under the Human Rights Act 1998? Yes No
Particulars of claim

1. At all material times the Claimant has been in business designing bespoke computer systems for other businesses, and the Defendant has been in business selling angling equipment, and has operated a telephone sales department.
2. By an oral contract ('the Contract') made at the Defendant's offices by Mrs Lisa Stephenson acting on behalf of the Claimant and Mr James Lomax acting on behalf of the Defendant on 3 September 2008 and evidenced in writing by letters (true copies of which are served with these Particulars of Claim) from the Claimant to the Defendant dated 5 September 2008 and from the Defendant to the Claimant dated 17 September 2008, the Claimant agreed to design and supply certain computer equipment and software to the Defendant being a bespoke computer order processing system for the Defendant's business (together referred to as 'the computer system').

Figure 8.1 *continued*

3. There were express terms of the Contract that:
   (a) the equipment and services provided under the Contract would be paid for by the Defendant at rates set out in the Claimant's price list dated 5 June 2008, a true copy of which is served with these Particulars of Claim;
   (b) the Defendant would pay the Claimant for the equipment and services provided under the Contract within 30 days of being invoiced;
   (c) subject to sub-paragraph (b) above, an initial sum of £50,000 would be paid by the Defendant to the Claimant on 4 December 2008 on account of the sums payable under the Contract; and
   (d) payment of the initial sum of £50,000 was a condition precedent to the Claimant's obligation to deliver the computer system.
4. In performance of the Contract the Claimant developed a bespoke computer system for the Defendant, and since 8 January 2009 has been ready and able to deliver the computer system to the Defendant.
5. In breach of the initial payment obligation pleaded in paragraph 3(c) above the Defendant has failed and/or refused to pay all or any of the initial sum of £50,000 whether on 4 December 2008 or at all.
6. The Claimant's claim is for £63,372.50 being the price of goods and services provided or ready to be provided by the Claimant to the Defendant, full particulars of which are given in the invoices detailed below, true copies of which are served with these Particulars of Claim.
7. Alternatively, the Defendant is in breach of the express term set out in paragraph 3(c) above by failing to pay the initial sum of £50,000 by 4 December 2008 or at all, and is thereby in breach of the condition precedent set out in paragraph 3(d) above.

PARTICULARS

4 October 2008	To Invoice No: 3510	£8,000.00
13 November 2008	To Invoice No: 3831	£17,494.75
17 December 2008	To Invoice No: 4023	£28,800.00
4 February 2009	To Invoice No: 4169	£9,077.75
		£63,372.50

8. Alternatively, the failure to pay combined with a letter from the Defendant dated 18 February 2009 purporting to delay implementation until 2010, and a telephone conversation on 21 February 2009 between Mrs Stephenson and Mr Lomax in which Mr Lomax said the Defendant did not have the money to pay the Claimant's invoices, constituted a repudiatory breach by the Defendant which the Claimant accepted by a letter from its solicitor to the Defendant dated 4 April 2009 or by service of the Claim Form in these proceedings.
9. Alternatively to the Defendant's liability to pay the amounts stated in the Claimant's invoices as set out in paragraph 6 above, by reason of the matters set out above the Claimant has lost the benefit of the Contract and lost the costs in developing the computer system and acquiring software and equipment for the computer system, and has thereby suffered loss and damage.

PARTICULARS

Cost of developing the computer system	To be assessed
Loss on software and equipment acquired for the computer system	To be assessed

Figure 8.1 *continued*

10. Further, the Claimant is entitled to interest at the rate of 8% per annum on the sum of £63,372.50 from 5 March 2009 to 22 September 2010 being 1 year 201 days amounting to £7,861.66 and continuing at the daily rate of £13.88, alternative on the sums found to be due for such periods as the Court may think just pursuant to the Senior Courts Act 1981, section 35A.
11. The parties have complied with the requirements of PD Pre-action conduct.

AND the Claimant claims:

(1) The sum of £63,372.50;
(2) Alternatively, damages for repudiation of the Contract;
(3) Interest of £7,861.66 alternatively to be assessed pursuant to the Senior Courts Act 1981, section 35A.

A. BARRISTER

Statement of Truth

- (I believe) (The Claimant believes) that the facts stated in these particulars of claim are true.
- I am duly authorized by the Claimant to sign this statement.

Full name

Name of Claimant's solicitor's firm: Messrs Smallwood & Co

Signed: Position or office held:
- (Claimant) (Litigation friend) (Claimant's solicitor) (if signing on behalf of firm or company)
- *delete as appropriate*

Address for Service
Messrs Smallwood & Co of 4 Market Place, Corby, Northamptonshire, NN17 6AL.
Claimant's solicitor's address to which documents should be sent if different from overleaf. If you are prepared to accept service by DX, fax, or e-mail, please add details.

8.03 The statement of value will give the amount sought if the claim can be specified, including a statement of accrued interest. This is particularly aimed at debt claims, but many district judges are of the view that a claimant can specify the amount sought in a damages claim by putting a figure on the amount of damages claimed. In cases where damages are to be decided by the court, the statement of value must state whether it is expected that the amount that will be recovered is no more than £5,000; between £5,000 and £25,000; or more than £25,000. As will be seen in Chapter 14, these are the bands used for case management track allocation. In some cases all that can be said is that the amount cannot be stated. In personal injuries claims the statement of value must say whether the general damages expected for pain, suffering, and loss of amenity are below or above £1,000 (which is also a threshold used for track allocation purposes).

8.04 A claim form in the Commercial Court (form N1(CC)) should be marked 'Queen's Bench Division, Commercial Court' in the top right-hand corner (PD 58, para 2.3). A statement of value is not required in the Commercial Court r 58.5(2)), but claims for interest must be set out both on the claim form and the particulars of claim r 58.5(3)). If the particulars of claim are not contained in or served with the claim form, the N1(CC) must state that if an acknowledgment of service is filed indicating an intention to defend, particulars of claim will follow r 58.5(1)(a)).

Figure 8.2 Form N1(CC) Commercial Court claim form

Claim Form

In the High Court of Justice
Queen's Bench Division
Commercial Court
Royal Courts of Justice

	for court use only
Claim No.	
Issue date	

Claimant(s)
SECURE BANK PLC

SEAL

Defendant(s)
LANDMARK TRADERS GRIMSTEAD LIMITED

Name and address of Defendant receiving this claim form

LANDMARK TRADERS GRIMSTEAD LIMITED
Unit 6 Biscay Trading Estate
Epsom
Surrey
KT3 8DN

Amount claimed	£394,450.95
Court fee	£1,530
Solicitor's costs	TBA
Total amount	

The court office at the Admiralty and Commercial Registry, Royal Courts of Justice, Strand, London WC2A 2LL is open between 10 am and 4.30 pm Monday to Friday. When corresponding with the court, please address forms or letters to the Court Manager and quote the claim number.

N1(CC) Claim form (CPR Part 7) (03.02)

Figure 8.2 *continued*

Claim No.

Brief details of claim

The claim is for £394,450.95 being the amount payable under a bill of exchange of £385,000 drawn by the Defendant on Carstairs Bank Plc in favour of Heathmarket Import and Export Limited and payable on [date] ("the bill of exchange") plus interest on that sum at 8% per annum for 112 days amounting to £9,450.95 by way of damages under the Bills of Exchange Act 1882, section 57 or as interest pursuant to the Supreme Court Act 1981, section 35A to the date of issue of this claim and continuing at the daily rate of £84.38. The bill of exchange was delivered to and paid by the Claimant, but was dishonoured when the Claimant presented it for payment at Carstairs Bank Plc after payment had been countermanded by Heathmarket Import and Export Limited. In the circumstances the Claimant is entitled to the sums claimed as the holder in due course of the bill of exchange.

Particulars of claim (*attached)(*will follow if an acknowledgment of service is filed that indicates an intention to defend the claim)

Statement of Truth

*(I believe)(The Claimant believes) that the facts stated in this claim form *(and the particulars of the claim attached to this claim form) are true.

* I am duly authorised by the claimant to sign this statement

Full name ____________________

Name of *(claimant)('s solicitor's firm) Messrs Pamsons

signed ____________________ position or office held ____________________

*(Claimant)('s solicitor) (if signing on behalf of firm, company or corporation)

delete as appropriate

Messrs Pamsons, 18 High Street, London EC1A 6FB

Claimant's or solicitor's address to which documents or payments should be sent if different from overleaf including (if appropriate) details of DX, fax or e-mail.

A fee is payable based on the stated value of the claim and accrued interest. There is nothing to prevent a claimant stating a value below the full potential loss, even though the effect may be that a smaller fee will be payable (*Khiaban v Beard* [2003] 1 WLR 1626). 8.05

B JURISDICTIONAL ENDORSEMENTS

In claims in the High Court, the claim form must, unless the claim is for a specified amount, be endorsed with either: 8.06

(a) a statement that the claimant expects to recover more than £25,000 (or more than £50,000 in personal injuries claims); or
(b) a statement that a named enactment provides that the claim may be commenced only in the High Court; or
(c) a statement that the claim is for a named specialist High Court list, or the claim form must comply with the requirements laid down in a practice direction for one of the specialist lists.

Examples are: 'I expect to recover more than £25,000'; 'My claim includes a claim for personal injuries and the value of the claim is £50,000 or more'. 8.07

C PARTICULARS OF CLAIM

Particulars of claim is the term used to describe the formal written statement setting out the nature of the claimant's case together with the nature of the relief or remedy sought from the defendant. It can be included in the claim form (on the reverse of the form), or be set out in a separate document. If a separate document is used it must be served either with the claim form, or within 14 days after service of the claim form (CPR, r 7.4(1)), and in any event within the period of validity of the claim form (usually four months from issue: see CPR, r 7.4(2)). In the Commercial Court, particulars of claim which are not served with the claim form must be served within 28 days of filing of the acknowledgment of service r 58.5(1)(c)). If the particulars of claim are to be set out in a separate document, the claim form must state that the particulars are either attached or will follow. Further information regarding the contents of particulars of claim can be found in Chapter 13. 8.08

D ISSUING A CLAIM FORM

Procedure on issuing a claim

The claimant's solicitors will make sufficient copies of the claim form for themselves, the court, and each defendant. They retain one, and send the others to the court office, together with the prescribed fee, under cover of a letter asking for the claim to be issued. Alternatively, 8.09

the claimant's solicitors may attend personally at the court office to ensure the claim is issued, which may be sensible if time is short. If the documents are sent by post, the court office stamps the covering letter when it is received. The court issues the claim by sealing the claim forms, and enters details of the claim in its records. On issuing the claim the court will allocate a claim number to the case, which it endorses on the claim forms. The court then sends a form called a notice of issue (forms N205A to N205C) to the claimant's solicitors. This form tells the claimant the claim number, the date of issue, confirms receipt of the issue fee, and, if service is effected by the court, also confirms the date of service.

8.10 There are special provisions dealing with issuing claim forms when the Commercial Court office is closed: see PD 58, para 2.2 and app 3. There is also a scheme for the electronic issue and service of claim forms and the electronic filing of other documents in the specialist courts and Chancery Division (PD 5C).

Money claim online

8.11 Money claims with a value up to £100,000 where neither party is a child or protected party, and where certain other conditions set out in PD 7E, para 4 are satisfied, can be issued electronically using a scheme known as 'Money Claim Online', using **<http://www.moneyclaim.gov.uk>**. These claims are issued at Northampton County Court by sending the court service an online claim form and paying the issue fee electronically. The particulars of claim may be filed and served separately from the claim form, but, if endorsed on the claim form, must not exceed 1,080 characters. Service of the claim form is effected by the court, and is deemed to be effected on the fifth day after issue irrespective of whether that day is a business day or not (para 5.7). Defendants can respond either electronically or by using hard copies (para 7.1). If no response is obtained, judgment can be entered in default by filing an electronic request (para 11). Electronic claims are transferred to the defendant's home court on various events, including the filing of a defence (para 12).

E SERVICE

8.12 The current rules on service were introduced with effect from 1 October 2008. Under the current CPR there are two slightly different systems dealing with service within the jurisdiction. One deals with service of originating process (primarily this is the claim form, but also most of the other types of process described in Chapter 18: see CPR, r 6.2(c)), and the other deals with service of all other types of document used during the course of proceedings (such as statements of case, lists of documents, and application notices). There is a third system relating to service at the registered office of a company or LLP under the Companies Act 2006 (see 8.21). A fourth system deals with service outside the jurisdiction (see Chapter 10). Part 6 does not apply where other rules (such as those in Part 54 on judicial review) contain specific provisions on service r 6.1). Nor does Part 6 apply where a statute makes express provision about service r 6.1(a) and *Mucelli v Government of Albania* [2009] 1 WLR 276, HL). It is worth noting that 'service' deals with providing documents to the other side, and the related concept of 'filing' deals with providing documents to the court.

F SERVICE OF THE CLAIM FORM

Period of validity

Service of a claim form on a defendant in England and Wales must be effected within four months after the date of issue. Strictly, this means a claim form is valid for four months and a day (see *Smith v Probyn* (2000) *The Times*, 29 March 2000), so that a claim form issued on 8 May would still be valid on 8 September. The period of validity for service is six months if the defendant is to be served outside the jurisdiction (CPR, r 7.5(2)). Expiry of the period of validity is considered at 8.38. **8.13**

Documents to be served

The documents to be served comprise the sealed claim form, the particulars of claim (although these may follow), and a 'response pack'. The response pack consists of forms of acknowledgment of service, admission, defence, and counterclaim. Form N9 (see figure 8.3) is a combined cover sheet for the response pack and tear-off acknowledgment of service form. There is also a combined form of defence and counterclaim. There are two types of admission form and also two types of defence and counterclaim form. Forms N9A and N9B are for use in claims for specified amounts of money. Forms N9C and N9D are for use in claims for unspecified sums of money and in non-money claims. An example of form N9C is shown in figure 8.4 and an example of form N9D in figure 8.5. **8.14**

In personal injuries claims the particulars of claim will have to be accompanied by a medical report and schedule of loss and expense, and these must be served with the claim form if the particulars of claim are served at the same time. A notice of any funding arrangement under a CFA or ATE insurance should be served, if applicable. **8.15**

Methods of service

Permissible methods of service are set out in CPR, r 6.3(1), which provides: **8.16**

A claim form may be served by any of the following methods—

(a) personal service in accordance with r 6.5;

(b) first class post, document exchange or other service which provides for delivery on the next business day, in accordance with [PD 6A];

(c) leaving it at a place specified in rr 6.7, 6.8, 6.9 or 6.10 [the address at which the defendant may be served];

(d) by fax or other means of electronic communication in accordance with [PD 6A]; or

(e) any method authorized by the court under r 6.15 [alternative service].

Hierarchy of modes of service of claim forms

There is a hierarchy of methods and places of service for claim forms which is set out in CPR, rr 6.3 to 6.13. It is not open to a party to devise their own methods of bringing claims to the attention of the defendant (*Brown v Innovatorone plc* [2009] EWHC 1376 (Comm)). In this case the defendant's solicitor merely entered into correspondence on behalf of the defendant. This **8.17**

Figure 8.3 Form N9, including acknowledgment of service

Response pack

You should read the 'notes for defendant' attached to the claim form which will tell you when and where to send the forms

Included in this pack are:

- either **Admission Form N9A** (if the claim is for a specified amount)
  or **Admission Form N9C** (if the claim is for an unspecified amount or is not a claim for money)
- either **Defence and Counterclaim Form N9B** (if the claim is for a specified amount)
  or **Defence and Counterclaim Form N9D** (if the claim is for an unspecified amount or is not a claim for money)
- **Acknowledgment of service** (see below)

	Complete
If you admit the claim or the amount claimed and/or you want time to pay	the admission form
If you admit part of the claim	the admission form and the defence form
If you dispute the whole claim or wish to make a claim (a counterclaim) against the claimant	the defence form
If you need 28 days (rather than 14) from the date of service to prepare your defence, or wish to contest the court's jurisdiction	the acknowledgment of service
If you do nothing, judgment may be entered against you	

Acknowledgment of service

Defendant's full name if different from the name given on the claim form

Name of court	Northampton County Court
Claim No.	NN982645
Claimant (including ref.)	Phillippa May Myers
Defendant	Nigel James Staniforth

Address to which documents about this claim should be sent (including reference if appropriate)

Fox and Headley,
52 Higham Road,
Kettering,
Northants.

Postcode N N 1 6 2 C H

If applicable	
Telephone no.	01562 891 744
Fax no.	9945 Kettering 2
DX no.	NS/4774
Your ref.	

E-mail

Tick the appropriate box

1. I intend to defend all of this claim ☑
2. I intend to defend part of this claim ☐
3. I intend to contest jurisdiction ☐

(My) (Defendant's) date of birth is 1 4 / 0 5 / 1 9 7 8

If you file an acknowledgment of service but do not file a defence within 28 days of the date of service of the claim form, or particulars of claim if served separately, judgment may be entered against you.

If you do not file an application to dispute the jurisdiction of the court within 14 days of the date of filing this acknowledgment of service, it will be assumed that you accept the court's jurisdiction and judgment may be entered against you.

If served outside the jurisdiction see CPR rule 6.35 and 6.37(5).

Signed

(Defendant) (Defendant's solicitor) (Litigation friend)

Position or office held (if signing on behalf of firm or company)

Date __/__/____

The court office at

is open between 10 am and 4 pm Monday to Friday. When corresponding with the court, please address forms or letters to the Court Manager and quote the claim number.

N9 Response pack (10.08)

Figure 8.4 Form N9C Admission (unspecified amount non-money and return of good claims)

Admission (unspecified amount, non-money and return of goods claims)

In the	Oldham County Court
Claim No.	OL 73619
Claimant (including ref.)	William Lake
Defendant	Helen Russell

- Before completing this form please read the notes for guidance attached to the claim form. If necessary provide details on a separate sheet, add the claim number and attach it to this form.
- If you are not an individual, you should ensure that you provide sufficient details about the assets and liabilities of your firm, company or corporation to support any offer of payment made.

In non-money claims only

☐ I admit liability for the whole claim (Complete section 11)

In return of goods cases only

Are the goods still in your possession? ☐ Yes ☐ No

Part A Response to claim *(tick one box only)*

☐ I admit liability for the whole claim but want the court to decide the amount I should pay / value of the goods

OR

☑ I admit liability for the claim and offer to pay £3,500.00 in satisfaction of the claim *(Complete part B and sections 1 - 11)*

Part B How are you going to pay the amount you have admitted? *(tick one box only)*

☐ I offer to pay on (date)

OR

☑ I cannot pay the amount immediately because *(state reason)*

I cannot afford to pay.

AND

I offer to pay by instalments of £ 50.00 per month per (week)(month)

starting *(date)* in 4 weeks

1 Personal details

Surname: Russell

Forename: Helen

☐ Mr ☑ Mrs ☐ Miss ☐ Ms

☑ Married ☐ Single ☐ Other *(specify)*

Date of birth: 2 2 0 7 1 9 7 0

Address: 47 Outram Road, Oldham

Postcode: OL8 3WJ

Tel. no. 0161 290 9924

2 Dependants *(people you look after financially)*

Number of children in each age group

under 11: 2 | 11-15: | 16-17: | 18 & over:

Other dependants *(give details)*

3 Employment

☑ I am employed as a: Administrative Assistant

My employer is: Blackburn District Council

Jobs other than main job *(give details)*: None

☐ I am self employed as a

Annual turnover is.......................... £

☐ I am **not** in arrears with my national insurance contributions, income tax and VAT

☐ I am in arrears and I owe.......... £

Give details of:
(a) contracts and other work in hand
(b) any sums due for work done

☐ I have been unemployed for years months

☐ I am a pensioner

4 Bank account and savings

☑ I have a bank account

☐ The account is in credit by........ £

☑ The account is overdrawn by.... £ 2,780.00

☐ I have a savings or building society account

The amount in the account is.......... £

5 Residence

I live in ☐ my own property ☐ lodgings ☐ jointly owned house ☑ rented property ☐ council accommodation

N9C Admission (unspecified amount and non-money claims) (04.06) HMCS

Figure 8.4 *continued*

6 Income

My usual take home pay *(including overtime, commission, bonuses etc)*	£ 1,250 per m
Income support	£ nil per
Child benefit(s)	£ 120 per m
Other state benefit(s)	£ nil per
My pension(s)	£ nil per
Others living in my home give me	£ nil per
Other income *(give details below)*	
	£ per
	£ per
	£ per
Total income	**£** 1,370 **per** m

7 Expenses

(Do not include any payments made by other members of the household out of their own income)

I have regular expenses as follows:

Mortgage *(including second mortgage)*	£ per
Rent	£ 560 per m
Council tax	£ 65 per m
Gas	£ 40 per m
Electricity	£ 45 per m
Water charges	£ 26 per m
TV rental and licence	£ 20 per m
HP repayments	£ 120 per m
Mail order	£ 40 per m
Housekeeping, food, school meals	£ 520 per m
Travelling expenses	£ 40 per m
Children's clothing	£ 50 per m
Maintenance payments	£ per
Others *(not court orders or credit debts listed in sections 9 and 10)*	
	£ per
	£ per
	£ per
Total expenses	**£** 1,526 **per** m

8 Priority debts

(This section is for arrears only. Do not include regular expenses listed in section 7)

Rent arrears	£ 80 per m
Mortgage arrears	£ per
Council tax/Community Charge arrears	£ per
Water charges arrears	£ per
Fuel debts: Gas	£ per
Electricity	£ 10 per m
Other	£ per
Maintenance arrears	£ per
Others *(give details below)*	
	£ per
	£ per
Total priority debts	**£** 90 **per** m

9 Court orders

Court	Claim No.	£	per
Total court order instalments		**£**	**per**

Of the payments above, I am behind with payments to *(please list)*

10 Credit debts

Loans and credit card debts *(please list)*

Loan Credit Plc	£ 56 per m
	£ per
	£ per

Of the payments above, I am behind with payments to *(please list)*

11 Declaration

I declare that the details I have given above are true to the best of my knowledge

Signed

Position or office held (if signing on behalf of firm or company)

Date

Figure 8.5 Form N9D Defence and Counterclaim (unspecified amount non-money and return of good claims)

Defence and Counterclaim
(unspecified amount, non-money and return of goods claims)

Name of court	
Northampton County Court	
Claim No.	NN 982645
Claimant (including ref.)	Phillippa May Myers
Defendant	Nigel James Staniforth

- Fill in this form if you wish to dispute all or part of the claim and/or make a claim against the claimant (a counterclaim)
- You have a limited number of days to complete and return this form to the court.
- Before completing this form, please read the notes for guidance attached to the claim form.
- Please ensure that all the boxes at the top right of this form are completed. You can obtain the correct names and number from the claim form. The court cannot trace your case without this information.

How to fill in this form

- Set out your defence in section 1. If necessary continue on a separate piece of paper making sure that the claim number is clearly shown on it. In your defence you must state which allegations in the particulars of claim you deny and your reasons for doing so. If you fail to deny an allegation it may be taken that you admit it.
- If you dispute only some of the allegations you must
  - specify which you admit and which you deny; and
  - give your own version of events if different from the claimant's.
- If the claim is for money and you dispute the claimant's statement of value, you must say why and if possible give your own statement of value.

- If you wish to make a claim against the claimant (a counterclaim) complete section 2.
- Complete and sign section 3 before returning this form.

Where to send this form

- send or take this form immediately to the court at the address given on the claim form.
- Keep a copy of the claim form and the defence form.

Need help with your legal problems?

Community legal advice is a free confidential service, funded by legal aid. They can help you find the information and advice you need by putting you in touch with relevant agencies, helplines or local advice services. And if you are eligible for legal aid, the service can offer specialist legal advice over the telephone in cases involving: debt; housing; employment; benefits; and education

Call 0845 345 4 345 or www.communitylegaladvice.org.uk

1. Defence

1. Paragraph 1 of the Particulars of Claim is admitted.

2. Paragraph 2 of the Particulars of Claim is denied. The collision occurred as the Claimant was passing some parked cars on her nearside. The Claimant approached the Defendant who was driving in the opposite direction. The Claimant was driving too fast and failed to give way to the Defendant. The collision occurred because the Claimant drove her into the Defendant's car, having failed to wait in a safe place.

3. It is denied that the Defendant was negligent or that any negligence on the part of the Defendant that may be proved caused the collision, whether as alleged in paragraph 3 of the Particulars of Claim or at all, for the reasons set out in paragraph 2 and 4 of this Defence.

4. Further or alternatively, the collision was caused either wholly or in part by the negligence of the Claimant.

PARTICULARS OF NEGLIGENCE

The Claimant was negligence in that she:

(a) Drove too fast;
(b) Failed to give way to the Defendant's car;
(c) Failed to wait in a gap in the parked cars on the Claimant's side of the road where the Defendant's car would have passed safely;
(d) Failed to keep any or any proper lookout;
(e) Continued driving when there was insufficient room for her car;
(f) Drove too far over into the oncoming lane; and/or
(g) Failed to brake sufficiently or in time to avoid the collision.

5. The Claimant is required to prove the alleged or any personal injuries, loss and damage and the amounts claimed.

(continue over the page)

N9D Defence and Counterclaim (unspecified amount, non-money and return of goods claims) (04.08)

Figure 8.5 *continued*

Claim No.	NN 982645

Defence (continued)

2. If you wish to make a claim against the claimant (a counterclaim)

- To start your counterclaim, you will have to pay a fee. Court staff can tell you how much you have to pay.
- You may not be able to make a counterclaim where the claimant is the Crown (e.g. a Government Department). Ask at your local county court office for further information.

If your claim is for a specific sum of money, how much are you claiming? £

I enclose the counterclaim fee of £85.00

My claim is for *(please specify nature of claim)*

6. Damages for negligence being the cost of repairs to the Claimant's car, amounting to £2,100, and interest on the account awarded at 8% per annum under the County Courts Act 1984, s.69.

What are your reasons for making the counterclaim?
If you need to continue on a separate sheet put the claim number in the top right hand corner.

7. The Defendant repeats paragraphs 1 to 5 of the Defence.
8. By reason of the negligence of the Claimant as set out in paragraph 4 of the Defence, the Defendant has suffered loss and damage, being the costs of repairs to this car, registration number JH06 KJP, amounting to £2,100.
9. The Defendant claims interest at 8% per annum on the amount found due pursuant to the County Courts Act 1984, s. 69.

3. Signed - To be signed by you or by your solicitor or litigation friend.

*(I believe) (The defendant believes) that the facts stated in this form are true.
*I am duly authorised by the defendant to sign this statement.

**delete as appropriate*

Position or office held (If signing on behalf of firm or company)

Date __/__/____

Defendant's date of birth, if an individual 14/05/1978

Give an address to which notices about this case can be sent to you

Fox and Headley,
52 Higham Road,
Kettering, Northants.

Postcode NN16 2CH

If applicable	
Telephone no.	01562 891744
Fax no.	9445 Kettering 2
DX no.	

E-mail

is not the same as the situation set out in sub-para (b) below, which meant that sending the claim form to the solicitor was not effective service on the defendant. The prescribed hierarchy is:

(a) If an enactment, a provision of the CPR or any PD or court order requires personal service, that method must be used r 6.5(1)). Otherwise,
(b) If the defendant notifies the claimant in writing of the defendant's solicitor's address for service, or the defendant's solicitor notifies the claimant in writing that the solicitor is instructed by the defendant to accept service, the claim form must be served at the address of the defendant's solicitor r 6.7). The solicitor's business address for this purpose must be either within the jurisdiction r 6.7(1)) or within any EEA state r 6.7(2) and EC Directive 2006/123/EC).
(c) If mandatory personal service r 6.5) or mandatory service on the defendant's solicitor (r 6.7) do not apply, the claimant has the choice of serving a claim form either:
    (i) by personal service (r 6.5(2)); or
    (ii) at an address within the jurisdiction which the defendant has given for the purpose of service of the proceedings r 6.8); or
    (iii) by a contractually agreed method of service r 6.11); or
    (iv) where they apply, under the special rules dealing with service on the Crown r 6.10), or in accordance with r 6.12 on an agent of a principal who is outside the jurisdiction, or in accordance with r 6.13 if the defendant is a child or protected party.
(d) If mandatory personal service r 6.5) or mandatory service on the defendant's solicitor r 6.7) do not apply, and the defendant has not given an address for service r 6.8), the claim form may be served at the defendant's usual or last known address under r 6.9 [see 8.18 to 8.20].

Address where a defendant may be served

Rule 6.9 of the CPR sets out in tabular form the appropriate places of service for different types of party: see table 8.1. An address for service must include a full postcode, unless the court otherwise orders r 6.6(2)). For individuals it is their usual or last known residence. For limited liability companies it is their principal office or any place of business having a real connection with the dispute. The address used for service has to be within the jurisdiction r 6.6(1)). **8.18**

Defendant's residence

An address owned by someone else, but used occasionally by the defendant and other members of his family when they visited England, is not his residence for the purpose of CPR, r 6.9 (*Chellaram v Chellaram (No 2)* [2002] 3 All ER 17). Where the defendant does have a usual or last known residence within the jurisdiction, service at that address will be effective even if the defendant was temporarily abroad on the date of service (*City and Country Properties Ltd v Kamali* [2007] 1 WLR 1219). The address for a defendant who is a tenant of a room is the house address, not that of the room (*Akram v Adam* [2005] 1 WLR 2762). **8.19**

Last known address

8.20 As can be seen from table 8.1, a defendant may be served at a 'last known' residence or place of business. Provided the address used was at one time the defendant's residence (*Collier v Williams* [2006] 1 WLR 1945), and provided it is the last address known to the claimant as such, it follows from *Godwin v Swindon Borough Council* [2002] 1 WLR 997 and *Cranfield v Bridgegrove Ltd* [2003] 1 WLR 2441 that once it is proved that documents were sent or left there in accordance with one of the permitted methods of service (see 8.16), they will be deemed to have been served, and evidence will not be admissible to prove they were not received by the defendant (see 8.39 and 8.43). This is so only if the claimant has taken reasonable steps to find the defendant's current address (*Mersey Docks Property Holdings v Kilgour* [2004] BLR 412). Where, having made reasonable inquiries, the claimant discovers the defendant's current address, the claim form must be served at that address r 6.9(4)(a)). If those inquiries point to some other address or method by which service could be effected, the claimant must make an application for alternative service under r 6.15 (see 8.33). It is only where these alternatives are not available that service may be effected at an address where the defendant no longer resides. If, on making reasonable inquiries, the defendant is found to be living abroad, the claimant cannot comply with rr 6.6(1) and 6.9, and instead will have to attempt service outside the jurisdiction in accordance with the rules discussed in Chapter 10.

Service on companies and LLPs

8.21 Instead of serving a company under the CPR at its principal office or place of business having a real connection with the dispute, a company may be served at its registered office (Companies Act 2006, s 1139) or other address agreed by the company (Sch 4, para 4). Company addresses can be found at **<http://www.companieshouse.gov.uk>**. Service

Table 8.1 Addresses for service on different types of party

Nature of defendant to be served	Place of service
Individual	Usual or last known residence
Individual being sued in the name of a business	Usual or last known residence of the individual; or principal or last known place of business
Individual who is suing or being sued in the name of a partnership	Usual or last known residence of the individual; or principal or last known place of business of the partnership
Limited liability partnership	Principal office of the partnership; or any place of business of the partnership within the jurisdiction which has a real connection with the claim
Corporation (other than a company) incorporated in England and Wales	Principal office of the corporation; or any place within the jurisdiction where the corporation carries on its activities and which has a real connection with the claim
Company registered in England and Wales	Principal office of the company; or any place of business of the company within the jurisdiction which has a real connection with the claim
Any other company or corporation	Any place within the jurisdiction where the corporation carries on its activities; or any place of business of the company within the jurisdiction

under s 1139 must be at the company's registered office. Consequently, leaving the documents with a receptionist or security guard at the reception area of a managed building is not enough (*Amerada Hess v Rome* (2000) *The Times*, 15 March 2000) unless the company agrees to some such method of service (Companies Act 2006, Sch 4, para 8). Service under s 1139 is sanctioned under the CPR, r 6.3(2), as is the similar service on limited liability partnerships provision in the Companies Act 1985, s 727, by r 6.3(3). It is arguable that r 6.3(2) and (3) bring service at the registered office, etc. under the Companies Acts within the scheme of CPR, Part 6, so that the deemed date of service and other provisions in Part 6 apply in these situations. This would be a change from the pre-2008 version of Part 6, where service at a company's registered office was regarded as falling outside Part 6, so there was only a rebuttable presumption of deemed service under the Interpretation Act 1978 (*Cranfield v Bridgegrove Ltd* [2003] 1 WLR 2441). The difference is that there was no equivalent of r 6.3(2) or (3) in the pre-2008 version of Part 6.

Effecting service

Personal service

Personal service is effected by leaving the documents that have to be served with the defendant. Where the defendant is uncooperative, it is sufficient to mention the nature of the documents and to leave them reasonably near the defendant. It is also sufficient to hand them to the defendant, provided the defendant has them long enough to see what they are, even if the defendant then hands them back to the process server saying they are not being accepted (*Nottingham Building Society v Peter Bennett and Co* (1997) *The Times*, 26 February 1997). Personal service on a company means service on a person in a senior position, which in turn means a director, treasurer, secretary, chief executive, manager, or other officer (PD 6A, para 6.2). **8.22**

Personal service on a partnership where partners are sued in the name of the partnership is effected by leaving the claim form with a partner or a person having the control or management of the partnership business at its principal place of business (CPR, r 6.5(3)(c)). **8.23**

Post

It is to be noticed that under CPR, r 6.3(1)(b), any postal delivery method that involves next-business-day delivery is permitted. Royal Mail first-class post, special delivery 9.00 a.m., special delivery next day, 'same day', and recorded-signed for all meet this criterion. It is not restricted to Royal Mail delivery services, and other commercial operators may be used provided the method used involves next-working-day delivery. Documents sent by slower delivery methods, such as second-class post, are not served in accordance with the rules. Such service would be irregular, though it is possible (but not certain) that it would be validated under r 3.10. Postal service is effected by placing the document in a post box, or leaving it with or having it collected by the relevant service provider (PD 6A, para 3.1). **8.24**

Leaving the documents at the defendant's address

This may be done by inserting the documents through the letter box at the defendant's address or that of the defendant's solicitor (in accordance with rr 6.7, 6.8, 6.9, or 6.10), or **8.25** otherwise leaving the documents at that address (such as by entering an office and leaving the documents on the reception desk).

Document exchange (DX)

8.26 This is a system used by the great majority of solicitors and chambers, and a number of other businesses, for transporting documents between their offices. It only works between offices using the system. Members pay periodic lump sums for the service. Generally documents put into the document exchange system arrive the next business day, although there are occasional delays. It is a permissible method of service only if the defendant's address where they are to be served includes a DX number, or where the writing paper of the defendant or its solicitor includes a DX number, and they have not stated they are unwilling to be served by DX (PD 6A, para 2.1).

Electronic methods of service

8.27 Where a document is to be served electronically (including fax and e-mail), the party to be served, or its solicitor, must have previously indicated in writing that it is willing to accept service by this method (PD 6A, para 4.1).

8.28 Where electronic means are to be used for serving on a party (as opposed to a solicitor), the willingness to accept electronic service must be expressly given for this purpose, although including a fax or e-mail address on a statement of case will be taken as a sufficient indication (para 4.1(2)(c)). Including a fax number on the litigant's letterhead is not enough (*Molins plc v GD Spa* [2000] 1 WLR 1741). For electronic service on a solicitor, express agreement, including an electronic address on a statement of case, or including a fax number on the solicitor's writing paper constitute sufficient indications (para 4.1(2)). Including an e-mail address on a solicitor's writing paper only amounts to an agreement to service by this method if it is also stated that the e-mail address may be used for service (para 4.1(2)(b)). Where a party seeks to serve electronically, he should first inquire whether the recipient has any limitations on matters such as on the format of transmitted documents or the size of attachments (para 4.2). A party who, in an emergency facing an opponent, refuses to agree to electronic service is likely to have difficulty resisting an application for relief from sanctions (*RC Residuals Ltd v Linton Fuel Oils Ltd* [2002] 1 WLR 2782). On the other hand, despatching documents by fax without obtaining the defendant's prior agreement is more than a minor departure from the rules (*Kuenyehia v International Hospitals Group Ltd* (2006) *The Times*, 17 February 2006).

8.29 In order to comply with the requirement in CPR, r 6.6(1), that addresses used for service must be within the jurisdiction, any fax number given for the purpose of service must be at the address for service r 6.23(5)), and e-mail and other electronic identifications are deemed to be at the address for service r 6.23(6)). There is no need to serve an additional hard copy after using fax or electronic methods of service (PD 6A, para 4.3), because rr 6.14 and 6.26 give rise to an irrebuttable presumption of due service (see 8.39).

Contractual method of service

8.30 Where a contract contains a term providing that proceedings may be served in a particular way, and the claim form is limited to claims arising from that contract, service will be valid if effected in accordance with the contractual term (CPR, r 6.11). Standard-form contracts often contain such provisions, as do contracts involving international trade. If a contractual provision involves serving a party outside the jurisdiction, the rules on service outside the jurisdiction (see Chapter 10) must also be complied with (r 6.11(2)).

Ad hoc agreement on service

It was held in *Anderton v Clwyd County Council (No 2)* [2002] 1 WLR 3174 that the only legitimate methods of service are those laid down by CPR, Part 6 (and the Companies Act 2006). *Cranfield v Bridgegrove Ltd* [2003] 1 WLR 2441 at [81], [85], however, approved *Kenneth Allison Ltd v AE Limehouse Ltd* [1992] 2 AC 105, which held that an ad hoc agreement between the parties about the method of service is also effective. **8.31**

Usual method of service

Generally service will be by the court (CPR, r 6.4), but there are exceptions. In the Commercial Court the claim form is served by the claimant (PD 58, para 9). In general litigation, a party can take responsibility for effecting service by giving notice to the court r 6.4(1)(b)). Court service will generally be by first-class post (PD 6A, para 8.1). **8.32**

Alternative service

Sometimes it is not possible to effect service using the various methods set out above, or the reasonable steps taken to find the defendant where the claimant has only a 'last known' address discloses some other means that could be used to bring the claim to the defendant's attention. The defendant may be evading service, or prove difficult to find. In such cases it is sometimes possible to persuade the court to allow service by an alternative method or at an alternative place under CPR, r 6.15. The mere absence of prejudice to the defendant, however, is not a sufficient reason for making an order (*Brown v Innovatorone plc* [2009] EWHC 1376 (Comm)). Such orders can be made prospectively (r 6.15(1)), or retrospectively to approve steps already taken in attempting to effect service r 6.15(2)). **8.33**

An application for an alternative service order needs to be supported by written evidence which must: **8.34**

- state the reason alternative service is sought;
- state the proposed alternative method or place of service; and
- explain why it is believed service will be effective if the alternative method or place is used.

Examples of possible methods of alternative service are by advertisement in a newspaper; service by text message; and service on the defendant at the address of his or her insurer (*Gurtner v Circuit* [1968] 2 QB 587). In *Abbey National plc v Frost* [1999] 1 WLR 1080, which involved a claim against a solicitor, it was held that an order to effect alternative service of proceedings upon the Solicitors' Indemnity Fund would be allowed. An order for alternative service at an address within the jurisdiction will not be made if its purpose is to evade the restrictions on serving defendants outside the jurisdiction (for which, see Chapter 10) (*Knauf UK GmbH v British Gypsum Ltd* [2002] 1 WLR 907). **8.35**

Dispensing with service of the claim form

8.36 The court may dispense with service of the claim form if there are exceptional circumstances (CPR, r 6.16(1)). An application under this rule may be made at any time, may be made without notice, and must be supported by evidence r 6.16(2)).

8.37 There may be an exceptional case where there has been a minor departure from the rules on service *(Cranfield v Bridgegrove Ltd* [2003] 1 WLR 2441). An example is *Home Office v Dorgan* (one of the cases reported at [2002] 1 WLR 3174), where a service deadline by fax was missed by three minutes. This power may be used where one of the translations of the claim form is omitted in a case where service has to be effected outside the jurisdiction (*Phillips v Symes (No 3)* [2008] 1 WLR 180, HL). Common errors, such as serving by fax when the defendant has not consented to such service, are not sufficiently exceptional *(Kuenyehia v International Hospitals Group Ltd* (2006) *The Times*, 17 February 2006). Where a draft, unsealed, claim form was sent to the defendant's insurers during the period of validity, but service was not duly effected on the defendant, it could not be said that the circumstances were exceptional so as to justify dispensing with service (*Cranfield v Bridgegrove Ltd*).

Expiry of period of validity

8.38 Where a claim form is served within the jurisdiction, by CPR, r 7.5(1), the claimant must complete the step required for the method of service the claimant chooses to use by 12.00 midnight on the calendar day four months after the date of issue of the claim form. All the claimant has to do is to take the relevant step. Whether the deemed date of service (see 8.39) takes place later, or the claim form never arrives, or is delayed in transmission, is irrelevant. Table 8.2 sets out the step the claimant is required to take for each method of service.

Table 8.2 Step required for service under CPR, r 7.5(1)

Method of service	Step required
First-class post, DX, or other delivery service which provides for delivery on the next business day	Posting, leaving with, delivering to, or collection by the relevant service provider
Delivery of the document to or leaving it at the relevant place	Delivering to or leaving the document at the relevant place
Personal service under r 6.5	Completing the relevant step required by r 6.5(3)
Fax	Completing the transmission of the fax
Other electronic method	Sending the e-mail or other electronic transmission

G DEEMED DATE OF SERVICE OF THE CLAIM FORM

8.39 A claim form served in accordance with the above rules is deemed to be served on the second business day after completion of the step required by CPR, r 7.5 (see r 6.14). A 'business day' is any day except Saturday, Sunday, a bank holiday, Good Friday, and Christmas Day r 6.2(b)).

Rule 6.14 creates an irrebuttable presumption of law, which means evidence to contradict the deemed date of service is inadmissible. See 8.44.

H SERVICE OF DOCUMENTS OTHER THAN A CLAIM FORM

Service of documents other than the claim form within the jurisdiction is governed by CPR, rr 6.20 to 6.29. The normal rule is that the party has to serve the other side if it prepared the relevant document, and the court will do so if it prepared the document r 6.21). In either case the court can order otherwise. **8.40**

The available methods of service are the same as for claim forms r 6.20, and see 8.16). While personal service must be used if this is prescribed r 6.22, eg, for orders with penal notices, applications to commit), generally documents other than claim forms are served at the address the party gives as the address where they may be served. Claimants do this by stating their address on the claim form, and defendants do likewise by stating their address on the acknowledgment of service or defence. Where the party has a solicitor acting for them, the address is that of their solicitor r 6.23(2)). A litigant in person has to provide an address for service which must be within the jurisdiction r 6.23(3)). Any change to these addresses has to be notified to the court and other parties as soon as it takes place r 6.24). **8.41**

The court also has powers to order service of documents other than the claim form by alternative methods or at alternative places r 6.27), and to dispense with service of such documents r 6.28). See 8.33 to 8.37. **8.42**

I DEEMED DATE OF SERVICE (NON-CLAIM FORM DOCUMENTS)

By CPR, r 6.26, documents other than the claim form are deemed to be served on the day shown in table 8.3. **8.43**

The deemed dates of service set out in table 8.3 take effect on proving one of the prescribed methods of service, and cannot be displaced by evidence tending to prove some other date of actual receipt (*Godwin v Swindon Borough Council* [2002] 1 WLR 997; *Anderton v Clwyd County Council (No 2)* [2002] 1 WLR 3174). It will be noticed that the deemed dates of service set out in table 8.3 sometimes refer to 'days' and sometimes refer to 'business days'. 'Business days' are defined by r 6.2(b) as excluding Saturdays, Sundays, bank holidays, Christmas Day, and Good Friday. References in table 8.3 to 'days' are to calendar days (*Anderton v Clwyd County Council (No 2)*), so include weekends and public holidays. *Anderton v Clwyd County Council (No 2)* makes it clear that r 2.8, which excludes weekends and public holidays when calculating periods of less than five days, does not apply. This is because r 2.8 applies when calculating the time 'for doing any act'. Nothing is 'done' when calculating a deemed date: it is simply a fictitious date. **8.44**

Most of the entries in table 8.3 are self-explanatory. It will be noticed, however, that there is no reference in table 8.3 providing for different treatment of documents posted after the last collection on a day. This means, eg, that a document sent by first-class post on **8.45**

Table 8.3 Deemed dates of service

Method of service	Deemed day of service
First-class post (or other service which provides for delivery on the next business day)	The second day after it was posted, left with, delivered to, or collected by the relevant service provider provided that day is a business day; or if not, the next business day after that day
Document exchange	The second day after it was left with, delivered to, or collected by the relevant service provider provided that day is a business day; or if not, the next business day after that day
Delivering the document to or leaving it at a permitted address	If it was delivered to or left at the permitted address on a business day before 4.30 p.m., on that day; or in any other case, on the next business day after that day
Fax	If the transmission of the fax is completed on a business day before 4.30 p.m., on that day; or in any other case, on the next business day after the day on which it was transmitted
Other electronic method	If the e-mail or other electronic transmission is sent on a business day before 4.30 p.m., on that day; or in any other case, on the business day after the day on which it was sent
Personal service	If the document is served personally before 4.30 p.m. on a business day, on that day; or in any other case, on the next business day after that day

a Friday at 10 p.m. is deemed to be served on the Monday. It does not matter that this is after the last post on the Friday. The second day after Friday is the Sunday. As this is not a business day, service is deemed to occur on Monday, the next business day after the Sunday. A document posted on a bank holiday Monday (it does not matter that this is not a business day) is deemed to be served on the second day thereafter, which is Wednesday, which is a business day (PD 6A, para 10.7). These results cannot be rebutted by evidence to the contrary, even evidence that there is no postal collection after 10 p.m. (*Anderton v Clwyd County Council (No 2)*).

8.46 Service by fax is deemed to take effect the same day if the transmission is completed before 4.30 p.m. on a business day. Faxes sent after 4.30 p.m. or on non-business days are deemed to be served on the next business day. Evidence of the date of actual receipt is inadmissible.

8.47 The deeming provisions in rr 6.14 and 6.26 only apply where service is effected under Part 6. They do not apply where a document is served under a statute rather than under Part 6. For example, in *Mucelli v Government of Albania* [2009] 1 WLR 276, HL, a notice of appeal under the Extradition Act 2003 was sent by fax a few minutes after (what would now be 4.30 p.m. in r 6.26) on the final day for service, but was held to have been served in time because under the statute, service could be effected at any time up to midnight on the final day.

J CERTIFICATE OF SERVICE

8.48 A party effecting service is often required to file a certificate of service. For example, a claimant who serves the claim form is required to file a certificate of service within 21 days of service of the particulars of claim, unless all the defendants file acknowledgments of service within that time (CPR, r 6.17(2)). An example is shown in figure 8.6.

Figure 8.6 Certificate of service

Certificate of service

Name of court	Claim No.
Northampton County Court	10NN 982645
Name of Claimant	
Phillippa May Myers	
Name of Defendant	
Nigel James Staniford	

On what day did you serve? 27/04/2010

What documents did you serve? *Please attach copies of the documents you have not already filed with the court.* Claim Form

On whom did you serve? *(If appropriate include their position e.g. partner, director).*

How did you serve the documents? - *please tick the appropriate box*

- ☑ by first class post or other service which provides for delivery on the next business day
- ☐ by Document Exchange
- ☐ by delivering to or leaving at a permitted place *(see notes overleaf)*
- ☐ by fax machine (................time sent, where document is other than a claim form) *(you may want to enclose a copy of the transmission sheet)*
- ☐ by personally handing it to or leaving it with (................time left, where document is other than a claim form) *(please specify)*
- ☐ by other electronic means (................time sent, where document is other than a claim form) *(please specify)*
- ☐ by other means permitted by the court *(please specify)*

Give the address where service effected, include fax or DX number, e-mail address or other electronic identification: 62 Fox Lane, Corby, Northants.

Being the ☐ claimant's ☑ defendant's ☐ solicitor's ☐ litigation friend

- ☑ usual residence
- ☐ last known residence
- ☐ place of business
- ☐ principal place of business
- ☐ last known place of business
- ☐ principal office of the partnership
- ☐ principal office of the corporation
- ☐ principal office of the company
- ☐ other *(please specify)*

The date of service is *(see overleaf for guidance)* 29/04/2010

I believe that the facts stated in this certificate are true.

Full name

Signed

(Claimant) (Defendant) ('s solicitor) ('s friend)

Position or office held

(If signing on behalf of firm or company)

Date ☐☐/☐☐/☐☐☐☐

N215 Certificate of service (10.08)

K IRREGULAR SERVICE

8.49 A party who starts a claim using the wrong form, or relying on the wrong statutory provision, is likely to be granted permission to amend in order to deal with the claim justly (particularly if the defendants are not misled by the mistakes) (*Thurrock Borough Council v Secretary of State for the Environment, Transport and the Regions* (2000) *The Times*, 20 December 2000). Where service is attempted, but executed incorrectly, an application may be made under CPR, r 3.10 to remedy the error in the procedure. On such an application the court will consider whether the claimant has taken all reasonable steps to put the matter right once the problem was discovered (*Nanglegan v Royal Free Hampstead NHS Trust* [2002] 1 WLR 1043). Attempting to serve at the wrong address is an error of procedure which may be remedied by an order under either r 3.10 or the general power to make orders for furthering the overriding objective in r 3.1(2)(m) (*Nelson v Clearsprings (Management) Ltd* [2007] 1 WLR 962, at [48]). In *Phillips v Symes (No 3)* [2008] 1 WLR 180 the House of Lords said that an order under r 3.10 was probably appropriate where the package sent to the defendant (who was in Switzerland) in error failed to include the English language version of the claim form.

8.50 The position is different where the real problem is that the claimant has missed the four (or six) month period of validity for the claim form. The general position is that such cases have to be approached applying CPR, r 7.6. This rule, which is discussed in Chapter 9, is regarded as providing a complete code on extending the period of validity of claim forms (*Vinos v Marks & Spencer plc* [2001] 3 All ER 784 and *Godwin v Swindon Borough Council* [2002] 1 WLR 997). As a result, attempts made by claimants to use general powers in the CPR to rectify late or defective service (rr 3.1 extending time, 3.9 seeking relief from sanctions, and 3.10 correcting errors of procedure) have usually been rejected. If there are exceptional circumstances the court may, however, make an order for alternative service (see 8.33 to 8.35) or dispense with service (see 8.36).

L EUROPEAN ORDER FOR PAYMENT

8.51 Regulation (EC) No 1896/2006 of 12 December 2006 (the 'EOP Regulation') created a European order for payment ('EOP') procedure with effect from 12 December 2008. The EOP Regulation applies to civil and commercial matters in cross-border cases, whatever the nature of the court or tribunal, but with various exceptions set out in art 1. For this purpose, a cross-border case is one in which at least one of the parties is domiciled or habitually resident in a Member State other than the Member State of the court seised (art 3(1)). The EOP procedure is intended to simplify, speed up, and reduce the costs of litigation in cross-border cases concerning uncontested money claims. It also permits the free circulation of EOP orders throughout the Member States by laying down a common procedure for establishing liability to pay. Compliance with the EOP procedure renders unnecessary any intermediate proceedings in the Member State of enforcement prior to recognition and enforcement (recital 9). The EOP procedure is an additional and optional means of establishing liability, with claimants remaining free to resort to court proceedings under national law (recital 10).

An EOP case is started by filing an application form in form A, which must be completed in English or accompanied by a translation into English (PD 78, para 2.1). An EOP application made to the High Court will be assigned to the Queen's Bench Division, but that will not prevent the application being transferred where appropriate (para 2.2). The court seised of an application for an EOP application is required to examine the application form to decide whether the requirements set out in the EOP Regulation, arts 2, 3, 4, 6, and 7, are met and whether the claim appears to be founded (art 8). The application will be rejected if the requirements are not met (art 11). If the requirements are met, the court issues a European order for payment using standard form E (art 12(1)), which has to be served on the defendant together with a statement of opposition in standard form F. In the EOP, the defendant is given the choice of either: **8.52**

(a) paying the amount indicated in the order to the claimant; or
(b) filing at court within 30 days of service (art 16(2)) of the EOP the completed statement of opposition.

If a statement of opposition is entered within the 30-day time limit, the proceedings continue before the competent courts of the Member State of origin in accordance with the rules of ordinary civil procedure unless the claimant has explicitly requested that the proceedings be terminated in that event (art 17(1)). There are further detailed provisions in the EOP Regulation and in CPR, Part 78, and PD 78. **8.53**

M FILING

Most of the important documents used in litigation, such as the claim form, statements of case, and witness statements, have to be filed at court. The courts maintain their own files on every case that is issued, placing on the court file additional documents such as correspondence, notices of hearings, and court orders. Filing is a matter of delivering (not merely posting) the relevant documents to the court office (CPR, r 2.3(1)), and takes effect immediately if documents are delivered through the court's letter box, even if the court is closed at the time (*Van Aken v Camden London Borough Council* [2003] 1 WLR 684). **8.54**

Traditionally, filing is by lodging hard copies of the relevant documents at the court office. It is possible to file documents electronically, provided the court has an e-mail address listed at the court service website (<**http://www.hmcourts-service.gov.uk**>): see PD 5B. The facility is only available if no fee is payable for the step in question, and if certain technical rules set out in PD 5B are complied with. **8.55**

KEY POINTS SUMMARY

8.56

- Civil proceedings are commenced by issuing a claim form.
- Issue takes place when the claim form is sealed by the court.
- Details of the cause of action and remedies sought are contained in the particulars of claim. This may be endorsed on the claim form, attached to the claim form, or served separately.

- Service must be effected in accordance with the hierarchy of methods of service set out in Part 6 (personal service—service on the defendant's solicitor—service at the address given by the defendant—service at the defendant's usual address—service at the last known address).
- Domestic claim forms are valid for four months for the purpose of service. Where service is to be effected outside the jurisdiction, the period of validity is six months.
- The deemed dates of service create irrebuttable presumptions of due service on the dates set out in CPR, rr 6.14 and 6.26. This means evidence is not admissible to prove the document did not in fact arrive, or that it arrived on some other date.
- Where there are problems in effecting service, consideration should be given to seeking an order for service by an alternative method, or at an alternative place, or to dispense with service.
- The European order for payment is an alternative to normal civil proceedings, and is designed to provide a simple method of establishing liability in uncontested cross-border money claims.

9

RENEWAL OF PROCESS

As was seen in Chapter 8, after proceedings have been commenced by issuing a claim form or other originating process, they must be brought to the attention of the defendants or respondents by service. Generally, originating process remains valid for the purpose of service for a period of four months. A party bringing proceedings is entitled to make full use of the limitation period before issuing process, and, in addition, is entitled to wait until the final day of the period of validity before effecting service. Thus, it is possible for a defendant to be first informed of a claim by service of proceedings some months after the expiry of the limitation period. Of course, whether it is wise to delay service is another question. Service of proceedings marks a watershed in the litigation process. It is at this point that the defendant is put on formal notice that legal proceedings have been brought, and the time limit on service of proceedings is one which is relaxed with extreme caution. **9.01**

If there are good reasons for not effecting service of the claim form during its period of validity, an extension may be granted either by consent or on making a without notice application to the court. Consent for an extension is only effective if given by the written agreement of the parties (see CPR, r 2.11, and *Thomas v Home Office* [2007] 1 WLR 230). A court asked to give permission to extend the period of validity of a claim form will always bear in mind that it is contrary to general principle to allow stale claims to proceed. As Megaw J said in *Heaven v Road and Rail Wagons Ltd* [1965] 2 QB 355 at 366: **9.02**

> It is unfair to defendants, and it makes the administration of justice more uncertain, if litigation is delayed so that witnesses die or cannot be traced; or memories fade; and defendants are

> entitled to know definitely, at the expiry of some defined time, whether or not they are to be pursued in the courts.

Accordingly, the discretion to extend the period of validity of originating process is sparingly used.

A PERIODS OF VALIDITY

9.03 The rules are contained in CPR, r 7.5:

> (1) Where the claim form is served within the jurisdiction, the claimant must complete the step required in the following table [see table 9.1] in relation to the particular method of service chosen, before 12.00 midnight on the calendar day four months after the date of issue of the claim form.
>
> (2) Where the claim form is to be served out of the jurisdiction, the claim form must be served in accordance with Section IV of Part 6 within 6 months of the date of issue.

9.04 Although a claim form may be served on the day it is issued, the effect of r 7.5(1) is to disregard that day for the purpose of calculating the period of validity. Therefore, a claim form for service in England or Wales issued on 8 May would still be valid on 8 September, but will have expired on 9 September (see *Smith v Probyn* (2000) *The Times*, 29 March 2000). By r 2.8(5), when a period of time specified by the CPR for doing any act 'at the court office' ends on a day when that office is closed, the act is deemed to have been done in time if done on the next day on which the court office is open. This does not apply to service, because this has to be effected on the defendant, rather than at the court office (see *Re N (Infants)* [1967] Ch 512). This ought not to cause any difficulties, because all the claimant needs to do under r 7.5(1) is to take the action necessary under the claimant's control (such as posting, or completing the transmission of a fax) by midnight on the final day. It does not matter when the document actually arrives.

9.05 The six-month period of validity provided by r 7.5(2) applies whether or not permission is required for service abroad (see Chapter 10).

9.06 In *Payabi v Armstel Shipping Corporation* [1992] QB 907 the originating process was addressed to defendants in Liberia, but was marked 'Not for service out of the jurisdiction'. The claimants purported to serve the proceedings on the defendants' solicitors in London, pursuant to an agreement as to the place of service, five months after it had been issued. Hobhouse J held

Table 9.1 Step required by 12.00 midnight on the final day of validity

Method of service	Step required
First-class post, document exchange, or other service which provides for delivery on the next business day	Posting, leaving with, delivering to, or collection by the relevant service provider
Delivery of the document to or leaving it at the relevant place	Delivering to or leaving the document at the relevant place
Personal service under rule 6.5	Completing the relevant step required by rule 6.5(3)
Fax	Completing the transmission of the fax
Other electronic method	Sending the e-mail or other electronic transmission

that the six-month period only applies where service is actually effected abroad, and that therefore service on the facts was irregular.

No specific provision is made for petitions (the extended definition of 'claim' in r 6.2(c) only applies to Part 6). This is because the rules lay down a seven-day minimum period before the hearing for service and the date of the hearing should be fixed when the petition is presented. **9.07**

B POWER TO RENEW

It is provided by CPR, r 7.6, that: **9.08**

> (1) The claimant may apply for an order extending the period for compliance with rule 7.5.
> (2) The general rule is that an application to extend the time for compliance with rule 7.5 must be made—
> (a) within the period specified by rule 7.5; or
> (b) where an order has been made under this rule, within the period for service specified by that order.
> (3) If the claimant applies for an order to extend the time for service of the claim form after the end of the period specified by rule 7.5 or by an order made under this rule, the court may make such an order only if—
> (a) the court has failed to serve the claim form; or
> (b) the claimant has taken all reasonable steps to comply with rule 7.5 but has been unable to do so; and
> (c) in either case, the claimant has acted promptly in making the application.
> (4) An application for an order extending the time for compliance with rule 7.5—
> (a) must be supported by evidence; and
> (b) may be made without notice.

The form of CPR, r 7.6, shows that a different approach will be taken depending on whether or not the application to extend the period of validity of the claim form is made while the claim form is still valid. Rule 7.6 is intended to form a self-contained code on extending the validity of claim forms, and other powers in the CPR will either not be applied, or will be applied only in exceptional circumstances, to evade the restrictions in r 7.6. See the discussion at 8.33 to 8.37 and 8.49 to 8.50. **9.09**

Applications made during the period of validity

No criteria are laid down in r 7.6 itself indicating how the discretion to extend should be exercised where an extension to the period of validity is sought while the originating process is still valid. In *Hashtroodi v Hancock* [2004] 1 WLR 3206, the court felt it appropriate to give only general guidance on the principles to be applied under r 7.6(2), namely: **9.10**

(a) the discretion to extend the period of validity of a claim form should be exercised in accordance with the overriding objective; and
(b) the reason for the failure to serve within the specified period is a highly material factor. If there is a very good reason for the failure to serve, an extension will usually be granted.

If there is no more than a weak reason, the court is very unlikely to grant an extension (*Collier v Williams* [2006] 1 WLR 1945).

9.11 In *Hashtroodi v Hancock*, the court refused to grant an extension where the reason for failing to serve within the period of validity was the incompetence of the claimant's legal advisers. While it may be appropriate to grant an extension where there are problems in tracing the defendant for the purpose of service, it is inappropriate to do so where extra time is sought in a personal injuries claim to prepare the particulars of claim, schedule of loss and damage, and medical evidence (*Mason v First Leisure Corporation plc* (2003) LTL 30/7/03). It may be inappropriate to grant an extension of time even in cases of difficulty in effecting service if the problem is only discovered at the last moment because service is not attempted until a few days before the expiry of the period of validity (the old case of *Baker v Bowketts Cakes Ltd* [1966] 1 WLR 861). Traditionally, it has been felt inappropriate to grant extensions on the basis that serving proceedings might prejudice ongoing negotiations (*The Mouna* [1991] 2 Lloyd's Rep 221).

9.12 If an order for an extension is granted, the defendant does not get an opportunity to object until after the claim is served (see 9.20). If the court forms the view that the extension should not have been granted, one of the most important factors in deciding whether to set aside service is whether the defendant is prejudiced by the order granting the extension (*Mason v First Leisure Corporation plc*). This usually involves a careful consideration of the correspondence passing between the parties, and asking whether the defendant gave any encouragement to the claimant to incur expense in progressing the claim.

Applications made after the expiry of the period of validity

9.13 For applications after the claim form has expired, fairly exacting criteria have been laid down by r 7.6(3) (see 9.08). A case where the court fails to serve because it completely overlooks the claim form comes within r 7.6(3)(a) just as much as a case where the court tries unsuccessfully to effect service (*Cranfield v Bridgegrove Ltd* [2003] 1 WLR 2441). In this situation the court will usually grant an extension. Under r 7.6(3)(b) it will be seen that there should have been efforts to serve, and that there must be no unexplained delay in making the application (albeit the application is made after the expiry of the period of validity). In *Smith v Probyn* (2000) *The Times*, 29 March 2000, the claimant served proceedings on the defendant's solicitors in the mistaken belief that they were authorized to accept service, but having failed to obtain written confirmation that they were authorized as required at the time (see now r 6.7, discussed at 8.17). An extension was then sought, but was refused because there had been nothing to prevent personal service.

9.14 It is not all that likely that a claimant who has been making efforts to serve will simultaneously forget about the period of validity. However, r 7.6 will assist a claimant who tries to effect service, but who later discovers that the method used was ineffective (*Amerada Hess v Rome* (2000) *The Times*, 15 March 2000, discussed at 8.21). The rule is most likely to assist a claimant who believes the court is effecting service, and later discovers this is not the case.

C CLAIMS IN RESPECT OF CARGO

Claims in respect of cargo carried by sea are governed by the special one-year limitation period in the Hague–Visby Rules, art III, r 6. Once the year has elapsed, the claim is extinguished if proceedings have not been commenced (*Aries Tanker Corporation v Total Transport Ltd* [1977] 1 WLR 185). The effect is that there is no power to extend validity more than one year after accrual of the cause of action: *Payabi v Armstel Shipping Corporation* [1992] QB 907. **9.15**

D MULTIPLE DEFENDANTS

It was argued in *Jones v Jones* [1970] 2 QB 576 that where there are several defendants it is necessary to serve only one of them within the period of validity of the originating process, and that the others could be served at leisure at some later time. If the argument had been accepted, it would have meant that a second defendant could have been validly served several years after issue provided the first defendant had been served during the initial period of validity. The Court of Appeal held that the rule (as it then stood) was not capable of bearing such a construction, with the result that every defendant on whom it is intended to serve proceedings must be served during the period of validity. **9.16**

E EFFECT OF STAY

While a stay is in operation no steps may be taken in the claim other than an application to remove the stay. However, time continues to run for the purposes of the period of validity of the claim form (*Aldridge v Edwards* [2000] CPLR 349). **9.17**

F PROCEDURE ON SEEKING AN EXTENSION

Applications for renewal are of necessity made before the defendant is on the record, so must be made without notice, and the practice is that they are made without an oral hearing. The application notice must be supported by written evidence which should set out all the relevant circumstances. As the application is made without notice, the claimant must give full and frank disclosure of all material facts, including those going against the granting of the order. The written evidence should include the following details: **9.18**

(a) the date of accrual of the cause of action and, if it has passed, the date of expiry of the primary limitation period;
(b) the date of issue of the originating process;
(c) a full explanation of the reasons for not having served process;
(d) the period of the extension sought and the reasons for it;

(e) the dates and periods of any previous renewals; and
(f) if the application is made after the expiry of the period of validity of the originating process, a full explanation of the circumstances excusing the late application.

9.19 Once the order has been made, the application notice and evidence in support must be served with the order on the party against whom the order was sought, unless the court otherwise orders (CPR, r 23.9). The order will contain a notice informing the defendant of the right to apply to set aside the order granting the extension, and any application to set aside must be made within seven days of service of the order (r 23.10).

G CHALLENGING AN ORDER GRANTING AN EXTENSION

9.20 A defendant will learn that an extension has been granted when the claim form is served. The order granting the extension may be challenged, but the defendant will first have to acknowledge service of the proceedings, stating an intention to defend, and must then issue an application notice supported by written evidence asking for an order setting aside the order granting the extension. See 11.13.

10

SERVICE OUTSIDE THE JURISDICTION

Inevitably, there are a number of complexities where the intended defendant to proceedings lives outside the jurisdiction. At common law, an action *in personam* (ie, an action against a legal person as opposed to an action *in rem* against a ship or other property) could be brought only against a defendant served with process while in England or Wales. This, at least superficially, had the merit of ensuring the courts of this country did not purport to exert an exorbitant jurisdiction over defendants who were not amenable to the coercive powers of the courts. The superficiality stemmed from the fact that jurisdiction could be established by service on a defendant while on a temporary visit to this country (10.05ff) or by a foreign defendant submitting to the jurisdiction (10.07ff). In any event, the restrictive common law rule has been subject to a discretionary power to allow English proceedings against defendants outside the jurisdiction since the enactment of the Common Law Procedure Act 1852. This discretionary power is governed by CPR, r 6.36, and is discussed at 10.86ff. These rules will be referred to in this chapter as the common law rules. **10.01**

A significant departure from the common law rules was made by the enactment of the Civil Jurisdiction and Judgments Act 1982 ('CJJA 1982'), which by s 2 gave effect to the Brussels Convention on Jurisdiction and the Enforcement of Judgments in Civil and Commercial **10.02**

Matters 1968 ('Brussels Convention'). The Brussels Convention laid down a general rule that a defendant domiciled in a contracting State must be sued in the courts of that State (see 10.31). The contracting States to the Brussels Convention were the Member States of the European Union ('EU'). An almost identical Convention (the Lugano Convention) was then entered into between the EU States and the members of the European Free Trade Association ('EFTA'), and was brought into effect by the Civil Jurisdiction and Judgments Act 1991 ('CJJA 1991'). The states currently bound by the Lugano Convention are Denmark, Iceland, Norway, and Switzerland. On 1 March 2002, Council Regulation (EC) No 44/2001 ('the Judgments Regulation'), which covers all Member States of the EU and replaces the Brussels Convention, came into force. 'Judgments Regulation' is the abbreviation used in CPR, r 6.31(d), for Council Regulation (EC) No 44/2001. All books and law reports up to 2008 called it the Jurisdiction Regulation. The CJJA 1982 has been amended by the Civil Jurisdiction and Judgments Order 2001 (SI 2001/3929), making the amendments necessary to give effect to the Judgments Regulation. The UK itself is divided into 'parts' (England and Wales, Scotland, and Northern Ireland), and a separate Modified Convention, set out in the CJJA 1982, Sch 4, allocates jurisdiction between the courts of each part. The Modified Convention does not apply to the Channel Islands, etc. (which will not be considered further here). The current position regarding service outside the jurisdiction and reciprocal enforcement is set out in table 10.1.

10.03 The Brussels, Lugano, and Modified Conventions, and also the Judgments Regulation, are in substantially the same terms as each other (but with some numbering and other small variations). In this chapter all references will be to the Judgments Regulation, as it is the most important of these instruments, but it should be kept in mind that cases decided under the Brussels Convention will refer to the old article numbers.

10.04 Where a claim can be brought in the courts of more than one country, there is a general concern that it should be brought in the courts of the most appropriate country. The courts are also concerned that the same dispute should not be litigated in several countries at the same time, with the risk of irreconcilable judgments and difficulties regarding the recognition of judgments for enforcement purposes. These problems are addressed under the common law rules by the courts' powers to stay English proceedings on the ground of *forum non conveniens* (see 10.111) and to grant injunctions to restrain foreign proceedings (see 10.111ff). Similar problems in Judgments Regulation cases are dealt with by requirements that courts other than the one first seised of the matter must either decline jurisdiction or stay their proceedings (see 10.78–10.83). Determining the system of law to be applied to resolve an action where one or more of the parties is foreign is a matter of private international law. As such it is outside the scope of this book, and specialist works should be consulted.

Table 10.1 Countries governed by different jurisdiction instruments

Countries	Governing Jurisdiction Instrument
Denmark, Iceland, Norway, and Switzerland	Lugano Convention
Austria, Belgium, Bulgaria, Cyprus, Czech Republic, Estonia, Finland, France, Germany, Greece, Hungary, Ireland, Italy, Latvia, Lithuania, Luxembourg, Malta, Netherlands, Poland, Portugal, Romania, Slovakia, Slovenia, Spain, Sweden, and the UK	Judgments Regulation (also known as the Jurisdiction Regulation)
Other 'parts' of the UK	CJJA 1982, Sch 4 as substituted by SI 2001/3929, Sch 2

A SERVICE ON A FOREIGN DEFENDANT WITHIN THE JURISDICTION

Under the common law rules, a foreign defendant is amenable to the jurisdiction of the courts in this country if process is served upon the defendant within the jurisdiction. Applying this rule, jurisdiction was established in *Maharanee Seethaderi Gaekwar of Baroda v Wildenstein* [1972] 2 QB 283, where the proceedings were served on the defendant while on a temporary visit to this country to attend the Ascot Races. This rule has been abolished for cases governed by the Judgments Regulation, which by art 3(2) provides that jurisdiction against EU defendants cannot be founded by service during the defendant's temporary presence in the country. It is possible to issue a claim form against a foreign defendant marked 'Not to be served out of the jurisdiction'. The intention when this is done is usually either to effect service on the defendant during a temporary visit to this country (unless the defendant lives in the EU) or to secure the defendant's agreement to service within the jurisdiction (often on English solicitors). The period of validity of an originating process intended to be served within the jurisdiction is four months, not six (CPR, r 7.5(1) and (2)). **10.05**

If a domestic claim form has been issued, and it is later discovered that the defendant is outside the jurisdiction, or if a claim form marked 'Not to be served out of the jurisdiction' cannot be served within the jurisdiction for any reason, the proper procedure is to apply for permission to issue a concurrent claim form for service outside the jurisdiction (a matter of practice not expressly covered by the CPR). **10.06**

B SUBMISSION TO THE JURISDICTION

Regardless of whether the court would otherwise have jurisdiction, a defendant may submit to the jurisdiction of the courts of this country. It may be that a defendant recognizes the advantages of litigating in England, and will agree to English proceedings being served at the offices of a solicitor in England. Alternatively, a domestic claim form may be sent to a defendant outside the jurisdiction in breach of the rules requiring permission to serve (see 10.86ff), and the defendant proceeds to contest the claim on its merits without objecting to the defects in service. In the absence of any express agreement to submit to the jurisdiction, it is a question whether the defendant's conduct, when viewed objectively in the context of all the circumstances of the case, is inconsistent with maintaining an objection to the jurisdiction of the court. What the defendant should do is to acknowledge service and make an application under CPR, Part 11, disputing the jurisdiction of the court within 14 days of acknowledging. If an application is made within this time, conduct will be treated as a submission to the jurisdiction only if it is wholly unequivocal (see 11.13–11.18). **10.07**

A claimant who has commenced proceedings gives the court jurisdiction to hear a counterclaim. **10.08**

C CASES OUTSIDE THE GENERAL RULES

10.09 Certain types of proceedings affect rights *in rem*. Both under the common law rules and under the Jurisdiction Regulation special rules govern where many of these types of proceedings must be litigated. The main policy consideration justifying these special rules is that rights *in rem* are often protected by detailed national laws, and the courts of the country in question are in the best position to apply them.

Under the common law rules

Land disputes

10.10 Claims founded on a dispute as to the title to, or possession of, land must be brought in the courts of the country where the land is situated. The authority for this is *British South Africa Co v Companhia de Moçambique* [1893] AC 602 as interpreted by later decisions. Where a question concerning the title of foreign land is no more than a collateral issue in a claim, the rule does not prevent the courts in this country exercising jurisdiction (see *St Pierre v South American Stores (Gath and Chaves) Ltd* [1936] 1 KB 382 and, in relation to actions for trespass, CJJA 1982, s 30). It was established by *Penn v Lord Baltimore* (1750) 1 Ves Sen 444 that the rule can be circumvented if the defendant is subject to the general jurisdiction of the courts in this country, such as through presence here, and if the claim can be framed so as to impose a personal obligation on the defendant. An example is a claim for rent due under a lease of foreign land (*St Pierre v South American Stores (Gath and Chaves) Ltd*).

Intellectual property

10.11 Claims founded on the validity or infringement of foreign copyrights, trade marks, and patents have to be brought in the country where they are registered (*Tyburn Productions Ltd v Conan Doyle* [1991] Ch 75). This is a recent extension of the preceding rule, and it is possible that it is restricted to cases where an English judgment would not be recognized in the country of registration.

Divorce, nullity, and judicial separation

10.12 Under the Domicile and Matrimonial Proceedings Act 1973, s 5(2), the courts in England have jurisdiction over proceedings for divorce, nullity, and judicial separation if either of the parties to the marriage, at the time the proceedings are commenced, either:

(a) is domiciled in England; or
(b) has been habitually resident in England for the previous year.

10.13 No permission is required for service abroad of family proceedings. A translation must be provided if the respondent does not understand English, and an enhanced period must be allowed for giving notice of intention to defend (Family Proceedings Rules 1991 (SI 1991/1247), r 10.6).

Insolvency proceedings

10.14 Service outside the jurisdiction of any document in proceedings under the Insolvency Act 1986 or the Insolvency Rules 1986 is not governed by the rules in CPR, Part 6, but by the Insolvency Rules 1986 (SI 1986/1925), r 12.12.

Proceedings under the 1986 Act or Rules, apart from petitions to wind up solvent companies, are outside the scope of the Judgments Regulation (by art 1 of the Regulation). A winding-up petition presented by the Secretary of State in the public interest under the Insolvency Act 1986, s 124A, is also outside the scope of the Regulation, even if the company sought to be wound up is solvent (*Re a Company (No 007816 of 1994)* [1995] 2 BCLC 539 at 541; *Re Senator Hanseatische Verwaltungsgesellschaft mbH* [1996] 2 BCLC 562). **10.15**

Exclusive jurisdiction under the Jurisdiction Regulation

Article 22 of the Judgments Regulation allocates exclusive jurisdiction, regardless of the domicile of the parties, over five categories of cases. The courts of the contracting States are required, of their own motion, to declare they have no jurisdiction in these cases (art 25). 'Regardless of domicile' in the opening words of art 22 are not an attempt to exclude the jurisdiction of courts in non-Member States, and are intended to apply only as between the courts of member states (*Choudhary v Bhatter* [2009] EWCA Civ 1176). They do not create an 'extra-EU jurisdiction' or 'universal international jurisdiction' (*Lucasfilm Ltd v Ainsworth* [2010] FSR 10 at [129], [183]). **10.16**

Land

Article 22(1) provides that proceedings which have as their object rights *in rem* in immovable property or tenancies of immovable property are subject to the exclusive jurisdiction of the courts of the contracting State in which the property is situated. This is subject to an exception in respect of actions concerning tenancies between natural persons domiciled in the same country for temporary private use for periods of up to six months, which may be brought in the country where the defendant is domiciled. **10.17**

Regarding rights *in rem*, the article has been interpreted by the ECJ in *Reichert v Dresdner Bank* (Case C–115/88) [1990] ECR I–27 as being restricted to actions to determine the extent, content, ownership, or possession of immovable property, or the existence of other rights *in rem* therein. In *Webb v Webb* (Case C–294/92) [1994] QB 696 an apartment in France had been bought in the defendant's name with money provided by the claimant. An action was brought in England claiming a declaration that the property was held on an express or resulting trust for the claimant. It was held, by reasoning analogous to that in *Penn v Lord Baltimore* (1750) 1 Ves Sen 444 (see 10.10), that the claim affected the defendant's obligations *in personam* and did not have as its object rights *in rem*, and so was outside the scope of art 22. **10.18**

Conversely, the provision regarding tenancies has been construed widely. It covers cases where the existence of a lease is disputed (*Sanders v Van der Putte* (Case 73/77) [1977] ECR 2383) and to any dispute concerning the respective obligations of the parties under a lease (*Rösler v Rottwinkel* (Case 241/83) [1986] QB 33). It therefore applies to claims in respect of unpaid rent and other breaches of covenant under a lease. There are limits, however. In *Jarrett v Barclays Bank plc* [1999] QB 1, claims by consumers against the bank under the Consumer Credit Act 1974 arising out of loans to purchase timeshares in properties in Portugal did not have as their object tenancies in immovable property. The foundation of the claims was the loan agreement, and so the claims were not prevented by art 22 from being commenced in England. **10.19**

Companies and associations

10.20 Article 22(2) provides that proceedings having as their object the validity of the constitution, nullity, or dissolution of companies or associations of legal or natural persons, or of their organs, must be brought in the country where the relevant body has its 'seat'. This is the country where the company or association was incorporated or formed, or where its central management and control are exercised (CJJA 1982, s 43(2)). A dispute over the composition of the board of a company falls within art 22(2) even where the dispute arises out of the interpretation of a shareholders' agreement (*Speed Investments Ltd v Formula One Holdings Ltd* [2005] 1 BCLC 455). In *Newtherapeutics Ltd v Katz* [1991] Ch 226 the claimant company, which was registered in England, brought a claim in England against a French director claiming:

(a) that certain transactions were signed by the defendant without the approval of a meeting of the board of directors; and
(b) that the transactions were such that no reasonable directors could properly have entered into.

10.21 The first of these was held to be within the exclusive jurisdiction of the courts in England as it concerned the validity of a decision of one of the company's organs, whereas the second claim fell outside art 22(2). The question then was whether the action had as its 'object' the validity of the decision of one of its organs. This depended on which of the two claims was the principal claim. In the circumstances of the case this was held to be the first claim, so the action was properly brought in England.

Public registers

10.22 Article 22(3) gives exclusive jurisdiction over proceedings concerning the validity of entries in a public register to the courts of the State where the register is kept.

Intellectual property

10.23 Article 22(4) gives exclusive jurisdiction over proceedings concerning the registration or validity of patents, trade marks, designs, and similar rights to the courts of the State where the property in question has been registered or where registration has been applied for. This does not extend to claims for infringement of patents, which are claims in tort and may be brought in accordance with art 5(3) (see 10.61ff).

Enforcement of judgments

10.24 Article 22(5) gives exclusive jurisdiction in enforcement proceedings to the courts of the State in which the judgment is to be enforced.

D JURISDICTION UNDER THE JUDGMENTS REGULATION

10.25 The Judgments Regulation is designed to determine the international jurisdiction of the courts of the Member States, to facilitate recognition, and to introduce a simple procedure for securing the international enforcement of judgments. Enforcement under the Judgments Regulation is considered at 44.58ff.

The main rule (see 10.31) is that a claim must be brought in the courts of the country where the defendant is domiciled. However, there are many exceptions (see 10.39–10.77). Where the Judgments Regulation applies to a defendant outside the jurisdiction, English proceedings may be issued and served without permission. As there is a possibility that the courts of more than one country might have jurisdiction over such a case, provision has been made for jurisdiction being declined or subsequent claims being stayed (see 10.78–10.83). **10.26**

Questions as to the interpretation of the Judgments Regulation may be referred to the European Court of Justice. Where an English court has to construe the Convention it must apply the principles laid down by, and any relevant decision of, the ECJ. It may also consider (but is not bound by) the reports prepared by Mr P. Jenard and Professor P. Schlosser (CJJA 1982, s 3). The Judgments Regulation is not intended to be construed as if it were an English statute. Rather, it is necessary to consider the overall objectives and scheme of the Regulation, and also the policy behind the provision in question. As explained by Lord Diplock in *Henn v Director of Public Prosecutions* [1981] AC 850: **10.27**

> The European Court, in contrast to English courts, applies teleological rather than historical methods to the interpretation of the Treaties and other Community legislation. It seeks to give effect to what it conceives to be the spirit rather than the letter of the Treaties; sometimes, indeed, to an English judge, it may seem to the exclusion of the letter. It views the Communities as living and expanding organisms and the interpretation of the provisions of the Treaties as changing to match their growth. For these reasons the European Court does not apply the doctrine of precedent to its own decisions as rigidly as does an English court.

It is important that the Judgments Regulation is interpreted in the same way in all the Member States. Obviously, there are many differences in the domestic laws applied in the various Member States, particularly between the civil and common law systems. The ECJ has therefore regularly decided that legal concepts used in the Judgments Regulation must be given a 'Community meaning'. This involves attempting to discover shared principles, a far from simple task. **10.28**

Scope of the Judgments Regulation

By art 1 the Judgments Regulation applies to civil and commercial proceedings whatever the nature of the court or tribunal. It does not apply to revenue, customs, social security, insolvency, arbitration (because this is covered by the New York Convention, 1958, see *Marc Rich & Co AG v Società Italiana Impianti PA* (Case C–190/89) [1991] ECR I–3855), or administrative matters, nor to proceedings relating to the status or legal capacity of natural persons, rights in property arising out of a matrimonial relationship (which are governed by Council Regulation (EC) No 2201/2003, *Proceedings brought by C* (Case C–435/06) [2008] Fam 27), wills, or succession. Consequently, it does not apply to a claim by or against a public law body concerning the exercise of its public powers (*Grovit v De Nederlandsche Bank NV* [2008] 1 WLR 51). **10.29**

It is substantive jurisdiction that is determined by the jurisdictional provisions of the Judgments Regulation. This stems from the word 'sued' in art 2(1) (see 10.31). It means that a court with jurisdiction over the substantive claim also has jurisdiction to grant interim or **10.30** ancillary orders in the claim (*Masri v Consolidated Contractors International (UK) Ltd (No 4)* [2009] 2 WLR 699).

Domicile

The general rule

10.31 The general rule laid down by the Judgments Regulation is that proceedings must be brought in the courts of the country where the defendant is domiciled. Article 2(1) provides:

> Subject to this Regulation, persons domiciled in a Member State shall, whatever their nationality, be sued in the courts of that Member State.

10.32 Domicile is defined for the purposes of the Convention by the CJJA 1982, ss 41 to 46. The domicile of individuals is governed by s 41, which provides in subsection (2):

> An individual is domiciled in the United Kingdom if and only if—
> (a) he is resident in the United Kingdom; and
> (b) the nature and circumstances of his residence indicate that he has a substantial connection with the United Kingdom.

10.33 By s 41(6) an individual is presumed to have a substantial connection with the United Kingdom after being resident in the United Kingdom for three months. Being a resident is not the same as having a residence in the jurisdiction (*Cherney v Deripaska* [2007] 2 All ER (Comm) 785 at [16]). An individual is resident for this purpose if he has a settled or usual place of abode within the jurisdiction. This requires some degree of permanence or continuity (*Bank of Dubai Ltd v Abbas* [1997] IL Pr 308). It is possible to be resident in more than one place at any one time (*Foote Cone and Belding Reklam Hizmetleri AS v Theron* [2006] All ER (D) 253). In the latter case the defendant was held to be resident in the jurisdiction because his wife was permanently living in a house in London, he occupied the house on regular monthly visits of at least a week, and his passport showed him as permanently resident here. In *Cherney v Deripaska* the defendant spent 57 per cent of his time at an address in Russia, about 5 to 7 per cent of his time at an address in London (spending mostly single nights there on an irregular basis), and had several other homes in other countries. He was held not to be resident in the jurisdiction.

10.34 By art 60, a corporation is domiciled where it has its 'seat', central administration, or principal place of business. A company's seat is its registered office or, if it does not have one, the place where it was incorporated. A company's 'principal place of business' is the place at the heart of its operations (*King v Crown Energy Trading AG* (2003) *The Times*, 14 March 2003), or where it is controlled and managed (*Ministry of Defence and Support for the Armed Forces of the Islamic Republic of Iran v FAZ Aviation Ltd* [2008] 1 All ER (Comm) 372).

10.35 The time for judging whether there is a defendant domiciled within the jurisdiction for the purposes of art 6 is the date of issue, not the date of service: *Canada Trust Co v Stolzenberg (No 2)* [2002] 1 AC 1.

Exceptions to the rule that jurisdiction is based on domicile

10.36 Although art 2 lays down the general rule, a claimant often has a choice of forum under the Judgments Regulation. This is because, in a wide variety of cases, the claimant is given the option of suing in another country. Article 3 provides that 'persons domiciled in a Member State may be sued in the courts of another Member State only by virtue of the rules set out in sections 2 to 7 of this Chapter'. These sections encompass arts 5 to 24 of the Judgments Regulation. Article 22 was considered at 10.16. Articles 5 to 21 and 23 and 24 will be considered at 10.39–10.77.

The basic scheme, as confirmed by CPR, r 6.33, is that the courts of England and Wales will have jurisdiction to hear and determine a claim under the Judgments Regulation if: **10.37**

(a) the case falls within one of the provisions set out in arts 5 to 24;
(b) there are no proceedings pending involving the same claim in another Member State; and
(c) the defendant is domiciled in a Member State.

However, the requirement of having a defendant domiciled in a Member State is dispensed with in cases falling within art 22 (exclusive jurisdiction: see 10.16) and is modified in art 23 cases (jurisdiction clauses: see 10.53ff), where the requirement is that *any* one of the parties must be domiciled in a Member State. **10.38**

Contract

Main provision

Article 5(1)(a) provides in part that a person domiciled in one Member State may alternatively 'be sued in matters relating to a contract, in the courts for the place of performance of the obligation in question'. **10.39**

In *Arcado Sprl v Haviland SA* (Case 9/87) [1988] ECR 1539 the ECJ confirmed that the phrase 'matters relating to a contract': **10.40**

> ...is to be regarded as an independent concept which, for the purpose of the application of the Convention, must be interpreted by reference principally to the system and objectives of the Convention in order to ensure that it is fully effective.

In *Kalfelis v Bankhaus Schröder, Münchmeyer, Hengst & Co* (Case 189/87) [1988] ECR 5565 the ECJ laid down the general principle that the special jurisdiction given by art 5 must be interpreted restrictively as it derogates from the principle that jurisdiction is vested in the courts of the country where the defendant is domiciled. An earlier decision of the ECJ, *Martin Peters Bauunternehmung GmbH v Zuid Nederlandse Aannemers Vereniging* (Case 34/82) [1983] ECR 987, decided that, as membership of an association creates close links between members of the same kind as those between the parties to a contract, jurisdiction over a dispute between an association and one of its members could be given by art 5(1). The effect is that art 5(1) can be invoked where either there is a contractual relationship giving rise to an actual contract, or there is a consensual obligation similar to a contract giving rise to a comparable obligation. **10.41**

In *Kleinwort Benson Ltd v Glasgow City Council* [1999] 1 AC 153, the House of Lords held that restitutionary claims based on void contracts did not fall within art 5(1). Where the only connection with this country is an alleged non-disclosure or misrepresentation in relation to the making of a contract, jurisdiction may be given by art 5(1). This is because **10.42** contractual 'obligations' within the meaning of art 5(1) can arise under the general law as well as under the terms of a contract. In the case of a non-disclosure, the obligation in question is to disclose, and jurisdiction will be given under art 5(1) to the courts for the country where the disclosure should have been made (*Agnew v Länsförsäkringsbolagens AB* [2001] 1 AC 223).

10.43 In *Effer SpA v Kantner* (Case 38/81) [1982] ECR 825 the ECJ held that art 5(1) applies even where the existence of the contract on which the claim is based is disputed by the defendant. Otherwise, a defendant could oust the jurisdiction granted by art 5(1) merely by saying there is a dispute. This decision was interpreted by the Court of Appeal in *Tesam Distribution Ltd v Schuh Mode Team GmbH* [1990] ILPr 149 as meaning that a court cannot accept jurisdiction under art 5(1) on the mere assertion or pleading of the claimant. There must be evidence from which it would be proper to conclude that a contract existed and that the place of performance was the country in which the action was brought. This concept was also applied by the Court of Appeal in *Boss Group Ltd v Boss France SA* [1997] 1 WLR 351 where Saville LJ's judgment is to the effect that a claimant relying on art 5(1) does not have to establish finally and conclusively that the place of performance of the obligation was in England, but does have to establish a 'good arguable case that that was so'.

10.44 If art 5(1) applies, proceedings may be brought in the courts of 'the place of performance of the obligation in question'. In *Etablissements A de Bloos Sprl v SCA Bouyer* (Case 14/76) [1976] ECR 1497 the ECJ held that the 'obligation' in art 5(1) refers to the contractual obligation forming the basis of the legal proceedings. In contracts for the sale of goods the place of performance is where the goods were or should have been delivered, and in contracts for the provision of services it is where the services were or should have been provided (art 5(1)(b)). In an international sale of goods on FOB terms, delivery takes place on shipment (Sale of Goods Act 1979, s 32(1) and *Scottish and Newcastle International Ltd v Othon Ghalanos Ltd* [2008] Bus LR 583). Where goods are to be delivered to a number of locations, the place of performance is the principal place of delivery determined by economic considerations (*Color Drack GmbH v Lexx International Vertriebs GmbH* (Case C–386/05) [2008] 1 All ER (Comm) 168). In *Medway Packaging Ltd v Meurer Maschinen GmbH & Co KG* [1990] 2 Lloyd's Rep 112 an English claimant brought a claim in England against a German defendant alleging the defendant had repudiated an exclusive distribution agreement without giving reasonable notice. It was held, first, that the defendant's alleged obligation to give due notice terminating the contract had to be performed at the claimant's place of business in England. Secondly, the agreement granting the claimant exclusive rights to distribute the defendant's machines was essentially negative in character, and could be broken in either England or Germany. That was held to be sufficient to give the courts in England jurisdiction under art 5(1).

10.45 Where a claimant brings a claim concerning a number of obligations under a single contract, it is the principal obligation that determines jurisdiction under art 5(1) (*Shenavai v Kreischer* (Case 266/85) [1987] ECR 239). This was applied in *Union Transport plc v Continental Lines SA* [1992] 1 WLR 15, where the claimant had claims under a voyage charter for failing to nominate a vessel (which was to be performed in England) and for failure to provide a vessel (which was to be performed in the USA). It was held that nominating a vessel was the principal obligation as it triggered the other contractual obligations, and therefore proceedings had validly been brought in England.

Contracts of employment

Articles 18 and 19 provide that in matters relating to individual contracts of employment, an employer may be sued in the Member State where he is domiciled or in the courts where the employee habitually carries or carried out his work, or if the employee does not habitually carry out his work in any one country, the employer may also be sued in the courts for the place where the business which engaged the employee was or is now situated. **10.46**

Allowing an employee to sue in the country where he or she is employed is in accordance with one of the policies of the Convention, namely, the protection of the weaker party in contractual relationships. This was emphasized by *Mercury Publicity Ltd v Wolfgang Loerke GmbH* (1991) *The Times*, 21 October 1991, where the Court of Appeal said the rule was restricted to relationships of master and servant of a personal nature, and refused to extend the rule to a contract of commercial agency. Employees can only be sued where they are domiciled (art 20). **10.47**

Consumer contracts

Articles 15 to 17 apply to consumer contracts, ousting the special jurisdiction granted by art 5(1). Again, these provisions are designed to protect the weaker party to certain contracts. A restrictive meaning has been given by art 15 to the term 'consumer contract'. To qualify as a consumer a party must not have entered the contract in the course of a trade or profession. A contract having a mixed consumer and business purpose is treated as a consumer contract only if the business purpose is negligible (*Gruber v Bay Wa AG* (Case C–464/01) [2005] ECR I–439; [2006] QB 204). The contract must also be: **10.48**

(a) for the sale of goods on instalment credit terms; or
(b) for a loan repayable by instalments, or for any other form of credit, made to finance the sale of goods; or
(c) concluded with a person who pursues commercial or professional activities in the consumer's Member State, or directs such business to the consumer's Member State (such as through advertising).

By art 16, a consumer acting as a claimant may bring proceedings in the courts where either party is domiciled, but a consumer may be sued only in the courts of the country in which he or she is domiciled. **10.49**

Insurance contracts

Jurisdiction in insurance matters is governed by arts 8 to 14, and art 5(1) is ousted. Articles 8 to 14 are designed to protect the insured, who is regarded as being the weaker party in insurance matters. It is not always the case that an insured will be in a weaker negotiating position than the insurer, especially where the insured is a large commercial corporation. Nevertheless, the Court of Appeal held in *New Hampshire Insurance Co v Strabag Bau AG* [1992] 1 Lloyd's Rep 361 that the concept of 'matters relating to insurance' in the Jurisdiction Regulation has to be given a literal interpretation, and is not restricted to insurance for domestic or private purposes. However, reinsurance contracts are outside the scope of arts 8 to 14 (see the Schlosser report, para 151, and *Agnew v Länsförsäkringsbolagens AB* [2001] 1 AC 223) on the basis that the parties to such transactions do not need special protection. **10.50**

By arts 9 and 10 an insurer domiciled (or having a branch, agency, or establishment) in a Member State may be sued: **10.51**

(a) in the courts of the State where it is domiciled; or

(b) in the courts of the State where the insured is domiciled, provided that State is a Member State; or
(c) if there are co-insurers, in the courts of a Member State where proceedings have been brought against the leading insurer; or
(d) if the case involves liability insurance or insurance over immovable property, in the courts for the place where the harmful event occurred.

10.52 The insured is protected by art 12, which provides that an insurer may bring proceedings only in the courts of the country where the insured is domiciled.

Jurisdiction agreements

10.53 Article 23(1) of the Judgments Regulation provides:

> If the parties, one or more of whom is domiciled in a Member State, have agreed that a court or the courts of a Member State are to have jurisdiction to settle any disputes which have arisen or which may arise in connection with a particular legal relationship, that court or those courts shall have exclusive jurisdiction. Such an agreement conferring jurisdiction shall be either—
>
> (a) in writing or evidenced in writing, or
> (b) in a form which accords with practices which the parties have established between themselves, or
> (c) in international trade or commerce, in a form which accords with a usage of which the parties are or ought to have been aware and which in such trade or commerce is widely known to, and regularly observed by, parties to contracts of the type involved in the particular trade or commerce concerned.

10.54 Under the first sentence, the parties must have 'agreed' to give jurisdiction to the courts of a contracting State. *Dresser UK Ltd v Falcongate Freight Management Ltd* [1992] QB 502 concerned a jurisdiction clause in a bill of lading relied on by a bailor of goods against a sub-bailee. Bingham LJ said that the article demands a contract between the parties. Consequently, the clause would operate between the immediate parties to the bill, and between an agent and an immediate party. It would also operate between an immediate party and a party to whom all the rights and obligations under the contract of carriage have been assigned (*Partenreederei ms Tilly Russ v Haven & Vervoebedriff Nova NV* (Case 71/83) [1985] QB 931). However, the relationship between a bailor and a sub-bailee does not depend on agreement, so the clause did not satisfy the requirements of art 23(1). In *Powell Duffryn plc v Petereit* (Case C–214/89) [1992] ECR I–1745 the ECJ held that a jurisdiction clause in the articles of association of a company was to be regarded as being part of a contract for the purposes of art 23(1) as between the company and the shareholders and also between the shareholders *inter se*.

10.55 Whether proceedings fall within a jurisdiction clause for the purposes of art 23 is a matter of construction, but such clauses should be construed liberally in accordance with what rational businessmen would have intended (*Fiona Trust and Holding Corp v Privalov* [2007] Bus LR 1719). It was decided by the ECJ in *Meeth v Glacetal Sàrl* (Case 23/78) [1978] ECR 2133 that a clause providing that the parties could be sued only in the courts of their respective countries was within art 23(1), despite the risk that two countries could have 'exclusive' jurisdiction if both parties decided to sue. This decision was applied in *Kurz v Stella Musical Veranstaltungs GmbH* [1992] Ch 196, where it was held that a clause giving both parties a choice of suing in either England or Germany was effective under art 23(1). This may be contrasted with *Dresser UK Ltd v Falcongate Freight Management Ltd*, where the Court of Appeal applied the *contra proferentem* rule of construction so as to restrict the scope of an ambiguous jurisdiction clause.

The second sentence of the article lays down certain requirements as to the form of jurisdiction clauses. A distinction is drawn between international trading and commercial contracts and, on the other hand, more general contracts. A jurisdiction clause in a general contract must be in writing or evidenced in writing, or else accord with the practices of the parties. The ECJ held in *Colzani v Rüwa* (Case 24/76) [1976] ECR 1831 that if the jurisdiction clause is contained in written standard terms, the contract must contain an express reference to those standard terms. General words of incorporation may be sufficient for the purposes of art 23(1)(a) provided the words are clear and precisely demonstrate a consensus that the jurisdiction clause be incorporated into the contract (*AIG Europe SA v QBE International Insurance Ltd* [2002] 2 All ER (Comm) 622). In international trade or commerce, a jurisdiction clause may alternatively be in a form which accords with a widely known usage in that trade or commerce of which the parties are or ought to have been aware. **10.56**

Article 23(3) provides: **10.57**

> Where such an agreement is concluded by parties, none of whom is domiciled in a Member State, the courts of other Member States shall have no jurisdiction over their disputes unless the court or courts chosen have declined jurisdiction.

Where at least one of the parties is domiciled in a Member State, art 23(1) provides that the nominated courts have exclusive jurisdiction. Where none of the parties is domiciled in a Member State, a jurisdiction clause has the effect of preventing the courts of Member States other than those nominated from having jurisdiction unless the nominated courts have declined jurisdiction. **10.58**

Restrictions on jurisdiction clauses

Parties are not completely free to confer jurisdiction by means of jurisdiction clauses. The following restrictions should be noted: **10.59**

(a) a jurisdiction clause cannot override exclusive jurisdiction conferred by art 22 (for which, see 10.16); or the rules on *lis pendens* (see 10.78) (*Erich Gasser GmbH v MISAT Srl* (Case C–116/02) [2005] QB 1);
(b) a jurisdiction clause inserted for the benefit of one party may be waived by that party;
(c) in claims relating to individual contracts of employment, consumer contracts, and insurance contracts, jurisdiction agreements are effective only (in broad terms) if entered into after the dispute has arisen or if invoked by the employee, consumer, or insured (see arts 13, 17, and 21); and
(d) submission to the jurisdiction (see 10.07) overrides a jurisdiction clause (*Elefanten Schuh GmbH v Jacqmain* (Case 150/80) [1981] ECR 1671).

Maintenance

Article 5(2) provides that, in matters relating to maintenance, as an alternative to bringing proceedings in the debtor's country of domicile, proceedings may be brought in the courts where the creditor is domiciled or habitually resident or, if the matter is ancillary to proceedings concerning the status of a person, in the court which has jurisdiction to entertain those proceedings (unless that jurisdiction is based solely on nationality). This provision, **10.60** like several already considered, is designed to protect the financially dependent and hence weaker party.

Tort

10.61 A claim in tort may be brought in the country either where the defendant is domiciled or where the harmful event occurred or may occur (art 5(3)).

10.62 Like matters relating to contract (10.39ff), it is important that this provision should be construed consistently in all the Member States despite differences in the types of conduct regarded as tortious in the various countries. Accordingly, the ECJ in *Kalfelis v Bankhaus Schröder, Münchmeyer, Hengst & Co* (Case 189/87) [1988] ECR 5565 decided that 'tort' must be regarded as an autonomous concept which is to be interpreted by reference to the scheme and objectives of the Jurisdiction Regulation.

10.63 Also on the same lines as jurisdiction in contract under art 5(1), the Court of Appeal in *Mölnlycke AB v Procter and Gamble Ltd* [1992] 1 WLR 1112 held that the court has power to filter off frivolous or vexatious use of the jurisdiction given by art 5(3) by insisting that the claimant must establish a good arguable case on the merits.

10.64 As to what is meant by the independent concept of tort, the ECJ in the *Kalfelis* case said:

> ...the term 'matters relating to tort, delict or quasi-delict' within the meaning of article 5(3) of the Convention must be regarded as an independent concept covering all actions which seek to establish the liability of a defendant and which are not related to a 'contract' within the meaning of article 5(1).
>
> ...it must be observed...that the 'special jurisdictions' enumerated in articles 5 and 6 of the Convention constitute derogations from the principle that jurisdiction is vested in the courts of the State where the defendant is domiciled and as such must be interpreted restrictively. It must therefore be recognised that a court which has jurisdiction under article 5(3) over an action in so far as it is based on tort or delict does not have jurisdiction over that action in so far as it is not so based.

10.65 The first half of this passage has been frequently misunderstood as meaning that art 5(3) is a catch-all provision. Such an interpretation is inconsistent with the second half of the quotation. In fact, the word 'liability' in the first passage must be understood as connoting liability within the scope of art 5(3). 'Mainstream' torts, such as negligence, nuisance, defamation, and patent infringement, all come within the definition.

10.66 The special jurisdiction granted by art 5(3) is allocated to the place where the harmful event occurred. It was held by the ECJ in *Handelskwekerij G J Bier BV v Mines de Potasse d'Alsace SA* (Case 21/76) [1978] QB 708 that this gives the claimant the option of commencing proceedings either in the country where the wrongful act or omission took place, or in the country where the damage occurred. In negligent misstatement cases this will be the place where the statement was made rather than where it was received (*Domicrest Ltd v Swiss Bank Corporation* [1999] QB 548). In a personal injuries claim the harmful event will be the original accident. Under French law it is possible to bring more than one claim arising out of a single accident if the claimant suffers a subsequent deterioration, but this does not entitle a claimant in this position to bring the second claim in England because the 'harmful event' remains the original accident (*Henderson v Jaoun* [2002] 1 WLR 2971). The place where the damage occurred is not the place where the damage was quantified or where steps were taken to mitigate the effects of the wrongful conduct of the defendant (*Netherlands v Rüffer* (Case 814/79) [1980] ECR 3807). Further, the 'place where damage occurred' cannot be construed as encompassing any place where adverse consequences of an event which have already caused actual damage elsewhere could be felt (*Marinari v Lloyds Bank plc* (Case C–364/93) [1996] QB 217). It therefore does not include a place where a claimant claimed to have suffered loss consequential on initial damage suffered in another contracting State.

10.67 These principles were applied in *Shevill v Presse Alliance SA* (Case C–68/93) [1995] 2 AC 18, ECJ; [1996] AC 959, HL. The claimants commenced an action in England against a French defendant complaining that they had been libelled in one of the defendant's newspapers. The newspaper had a daily circulation of 200,000 copies in France, and about 250 copies in England. Their particulars of claim relied only on publication in England. It was held that as the 'harmful event' in art 5(3) included the place where the damage was suffered, the action had been validly brought in England, although the English courts had jurisdiction solely in respect of the harm caused in England.

Criminal compensation

10.68 Where a civil claim is made based on an act giving rise to criminal proceedings, jurisdiction is given by art 5(4) to the courts of the country dealing with criminal proceedings.

Branches, agencies, and establishments

10.69 Article 5(5) provides that alternative jurisdiction is given as regards disputes arising out of the operations of a branch, agency, or other establishment to the courts for the place in which the branch, agency, or other establishment is situated. This provision has been restrictively interpreted. From the Jenard Report and the opinion of the Advocate General in *Etablissements A de Bloos Sprl v SCA Bouyer* (Case 14/76) [1976] ECR 1497 it is accepted that the branch, agency, or other establishment referred to must be that of the proposed defendant, and the claimant's arrangements in this respect are irrelevant. Further, the mere fact that some person in the country where the claimant wishes to commence proceedings acted as the proposed defendant's agent for the purposes of the law of agency is not enough, on its own, to satisfy art 5(5). 'Agency' must be interpreted *eiusdem generis* with 'branch' and 'establishment'. The effect is that art 5(5) is dealing with emanations of the defendant's business which are subject to the defendant's control and which give the defendant a corporate presence within the relevant jurisdiction. Even if the defendant does have a branch, agency, or establishment within the meaning of art 5(5), it is further necessary that the dispute must arise out of the activities of that branch, agency, or establishment. This will comprehend, according to *Somafer SA v Saar-Ferngas AG* (Case 33/78) [1978] ECR 2183, the following types of activities by the branch, agency, or establishment:

(a) management matters, such as the local engagement of staff;
(b) contractual undertakings given in the name of the parent;
(c) tortious and other non-contractual liability.

10.70 If a dispute arises out of the operations of a branch, there is no further requirement that the obligation in question must be performed in the State where the branch is situated, provided there is a nexus between the operations of the branch and the dispute which renders it natural to describe the dispute as one arising out of the activities of the branch (*Anton Durbeck GmbH v Den Norske Bank ASA* [2003] QB 1160). So, in *Lloyd's Register of Shipping v Société Campenon Bernard* (Case C–439/93) [1995] ECR I–961 the claimant entered into a contract with the French branch of the defendant under which the defendant agreed to do certain work in Spain. The work was carried out by the defendant's Spanish branch. A dispute arose, and proceedings were commenced in France, the claimant relying on art 5(5). The ECJ held the proceedings had been validly commenced in France, and there was no requirement in art 5(5) for performance to be in the State where proceedings were commenced.

Trusts

10.71 A settlor, trustee, or beneficiary of a trust created by the operation of a statute, or by a written instrument, or created orally and evidenced in writing, may be joined as a party to proceedings brought in the courts of the country where the trust is domiciled (art 5(6)). This form of wording excludes implied and constructive trusts, and a person with power to appoint who will take assets under a trust is not a 'trustee' for this purpose unless expressly named as trustee (*Gomez v Gomez-Monche Vives* [2009] 2 WLR 950). A trust is domiciled in England if English law is the system of law with which the trust has its closest and most real connection (CJJA 1982, s 45(3)).

Salvage and freight

10.72 Under art 5(7) claims for freight or salvage of cargo may be brought where the freight or cargo has been or could be arrested.

Co-defendants

10.73 It is provided by art 6(1), that:

> a person domiciled in a Member State may also be sued, where he is one of a number of defendants, in the courts for the place where any one of them is domiciled provided the claims are so closely connected that it is expedient to hear and determine them together to avoid the risk of irreconcilable judgments resulting from separate proceedings.

10.74 The first precondition is that there must be a valid claim against the defendant domiciled within the jurisdiction (*The Rewia* [1991] 2 Lloyd's Rep 325). It is then necessary to consider whether the joinder is valid. The nature of the connection justifying joinder of a defendant not domiciled in England is given an independent Community meaning, and it is not necessarily enough that the joinder satisfies CPR, r 19.1 (for which, see 17.51–17.53) (*Kalfelis v Bankhaus Schröder, Münchmeyer, Hengst & Co* (Case 189/87) [1988] ECR 5565). According to the ECJ, the proper use of art 6(1) is to avoid the risk of irreconcilable judgments and to prevent related actions proceeding in different contracting States. This concept is wide enough to cover situations where there are two sets of proceedings in England based on the same breach, one against defendants domiciled in England, and the other against defendants domiciled in another Member State (*Masri v Consolidated Contractors International (UK) Ltd* [2006] 1 WLR 830).

In *Société Commerciale de Réassurance v ERAS (International) Ltd (No 2)* [1995] 2 All ER 278 Potter J held there was no requirement in art 6(1) for the 'defendants' (in this case four claimants in four separate claims) to be jointly liable, or even that the defendants be sued in the same claim. The applicant was seeking identical injunctions against each of the claimants to restrain their proceedings based upon similar acts on the part of each of them, and his Lordship held he was permitted to take a broad view of what was meant in *Kalfelis* as to the risk of irreconcilable judgments. On this basis it was held that the High Court had jurisdiction over all the claimants. This is inconsistent with the decision at first instance of Hirst J in *Barclays Bank plc v Glasgow City Council* [1993] QB 429, where it was held that a number of closely connected, but technically separate, claims did not come within art 6(1). Whichever decision is correct, it is arguable that consolidated claims satisfy the requirements of art 6(1). **10.75**

In *Gascoine v Pyrah* (1991) *The Times*, 26 November 1991 the second defendant, a German veterinary surgeon, was struck out of an English claim against an English defendant over the sale of a horse. The reasons for doing so were that the place of performance of the principal obligation was Germany, the event causing the damage occurred in Germany, and there was no real risk of irreconcilable judgments if the first defendant was sued in England and the second defendant was sued in Germany. **10.76**

Counterclaims and additional claims under Part 20

By art 6(2) and (3), counterclaims arising from the same facts as those founding the claim and additional claims under Part 20 may be brought in the court in which the claimant's claim is pending. In *Kinnear v Falconfilms NV* [1996] 1 WLR 920 a claim was commenced in England by the administrators of an actor's estate against a film company claiming damages arising out of a riding accident during the shooting of a film in Spain. The film company issued an additional claim seeking an indemnity or a contribution against the Spanish hospital that treated the actor, claiming that the actor's death was caused by the negligence of the hospital. It was held that the hospital could be brought in as a third party in the English proceedings, because the nexus required for bringing claims against third parties under CPR, Part 20 (see Chapter 18), was in practical terms sufficient to satisfy the requirements of the special jurisdiction conferred by art 6(2). Contribution notices are not claim forms and therefore cannot be served outside the jurisdiction (*Knauf UK GmbH v British Gypsum Ltd* [2002] 2 Lloyd's Rep 416). **10.77**

Lis pendens

Article 27 provides: **10.78**

> Where proceedings involving the same cause of action and between the same parties are brought in the courts of different Member States, any court other than the court first seised shall of its own motion stay its proceedings until such time as the jurisdiction of the court first seised is established.
>
> Where the jurisdiction of the court first seised is established, any court other than the court first seised shall decline jurisdiction in favour of that court.

10.79 This article is designed to prevent parallel proceedings before the courts of different contracting States, and to avoid the conflicts that might otherwise result. It is to be interpreted broadly, and covers all situations of *lis pendens*, irrespective of the parties' domicile (*Overseas Union Insurance Ltd v New Hampshire Insurance Co* (Case C–351/89) [1992] QB 434). The phrase 'proceedings involving the same cause of action' must be given an independent Community meaning (*Gubisch Maschinenfabrik KG v Palumbo* (Case 144/86) [1987] ECR 4861). The article obviously covers the situation where a claimant brings identical proceedings in two countries. It also covers the situation where a claimant brings proceedings in one country for a declaration that there has been no breach of a contract and the defendant to that action brings proceedings in another country claiming damages for breach of that contract (see *The Maciej Rataj* (Case C–406/92) [1999] QB 515). It even covers a case where one party to a contract brings a claim for rescission of a contract and the other party to the contract brings proceedings in another country to enforce the same contract. However, art 27 operates only to the extent that the parties to the second claim are the same as those in the first, or, if technically different, where their interests are identical and indissociable (*Drouot Assurances SA v Consolidated Metallurgical Industries (CMI Industrial Sites)* (Case C–351/96) [1999] QB 497).

10.80 Priority under art 27 is given to the court 'first seised'. This occurs when documents capable of being served are lodged with the court to institute proceedings (*Kolden Holdings Ltd v Rodette Commerce Ltd* [2008] Bus LR 1051). An English court becomes seised when a claim form (or other originating process) is lodged at court for issue, provided the claimant does not subsequently fail to effect service (art 30(1)). Slightly different rules apply in some other Regulation States (art 30(2)) where domestic law requires the originating process to be served before being lodged in court. In such cases the court becomes seised when the document is received by the authority responsible for service, provided the claimant has not subsequently failed to take any required steps to lodge the document with the court. Where there has been a defective attempt to serve English proceedings, the English court can use its powers to cure irregularity (CPR, r 3.10) or to dispense with service (r 6.16) even though the effect is to constitute the English court as the court first seised (*Phillips v Symes (No 3)* [2008] 1 WLR 180).

10.81 Where proceedings are brought in one country, and the defendant to that action brings a second action in another country and alleges that the courts of the country first seised have no jurisdiction under the Jurisdiction Regulation, the second court may either decline jurisdiction or stay its proceedings to await the outcome of any challenge made to the jurisdiction of the first court. What the second court is not allowed to do is to investigate the jurisdiction of the first court (*Overseas Union Insurance Ltd v New Hampshire Insurance Co)*. This is so even where there is a choice of forum clause conferring jurisdiction on the second court, and even where there are excessive delays in the first court (*Erich Gasser GmbH v MISAT Srl* (Case C–116/02) [2005] QB 1).

Related actions

10.82 Article 28 provides:

(1) Where related actions are brought in the courts of different Member States, any court other than the court first seised may stay its proceedings.

(2) Where these actions are pending at first instance, any court other than the court first seised may also, on the application of one of the parties, decline jurisdiction if the court seised has jurisdiction over the actions in question and its law permits the consolidation thereof.
(3) For the purposes of this article, actions are deemed to be related where they are so closely connected that it is expedient to hear and determine them together to avoid the risk of irreconcilable judgments resulting from separate proceedings.

Article 28 is dealing with the area between situations where two claims are the same (where the second claim must be stayed under art 27) and situations where it is right for two claims to proceed at the same time. In considering whether to grant a stay, the court must apply the simple test set out in the article, which is designed to cover a range of circumstances. A stay was granted in *Sarrio SA v Kuwait Investment Authority* [1999] 1 AC 32, where there was an overlap between the issues raised in insolvency proceedings in Spain and later proceedings in England claiming damages for negligent misrepresentation. It would cover an action *in rem* and an action *in personam* in respect of the same loss, where technically the parties are not the same (*The Sylt* [1991] 1 Lloyd's Rep 240). It was conceded in *Dresser UK Ltd v Falcongate Freight Management Ltd* [1992] QB 502 that it would cover proceedings for limitation of liability for loss of cargo at sea and an action claiming damages for the loss of the same cargo. Once it is held that proceedings are related, the court has a discretion whether to grant a stay, but it will be unusual for the stay to be refused (*The Linda* [1988] 1 Lloyd's Rep 175). **10.83**

Interim relief

The CJJA 1982, s 25(1), confers on the High Court in England power to grant interim relief in the absence of substantive proceedings, where proceedings have been or will be commenced in another State. The principle underpinning s 25 is that the court should assist the courts of other jurisdictions by providing such interim relief as would be available if it were itself seised of the substantive proceedings (*Refco Inc v Eastern Trading Co* [1999] 1 Lloyd's Rep 159; *Kensington International Ltd v Congo* [2008] 1 WLR 1144). The power to grant interim relief extends to any proceedings in any state, regardless of whether it is a Brussels or Lugano contracting state or whether the proceedings fell within the scope of the Conventions or the Jurisdiction Regulation (Civil Jurisdiction and Judgments Act 1982 (Interim Relief) Order 1997 (SI 1997/302)). This solves the difficulty encountered in *The Siskina* [1979] AC 210 (see 35.28, 35.29), where the House of Lords held that the English courts had no power to grant a freezing injunction over assets within the jurisdiction in the absence of a cause of action justiciable here, because a freezing injunction is a form of relief, not a substantive cause of action. Detailed consideration of s 25 can be found at 36.10 and 36.17. **10.84**

Procedure on commencing proceedings pursuant to the Judgments Regulation

Where proceedings can be served outside the jurisdiction pursuant to the provisions of the Brussels, Lugano, or Modified Convention, or the Judgments Regulation, service may be effected without the permission of the court (CPR, r 6.33). The claimant is required to file a notice in form N510 with the claim form containing a statement of the grounds on which **10.85** the claimant is entitled to serve the claim form outside the jurisdiction (r 6.34 and PD 6B, para 2.1). The N510 has to be served with the claim form (r 6.34(1)(b)).

E ASSUMED JURISDICTION

10.86 The rules discussed in this section deal with the situation where it is desired to serve English proceedings on a defendant living in a country outside the scope of the Jurisdiction Regulation and Brussels and Lugano Conventions. If service is to be effected out of the jurisdiction in such a country, permission must first be obtained from the English court. Unless permission is obtained, and if the defendant's address is outside the jurisdiction, when the claim form is issued it will be stamped 'not for service out of the jurisdiction'.

Basic principles governing applications for permission

10.87 The requirements that need to be satisfied if the English courts are to grant permission to serve proceedings outside the jurisdiction under the court's assumed jurisdiction are those laid down by the House of Lords in *Seaconsar Far East Ltd v Bank Markazi Jomhouri Islami Iran* [1994] 1 AC 438 as altered by what is now CPR, r 6.37. Applications for permission to serve outside the jurisdiction made between four and six months after issue are governed by rr 6.36 and 6.37, not the rules on extending validity of claim forms in r 7.6 (*Anderton v Clwyd County Council (No 2)* [2002] 1 WLR 3174). The intending claimant must establish that:

(a) There is a good arguable case that the court has jurisdiction within one of the 20 grounds set out in PD 6B, para 3.1 (r 6.36). These are discussed at 10.91. The need to show a good arguable case is not as strict a requirement as satisfying the court to the civil standard of proof (*Agrafax Public Relations Ltd v United Scottish Society Inc* (1995) *The Times*, 22 May 1995).
(b) The claim has a reasonable prospect of success (r 6.37(1)(b)). This is the same as the test applied for summary judgment and setting aside default judgments.
(c) The case is a proper one for service outside the jurisdiction. This is considered further at 10.99–10.101.

10.88 Obviously, putting a person in an overseas country to the inconvenience of defending a claim in this country is a serious matter, so the courts have always exercised the power to allow service abroad with caution.

Procedure on seeking permission

10.89 As there is no defendant on the record, an application for permission to serve a claim form out of the jurisdiction should be made without notice. While permission should be sought before the claim is served, it is possible to grant retrospective permission (*Nesheim v Kosa* (2006) LTL 4/10/06). There will be no hearing. In the RCJ, a copy of the application notice and evidence in support should be left in the Master's Support Unit, room E16.

The evidence must state, according to CPR, r 6.37(1): 10.90

(a) the grounds on which the application is made and the paragraphs of PD 6B, para 3.1 relied upon;
(b) that in the witness's belief, the claimant has a reasonable prospect of success;
(c) the defendant's address or, if unknown, in what place or country the defendant is or can probably be found; and
(d) where the application is made under para 3.1(3) (that the defendant is a necessary or proper party), the grounds for believing that there is a real issue between the claimant and the existing defendant which it is reasonable for the court to try.

Grounds for granting permission

As mentioned in 10.87, the grounds on which permission may be granted for service outside the jurisdiction on defendants outside the Convention countries are set out in PD 6B, para 3.1. There are 20 permitted grounds, which include cases where: 10.91

(4) a claim is made for a remedy against a person domiciled within the jurisdiction;
(5) a claim is made for an injunction ordering the defendant to do or refrain from doing an act within the jurisdiction;
(6) a claim is made against a defendant on whom the claim form has been or will be served and there is between the claimant and the defendant a real issue which it is reasonable for the court to try, and the claimant wishes to serve the claim form on another person who is a necessary or proper party to that claim;...
(7) a claim is made for an interim remedy under CJJA 1982, s 25(1);
(8) a claim is made in respect of a contract where the contract:
  (a) was made within the jurisdiction;
  (b) was made by or through an agent trading or residing within the jurisdiction;
  (c) is governed by English law; or
  (d) contains a term to the effect that the court shall have jurisdiction to determine any claim in respect of the contract;
(9) a claim is made in respect of a breach of contract committed within the jurisdiction;
(10) a claim is made for a declaration that no contract exists where, if the contract were found to exist, it would comply with the conditions set out in paragraph (6);
(11) a claim is made in tort where:
  (a) damage was sustained within the jurisdiction; or
  (b) the damage sustained resulted from an act committed within the jurisdiction.

General interpretation

The grounds in PD 6B, para 3.1, have been regularly amended over the years. The rule was reformulated in 2000 and 2008, so some caution is necessary with earlier case law. 10.92

As these provisions allow the court to exercise an exorbitant jurisdiction, they are to be strictly construed in favour of the overseas party (*The Hagen* [1908] P 189). Service out is not allowed unless the claim falls into one or other of the grounds set out in PD 6B, para 3.1 (*Holland v Leslie* [1894] 2 QB 346), and there must be a good arguable case that this is so. 10.93

Although the claimant can choose which ground or grounds to rely on (*Matthews v Kuwait Bechtel Corporation* [1959] 2 QB 57), the claimant must specifically state those grounds in the evidence in support of the application, and will not be permitted to raise alternative grounds on a defendant's application to discharge the order granting permission (*Metall und Rohstoff AG v Donaldson Lufkin and Jenrette Inc* [1990] 1 QB 391). While some cases, such as *Johnson v Taylor Bros and Co* [1920] AC 144, say that the case must fall within the overall purposes of the relevant ground, not merely its strict letter, there are other cases, such as *Sharab v Prince Al-Waleed bin Talal bin Abdal-Aziz-Al-Saud* [2009] 2 Lloyd's Rep 160, which say there is no need to come within the spirit of the relevant sub-paragraph as well as its letter.

Injunctions

10.94 The injunction referred to in PD 6B, para 3.1(2), has to be final as opposed to interim (*The Siskina* [1979] AC 210). The injunction must be the real form of relief sought, and must not simply be tacked on in order to found jurisdiction (*Rosler v Hilbery* [1925] Ch 250).

Necessary or proper party

10.95 PD 6B, para 3.1(3) may be compared with art 6(1) of the Judgments Regulation (see 10.73–10.76). The claimant's evidence must set out the grounds for believing that there is a real issue which the court may reasonably be asked to try between the claimant and the defendant who has already been served. Once this has been established, the claimant must further show that the second defendant is a necessary or proper party to the claim. There is particular reluctance to allow service under this paragraph given its anomaly (in relation to the other grounds) in not being founded upon any territorial connection between the claim and the jurisdiction of the English courts (*Multinational Gas and Petrochemical Co v Multinational Gas and Petrochemical Services Ltd* [1983] Ch 258). An example of where it might be used is where a partnership has been served in England, and it is sought to serve a foreign partner (*West of England Steamship Owners' Protection and Indemnity Association Ltd v John Holman and Sons* [1957] 1 WLR 1164).

Contract

10.96 Whether a contract was made within the jurisdiction depends on general contractual principles (see *Brinkibon Ltd v Stahag Stahl und Stahlwarenhandelsgesellschaft mbH* [1983] 2 AC 34). This case involved an exchange of telexes between parties in different countries. It was held that the contract was made in the country where the telex accepting the offer was received. A contract made within the jurisdiction which is subsequently amended outside the jurisdiction still comes within PD 6B, para 3.1(6)(a) unless the amendment substitutes a new contract (*BP Exploration Co (Libya) Ltd v Hunt* [1976] 1 WLR 788). Unlike the Judgments Regulation, art 5(5) (see 10.69), PD 6B, para 3.1(6)(b) is given a wide interpretation, and even includes a case where the defendant's London agent merely sent the claimant the defendant's price list and forwarded the claimant's order to the defendant (*National Mortgage and Agency Co of New Zealand Ltd v Gosselin* (1922) 38 TLR 832). The 'agent', however, must be that of the defendant, not the claimant (*Union International Insurance Co Ltd v Jubilee Insurance Co Ltd* [1991] 1 WLR 415). There is no equivalent to PD 6B, para 3.1(6)(c), that the contract is governed by

English law, in the Judgments Regulation. An express term to this effect should not cause difficulties. An implication that a contract is governed by English law may arise by course of dealings where earlier transactions between the parties were governed by English law (*Banque Paribas v Cargill International SA* [1992] 1 Lloyd's Rep 96). An express jurisdiction clause (PD 6B, para 3.1(6)(d)) will almost always be given effect by the courts (compare 10.53ff), but there are sometimes questions whether the claimant is a party entitled to rely on the clause in cases where there are interlocking contracts (see, eg, *The Mahkutai* [1996] AC 650).

PD 6B, para 3.1(7), breach within the jurisdiction, should be compared with the Judgments Regulation, art 5(1) (see 10.39ff). Where the breach consists of a failure to perform a contractual obligation, it is necessary to find the place where performance should have taken place (*Brinkibon Ltd v Stahag Stahl etc.*). **10.97**

Tort

Jurisdiction in tort under PD 6B, para 3.1(9), is in the same terms as the Judgments Regulation, art 5(3) (see 10.61ff). Jurisdiction may be founded either on the basis of damage being suffered in England or through the tortious act being committed in England. In *Booth v Phillips* [2004] 1 WLR 3292 it was held that damage under PD 6B, para 3.1(9) refers to physical or economic harm suffered by the claimant. It is enough if some damage is suffered within the jurisdiction, and there is no requirement that the damage within the jurisdiction must complete the cause of action. In *Ashton Investments Ltd v Rusal* [2007] 1 Lloyd's Rep 311 the defendant was alleged to have hacked into a computer server in London from outside the jurisdiction. It was held the damage was sustained and the relevant act was committed within the jurisdiction. If separate acts constituting a single tort are committed here and abroad, the question is whether the tort was in substance committed within the jurisdiction (*Metall und Rohstoff AG v Donaldson Lufkin and Jenrette Inc* [1990] 1 QB 391). **10.98**

Forum non conveniens

The need to show that the case is a proper one for service outside the jurisdiction also manifests itself in the court's discretion to refuse permission on the basis of *forum non conveniens*. The leading case is *Spiliada Maritime Corporation v Cansulex Ltd* [1987] AC 460. The claimant shipowner sought permission to serve English proceedings on Canadian sulphur exporters, claiming damages in respect of severe corrosion to the hold of the claimant's ship, the *Spiliada*, allegedly caused by a cargo of wet sulphur. An almost identical claim, *The Cambridgeshire*, had just reached trial in England. The defendants in both claims were the same, and the claimants in both claims had the same insurer (through subrogation, the insurer rather than the nominal claimants had the real interest in bringing the actions). *The Cambridgeshire* was in the nature of a test case. The scientific investigations made approached the limits of scientific knowledge. The claimant's experts came from England, whereas the defendant had instructed two English and four foreign experts. A total of 15 counsel were instructed, each being armed with 75 files of evidence and documents, and the trial was estimated for six months. Many of the potential witnesses of fact would be Canadian, but many witnesses would come from other places (the *Spiliada* was registered in Liberia). On the facts, the extent and depth of preparation undertaken in *The* **10.99**

Cambridgeshire proceedings, and the fact that English law was the proper law of the contract, meant that England was the appropriate forum, and permission to serve outside the jurisdiction was granted.

10.100 Lord Goff of Chieveley laid down the general principle that the court has to identify the forum in which the case can be most suitably tried in the interests of all the parties and for the ends of justice. The burden of proof rests on the claimant to show that England is clearly the most appropriate place for the trial of the action. An overly technical approach to using the language from *Spiliada Maritime Corporation v Cansulex Ltd* is not necessary where the judge is experienced and where it is clear the correct principles have been applied (*Novus Aviation Ltd v Onur Air Taşimacilik Aş* [2009] 1 Lloyd's Rep 576). Whether the emphasis is on the appropriate forum or the natural forum, or the forum in which the case might be suitably tried in the interests of the parties and for the ends of justice, or the forum with which the claim has its most real and substantial connection, the same matters have to be considered. These include the availability of witnesses, the governing law, the residence and/or places of business of the parties, and the ground in PD 6B, para 3, relied upon. Other factors include the languages used by the witnesses and courts, and the relative ease of enforcement of any judgment both in this and the proposed jurisdiction (*Sharab v Prince Al-Waleed bin Talal bin Abdal-Aziz-Al-Saud* [2009] 2 Lloyd's Rep 160). The availability of public funding is, however, irrelevant: see *Connelly v RTZ Corporation plc* [1996] QB 361.

10.101 The weight to be attached to the relevant factors depends on all the circumstances of the case. As Lord Goff said in *The Spiliada*:

> ...the defendant's place of residence may be no more than a tax haven to which no great importance should be attached. It is also significant to observe that the circumstances specified in [PD 6B, para 3.1], as those in which the court may exercise its discretion to grant leave to serve proceedings on the defendant outside the jurisdiction, are of great variety, ranging from cases where, one would have thought, the discretion would normally be exercised in favour of granting leave (eg, where the relief sought is an injunction ordering the defendant to do or refrain from doing something within the jurisdiction) to cases where the grant of leave is far more problematical. In addition, the importance to be attached to any particular ground invoked by the plaintiff may vary from case to case. For example, the fact that English law is the putative law of the contract may be of very great importance (as in *BP Exploration Co. (Libya) Ltd v Hunt* [1976] 1 WLR 788, where, in my opinion, Kerr J rightly granted leave to serve proceedings on the defendant out of the jurisdiction); or it may be of little importance as seen in the context of the whole case.

F SERVICE ABROAD

Effecting service abroad

10.102 The general rule is that service abroad must be effected in accordance with the law of the country where it is sought to effect service.

10.103 In practice, service out of the jurisdiction may be effected either through diplomatic channels or, where permitted under local law, informally by the claimant.

Service through diplomatic channels under the Hague Convention

The United Kingdom, together with the other countries listed in table 10.2, is a party to the Hague Convention on the Service Abroad of Judicial and Extra-judicial Documents in Civil or Commercial Matters (1965) ('the Hague Convention'). The Hague Convention, however, gives way to the EU Service Regulation (see 10.106). Each contracting state has designated a central authority to receive and transmit requests for service from other contracting states. A claim form may be served in another contracting state either through the central authority in the state in question, or, if permitted by the law of that country, through the judicial authorities of that country or the British consular authority in that country. **10.104**

Table 10.2 Contracting States to the Hague Convention other than Service Regulation States

Albania, Anguilla, Antigua, Argentina, Aruba, Bahamas, Barbados, Belarus, Bermuda, Botswana, British Virgin Islands, Bulgaria, Canada, Cayman Islands, China, Croatia, Denmark, Egypt, Falkland Islands, Gibraltar, Guernsey, Hong Kong, India, Isle of Man, Israel, Japan, Jersey, Korea, Kuwait, Macau, Malawi, Mexico, Monaco, Montserrat, Norway, Pakistan, Pitcairn, Romania, Russian Federation, San Marino, Seychelles, Sri Lanka, St Helena, St Vincent, Switzerland, Turkey, Turks and Caicos Islands, Ukraine, United Kingdom, United States of America, Venezuela

The following documents should be filed at the Foreign Process Department, RCJ, room E02 for onward transmission via the Parliamentary Under-Secretary of State to the Foreign Office, to the central authority in the receiving country (CPR, rr 6.43, 6.45 and PD 6B, paras 4.1, 4.2): **10.105**

(a) a request for service of the claim form, specifying the method of service to be used under r 6.42;
(b) a copy of the claim form, plus a duplicate for every defendant to be served;
(c) particulars of claim, and documents accompanying the claim form, and duplicates for every defendant to be served;
(d) the response pack, amended to show the relevant deadline for filing the acknowledgment and/or the defence, for each defendant to be served;
(e) translations into the language of the country where service is to be effected (if English is not an official language) of the claim form, particulars of claim, and response pack, accompanied by a statement by the translator that each is a correct translation;
(f) some countries require a legalization of documents to be served, and some require a formal letter of request signed by the Senior Master; and
(g) an undertaking to be responsible for the expenses incurred by the Foreign and Commonwealth Office or foreign judicial authority (r 6.46).

Service under the Service Regulation

Council Regulation (EC) No 1348/2000 ('the Service Regulation') applies to all EU Member States apart from Denmark, and supersedes all previous service treaties for its members. The Royal Courts of Justice, Foreign Process Department, is the transmitting and receiving agency for England and Wales under the Service Regulation. Claimants serving process in Member States need to file the claim form and translations at the Foreign Process Department, which will transmit the documents to the receiving agency of the country in question. The receiving **10.106** agency then serves the documents on the defendants. The intention is that the whole process should take no more than a month (reg 7(2)).

Other methods of service out of the jurisdiction

10.107 There are a number of countries, mainly in Europe, with which the United Kingdom has bilateral civil procedure conventions. Process may be served in these countries through their judicial authorities, or through the British consular authority in that country, subject to local laws, in much the same way as described in 10.104. If there is no bilateral convention with the country where service has to be effected, it is still possible to use British consular authorities or seek the assistance of the government of the country in question, but there is a greater risk that these methods will be contrary to local law. In practice, lawyers in the country in question are usually appointed as agents to advise and effect service.

Responding to a claim served out of the jurisdiction

10.108 Enhanced periods for responding to claims served out of the jurisdiction are provided by CPR, rr 6.35 and 6.37(5). If the defendant is in an EU Member State, the time for acknowledging service or filing the defence is 21 days from the date of service of the particulars of claim. Such a defendant who acknowledges service first has a total of 35 days from the date of service of the particulars of claim in which to file the defence. Defendants who are in countries or territories outside the Member States have even longer periods in which to respond, with different periods being laid down in PD 6B for different countries depending on how remote they are.

G JUDGMENT IN DEFAULT

10.109 No special rule applies in cases of assumed jurisdiction regarding entering judgment in default other than the need for waiting for the enhanced period laid down for responding to the claim.

10.110 Where service outside the jurisdiction has been effected without permission under the Judgments Regulation, judgment in default can be entered only by application under CPR, Part 12 (CPR, r 12.10(b)(i)). Where service was effected under the Service Regulation default judgment cannot be entered until it is established that the documents were served in accordance with the internal law of the receiving State or were actually delivered to the defendant or to the defendant's residence, and that the defendant has had sufficient time to defend the claim (Service Regulation, art 19).

H STAYS ON THE GROUND OF *FORUM NON CONVENIENS*

10.111 English proceedings can be served as of right on a defendant within the jurisdiction irrespective of the degree of connection with this country of the defendant or the cause of action (see 10.07–10.08). A claim form for an Admiralty claim *in rem* may be served within the jurisdiction on a ship or sister ship while at port in the country, even if there is absolutely no other connection with this country.

To prevent completely unsuitable claims proceeding, the courts have a discretion to stay English proceedings on the principle of *forum non conveniens*. The leading case is *Spiliada Maritime Corporation v Cansulex Ltd* [1987] AC 460. The principles applied are the same as on applications for permission under PD 6B, para 3.1, but the burden of proof is reversed. **10.112**

Appropriate forum

In *Spiliada Maritime Corporation v Cansulex Ltd* [1987] AC 460 Lord Goff of Chieveley said: **10.113**

> The basic principle is that a stay will only be granted on the ground of *forum non conveniens* where the court is satisfied that there is some other available forum, having competent jurisdiction, which is the appropriate forum for the trial of the action, i.e. in which the case may be tried more suitably for the interests of all the parties and the ends of justice.

The burden of proof rests on the defendant to show there is some other clearly more appropriate forum. If there is no other more suitable forum, the stay should usually be refused. So, eg, in *The Vishva Abha* [1990] 2 Lloyd's Rep 312 the owners of cargo on board a ship named the *Dias* made a claim *in rem* against the owners of a ship named the *Vishva Apurva*. The collision happened on the high seas. The only connection with England other than the fact that the defendant's ship was arrested here was that the defendant's ships regularly docked in this country. The suggested alternative forum was South Africa, on the ground that the *Dias* had been arrested there in litigation between the owners of the two ships. The only connection with South Africa was that proceedings had been served there while the *Dias* was in port. It was pure chance that litigation was pending in South Africa over the same collision as opposed to any other country, so there was no other distinctly more appropriate forum. **10.114**

In considering whether there is an alternative forum, the court will look for the country 'with which the action has the most real and substantial connection' (*The Abidin Daver* [1984] AC 398 *per* Lord Keith of Kinkel). Sometimes, the natural forum of the action will be obvious. In *MacShannon v Rockware Glass Ltd* [1978] AC 795, a Scots employee sued his employer, which was registered in England, in respect of an accident in Scotland. All the witnesses lived in Scotland. Clearly, Scotland was the natural forum. *Gulf Oil 'Belgian' SA v Finland Steamship Co Ltd* [1980] 2 Lloyd's Rep 229 arose from a collision between two ships in Swedish waters caused by a misunderstanding between two Swedish pilots speaking in Swedish by VHF radio. It was patently obvious that the case should be tried in Sweden. The places of residence or business of the parties must be considered. A stay will more readily be granted if service was effected during a temporary visit to England and Wales. On the other hand, where the defendant has an established place of business within the jurisdiction, very clear and weighty grounds must be shown for refusing to exercise jurisdiction (*Banco Atlantico SA v British Bank of the Middle East* [1990] 2 Lloyd's Rep 504). The court will also consider the availability of factual and expert witnesses, the law governing the dispute, and whether the parties have conferred jurisdiction on any particular court. Usually, it is best for proceedings to be continued in the country whose law governs the dispute (*Standard Steamship Owners' Protection and Indemnity Association (Bermuda) Ltd v Gann* [1992] 2 Lloyd's Rep 528). An alternative forum **10.115** which simply applies its own laws irrespective of the generally accepted rules on the conflict of laws is unlikely to be regarded as a suitable alternative (*Banco Atlantico SA v British Bank of the Middle East*). Convincing reasons must usually be shown before the court will go behind an express agreement between the parties as to jurisdiction (*Kuwait Oil Co (KSC) v Idemitsu Tankers KK* [1981] 2 Lloyd's Rep 510).

Reasons of justice

10.116 If there is some more appropriate forum, the court may refuse a stay if, in all the circumstances of the case, justice requires that a stay should not be granted (*Spiliada Maritime Corporation v Cansulex Ltd* [1987] AC 460). The burden of proof regarding showing some reason for not granting a stay despite there being some more suitable forum is on the claimant. A stay may be refused, eg, where the claimant has cogent evidence that justice will not be done in the foreign jurisdiction (*The Abidin Daver* [1984] AC 398). However, a fear that justice will not be done in the claimant's own country, if that is the appropriate forum, is irrelevant (*Jeyaretnam v Mahmood* (1992) *The Times*, 21 May 1992).

Legitimate personal or juridical advantage

10.117 There are many cases where a claimant can secure some advantage by commencing proceedings in one jurisdiction rather than another. Examples include the measure of damages, the vigour of the procedures on disclosure, the power to award interest, and the length of the limitation period. Generally, an advantage to the claimant will give rise to an equal disadvantage to the defendant. Stays have been granted in cases where doing so deprives the claimant of some advantage, as in *Trendtex Trading Corporation v Crédit Suisse* [1982] AC 679. Generally, the court seeks to do 'practical justice' between the parties (see Lord Goff of Chieveley in *Spiliada Maritime Corporation v Cansulex Ltd* [1987] AC 460), being less worried about depriving a claimant of a benefit secured by 'forum shopping'. Any injustice that may be caused by granting a stay may be avoided by making the order subject to conditions. For example, a stay may be granted in favour of a jurisdiction with a shorter limitation period on condition that the defendant shall waive any limitation defence. Indeed, the parties may try to pre-empt arguments along these lines by voluntarily undertaking not to take advantage of procedural differences in advance of the hearing for the stay.

Judgments Regulation cases

10.118 The CJJA 1982, s 49, provides that nothing in the Act shall prevent the court from staying proceedings on the ground of *forum non conveniens* or otherwise, where to do so is not inconsistent with the Judgments Regulation. This means that there is no power to stay where that is inconsistent with the Judgments Regulation. Generally, the Judgments Regulation provides a complete code, so a stay would be inconsistent with the Judgments Regulation. Where the defendant is domiciled in England, but the dispute as to jurisdiction is between the courts of this country and the courts of a non-Member State, English proceedings may be stayed on the ground of *forum non conveniens* (*Re Harrods (Buenos Aires) Ltd* [1992] Ch 72).

I INJUNCTIONS TO RESTRAIN FOREIGN PROCEEDINGS

In rare circumstances, an English court may grant an injunction restraining the institution or continuance of foreign proceedings. Such injunctions do not infringe art 6 of the European Convention on Human Rights, provided a fair trial is available somewhere (*OT Africa Line Ltd v Hijazy* [2001] 1 Lloyd's Rep 76). Such an injunction is granted only when it is required for the ends of justice (*Castanho v Brown and Root (UK) Ltd* [1981] AC 557). The injunction is directed to a party, not to the foreign court, so is available only against a party who is amenable to the jurisdiction of the English courts. It is a jurisdiction which must be exercised with a great deal of caution. The leading case is *Société Nationale Industrielle Aérospatiale v Lee Kui Jak* [1987] AC 871. The principle laid down was that where a remedy for a particular wrong is available both in England and in a foreign country, an injunction will be granted to restrain the foreign proceedings only if pursuit of those proceedings would be vexatious and oppressive. This presupposes that England is the natural forum for the trial. Account must be taken of the balance of injustice to the parties depending on whether the injunction is either granted or refused, bearing in mind the possibility of removing any injustice by the imposition of suitable terms or the giving of undertakings. **10.119**

The facts were that the deceased, who had lived in Brunei, was killed in a helicopter crash in Brunei. A government report concluded that the accident was caused by metal debris in the rotating assembly. The administrators of the deceased's estate started proceedings, *inter alia*, against the manufacturer of the helicopter and the maintenance company in both Brunei and Texas. The maintenance company had been served with a contribution notice in Brunei where it did not object to the jurisdiction of the court, but was vigorously resisting the jurisdiction of the court in Texas. Brunei was obviously the natural forum for the action, but an injunction could be granted only if the proceedings in Texas were vexatious or oppressive. Vexation on the ground that under Texan law there was strict liability and punitive damages was neutralized by undertakings by the claimants that neither of these would be pursued. However, there was a distinct possibility that the defendants would be unable to claim a contribution from the maintenance company in Texas, whereas they could in Brunei, with the result that the proceedings in Texas could be described as oppressive. An injunction was granted. **10.120**

In *Turner v Grovit* (Case C–159/02) [2005] AC 101, the Court of Justice of the European Communities held that it is inconsistent with the Judgments Regulation for the courts in England to restrain defendants from commencing or continuing proceedings in another Member State even when those defendants are acting in bad faith with the purpose of frustrating proceedings properly before the English courts. In the same way it is contrary to the Judgments Regulation for the court in a second Member State to grant an injunction to restrain proceedings in a first Member State on the ground that those proceedings would be contrary to an arbitration agreement (*West Tankers Inc v Riunione Adriarica Di Sicurita Spa* (Case C–185/07) [2009] 1 AC 1138). **10.121**

An application for an anti-suit injunction should be made promptly. It is unlikely to be granted once judgment has been obtained in the foreign claim, or where it has been allowed to continue almost to the point of judgment (*Toepfer International GmbH v Molino Boschi Srl* **10.122**

[1996] 1 Lloyd's Rep 510). On the other hand, the foreign action must be more than merely anticipated (*Pan American World Airways v Andrews* 1992 SLT 268).

KEY POINTS SUMMARY

10.123

- Generally proceedings have to be served within the jurisdiction. There always has to be a sound basis before proceedings can be served outside the jurisdiction.
- Where the defendant is domiciled in the EU, the general rule is that they must be sued in the country where they are domiciled.
- If jurisdiction can be established against an EU defendant (such as under arts 5 or 6 of the Judgments Regulation):
  - (a) the claimant can choose whether to sue in England (under arts 5 or 6) or in the defendant's country of domicile (under art 2); and
  - (b) English proceedings may be served without permission.
- If jurisdiction can be established against a defendant who is outside the EU under CPR, r 6.36 and PD 6B, para 3.1, proceedings can be served outside the jurisdiction only with the permission of the court.
- The times for responding to claims served outside the jurisdiction are extended (to take into account the realities of postal delivery).
- If a defendant outside the jurisdiction does not respond to the claim, judgment in default can be entered in the usual way if permission to serve outside the jurisdiction was obtained (because the defendant is outside the EU), but permission to enter judgment in default must be sought if the defendant was served without permission under the Judgments Regulation.

11

RESPONDING TO A CLAIM

A defendant who intends to contest proceedings must respond to the claim by filing an acknowledgment of service and/or by filing a defence. Defended claims become subject to the court's case management system, with the court sending allocation questionnaires to the parties, followed by a procedural judge allocating the claim to a case management track (see Chapter 14) and giving directions for the future conduct of the claim. If a defendant fails to make any response to a claim the usual result is that a default judgment will be entered within a relatively short period after service (see Chapter 12). There are cases where the defendant has no real answer to a claim, but may want time to pay. This is considered at 11.04–11.06. There are other cases where the defendant objects to the jurisdiction of the court. These cases are considered at 11.13–11.18. **11.01**

A TIME FOR RESPONDING

For claims governed by the main provisions of the CPR, the event that starts time running against the defendant for the purpose of responding to the claim is service of the particulars **11.02** of claim (CPR, r 9.1(2)). The defendant has 14 days from the date of service of the particulars of claim (see r 10.3(1), r 14.2(1), and r 15.4) to do one of the following:

(a) file or serve an admission; or
(b) file a defence (which may be combined with making a counterclaim); or
(c) file an acknowledgment of service r 9.2).

11.03 This means that the defendant is under no immediate obligation to respond to proceedings if the claim form is served with particulars of claim to follow (CPR, r 9.1(2)). A claim form may be served on which are set out the particulars of claim (as in figure 8.1), or the particulars of claim may form a separate document which may be served either with the claim form or later. Where the claim form and the particulars of claim are separate documents, the particulars should be served within 14 days of the claim form and in any event during the period of validity of the claim form r 7.4).

B ADMISSIONS

11.04 A defendant who admits the claim is normally best advised to complete the admission form included in the response pack. As mentioned at 8.14, there are two types of admission form. N9A is used in claims for specified sums of money, and N9C is for use in claims for unspecified amounts of money, non-money claims, and claims for the return of goods. An example of form N9C was illustrated in figure 8.4. The form allows the defendant to admit either the whole claim or just a part. If the whole claim is admitted, the defendant needs to decide about payment. If the whole sum is paid within 14 days of service of the claim form, the defendant's liability for the claimant's costs will be limited to certain fixed sums laid down in CPR, Part 45. This assists the defendant, because fixed costs are considerably lower than the sums recoverable in contested litigation.

11.05 If the defendant needs time to pay, the admission form allows him to make an offer to pay by instalments. If this is done, the defendant must also complete a large number of questions set out in the form dealing with the defendant's personal and financial circumstances. The form will be sent to the claimant. The claimant will then consider the offer, and, if it is acceptable, will notify the court and a judgment will be entered for payment by the instalments offered by the defendant. If the claimant does not agree to the offer to pay by instalments, the rules make provision for the rate of payment to be determined by the court.

11.06 A defendant can also use the admission form to make a partial admission, denying the rest of the claim. The part that is denied has to be dealt with in a defence, which should be filed at court with the admission form. Again, if this happens the claimant is asked whether the partial admission is acceptable, and if so a judgment will be entered in that sum.

11.07 Formal and informal admissions are considered further at 34.02–34.04.

C DEFENCES

11.08 A defendant disputing a claim must file a defence. One of the forms in the response pack is a form of defence and counterclaim, there being different forms for claims for specified amounts (form N9B) and for unspecified and non-money claims (form N9D). An example of form N9D was given at figure 8.5. It has spaces where the defendant can set out the reasons why the claim is disputed, and also for details of any counterclaim. Alternatively, the defendant can draft a defence using ordinary paper, see figure 13.3. This is recognized by PD 15, para 1.3, which provides merely that a defence 'may' be set out in the response pack form. This alternative is often used by lawyers acting for clients, because well-drafted defences tend to set out the facts in some detail, and the space on the form is quite limited. Consideration of what needs to go into defences and counterclaims is given in Chapter 13.

D ACKNOWLEDGMENT OF SERVICE

Acknowledgments of service are used if the defendant is unable to file a defence in the time limited, or if the defendant intends to dispute the court's jurisdiction. By acknowledging service a defendant is given an extra 14 days for filing the defence, so that the defence need not be served until 28 days after service of the particulars of claim (CPR, r 15.4(1)(b)). **11.09**

The acknowledgment of service form is combined with the cover sheet of the response pack (form N9): see figure 8.3. The intention is that the defendant will cut the form along the line one-third the way down the page, and return the lower two-thirds to the court. It has a heading setting out the court, claim number, and the parties. If the defendant has been misnamed, the correct name should be inserted in the space provided. A defendant who is an individual must state his date of birth (PD 16, para 10.7). The defendant's address for service, which must be within the jurisdiction, must be provided. If the defendant is acting by a solicitor, the address for service will be the solicitor's address. The defendant must tick a box indicating whether the whole of the claim is to be defended or just a part, or whether the court's jurisdiction will be contested. The form is then signed, dated, and returned to the court. Two or more defendants acting through the same solicitors need file only a single acknowledgment of service (PD 10, para 5.3). **11.10**

Once the acknowledgment of service has been filed, the court must notify the claimant in writing (CPR, r 10.4). This is normally done by sending a copy of the form to the claimant's solicitor. **11.11**

E AGREED EXTENSIONS

The parties may agree to extend the time for serving a defence, but any agreement can be for only a maximum of a further 28 days (CPR, r 15.5(1)). The defendant has to notify the court in writing of the agreed extension. The restricted period for agreed extensions is to ensure the court retains control over proceedings in accordance with its case management functions. **11.12**

F DISPUTING SERVICE OR THE COURT'S JURISDICTION

11.13 As indicated at 11.09, a defendant disputing service or the court's jurisdiction must return the acknowledgment of service form to the court within 14 days after service of the particulars of claim indicating that jurisdiction is being challenged by ticking the relevant box on the form (CPR, r 11(2)). Part 11 is not limited to disputes over the court's territorial jurisdiction (Chapter 10), but also applies where the defendant disputes the court's power or authority to try the claim (*Hoddinott v Persimmon Homes (Wessex) Ltd* [2008] 1 WLR 806). Examples are where the defendant seeks to stay court proceedings under the Arbitration Act 1996, s 9, or to dispute an order extending the period of validity of a claim form (Chapter 9). Conversely, a dispute that amounts to a procedural defence, such as the expiry of limitation (Chapter 7), or that the claim has no real prospect of success (Chapter 21), do not engage Part 11 (*Dunn v Parole Board* [2009] 1 WLR 728).

11.14 Within the next 14 days after acknowledging service, the defendant must issue an application notice seeking an order declaring that the court has no jurisdiction or should not exercise any jurisdiction it might have r 11(1) and (4)). The court has a discretion to extend this 14-day period (*Sawyer v Atari Interactive Inc* [2005] EWHC 2351 (QB)), but a failure to apply within the time limit may be taken as a submission to the jurisdiction (*Maple Leaf Macro Volatility Master Fund v Rouvroy* [2009] 2 All ER (Comm) 287, at [187], unaffected by the appeal at [2009] EWCA Civ 1334). If the defendant disputes the court's jurisdiction, there is no need to serve a defence until after the application is determined. If the application is successful the court may make consequential directions setting aside the claim form, or service, or discharging prior orders, or staying the proceedings r 11(6)). If the application fails, the defendant is given 14 days from the date of the hearing to file a second acknowledgment of service r 11(7)(b)), after which the claim proceeds in the usual way, but with the court giving directions for filing and serving the defence, followed by track allocation or judgment in default.

11.15 Applications disputing the court's jurisdiction are sometimes met by arguments that the defendant has submitted to the court's jurisdiction, or has waived any irregularity in service. As mentioned at 10.07, in the absence of any express agreement to submit to the jurisdiction, it is a question whether the defendant's conduct, when viewed objectively in the context of all the circumstances of the case, is inconsistent with maintaining an objection to the jurisdiction of the court. If an application disputing the court's jurisdiction is made within the 14 days allowed by r 11(4), conduct will be treated as a submission to the jurisdiction only if it is wholly unequivocal.

11.16 For example, a defendant who has applied to dispute jurisdiction who attends before a judge to challenge a freezing injunction obtained without notice has not thereby unequivocally submitted to the jurisdiction, unless he also agrees to an order regulating his position pending trial (*SMAY Investments Ltd v Sachdev* [2003] 1 WLR 1973). Making an application for 'directions' is also equivocal, because the directions could have been for a stay of the proceedings (*Patel v Patel* [2000] QB 551).

11.17 If an application disputing jurisdiction is not made within the 14-day period, a defendant may be held to have submitted to the jurisdiction by:

(a) instructing a solicitor to accept service in the jurisdiction (*Manta Line Inc v Sofianites* [1984] 1 Lloyd's Rep 14); or

(b) appearing to contest the merits. An example is *Marc Rich & Co AG v Società Italiana Impianti PA (No 2)* [1992] 1 Lloyd's Rep 624, where the defendant was held to have submitted to the jurisdiction of the courts in Italy by delivering a statement of case disputing the merits of the claim.

A similar principle applies in Judgments Regulation cases, where art 24 provides that the courts of a Member State have jurisdiction where the defendant 'enters an appearance' unless the appearance is entered to contest jurisdiction. The reference to entering an appearance is to acknowledging service or filing a defence. From *Elefanten Schuh GmbH v Jacqmain* (Case 150/80) [1981] ECR 1671 (ECJ), it appears that a defence contesting jurisdiction and the merits in the alternative does not constitute a submission to the jurisdiction. However, it is not possible to submit to the jurisdiction of a court where the courts of another country have exclusive jurisdiction under art 22. **11.18**

G TRANSFER

There is an automatic transfer provision (CPR, r 26.2) for defended claims for specified sums of money against individuals, which are transferred to the defendant's home court. Transfers in other cases are governed by CCA 1984, ss 40 and 42 and by CPR, Part 30. Non-automatic transfers are usually dealt with in case management directions at the allocation stage, so will be considered at 14.06–14.09. **11.19**

H SPECIALIST CLAIMS

Different rules apply in relation to responding to claims in specialist proceedings. In the TCC, eg, the general rules on issuing, service, and responding apply (CPR, r 60.3), except that claims are brought in one of the specialist TCC courts r 60.4) and must be marked 'Technology and Construction Court' in the second line in the top right-hand corner (PD 60, para 3.2). This means that defendants must respond after service of the particulars of claim in the usual way by acknowledging service and filing a defence. However, once an acknowledgment of service or defence is filed the court will fix a case management conference (PD 60, para 8.1), after which the court exerts even greater control of the litigation than in usual multi-track claims. **11.20**

The Admiralty Court has many forms of its own (forms ADM1 to ADM21). There are three different Admiralty Court claim forms (for Admiralty claims *in rem*, Admiralty limitation claims, and other Admiralty claims), a prescribed form for collision claim statements of case, and special acknowledgment of service forms. Different special rules apply to different types of Admiralty claims. For example, the particulars of claim for Admiralty claims *in rem* must be contained in the claim form or served within 75 days of the claim form r 61.3(3)), the claim form must be served within 12 months of issue r 61.3(5)), and an acknowledgment must be filed within 14 days of service of the claim form (rather than the particulars of claim) (r 61.3(4)). This means that judgment in default can be obtained in claims *in rem* in default of either an acknowledgment of service or a defence r 61.9(1)). **11.21**

11.22 There are also various specialist forms for use in the Commercial Court. There are standard Commercial Court claim forms (form N1(CC)), and also special Commercial Court Part 8 claim forms (N208(CC)), additional claim forms (N211(CC)), and arbitration claims claim forms (N8), together with Commercial Court acknowledgment of service forms (N9(CC), N210(CC), and N213(CC)). A Commercial Court claim need not include a statement of value r 58.5(2)). In a Part 7 Commercial Court claim, the particulars of claim can be contained in or served with the claim form, otherwise the particulars of claim must be served within 28 days of filing an acknowledgment of service indicating an intention to defend r 58.5(1)). An acknowledgment of service is required within 14 days of service of the claim form in every case, even where the claim form is served without particulars of claim r 58.6). Default judgment may be obtained without filing particulars of claim if the defendant fails to acknowledge service r 58.8).

11.23 In addition to the specialist provisions in the CPR, reference should be made to the specialist court guides: see BCP app 3.

KEY POINTS SUMMARY

11.24
- In non-specialist Part 7 claims (typical litigation), the defendant must respond by acknowledging service or filing a defence within 14 days of service of the particulars of claim.
- Filing an acknowledgment of service extends the period for responding to 28 days.
- These periods can be extended by agreement or court order.
- In Commercial Court claims the defendant is required to acknowledge service of the claim form, even where this does not include particulars of claim.
- There are different boxes on the acknowledgment of service form (figure 8.3) for defending on the merits and for contesting jurisdiction.

12

DEFAULT JUDGMENT

Judgment in default may be entered where the defendant fails to defend a claim. It produces a judgment in favour of a claimant without holding a trial. The procedure is designed to prevent unnecessary expenditure of time, money, and court resources in protracted litigation over undefended claims. It is appropriate where the defendant is not defending on the merits. **12.01**

A large proportion of the claims brought in the civil courts are little more than debt recovery actions. Often, there is no dispute that the defendant has purchased goods or agreed to pay for services provided by the claimant, and has not paid for them. In fact there are hundreds of thousands of cases each year where proceedings are issued and served, and then are simply ignored by the defendants. Once the time for responding to the claim has elapsed, the claimant will think about entering judgment in default. **12.02**

Actually entering a judgment in default is usually a purely administrative matter, and involves no consideration by the court of the merits of the claim. All the claimant usually has to do, once the time for responding to the claim has elapsed, is to return a request form to the court asking for judgment to be entered. This will then be acted upon by the administrative staff at the court, and a judgment will be entered. Such a judgment binds the **12.03** defendant just as much as if it had been entered after a contested trial, and may be enforced in the normal way. However, it does not give rise to an estoppel *per rem judicatam* and may be set aside if the defendant can show a real prospect of defending the claim (see 12.32).

A TIME WHEN DEFAULT JUDGMENT MAY BE ENTERED

Part 7 claims

12.04 A defendant to a Part 7 claim (ie, an ordinary non-specialist claim) who has been served with the particulars of claim has 14 days from the effective date of service to make a response (CPR, r 10.3). Slightly longer periods are allowed where proceedings are served outside the jurisdiction. A response may be by filing an acknowledgment of service or a defence. The 14 days are calculated using the ordinary rules on calculating the effective date for service, for which see Chapter 8. Consequently, a defendant cannot be in default until that time has elapsed. For non-specialist Part 7 claims, a defendant cannot be in default if a claim form is served without particulars of claim until the particulars of claim are actually served. In such cases, time starts running for default judgment purposes only from the effective date of service of the particulars of claim.

12.05 A defendant who has taken the precaution of acknowledging service has a total of 28 days from the effective date of service of the particulars of claim in which to serve a defence and prevent judgment being entered in default (CPR, r 15.4).

12.06 For ordinary claims r 12.3 allows a claimant to enter a default judgment in the following circumstances:

(a) if the defendant has not filed an acknowledgment of service or a defence to the claim (or any part of the claim), and 14 days have expired since service of the particulars of claim; or
(b) if the defendant has filed an acknowledgment of service but has not filed a defence, and 28 days have expired since service of the particulars of claim.

12.07 These periods can be extended, either by agreement (for a further period of up to 28 days: r 15.5) or by order of the court. Extensions of time are granted quite readily in complicated cases or where there are genuine reasons for not being able to file a defence within the time limited by the rules. Obviously, where an extension has been granted, default judgment may be entered only once the extended period has expired (r 12.3). Similarly, time does not run during the period of any stay of the proceedings (see 22.47ff and *Roundstone Nurseries Ltd v Stephenson Holdings Ltd* [2009] EWHC 1431 (TCC)).

Commercial and mercantile claims

12.08 In every claim proceeding in the Commercial Court and the mercantile courts, after service of the claim form (whether with or without particulars of claim) the defendant must file an acknowledgment of service (CPR, rr 58.6(1) and 59.5(1)). This means that default judgments can be obtained in these courts:

(a) if the defendant fails to acknowledge service within 14 days of service of the claim form; or

(b) if the defendant fails to file and serve a defence within 14 days of service of the particulars of claim.

In the Commercial Court the procedure for entering default judgment is the same as the normal rules described at 12.13ff. In the mercantile courts, judgment in default of an acknowledgment of service can only be entered on making an application (without notice) to the court (r 59.7). **12.09**

B EXCLUDED CASES

Part 8 claims and petitions

Judgment in default is not available in Part 8 claims (see CPR, r 12.2(b)). The procedure relating to petitions does not include acknowledging service or serving defences, so default judgments are not available in this form of litigation either. **12.10**

Excluded Part 7 claims

Default judgments are not available in a number of Part 7 claims even if the defendant fails to respond to the claim. Excluded cases where the nature of the proceedings is a bar to obtaining a default judgment are set out in CPR, r 12.2, and PD 12, paras 1.2 and 1.3, as follows: **12.11**

(a) claims for the delivery of goods subject to an agreement regulated by the Consumer Credit Act 1974;
(b) claims for provisional damages;
(c) claims governed by certain specialized procedures which do not include a requirement to file a defence or acknowledgment of service, or which provide special rules for obtaining default judgments. Cases falling into this subcategory are:
    (i) admiralty proceedings;
    (ii) arbitration proceedings;
    (iii) possession claims; and
    (iv) contentious probate proceedings.

Claims excluded by reason of steps taken

In certain circumstances, some step taken by the defendant will prevent the claimant entering judgment in default. Cases in this category are set out in CPR, r 12.3(3), which says that a claimant may not obtain a default judgment if: **12.12**

(a) the defendant has applied for summary judgment under Part 24, or to strike out the claim under r 3.4, and that application has not been disposed of;
(b) the defendant has satisfied the whole claim (including any claim for costs) on which the claimant is seeking judgment; or
    (i) the claimant is seeking judgment on a claim for money; and

(ii) the defendant has filed or served on the claimant an admission under r 14.4 or 14.7 (admission of liability to pay all of the money claimed) together with a request for time to pay.

C ENTERING DEFAULT JUDGMENT

Money claims and claims for delivery of goods

12.13 In claims seeking to recover money and/or the delivery of goods (provided the defendant has the alternative of paying the value of the goods), which are by far the most common types of cases, default judgments are available simply by filing a standard-form request. The claimant entering the judgment sends the form to the court office and a member of the court staff will enter the judgment. There is no hearing and no question of trying to persuade the court to enter judgment.

12.14 When proceedings are issued the court will send the claimant a notice of issue. There are three different forms of notice of issue: one for specified money claims, another for unspecified money claims, and the third for non-money claims. The two money claim notices (forms N205A and N205B) include a tear-off section for the request for judgment. In the top part of the form the court staff enter the claim number, the date of issue, and the dates when the claim form was posted to the defendant, the deemed date of service, and the date by which the defendant has to respond. All the claimant has to do is wait until the time for responding has elapsed, then, if the claim is for a specified sum of money, tick a box saying the defendant has failed to respond, enter the defendant's date of birth (if known) and details of the judgment sought. This involves calculating the amount owed together with interest and fixed costs (as set out in the CPR), and deciding whether to ask for the whole sum to be paid immediately or by stated instalments. The request form is then signed, dated, and returned to the court. In claims for unspecified sums, all the claimant has to do, once the time for responding has elapsed, is to sign and date the request form, and return it to the court.

12.15 If the particulars of claim were served by the claimant, judgment in default cannot be obtained unless a certificate of service (see figure 8.6) has been filed: CPR r 6.17(2)(b) and PD 12, para 4.1. There is no need for such a certificate if service is effected by the court (r 6.17(1)).

Non-money claims

12.16 Default judgments in non-money and non-recovery of goods claims (principally these will be cases where some form of equitable relief is sought, such as injunctions) have to be applied for. In other words, where equitable relief is sought and the defendant does not defend the claim, a judgment can be obtained only at a hearing before a master, district judge, or judge who will decide whether to exercise the court's discretion to grant the relief sought.

12.17 Chapter 19 describes how to make applications. The application will be made by issuing an application notice, which must state the defendant's date of birth (if known), and must be supported by written evidence. The evidence should include a certificate of service if the particulars of claim were served by the claimant. There is no need to serve the evidence in support on any defendant who did not acknowledge service (CPR, r 12.11(2)). This means that a defendant who acknowledged service but failed to file a defence has to be served with the evidence in support. Although the evidence in support in many cases does not need to be served on the defendant, the defendant should in all cases (other than service outside the jurisdiction, category (a) below) be given notice of the application itself by being served with the application notice (PD 12, para 5.1).

A defendant may seek to prevent judgment being entered in default by filing or seeking to file an acknowledgment of service or a defence on or just before the return day for the claimant's application. Where this happens the defendant should issue a cross-application for an extension of time. Whether permission will be granted is a matter for the court's discretion, but normally it will be exercised in favour of extending time (*Coll v Tattum* (2001) *The Times*, 3 December 2001). **12.18**

Money and goods claims where permission is required

Within the context of claims seeking money or recovery of goods, there are a number of exceptional cases where default judgments cannot be entered by filing a request, but only by obtaining permission after making an application. These are: **12.19**

(a) Where the claim form was served out of the jurisdiction without permission under the Brussels or Lugano Conventions or Judgments Regulation on a defendant domiciled in a contracting state (these are EU countries plus three others) (see CPR, r 12.10(b)). Service outside the jurisdiction was considered in Chapter 10. Where service is effected outside the jurisdiction under the Service Regulation (see 10.106), judgment in default cannot be given until it is established that service was effected by a method prescribed by the internal law of the receiving State or that the documents were actually delivered to the defendant or to his residence by another method provided by the Service Regulation (Service Regulation, art 19). The claimant's evidence in support of the application for judgment must establish that the claim is one that the English court has power to hear and decide, that no other court has exclusive jurisdiction, and that the claim form has been properly served in accordance with the Convention or Regulation (PD 12, para 4.3). The evidence in this particular case must be on affidavit (rather than the usual witness statement format) (PD 12, para 4.5).

(b) Where the defendant is a child or protected party (CPR, r 12.10(a)(i)). Before applying for judgment the claimant must apply for the appointment of a litigation friend to represent the person under disability. On the application for judgment the evidence must satisfy the court that the claimant is entitled to the judgment sought (PD 12, para 4.2).

(c) Where the claim is for or includes costs other than fixed costs (CPR, r 12.9).

(d) Where the claim is brought by one spouse against the other on a claim in tort (CPR, r 12.10(a)(ii)).

(e) Where the claim seeks delivery-up of goods where the defendant is not to be allowed the alternative of paying their value. Relief in this form, unlike other types of delivery orders which may be asked for in claims relating to goods, is discretionary (see the Torts (Interference with Goods) Act 1977), which is why an application must be made. The evidence in support must identify the goods and say where the goods are believed to be kept and why the claimant says an order for specific delivery should be granted (PD 12, para 4.6). Usually this will have to be because of the rare or irreplaceable nature of the goods concerned.

D FINAL JUDGMENT AND JUDGMENT FOR AN AMOUNT TO BE DECIDED

12.20 There are two main types of judgment obtainable in money claims. The best type is a final judgment, which will require the defendant to pay a set amount of money usually within 14 days. Apart from giving the defendant a limited amount of time to raise the money, this type of judgment allows the claimant to recover the whole sum straight away or to apply to enforce if the defendant does not pay.

12.21 The other type is a judgment for damages to be decided by the court. There are variations on this form of judgment, such as judgments for the value of goods to be decided by the court and judgment for the amount of interest to be decided by the court. This type of judgment is sometimes called an 'interlocutory judgment', and the rules occasionally refer to this type of judgment as a 'relevant order'. This second type of judgment means that liability has been established and will not be considered any further, but all questions relating to the amount of damages or interest payable, or the value of the goods, have yet to be determined.

12.22 Final judgment will be entered in claims for specified sums (CPR, r 12.5), whereas judgment for damages to be decided will be entered in claims for unspecified amounts. There is some doubt as to what is meant by 'specified'. It could mean simply that the claim form has set out a specified sum sought by the claimant. Alternatively, it could mean the same thing as a liquidated demand. Liquidated demands are claims such as for the repayment of a loan or bank overdraft, or for the price of goods or services, or for rent. For each of these the amount claimed is fixed by the underlying agreement between the parties. This is so even though the amount may need to be calculated, such as the interest payable on the overdraft, or the rent payable over a period of time. Liquidated demands are usually contrasted with claims for unliquidated damages, such as for personal injuries or for the unsatisfactory quality of goods sold. Valuing an unliquidated claim requires an exercise of judicial judgment. Consequently, one school of thought takes the view that all damages claims are unspecified, and so default judgments in these cases should be for damages to be decided. However, the other school of thought takes the view that if the claimant spells out in the particulars of claim the amount of damages claimed the claim becomes one for a specified amount, so that a final judgment can be obtained.

E PROCEDURE FOR DECIDING THE AMOUNT OF DAMAGES

12.23 When the court enters a default judgment of the second type for damages or interest to be decided, or for the value of goods to be decided by the court, it will give any directions it considers appropriate. Further, if it thinks it appropriate, it will also allocate the claim to a case management track (CPR, r 12.7). Alternatively, the court may list the matter for a disposal hearing, or will stay the action while the parties try to settle the case using ADR or other means.

The orders being considered here are described as 'relevant orders' by PD 26, para 12. In addition to being one of the possibilities on obtaining a default judgment, they may also be made on entry of judgment on an admission; on the striking-out of a statement of case; on a summary judgment application; on the determination of a preliminary issue or on a split trial as to liability; or even by consent or at trial. **12.24**

Disposal hearings

At a disposal hearing the court will either give directions or decide the amount payable (PD 26, para 12.4(2)). Relevant orders made by entry of default judgment without a hearing are usually dealt with in this way. **12.25**

If the case is listed for a disposal hearing and the claim is worth less than £5,000, the court will usually allocate it to the small claims track (for costs purposes) and decide the amount payable there and then (PD 26, paras 12.3(1), 12.4(3)). If the financial value of the claim is more than £5,000 the court may still determine the amount payable at the disposal hearing, but in these cases the ordinary costs rules will apply. In cases determined at disposal hearings evidence may, unless the court otherwise directs, be adduced under CPR, r 32.6 (see PD 26, para 12.4(4)). This means that reliance may be placed on the matters set out in the particulars of claim (provided it is verified by a statement of truth) or by witness statement. The evidence relied upon must be served on the defendant at least three clear days before the disposal hearing. **12.26**

Allocating relevant order cases to tracks

Allocating a case to the fast track or multi-track after a relevant order has been made should happen only if the amount payable is genuinely disputed on grounds that appear to be substantial (PD 26, para 12.3(2)). Track allocation is considered further in Chapter 14. **12.27**

Hearing to assess damages

Generally, hearings to assess damages will be listed before masters and district judges irrespective of the amount in issue (PD 26, para 12.6), but the court may give directions specifying the level or type of judge who is to deal with the case (PD 26, para 12.2(2)). Other directions made will include a timetable for disclosure of documents, the exchange of witness statements, and for the admission of expert evidence and disclosure of reports from experts. Hearings to assess damages are trials, and so trial bundles and formal evidence are required. On an assessment of damages the defendant can raise any point which goes to quantification of the damage, provided that it is not inconsistent with any issue settled by the judgment (*Lunnun v Singh* [1999] CPLR 587). Where judgment for damages to be assessed was entered after the court rejected a defence that the claimant was guilty of gross misconduct disentitling him to any damages, it was still open for the defence to raise mitigation of damages on the assessment (*Pugh v Cantor Fitzgerald International* [2001] CPLR 271). **12.28**

F SETTING ASIDE DEFAULT JUDGMENTS

12.29 The CPR, rr 13.2 and 13.3, provide grounds on which the court either may or must set aside or vary judgments entered in default. The court may exercise these powers either on an application made by the defendant or of its own motion. Litigation is not a game of 'snap', and it has long been recognized that the court needs to have the power to set aside judgments entered without a full consideration of the merits of the claim.

Setting aside as of right

12.30 In limited circumstances the court *must* set aside a default judgment. This is restricted to certain cases where the default judgment was wrongly entered (CPR, r 13.2). There is a restrictive definition for this, limited to:

(a) situations where the essential conditions about failing to acknowledge service or defend, or the relevant time having elapsed, are not satisfied; or
(b) the claim was satisfied before judgment was entered; or
(c) the defendant had already applied for summary judgment or to strike out the claim; or
(d) the defendant had already filed an admission requesting time to pay.

12.31 Judgment was set aside as of right under para (a) in *Crédit Agricole Indosuez v Unicof Ltd* (2003) LTL 4/2/03. The claimant purported to serve the claim form by leaving it with the defendant's company secretary in Kenya, whereas service in Kenya had to be by leaving the claim form at the company's registered office. As the claim form had not been served, the defendant was entitled to have the judgment set aside. Judgment was also set aside as of right in *Intense Investments Ltd v Development Ventures Ltd* [2005] BLR 478, because it had been entered by the request method (see 12.13–12.15) in circumstances where the application method (see 12.16–12.18) should have been used.

Discretion to set aside

12.32 In other cases, the court will set aside or vary a default judgment only if the defendant 'has a real prospect of successfully defending the claim' or 'it appears . . . there is some other good reason why . . . the defendant should be allowed to defend the claim', taking into account whether the application to set aside has been made promptly (CPR, r 13.3).

Setting aside on the merits

12.33 In *Thorn plc v MacDonald* [1999] CPLR 660, the Court of Appeal approved the following principles:

(a) While the length of any delay in making the application must be taken into account, any pre-action delay is irrelevant. An application may be 'prompt' even if it was made several weeks after the default judgment was entered, if, for example, evidence had to be obtained from overseas (*Shandong Chenming Paper Holding Ltd v Saga Forest Carriers Intl AS* [2008] EWHC 1055 (Comm)).

(b) Any failure by the defendant to provide a good explanation for the delay is a factor to be taken into account, but is not always a reason to refuse to set aside.
(c) The primary considerations are whether there is a defence with a real prospect of success, and that justice should be done. The question whether there is a defence with a real prospect of success is the same as on applications for summary judgment (*ED & F Man Liquid Products Ltd v Patel* [2003] CPLR 384), and is discussed in detail at 21.15–21.45.
(d) Prejudice (or the absence of it) to the claimant also has to be taken into account.

The written evidence in support of the application to set aside will have to address these factors, and in particular the alleged defence on the merits, the reasons for not responding to the claim in time, and the explanation for any delay in making the application to set aside. **12.34**

Some other good reason

Defendant unaware of the proceedings

Once it is proved (such as by a certificate of service) that proceedings have been served by one of the methods prescribed by the CPR, service is deemed to take effect on the date laid down by r 6.14 (see 8.39), and evidence to prove the contrary is not admissible (see 8.44). This is so even if the documents are returned undelivered provided they were sent to the correct address for service. Where a default judgment has been entered after the expiry of 14 days from the deemed date of service in a case where the defendant did not in fact receive the proceedings, setting aside is subject to the court's discretion rather than as of right (*Godwin v Swindon Borough Council* [2002] 1 WLR 997). Such a defendant will either have to show a defence with a real prospect of success, or rely on non-service as 'some other good reason' for setting aside the judgment. According to May LJ this may arise where a defendant would have paid instead of having an embarrassing judgment entered, and it may give grounds for departing from the usual rule of the defendant being ordered to pay the costs thrown away (see 12.38). Requiring a defendant who is deemed to have been served to show a defence with a real prospect of success or some other good reason before setting aside does not infringe the European Convention on Human Rights, art 6(1) (*Akram v Adam* [2005] 1 WLR 2762). It would be wrong to give too much weight to the comment of Mummery LJ in *Raja v Van Hoogstraten (No 9)* [2009] 1 WLR 1143, at [84] that in cases where the defendant is unaware of the proceedings any default judgment should be set aside unless there are exceptional circumstances, as the case was about a different provision in the CPR (r 23.10). **12.35**

Claimant's conduct amounting to a good reason

It can be relevant for the court to consider the conduct of the parties in deciding whether there is some other good reason for setting aside a default judgment (*Hart Investments Ltd v Fidler* [2007] BLR 30). There may be a good reason for setting aside where the conduct in entering the judgment is regarded as unreasonable, such as where the claimant takes advantage of a mutual failing to extend a stay (*Roundstone Nurseries Ltd v Stephenson Holdings Ltd* [2009] EWHC 1431 (TCC)). **12.36**

Discretion where defendant outside jurisdiction

12.37 Where service was effected outside the jurisdiction under the Service Regulation (see annex to PD 6B), the court has power under the Service Regulation, art 19(4), to relieve the defendant from the effect of any judgment entered in default if:

(a) the defendant, without any fault on his part, did not have knowledge of the documents served in sufficient time to defend; and
(b) the defendant discloses a *prima facie* defence to the claim on its merits.

Setting aside on conditions

12.38 If the court sets aside a default judgment, it may do so on terms (CPR, r 3.1(3)). Conditions imposed on setting aside a default judgment are not intended to punish the defendant, but to ensure that justice is achieved between the parties (*Hussain v Birmingham City Council* [2005] EWCA Civ 1570). In most cases the defaulting defendant will be ordered to pay the claimant's costs thrown away. In addition, the court may consider imposing a condition that the defendant must pay a specified sum of money into court to await the final disposal of the claim. The sum paid into court makes it easy for the claimant to recover any sum found due at trial, and also operates as a secured fund if the defendant becomes insolvent (*Re Ford* [1900] 2 QB 211).

12.39 In deciding whether to impose such a condition, the court will consider factors such as whether there was any delay in applying to set aside, doubts about the strength of the defence on the merits, and conduct of the defendant indicating a risk of dissipation of assets (see *Creasey v Breachwood Motors Ltd* [1993] BCLC 480). As to the amount, this is in the court's discretion, which should be exercised applying the overriding objective. However, a condition requiring payment into court of a sum that the defendant will find impossible to pay ought not to be ordered (*M V Yorke Motors v Edwards* [1982] 1 WLR 444, HL), as that would be tantamount to refusing to set aside.

G STAY OF UNDEFENDED CASES

12.40 If none of the defendants to a claim file admissions or defences, the claimant should generally enter judgment in default shortly after the time for filing has elapsed, but in any event within six months of the period for filing the defence. Once the six months have elapsed, the claim is automatically stayed by virtue of CPR, r 15.11.

12.41 Any party may apply to lift the stay. This is done by making an application in accordance with the procedure discussed in Chapter 20, giving the reason for the delay in proceeding with or responding to the claim (PD 15, para 3.4). In considering whether to lift the stay the court will apply the criteria for granting relief from sanctions in r 3.9, which are discussed at 28.24–28.30: see *Audergon v La Baguette Ltd* [2002] CPLR 192.

KEY POINTS SUMMARY

- Judgment in default may be entered once the period for responding to a claim has elapsed. **12.42**
- In money claims, default judgment is usually entered simply by filing a certificate of service and a request for judgment.
- In non-money claims (mostly claims for equitable relief) and certain exceptional cases (such as where the defendant is a child or patient), a formal application must be made for default judgment.
- Final judgment will be entered in money claims for specified amounts.
- In money claims where the amount sought is unspecified, any default judgment will be for damages to be decided by the court.
- A default judgment which is entered irregularly (eg, prematurely) will be set aside as of right.
- A regular default judgment will only be set aside if there is a defence with a real prospect of success or some other good reason for allowing the defendant to defend the claim.
- Conditions as to costs and paying money into court may be imposed if a default judgment is set aside.

13

STATEMENTS OF CASE

13.01 The early stages of a common law action commenced by ordinary claim form are dominated by the exchange of statements of case by the respective parties. Statements of case are formal documents used in litigation to define what each party says about the case. They have a number of functions, including:

(a) Informing the other parties of the case they will have to meet. This helps to ensure neither party is taken by surprise at trial.
(b) Defining the issues that need to be decided. This helps to save costs by limiting the investigations that need to be made and the evidence that needs to be prepared for the trial, and also helps to reduce the length of trials.
(c) Providing the judges dealing with the case (both for case management purposes and at trial) with a concise statement of what the case is about.

13.02 'Statements of case' include all the following documents:

(a) the claim form;
(b) particulars of claim where this document is not included in a claim form;
(c) defence;
(d) counterclaim;
(e) additional claims under Part 20 (which will be considered further in Chapter 18);

(f) reply to defence;
(g) Scott schedules (*Easygroup IP Licensing Ltd v Easyjet Airline Co Ltd* [2009] EWHC 1386 (Ch)); and
(h) any further information given in relation to the above whether voluntarily or by court order (see Chapter 16).

The equivalent documents in judicial review proceedings are also statements of case (*R (Corner House Research) v Director of the Serious Fraud Office* [2008] EWHC 246 (Admin)). Before the modernization of insolvency practice made by the Insolvency (Amendment) Rules 2010 (SI 2010/686), winding-up petitions (see Chapter 19) were not regarded as statements of case (*Investment Invoice Financing Ltd v Limehouse Board Mills Ltd* [2006] 1 WLR 985). Now that winding-up petitions have to be verified by a statement of truth (IR 1986, r 4.12) they too should be regarded as statements of case. **13.03**

Statements of case in Part 7 claims are served in sequence, with the claimant serving particulars of claim first, followed by a defence from the defendant, then possibly a reply from the claimant. They are often the first documents read by a judge, and obviously it is wise to give a good impression by ensuring they are well drafted. Also, a party may be prejudiced on the substantive issues in the claim if they are not adequately set out in the statements of case, particularly if the court refuses permission to amend (a topic considered in Chapter 15). **13.04**

A FORM OF STATEMENTS OF CASE

Physical form

A statement of case, like all other court documents, should be on A4 paper (unless the form of the document makes this impractical), of durable quality, and with a margin of at least 35 mm (PD 5A, para 2.2). It must be fully legible, and should normally be typed. It should be securely bound together in a manner that will not hamper filing (if this is not possible, each page should include the claim number). A statement of case exceeding 25 pages must be accompanied by a short summary (PD 16, para 1.4). **13.05**

Heading

A statement of case starts with a heading. This will include the name of the court in which the claim is proceeding, such as by the words 'IN THE COUNTY COURT' or 'IN THE HIGH COURT OF JUSTICE'. In High Court cases this is followed by the Division (QBD, ChD, or FamD). Claims in a specialist court then identify that court. Traditionally this information is set out in the top left-hand corner. Traditionally, the claim reference number will appear in the top right-hand corner. This is the number allocated to the claim by the court when it is issued. County court claim numbers consist of a year reference, followed by a two-letter identification code for the issuing court, then the individual claim number. **13.06**

There then follows the title of the proceedings. The word 'BETWEEN' appears on the left-hand side underneath the name of the court. This is followed by the names of the parties down the centre of the page, with the claimants' names first, and the word 'Claimants' on the right-hand **13.07** side of the page, followed by the names of the defendants, and the word 'Defendants' on the right-hand side of the page. The defendants are separated from the claimants by the word 'and'. Multiple claimants or defendants are usually numbered '(1)', '(2)', etc. to the left of their names. Rules on how to name different types of party can be found in 17.04ff.

13.08 After setting out the names of the parties the heading will state the form of statement of case, such as 'PARTICULARS OF CLAIM', 'DEFENCE', or 'REPLY', usually in the centre of the page and between horizontal straight lines.

Contents

13.09 A claim form need only contain a concise statement of the nature of the claim (CPR, r 16.2(1)(a)). This imposes an obligation to inform the defendant in the simplest terms of the case the defendant has to meet (*Adams v Thomson Holidays Ltd* [2009] EWHC 2559 (QB)). Other statements of case should set out sufficient details of the facts relied upon for the other parties to know the case that is being advanced and for the court to be able to see what the issues are. Pages should be numbered consecutively, and the text should be divided into numbered paragraphs. All numbers and dates must be expressed as figures (PD 5A, para 2.2). The allegations should be stated in a summary form, and as briefly as the nature of the case permits. This means that all the elements necessary for establishing a cause of action or defence must be set out in the statement of case, and if even a single essential allegation is omitted, the statement of case will be amenable to being struck out (see Chapter 22, and *Bruce v Odhams Press Ltd* [1936] 1 KB 697). General allegations have to be supported by particulars. Commonly occurring examples are particulars of negligence, of breach of statutory duty, of breach of contract, and of loss and damage. An allegation of 'systematic overcharging' had to be supported by particulars of the supposed system (*Clyde and Co LLP v New Look Interiors of Marlow Ltd* [2009] EWHC 173 (QB)). Further, sufficient background facts should be included so that a judge reading the statement of case for the first time will be able to understand the essential factual basis of the claim or defence.

13.10 A party may refer to any point of law on which the claim or defence is based (PD 16, para 13.3(1)). A statement of case may (not must) give the name of any witness intended to be called (para 13.3(2)). The claim form or particulars of claim should state whether the parties have complied with any relevant pre-action protocol (PD Pre-action conduct, para 9.7).

13.11 Generally, a party will comply with its obligations when drafting a statement of case if it sets out the facts of its claim or defence, and avoids setting out the evidence it intends to adduce to prove its case. Material documents should in general simply be referred to, but with sufficient detail to enable them to be identified. Quoting from documents is necessary in libel and misrepresentation claims to identify the words complained of. Quoting can also be useful in other cases (see *Morris v Bank of America National Trust* [2000] 1 All ER 954), but can be counter to the overriding objective, particularly where the quotations are lengthy or numerous.

13.12 The ultimate purpose of statements of case is to inform the other party of the case against him (*Conticorp SA v Central Bank of Ecuador* [2007] UKPC 40). The pleading in this case was regarded as being sufficient even though the issues were convoluted, because they were not in doubt, partly because of further information (see Chapter 16) which had been provided. An issue may also be sufficiently pleaded without express allegations provided the allegations which are pleaded raise the issue by clear implication (*Sinclair Investment Holdings SA v Versailles Trade Finance Ltd* [2006] 1 BCLC 60). On the other hand, a claim making broad, unfocussed, and unparticularized allegations was struck out in *English, Welsh and Scottish Railway Ltd v Goodman* (2007) LTL 9/5/2007. A 221-page particulars of claim was struck out in *Dunn v Glass Systems (UK) Ltd* (2007) LTL 23/7/2007 because it was excessively long, contained details which were irrelevant to the cause of action, and contained a large number of incomprehensible terms.

There is no need to anticipate the other side's statement of case, so a claimant generally should not answer possible lines of defence in the particulars of claim (this is the function of the reply). One well-settled exception to this relates to personal injuries claims issued more than three years after the relevant accident, where it is usual in the particulars of claim to give the grounds for alleging that the claimant can take the benefit of the Limitation Act 1980, s 14 or 33 (see 7.28 and 7.54ff). Facts presumed by law to be true need not be set out in the statement of case of the party relying on the presumption. **13.13**

There is no objection to a claimant advancing alternative claims, provided the alternative sets of facts are clearly stated. In such cases the claimant can sign the statement of truth, which has the effect of stating the claimant's honest belief that on either one set of facts or the other his claim is made out. What is not permitted is a unified claim with contradictory facts, because in such a case the claimant cannot honestly sign a statement of truth (*Clarke v Marlborough Fine Art (London) Ltd* [2002] 1 WLR 1731). The dividing line between these two concepts has to be drawn applying the overriding objective. An alternative claim that is wholly speculative will not be allowed. On the other hand, a claimant will be allowed to plead different versions of how an incident happened where he has no personal knowledge of the material events, and has to rely on independent witnesses who give different versions of the facts. Another example is where the claimant, perhaps through having honestly convinced himself of the truth of his version of events as set out in the particulars of claim, gives evidence, but a different version of events emerges from the body of evidence at the trial. Permission is often given in such cases to plead the version that has emerged at trial. See *Binks v Securicor Omega Express Ltd* [2003] 1 WLR 2557. It is improper to set out facts in a statement of case which are contrary to the known and uncontested documentary evidence (*Re Unisoft Group Ltd (No 3)* [1994] 1 BCLC 609 at 618). **13.14**

Supporting documentation

The parties are permitted to attach or serve with their statements of case copies of any documents which are considered necessary for the claim or defence (PD 16, para 13.3(3)). Documents served with a statement of claim may include experts' reports (and in personal injuries claims medical reports about the alleged injuries should be served with the particulars of claim: para 4.3). In contract claims based on written agreements copies of the agreement or documents constituting the agreement must be attached to or served with the particulars of claim (para 7.3). **13.15**

Final endorsements

13.16 A statement of case must bear the signature of the legal representative who drafted it. The engrossed version of a draft settled by counsel usually has counsel's name in capitals at the end of the draft, and is signed by the solicitor who has conduct of the case. A solicitor or employee of a firm of solicitors should sign in the firm's name (PD 5A, para 2.1). Litigants in person sign their own statements of case. Particulars of claim and defences should give an address for service, which should be within the jurisdiction, in order to comply with CPR, r 6.5(2).

Statement of truth

13.17 Every statement of case should be verified by a statement of truth (CPR, r 22.1(1)(a)). This states that the facts set out in the statement of case are believed to be true. The purpose of the statement of truth is to eliminate claims in which a party had no honest belief and to discourage claims unsupported by evidence which are put forward in the hope that something may turn up on disclosure or at trial (*Clarke v Marlborough Fine Art (London) Ltd* [2002] 1 WLR 1731). When a statement of case is amended, the court may dispense with reverification (r 22.1(2)). This power may be exercised where a party relies, in the alternative, on facts asserted by the other side which are inconsistent with the facts he relies on for his primary case (*Binks v Securicor Omega Express Ltd* [2003] 1 WLR 2557). The statement of truth must generally be signed by the party on whose behalf the statement of case has been drafted, or by that party's legal representative (r 22.1(6)). Any failure to include a statement of truth may result in an application for an unless order, with striking out as the sanction (PD 22, para 4.2).

13.18 Any person who makes, or causes to be made, a false statement in a document verified by a statement of truth without an honest belief in its truth may be punished for contempt of court (CPR, r 32.14(1)). However, proceedings for contempt under this rule may be brought only by the Attorney-General or with the permission of the court (r 32.14(2)). A party intending to make such an application should give advance warning to the maker of the statement, but such warning should not be given until after that person has given evidence (*KJM Superbikes Ltd v Hinton* [2009] 1 WLR 2406). The question on an application for permission is whether the matter is sufficiently serious that committal proceedings will be in the public interest (*KJM Superbikes Ltd v Hinton*). At the committal hearing the falsity and lack of honest belief have to be proved beyond reasonable doubt (*Kirk v Walton* [2009] EWHC 703 (QB)).

B PARTICULARS OF CLAIM

Contents

13.19 The particulars of claim will set out the claimant's causes of action and the relief or remedy claimed. As mentioned at 13.09, the particulars of claim must set out the essential elements of the causes of action asserted. The particulars must also set out the facts giving rise to the dispute, and must cover the facts which are the essential elements, as a matter of law, of the cause of action on which the case is based. For certain categories of claim (such as personal injuries claims, fatal accidents, hire-purchase claims, claims raising human rights issues, and claims for the recovery of land) PD 16 sets out details that need to be included in the particulars of claim. An example of particulars of claim in a personal injuries claim can be seen in figure 13.1. An example of particulars of claim incorporated into a claim form in a breach of contract claim can be seen in figure 8.1. In contractual claims the particulars of claim should state whether the agreement was written or oral, its date, and who acted for each side in forming the contract. Written contracts must be attached to or served with the particulars of claim, and in oral contracts the particulars must include the contractual words used, who said them, to whom, when and where (PD 16, paras 7.3, 7.4).

Figure 13.1 Particulars of Claim

IN THE NORTHAMPTON COUNTY COURT Claim No 10NN98264

BETWEEN:—

PHILLIPPA MAY MYERS Claimant

and

NIGEL JAMES STANIFORTH Defendant

PARTICULARS OF CLAIM

1 On 17 July 2008 the Defendant was driving a car registration number CY06 733 JLF west along the A427 near Weldon, Northamptonshire, and the Claimant was driving her car registration number PD03 KWM east along the A427 travelling towards the Defendant's car.

2 As the Defendant approached the Claimant's car he was in the process of overtaking a line of vehicles. At this location the A427 is a single lane carriageway, and the Defendant was therefore driving in the oncoming lane.

3 The Defendant failed to return to his own lane, and collided with the Claimant's car ('the collision').

4 The collision was caused by the negligence of the Defendant.

PARTICULARS OF NEGLIGENCE

The Defendant was negligent in:

(a) failing to keep any or any proper look-out;
(b) failing to see the Claimant's car, or to notice or take account of the presence or approach of the Claimant's car;
(c) driving on the wrong side of the road when it was unsafe to do so;
(d) overtaking when it was unsafe to do so;
(e) driving too fast in the circumstances;
(f) failing to give precedence to the Claimant's vehicle; and/or
(g) failing to stop, slow down, or steer so as to avoid the collision.

5 As a result of the matters set out above the Claimant has suffered personal injuries, pain, suffering, loss, and damage.

PARTICULARS OF INJURY

The Claimant, who was born on 14 July 1972 and was aged 36 years at the date of the collision, suffered:

(a) fractured right fibula and tibia;
(b) whiplash injuries to her cervical spine;

Figure 13.1 *continued*

(c) multiple cuts, abrasions, and bruises;
(d) nervous reaction involving flashbacks, disturbance of sleep, and panic attacks.

Further particulars of the Claimant's injuries are given in the medical report of Mr S Long served with these particulars of claim.

PARTICULARS OF LOSS AND DAMAGE

The Claimant's losses are set out in the Schedule of Past and Future Loss and Expense served with these particulars of claim.

6 Further, the Claimant is entitled to interest pursuant to the County Courts Act 1984, section 69:

(a) upon special damages at the full relevant special account rates from the date of accrual of each item of non-recurring special damage and at half the relevant special account rates for the period of each item of recurring special damage; and
(b) upon general damages at the rate of 2 per cent per annum from the date of service of the claim form,

until the date of judgment or earlier payment.

7 The parties have complied with the requirements of the Pre-action Protocol for Personal Injury Claims.

AND the Claimant seeks:

(1) Damages;
(2) Interest pursuant to the County Courts Act 1984, section 69.

Statement of Truth

(I believe) (The Claimant believes) that the facts stated in these particulars of claim are true.

I am duly authorized by the Claimant to sign this statement.

13.20 In addition to setting out the cause of action relied upon, particulars of claim must include details of the remedies being claimed. Thus particulars of claim must contain details of any claim for aggravated or exemplary damages, any claim for provisional damages, and any other remedy sought. Particulars of claim must also give full details of any interest claimed, including the rate, period covered, and the authority for claiming it. Interest claims are most often based on the CCA 1984, s 69, the SCA 1981, s 35A, or the Late Payment of Commercial Debts (Interest) Act 1998. See BCP, Chapter 62.

13.21 The form for the statement of truth required for particulars of claim is:

> I believe [The Claimant believes] that the facts stated in these particulars of claim are true.

Personal injuries claims

13.22 Particulars of claim in personal injuries claims must, in addition to stating the basis of the claim, state the claimant's date of birth and give brief details of the injuries sustained (PD 16, para 4.1).

Further, the claimant must attach a schedule of details of any past and future expenses and losses that are claimed (para 4.2), which must also be verified by a statement of truth. A simple example is given in figure 13.2. A medical report should be attached to or served with the particulars of claim dealing with the injuries sustained (para 4.3). **13.23**

Recovery of land

In claims for the recovery of land the particulars of claim must identify the land sought to be recovered, state whether the claim relates to residential premises, give details of any tenancy agreement, information about any mortgage, and various other details as set out in PD 55A, paras 2.1 to 2.7. There are prescribed forms for particulars of claim in several types of claim for the recovery of land, such as N119, which is the prescribed form of particulars of claim for possession claims for rented property. This document is three pages long, and divided into ten paragraphs with boxes to be completed with information about the tenancy and the tenant. **13.24**

Human rights points

Where a party seeks to raise a human rights point, the particulars of claim (and any other type of statement of claim or appeal notice filed on behalf of that party) must set out precise details of the Convention right relied upon. It must also give details of the alleged infringement and it must state the relief sought (PD 16, para 15.1). **13.25**

Service

Particulars of claim must be served within 14 days of service of the claim form. Additionally, service of the particulars of claim must be within the period of validity of the claim form (CPR, r 7.4(2)). If they are served separately from the claim form, the claimant must file a copy together with a certificate of service within seven days of service (r 7.4(3)). **13.26**

Where a claimant is late in serving the particulars of claim, the court has a general discretion under r 3.1(2)(a) to extend time. This is so even where the delay extends beyond the period of validity of the claim form, and such applications are not bound by the requirements in r 7.6(3), discussed at 9.13 (*Totty v Snowden* [2002] 1 WLR 1384). **13.27**

C DEFENCE

General

The defence is intended to answer the allegations made in the particulars of claim. Like all other statements of case, a defence must contain a statement of truth. The defence must be filed at court (CPR, r 15.2) and served on every other party (r 15.6) within 14 days of service of the particulars of claim, or 28 days if the defendant has acknowledged service. Several defendants with the same interest in a claim may serve identical defences, in which case they **13.28** must act by the same solicitors and instruct the same counsel at trial. Defendants who serve different defences may instruct the same or different lawyers.

Figure 13.2 Schedule of special damages

IN THE NORTHAMPTON COUNTY COURT — Claim No 10NN98264

BETWEEN

PHILLIPPA MAY MYERS — Claimant

and

NIGEL JAMES STANIFORTH — Defendant

SCHEDULE OF PAST AND FUTURE LOSS AND EXPENSE AT 25 MAY 2010

ITEM	AMOUNT
1 Before the accident on 17 July 2008 the Claimant was employed as a data analyst with a salary of £1,213 per month net. The Claimant has been unable to return to work, and her contract of employment was terminated with effect from 1 September 2008. She has been unable to find employment and has been unemployed for 1 year, 7 months, 21 days.	£23,956.75
2 Continuing loss of earnings at the rate of £1,213 net per month.	
3 The Claimant's salary in her former employment as a data analyst was subject to upwards annual review on 1 January each year. She accordingly has a continuing loss in the net amount of each annual review, full particulars of which will be given on disclosure of documents.	
4 Damaged clothing comprising:	
Dress	£45.99
Cardigan	£29.99
Shoes	£27.49
Watch	£54.00
Sub-total	£157.47
5 Travel to hospital outpatients department	£35.00
6 Prescriptions: 4 at £7.10	£28.40

Statement of Truth

I believe that the facts stated in this schedule of past and future loss and expense are true.

Signed:

Dated:

Answering the particulars of claim

13.29 By CPR, r 16.5(1), a defence must state:

(a) which allegations in the particulars of claim are denied. Denials are used for any facts which, if they had occurred, would have been within the defendant's knowledge. This covers cases where the defendant has an alternative version of the events, and also cases where the defendant deduces that the particulars of claim must be wrong because if they were correct the defendant would know about the matter;

(b) which allegations the defendant is unable to admit or deny, but which he requires the claimant to prove. It is inappropriate to make a non-admission on a matter on which the defendant must have personal knowledge. Such a matter must either be admitted or denied with reasons (*Ciccone v Associated Newspapers Ltd* [2009] EWHC 1108 (Ch)); and

(c) which allegations are admitted. Facts which are admitted are no longer in issue, and evidence on them will not be received at trial. It is an abuse not to admit facts demonstrably known to be true to the defendant (*Newland v Boardwell* [1983] 1 WLR 1453).

Any specific allegation that is not answered will be taken to be put in issue if the general nature of the defence on the issue appears from what is said in the defence. Otherwise the issue is deemed to be admitted (CPR, r 16.5(3) and (5)). Where a paragraph in the particulars of claim sets up a contention followed by a number of sub-paragraphs, each containing allegations of fact, a general response to the main allegation without responding to the individual sub-paragraphs may be inadequate, depending on the circumstances and how important the allegations are (*Ciccone v Associated Newspapers Ltd*, where further particulars were required). The amount of any money claim is deemed to be in dispute unless expressly admitted. If the claimant's statement of value is disputed, the defendant must say why and, if able to, give a counter-estimate (r 16.5(6)). **13.30**

Any denial of an allegation in the particulars of claim must be backed up by reasons in the defence. A defendant who intends to put forward a different version of events from the one advanced by the claimant has to state the alternative version in the defence (r 16.5(2)). A denial must go to the root of the allegation in the particulars of claim, and must not be evasive. An equivocal denial may be taken by the court to be an admission. For example, stating that 'the terms of the arrangement were never definitely agreed upon as alleged' was held to be evasive and to be an admission that an arrangement was made in *Thorp v Holdsworth* (1876) 3 ChD 637. A denial that follows the wording of the particulars of claim too closely may result in a pregnant negative—a denial pregnant with an unstated affirmative case. For example, in *Pinson v Lloyds and National Provincial Foreign Bank Ltd* [1941] 2 KB 72 the claimant stated that the defendants had 'effected purchases and sales without having been authorised to do so'. The defendants denied that 'they effected purchases or sales without having been authorised by the [claimant] to do so'. This was embarrassing, because it could have been a denial that the defendants entered into the transactions at all, or it could have been a denial of lack of authority pregnant with an affirmative case that they had the claimant's authority. **13.31**

Any affirmative case and any defences must be expressly set out. Each defence should be set out in a separate paragraph. The defence must specifically set out any matter, such as performance, release, expiry of limitation, fraud, or illegality, which is a defence to the claim, or which might take the claimant by surprise, or which raises issues of fact not included in the particulars of claim. Failing to set out such matters may debar the defendant from raising them at trial (*Shell Chemicals UK Ltd v Vinamul Ltd* (1991) *The Times*, 7 March 1991, CA). Similarly, any matters in mitigation, limitation, or reduction of damages must be expressly stated. Where the defendant is an individual, his date of **13.32** birth must be stated in the defence (PD 16, para 10.7). A precedent defence is illustrated at figure 13.3.

Figure 13.3 Defence

IN THE HIGH COURT OF JUSTICE Claim No. HQ10 87105
QUEEN'S BENCH DIVISION
BETWEEN:—

STEPHENSON HYPERLINKS PLC Claimant

—and—

LOMAX FISHING EQUIPMENT LIMITED Defendant

DEFENCE

1 Paragraph 1 of the Particulars of Claim is admitted.

2 Save that it is denied that there was a contract concluded between the parties, paragraph 2 of the Particulars of Claim is admitted. The conversation on 3 September 2008 and the letters dated 5 September 2008 and 17 September 2008 were only negotiations between the parties, and there was no final agreement either on these occasions or at all.

3 By reason of the matters set out in paragraph 2 above, paragraphs 3 and 7 of the Particulars of Claim are denied.

4 Save that the Claimant is required to prove that it developed a bespoke or any computer system for the Defendant, paragraph 4 of the Particulars of Claim is denied for the reasons set out in paragraph 2 above.

5 Save that it is admitted that the Claimant sent the invoices listed in paragraph 6 of the Particulars of Claim to the Defendant, paragraphs 5 and 6 of the Particulars of Claim are denied for the reasons set out in paragraph 2 above.

6 Save that it is admitted the Defendant sent a letter to the Claimant dated 18 February 2009 and that the Defendant received a letter from the Claimant's solicitors dated 6 April 2009, paragraph 8 of the Particulars of Claim is denied. The letter of 18 February 2009 was part of continuing negotiations under which the Defendant told the Claimant that no work on the proposed computer system should be done until 2010. The letter dated 6 April 2009 did not operate as an acceptance of a repudiatory breach because there was no contract and there was no breach. Although there was a telephone conversation in February 2009 (the precise date of which the Claimant is required to prove), in the conversation Mr Lomax told Mrs Stephenson that the Claimant's invoices had been raised wrongly because there was no agreement.

7 By reason of the matters set out above, paragraph 9 of the Particulars of Claim is denied.

8 Paragraph 11 of the Particulars of Claim is admitted.

D. COUNSEL

Statement of Truth

[I believe] [The Defendant believes] that the facts stated in the defence are true.

Signed

Dated

Fox and Headley, of 52 Higham Road, Kettering, Northants, NN16 2CH, Solicitors for the Defendant.

D COUNTERCLAIM

A defendant with a cause of action against the claimant can raise it either by bringing separate proceedings or by counterclaiming in the present proceedings. The subject matter of a counterclaim need not be of the same nature as the original claim, or even analogous to it. The only limitation is that the parties to the counterclaim have to sue and be sued in the same capacities as they appear in the main claim. A counterclaim is in substance a separate claim. Safeguards against misuse of the right to counterclaim are provided by the court's case management powers in CPR, rr 1.4 and 3.4, either to strike out the counterclaim, or to order it to be tried separately. On an application to strike out a counterclaim, the court's discretion ought to be exercised, according to Lightman J in *Ernst and Young v Butte Mining plc (No 2)* [1997] 1 WLR 1485, with a view to limiting the use of the procedure of counterclaiming to cases where it is procedurally convenient. A lack of mutuality between the claim and counterclaim is a weighty factor in favour of striking out the counterclaim. **13.33**

Assuming there is a defence, the statement of case is known as a defence and counterclaim. A counterclaim must comply with the rules relating to particulars of claim. It can be made using one of the forms included in the response pack. It must be verified by a statement of truth. A counterclaim may be made without permission if filed with the defence (CPR, r 20.4(2)(a)). An issue fee based on the full value of the counterclaim is payable, and a copy of the additional claim form must be served on every other party when the defence is served (r 20.8(1)(a)). **13.34**

E REPLY AND DEFENCE TO COUNTERCLAIM

A reply may be used to narrow the issues by making admissions, or to assert an affirmative case in answer to the defence. However, it cannot make any allegations inconsistent with the particulars of claim (which should be raised by amending the particulars of claim). Where the defendant has made a counterclaim the claimant must serve a defence to counterclaim, which must comply with the rules relating to defences. If combined with a reply the statement of case is called a reply and defence to counterclaim. **13.35**

A reply must be filed within the time limited for filing allocation questionnaires, which is stated in the form and happens shortly after filing the defence. Like other statements of case the reply must be verified by a statement of truth. **13.36**

F SUBSEQUENT STATEMENTS OF CASE

Statements of case after the reply are exceptionally rare. The statement of case after a reply is a rejoinder, followed by a surrejoinder and a rebutter. **13.37**

G DISPENSING WITH STATEMENTS OF CASE

13.38 The court has a power to order a claim to continue without any further statements of case (CPR, r 16.8). This may be appropriate in cases involving points of law or construction which do not raise issues of fact.

Figure 13.4 Diagram illustrating early stages in litigation

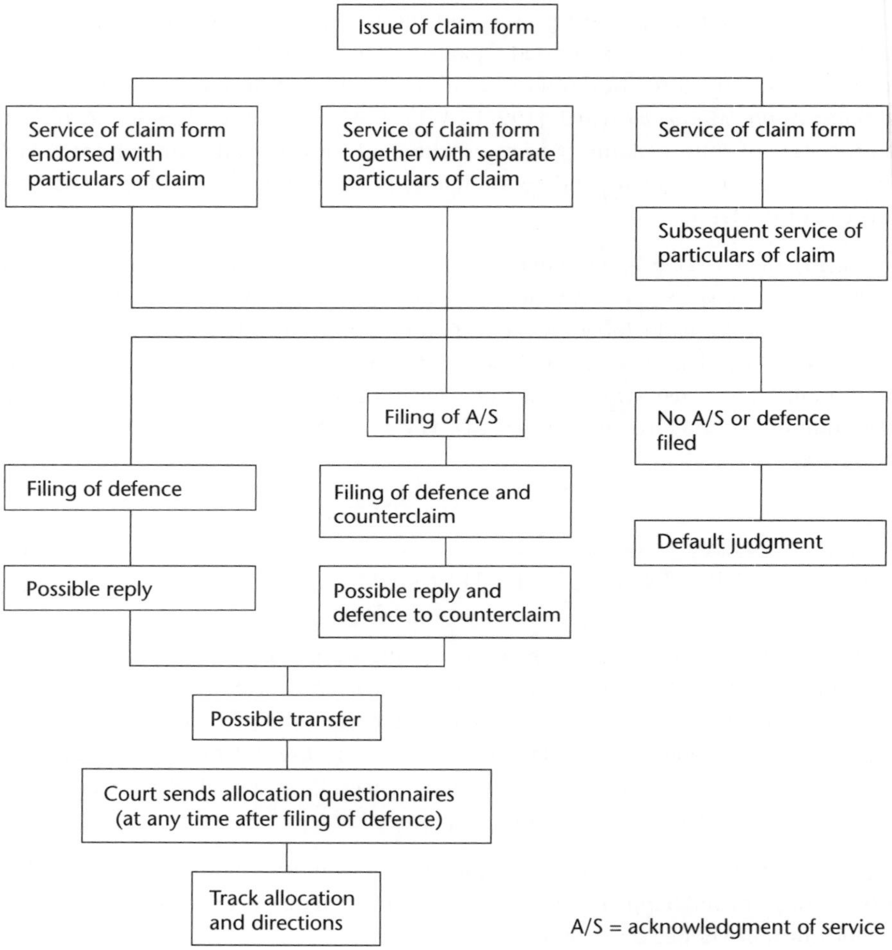

H INTERRELATION WITH CASE MANAGEMENT

13.39 Filing of the defence triggers the start of standard case management intervention by the court in the form of sending out allocation questionnaires. This is the first step in the track allocation process, and leads also to the court making case management directions.

These topics will be considered further in Chapter 14. The overall scheme is shown in figure 13.4.

I USE OF STATEMENTS OF CASE AT TRIAL

As part of the purpose of statements of case is to define the issues in the claim, a party is quite justified in omitting to prove matters which could be relevant to the case for the other side, but are not in the party's own statements of case. Indeed, strictly, evidence on matters that have not been included in statements of case should not be adduced, and the judge must not give judgment relying on issues that are not in the statements of case (see *Lipkin Gorman v Karpnale Ltd* [1989] 1 WLR 1340). Despite this there have been times when the courts have appeared to take a fairly relaxed view about defects in the parties' statements of case, but authorities such as *Hockaday v South West Durham Health Authority* [1994] PIQR P275 and *Bagnall v Hartlepool Borough Council* [1995] PIQR P1 have insisted on the importance of properly stating the case and defence to be presented at trial. An example is *Larner v British Steel plc* [1993] 4 All ER 102, where an injured claimant alleged that his employer was liable for breach of statutory duty under the Factories Act 1961, s 29 (now repealed), for failing to ensure his workplace was made and kept safe. An employer was liable under this section only in so far as it was reasonably practicable to make the premises safe. Lack of reasonable practicability was a matter of defence, and the employer was held entitled to advance this defence only if it had been expressly pleaded. **13.40**

If it appears that the statements of case do not adequately set out the case for either or both parties, it is usually possible to obtain permission to amend even during the trial. However, as will be seen in Chapter 15, certain types of amendment cannot be made after the relevant limitation period has expired, and, even if the court has a discretion to allow an amendment, there are circumstances in which late amendments will not be allowed. **13.41**

14

TRACK ALLOCATION AND CASE MANAGEMENT

14.01 Judicial case management of civil litigation is one of the central planks of the CPR. In exercising their powers to manage cases, the courts will be seeking to secure the overriding objective of the CPR of ensuring that cases are dealt with justly. Rule 1.1(2) provides that dealing with cases justly includes ensuring that they are dealt with expeditiously and fairly, allotting to them an appropriate share of the court's resources, and ensuring they are dealt with proportionately, bearing in mind factors such as the importance and complexities of the issues and the value of the claim. This will include identifying the issues in the case, summarily disposing of some issues and deciding the order in which other issues are to be resolved, fixing timetables for the procedural steps in preparing cases for trial, and limiting evidence, particularly documentary and expert evidence.

14.02 To assist with this process defended claims are assigned to one of three 'tracks'. The smallest and simplest cases are assigned to the 'small claims track'. Cases expected to last one day or less and with a value in the range of £5,000 to £25,000 are usually allocated to the 'fast track' with standard directions and tight timetables of up to 30 weeks for completion of the interim stages before trial. Larger and more important cases are assigned to the 'multi-track'. Cases on the multi-track have widely differing values and complexity, and the courts are given a great deal of flexibility in the way they can manage these cases commensurate with the particular features of each case. Multi-track cases are dealt with mainly at civil trial centres, and are usually transferred to such locations at an early stage.

To ensure that case management is proportionate, there is active judicial intervention only to the extent cases require it. Basic management, with a fixed timetable and standard procedure, is used wherever possible, on the multi-track as well as on the fast track. Directions may be given without hearings and by consent. The CPR give the courts powers to hold four types of procedural hearing (allocation hearings, case management conferences, hearings at the pre-trial checklist stage—sometimes known as 'listing hearings'—and pre-trial reviews). The majority of defended cases will proceed between the filing of a defence and trial with directions in a more or less standard form, but tailored to the needs of the particular case, without the need for the parties to attend court for a directions hearing, with case management hearings restricted to the more difficult and important cases. **14.03**

A PROCEDURAL JUDGES

Case management decisions may, by CPR, r 2.4, be taken by any judicial officer, whether a district judge, master, or judge, subject to any specific contrary provision in any enactment, rule, or practice direction. However, PD 29, para 3.10, says (in relation to multi-track cases) that masters will in general perform case management functions in the Royal Courts of Justice, district judges in district registry matters, and either district judges or circuit judges in county court cases. PD 2B enables masters and district judges to deal with all types of application, but with express exceptions set out in the practice direction. Exceptions include most interim injunction applications and applications affecting the liberty of the subject, which must be dealt with by a judge. **14.04**

Cases in the Chancery and Queen's Bench Divisions are assigned to individual masters (PD 2B, para 6.1), although from time to time hearings may be dealt with by other masters or deputies as the circumstances may require, and cases may be transferred from one master to another. Important cases in the Commercial Court are allocated to a management team of two designated judges (*Commercial Court Guide*, para D 4.1). **14.05**

B TRANSFER TO APPROPRIATE COURT

Subject to the rules relating to commencing proceedings in the High Court, a claimant has a free choice of which court to use when commencing proceedings. Defended money claims are automatically transferred to the defendant's home court (CPR, r 26.2, and see 11.19). If automatic transfer does not apply, the first discretionary case management intervention may be to transfer the case to the most appropriate court. **14.06**

14.07 If a case has been started in the wrong court, the court may order it to be transferred to the correct court, may allow it to continue where it is, or may strike it out (CPR, r 30.2(2), and see 2.35).

14.08 Cases started in the correct court which are not covered by the automatic transfer rule may be transferred to the High Court or county court, between county courts or district registries, and between Divisions, and to and from specialist courts, at the court's discretion. A case may be transferred to a county court even though its value exceeds the relevant county court limit (*National Westminster Bank plc v King* [2008] Ch 385). Criteria for deciding whether to transfer are set out in the Jurisdiction Order of 1991 and in r 30.3(2). These criteria include the value of the claim, the simplicity or complexity of the facts and issues, the importance of the case, whether it would be more convenient to try the case in another court, and the availability of specialist judges.

14.09 Cases commenced in courts that are not civil trial centres (such courts are described as 'feeder courts') are considered by a procedural judge when defences are filed. If it appears that the case is suitable for allocation to the multi-track, the district judge will normally make an order allocating the case to the multi-track, will give case management directions, and transfer the claim to a civil trial centre (PD 26, para 10.2(5)). Exceptionally, a case may be allocated to the multi-track and be retained in a feeder court. This will happen where it is envisaged that there may need to be more than one case management conference and the parties or their legal advisers are located inconveniently far from the designated civil trial centre (PD 26, para 10.2(10)) or where pressure of work in the trial centre has led to the designated civil judge approving retention of the case by the feeder court. If it is not possible to decide whether a case should be allocated to the fast or multi-track, the procedural judge will either hold an allocation hearing at the feeder court, or transfer the case to a civil trial centre for the allocation decision to be made there (paras 10.2(6) and (8)).

C TRACK ALLOCATION

14.10 Every defended claim has to be allocated to one of the three tracks (small claims track, fast track, multi-track) by an order by a procedural judge. To assist the court the parties are usually required to file allocation questionnaires in form N150 shortly after defences are filed, to provide the court with additional information about the progress that has been made to date in seeking a resolution with the other parties and in preparing the evidence for trial, and also with information relevant to the likely length of the trial and about costs.

14.11 At the same time, the parties are required, in claims outside the financial scope of the small claims and fast tracks, to file and serve estimates of their costs following Precedent H in the schedule to PD Costs (PD Costs, para 6.4(1)).

Time when track allocation is decided

14.12 The usual position is that the procedural judge will decide which track to allocate a case to when every defendant has filed an allocation questionnaire, or when the period for filing allocation questionnaires has expired, whichever is the sooner (CPR, r 26.5(1)). Although the rule mentions only questionnaires filed by defendants, it is to be expected that the court will wait for the claimant's questionnaire if the specified period has not expired. There are some additional provisions dealing with track allocation in special cases, as follows:

(a) In cases where there is a stay for settlement (see 14.40), allocation is dealt with at the end of the period of the stay (r 26.5(2)).
(b) In cases which are automatically transferred, allocation decisions are taken after the transfer takes place and are made by a procedural judge of the destination court.
(c) In cases which could be allocated either to the fast track or to the multi-track, allocation decisions are usually taken in the court where the proceedings are commenced, but occasionally they will be transferred to the appropriate civil trial centre for allocation and directions.
(d) Where a claimant enters a default judgment for an amount of money to be decided by the court or for the value of goods or the amount of interest to be decided by the court, the case will not be 'defended', in that a defence will not have been filed. These cases therefore are not governed by the standard track allocation provisions. Instead, when judgment is entered the court will give any necessary directions and will, if appropriate, allocate the case to one of the three tracks (r 12.7(2)(b)). These cases are considered further at 12.23ff.
(e) When judgment is entered for damages to be decided on an admission by the defendant in a claim for money that has not been specified, then, as in (d), the court will give any necessary directions and, if appropriate, allocate the case to one of the three tracks (r 14.8). These cases are also considered at 12.23ff.
(f) Part 8 claims are treated as allocated to the multi-track (r 8.9(c)).
(g) Stage 3 RTA protocol cases (see Chapter 6) are treated as not allocated to any track (PD 8B, para 17.1).
(h) Most types of specialist proceedings are treated as allocated to the multi-track. This includes claims allocated to the Technology and Construction Court (r 60.6), proceedings in the Commercial List in the Queen's Bench Division (r 58.13(1)), claims retained in the Chancery Division (Chancery Guide, para 2.5), claims in the Patents Court (r 63.7(1)), admiralty proceedings (PD 61, para 2), mercantile claims (r 59.11), arbitration claims (r 62.7(1)), directors disqualification proceedings (PD Directors Disqualification Proceedings, para 2.1), and insolvency proceedings (Insolvency Rules 1986 (SI 1986/1925), r 7.51A(3)).

Allocation questionnaires

When a defendant files a defence (or, in the case of multiple defendants, when they have all filed defences or the time limited for doing so has expired), the court will serve allocation questionnaires in form N150 (as shown in figure 14.1) on each party, or will make a direction dispensing with the need for questionnaires (CPR, r 26.3(1) and (2)). Questionnaires may be dispensed with if there has already been an application, such as for summary judgment, which has been treated as an allocation hearing (PD 26, para 2.4). The obligation of serving allocation questionnaires rests with the court where proceedings were commenced, even in claims that are automatically transferred to the defendant's home court. **14.13**

Figure 14.1 Form N150 Allocation questionnaire

Allocation questionnaire

To be completed by, or on behalf of,

Stephenson Hyperlinks Plc

who is [1st][2nd][3rd][ ][Claimant][Defendant]
[Part 20 claimant] in this claim

Name of court	High Court of Justice Queen's Bench Division
Claim No.	10Q 87105
Last date for filing with court office	08.11.2010

Please read the notes on page six before completing the questionnaire.

You should note the date by which it must be returned and the name of the court it should be returned to since this may be different from the court where the proceedings were issued.

If you have settled this claim (or if you settle it on a future date) and do not need to have it heard or tried, you must let the court know immediately.

Have you sent a copy of this completed form to the other party(ies)? ☑ Yes ☐ No

A Settlement

Under the Civil Procedure Rules parties should make every effort to settle their case before the hearing. This could be by discussion or negotiation (such as a roundtable meeting or settlement conference) or by a more formal process such as mediation. The court will want to know what steps have been taken. Settling the case early can save costs, including court hearing fees.

For legal representatives only

I confirm that I have explained to my client the need to try to settle; the options available; and the possibility of costs sanctions if they refuse to try to settle. ☑

For all

Your answers to these questions may be considered by the court when it deals with the questions of costs: see Civil Procedure Rules Part 44.3 (4).

1. **Given that the rules require you to try to settle the claim before the hearing, do you want to attempt to settle at this stage?** ☑ Yes ☐ No
2. **If Yes, do you want a one month stay?** ☑ Yes ☐ No
3. **Would you like the court to arrange a mediation appointment?** ☐ Yes ☑ No
   (A fee will be payable to the mediation provider appointed by the National Mediation Helpline.)
4. **If you answered 'No' to question 1, please state below the reasons why you consider it inappropriate to try to settle the claim at this stage.**

Reasons:

N150 Allocation questionnaire (04.08) 1

Figure 14.1 *continued*

Experts

Do you wish to use expert evidence at the trial or final hearing? ☑ Yes ☐ No

Have you already copied any experts' report(s) to the other party(ies)? ☑ None yet obtained ☐ Yes ☐ No

Do you consider the case suitable for a single joint expert in any field? ☑ Yes ☐ No

Please list any single joint experts you propose to use and any other experts you wish to rely on. Identify single joint experts with the initials 'SJ' after their name(s).

Expert's name	Field of expertise (eg. orthopaedic surgeon, surveyor, engineer)
Mr Jonathan Cousins	Computer software design

Do you want your expert(s) to give evidence orally at the trial or final hearing? ☑ Yes ☐ No

If Yes, give the reasons why you think oral evidence is necessary:

The claim raises difficult technical issues as to the nature of the equipment, software and services required under the contract, and the trial judge is likely to find it essential to have an independent technical expert available in court to assist in understanding these issues.

Track

Which track do you consider is most suitable for your claim? Tick one box

☐ small claims track
☐ fast track
☑ multi-track

If you have indicated a track which would not be the normal track for the claim, please give brief reasons for your choice

3

Figure 14.1 *continued*

E Trial or final hearing

How long do you estimate the trial or final hearing will take? 2 days | 0 hours | 0 minutes

Are there any days when you, an expert or an essential witness will not be able to attend court for the trial or final hearing? ☑ Yes ☐ No

If Yes, please give details

Name	Dates not available
Mr Jonathan Cousins	See attached list

F Proposed directions *(Parties should agree directions wherever possible)*

Have you attached a list of the directions you think appropriate for the management of the claim? ☑ Yes ☐ No

If Yes, have they been agreed with the other party(ies)? ☐ Yes ☑ No

G Costs

Do not complete this section if you have suggested your case is suitable for the small claims track or you have suggested one of the other tracks and you do not have a solicitor acting for you.

What is your estimate of your costs incurred to date? £9,000.00

What do you estimate your overall costs are likely to be? £30,000.00

In substantial cases these questions should be answered in compliance with CPR Part 43

H Fee

Have you attached the fee for filing this allocation questionnaire? ☑ Yes ☐ No

An allocation fee is payable if your claim or counterclaim exceeds £1,500.

Additional fees will be payable at further stages of the court process.

4

Figure 14.1 *continued*

I Other information

Have you attached documents to this questionnaire? ☑ Yes ☐ No

Have you sent these documents to the other party(ies)? ☐ Yes ☑ No

If Yes, when did they receive them?

Do you intend to make any applications in the immediate future? ☐ Yes ☑ No

If Yes, what for?

In the space below, set out any other information you consider will help the judge to manage the claim.

We are seeking to agree with the Defendant the appointment of Mr Jonathan Cousins as a jointly instructed computer systems design expert.

Although documents were exchanged pursuant to Practice Direction Pre-action Conduct before proceedings were issued, and some contractual documents were served with the Particulars of Claim, we consider that full standard disclosure should be ordered.

Signed

[Counsel] [Solicitor] [for the][1st][2nd][3rd][ ]
[Claimant] [Defendant] [Part 20 claimant]

Date

Please enter your name, reference number and full postal address including (if appropriate) details of telephone, DX, fax or e-mail

Smallwood & Co 4 Market Place Corby Northamptonshire		If applicable
	Telephone no.	01562 384500
	Fax no.	01562 384572
	DX no.	87456 Corby
Postcode N N 1 7 6 A L	Your ref.	GS/89734

E-mail

5

14.14 The allocation questionnaire form will state the date by which it must be filed, which should be at least 14 days after the date it is deemed to have been served on the party in question. This date cannot be varied by agreement between the parties (CPR, r 26.3(6A)). A fee is payable by the claimant when the questionnaire is filed. No fee is payable in Part 8 claims or claims having a value below £1,500.

14.15 The parties are encouraged to consult one another and cooperate in completing their allocation questionnaires, and also in deciding on any additional information, which may include suggested directions, they may send to the court with their questionnaires (PD 26, para 2.3). However, they should not allow consultation to delay filing of their questionnaires.

14.16 Allocation questionnaires are not, in general, used in specialist cases automatically allocated to the multi-track. Each specialist court has its own procedure dealing with case management at the allocation stage. In the Technology and Construction Court, the court will send the parties a case management questionnaire and a case management directions form (see PD 60, para 8.2 and apps A and B). In the Commercial Court, after service of the defence, the legal representatives for each party must liaise for the purpose of preparing a short case memorandum and an agreed list of important issues (with a separate section dealing with matters which are common ground between all or some of the parties), and the claimant's solicitors must prepare a case management bundle (*Commercial Court Guide*, paras D5.1, D6.1, and D7.1). The claimant must apply for a case management conference within 14 days after service of the last defence to ensure this takes place as soon as practicable (r 58.13(3); PD 58, para 10.2). Seven days before the case management conference each party must file a completed case management information sheet, in the form set out in the *Commercial Court Guide* and it is this form that takes the place of the allocation questionnaire (para D8.5, and see figure 14.2). On the other hand, allocation questionnaires are used in Chancery Division cases despite the fact these cases are automatically allocated to the multi-track.

Failure to file an allocation questionnaire

14.17 If a party fails to file an allocation questionnaire, the court may give any direction it considers appropriate (CPR, r 26.5(5)). The court's response may well depend on whether the other parties have filed their questionnaires. If they have, the party in default can hardly complain if allocation and directions decisions are made based entirely on the information given by the other parties. If the court decides it does not have enough information, it will list the matter for an allocation hearing (PD 26, para 2.5(2)(b)), and will almost certainly order the costs of the hearing to be paid by the party in default on the indemnity basis, usually with a summary assessment of those costs and an order for them to be paid forthwith or within a stated period (PD 26, para 6.6(2)). If all the parties are in default, the file will be referred to the judge, who will usually order that, unless allocation questionnaires are filed within three days from service of the order, the claim and any counterclaim will be struck out (PD 26, para 2.5(1)).

Figure 14.2 Commercial Court case management information sheet

Party lodging information sheet:

Name of solicitors:

Name(s) of advocates for trial:

Figure 14.2 *continued*

[Note: This Sheet should normally be completed with the involvement of the advocate(s) instructed for trial. If the claimant is a litigant in person this fact should be noted at the foot of the sheet and proposals made as to which party is to have responsibility for the preparation and upkeep of the case management bundle.]

(1) By what date can you give standard disclosure?

(2) In relation to standard disclosure, do you contend in relation to any category or class of document under rule 31.6(b) that to search for that category or class would be unreasonable? If so, what is the category or class and on what grounds do you so contend?

(3) Is specific disclosure required on any issue? If so, please specify.

(4) By what dates can you (a) give specific disclosure or (b) comply with a special disclosure order?

(5) May the time periods for inspection at rule 31.15 require adjustment, and if so by how much?

(6) Are amendments to or is information about any statement of case required? If yes, please give brief details of what is required.

(7) Can you make any additional admissions? If yes, please give brief details of the additional admissions.

(8) Are any of the issues in the case suitable for trial as preliminary issues?

(9) (a) On the evidence of how many witnesses of fact do you intend to rely at trial (subject to the directions of the Court)? Please give their names, or explain why this is not being done.
- (b) By what date can you serve signed witness statements?
- (c) How many of these witnesses of fact do you intend to call to give oral evidence at trial (subject to the directions of the Court)? Please give their names, or explain why this is not being done.
- (d) Will interpreters be required for any witness?
- (e) Do you wish any witness to give oral evidence by video link? Please give his or her name, or explain why this is not being done. Please state the country and city from which the witness will be asked to give evidence by video link.

(10) (a) On what issues may expert evidence be required?
- (b) Is this a case in which the use of a single joint expert might be suitable (see rule 35.7)?
- (c) On the evidence of how many expert witnesses do you intend to rely at trial (subject to the directions of the Court)? Please give their names, or explain why this is not being done. Please identify each expert's field of expertise.
- (d) By what date can you serve signed expert reports?
- (e) When will the experts be available for a meeting or meetings of experts?
- (f) How many of these expert witnesses do you intend to call to give oral evidence at trial (subject to the directions of the Court)? Please give their names, or explain why this is not being done.
- (g) Will interpreters be required for any expert witness?
- (h) Do you wish any expert witness to give oral evidence by video link? Please give his or her name, or explain why this is not being done. Please state the country and city from which the witness will be asked to give evidence by video link.

Figure 14.2 *continued*

(11) What are the advocates' present provisional estimates of the minimum and maximum lengths of the trial?

(12) What is the earliest date by which you believe you can be ready for trial?

(13) Is this a case in which a pre-trial review is likely to be useful?

(14) Is there any way in which the Court can assist the parties to resolve their dispute or particular issues in it without the need for a trial or a full trial?

(15) (a) Might some form of Alternative Dispute Resolution procedure assist to resolve or narrow the dispute or particular issues in it?
(b) Has the question at (a) been considered between the client and legal representatives (including the advocate(s) retained)?
(c) Has the question at (a) been explored with the other parties in the case?
(d) Do you request that the case is adjourned while the parties try to settle the case by Alternative Dispute Resolution or other means?
(e) Would an ADR order in the form of Appendix 7 to the *Commercial Court Guide* be appropriate?
(f) Are any other special directions needed to allow for Alternative Dispute Resolution?

(16) What other applications will you wish to make at the Case Management Conference?

(17) Does provision need to be made in the pre-trial timetable for any application or procedural step not otherwise dealt with above? If yes, please specify the application or procedural step.

(18) Are there, or are there likely in due course to be, any related proceedings (e.g. a Part 20 claim)? Please give brief details.

[Signature of solicitors]

Note: This information sheet must be lodged with the Clerk to the Commercial Court at least 7 days before the Case Management Conference (with a copy to all other parties): see section D8.5 of the *Commercial Court Guide*.

Non-payment of the allocation fee

14.18 Rule 3.7 of the CPR provides that claims will be struck out automatically if allocation or listing fees are not paid after due warning, which the court gives by sending the claimant a form N173. PD 3B says that if a claim is struck out, the court will send the defendant a notice which will explain the effect of r 25.11, which provides that any interim injunction will cease to have any effect after 14 days unless the claimant applies to reinstate the claim. This notice will prompt most defendants to apply for their costs against the defaulting claimant. Once the claim has been struck out the court retains a power to reinstate it (r 3.7(7)), and on such an application the court will apply the criteria set out in r 3.9 relating to applications for relief from sanctions (see 28.25ff). However, any order for reinstatement will be made conditional on the fee being paid within two days of the order if the claimant is present at the hearing, otherwise within seven days of service of the order.

Allocation hearing

14.19 The court may hold an allocation hearing if it thinks it is necessary (CPR, r 26.5(4)). Alternatively, the court may treat any other interim hearing as an allocation hearing, the most likely candidates being applications for summary judgment and interim injunctions. At such a hearing the procedural judge will consider which track will be most suitable for the case, and give suitable case management directions. Consequently, the person attending must be familiar with the case, be able to provide the court with the information it is likely to require, and have sufficient authority to deal with any issues that are likely to arise (PD 26, para 6.5).

D ALLOCATION RULES

The primary rules for track allocation are based on the financial value of the claim. This is the monetary value of the claim disregarding any amount not in dispute, any claim for interest or costs, and also disregarding any allegation of contributory negligence (CPR, r 26.8(2)). It is for the court to assess the value of the claim, though it will take into account the way in which the claim is formulated in the particulars of claim and any information given in the allocation questionnaire. Any sum for which the defendant does not admit liability is in dispute, but the court will not regard the following as in dispute (PD 26, para 7.4): **14.20**

(a) sums for which summary judgment on a part of a claim has been entered;
(b) any distinct items in the claim for which the defendant has admitted liability; and
(c) any distinct items in the claim which have been agreed between the parties.

Generally claims are allocated in accordance with their financial value, but a claim may be allocated to a track which is not the one normally appropriate to its value if the procedural judge decides that it can be dealt with more justly on that other track, taking into account a number of factors set out in CPR, r 26.8 (see 14.30). However, a claim will not be allocated to a lower track than its financial value would indicate was appropriate, unless all the parties consent to the lower track allocation (r 26.7(3)). **14.21**

Small claims track

The small claims track is intended to provide a proportionate procedure for the most straightforward types of cases, such as consumer disputes, small accident claims, disputes about the ownership of goods, and certain landlord and tenant cases. This is the normal track for defended claims with a value not exceeding £5,000 (CPR, r 26.6(3)). **14.22**

Although most claims under £5,000 will end up in the small claims track, the following types of claim will not normally be allocated there even if they have a value under £5,000: **14.23**

(a) personal injuries cases where the value of the claim for pain, suffering, and loss of amenity exceeds £1,000 (r 26.6(1)(a) and (2));
(b) claims by tenants of residential premises seeking orders that their landlords should carry out repairs or other works to the premises where the value of the claim exceeds £1,000 (r 26.6(1)(b));
(c) claims by residential tenants seeking damages against their landlords for harassment or unlawful eviction (r 26.7(4)); and
(d) claims involving a disputed allegation of dishonesty (PD 26, para 8.1(1)(d)).

14.24 Even if the claim is worth less than £5,000 there may be other reasons why it should not be allocated to the small claims track. One relates to expert evidence, which is not allowed in small claims track cases, either by calling an expert at the hearing or simply relying on an expert's report, unless the court gives permission (CPR, r 27.5).

14.25 If the claim is worth more than £5,000, the parties may consent to it being allocated to the small claims track (rr 26.7(3) and 27.14(5)). However, the court retains control, and may refuse to allocate the case in accordance with the parties' wishes if it feels the case is not suitable for the small claims track (PD 26, para 8.1(2)(b)). For example, it is unlikely to agree to a case being allocated to the small claims track if the hearing is likely to take more than a day (PD 26, para 8.1(2)(c)). If the court agrees with the parties and allocates the case to the small claims track, the case is treated for the purposes of costs as a small claims track case, unless the parties agree that the fast track costs rules are to apply (CPR, r 27.14(5)).

Fast track

14.26 The fast track is the normal track for cases broadly falling into the £5,000 to £25,000 bracket, and which can be disposed of by a trial which will not exceed a day. There are therefore two factors for deciding whether the fast track is the normal track for defended cases that are not allocated to the small claims track. The first factor, value (CPR, r 26.6(1) to (4)), is to the effect that the following cases will normally be allocated to the fast track:

(a) personal injuries cases with a financial value between £5,000 and £25,000;
(b) personal injuries cases with an overall value under £5,000, but where the damages for pain, suffering, and loss of amenity are likely to exceed £1,000;
(c) claims by residential tenants for orders requiring their landlords to carry out repairs or other work to the premises where the value of the claim is between £1,000 and £25,000;
(d) claims by residential tenants for damages against their landlords for harassment or unlawful eviction where the value of the claim does not exceed £25,000; and
(e) other categories of cases where the value of the claim is between £5,000 and £25,000.

14.27 The second factor, disposal at trial (r 26.6(5)), is to the effect that cases falling within the normal limits for allocation to the fast track must also be likely to be disposed of by a trial lasting no more than a day, and with oral expert evidence limited to experts in no more than two expert fields and to one expert per field of expertise. The possibility that the trial might last longer than a day (which in this context means five hours) is not necessarily a conclusive reason for allocating a case to the multi-track (PD 26, para 9.1(3)(c)), though in practice such cases are almost always so allocated.

Multi-track

14.28 The multi-track is the normal track for claims not falling within the rules in 14.20, 14.23, and 14.26 for allocation to either the small claims or fast track (CPR, r 26.6(6)). Typically these will be cases involving claims exceeding £25,000, and cases worth less than that sum where the trial is likely to exceed a day. Part 8 claims and specialist proceedings are usually treated as allocated to the multi-track (see 14.12).

Claims with no financial value

Claims with no financial value will be allocated to the track which the procedural judge considers to be most suitable to enable it to be dealt with justly, taking into account the factors discussed at 14.30 (CPR, r 26.7(2)). In these cases the importance of careful completion of the allocation questionnaire cannot be over-emphasized. **14.29**

Discretionary factors

In addition to the financial value of the claim (if it has one), when deciding which track to allocate it to the court is required to have regard to the following factors (CPR, r 26.8): **14.30**

(a) the nature of the remedy sought;
(b) the likely complexity of the facts, law, or evidence. Low-value claims in emerging areas may be suitable for the multi-track (*Kearsley v Klarfeld* [2006] 2 All ER 303);
(c) the number of parties or likely parties;
(d) the value of any counterclaim or other additional claim and the complexity of any matters relating to those claims (the court will not aggregate the sums claimed in the claim, counterclaim, and so on, but will generally simply look at the value of the largest of the cross-claims: PD 26, para 7.7);
(e) the amount of oral evidence which may be required;
(f) the importance of the claim to persons who are not parties to the proceedings;
(g) the views expressed by the parties, which will be regarded as important, though not binding on the court (PD 26, para 7.5); and
(h) the circumstances of the parties.

Applying these factors, the following types of cases will usually be allocated to the multi-track even if the amount at stake is within the normal financial value for allocation to the fast track: **14.31**

(a) cases involving issues of public importance;
(b) test cases;
(c) medical negligence cases; and
(d) cases where there is a right to trial by jury, including deceit cases.

E TRIAL IN THE ROYAL COURTS OF JUSTICE

In principle only the most important cases should be managed and tried in the Royal Courts of Justice as opposed to another civil trial centre. Thus, in general, cases with an estimated value of less than £50,000 will be transferred out of the Royal Courts of Justice to a county court (PD 29, para 2.2). **14.32**

F NOTICE OF ALLOCATION

14.33 After the court has decided on the track to which a case is allocated, it will send a notice of allocation to the parties, together with copies of all relevant allocation questionnaires and further information provided by the other parties (CPR, r 26.9). Several forms of notice of allocation have been devised for different circumstances. There are four different forms for cases allocated to the small claims track (N157 to N160), one for the fast track (N154), and one for the multi-track (N155). Each has a space for allocation directions and for the judge's reasons for the allocation decision.

G ALLOCATION DIRECTIONS

14.34 The type of directions the court will make at the allocation stage depends on which track the case is allocated to, and the circumstances of the case. Typically the court will make standard directions in small claims track cases (see Chapter 25). In fast track cases there are more highly developed standard directions. In both fast track and multi-track cases the court will consider making directions covering disclosure of documents, exchange of witness statements, disclosure of experts' reports and narrowing the expert evidence issues, and listing the claim for trial. In multi-track cases the court will also consider whether to convene a case management conference or a pre-trial review. These matters are considered in more detail in Chapters 26 and 27.

14.35 When making directions the court will be astute to apply the overriding objective. It will seek to ensure that the case is prepared properly so that the claim can be determined justly, but it will also seek to avoid unnecessary expense. Where appropriate it will use its power under CPR, r 32.1, to control the evidence that is prepared. This rule gives the court a wide-ranging power to give directions about the issues on which it requires evidence, the nature of the evidence which it requires to decide those issues, and the way in which the evidence is to be placed before the court. The power under the rule may be used to exclude evidence that would otherwise be admissible (r 32.1(2); *Grobbelaar v Sun Newspapers Ltd* (1999) *The Times*, 12 August 1999).

H CHANGING TRACKS

14.36 After a claim has been allocated to a track the court may make a subsequent order reallocating it to a different track (CPR, r 26.10). Where a claim was initially allocated to the small claims track, and is later reallocated to another track, the small claims costs restrictions cease to apply from the date of reallocation (r 27.15).

14.37 A party who is dissatisfied with an allocation decision may challenge the decision either by appealing up to the next higher court or by making an application back to the judge who made the initial decision (PD 26, para 11.1(1)). Applications should be used where the decision was made without any hearing of which the party was given due notice or if there has been a material change of circumstances. If the party was present, represented, or given due notice of the hearing where the decision was made, the only appropriate route is by way of appeal (PD 26, paras 11.1 and 11.2).

If an additional claim under Part 20 is issued, it may be necessary to redetermine the most **14.38** suitable track for the proceedings. Mere issue of an additional claim will not have this effect, but where a defence to an additional claim has been filed the proceedings will be reconsidered by the procedural judge to determine whether the claim should remain on its existing track (particularly in cases on the small claims and fast tracks) and whether there needs to be any adjustment to the timetable. At the same time the procedural judge will consider whether the additional claim should be dealt with separately from the main claim.

If the value of a claim is substantially increased on an amendment to the statement of **14.39** case the claim will usually be reallocated. However, permission to amend may be refused if reallocating will involve aborting a trial where a fast track claim is being tried by a district judge, and the amendment will bring the claim into the multi-track (*Maguire v Molin* [2003] 1 WLR 644).

I ADR AND STAYS TO ALLOW FOR SETTLEMENT

One of the court's case management functions is to help the parties to settle the whole **14.40** or part of the case (CPR, r 1.4(2)(f)), and another is to encourage the parties to use alternative dispute resolution (ADR) procedures if appropriate and to facilitate the use of such procedures (r 1.4(2)(e)). Lawyers on both sides are obliged to consider alternatives to litigation, such as mediation, and to resort to proceedings only where this is really unavoidable (*Cowl v Plymouth City Council* (2001) *The Times*, 8 January 2002). The pre-action protocols (see Chapter 5) require all potential litigants to at least consider possible ADR methods of achieving a settlement before commencing proceedings. It may be that ADR has not been attempted before a case reaches the track allocation stage of litigation. Where there is a chance that ADR or further negotiation may result in a settlement, the CPR give the court the power to order a stay of proceedings for the possible settlement of the case.

The allocation questionnaire allows a party to include a request for the proceedings to be **14.41** stayed while the parties try to settle the case. If all the parties make such a request, or if the court on its own initiative considers that such a stay would be appropriate, a direction will be made staying the proceedings for one month, or such specified period as the court considers appropriate (r 26.4(2)). The court has power to extend the stay for such specified period as it thinks appropriate (r 26.4(3)), which it will generally exercise on receipt of a letter from either party confirming that the extension is sought with the agreement of all the parties and giving a reasonable explanation of the steps being taken and the identity of the mediator or expert assisting with the process (PD 26, para 3.1(1)). Extensions will not usually exceed four weeks at a time unless there are clear reasons to justify a longer time. During the period of such a stay the claimant is under a duty to inform the court if a settlement is reached (CPR, r 26.4(4)). If, by the end of the defined period of the stay, the claimant has not told the court that the case has been settled, the court will give such directions for the management of the case as it considers appropriate, including allocating it to an appropriate track (rr 26.4(5) and 26.5(2)). The periods of stays under these rules are carefully restricted so as to prevent the procedure being used to secure protracted 'authorized' delays after proceedings are commenced, under the guise of attempting to settle.

J SUBSEQUENT CASE MANAGEMENT

14.42 Chapters 25 to 27 deal in more detail with the further progress of cases on each of the three case management tracks following allocation. Figure 14.3 shows the routes which cases may take from either a defence being filed or a 'relevant order' being made up to the decision to allocate the case to a case management track. Figure 14.4 shows in broad terms what happens to cases on the three case management tracks from the time they are allocated to a track until trial.

Figure 14.3 Routes to making track allocation decision

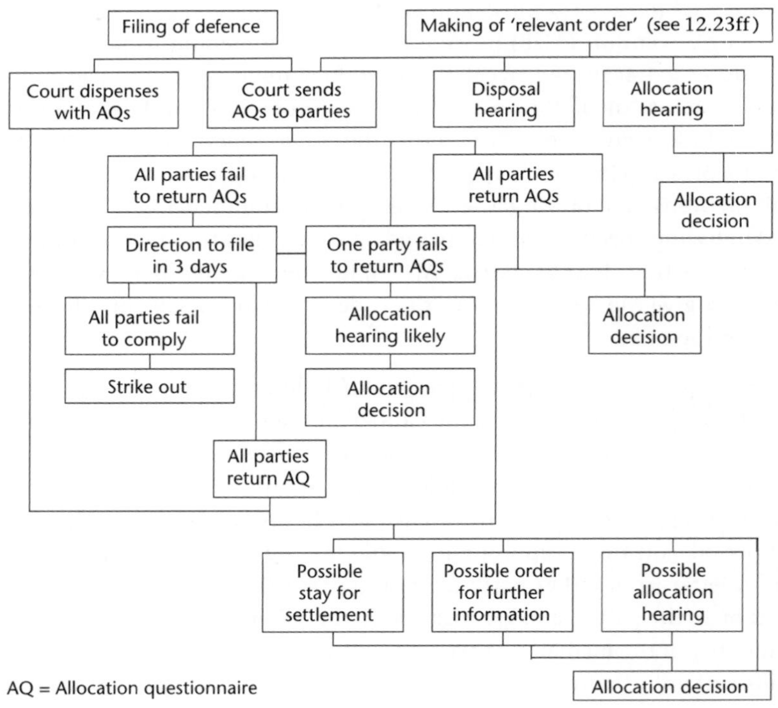

Figure 14.4 The case management tracks

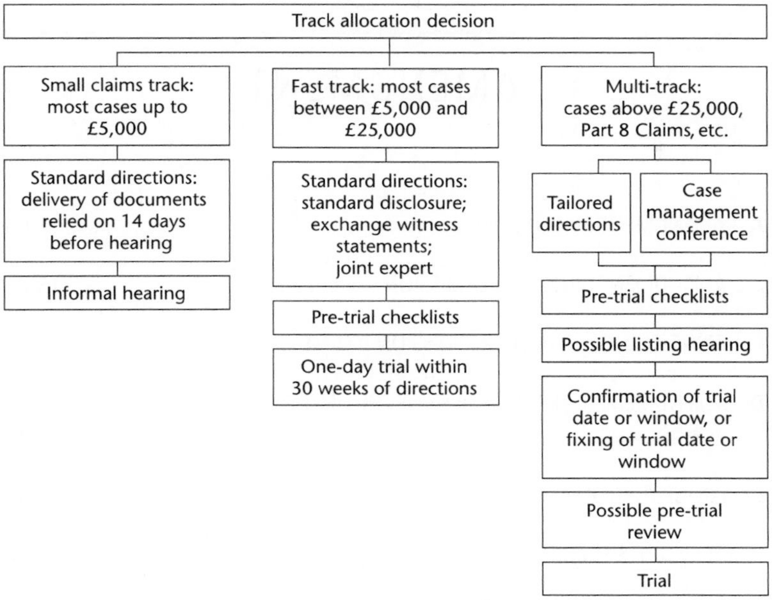

KEY POINTS SUMMARY

- Claims not exceeding £5,000 are usually allocated to the small claims track. **14.43**
- Claims between £5,000 and £25,000 are usually allocated to the fast track.
- Claims over £25,000 and specialist court cases are usually allocated to the multi-track.
- Strictly, the allocation procedure applies in defended cases. Claims where there is default judgment for damages to be assessed may be, but often are not, allocated to a track.
- In general litigation, allocation takes place through the allocation questionnaire procedure.
- In Commercial Court claims a case management information sheet is used instead of the allocation questionnaire.
- At the track allocation stage, the court will give directions laying down a timetable of steps to be taken to prepare the case for trial and for the exchange of evidence.
- Directions may be given without a hearing.
- Particularly in multi-track cases, directions may be given at a case management conference.

15

AMENDMENT

15.01 Changes in the parties' knowledge of a case as it progresses and straightforward drafting errors make it necessary on occasion to make amendments to their statements of case. The underlying principle is that all amendments should be made which are necessary to ensure that the real question in controversy between the parties is determined, provided such amendments can be made without causing injustice to any other party.

15.02 Amendments are allowed either:

(a) with the consent of the other parties (see 15.04); or
(b) in the absence of consent and without the need for permission from the court, provided the amendment is made before the statement of case is served (see 15.05–15.07); or
(c) with the permission of the court. Usually permission is granted, but on terms as to the payment of the costs occasioned by the amendment (see 15.08–15.25). However, there may be problems in making an application to amend in the later stages of proceedings (see 15.14–15.18) or after the expiry of the limitation period (see 15.26–15.45).

15.03 Not every minor development needs to be reflected in an amendment to the statements of case. So, eg, in personal injuries cases it is not necessary to amend each time the claimant's medical condition changes or updating medical reports are obtained (*Owen v Grimsby and Cleethorpes Transport* [1992] PIQR Q27, CA).

A AMENDMENT BY CONSENT

15.04 Any statement of case can be amended at any stage of the proceedings with the written consent of all the parties (CPR, r 17.1(2)(a)).

B AMENDMENT WITHOUT PERMISSION

Amendments that can be made without permission

By CPR, r 17.1(1), a party is allowed to amend a statement of case at any time before it has been served on any other party. As we have seen at the beginning of Chapter 13, the term 'statements of case' is defined as the claim form, particulars of claim, the defence, reply, additional claims under Part 20, and any further information given in relation to them (r 2.3(1)). Once it has been served, a statement of case can be amended only with the consent of the other parties or the permission of the court. The right to amend without permission is therefore largely restricted to amendments to the claim form and particulars of claim in the period between issue and service, which could be as long as four months. Other statements of case could be amended without permission in the period between filing and service, but in most cases this will be a very short period of time. **15.05**

Amendments made before service can be as wide-ranging as may be desired, including adding, removing, or substituting parties (CPR, r 19.4(1)), and even deleting and replacing the whole of the original text, and still will not require the court's permission (r 17.1(3)). However, amendments to the particulars of claim of this nature before service of the particulars of claim may require consent or permission if the claim form has already been served, because (for example) amendments to the parties in the particulars of claim will involve consequential amendments to the claim form and, if the claim form has been served, consent or permission will be required for the amendment to the claim form. **15.06**

Objecting to amendments made without permission

A party served with a statement of case amended without permission can object to the amendment by issuing an application notice seeking an order disallowing the amendment pursuant to CPR, r 17.2. Such an application should be made within 14 days of service of the amended statement of case (r 17.2(2)). The general approach is to disallow amendments made without permission if permission would not have been granted had an application needed to be made (for which, see 15.08–15.25). **15.07**

C PRINCIPLES GOVERNING PERMISSION TO AMEND

The courts have power under CPR, r 17.1(2)(b), to allow the amendment of a statement of case. The rule simply says that amendments may be made with the permission of the court, without saying how the discretion will be exercised. A court asked to grant permission to amend will therefore base its decision on the overriding objective. Generally, disposing of a case justly will mean that amendments should be allowed to enable the real matters in controversy between the parties to be determined. The usual costs rule is that the party granted permission to amend must pay the other parties their 'costs of and caused by' the amendment (see 15.19). **15.08**

15.09 There is a public interest in allowing a party to deploy its real case, provided it is relevant and has a real prospect of success (a concept discussed at 21.16–21.45): *Cook v News Group Newspapers Ltd* (2002) LTL 21/5/02.

15.10 In *Clarapede and Co v Commercial Union Association* (1883) 32 WR 262, CA, Brett MR went so far as to say:

> However negligent or careless may have been the first omission, and however late the proposed amendment, the amendment should be allowed if it can be made without injustice to the other side. There is no injustice if the other side can be compensated in costs.

15.11 The principles in this and some of the following cases were approved in the post-CPR case of *Charlesworth v Relay Roads Ltd* [2000] 1 WLR 230, where Neuberger J described them as representing a fundamental assessment of the functions of the court and having a universal and timeless validity.

Merits of the amended case

15.12 As the party seeking permission to amend needs the exercise of the court's discretion, the court is obviously competent to refuse to exercise its powers if the proposed amendment will serve no useful purpose. A proposed amendment will be refused where the amended case has no real prospect of success (*Oil & Mineral Development Corporation Ltd v Sajjad* (2001) LTL 3/12/01; *Clarke v Slay* (2002) LTL 25/1/02). Amendments were refused in *TG Can Ltd v Crown Packaging UK plc* [2007] EWHC 1271 (QB) where the claimant sought to add implied terms to the particulars of claim. The court held that there was no basis, such as to give business efficacy to the contract, for implying the proposed terms. As with many other interim applications, the evidence on the merits of the substantive claim will usually be incomplete and untested by cross-examination. It will be inappropriate to refuse an amendment on the merits if, eg, one of the main issues turns on a disputed oral conversation, because that is a matter to be determined at trial (*Young v J R Smart (Builders) Ltd (No 2)* (2000) LTL 7/2/00).

15.13 It was an old general rule that the claimant needed to have an existing cause of action on the date the originating process was issued. If not, the proceedings were incurably bad (*Vax Appliances Ltd v Hoover plc* [1990] RPC 656). The modern approach is more flexible, with amendments being granted in accordance with the justice of the case. There is no longer any absolute rule of law or practice which precludes an amendment to rely on a cause of action which has arisen after the commencement of the proceedings where otherwise the claim would fail (*Maridive & Oil Services (SAE) v CNA Insurance Co (Europe) Ltd* [2002] 2 Lloyd's Rep 9).

Late amendments

15.14 In *Ketteman v Hansel Properties Ltd* [1987] AC 189, HL, one of the defendants, who had previously been defending the action on its merits, applied at trial during the closing speeches to amend its defence to plead that the action was time-barred under the Limitation Act. Lord Griffiths, commenting on the decision in *Clarapede and Co v Commercial Union Association* (1883) 32 WR 262 cited above said:

> ...whatever may have been the rule of conduct a hundred years ago, today it is not the practice invariably to allow a defence which is wholly different from that pleaded to be raised

> by amendment at the end of the trial even on terms that an adjournment is granted and that the defendant pays all the costs thrown away. There is a clear difference between allowing amendments to clarify the issues in dispute and those that permit a distinct defence to be raised for the first time.

Lord Griffiths went on to say that the court must consider where justice lies, and that there may be many factors that bear on the exercise of the court's discretion. These include a legitimate expectation that the basis of a claim will not be fundamentally changed at the last moment, and the adverse effect on other litigants of lost judicial time through avoidable adjournments. Accordingly, the amendment was refused. **15.15**

It follows from the speech of Lord Griffiths in *Ketteman v Hansel Properties Ltd* that it may be perfectly proper to allow a late amendment for the purpose of clarifying the issues between the parties. Where this is done to reflect a version of the facts that only emerges with the evidence at the trial, an amendment is generally permitted as this accords with the overriding objective (*Binks v Securicor Omega Express Ltd* [2003] 1 WLR 2557). **15.16**

It is important to note that the factors emphasized by the House of Lords in *Ketteman v Hansel Properties Ltd* apply only to applications made at a very late stage. In *Easton v Ford Motor Co Ltd* [1993] 1 WLR 1511, the claimant sued the defendant for breach of contract in relation to an employee suggestion scheme. The defendant initially defended on the ground that the claimant's suggestion was not novel. Then, over five years after the proceedings had been issued, the defendant applied to amend its defence to add that under the scheme the committee which scrutinized suggestions had the final say and could not be challenged. Although the claim had been pending for a considerable period of time, it was nowhere near ready for trial. In those circumstances, the Court of Appeal decided that the normal rule under *Clarapede and Co v Commercial Union Association* applied, and as the proposed amendment did not cause any injustice, as it did not of itself raise any need for new evidence, it was allowed. **15.17**

It will be seen from the above that, when faced with late amendments, the court has to balance a number of factors. These include the exact stage reached in the proceedings, how great a change is made in the issues by the proposed amendments, whether the other side is taken by surprise, whether an adjournment to the trial will be necessary, and whether there is any prejudice to the other side. Thus, in *Willis v Quality Heating Services Ltd* (2000) LTL 24/3/00, CA, an amendment was allowed three weeks before trial. The claim originally alleged that the claimant had suffered a back injury from two specific incidents at work. The amended claim alleged the claimant's back was injured through being required to lift heavy loads throughout his employment. While this should have been pleaded much earlier, the wider basis of the claim had been foreshadowed in other documents served by the claimant, and allowing the amendment accorded with the overriding objective of dealing with the case justly. Likewise, seeking permission to argue an unpleaded point which is raised for the first time at or shortly before the hearing will generally be granted, as refusing may be an unduly harsh penalty and represent a windfall to the other side (*E I Du Pont de Nemours and Co v S T Dupont* (2003) *The Times*, 28 November 2003). Conversely, lateness, combined with a weak case, albeit one with some prospect of success, resulted in permission being denied in *Savings and Investment Bank Ltd v Fincken* [2004] 1 WLR 667. **15.18**

Costs of amendment

15.19 The usual rule is that where an amendment is allowed, the party seeking to amend must pay the other side the costs of and occasioned by the amendment (*Lidl UK GmbH v Davies* [2008] EWCA Civ 976). These costs will comprise the correspondence relating to the application to amend, preparation for and attendance at the application, and the costs relating to any consequential amendment of subsequent statements of case (PD Costs, para 8.5). Generally, consent (see 15.04) should be given for any amendment sought by the other side in order to save costs unless there are substantial grounds for objecting. An unreasonable refusal to consent may result in the loss of the usual costs order against the party applying to amend (*La Chemise Lacoste SA v Sketchers USA Ltd* (2006) LTL 24/5/06).

15.20 A very late amendment may be allowed with an appropriately onerous order as to costs. In *Beoco Ltd v Alfa Laval Co Ltd* [1995] QB 137, CA, the claimant was allowed to make a fifth amendment to its statement of case on the sixth day of the trial. The proposed amendment pleaded an alternative claim against the first defendant which could not be brought by separate proceedings. Disallowing the amendment would therefore have caused real prejudice to the claimant. However, the previously pleaded case against the first defendant was weak (and in the event failed at trial), and the first defendant had decided against protecting itself by making a payment into court (for which, see Chapter 42). To avoid injustice to the first defendant, the claimant (who won on the amended claim) was ordered to pay the first defendant's costs up to the date of the amendment and 85 per cent of its costs thereafter. Such a penal approach is not always correct. In *Professional Information Technology Consultants Ltd v Jones* (2001) LTL 7/12/01, the claim succeeded on the basis of a late amendment, but this was reflected by simply reducing the costs of the claim recovered by the claimant by one-third.

Addition, removal, and substitution of parties

15.21 One of the most fundamental types of amendment is where it is proposed to make a change in the parties to the claim. Sometimes this is little more than a technicality, such as where the amendment seeks to correct a mistake in the name of one of the parties if no one has been misled by the way that party was originally named (this is not uncommon when suing businesses, which sometimes trade through limited liability companies with similar names, and which sometimes appear to be partnerships when in fact they are companies). At the other end of the scale are cases where, late in the litigation process, the claimant realizes that a completely new party needs to be added to the claim, in which event all the stages in the claim will have to be repeated with the new party.

15.22 The main test of whether a change involving the addition or substitution of a party may be made is whether the amendment is 'desirable': see CPR, r 19.2(2) to (4). Nobody, however, may be added as a claimant unless he or she consents in writing and the consent is filed at court (r 19.4(4)). A person who refuses to consent to being added as a claimant may be added as a defendant, unless the court orders otherwise (r 19.3(2)). Further, the court's permission is always required to remove, add, or substitute a party, unless the claim form has not been served (r 19.4(1)).

Rule 19.2 of the CPR provides, so far as is material: 15.23

(2) The court may order a person to be added as a new party if—
   (a) it is desirable to add the new party so that the court can resolve all matters in dispute in the proceedings; or
   (b) there is an issue involving the new party and an existing party which is connected to the matters in dispute in the proceedings, and it is desirable to add the new party so that the court can resolve that issue.

(3) The court may order any person to cease to be a party if it is not desirable for that person to be a party to the proceedings.

(4) The court may order a new party to be substituted for an existing one if—
   (a) the existing party's interest or liability has passed to the new party; and
   (b) it is desirable to substitute the new party so that the court can resolve the matters in dispute in the proceedings.

The rule is designed to prevent claims being defeated on technical grounds relating to the parties which have or should have been joined. This is in accordance with the statutory objective in the SCA 1981, s 49(2), of ensuring that all matters in dispute between the parties are completely and finally determined, and of avoiding all multiplicity of proceedings. The discretion granted under the rule is applied in accordance with the overriding objective along similar lines to those discussed at 15.08–15.18 above. As with other amendments, permission is usually granted on terms that the amending party must pay the costs of and arising from the amendment. 15.24

Adding defendants close to the expiry of limitation

A person added as a defendant by amendment becomes a party for the first time when the amended proceedings are served (*Ketteman v Hansel Properties Ltd* [1987] AC 189, HL). This is important in cases where amendments are sought close to the expiry of a limitation period, because if service is to be effected after limitation expires, the additional requirements discussed at 15.26–15.45 will also need to be fulfilled if permission to amend is to be granted (*Bank of America National Trust and Savings Association v Chrismas* [1994] 1 All ER 401). Consequently, if an order to add a new party is made close to the expiry of limitation where the conditions for amendments after the expiry of limitation do not apply, the order granting permission to amend should impose a condition that service on the additional defendants must be effected before the expiry of the limitation period. If the application is heard after the limitation period has expired, the court is obliged to apply the more exacting after-expiry of limitation requirements (*Welsh Development Agency v Redpath Dorman Long Ltd* [1994] 1 WLR 1409). 15.25

D AMENDMENT AFTER THE EXPIRY OF THE LIMITATION PERIOD

An amendment to add or substitute a new party or a new cause of action is deemed to be a separate claim and to have been commenced on the same date as the original proceedings (LA 1980, s 35(1) and (2)). Consequently, if the original proceedings were commenced 15.26

within the relevant limitation period, and an amendment is allowed adding a party or cause of action after the expiry of the limitation period, the defendant will be deprived of the limitation defence, and will usually suffer injustice not compensable by an order for costs. The usual rule, therefore, is that such amendments are not permitted (LA 1980, s 35(3)). There are, however, a number of exceptions which are considered below. It seems that if there is a dispute about whether a limitation period has expired, the test is whether the claim is unarguably time-barred (*Leicester Wholesale Fruit Market Ltd v Grundy* [1990] 1 WLR 107, CA).

15.27 The statutory relation back in the LA 1980, s 35(1), applies only to the procedural time bars in the LA 1980. It does not apply to contractual or substantive time limits, like that in the Hague–Visby Rules, art III, rule 6, which have the effect that on expiry of the period laid down the claimant's cause of action ceases to exist (*Payabi v Armstel Shipping Corporation* [1992] QB 907). Likewise, defective product claims against the producer under the Consumer Protection Act 1987 are extinguished on the expiry of the 10-year limitation period in the LA 1980, s 11A(3) (giving effect to Directive 85/374, art 11). This means that generally the producer cannot be substituted as a defendant after this period has expired (*O'Byrne v Aventis Pasteur SA* Case C-358/08 *The Times*, 9 December 2009; [2010] UKSC 23).

Amendment of parties after the limitation period

15.28 The addition or substitution of new parties after the expiry of any limitation period is permitted only if it is necessary for the determination of the original action (LA 1980, s 35(5)(b)). An amendment to add an alternative claim against a new party is not 'necessary' for this purpose (*Martin v Kaisary* [2006] PIQR P5). There are a number of circumstances, which are discussed at 15.29–15.43, where amendments to the parties may be allowed despite the expiry of the limitation period. Unless the case falls into one of these categories, an amendment to the parties after the expiry of the limitation period cannot be allowed even if it is 'necessary' in the colloquial meaning of that word.

Assignment or transmission of interest

15.29 Rule 19.2(4) of the CPR provides that the court may make an order for a new party to be substituted for an existing party if:

(a) the existing party's interest or liability has passed to the new party; and
(b) it is desirable to substitute the new party so that the court can resolve the matters in dispute in the proceedings.

15.30 This rule allows claims in which the interest of a party has been assigned, transmitted, or devolved on another to be carried on by the person now having an interest in the dispute. This may occur, eg, if the original party dies so that his or her interest passes to executors or administrators, or where the original party's interest is assigned to another person. Once limitation has passed, substitution of the new party may be allowed if the original party's interest has passed to the new party on the original party's death or bankruptcy (CPR, r 19.5(3)(c)). In *Finlan v Eyton Morris Winfield (A Firm)* [2007] 4 All ER 143, an amendment was allowed after the expiry of limitation to substitute an assignment of the cause of action which was executed after the claim form was issued.

Correcting a genuine mistake

One of the grounds on which the addition or substitution of a new party after the expiry of limitation will be regarded as 'necessary' within the meaning of the LA 1980, s 35, is where the new party is substituted for a party whose name was given in mistake for the new party's name (s 35(6)(a)). Rules of court can be made for allowing such an amendment, which may impose further restrictions (s 35(4)). There are two provisions in the CPR dealing with this situation, which have to be read together, namely: **15.31**

(a) CPR, r 19.5(3)(a), which provides that the addition or substitution of a party will be necessary (for the purposes of LA 1980, s 35) if the new party is to be substituted for a party who was named in the claim form in mistake for the new party; and
(b) CPR, r 17.4(3), which provides that the court may allow an amendment to correct a mistake as to the name of a party, but only where the mistake was genuine and not one which would cause reasonable doubt as to the identity of the party in question. This applies where the amendment does not involve substituting a new party, but is limited to correcting the name of the original party.

Courts dealing with applications under r 19.5(3)(a) apply the same principles as those governing the now repealed RSC ord 20, r 5 (see *Adelson v Associated Newspapers Ltd* [2008] 1 WLR 585). Accordingly, in these applications: **15.32**

(a) the court must be satisfied that the person who made the mistake, directly or through an agent, was the person responsible for issuing the claim form (r 19.5(3)(a));
(b) the applicant has to show that, had the mistake not been made, the new party would have been named in the claim form;
(c) the mistake has to be as to the name of the party rather than as to the identity of the party (*The Sardinia Sulcis* [1991] 1 Lloyd's Rep 201);
(d) no injustice should be caused if the application is granted. Often there will be a connection between the party named in the claim form and the party to be substituted (although this is not a requirement), and often the party intended to be substituted will have been aware of the proceedings (again this is not a formal requirement). If the party to be substituted was unaware of the claim, the court is likely to exercise its discretion against granting the application (*Horne-Roberts v SmithKline Beecham plc* [2002] 1 WLR 1662); and
(e) all that is permitted is a substitution of parties, not the addition of an extra party (*Broadhurst v Broadhurst* [2007] EWHC 1828 (Ch)).

Under CPR, r 17.4(3), whether a mistake would cause reasonable doubt as to the identity of the party intending to sue has to be determined objectively having regard to what is said in the claim form in the light of what was known by the defendant and the context in which the claim was made (*ABB Asea Brown Boveri Ltd v Hiscox Dedicated Corporate Member Ltd* [2007] EWHC 1150 (Comm)). A description of the role played by the claimant in the particulars of claim attached to the claim form may be sufficiently clear to avoid such doubt (*International Bulk Shipping and Services Ltd v Minerals and Metals Trading Corp of India* [1996] 1 All ER 1017). **15.33**

Claim cannot properly be carried on without the new party

15.34 Once a limitation period has expired, the addition or substitution of a new party may also be regarded as 'necessary' within the meaning of the LA 1980, s 35, where the original claim cannot be maintained by or against an existing party unless the new party is joined or substituted as a claimant or defendant (s 35(6)(b)). This provision may also be subject to further restrictions imposed by rules of court (s 35(4)).

15.35 The relevant rule is CPR, r 19.5(3)(b), which provides that amendments under s 35(6)(b) may be made when claims cannot 'properly be carried' on without the amendment. Some commentators have said that the rule gives a general discretion to the court to consider whether evading the provisions of the LA 1980 by amendment would be 'proper'. However, this cannot be correct, because rules of court made under the LA 1980, s 35(4), can impose further restrictions going beyond s 35(6), but cannot relax the basic requirements of that subsection. The phrase 'cannot properly be carried on' in r 19.5(3)(b) therefore cannot be any wider than the phrase 'cannot be maintained' in s 35(6). So, in *Roberts v Gill and Co* [2009] 1 WLR 531 permission to amend to add a claim in the claimant's capacity as a personal representative in addition to his existing claim in his personal capacity was refused, because the personal claim could be properly carried on without adding the new claim.

15.36 Situations within r 19.5(3)(b) are probably similar to those set out in the pre-1999 RSC, ord 15, r 6(6). This set out five categories of cases where errors in naming parties gave rise to a legal bar to obtaining a remedy, and it was only in these five categories where it was considered 'necessary' (the same word used in the present rules in r 19.5(2)(b) in this context) to add a party once limitation had expired (a view which is strongly supported by *Merrett v Babb* [2001] QB 1174). The old categories were where:

(a) the new party was a necessary party to the claim in that property is vested in him at law or in equity and the claimant's proceedings asserting an equitable interest in that property were liable to be defeated unless the new party was joined, or
(b) the relevant cause of action was vested in the new party and the claimant jointly but not severally, or
(c) the new party was the Attorney-General and the proceedings should have been brought by relator proceedings in his name, or
(d) the new party was a company in which the claimant was a shareholder and on whose behalf the claimant was suing to enforce a right vested in the company, or
(e) the new party was sued jointly with the defendant and was not also liable severally with him and failure to join the new party might render the claim unenforceable.

15.37 It will be appreciated that these categories were rather restricted. A right or liability would be vested in persons jointly but not severally (grounds (b) and (e) above) where, eg, a contract by its terms was made jointly between numerous persons (see, eg, *Roche v Sherrington* [1982] 1 WLR 599). Another example was the joint liability of partners in respect of contracts entered into on behalf of the partnership under the Partnership Act 1890, s 9. An example under (c) was an action in respect of public nuisance, which had to be brought on the relation of the Attorney-General. Paragraph (d) was intended to assist in cases falling foul of the rule in *Foss v Harbottle* (1843) 2 Hare 461.

Alteration of capacity

An amendment may be allowed after the expiry of the limitation period to alter the capacity in which a party claims. This applies whether the new capacity is one which that party had at the date the proceedings were commenced or is one acquired thereafter (CPR, r 17.4(4)). 'Capacity' in this rule is used in the sense of legal competence or status to bring or defend a claim. It could not be used where a claimant wrongly issued proceedings in her own right (because the cause of action had vested in her trustee in bankruptcy), and thereafter took an assignment from the trustee, and asked for permission to amend to plead the assignment. This was because both before and after the proposed amendment the claimant was purporting to sue in her personal capacity, so there was no 'alteration of capacity' (*Haq v Singh* [2001] 1 WLR 1594). **15.38**

Personal injuries cases

The LA 1980, s 35(3), provides that an amendment may be allowed after the expiry of the primary limitation period in a personal injuries case, provided the court makes a direction under the LA 1980, s 33 (for which see 7.54–7.62). This provision is incorporated into the CPR in r 19.5(4)(a). In *Howe v David Brown Tractors (Retail) Ltd* [1991] 4 All ER 30 the Court of Appeal held that an amendment to add a party under what is now r 19.5(4)(a) could be made only if an application to disapply the usual three-year limitation period under the LA 1980, s 33, had already been made and granted, or if a s 33 application was made at the same time as the application to amend. This has been reversed by r 19.5(4)(b), which provides that an amendment may be allowed if a s 33 issue is directed to be determined at trial. **15.39**

Amendment of causes of action after the expiry of the limitation period

Amendments to add causes of action are generally not allowed once limitation has expired. An amendment to plead consequential loss in a professional negligence claim was interpreted as simply adding a new head of damage, so was not a new cause of action in *Harland and Wolff Pension Trustees Ltd v Aon Consulting Financial Services Ltd* [2010] ICR 121. However, making an amendment to justify a claim on a different factual basis amounts to making a new claim even if the sum claimed remains unchanged (*Seele Austria GmbH and Co KG v Tokio Marine Europe Insurance Ltd* [2009] BLR 481). Exceptions where a new cause of action may be added to an existing claim after the relevant period of limitation has expired are: **15.40**

(a) where the claim is in respect of personal injuries and the court makes a direction under the LA 1980, s 33, that the usual limitation period shall not apply (LA 1980, s 35(3));
(b) where the new cause of action is an original set-off or counterclaim (LA 1980, s 35(3)). An original set-off or counterclaim is one made by an original defendant who has not previously pleaded a counterclaim, and the counterclaim must be made against the original claimant (see *Kennett v Brown* [1988] 1 WLR 582, which is still good law on this point). An original counterclaim brought after limitation should not be allowed if the counterclaim is being used offensively, or if it is radically different from the existing claim (*Law Society v Shah (No 2)* [2009] 1 WLR 2254). If bringing a counterclaim in effect evades an accrued limitation period, the claimant should consider making an application to strike

out the counterclaim under CPR, r 3.4 (*Ernst and Young v Butte Mining plc (No 2)* [1997] 1 WLR 1485); and

(c) where the new cause of action arises out of the same facts or substantially the same facts as are already in issue in the original claim (LA 1980, s 35(5)(a) and CPR, r 17.4).

Same or substantially the same facts

15.41 Whether amendments involve the same or substantially the same facts as those already in issue is largely a matter of impression. In deciding whether the new cause of action arises out of substantially the same facts as those originally pleaded it is necessary to identify '. . . the bare minimum of essential facts abstracted from the original pleading [and to compare that] with the minimum as it would be constituted under the amended pleading' (*P&O Nedlloyd BV v Arab Metals Co* [2007] 1 WLR 2483 at [14], applying the similar test from *Smith v Henniker-Major* [2003] Ch 182). An amendment adding a new duty or obligation usually raises a new cause of action, whereas pleading additional facts, or better particulars, allegedly constituting a breach of the duty already pleaded, usually will not (*Darlington Building Society v O'Rourke James Scourfield* [1999] PNLR 365). If the new plea introduces an essentially distinct allegation, it will be a new cause of action. Where the only difference between the original case and the case set out in the proposed amendments is a further instance of breach, or the addition of a new remedy, there is no addition of a new cause of action.

15.42 In *Goode v Martin* [2002] 1 WLR 1828, the claimant sought permission to amend her claim after the expiry of limitation to plead that on the alternative version of the facts pleaded in the defence, the defendant would still be liable to her. The judge held that there was no power to allow the amendment, because r 17.4(2) allows such amendments if the new claim arises out of the same or substantially the same facts 'as a claim in respect of which [the claimant] has already claimed', and the facts relied upon were pleaded by the defendant. The Court of Appeal held that the Human Rights Act 1998, s 3, allowed it to read the words 'are already in issue on' into this rule, with the effect that the court had power to allow the amendment as it was based on facts put in issue by the defence. It also allows a claimant to adopt facts after the expiry of limitation which had been pleaded by one defendant by amending the particulars of claim against another defendant (*Charles Church Developments Ltd v Stent Foundations Ltd* [2007] 1 WLR 1203).

15.43 In *Hancock Shipping Co Ltd v Kawasaki Heavy Industries Ltd* [1992] 1 WLR 1025, CA, permission to amend the particulars of claim was sought three years after service of the original statement of case, and after the limitation period had expired. In considering whether it is just to allow an amendment in such circumstances, the court held that it had to take into account that granting permission will deprive the defendant of an accrued limitation defence, but could exercise its discretion to allow the amendment in the light of all the relevant factors. An important factor is the degree to which the defendant is prejudiced in being unable to investigate the facts of the new claim through the disappearance of evidence. The Court of Appeal in *Hancock Shipping Co Ltd v Kawasaki Heavy Industries Ltd* disallowed certain of the proposed amendments on the ground that the defendant would be prejudiced through the loss of evidence, but allowed certain other amendments which were closely related to the claim already made as there was likely to be little prejudice through the loss of evidence.

Amendments after the limitation period affecting accrued rights

A defendant will not be given permission to amend where the effect of the proposed amendment is to transfer responsibility for the claim on to a non-party who cannot be sued by the claimant as a result of the expiry of the relevant limitation period. An example is *Cluley v R L Dix Heating* (2003) LTL 31/10/03, where the claimant sued for breach of contract. After the expiry of the limitation period, the defendant sought to amend its defence, which had admitted the contract but denied breach, to plead that there was no contract with the claimant and that the claimant should have sued other parties. Suing the other parties was no longer viable because of the expiry of limitation. Permission to amend was refused, because even an order for costs could not put the claimant into the same position as if the proposed defence had been pleaded at the proper time. **15.44**

Much depends on whether the defendant has been at fault in not pleading the proposed defence at the proper time. So, in *Weait v Jayanbee Joinery Ltd* [1963] 1 QB 239, CA, through no fault of their own, the defendants discovered after the expiry of the limitation period that the claimant's injuries were probably worse than they should have been through the intervening negligence of the doctor who treated the claimant. An amendment to the defence to plead the doctor's negligence was allowed, despite the fact that the claimant could not make a claim against the doctor as that claim was time-barred. Further, an amendment blaming a non-party may be allowed if it alleges facts within the knowledge of the claimant, since in such a case the claimant is prejudiced by his or her own failure to sue the non-party in time, rather than by some line of defence being made known at a late stage. **15.45**

E PROCEDURE ON AMENDING

Making the amendment

Words added to a document are written or typed in red ink, and words deleted are struck through in the same colour. Reamendments are made in green ink, and subsequent amendments in violet, then yellow. If the amendments cannot be conveniently incorporated into the original document, a fresh document should be prepared. However, there are two other options: **15.46**

(a) using a monochrome typeface, but with a numeric code indicating the amendments (PD 17, para 2.2(2)); or
(b) simply retyping the document incorporating the changes and omitting deleted text (PD 17, para 2.2).

The court may, if it thinks it desirable, direct that the amendments be shown in one or other of the ways described above.

15.47 If there is a substantial change the document should be reverified by a statement of truth (PD 17, para 1.4). The amended statement of case should be endorsed 'Amended [Particulars of Claim] by Order of District Judge [name of judge] dated [date]'.

Applying for permission

15.48 A party seeking permission to amend must issue an application notice. An application may be made by an existing party or by a person who wishes to become a party (CPR, r 19.4(2)). There is an express provision requiring evidence in support of an application under r 19.2(4) for the substitution of a new party where an existing party's interest has passed (eg, on death), and that type of application can be made without notice (r 19.4(3)). Any other type of application for addition or substitution does not strictly have to be supported by written evidence, though the circumstances may make this desirable. This is particularly so in applications where the expiry of the limitation period is relevant. The proposed amended statement of case must be filed with the application (PD 17, para 1.2(2)).

15.49 Applications for permission to amend are usually made on notice to all other parties. As indicated earlier in this chapter, applications in the later stages of litigation can be made to the trial judge. Otherwise they tend to be dealt with by district judges and masters as part of the case management functions of the court.

Procedure after permission is granted

15.50 If permission to amend is granted by the court, the order will be drawn up and served in the usual way on the parties. If the order provides for the addition, removal, or substitution of a party, the order must also be served on the party affected by the order (CPR, r 19.4(5)). Court fees are also payable when new parties are brought in.

15.51 Any order granting permission to make an amendment may include consequential directions, particularly regarding amendments to other statements of case, and perhaps altering any existing directions timetable. Where an amendment involves the addition, removal, or substitution of a party, CPR, r 19.4(6) and PD 19A, para 3.2 provide that consequential directions may also deal with:

(a) filing and serving of the amended claim form and particulars of claim on any new defendant, usually within 14 days;
(b) serving other relevant documents on the new party;
(c) providing the new defendant with a response pack for the purpose of admitting, defending, or counterclaiming;
(d) serving the order on all parties and any other person affected by it; and
(e) the management of the proceedings.

KEY POINTS SUMMARY

15.52
- Permission to amend is required if the statement of case has been served.
- Normally, consent from the other parties is an alternative to seeking the court's permission to amend.

- Normally, permission is granted on condition that the party amending pays the costs of and occasioned by the amendments.
- Late amendments are sometimes disallowed.
- The statutory relation back in the Limitation Act 1980, s 35, means that there are restrictions on amending after limitation has expired.
- Amendments after the expiry of limitation to change parties are usually allowed only if there was a mistake.
- Amendments after limitation to change causes of action are usually restricted to cases where the new case arises out of facts which are the same or substantially the same as those already in issue.

16

REQUESTS FOR FURTHER INFORMATION

16.01 Sometimes a party will take the view that the statement of case provided by the other side is not as clear as it should be, or fails to set out the other side's case with the precision that would be expected. In such cases a request may be made for further information about the facts on which the other side's case is based. Generally it is to be expected that such requests should be made shortly after the relevant statement of case is served.

16.02 The situation described in the previous paragraph is in fact just one of the situations in which it may be appropriate for a request to be made for further information, and is not limited to deficiencies in the other side's statement of case. Further information can also be sought to clarify any matter in dispute, or to seek information about any such matter, even though the point in question is not contained in or referred to in a statement of case (CPR, r 18.1). The procedure can therefore be used to try to find out about facts that might be expected to be contained in the witness statements (in which case the application would normally be expected to be made after the exchange of witness statements).

16.03 The procedure can also be used by the court of its own initiative for a variety of purposes, including court-led inquiries into the facts relied upon by a party and requests aimed at finding out information for case management purposes. It is doubtful whether the request procedure can be used to seek information on the nature and extent of the insurance cover available to meet a claim, even in cases where it would be irrational to devote a great deal of costs on investigating quantum if the resources available to the defendant are limited (*West London Pipeline and Storage Ltd v Total UK Ltd* [2008] 1 CLC 935, disapproving *Harcourt v FEF Griffin* [2007] PIQR Q177).

A THE REQUEST FOR FURTHER INFORMATION

Format of the request

A party seeking clarification or information is, in PD 18, called the first party, and the party from whom the clarification or information is sought is called the second party. The first party should serve the second party with a written request for the clarification or information sought, stating a date by which the response to the request should be served. If practicable the request should be served by e-mail (PD 18, para 1.7). The date must allow the second party a reasonable time to respond. Such a request is known as a preliminary request, and is served without the need for a prior court order or direction. **16.04**

A request should be concise and strictly confined to matters which are reasonably necessary and proportionate to enable the first party to prepare its own case or to understand the case that has to be met (PD 18, para 1.2). A request may be made by letter if the text of the request is brief and the reply is likely to be brief. If a request is made by letter, it must contain a clear statement that it contains a request under CPR, Part 18, and the letter must be limited to dealing with the request under Part 18 (PD 18, para 1.5). **16.05**

More complex requests resemble statements of case: see figure 16.1. Technically, requests are not statements of case but merely lists of questions, so are not verified by statements of truth. Most requests leave no space for answers, which appear in a separate response document. Alternatively, a request may be prepared in such a way that the response may be given on the same document. In a request in this form the text of the request appears as the left-hand half of each sheet, so that the text of each response can then be inserted on the right. A party serving a request in this form must serve two copies on the second party (PD 18, para 1.6(2)(c)). **16.06**

Requests must, so far as possible, be made in a single comprehensive document, and not made piecemeal (PD 18, para 1.3). **16.07**

Contents of the request

A request for information, whether made by letter or separate document, must, by PD 18, para 1.6: **16.08**

(a) be headed with the name of the court, the title of the claim, and the claim number;
(b) state in its heading that it is a request made under Part 18;
(c) state the date on which it is made;
(d) where the request relates to a document (such as a statement of case or witness statement), identify that document and, if relevant, the paragraph or words to which it relates;
(e) set out in separate numbered paragraphs each request for information or clarification; and
(f) state the date by which the first party expects a response to the request.

Figure 16.1 Request for further information

IN THE HIGH COURT OF JUSTICE
QUEEN'S BENCH DIVISION
BIRMINGHAM DISTRICT REGISTRY
MERCANTILE COURT
BETWEEN

Claim No 10BM 47644

GREMMEL ENGINEERING LIMITED — Claimant

and

MARKWARD IMPORTS LIMITED — Defendant

REQUEST FOR FURTHER INFORMATION OF THE PARTICULARS OF CLAIM AND CLARIFICATION UNDER PART 18

Made on behalf of Markward Imports Limited (the first party) to Gremmel Engineering Limited (the second party) dated 18 August 2010.

Under paragraph 2

Of: '... by an agreement made on 10 November 2008 the Defendant agreed with the Claimant to sell and supply 4,000 metric tonnes of steel rods...'

Requests

1. Was the alleged agreement written or oral?
2. If it was written, please identify the document or documents in which it was made, and provide copies in accordance with Practice Direction 16, paragraph 7.3.
3. If it was oral, please state:
   (a) where the agreement was made; and
   (b) as precisely as possible the words used.

Clarification of the Claimant's case

Request

4. Is it alleged that the agreement alleged in paragraph 2 of the Particulars of Claim was made under the framework agreement as set out in paragraphs 5 and 6 of the Defence?

Take notice that these requests are to be answered no later than 4.00 p.m. on 8 September 2010.

Dated 18 August 2010 by Messrs Whitely & Hilt of 34 St Andrews Road, Birmingham, B1 9FP, solicitors for the Defendant.

B THE RESPONSE

16.09 If the request is in the format having the requests on the left of the page with the responses to be entered on the right-hand side, the second party may use the document supplied for the purpose for the response. Otherwise, a response must, by PD 18, para 2.3:

(a) be headed with the name of the court and the title and number of the claim;
(b) in its heading identify itself as a response to that request;
(c) repeat the text of each separate paragraph of the request and set out under each paragraph the response to it; and
(d) have attached to it a copy of any document not already in the possession of the first party which forms part of the response.

An example of a response is given at figure 16.2.

Under the old rules, and presumably this holds good under the CPR, it was regarded as improper for the response to a request to set out matters in answer that departed from the second party's earlier statement of case (*Re Unisoft Group Ltd (No 3)* [1994] 1 BCLC 609). **16.10**

The second party must serve the response on the first party, and must file at court and serve on every other party a copy of the request and of the response (PD 18, para 2.4). Unlike requests, responses are statements of case and should be verified by a statement of truth (para 3). **16.11**

Figure 16.2 Response to request for further information

IN THE HIGH COURT OF JUSTICE Claim No 10BM 47644
QUEEN'S BENCH DIVISION
BIRMINGHAM DISTRICT REGISTRY
MERCANTILE COURT
BETWEEN

GREMMEL ENGINEERING LIMITED Claimant

and

MARKWARD IMPORTS LIMITED Defendant

FURTHER INFORMATION OF THE PARTICULARS OF
CLAIM AND CLARIFICATION UNDER PART 18

This further information of the Particulars of Claim and clarification is given by the Claimant to the Defendant pursuant to the Request dated 18 August 2010 made by the Defendant.

Under paragraph 2

Of: '... by an agreement made on 10 November 2008 the Defendant agreed with the Claimant to sell and supply 4,000 metric tonnes of steel rods ...'

Request

1. Was the alleged agreement written or oral?

Response

Written.

Request

2. If it was written, please identify the document or documents in which it was made, and provide copies in accordance with Practice Direction 16, paragraph 7.3.

Figure 16.2 *continued*

Response
The Claimant's purchase order dated 29 October 2008 and an e-mail from the Defendant to the Claimant dated 8 November 2008, copies of which are attached to this Response.

Request

3. If it was oral, please state:
   (a) where the agreement was made; and
   (b) as precisely as possible the words used.

Response

Not applicable.

Clarification of the Claimant's case

Request
4. Is it alleged that the agreement alleged in paragraph 2 of the Particulars of Claim was made under the framework agreement as set out in paragraphs 5 and 6 of the Defence?

Response

No.

Statement of truth
- (I believe) (The Claimant believes) that the facts stated in this response to a request for further information are true.
- I am duly authorized by the Claimant to sign this statement.

Full name:

Name of Claimant's solicitor's firm: Messrs Young & Thompson

Signed: Position or office held:

- (Claimant) (Litigation Friend) (if signing on behalf of firm or company) (Claimant's solicitor)
- *delete as appropriate*

Dated 1 September 2010, by Messrs Young & Thompson, of 40 High Street, Barnet EN10 4SL, solicitors for the Claimant.

C OBJECTING TO REQUESTS

16.12 If the second party objects to answering a request, or if the second party considers the time given by the first party to be too short, the second party should inform the first party of the objection promptly and within the time stated for the response given by the first party (PD 18, para 4.1). Objections could include the disproportionate nature of the request, or that it infringes privilege or otherwise infringes the overriding objective.

Objections to providing further information must be made in writing, and must state the reasons for taking the objection. Where the complaint is that the time given by the first party is too short, the objection must give a date by which the second party expects to have responded. **16.13**

D ORDERS FOR RESPONSES

If a request for further information is not responded to, the first party is entitled to apply to the court for an order requiring the second party to reply in a stated period of time. Applications are made in the usual way under CPR, Part 23 (see Chapter 20). The first party will issue an application notice, which must generally be served on the second party at least three clear days before the return day. The application notice will either set out or have attached to it the text of the order sought. This must set out the matters in respect of which further information is sought (PD 18, para 5.2), and this can usually best be done by reference to the request previously served upon the second party. **16.14**

Both parties should consider whether they will serve evidence in support or in opposition to the application (PD 18, para 5.4). If the first party has not served a preliminary request on the second party, the reasons for not doing so should be dealt with in the written application or evidence in support. If a preliminary request was made, the notice or evidence in support should describe the response, if any, received from the second party (para 5.3). **16.15**

There is no need to inform the second party of the application for such an order if the second party failed to make any response at all to the preliminary request within the time stated by the first party, and provided at least 14 days have passed since the request was served (PD 18, para 5.5). **16.16**

E PRINCIPLES

As previously mentioned at 16.05, a request for further information should be concise and strictly confined to matters which are reasonably necessary and proportionate to enable the first party to prepare its own case or to understand the case that must be met. **16.17**

Under the old system, there was always the suspicion that many requests for further and better particulars and interrogatories, the procedures replaced by requests for further information, were mainly designed to rack up costs or to make it difficult for the other party to answer, so that applications for 'unless' orders (orders with sanctions) could be made. Applying the overriding objective and as PD 18, para 1.2 makes clear, any requests made for information should be reasonably necessary and proportionate. A request for further information may be the proportionate method for dealing with a statement of case which does not provide full information, rather than the more drastic approach of applying to strike out (*Deutsche Morgan Grenfell Group plc v Inland Revenue Commissioners* [2007] 1 AC 558, HL). **16.18**

Requests related to statements of case

16.19 Particulars of claim and other statements of case should contain a *concise* statement of the facts relied upon (CPR, r 16.4(1)(a); *McPhilemy v Times Newspapers Ltd* [1999] 3 All ER 775). The statements of case should therefore set out the parameters of the case that is being advanced by each party. They identify the issues and the extent of the dispute between the parties, and should make clear the general nature of the case of the pleader.

16.20 In *McPhilemy v Times Newspapers Ltd*, Lord Woolf MR pointed out that excessive detail in the statements of case can obscure the issues rather than providing clarification. Further, after disclosure of documents and the exchange of witness statements the statements of case frequently become of only historical interest. Unless there is some obvious purpose to be served by fighting over the precise terms of a statement of case, contests over its terms are to be discouraged.

Clarification requests

16.21 Requests for further information about statements of case (see 16.19–16.20) are met far more frequently than general requests for clarification (see request 4 in figure 16.1). Requests of this second type are aimed at clarification of the facts relating to the issues in the case without being tied to the wording of the other side's statement of case. They can be useful, but can be time-consuming and expensive diversions from sensible preparation of the case. This type of request therefore tends to be carefully policed by the courts.

16.22 There are a number of well-established reasons for disallowing requests for clarification:

(a) 'Fishing' requests. A request is fishing if the party making it does not have evidence supporting the cause of action or defence being put forward, but hopes something may turn up in response to the request (*Best v Charter Medical of England Ltd* (2001) *The Times*, 19 November 2001).

(b) Requests put for an unfair purpose. An example was *Lovell v Lovell* [1970] 1 WLR 1451, where the purpose behind asking a particular request was to obtain a written acknowledgment of a debt for the purpose of the Limitation Act 1980, s 29 (see 7.51).

(c) Oppressive requests. These ask for information going beyond the level of detail that can reasonably be expected (*White and Co v Credit Reform Association and Credit Index Ltd* [1905] 1 KB 653).

(d) Requests that are not precisely formulated (*Kirkup v British Rail Engineering Ltd* [1983] 1 WLR 1165).

(e) Where the request is not necessary for saving costs (see CPR, r 1.4(2)(h)). A common example is where the information sought is likely to be included under standard disclosure (see Chapter 29) or in exchanged witness statements (see Chapter 32), so the request duplicates steps that will be taken later in the proceedings. Whether this will be an effective answer depends on the circumstances of the case (*English, Welsh and Scottish Railway Ltd v Goodman* (2007) LTL 9/5/07).

F REQUESTS IN FREEZING INJUNCTIONS

By the CPR, r 25.1(1)(g), the court has the power to make orders directing a party to provide information about the location of relevant property or assets, or to provide information about relevant property or assets which are or may be the subject of an application for a freezing injunction. For this purpose, relevant property means property (including land) which is the subject of a claim or as to which any question may arise on a claim (r 25.1(2)). Clauses 9 and 10 of the standard-form freezing injunction order in PD 25A require defendants served with freezing injunctions to provide the claimant's solicitors with details of all their assets, which must be confirmed by evidence on affidavit. A defendant will normally be required to provide this information even if there is a pending application to set aside the freezing injunction (*Motorola Credit Corporation v Uzan* [2002] 2 All ER (Comm) 945). Clauses 18 and 19 of the standard-form search order in PD 25A require defendants immediately to provide information about the listed items being searched for, which again must be confirmed by affidavit. **16.23**

G COLLATERAL USE

Rule 18.2 of the CPR says that the court may direct that information provided either voluntarily or after an order must not be used for any purpose other than for the proceedings in which it is given. Consideration should be given to asking for such a direction whenever sensitive information is to be given in answer to a request for information. See also the discussion in relation to disclosure at 29.78–29.80. **16.24**

17

PARTIES AND JOINDER

17.01 As the remedies granted by the courts are generally effective only as between the parties, it is important to take care when drafting proceedings that no mistakes are made over the parties to be brought in. Although it is possible to correct most mistakes by amendment at a later stage, the passing of a limitation period may prevent this, and, in any event, avoidable amendments will be penalized in costs and may weaken the credibility of the case at trial.

17.02 This chapter will first look at the rules relating to different classes of party, and will then consider the rules governing multi-party litigation.

A DESCRIPTION OF PARTIES

17.03 The descriptions of the parties according to the nature of the court proceedings are set out in table 17.1.

Table 17.1 Descriptions of parties

Type of proceedings	Issuing party	Party served
Claim form	Claimant	Defendant
Interim application	Applicant	Respondent
Additional claim under Part 20	Defendant	Third (or Fourth, etc.) Party
Petition	Petitioner	Respondent
Bankruptcy	Petitioner	Debtor
Notice of appeal	Appellant	Respondent
Enforcement	Judgment creditor	Judgment debtor

B PARTICULAR CLASSES OF PARTY

Table 17.2 sets out the form of words to be used to describe different types of parties in the heading of statements of case and other court documents. Paragraphs 17.05–17.45 comment on the various rules. **17.04**

Table 17.2 Names of parties in court documents

Class of party	Examples of forms of words
Individuals	Mr HUGH TREVOR GROVES
change of name	Mrs JANE HALL (formerly Ms JANE OLD)
Children	Miss JANE OLD (a child, by Mrs CAROL OLD her litigation friend)
Child reaching full age	Miss JANE OLD (formerly a child but now of full age)
Protected party	Mr HENRY RIMMER by Ms MARY JONES his litigation friend
Partnership	HUNT & MURRAY (a firm)
Sole trader	Mr MARK ALAN WATSON, trading as FOREST SHOES
Corporation sole	MICHAEL, Bishop of Lincoln
Companies	
limited	CLARKE'S LINEN IMPORTS LIMITED
status unclear from name	CLARKE'S PROVIDENT (a company limited by guarantee)
in liquidation	BEN CLOVE LIMITED (in liquidation)
Bankrupts	The trustee of the estate of Mr HUGH TREVOR GROVES, a bankrupt
Deceased party	Mrs MARY JONES (executrix of the estate of Mr CLIVE DEAN deceased)
Deceased defendant, no grant of probate or administration	The personal representatives of Mr CLIVE DEAN deceased
Relator proceedings	The Attorney-General at the relation of Mr GAVIN WILSON
Representative proceedings	Mr HUGH TREVOR GROVES and Mr CLIVE DEAN on behalf of themselves and all other persons carrying on trade as fishermen in the parish of Holcombe
Intervention	(Miss MARY JONES intervening)

Individuals

Individuals should be given their full names and titles in all court documents. Initials may be used if these are all that is known, and it is also possible to commence proceedings using **17.05** only the defendant's surname. A litigant who changes their name, eg, on marriage, must file a notice of the change at the court office and serve it on the other parties.

Direct claims against motor insurers

17.06 The European Communities (Rights against Insurers) Regulations 2002 (SI 2002/3061) apply to claimants residing in a Member State of the EU or in Iceland, Liechtenstein, Norway, or Switzerland who are bringing proceedings in tort arising out of road accidents. They may issue proceedings against the insurer of the vehicle alleged to be responsible for the accident (reg 3) in addition to the existing right of action against the driver (reg 3(2)). An 'accident' for the purposes of the Regulations means an accident on a road or other public place in the United Kingdom caused by, or arising out of, the use of any insured vehicle (reg 2(1)). A 'vehicle' is any land-based vehicle other than a train which is normally based in the United Kingdom (reg 2(1)). A vehicle is 'insured' if there is a policy of insurance in force fulfilling the requirements of the Road Traffic Act 1988, s 145 (reg 2(3)).

Persons under disability

17.07 There are two categories of persons under disability: children and protected parties. Persons under 18 years of age are children. A protected party is a party, or intended party, who lacks capacity within the meaning of the Mental Capacity Act 2005 to conduct proceedings (CPR, r 21.1(2)(c), (d)). There is a presumption of full mental capacity, which is displaced where an individual has an impairment of their mind or brain which prevents them from being able to make relevant decisions (*Masterman-Lister v Brutton and Co (Nos 1 and 2)* [2003] 1 WLR 1511, Mental Capacity Act 2005, s 3).

Litigation friends

17.08 A person under disability must sue and be sued by a litigation friend (CPR, r 21.2), although the court may grant permission for a child to conduct proceedings without a litigation friend (r 21.2(3)). A child's litigation friend is normally a relative with no interest in the litigation adverse to that of the child. A deputy appointed by the Court of Protection under the Mental Capacity Act 2005 with power to conduct proceedings on the protected party's behalf is entitled to be their litigation friend in the relevant proceedings (r 21.4(2)).

17.09 A person may become a litigation friend without needing a court order by following the procedure in CPR, r 21.5. A deputy intending to act as a litigation friend for a protected party must file an official copy of the order of the Court of Protection when the claim form is issued or (if acting for a defendant) when he first takes a step in the proceedings (r 21.5(2)). In the absence of such a deputy, r 21.4(3) permits a person who can fairly and competently conduct proceedings on the protected party's behalf, who has no adverse interest, and who (if acting for a claimant) undertakes to pay any costs the protected party may be ordered to pay, to act as the protected party's litigation friend. Such a person needs to file and serve a certificate of suitability (r 21.5(3), (4)). Likewise, a person acting as a litigation friend for a child must file a certificate of suitability. An example of such a certificate is shown in figure 17.1. In addition, a litigation friend willing to act on behalf of a claimant has to undertake to pay any costs which the child or protected party may be ordered to pay in relation to the proceedings, subject to any right he may have to be repaid from the assets of the child or protected party (r 21.4(3)(c)). Undertakings are not required from litigation friends acting on behalf of defendants.

Figure 17.1 Certificate of suitability of litigation friend

Certificate of suitability of litigation friend

If you are acting

- **for a child,** you must serve a copy of the completed form on a parent or guardian of the child, or if there is no parent or guardian, the carer or the person with whom the child lives
- **for a protected party,** you must serve a copy of the completed form on one of the following persons with authority in relation to the protected party as: (1) the attorney under a registered enduring power of attorney (2) the donee of the lasting power of attorney; (3) the deputy appointed by the Court of Protection; or if there is no such person, an adult with whom the protected party resides or in whose care the protected party is. You must also complete a certificate of service (obtainable from the court office)

You should send the completed form to the court with the claim form (if acting for the claimant) or when you take the first step on the defendant's behalf in the claim together with the certificate of service (if applicable).

Name of court	Barnet County Court
Claim No.	10BT 54962
Claimant (including ref.)	Miss Jocelyn Griebart (a child by Mrs Elizabeth Jane Griebart)
Defendant (including ref.)	Mr Howard Morris

You do not need to complete this form if you are a deputy appointed by the Court of Protection with power to conduct proceedings on behalf of the protected party.

I consent to act as litigation friend for Jocelyn Griebart (claimant)(defendant)

I believe that the above named person is a

☑ child ☐ protected party *(give your reasons overleaf and attach a copy of any medical evidence in support)*

I am able to conduct proceedings on behalf of the above named person competently and fairly and I have no interests adverse to those of the above named person.

*I undertake to pay any costs which the above named claimant may be ordered to pay in these proceedings subject to any right I may have to be repaid from the assets of the claimant.

* delete if you are acting for the defendant

Please write your name in capital letters

☐ Mr ☑ Mrs ☐ Miss ☐ Ms ☐ Other ________

Surname Griebart

Forenames Elizabeth Jane

Address to which documents in this case are to be sent.

Whitely & Hilt
34 Brimsdown Road,
Barnet,
EN7 8RW

I certify that the information given in this form is correct

Signed ________

Date 14.09.2010

The court office at St Mary's Court, Regent's Park Road, London N3 1BQ

is open between 10 am and 4 pm Monday to Friday. When corresponding with the court, please address forms or letters to the Court Manager and quote the claim number.

N235 Certificate of suitability of litigation friend (10.07)

17.10 Where a party under a disability does not have a litigation friend, the court may appoint one on an application made by the person wishing to be the litigation friend or by a party (CPR, r 21.6). This may be necessary, eg, where the person under a disability is the defendant, because until a litigation friend is appointed no steps can be taken in the proceedings other than issuing and serving the claim form, and applying for the appointment of a litigation friend (r 21.3(2)(b)).

17.11 A child acting by a litigation friend should be referred to in the title to the proceedings as 'Master JOHN SMITH (a child by Mrs HELEN SMITH his litigation friend)'. A child acting without a litigation friend is referred to as 'Master JOHN SMITH (a child)'.

Child attaining 18 years

17.12 A child who is a party to proceedings and who reaches full age must serve on the other parties and file at court a notice stating that he or she is now over 18 and that the litigation friend's appointment has ceased (CPR, r 21.9). The notice must also give an address for service and state whether or not he or she intends to carry on being a party. Such a party who carries on will be described as 'Mr JOHN SMITH (formerly a child but now of full age)'. If the child (now of full age) fails to serve such a notice, the litigation friend can serve a notice to the effect that the child has reached full age and the appointment as litigation friend has ceased. A child claimant's litigation friend's liability in costs continues until notice is given to the other parties.

Protected party recovering

17.13 When a protected party regains or acquires capacity, the litigation friend's appointment continues until it is ended by a court order (CPR, r 21.9(2)). The application for such an order may be made by the former protected party, the litigation friend, or any party.

Service on person under disability

17.14 Originating process must be served on a child's parent or guardian or, if there is none, the person with whom the child resides or in whose care he or she is. In the case of a protected party, process must be served on the person with authority in relation to the protected party (the attorney under a registered enduring power of attorney, the donee under a lasting power of attorney, or the deputy appointed by the Court of Protection), failing which, on the adult with whom the protected party resides or in whose care he or she is (CPR, r 6.6).

Limitation

17.15 Periods of limitation do not run against persons under disability at the time the cause of action accrued: see 7.40.

Approval of settlements

17.16 Two regimes apply to applications for the court's approval of settlements of monetary claims by persons under disability. Under both regimes, until a proposed settlement is approved by the court there is no binding contract, and either party may back out of it (*Dietz v Lennig Chemicals Ltd* [1969] 1 AC 170; *Drinkall v Whitwood* [2004] 1 WLR 462). Where the settlement is agreed before proceedings are commenced the rules are permissive. Although this is the position in theory, in practice approval is always sought in order to give the defendant a valid discharge for the money paid and to ensure there can be no question of unfairness to the person under disability. Approval is sought by issuing a Part 8 claim form (CPR, r 21.10(2)).

The second regime is mandatory. A settlement reached after proceedings have been commenced must be approved by the court if it is to be valid. Approval is sought by issuing an ordinary application notice (CPR, r 21.10(1)). **17.17**

If a Part 8 claim is used, the claim form must set out details of the claim and also the terms of the settlement or compromise, or must have attached to it a draft consent order. Both types of application must be supported by written evidence. Information to be provided includes whether and to what extent the defendant admits liability, the age and any occupation of the child, the litigation friend's approval of the proposed settlement, and details of any relevant prosecution. In personal injuries claims the evidence must deal with the circumstances of the accident, and in many cases the police report must be obtained. Medical reports and a statement of past and future loss and expense must be made available to the court. In all except very clear cases a copy of an opinion from counsel on the merits of the settlement, together with the instructions (unless sufficiently set out in the opinion) must also be supplied to the court (PD 21, para 6.3). **17.18**

Most applications for approval are heard by masters and district judges sitting in private. The decision, however, will be pronounced in public in accordance with the European Convention on Human Rights, art 6(1). **17.19**

When considering the proposed settlement, the master or district judge has to weigh the claimant's prospects of success against the likely level of damages on full liability, and decide whether the proposed settlement is in the interests of the person under disability. If the court decides the settlement is not in the interests of the person under disability, the application is adjourned for the parties to negotiate new terms. **17.20**

If approval is given, directions are given as to how the money shall be dealt with (CPR, r 2.11). Where money is recovered by or on behalf of a protected party, before giving directions under r 21.11, the court must consider whether the protected party is a protected beneficiary (r 21.11(3)). This is a protected party who lacks capacity to manage and control money he recovers in the proceedings (r 21.1(2)(e)). If so, the Court of Protection has jurisdiction to make investment decisions in the best interests of the protected beneficiary. Otherwise, the court will itself administer and invest the fund. The court acts on the principle that such funds should be applied for the purpose for which the damages were awarded. So, eg, the court will be careful to avoid the money being applied for the general benefit of a child's family. **17.21**

Trusts and estates

Trustees, executors, and administrators should act jointly, and all should be named in any proceedings (as defendants if they will not consent to act as claimants). Regarding beneficiaries, it is provided by CPR, r 19.7A(1), that a claim may be brought by or against trustees, executors, or administrators without the need to join the beneficiaries. This is invariably the most convenient way of bringing proceedings, and where this is done any judgment or order in the claim is binding on the beneficiaries unless the court orders otherwise (r 19.7A(2)). **17.22**

Bankruptcy

17.23 A bankrupt's estate vests in the trustee in bankruptcy on the appointment of the trustee (Insolvency Act 1986, s 306), who becomes the person who should be named in litigation involving the bankrupt's estate. A bankrupt has no standing to make applications in litigation even in the period between the making of a bankruptcy order and the appointment of a trustee (*Dadourian Group International Inc v Simms* [2008] EWHC 723 (Ch)). By way of exception, claims for personal injuries and defamation remain vested in the bankrupt (see *Ord v Upton* [2000] Ch 352).

17.24 The heading in a claim involving a trustee in bankruptcy does not individually identify the trustee, but refers to the trustee simply by his office (see table 17.2 and the IA 1986, s 305(4)). Where a party becomes bankrupt during the currency of proceedings, the trustee in bankruptcy may be ordered to be substituted for the bankrupt (CPR, r 19.2(2)). Proceedings against a bankrupt may only be commenced with the court's permission (IA 1986, s 285(3)). Proceedings commenced without such permission are a nullity, and cannot be retrieved by granting retrospective permission (*Fusion Interactive Communication Solutions Ltd v Venture Investment Placement Ltd (No 2)* [2005] 2 BCLC 571).

Deceased parties

17.25 Generally, causes of action other than for defamation survive a claimant's death, and vest in the deceased's personal representatives, who should be named as parties in any litigation. Before the grant of letters of administration or probate there is a limited power for a person to take essential steps to preserve and protect the deceased's estate, but unless an application is necessary, the court will refuse to make an order without a grant (*Caudle v LD Law Ltd* [2008] 1 WLR 1540). Where a party dies during the currency of proceedings, the personal representatives may be ordered to be made parties by substitution (CPR, r 19.2(2)). In *Fielding v Rigby* [1993] 1 WLR 1355, CA, the named claimant issued proceedings claiming damages for injuries sustained in an accident, but died before the proceedings were served. Without amending the proceedings to name the personal representative as the claimant or obtaining an order to carry on, the claimant's personal representative served proceedings on the defendant, who then applied to have the claim struck out as a nullity. It was held that service had been merely irregular, and the defects were rectified under what is now r 3.10.

17.26 If a claim is brought against someone who was in fact dead when the claim was issued, it will be treated as if it was brought against the estate of the deceased (r 19.8(3)(b)). By way of exception to these general rules, in a claim where one of the persons having an interest in the claim has died and has no personal representatives, it is possible for any of the parties to apply to the court for an order that the claim may proceed in the absence of a person to represent the estate of the deceased (see r 19.8(1)(a)). If such an order is made, any judgment or order made in the claim will still bind the estate of the deceased (r 19.8(5)).

Partnerships

17.27 A partnership exists where a number of people carry on a business in common with a view of profit (Partnership Act 1890, s 1(1)). Every partner is an agent for the firm (s 5). In most situations a partnership will be bound by acts done on behalf of the firm (ss 6 and 10), and the individual partners will also be personally liable, either jointly or jointly and severally (ss 9 and 12). The partners who will be liable are those who were partners at the time of the relevant event.

Partnerships typically trade under a firm name. This often consists of the surnames of each of the partners, but many partnerships use a brand name, or words to describe their main business activities. By PD 7A, para 5A.3, where a partnership has a name, unless it is inappropriate to do so, claims must be brought in or against the name under which the partnership carried on business at the time the cause of action accrued. This is done by adding the words '(a firm)' after its name in the title to the proceedings. Use of the partnership name is simply the shorthand method of specifically naming as defendants (or claimants) each of the persons who were partners when the cause of action accrued (*Ernst and Young v Butte Mining plc (No 2)* [1997] 1 WLR 1485 *per* Lightman J). **17.28**

Service of process

A document may be served on partners by the usual methods: personal service, first-class post, by leaving it at the defendant's address, and, subject to certain conditions, through the document exchange, or by fax or other means of electronic communication (CPR, rr 6.3 to 6.9). For individuals suing or being sued in the name of a partnership, the place of service is their usual or last known residence, or the principal or last known place of business of the partnership (r 6.9(2)). Personal service on a partnership was considered at 8.23. **17.29**

Acknowledgment of service

PD 10, para 4.4, provides that where a claim is brought against a partnership: **17.30**

(a) service must be acknowledged in the name of the partnership on behalf of all persons who were partners at the time when the cause of action accrued; and
(b) the acknowledgment of service may be signed by any of those partners, or by any person authorized by any of those partners to sign it.

Disclosure of partners' names

Any party to a claim may make a request to the firm, stating the date when the relevant cause of action accrued, seeking details of the partners at that time. The partners are obliged to provide a 'partnership membership statement' within 14 days of receipt of such a request. This is a written statement of the names and last known places of residence of all the persons who were partners at the time the cause of action accrued (PD 7A, paras 5B.1 to 5B.3). **17.31**

Enforcement

A judgment obtained against a partnership may be enforced against any partnership property within the jurisdiction (PD 70, para 6A.1). Depending on the circumstances, it may also be enforced against a partner who acknowledged service as a partner, or a person who is found by the court to have been a partner at the relevant time (PD 70, paras 6A.2 to 6A.4). **17.32**

Companies

17.33 A registered company must be named using the full registered name. Where its legal status is not apparent from its name, eg, a company limited by guarantee or in liquidation, this must be included in the heading. Service on companies was considered at 8.21 and 8.22.

Representation of companies

17.34 Companies are artificial bodies, so need to act through directors or other duly authorized individuals. Where a director or some other individual appears for a company at a hearing, a written statement must be completed giving the company's full name, its registered number, the status of the representative within the company (such as being a director), and the date and form by which the representative was authorized to act for the company. For example: '22 September 2010: Board resolution dated 22 September 2010'. See PD 39A, para 5.2.

Overseas companies

17.35 A company incorporated outside Great Britain which establishes a place of business in Great Britain must register certain documents and particulars with the registrar of companies. Among these is a list of the names and addresses of persons resident in Great Britain authorized to accept service of process on the company's behalf (see the regulations to be made under the Companies Act 2006, s 1046). Documents may be served on an overseas company by leaving them at, or sending them by post to, the registered address of a person authorized to accept service. If there is no such person, or if service cannot be effected, the documents may instead be left at or sent to any place of business of the company within the United Kingdom (Companies Act 2006, s 1139(2)).

Companies in liquidation

17.36 The Insolvency Act 1986, s 130(2), provides that, when a winding-up order has been made or a provisional liquidator appointed, no proceedings shall be continued against the company or its property except by permission of the court and subject to such terms as the court may impose.

17.37 Once the liquidation is complete, the company involved will be dissolved. Although dissolution puts an end to the company's corporate existence, it may still be possible to bring a claim against it by applying to the court for an order for the restoration of the company to the register under the Companies Act 2006, s 1030. Such applications are made from time to time by claimants claiming damages for personal injuries against dissolved companies which were insured at the time of the accident. Section 1030(2) provides that no order shall be made if it appears 'that the proceedings would fail by virtue of any enactment as to the time within which proceedings must be brought'. In *Re Workvale Ltd* [1992] 1 WLR 416 a company was restored despite the fact that the primary limitation period had expired. The Court of Appeal held it was sufficient that the claimant had an arguable case for the exercise of the court's discretion to 'disapply' the usual three-year limitation period under the Limitation Act 1980, s 33 (discussed further at 7.54ff).

17.38 If a foreign company which is a party to litigation in England ceases to exist in its home jurisdiction but, under the doctrine of universal succession, all its assets and liabilities are transmitted to a successor company (eg, on merger) then the successor company may be substituted as a party under CPR, r 19.2(2): *Toprak Enerji Sanayi AC v Sale Tilney Technology plc* [1994] 1 WLR 840.

Bodies suing in their own names

The following bodies may sue and be sued in their own names: **17.39**

(a) Corporations other than registered companies. Service may be effected on the mayor, chairman, or president, or the town clerk, or other similar officer (PD 6A, para 6.2(2)). It was held in *Kuwait Airways Corporation v Iraqi Airways Co* [1995] 1 WLR 1147, HL, that a junior employee left in charge of the defendant's UK office was a 'similar officer' within the meaning of the predecessor to this provision.
(b) Trade unions and unincorporated employers' associations (Trade Union and Labour Relations (Consolidation) Act 1992, s 10).
(c) London boroughs (London Government Act 1963, s 1), metropolitan districts, and non-metropolitan counties and districts (Local Government Act 1972, s 2).
(d) Most central government departments: see the list published by the Minister for the Civil Service in the Annex to PD 19A. Proceedings involving the Crown are governed by the special code in CPR, Part 66 which gives the Crown a number of procedural privileges not enjoyed by other litigants.
(e) There are numerous quasi-governmental public bodies which are not formal Departments of State. These bodies will usually have an implicit power to bring proceedings to protect their special interests in the performance of their functions (*Broadmoor Hospital Authority v Robinson* [2000] QB 775).

Her Majesty's Attorney-General

In the following situations proceedings are brought in the name of or against the Attorney-General: **17.40**

(a) where a central government department is not mentioned on the Crown Proceedings Act 1947, s 17, list (see the Annex to PD 66);
(b) claims to enforce public rights in the absence of persons who have sustained special damage, such as to abate a public nuisance, or to compel the performance of a public duty, are the prerogative of the Attorney-General and are brought by relator proceedings in the name of the Attorney-General (*Emerald Supplies Ltd v British Airways plc* [2010] Ch 48 at [30]);
(c) in Chancery claims including the administration of a charity (PD 64B, para 4.4) or where a bequest could be construed as being charitable, but is not in favour of a registered charity, the Attorney-General is named to protect the charitable interest; and
(d) applications for vexatious litigant orders (see 17.46–17.47) are made by the Attorney-General.

Foreign parties

Proceedings, including additional claims under Part 20, cannot be brought by a person voluntarily resident in an enemy country. Foreign sovereigns, ambassadors, high commissioners **17.41** and their staffs, and certain other diplomatic staff cannot be sued in this country (State Immunity Act 1978; Diplomatic Privileges Act 1964, etc.). Where proceedings involving foreign parties do not contravene the above rules, it may be necessary to obtain permission to issue and serve proceedings: see Chapter 10. If English proceedings are commenced in a case with a foreign element, it is possible that they may be stayed under the doctrine of *forum non conveniens*: see 10.111ff.

Unincorporated associations

17.42 Social and sporting clubs, social societies, and other unincorporated associations have no separate legal personality and cannot be parties to proceedings in their own right. Where proceedings are necessary there are two main options. These are:

(a) Proceedings in the name of or against an individual member or members. This depends on a member or members being found with personal rights or liabilities which are reasonably similar to those asserted by or against the unincorporated association. The result is that members who are not made parties will have no direct interest in the proceedings.
(b) Representative proceedings (see 17.55–17.58). Such proceedings are usually brought in the name or names of one or more committee members of the association 'on behalf of [themselves] and all other members of the [name of the association]'.

17.43 Where the latter option is used when bringing proceedings, it is permissible for the claimants to state the association's principal address in the originating process rather than the named parties' home addresses (see *Hawkins v Black* (1898) 14 TLR 398, where claimants suing as representatives of the Honourable Society of the Middle Temple were allowed to give the 'Treasury, Middle Temple Lane' as their address).

17.44 It is possible that a proprietary club may be regarded as a partnership, with the result that it may be sued in its 'firm' name, for which see 17.28.

Persons unknown

17.45 Under the pre-CPR rules it was an almost invariable rule that proceedings and orders could only be granted against named parties (*Friern Barnet Urban District Council v Adams* [1927] 2 Ch 25). For some years there has been an exception for claims against trespassers (CPR, r 55.6). In *Bloomsbury Publishing Group Ltd v News Group Newspapers Ltd* [2003] 1 WLR 1633 (affirmed by *South Cambridgeshire District Council v Persons Unknown* (2004) *The Times*, 11 November 2004), the claimant was allowed to join 'person or persons unknown' as second defendants to a claim where an interim injunction was granted restraining disclosure of the contents of or information from a book prior to its publication date. Laddie J said the ban on claims against 'persons unknown' has not survived into the CPR, and that if somebody could be identified clearly enough, a court has the power to grant an injunction.

C VEXATIOUS LITIGANTS

17.46 A small minority of litigants misuse the freedom of access to the courts by launching large numbers of unmeritorious actions or numerous interim applications, causing a great deal of anxiety and trouble to their victims, and usually with little prospect of costs being recovered.

Where it is proved that a litigant 'has habitually and persistently and without reasonable cause' instituted vexatious proceedings or applications, the High Court is given power by SCA 1981, s 42, on the application of the Attorney-General, to make a civil proceedings order. A person subject to such an order is prevented from continuing or commencing or making applications in civil proceedings without the permission of the High Court. If permission is granted, the defendant to the new proceedings may apply to set aside the permission (PD 3A, para 7.9).

In slightly less serious cases the court may make a civil restraint order under CPR, r 3.11. **17.47** These come in three different forms (limited, extended, and general: see r 2.3(1)), and restrain a person from issuing claims or making applications in proceedings or courts defined in the order. They are used in particular where a litigant has a history of issuing claims or making applications which are totally without merit (PD 3C). Where a court strikes out a statement of case, or deals with an application or appeal, which it considers to be totally without merit, that fact must be recorded in the order it makes, and the court must consider whether it should make a civil restraint order (rr 3.3(7), 3.4(6), 23.12, 52.10(6)).

D JOINDER

As a general principle, SCA 1981, s 49(2), provides that every court exercising civil jurisdiction in England and Wales: **17.48**

> shall so exercise its jurisdiction in every cause or matter before it as to secure that, as far as possible, all matters in dispute between the parties are completely and finally determined, and all multiplicity of legal proceedings with respect to any of those matters is avoided.

The rules on joinder are designed to assist in this objective

Generally it is for the claimant to decide which causes of action to pursue in a claim and **17.49** which parties to claim against. A claim is sufficiently constituted if it asserts a single cause of action by a single claimant against a single defendant. If the claimant has more than one cause of action, it is possible to bring a separate claim for each. This will mean paying separate issue fees for each claim, is likely to be more expensive in costs if the factual issues are similar, runs the risk of irreconcilable judgments, and may give rise to problems of *res judicata*. It is obvious that if an accident gives rise to claims in negligence and breach of statutory duty then they should be brought by a single claim. Regarding parties, where rights are vested in persons jointly they must all be joined as claimants (or added as defendants if they will not consent to acting as claimants: CPR, r 19.3). Similarly, where liability is joint but not several everyone jointly liable must be made a defendant. Examples are trustees and personal representatives, joint tenants, and joint contractors. Where liability is several, or where a claimant has related causes of action against different persons, it may be possible to deal with all the causes in a single claim: see 17.51ff. Whether it is prudent to do so depends on a number of factors. For example, some of the possible defendants may be impecunious, or the evidence against some of the possible defendants may be weaker than against others.

Joinder of causes of action

17.50 Pursuing more than one cause of action in the same proceedings is permitted by CPR, r 7.3, which provides:

> The claimant may use a single claim form to start all claims which can be conveniently disposed of in the same proceedings.

Joinder of parties

17.51 It is provided in CPR, r 19.1, that:

> any number of claimants or defendants may be joined as parties to a claim.

17.52 Apart from the operation of the overriding objective, the only restriction against joinder of parties appears to be that there must be a cause of action against each of the parties joined. There is no jurisdiction under the rule to join people purely for the purpose of obtaining disclosure against them (*Douihech v Findlay* [1990] 1 WLR 269). Contrast the situation where there is a cause of action against the defendant, but the primary purpose in joining him is to obtain disclosure, and the special cases of *Norwich Pharmacal* and *Bankers Trust* orders (see 30.02ff and 30.14ff).

17.53 Joint claimants (but not co-defendants) must not have conflicting interests in the litigation, and must act by the same solicitors and counsel.

Discretion to order separate trials

17.54 Even if joinder is technically permissible within the above rules, the court has a discretionary power to order separate trials in order to ensure that the case proceeds quickly and efficiently (CPR, r 3.1(2)(i)).

E REPRESENTATIVE PROCEEDINGS

17.55 It is provided in CPR, r 19.6(1), that:

> where more than one person has the same interest in a claim—
>
> (a) the claim may be begun; or
> (b) the court may order that the claim be continued, by or against one or more of the persons who have the same interest as representatives of any other persons who have that interest.

17.56 By CPR, r 19.6(4), unless the court otherwise directs, any judgment or order made in representative proceedings is binding on all persons represented in the claim, but may be enforced by or against such a person only with the permission of the court.

17.57 According to *Duke of Bedford v Ellis* [1901] AC 1 and *Emerald Supplies Ltd v British Airways plc* [2010] Ch 48 persons will have the 'same interest' if:

(a) they have a common interest; and
(b) they have a common grievance;

(c) the relief sought is in its nature beneficial to all whom the claimant proposes to represent; and
(d) the criteria for inclusion in the class must not depend on the outcome of the claim itself, because in such a case the members of the class cannot be identified as having the same interest when the claim is begun.

It was held that six fruitgrowers were entitled to represent all other fruitgrowers claiming rights over stands at the defendant's market. However, if on analysis it appears that members of the class in fact have competing interests it will not be appropriate to allow representative proceedings (*Smith v Cardiff Corporation* [1954] 1 QB 210, CA). Whether it would be appropriate to allow a derivatives claim against directors depends on the exceptions to the rule in *Foss v Harbottle* (1843) 2 Hare 461 (see *Prudential Assurance Co Ltd v Newman Industries Ltd (No 2)* [1982] Ch 204 and CPR, r 19.9A). Representative defendants may be used, eg, in cases where numerous persons are alleged to be infringing the claimant's copyright (*EMI Records Ltd v Kudhail* [1983] Com LR 280, CA). **17.58**

F REPRESENTATION OF UNASCERTAINED PERSONS

In Part 8 claims to construe wills and trusts, and in proceedings involving the estates of deceased persons or trust property, where any person is an unborn person or cannot be easily ascertained or found, or there is a class of persons, some of whom are not yet born, or cannot easily be found or ascertained, or it would further the overriding objective (such as by saving costs) to make the order, the court may appoint one or more persons to represent those persons (CPR, r 19.7). Applications for representation orders are normally stated on the Part 8 claim form and orders are usually made on the hearing, although it is possible to apply earlier. If an order is made, any judgment is binding on the persons represented. **17.59**

G INTERVENTION

Under CPR, r 19.2(2), a non-party may intervene and be added as a party on the ground either: **17.60**

(a) that the presence of the intervener before the court is desirable to ensure that all matters in dispute can be resolved; or
(b) that there exists a question or issue between the intervener and an existing party which it would be desirable to determine at the same time as the existing claim.

Examples of where the court may exercise its discretion to allow a person to intervene include: **17.61**

(a) Cases where the intervener's legal, property, or financial rights will be directly affected. Thus, the Motor Insurers' Bureau may be allowed to intervene where a defendant in a personal injuries case arising out of a motor accident is untraced or uninsured, because the Bureau will be required to pay any damages awarded (*Gurtner v Circuit* [1968] 2 QB 587, CA).

(b) Where a private claim affects the prerogatives of the Crown or involves questions of public policy the Attorney-General may intervene. An example is *Re Westinghouse Electric Corporation Uranium Contract Litigation* [1978] AC 547, where the question was whether the extraterritorial effect of the US antitrust legislation was an infringement on the sovereignty of the United Kingdom.

(c) Where a member of a class which the claimant claims to represent disputes the claimant's entitlement to represent the class (*McCheane v Gyles (No 2)* [1902] 1 Ch 915).

H CONSOLIDATION

17.62 Closely connected claims may be ordered to be consolidated (CPR, r 3.1(2)(g)). This means that they will continue and be tried as if they were a single claim. Consolidation is likely to be convenient only where there is a strong overlap between two claims, or where there is a risk of irreconcilable judgments. Where there is minimal overlap, consolidation is inappropriate (*Law Debenture Trust Corporation (Channel Islands) Ltd v Lexington Insurance Co* (2001) LTL 12/11/01). In *IXIS Corporate and Investment Bank v Westlb AG* [2007] EWHC 1748 (Comm) the applicant was the claimant in one claim, and the defendant in another claim. The other parties in the two claims were different. Although there was a degree of overlap between the two cases, a trial date had been fixed in one case whereas the other had not reached the defence stage. It was therefore neither fair nor just to order consolidation.

17.63 A consolidation order can be made only if all the claims are before the court at the same time. Therefore applications will need to be made in each of the claims returnable at the same time, or a single application must be issued fully stating the titles of all the claims. If the order is made, one of the claims will be nominated as the lead claim, and consequential directions will be given for the future conduct of the other claims.

17.64 Alternatives to consolidating mentioned in the rules include ordering the claims to be tried by the same judge one after the other, and staying all but one of the claims until after the determination of that one.

I INTERPLEADER

17.65 Interpleader proceedings may be used in two circumstances. In the first, a person holding goods or money, or liable on a debt, is or expects to be sued by two or more persons making adverse claims to the property in question. For example, Nigel leaves a car with a garage for minor repairs. Before the work is completed, the garage receives a claim to the car from Janice who claims to be its true owner. The garage may not know who to deliver the car to, so may protect itself by commencing interpleader proceedings. In essence, interpleader proceedings enable the garage to bring both claimants before the court so that the issue as to ownership of the car can be determined as between Nigel and Janice.

In the second category, an enforcement officer or bailiff who has taken or intends to take goods in execution of a judgment (for which, see 44.08ff) receives a claim to those goods from a person other than the judgment debtor. The claimant is required to make the claim in writing stating the grounds relied on. Notice of the claim must be given to the judgment creditor by the enforcement officer or bailiff, and the judgment creditor must reply to the enforcement officer or bailiff within seven days (High Court, four days in the county courts) admitting or disputing the claim. A judgment creditor who admits the claim is not liable for any fees or expenses incurred after receipt of the notice. Where the judgment creditor disputes the claim, the enforcement officer or bailiff may apply for interpleader relief (RSC, ord 17, r 2, in CPR, Sch 1; CCR, ord 33, rr 1 to 4, in CPR, Sch 2). **17.66**

Mode of application

In the county courts, special claim forms are prescribed (form N88 for use in relation to execution and form N89 for other cases). In the High Court, RSC, ord 17, r 3(1), in CPR, Sch 1, provide that if proceedings have not been commenced against the person in possession of the property the application is made by claim form, and that if proceedings are already pending, the application is made by ordinary notice of application. The application must be served on the existing claimant if made in pending proceedings, and on all claimants to the property. **17.67**

Where the claim is not brought by an enforcement officer or bailiff, the application must be supported by evidence stating that the applicant: **17.68**

(a) claims no interest in the subject matter of the dispute other than for charges or costs;
(b) does not collude with any of the claimants to that subject matter; and
(c) is willing to pay or transfer that subject matter into court or to dispose of it as the court may direct.

A person making a claim in relation to the execution of a judgment debt is required to serve a witness statement or affidavit on the judgment creditor and the enforcement officer or bailiff specifying any money or goods claimed and setting out the grounds of the claim (RSC, ord 17, r 3(6), in CPR, Sch 1; compare CCR, ord 33, r 10, in CPR, Sch 2). **17.69**

Powers of the court on the hearing

On the return day the court has the following powers: **17.70**

(a) if the application was made in pending proceedings, it may order that any interpleader claimant be made a defendant in the claim in addition to or in substitution for the applicant in the interpleader proceedings;
(b) it may order that an issue be stated and tried between the claimants, with a direction as to which of the parties is to be the claimant and which the defendant;
(c) where all the parties claiming the money or property consent, or any of them so requests, or where the question at issue is one of law and the facts are not in dispute, it may determine the question at issue summarily and make an order accordingly on such terms as may be just; and

(d) where a party claiming the money or property fails to attend, it may make an order declaring they are forever debarred from bringing the claim against the applicant in the interpleader proceedings. Such an order does not affect the rights of claimants between themselves.

Where an issue needs to be tried

17.71 Where the issue cannot be determined on the first return day, the court will usually make directions designed to release the stakeholder at the earliest opportunity. If the property in dispute is money it will usually be ordered to be paid into court. If the property is goods, directions will provide for its safe custody or sale under RSC, ord 17, rr 6 or 8, in CPR, Sch 1; or CCR, ord 33, r 9, in CPR, Sch 2. Disclosure takes place with such modifications as may be necessary (RSC, ord 17, r 10). Trial will follow in much the usual way (RSC, ord 17, r 11), but the parties may well agree to trial by a master in order to save costs.

J ASSIGNMENT

17.72 It is provided in CPR, r 19.2(4), that:

> the court may order a new party to be substituted for an existing one if—
> (a) the existing party's interest or liability has passed to the new party; and
> (b) it is desirable to substitute the new party so that the court can resolve the matters in dispute in the proceedings.

17.73 Permission from the court is required if the substitution is sought after the proceedings have been served (r 19.4(1)). An application for a substitution order may be made without notice, but must be supported by evidence (r 19.4(3)). The evidence must show the stage the claim has reached, and set out the details of how the interest or liability was transferred (PD 19A, para 5.2). Where substitution of a claimant is sought, the signed consent of the proposed new claimant must be filed with the court (CPR, r 19.4(4)). If the order is granted, it must be served on all the existing parties and anyone else whom it affects (r 19.4(5)). The court may also make consequential directions regarding service of statements of case and other documents, and for the management of the claim (r 19.4(6)).

K GROUP LITIGATION

17.74 Where a number of claims give rise to common or related issues of fact or law, the court may make a group litigation order ('GLO'): see CPR, rr 19.10 and 19.11. A GLO can be made only with the consent of a senior judge (Lord Chief Justice for QBD claims; Vice-Chancellor for ChD claims, and Head of Civil Justice for county courts): PD 19B, para 3.3. These orders are most likely to be made where a number of claims are made arising out of a disaster (such as a serious public transport accident) or where a number of claims are made against a manufacturer having a common cause (such as claims arising out of the side-effects of a medication). If a GLO is made it will:

(a) contain directions about maintaining a group register of the claims governed by the GLO;
(b) specify the GLO issues to be dealt with under the group litigation and identify the claims which can be managed under the GLO; and
(c) specify the court that will manage the group litigation.

Further directions made under a GLO include directing that group claims must be transferred to the management court; that certain details must be included in particulars of claim to show that the criteria for entry of the claim on that group register have been met; that future claims raising GLO issues must be commenced in the management court; that one or more of the claims shall proceed as test cases; and that the others shall be stayed until further order. Documents disclosed (see Chapter 29) in a GLO claim are treated as disclosed to all the parties on the group register (CPR, r 19.12(4)), unless the court otherwise orders. Any judgment or order made in a claim on the group register is binding on the parties to all the other claims, unless the court otherwise orders (r 19.12(1)(a)). The court may give directions as to the extent that an order or judgment shall bind the parties to claims added to the group register after the order or judgment was made or given (r 19.12(1)(b)). **17.75**

Regarding costs, the usual rule in CPR, r 48.6A, is that where a group litigant is the paying party, he will, in addition to any costs he is liable to pay to the receiving party, be liable for: **17.76**

(a) the individual costs of his own claim; and
(b) an equal proportion, together with the other group litigants, of the common costs, which are the costs incurred in relation to the GLO issues, costs incurred in a test claim, and costs incurred by the lead solicitor in administering the group litigation.

KEY POINTS SUMMARY

- There are technical rules for how litigants must be named. The key is being accurate, so there is no doubt as to who is named. **17.77**
- Special care must be taken with companies, etc. This may simply be a case of ensuring it is correctly identified as 'Limited', 'PLC', 'LLP', etc. Note also that every registered company has a name which is unique to itself, and that many companies have very similar names.
- Initially it is for the claimant to decide who should be parties to a claim, and on which causes of action to raise. Defendants can object if the choice results in inconvenience. Defendants can add parties by making additional claims (see Chapter 18), and outsiders can apply to intervene.
- Certain parties have protections not enjoyed by other litigants. Primary examples are children and protected parties, and to a lesser extent, the Crown.
- Special rules apply to other types of party, such as bankrupts, partnerships, companies, and trusts.

18

ADDITIONAL CLAIMS UNDER PART 20

A NATURE OF ADDITIONAL CLAIMS

18.01 A defendant to an existing claim is permitted, within certain limits, to bring a claim against a third party. Usually, the Part 20 procedure is invoked to pass the defendant's liability on to the third party. A defendant with a cause of action against a third party has the alternative option of commencing separate proceedings. However, it will often be more convenient to bring what is called an 'additional claim' under Part 20, because this tends to keep costs to a minimum, avoids multiple proceedings, and avoids the danger of inconsistent judgments.

18.02 Like an ordinary claim, an additional claim is brought by issuing a claim form in the court office, but a special form has to be used (see figure 18.1). Once served, the third party becomes a party to the claim with the same rights to defend as if duly sued in the ordinary way by the defendant. Although related to the main action between the claimant and the defendant, to a large extent additional claims have a life of their own independent of the main claim.

B RELATED PROCEDURES

A defendant who blames or has a claim against another person needs to decide on the most appropriate way of proceeding. The following situations should be distinguished from each other and from additional claims under Part 20: **18.03**

(a) When the defendant blames someone else and claims to have no personal responsibility for the claimant's damage, the matter should be pleaded in the defence, and an additional claim is inappropriate. Examples are: where a defendant is sued in respect of a road traffic accident and alleges the accident was wholly the responsibility of someone else (claimant, co-defendant, or non-party); where a defendant is sued for breach of contract and alleges he was acting, as known by the claimant, as agent for his principal; and where a defendant is sued for breach of contract and relies on an exclusion clause absolving him from liability in respect of a breach caused by the fault of a subcontractor.
(b) A defendant with a cross-claim against the claimant may either counterclaim in the present proceedings or commence separate proceedings. Counterclaiming usually has the advantage in costs. Counterclaims are discussed at 13.32–13.33. Rather confusingly, the rules governing counterclaims are also found in CPR, Part 20.
(c) A defendant with a cross-claim against the claimant and a non-party either jointly or severally may bring that claim by counterclaim, the non-party being brought in as a third party, a situation considered at 18.05–18.06.
(d) A defendant who blames or has a claim against another party (invariably a co-defendant) may issue a type of additional claim which is unofficially referred to as a contribution notice: see 18.30–18.31. For example, one of several co-defendants sued in respect of a road traffic accident may deny liability, but accept there is a possibility that the court might find him partly to blame for the claimant's injuries. In such circumstances it may be appropriate for the defendant to seek a contribution towards any damages that he may be ordered to pay from some or all of the co-defendants by serving contribution notices.
(e) A defendant who wishes to have some legal or factual question that arises in the existing proceedings brought by the claimant resolved also between him and some non-party has the option of commencing separate proceedings or seeking an order that the non-party be joined to the existing claim under CPR, r 19.2(2)(b) (see 18.18).

C SCOPE OF PART 20

The situations in which a defendant may bring an additional claim are set out in CPR, r 20.2. There are three types of such claims: **18.04**

(a) counterclaims brought by the defendant against the claimant (as discussed at 13.32–13.33), and counterclaims against the claimant and a third party (discussed at 18.05–18.06);
(b) claims brought by the defendant seeking a contribution (see 18.07–18.09), or an indemnity (see 18.10–18.13), or some other remedy (see 18.14–18.15), either from an existing party (also known as a contribution notice), or against a non-party (a true third-party claim); and
(c) claims brought by third parties against other persons (whether parties or not), which are referred to as fourth-party (etc.) proceedings.

Counterclaims against the claimant and another person

18.05 The rules on counterclaims are to be found in Part 20 of the CPR, but they are treated very differently from true third-party claims. The straightforward situation of a defendant counterclaiming against a claimant has already been mentioned. A rather more complex situation is where the defendant wants to make a counterclaim against the claimant and someone else. Before making such a counterclaim the defendant must obtain an order from the court adding the new party to the proceedings as an additional party (CPR, r 20.5). An application for such an order may be made without notice, and a draft of the proposed statement of case must be filed with the application notice (PD 20, para 1.2). The evidence in support of the application has to set out the stage reached in the main claim, the nature of the claim against the new party, and a summary of the facts on which that claim is based.

18.06 If an order is made adding the new party (who is referred to as the 'third party'—see PD 20, para 7.4(c)—although their role is as a defendant to the counterclaim), the court will also give directions for managing the case. These are likely to include provision for service of all statements of case on the third party together with a response pack and a time for responding to the counterclaim, the role the third party can play at trial, as well as the usual matters such as disclosure of documents, witness statements etc. In the title to the proceedings the various parties are described as follows:

Miss CAROL CARTER	Claimant
and	
Mr DAVID DEAN	Defendant
and	
Mr NORMAN PARR	Third Party

As with other counterclaims, a counterclaim against a third party needs to be issued and an issue fee must be paid (together with a fee for adding the third party).

Contribution

18.07 Typically, a right to a contribution arises in situations where there are joint tortfeasors, joint contractors, joint sureties, joint debtors, or joint trustees. Further, by the Civil Liability (Contribution) Act 1978, s 1(1): '...any person liable in respect of any damage suffered by another person may recover contribution from any other person liable in respect of the same damage (whether jointly liable with him or otherwise)'. The 'damage' referred to is damage suffered by the claimant. It is the wrong causing the injury: it is not referring to the injury itself (*Jameson v Central Electricity Generating Board* [1998] QB 323). Note also that the word used is 'damage' rather than 'damages' (see *Birse Construction Ltd v Haiste Ltd* [1996] 1 WLR 675). The 1978 Act extends the reach of the contribution principle to cover cases whatever the legal basis of the liability, whether in tort, breach of contract, breach of trust, or otherwise (see s 6(1)).

18.08 In deciding whether the defendant and the third party are 'liable for the same damage', the words from s 1(1) must be given their natural and ordinary meaning, without any restrictive or expansive gloss (*Royal Brompton Hospital NHS Trust v Hammond* [2002] 1 WLR 1397). The words do not cover damage which is merely substantially or materially similar (*per* Lord Steyn). The defendants in *Royal Brompton Hospital NHS Trust v Hammond* were architects who were sued by the hospital for negligently issuing certificates to building contractors, the effect of which was to give the contractors a defence to a claim the hospital had against the contractors for breach of contract for delays in completing building work. It was held that the hospital's claims against the contractors and against the architects were different, so the architects could not claim a contribution against the contractors. In *Charter plc v City Index Ltd* [2008] Ch 313 it was held that, while a contribution could be claimed for breach of trust to make good the claimant's loss, a claim for an account of profits arising from a breach of trust falls outside s 1(1). If the third party has no liability to the claimant, such as through a term in a contract absolving the third party from liability, the defendant cannot claim contribution from the third party (*Co-operative Retail Services Ltd v Taylor Young Partnership Ltd* [2002] 1 WLR 1419).

The extent of the contribution that may be claimed depends on the nature of the case. In equity, the usual principle is one of equality. In the case of joint tortfeasors contributions are assessed on the basis of causation and blameworthiness. Usually the court attributes a percentage of blame to each party, but in a suitable case can order a party to make a 100 per cent contribution (*Re-Source America International Ltd v Platt Site Services Ltd* (2004) 95 Con LR 1). **18.09**

Indemnity

Whereas a right to a contribution has the effect of sharing the responsibility for the liability to the claimant, the effect of an indemnity is that the defendant can recover the entirety of his liability to the claimant from the third party. Entitlement to an indemnity may arise by contract, under statute, or by virtue of the relationship between the parties. **18.10**

A common instance of indemnities arising by contract is the contract of insurance. A defendant sued in respect of an insured risk could issue an additional claim seeking an indemnity against the insurer, although this will be unnecessary if the insurer accepts liability. More generally, whether in any individual case there is a contractual indemnity depends on the express terms of the contract. **18.11**

An example of a statutory indemnity is provided by the Law of Property Act 1925, s 76(1)(D) and Sch 2, part IV. This relates to a conveyance by way of mortgage of freehold property subject to a rent or of leasehold property. In such a conveyance the statute implies a covenant to indemnify the mortgagee against all claims, damages, and costs incurred by reason of any non-payment of the rent or non-observance of any provision in the lease. **18.12**

Indemnities arising by virtue of the relationship between the parties depend on the substantive law. Thus, a principal is required to indemnify an agent in respect of liabilities incurred by the agent when acting within authority. Similarly, a surety who is sued may claim an indemnity from the principal debtor. Where one of several trustees has misapplied trust funds for personal use it is possible for all the trustees to be liable for breach of trust, but the trustee guilty of misapplying the funds may be required to indemnify the others. **18.13**

Some other remedy

Rule 20.2(1)(b) of the CPR also allows additional claims to be made against third parties seeking 'some other remedy' beyond a contribution or indemnity. On the face of them these are wide words, and clearly some limitation has to be applied, otherwise they would allow **18.14** the defendant to make an additional claim against anyone for any type of remedy whether connected to the original claim or not. Restrictions are to be found in r 20.9, which sets out the factors the court should take into account when considering whether to dismiss an additional claim, or to order it to be dealt with as a separate claim (see 18.20–18.23). These factors include the degree of connection between the original claim and the additional claim, and also whether the remedy sought in the additional claim is substantially the same as the remedy sought in the original claim. Without a substantial connection between the two claims, it will usually be inconvenient for them to be dealt with at the same time.

18.15 One everyday situation is where a claimant seeks damages for personal injuries against the defendant arising out of a road traffic accident. The defendant claims the accident was at least partly the fault of the third party, another driver. In addition to seeking a contribution in respect of the claim against him (see 18.07–18.09), the defendant could also claim damages for his or her own personal injuries as related relief against the third party.

Related question

18.16 As mentioned at para 18.03, point (e), above, there are situations where a defendant wishes to have an issue that arises between him and the claimant decided also as between him and a non-party. One of the reasons for this being desirable is that, unless the issue is decided in proceedings to which all those affected by the decision are parties, those who are not parties to the first claim that goes to final determination will not be bound by the result. They may therefore seek to persuade another court that the issue should be decided differently. A defendant caught in the middle may find that the issue is decided against him, with opposite results, in two sets of proceedings. To avoid this happening it is desirable that all those affected are made parties to the first claim.

18.17 An example of where this may arise is a claim for breach of a construction contract where the defendant is the main contractor. If the defence is that the contract has been frustrated, it may be appropriate for the frustration question to be determined also as between the defendant and any subcontractors. Another example is where a defendant is sued for the delivery up of goods which the claimant alleges have been stolen. If the defence is that one of the exceptions to the *nemo dat* rule applies, the defendant may want that issue determined also as between the defendant and the third party from whom the goods were bought.

18.18 One way of avoiding the risk of irreconcilable judgments is by joining the other persons affected by the issue to the original claim under CPR, r 19.2(2)(b). This allows parties to be joined to existing proceedings on the ground that there is an issue between the defendant and the new party which is connected to the matters in dispute and it is desirable to add the new party to resolve that issue.

18.19 A strict reading of the rules suggests that this is the only procedural method for dealing with related questions, other than by commencing separate claims. Under the old rules, however, related questions were often dealt with by raising them in third-party claims, and many practitioners continue using additional claims for this purpose. Some support for this use of additional claims can be found in r 20.9(2)(c) (see 18.20–18.23), but this arises only when the court is considering whether an additional claim should be allowed to continue. It should not be regarded as increasing the scope of Part 20 (see r 20.2, where the determination of related questions is not mentioned).

Discretion

Even if a claim falls within the grounds set out in CPR, r 20.2, the court retains a discretion whether to allow the additional claim to continue. An objection to the continuation of third-party proceedings should normally be taken when the court considers the future conduct of the case following the filing of the defence to the additional claim. **18.20**

In *Chatsworth Investments Ltd v Amoco (UK) Ltd* [1968] Ch 665, Russell LJ said that the court has to take a wide approach, and must ask whether the additional claim in question accords with the general functions of third-party proceedings. These functions were set out by Scrutton LJ in *Barclays Bank Ltd v Tom* [1923] 1 KB 221, at 224, as follows: **18.21**

(a) to safeguard against differing results, and to ensure the third party is bound by the decision between the claimant and the defendant. If instead separate proceedings are taken, the court hearing the second action is not bound by the decision in the first action;
(b) to ensure the question between the defendant and the third party is decided as soon as possible after the decision between the claimant and the defendant; and
(c) to save the expense of two trials. A party commencing separate proceedings unnecessarily where an additional claim could have been used may be penalized in costs.

These ideas are largely reflected in CPR, r 20.9(2), which provides that, in deciding whether to grant permission to allow an additional claim to be made (where permission is needed: see 18.34), or to dismiss an additional claim at a later stage, the matters the court will take into account include: **18.22**

(a) the degree of connection between the additional claim and the main claim;
(b) whether the defendant is seeking substantially the same remedy as is being claimed by the claimant; and
(c) whether the additional claim raises any question connected with the subject matter of the main claim.

Examples under the old rules include *Chatsworth Investments Ltd v Amoco (UK) Ltd*, where the additional claim was dismissed because the disputes in the original claim and the additional claim were in reality independent of each other. Additional claims have also been dismissed where all the matters arising between the various parties could not be resolved in one trial (*Schneider v Batt* (1881) 8 QBD 701, CA) and where the third party faced difficulties in investigating the alleged facts and a fixed trial date would have had to be vacated (*Courtenay-Evans v Stuart Passey and Associates* [1986] 1 All ER 932). **18.23**

D STATEMENTS OF CASE IN ADDITIONAL CLAIMS

Claim form in additional claims

There are prescribed forms for use in additional claims. Form N211 is used in general litigation, and form N211CC is the equivalent claim form for use in the Commercial Court. **18.24**

Particulars of additional claim

18.25 The title to an additional claim includes details of the court and claim number. It then has a list of all the parties, giving each party a separate description (PD 20, para 7.2). Claimants and defendants in the original claim are called 'claimants' and 'defendants' in the additional claim, a position that does not change even if they acquire an additional procedural status (para 7.3). The first additional party is called the 'third party'. Subsequently added parties are the 'fourth party', 'fifth party', etc., in the order in which they are joined to the proceedings (para 7.4). If an additional claim is brought against more than one party jointly, they are known as the 'first-named third party' and 'second-named third party', etc. (para 7.5). If an additional party ceases to be a party, all the remaining parties retain their existing nominal status (para 7.9).

18.26 The name of the statement of case, which is traditionally set out in tramlines beneath the parties in the title, must reflect the nature of the document and its relation to the parties. For example, a 'defendant's additional claim against third party' is an additional claim brought by the defendant against a single additional party, the third party.

18.27 It is established drafting practice to set out in the opening paragraphs of the particulars of an additional claim summaries of the original and any existing additional claims. These paragraphs also state that copies of the previous statements of case are being served with the present statement of case (in compliance with r 20.12), and (usually) deny the claim made against the drafting party. This provides a context for the rest of the statement of case against the additional party, and also allows certain terms to be defined for use in the rest of the draft.

Subsequent statements of case

18.28 A third party seeking to defend against an additional claim will file and serve a 'third party's defence to defendant's additional claim'. It should be drafted in accordance with the principles discussed for normal defences at 13.28ff.

18.29 In proceedings where there are fourth or subsequent parties, they should be referred to in the text of statements of case, witness statements, etc., by name, suitably abbreviated if appropriate (para 7.11). If parties have similar names, suitable distinguishing abbreviations should be used. An example can be seen in figure 18.1.

Figure 18.1 Third party's additional claim against fourth party

IN THE HIGH COURT OF JUSTICE   Claim No. HQ10X 96789

QUEEN'S BENCH DIVISION

BETWEEN:—

CHEDISTON WHOLESALE LIMITED   Claimant

—and—

LINSTEAD FRUITGROWERS LIMITED   Defendant

—and—

Figure 18.1 *continued*

METFIELD WHOLESALERS LIMITED	<u>Third Party</u>
—and—	
HARVEY & Co (a Firm)	<u>Fourth Party</u>

THIRD PARTY'S ADDITIONAL CLAIM AGAINST FOURTH PARTY

1 In its claim against the Defendant the Claimant claims damages and interest pursuant to the Senior Courts Act 1981, section 35A, for alleged breach of a contract in writing dated 13 June 2008 ('the third contract') for the sale of 500 tonnes of Metfield dessert pears ('the goods'). Copies of the third contract, Claim Form, and Particulars of Claim are served with these particulars of additional claim.

2 The Defendant denies it is liable to the Claimant on the grounds set out in the Defence, a copy of which is served with these particulars of additional claim.

3 In its additional claim against the Third Party, the Defendant claims damages and interest pursuant to the Senior Courts Act 1981, section 35A, for alleged breach of a contract in writing dated 5 June 2008 ('the second contract') for the goods. Copies of the second contract, Additional Claim Form, and Defendant's Additional Claim against Third Party are served with these particulars of additional claim.

4 The Third Party denies it is liable to the Defendant on the grounds set out in the Third Party's Defence to Defendant's Additional Claim, a copy of which is served with these particulars of additional claim. If, contrary to the Third Party's Defence to Defendant's Additional Claim, the Third Party is held liable in whole or in part to the Defendant, the Third Party claims against the Fourth Party ('Harvey &Co')[to be indemnified against] [alternatively, a contribution towards] [its liability, if any, to the Defendant][damages and interest pursuant to the Senior Courts Act 1981, section 35A, for alleged breach of a contract in writing dated 26 May 2008 ('the first contract') for the goods] for the reasons set out below.

5 [Continue with details of the claim against the Fourth Party as in normal particulars of claim.]

Statement of Truth

(I believe) (The Third Party believes) that the facts stated in this third party's additional claim against fourth party are true.

I am duly authorized by the Third Party to sign this statement.

Full name

Name of Third Party's solicitor's firm Boardman, Phipps & Co.

Signed

Dated

E CONTRIBUTION NOTICES

18.30 A defendant who has an additional claim against another defendant may issue a contribution notice under CPR, r 20.6. A defendant must, by r 20.6(2), obtain permission to file and serve a contribution notice unless this is done either:

(a) with that defendant's defence; or
(b) if the claim for the contribution or indemnity is against a defendant added to the claim after the original defence was filed, within 28 days after the new defendant filed its defence.

A contribution notice follows the same general form as described above.

18.31 Issuing a contribution notice inevitably involves incurring costs. If the defendant claims a contribution (and no other relief) under the Civil Liability (Contribution) Act 1978, s 1, against a co-defendant who is jointly liable for the damage sustained by the claimant, the trial judge has power under s 2 of the same Act to apportion liability between them and to order them to contribute between each other even in the absence of a contribution notice. Accordingly, in these circumstances the practice is not to issue a contribution notice, but simply to write to the co-defendant warning of the intention to ask for such an order. Indeed, in such cases, costs will usually be disallowed if a contribution notice is issued: see *Croston v Vaughan* [1938] 1 KB 540, CA. However, if a defendant seeking contribution from a co-defendant in addition wishes to obtain disclosure of documents or to seek further information under Part 18 from the co-defendant, a contribution notice should be served (*Clayson v Rolls Royce Ltd* [1951] 1 KB 746, CA).

F PROCEDURE

Limitation

18.32 For limitation purposes an additional claim is commenced when the claim form in the additional claim is issued by the court. See the LA 1980, s 35(1)(a), CPR, r 20.7(2), and the discussion at 7.39.

Contribution notices

18.33 These may be issued at any time (CPR, r 20.8(2)). They must be served, using the usual rules on service, on the other defendant (r 20.6). Contribution notices are not claim forms, so permission cannot be sought to serve one outside the jurisdiction (see 10.77 and *Knauf UK GmbH v British Gypsum Ltd* [2002] 2 Lloyd's Rep 416). A defendant who acknowledges service is required by r 6.23(1), (2), to provide an address for service within the United Kingdom, and it is this address which is used for serving contribution notices.

Additional claims against non-parties

Permission to issue

Permission to issue an additional claim form against a non-party is not required if it is issued before or at the same time as the defence to the original claim is filed (CPR, r 20.7(3)(a)). Once the defence has been filed, permission must be sought. Permission is usually sought without giving notice to any of the existing parties or anyone else (r 20.7(5)). The application notice has to be supported by evidence setting out the stage the main claim has reached together with a timetable of the claim to date; the nature of the additional claim; the facts on which it is based; and the name and address of the proposed third party (PD 20, para 2.1). Where delay has been a factor an explanation for the delay should be included. The discretionary factors discussed at 18.20–18.23 will be applied on the application for permission (r 20.9). *Borealis AB v Stargas Ltd* (2002) LTL 9/5/02 was a complex multi-party claim. There was a counterclaim against the claimant, and the claimant had sought to bring an additional claim against a non-party, SA, to contribute towards any liability on the counterclaim. The claimant's additional claim was set aside by the House of Lords in March 2001. In September 2001 there was a case management conference and a trial was fixed for July 2002. In March 2002 the defendant, for the first time, sought to bring an additional claim against SA to contribute towards any liability the defendant might have. Although it was held that the defendant had a good arguable case on its additional claim, permission was refused because there was an inexcusable delay of a year after the House of Lords decision, and granting permission would have resulted in the trial being vacated. If the court grants permission, it will at the same time give directions as to service of the additional claim form (r 20.8(3)). **18.34**

Service

The additional claim form must be served within 14 days of being issued (CPR, r 20.8(1)(b)). An additional claim form must be served with a response pack of forms for acknowledging service, admitting, and defending the claim. It must also be served with copies of all the statements of case already served in the proceedings (r 20.12). A copy of the additional claim form must also be served on all other existing parties. **18.35**

The third party becomes a party to the proceedings once served with the additional claim form (r 20.10). **18.36**

Default judgment

The general rules set out in the CPR apply to additional claims (CPR, r 20.3), and these include the provisions relating to default judgments (discussed in Chapter 12). If the third party fails to file a defence or acknowledge service within the 14-day period, the defendant may obtain a default judgment. In an additional claim seeking simply an indemnity or a contribution, default judgment is entered by filing a request for judgment, and the third party will be deemed to admit the additional claim and will be bound by any judgment or decision in the main proceedings which may be relevant to the additional claim. If the additional claim seeks some other remedy against the third party, the defendant will have to apply for judgment, though this may be done without notice (CPR, r 20.11). **18.37**

Case management

18.38 Where a defence is filed to an additional claim, the court will consider the future conduct of the proceedings and give appropriate directions (CPR, r 20.13). In doing so, the court will ensure that, as far as possible, the claim and additional claim are managed together (r 20.13(2)). Usually a case management hearing will be convened (PD 20, para 5.1), with notice being given to all affected parties. The court may use this hearing as a forum for summarily dismissing the additional claim, or for entering summary judgment (para 5.3). More usually it will give directions:

(a) as to the way in which the claims, issues, and questions raised in the additional claim should be dealt with;
(b) as to the part, if any, that the third party will take at the trial of the original claim;
(c) as to the extent to which the third party will be bound by any judgment or decision made in the original claim; and
(d) as to further case management matters, such as disclosure of documents, exchange of witness statements, experts, trial estimates, and the trial date or window.

G RELATION TO THE MAIN CLAIM

18.39 Although it is procedurally connected with the main claim, an additional claim is in many respects a separate claim. Settlement, dismissal, or striking-out of the main claim will not usually terminate third-party proceedings (*Stott v West Yorkshire Road Car Co Ltd* [1971] 2 QB 651, CA). Whether there is any point in continuing an additional claim after the termination of the main claim depends on the nature of the third-party relief claimed. If the defendant claims an indemnity or contribution from the third party and the main claim is dismissed or struck out, the additional claim will end as its basis has gone. However, if the main claim is settled, the question whether the third party must contribute or indemnify remains alive, so the additional claim will continue. Further, if the defendant is claiming related relief, or is seeking the determination of a related question, again the additional claim will continue for that to be resolved.

KEY POINTS SUMMARY

18.40
- An additional claim typically will seek to pass any liability established against the defendant to a third party.
- This is achieved by seeking indemnities, contributions, or related remedies against the third party.
- A third party may in turn seek to pass on its liability to a fourth party, and so on.
- Permission to issue an additional claim is not required if the additional claim is issued before or at the same time as the defendant files its defence.

- An additional claim operates as a separate claim within the original claim. It is commenced by issuing an additional claim form, the defendant's case against the third party must be set out in a statement of case, the third party must be served with a response pack (and must file a defence to the additional claim), and the court will case-manage the additional claim.

19

PART 8 CLAIMS AND PETITIONS

19.01 Part 8 claims and petitions are forms of originating process. They can be used only for commencing certain specific types of proceedings as expressly provided by the statute, procedural rules imposed by statutory instrument, or rules of court governing the type of proceedings in question.

19.02 Often, the provisions requiring a certain type of application to be made by Part 8 claim form or petition will lay down additional procedural requirements. These additional procedural requirements usually specify whether there must be written evidence in support, and may also lay down various matters that must be included in that evidence. Sometimes detailed codes of procedure are laid down for specific types of proceedings. A highly modified Part 8 procedure is laid down for Stage 3 of the RTA protocol for determining the amount of damages in low value RTA cases (see Chapter 6).

19.03 Most types of proceedings which have to be brought by either Part 8 claim form or petition are very narrow and specialized, but some are of great importance. The most important types of proceedings which must be commenced by petition are those for divorce, judicial separation, bankruptcy, and the winding-up of companies. Detailed rules apply to these forms of petition. Petitions for winding-up of companies are considered at 19.15ff by way of illustration.

19.04 In addition, there are a number of miscellaneous forms of originating process referred to in various of the old RSC and CCR provisions preserved in Schs 1 and 2 to the CPR. These are mostly highly specialized and will not be considered further here.

A PART 8 CLAIMS

19.05 The main type of originating process under the CPR is the Part 7 claim form previously discussed in Chapter 8. That type of claim form is used for almost all types of proceedings where there is likely to be a dispute of fact. The issues raised in such claims are defined in written statements of case that have to be served and filed by each party (see Chapter 13).

An alternative procedure for bringing a claim is that laid down in CPR, Part 8. A claim brought under Part 8 has its own 'Part 8 claim form' (form N208). Part 8 claims are for use where there is no substantial dispute of fact (CPR, r 8.1(2)(a)). One example is a claim brought by a trustee or executor seeking the court's ruling on the true meaning of a clause in a trust deed or will. In such a case the court is simply being asked to construe a document, and there should be no dispute of fact. A Part 8 claim can be used for some applications pursuant to statute or statutory instrument. For example, Part 8 claims are used for approval of children's settlements where proceedings have not been commenced (r 21.10(2)). A detailed list of applications under various statutes which must be commenced using the Part 8 procedure, can be found in the table following PD 8A, para 9.4. **19.06**

Issue and service

A Part 8 claim form must be in form N208 (form N208(CC) in the Commercial Court). It must state that Part 8 applies, and must set out the question the claimant wants the court to decide or the remedy sought. If the claim is brought pursuant to statute the relevant statute must be stated (CPR, r 8.2). Otherwise, a Part 8 claim form looks very much like an ordinary claim form. **19.07**

Where it appears to a court officer that a claim has been inappropriately issued using the Part 8 procedure, the claim may be referred to a judge to decide how the case should be dealt with (PD 8A, para 3.4). A procedural judge may at any stage order the claim to continue as a Part 7 claim, and where this happens the court will issue directions and allocate the claim to a track (para 3.5). **19.08**

The normal rules relating to service apply to Part 8 claims: see Chapter 8. **19.09**

Evidence in support and reply

Any evidence the claimant relies upon must be filed and served with the claim form (CPR, r 8.5(1) and (2)). This can be in the form of witness statements or affidavits (PD 8A, para 7.2). After the claim form has been issued and served, any defendants have 14 days to acknowledge service (r 8.3(1)). An acknowledgment of service should be on the prescribed form (form N210). Defendants must file their evidence when they acknowledge service. The claimant may file and serve evidence in reply within 14 days thereafter (r 8.5(5) and (6)). **19.10**

Case management

Part 8 claims are treated as allocated to the multi-track (CPR, r 8.9(c)), although the court may override this and allocate the claim to a track (PD 8A, para 8.2). The court may give directions for managing the claim either immediately on being issued or later, and on an application by a party or of its own initiative (PD 8A, para 6.1). In claims where there is no dispute, such as child and protected party settlements, and in other cases where it is convenient (such as mortgage possession claims), the court will usually fix a hearing date when the claim is issued. Where the court does not fix a date for the hearing, it will give directions for the disposal of the claim as soon as practicable after the defendant has acknowledged service, or **19.11** after the period for acknowledging service has expired (PD 8A, para 6.2). If the case merits it, the court will convene a directions hearing (para 6.4).

B PETITIONS

19.12 As mentioned earlier in this chapter, typical examples of petitions are those for divorce, judicial separation, bankruptcy of individuals, and winding-up of companies. Matrimonial petitions are governed by the Family Proceedings Rules 1991 (SI 1991/1247). Insolvency petitions are governed by the Insolvency Rules 1986 (SI 1986/1925) ('IR 1986') (which are likely to be replaced in the near future). Petitions are almost unknown, especially in the county courts, outside these areas. The procedure to be followed on general-form petitions, such as election petitions under the Representation of the People Acts, is considered in this section.

Form of petitions

19.13 Petitions must be in form N200. A replica of the royal arms must be printed or embossed at the head of the first page. The title identifies the court in which the petition is to proceed. The next line says the petition is brought 'In the matter of' the Act which gives the court power to entertain the proceedings. It may also state it is brought 'In the matter of [an identified trust, settlement, company or property]'. Like a statement of case, the body of the petition states, usually in several numbered paragraphs, the grounds on which the petitioner claims to be entitled to an order from the court. It then includes a concise statement of the relief or remedy claimed. It will conclude with a statement of the names of the persons, if any, who are intended to be served with the petition, and the addresses of the petitioner and the petitioner's solicitors. A High Court petition may be commenced either in London or in one of the Chancery district registries.

Subsequent steps

19.14 On issuing a petition the proper officer of the court will fix a date for the hearing. This may be the final hearing or a directions hearing. Evidence at the hearing is usually taken by witness statement or affidavit.

C WINDING-UP PETITIONS

19.15 Proceedings for the compulsory winding-up of companies are governed by the Insolvency Act 1986 ('IA 1986') and the IR 1986. The IA 1986, s 122(1), sets out the grounds for making an order for the compulsory winding-up of a company, the one most commonly invoked being that the company is unable to pay its debts as they fall due. A company is deemed, by virtue of the IA 1986, s 123, to be unable to pay its debts if, *inter alia*:

(a) It has been served with a statutory demand for a debt exceeding £750 and it has failed to pay or compound for it within 21 days after service. An example of a statutory demand is shown in figure 19.1.

(b) Judgment has been entered against it and execution has been returned unsatisfied in whole or in part.

Figure 19.1 Statutory demand

STATUTORY DEMAND

WARNING

- This is an IMPORTANT document.
- This demand must be dealt with WITHIN 21 DAYS after its service upon the company or a winding-up order could be made in respect of the company.
- Please read the demand and notes carefully.

NOTES FOR THE CREDITOR

- If the creditor is entitled to the debt by way of assignment, details of the original creditor and any intermediary assignees should be given in part B on page 3.
- If the amount of debt includes interest not previously notified to the company as included in its liability, details should be given, including the grounds upon which interest is charged. The amount of interest must be shown separately.
- Any other charge accruing due from time to time may be claimed. The amount or rate of the charge must be identified and the grounds on which it is claimed must be stated.
- In either case the amount claimed must be limited to that which has accrued due at the date of the demand.
- If the signatory of the demand is a solicitor or other agent of the creditor the name of his/her firm should be given.

DEMAND

TO FOTHERGILL (GR) & CO. LIMITED

Address: 31 Jebson Avenue, Swindon, Wiltshire SN1 5ES

This demand is served on you by the creditor:

Name: Roberts (HKT) Machine Tools Limited

Address: 64 Victoria Street, Birmingham B8 9JY

The creditor claims that the company owes the sum of £85,732.90, full particulars of which are set out on page 2.

The creditor demands that the company do pay the above debt or secure or compound for it to the creditor 's satisfaction.

Signature of individual

Name HOWARD KENNETH THOMAS ROBERTS

(BLOCK LETTERS)

Date: 05 May 2010

Position with or relationship to creditor: Director

Figure 19.1 *continued*

I am duly authorized to make this demand on the creditor's behalf.

Address: 7 Burnham Grove, Birmingham B5 7DP

NB THE PERSON MAKING THIS DEMAND MUST COMPLETE THE WHOLE OF THIS PAGE, PAGE 2 AND PARTS A AND B (AS APPLICABLE) ON PAGE 3.

PARTICULARS OF DEBT

11.2.2010 Machine tools. Invoice RB 45782

3 of lathes model GH Mk 456/2;

1 of guillotine model Mk VI;

2 of burners model 3429193.

	£72,964.17
VAT at 17.5%	£12,768.73
	Total £85,732.90

PART A

The individual to whom any communication regarding this demand may be addressed is:

Name HOWARD KENNETH THOMAS ROBERTS

(BLOCK LETTERS)

Address: 7 Burnham Grove, Birmingham B5 7DP

Telephone no. 0121 853 9483

Reference RB 45782

PART B

For completion if the creditor is entitled to the debt by way of assignment

	Name	Date of Assignment
Original Creditor		
Assignees		

HOW TO COMPLY WITH A STATUTORY DEMAND

If the company wishes to avoid a winding-up petition being presented it must pay the debt shown on page 1, particulars of which are set out on page 2 of this notice, within the period of 21 DAYS AFTER its service upon the company. Alternatively, the company can attempt to come to a settlement with the creditor. To do this the company should:

- inform the individual named in Part A above immediately that it is willing and able to compound for the debt to the creditor's satisfaction.

If the company disputes the demand in whole or in part it should contact the individual named in Part A immediately.

Figure 19.1 *continued*

REMEMBER! THE COMPANY HAS ONLY 21 DAYS AFTER THE DATE OF SERVICE ON IT OF THIS DOCUMENT BEFORE THE CREDITOR MAY PRESENT A WINDING-UP PETITION.

NOTE: the company has the right to make an application to the court for an injunction restraining the creditor from presenting or advertising a petition for the winding-up of the company.

A number of persons have *locus standi* to petition for the winding-up of a company. These include the company itself, its directors, or the Secretary of State, but most petitions are brought by unpaid creditors. The petition must be brought in the High Court if the company has paid-up share capital in excess of £120,000, otherwise there is concurrent jurisdiction between the High Court and the county courts (IA 1986, s 117). Certain county courts have been nominated to deal with insolvency matters. Although most companies fall below the £120,000 threshold, in practice a very large proportion of winding-up petitions are commenced in the High Court. High Court petitions are presented in the Companies Court of the ChD. **19.16**

Commencement

The petitioner must pay the court fee (currently £190) and must also deposit the sum of £715 to cover the official receiver's fees. The petition must be in form 4.2 of the IR 1986, Sch 4. A petition based on the statutory demand in figure 19.1 is illustrated in figure 19.2. The petition is filed at court, and an additional copy must be provided for service on the company. The court seals the petition and endorses it with the hearing date. **19.17**

Figure 19.2 Winding-up petition

<u>IN THE HIGH COURT OF JUSTICE</u> No 9452 of 2010

<u>CHANCERY DIVISION</u>

<u>COMPANIES COURT</u>

IN THE MATTER of G R Fothergill & Co. Limited

AND IN THE MATTER of the Insolvency Act 1986

To Her Majesty's High Court of Justice

The petition of H K T Roberts Machine Tools Limited of 64 Victoria Street, Birmingham B8 9JY.

1 G R Fothergill & Co. Limited (hereinafter called 'the company') was incorporated on 4 November 1988 under the Companies Act 1985 as a company limited by shares.

2 The registered office of the company is at 31 Jebson Avenue, Swindon, Wiltshire SN1 5ES.

3 The nominal capital of the company is £5,000 divided into 5,000 shares of £1 each. The amount of the capital paid up or credited as paid up is £3,000.

4 The principal objects for which the company was established are to carry on business as motor component manufacturers and other objects stated in the memorandum of association of the company.

Figure 19.2 *continued*

5 The company is indebted to the Petitioner in the sum of £85,732.90 in respect of machine tools sold and delivered by the Petitioner to the company on 11 February 2010.

6 On 5 May 2010 the Petitioner served on the company by leaving it at the company's registered office a demand requiring the company to pay the said sum, which demand was in the prescribed form.

7 Over 3 weeks have now elapsed since the Petitioner served the said demand, but the company has neglected to pay or satisfy the said sum or any part thereof or to make any offer to the Petitioner to secure or compound the same.

8 The Company is not an insurance undertaking; a credit institution; collective investment undertaking or an investment undertaking providing services involving the holding of funds or securities for third parties as referred to in Article 1.2 of the EC Regulation.

9 The EC Regulation on Insolvency Proceedings apply and these proceedings will be main proceedings as defined in Article 3 of the EC Regulation.

10 The Company is unable to pay its debts.

11 In the circumstances it is just and equitable that the company should be wound up.

The Petitioner therefore prays as follows:

(1) that R Fothergill & Co. Limited may be wound up by the Court under the provisions of the Insolvency Act 1986; or
(2) that such other order may be made as the Court thinks fit.

Note: It is intended to serve this petition on G R Fothergill & Co. Limited.

Statement of Truth

I believe that the facts stated in this petition are true.

I am duly authorized by the petitioner to sign this statement.

Signed: Howard Roberts

Office held: Director of HKT Roberts Machine Tools Limited

(if signing on behalf of a company)
Dated: 6 July 2010

ENDORSEMENT

This petition having been presented to the Court on 7 July 2010 will be heard at the Royal Courts of Justice, Strand, London WC2A 2LL on:

Date: 13 October 2010

Time: 10.30 hours (or as soon thereafter as the petition can be heard).

The solicitor to the Petitioner is:

Messrs Collins, Brown and Heath, of 7 Ingrave Road, Birmingham B5 8EP.

Figure 19.2 *continued*

Telephone: 0121 215 8349

Reference: JGB/R93

Service

Service of the petition must be effected at the company's registered office. Under the IR 1986, r 4.8, service is effected either by: **19.18**

(a) handing the documents to a person who acknowledges himself to be, or who is to the best of the server's knowledge, information, and belief, a director, officer, or employee of the company; or
(b) handing the documents to a person who acknowledges himself to be authorized to accept service on the company's behalf; or
(c) (where no such person as mentioned above is available) depositing the documents in a place at the registered office where they are likely to come to the notice of a person attending the office.

If none of the above methods is practicable, service may be effected at the company's principal place of business, or on one of its directors or officers. Otherwise, an order for substituted service may be sought. **19.19**

After service the petitioner is required to file a certificate of service, which must specify the manner in which service was effected. **19.20**

Advertisement

A petitioning creditor does not petition for his or her personal benefit only, but as a member of the class of creditors. Advertising the petition notifies other creditors and gives them an opportunity to appear at the hearing to support or oppose the making of a winding-up order. It also notifies persons who may have dealings with the company. By virtue of the IA 1986, s 127, if a winding-up order is eventually made any dispositions of the company's property after the date of presentation of the petition are avoided unless validated by the court. For this reason, banks and other traders may refuse to do further business with the company after becoming aware that a petition has been presented. Consequently, advertisement is regarded as a serious step. **19.21**

The advertisement must be in form 4.6 of the IR 1986, Sch 4. It contains details of the company and the hearing date, and invites creditors to give notice of their intention to appear at the hearing to the petitioner's solicitor by 4 p.m. on the day before the hearing. It must appear in the *Gazette* at least seven business days after service of the petition on the company, and at least seven business days before the hearing (IR 1986, r 4.11). **19.22**

Certificate of compliance

No later than 4.30 p.m. on the Friday before the hearing the petitioner must file in court a certificate of compliance in form 4.7 of the IR 1986, Sch 4. This gives the dates of presenting the petition, service, advertisement, and hearing. A copy of the advertisement must be filed with the certificate. **19.23**

Disputes by the company

19.24 There are three courses open to a company which disputes the debt which founds a petition:

(a) apply for an injunction to restrain the petition (and/or advertisement) (for which, see 35.82); or
(b) apply to strike out the petition as an abuse of process (for which, see 22.21); or
(c) file a witness statement in opposition to the petition not less than five business days before the hearing showing at least an arguable dispute that the debt is presently owing.

A genuine dispute over a debt must be resolved by an ordinary QBD claim. If it is not clear that the alleged debt is presently owing, the winding-up petition will be dismissed.

Supporting and opposing creditors

19.25 Supporting and opposing creditors who intend to appear at the hearing should give notice to that effect to the petitioner's solicitors in form 4.9 in the IR 1986, Sch 4, by 4 p.m. on the day before the hearing. Thereafter, the petitioner's solicitors will compile a list of appearances in form 4.10 of the IR 1986, Sch 4, giving details of all creditors who duly gave notice. The list has to be handed in to the court on the day of the hearing (IR 1986, r 4.17).

Hearing

19.26 High Court winding-up petitions are heard by the registrar on Wednesdays in open court. At the hearing the court has power to dismiss the petition, adjourn the hearing conditionally or unconditionally, make interim orders or any other order it thinks fit (IA 1986, s 125). If all the necessary steps have been taken and all the paperwork is in order, an undefended hearing will take a matter of seconds and the winding-up order is made as of right. A typical submission made by counsel for the petitioner is:

> Sir, this is a trade creditor's petition in the sum of £85,732 odd. So far as I am aware the company does not appear and the lists are negative. My application is for the usual compulsory order, main proceedings.

19.27 This submission indicates the nature of the petition, that the company is not represented in court to dispute the debt (see 19.24), that no creditors have given notice of their intention to appear, and that therefore there are no entries on the list of appearances (see 19.25), and asks the court to make a winding-up order in the usual terms (see figure 19.3). The reference to 'main proceedings' is to Council Regulation (EC) No 1346/2000, which provides that the main insolvency proceedings in relation to a debtor in the EU (other than Denmark) should be presented in the EU State where the centre for the debtor's main interests is situated. Paragraphs 8 and 9 of the petition (see figure 19.2) deal with the same Regulation.

19.28 Defects in the procedure or paperwork fall into three categories. Minor defects may be waived by the court and a winding-up order will still be made. Whether a defect is sufficiently minor to be waived is a question of degree, with much turning on whether the company or other creditors could have been prejudiced or misled. For example, a non-misleading typing error might be waived, but a failure to state the method of service in the affidavit of service is likely to lead to an adjournment. If there is a defect which is not capable of remedy, the petition will be dismissed. An example would be advertising the petition before service on the company.

Figure 19.3 Winding-up order

IN THE HIGH COURT OF JUSTICE No 9452 of 2010

CHANCERY DIVISION

COMPANIES COURT

Mr Registrar Young

Wednesday 13 October 2010

IN THE MATTER of G R Fothergill & Co. Limited

AND IN THE MATTER of the Insolvency Act 1986

Upon the petition of a creditor of the company presented to this court on 7 July 2010

And upon hearing counsel for the Petitioner and no one appearing for and on behalf of the said Respondent company

And upon reading the evidence

It is ordered that G R Fothergill & Co. Limited be wound up by this court under the provisions of the Insolvency Act 1986.

And the court being satisfied on the evidence that the EC Regulation does apply and that these proceedings are main proceedings as defined in Article 3 of the EC Regulation.

And it is ordered that the costs of H K T Roberts Machine Tools Limited of the said petition be paid out of the assets of the company.

Dated 13 October 2010

Note: One of the official receivers attached to the court is by virtue of this order liquidator of the company.

Liquidation

If a winding-up order is made, the court notifies the official receiver who becomes the liquidator of the company. If the company has insufficient assets to cover the costs of winding up, the official receiver may apply for an early dissolution under the IA 1986, s 202. Otherwise, the liquidator's task is to get in the assets of the company and to pay its creditors in accordance with their respective priorities. When this has been done, the liquidator files a report with the registrar of companies, and the company is dissolved three months later. **19.29**

20

INTERIM APPLICATIONS

20.01 It is often necessary or desirable to seek orders and directions from the court in advance of the final, substantive, hearing of a case. Directions are made in most defended cases at the track allocation stage, which is usually a few weeks after proceedings are served (Chapter 14). Directions are formal requirements laid down by the court, usually a district judge or master, dealing with matters such as the times by when evidence must be exchanged between the parties and setting a timetable for preparing the case for trial.

20.02 Orders are usually made by district judges and masters, although several types of order can be granted only by judges. An order is a formal decision by the court granting a remedy or relief to a party, usually in the stages before the final determination of a case. Interim orders are also sometimes made after the substantive hearing of a claim, and sometimes the relief granted at trial includes various types of orders. Interim orders, eg, include remedies such as interim injunctions (Chapter 35) and security for costs (Chapter 24); they may impose a sanction on a party who fails to keep to the timetable laid down by a previous order giving directions (Chapter 28) or may grant permission to renew the claim form (Chapter 9) or to amend a statement of case (Chapter 15).

20.03 Orders are usually sought on an application made by one of the parties, and are usually made 'on notice', giving the other side an opportunity to argue against the order being made. However, orders can be made by the court of its own initiative, or on an application listed by the court of its own initiative, and in certain circumstances an application can be made 'without notice' to the other parties.

Parties seeking interim orders or directions on notice have to issue an application notice in form N244, pay a court fee, and often have to provide written evidence in support. In general the documentation must be served on the other parties at least three clear days before the return date (when the application will be heard). Generally, service must be effected by the applicant, although the court may order otherwise (CPR, r 6.21(1)). **20.04**

Once an interim order has been obtained, it must be drawn up, a topic discussed at 41.39ff. **20.05**

A JURISDICTIONAL RULES

Court

In general an application must be made to the court where the claim is presently being dealt with. This will be the court where the proceedings were commenced (CPR, r 23.2(1)), unless: **20.06**

(a) the claim has been transferred (r 23.2(2));
(b) the claim has been listed for trial at another court, in which event the application should be made to the trial court (r 23.2(3)); or
(c) the application is made after judgment, in which event the application may need to be made to the court dealing with enforcement (r 23.2(5)).

An application for pre-action remedies (such as some injunction, freezing injunction, and search order applications) should be made to the court where the substantive proceedings are likely to be brought, unless there is a good reason for applying to another court (r 23.2(4)). Freezing injunctions and search orders must (except in limited circumstances) be applied for in the High Court (County Court Remedies Regulations 1991 (SI 1991/1222)). **20.07**

Judge

Unless otherwise provided for by an Act, rule, or practice direction, interim applications can be dealt with by judges, masters, and district judges (CPR, r 2.4). The most significant exceptions are freezing injunctions and search orders, which are dealt with by High Court judges, and ordinary interim injunctions, which are generally dealt with by a judge who would have jurisdiction to try the claim (see PD 25A, para 1; PD 2B, para 2.2). In the county courts this means that circuit judges will deal with interim injunction applications in most multi-track claims, but district judges may hear such applications in small claims and fast track cases, and also in a number of other types of claim, such as for the recovery of land (PD 2B, para 11.1). High Court masters and district judges may grant interim injunctions by consent, in connection with charging orders and receivers, and in aid of execution. **20.08**

Applications in the Commercial Court are dealt with by a Commercial Judge (PD 58, para 1.2). Applications to the judge in the Chancery Division (judge's applications) are made to the Chancery Applications Judge. An application notice must be used, which should usually state that it is to be heard by 'the Chancery Applications Judge'. **20.09**

In the Chancery and Queen's Bench Divisions there are arrangements for assigning claims to individual masters. Once assigned a claim may be transferred to another master, and the fact **20.10** that a claim has been assigned does not prevent it being dealt with by another master (PD 2B, para 6.2). However, the usual rule is that once a claim is assigned all applications in that claim will be dealt with by the assigned master.

B TIME TO APPLY

20.11 The basic rules are that interim applications should be made as early as possible (PD 23A, para 2.7), but after the party making the application has come on to the court record. For a claimant this is after proceedings are issued, and for a defendant it is after service is acknowledged or a defence is filed (CPR, r 25.2(2)).

C PRE-ACTION INTERIM REMEDIES

20.12 A claimant may exceptionally make an application for an interim order before the commencement of proceedings (see CPR, r 25.2(2)(b)) if either:

(a) the matter is urgent; or
(b) it is otherwise desirable to grant the interim remedy before the claim is brought in the interests of justice.

20.13 The courts may thus entertain pre-commencement applications for urgent interim injunctions (such as some libel cases where publication is threatened within hours of the applicant finding out about the matter) and some applications for freezing injunctions and search orders.

20.14 If a pre-action interim remedy is granted, the court should give directions requiring a claim to be commenced (r 25.2(3)). Rule 25.2(4) points out that such directions need not be given where an order is made for pre-action disclosure or inspection under the SCA 1981, s 33, or the CCA 1984, s 52 (see Chapter 30). This is because such an order may result in the applicant deciding not to bring substantive proceedings at all, as recognized in *Dunning v United Liverpool Hospitals' Board of Governors* [1973] 1 WLR 586. Normally directions for bringing substantive proceedings are made in other types of pre-action order.

D OBLIGATION TO APPLY EARLY

20.15 The obligation to apply early for an interim remedy stems from the overriding objective, which includes ensuring that cases are dealt with expeditiously (CPR, r 1.1(2)(d)).

20.16 Parties should normally notify the court of any intention to apply for interim relief which may dispose of the case or reduce the issues or amount in dispute, when they file their allocation questionnaires (PD 26, para 2.2(3)).

In multi-track cases the appropriate time to consider most forms of interim relief, if possible, is the first case management conference. A party that wishes to invite the court to make directions or orders of types not usually dealt with in case management conferences, and which are likely to be opposed, is required by PD 29, para 5.8, to issue and serve an application returnable at the same time as that set for the case management conference (with a time estimate if it is clear that the time originally allowed for the case management conference will be insufficient, so a fresh date can be fixed). Paragraph 3.8 expressly says that applications in multi-track cases must be made as early as possible so as to minimize the need to change the directions timetable, and an application to vary a directions timetable laid down by the court (perhaps on its own initiative) must ordinarily be made within 14 days of service of the directions (para 6.2). **20.17**

There are some express restrictions in the CPR about when some types of application can be made. Examples include summary judgment, which can be applied for only after the defendant has acknowledged service or entered a defence (r 24.4(1)), and interim payments, where a similar restriction applies (r 25.6(1)). Nevertheless, summary judgment (and striking-out) applications should normally be made on or before filing of allocation questionnaires (PD 26, para 5.3(1)). **20.18**

Of course the need for an interim remedy may not become apparent until some later stage. Rule 25.2(1)(b) of the CPR provides that applications can be made even after final judgment has been given. Where it becomes necessary to make an application shortly before trial, it should be dealt with on the pre-trial review if there will be one (there is a pre-trial review about eight to ten weeks before the trial in some multi-track cases: see 27.28). If this is not possible, another option is to make the application at the start of the trial itself. **20.19**

E APPLICATIONS WITHOUT NOTICE

Procedure on without-notice applications

The general rule is that all applications must be made on notice to the other parties (CPR, r 23.4(1)). It is wrong, eg, to apply for an 'unless order' (see 28.12ff) without notice (*Irwin Mitchell Solicitors v Patel* (2003) LTL 15/4/03). Applications can be made without notice only where permitted by a provision in the CPR, a practice direction, or a court order (r 23.4(2)). For example, applications to extend the time for serving a claim form (renewal of process) are permitted without notice (r 7.6(4)), as are applications for permission to issue additional claims after filing of the defence (r 20.7(5)). These are both examples of applications where the opposite party will not be on the court record when the application is made. Other situations where applications may be made without giving notice to the other parties are: **20.20**

(a) Where the application arises in urgent circumstances, so there is no practical possibility of giving the required minimum of three clear days' notice to the other side. In cases of this sort informal notification should be given to the other parties unless the circumstances require secrecy (PD 23A, para 4.2).

(b) Where a party decides to make an application at a hearing that has already been fixed, but there is insufficient time to serve an application notice. In cases of this sort the applicant should inform the other parties and the court (preferably in writing) as soon as possible of the nature of the application, the reason for it, and then make the application orally at the hearing (PD 23A, para 2.10).

(c) Where the application depends on secrecy for its efficacy, such as most applications for freezing injunctions and search orders.

20.21 Like applications on notice, applications without notice should normally be made by filing an application notice (CPR, r 23.3(1)) in form N244, which must state the order being sought and the reasons for seeking the order (r 23.6). The application notice must also be signed, and include the title of the claim, its reference number, and the full name of the applicant. If the applicant is not already a party it should also give the applicant's address for service. If the applicant wants a hearing, that too must be stated (PD 23A, para 2.1). The application should normally be supported by evidence, which should, in addition to setting out the evidence in support of the relief sought, state the reasons why notice was not given (CPR, r 25.3(3)).

Hearing of without-notice applications

20.22 It follows from PD 23A, para 2.1 that an application without notice can be adjudicated upon with or without a hearing. Hearings of without-notice applications are technically in public (r 39.2), but usually take place in the judge's private room. Advocates have a duty to take a full note on any without-notice hearing, which should be provided to other persons affected by the order (*Cinpres Gas Injection Ltd v Melea Ltd* (2005) *The Times*, 21 December 2005). If the applicant is disappointed with an order made without a hearing, the application can be renewed to a judge at the same level as the one who dealt with the application on the papers (*Collier v Williams* [2006] 1 WLR 1945). The renewed application is dealt with at a hearing.

Duty of full and frank disclosure

20.23 There is a duty of full and frank disclosure in applications made without notice. It extends both to facts within the actual knowledge of the claimant and to facts which would have been known on the making of reasonable inquiries. If the applicant is found to be guilty of material non-disclosure, the order will ordinarily be discharged as of right regardless of the merits on the full facts: *R v Kensington Income Tax Commissioners, ex p Princess Edmond de Polignac* [1917] 1 KB 486. A breach of an advocate's duty to the court may also result in the loss of the order: *Sidhu v Memory Corporation plc* [2000] CPLR 171. Giving only one hour's notice for no good reason, combined with a failure to give full and frank disclosure, resulted in an interim injunction being discharged in *Kulkarni v Milton Keynes Hospital NHS Trust* [2008] LS Law Medical 494.

20.24 The duty is to disclose facts material to the matter being decided on the application. What is material depends on the nature of the application. Facts going to granting permission to serve outside the jurisdiction are not relevant on an application for permission to serve by an alternative method (*Albon (t/a NA Carriage Co) v Naza Motor Trading Sdn Bhd (No 2)* [2007] 1 WLR 2489 at [47]). Proper disclosure requires advocates to identify all relevant documents for the judge, taking the judge to the particular passages in those documents, and ensuring the judge is aware of the legal significance of the material (*R (Lawer) v Restormel Borough Council* [2008] HLR 20).

Full and frank disclosure in freezing injunction applications

Freezing injunction applications are considered in Chapter 36, and are invariably made without notice. To determine whether there has been a material non-disclosure on such an application, it is first necessary to consider the affidavit in support to see whether any adverse facts which the applicant either knew or could have discovered have been omitted. All material facts must appear in the affidavit itself, not in documents exhibited to it (see *National Bank of Sharjah v Dellborg* (1992) *The Times*, 24 December 1992). Secondly, it is necessary to consider whether anything omitted was 'material' in the sense that it would have affected the judgment of a reasonable tribunal when deciding whether to grant the freezing injunction in question: *Lloyds Bowmaker Ltd v Britannia Arrow Holdings plc* [1988] 1 WLR 1337. **20.25**

Facts are material if they are necessary to enable the court to exercise its discretion on a proper basis, bearing in mind the need to act fairly between the parties, the fact that the defendant has not been heard, and the inherent hardship and inconvenience caused by a freezing injunction. There is obviously a distinction between what are material facts and documents for the purposes of the application for the injunction and those which will be relevant at the trial of the claim, and a claimant should not feel it is necessary to exhibit more than a few key documents to the affidavit in support of the application without notice: *National Bank of Sharjah v Dellborg*. Instances where facts have been held to be material include: **20.26**

(a) mistakes in framing the cause of action: *Bank Mellat v Nikpour* [1985] FSR 87;
(b) failing to disclose the existence of proceedings in another country: *Behbehani v Salem* [1989] 1 WLR 723;
(c) failing to disclose weaknesses in the claimant's financial position, which are relevant to the value of the claimant's undertaking in damages and to the undertaking to indemnify third parties; and
(d) misstating the source of information included in the affidavits in support of the without-notice application (*St Merryn Meat Ltd v Hawkins* (2001) LTL 2/7/01, where it was said that the information was obtained using a bugged telephone in the claimants' offices, whereas in fact it was obtained using an interception device at the defendant's home).

The duty to make full and frank disclosure is a continuing one, so the applicant has a duty to bring to the attention of the court any material changes in the circumstances after a freezing injunction has been granted: *Commercial Bank of the Near East plc v A* [1989] 2 Lloyd's Rep 319. The duty continues to the first hearing on notice on most matters, but continues until the final disposal of the claim on the question of the applicant's financial circumstances (*Staines v Walsh* (2003) *The Times*, 1 August 2003). **20.27**

Finding a material non-disclosure is not necessarily the end of the matter. As Lord Denning said in *Bank Mellat v Nikpour*, at 90, 'It is not for every omission that the injunction **20.28** will be automatically discharged. A *locus poenitentiae* may sometimes be afforded.' In deciding what should be the consequences of any breach of duty, it is necessary to take into account all the relevant circumstances, including the gravity of the breach, the excuse or explanation offered, the severity and duration of any prejudice occasioned, and whether the consequences of the breach were remediable and had been remedied. The court must also apply the overriding objective and the need for proportionality: *Memory Corporation plc v Sidhu (No 2)* [2000] 1 WLR 1443, CA. It is important that the rule against material non-disclosure does not itself become an instrument of injustice: *Brink's Mat Ltd v Elcombe* [1988] 1 WLR 1350. The court has a discretion to continue the order or to make a new order on terms (such as on costs or payment of damages) 'if the original non-disclosure was innocent and if an injunction could properly be granted even had the facts been disclosed' (*per* Glidewell LJ in *Lloyds Bowmaker Ltd v Britannia Arrow Holdings plc*). 'Innocence' in this connection depends on whether the omission was made intentionally, but, of course, there are degrees of culpability. Much depends on the quality of the facts that have not been disclosed. Some facts are so important that the court will readily infer that the non-disclosure was deliberate. Others, being material but not central to the application, will be more readily forgiven. See the judgment of Woolf LJ in *Behbehani v Salem*.

Orders made without notice

20.29 Where an order is made against a person without notice, CPR, r 23.9(2), provides that the order must be served on that person together (unless the court orders otherwise) with the application notice and any evidence in support. The order must, by virtue of r 23.9(3), contain a statement to the effect that the person against whom it is made has a right to apply to set aside or vary the order within seven clear days of service of the order. Applications to set aside or vary are normally made back to the judge who made the original order.

F APPLICATIONS WITH NOTICE

Documentation

20.30 An interim application should normally be made by filing an application notice stating the order being sought and the reasons for seeking it (CPR, rr 23.3(1) and 23.6). The application notice must be signed, and should include the title of the claim, its reference number, and the full name of the applicant. If the applicant is not already a party it should also give the applicant's address for service. If the applicant wants a hearing, that too must be stated (PD 23A, para 2.1). The application should normally be supported by written evidence setting out the facts justifying the relief sought (CPR, r 25.3(2)). The notice must be filed at court together with the prescribed fee, and served as soon as possible thereafter (see 20.45). The standard form of application notice is form N244: see figure 20.1 (form N244(CC) is used in the Commercial Court: see figure 21.1).

Figure 20.1 Form N244 Application notice

Application notice

For help in completing this form please read the notes for guidance form N244Notes.

Name of court	Northampton County Court
Claim no.	10NN98264
Warrant no. (if applicable)	
Claimant's name (including ref.)	PHILLIPPA MYERS
Defendant's name (including ref.)	NIGEL STANIFORD
Date	23.6.2010

1. What is your name or, if you are a solicitor, the name of your firm?

   Messrs Wells, Wells & Co

2. Are you a ☐ Claimant ☐ Defendant ☑ Solicitor

   ☐ Other *(please specify)*

   If you are a solicitor whom do you represent? Defendant

3. What order are you asking the court to make and why?

   (1) That the judgment entered on 9 June 2010 be set aside
   (2) That the costs of this application be provided for.

   On the ground that the Defendant has a meritorious defence to this claim, and this application is made promptly after the judgment was entered.

4. Have you attached a draft of the order you are applying for? ☐ Yes ☑ No

5. How do you want to have this application dealt with? ☑ at a hearing ☐ without a hearing ☐ at a telephone hearing

6. How long do you think the hearing will last? 0 Hours 20 Minutes

   Is this time estimate agreed by all parties? ☐ Yes ☑ No

7. Give details of any fixed trial date or period: None

8. What level of Judge does your hearing need? District Judge

9. Who should be served with this application? Claimant

N244 Application notice (05.08) 1

Figure 20.1 *continued*

10. What information will you be relying on, in support of your application?

☑ the attached witness statement

☐ the statement of case

☐ the evidence set out in the box below

If necessary, please continue on a separate sheet.

Statement of Truth

(I believe) (The applicant believes) that the facts stated in this section (and any continuation sheets) are true.

Signed ______________________ Dated ______________

Applicant('s Solicitor)('s litigation friend)

Full name ______________________

Name of applicant's solicitor's firm ______________________

Position or office held ______________________

(if signing on behalf of firm or company)

11. Signature and address details

Signed ______________________ Dated ______________

Applicant('s Solicitor)('s litigation friend)

Position or office held Assistant Solicitor

(if signing on behalf of firm or company)

Applicant's address to which documents about this application should be sent

40 Station Road,
Corby,
Northamptonshire

Postcode NN15 8EX

If applicable	
Phone no.	01536 403 3278
Fax no.	01536 403 3608
DX no.	87933 Corby 1
Ref no.	9271/PDL

E-mail address ______________________

2

On receipt of the application notice the court may either notify the parties of the time and date of the hearing, or notify them that it proposes to consider the application without a hearing (PD 23A, para 2.3). 20.31

Evidence in support

The general rule is that applications for interim remedies must be supported by evidence (CPR, r 25.3(2)), but evidence in support is not required when applying for case management directions. Some judgement is required from lawyers when deciding whether they need evidence for their applications. PD 23A, para 9.1, specifically mentions that, as a practical matter, the court will often need to be satisfied by evidence of the facts that are relied on in support of, or for opposing, an application. 20.32

Four options are available to the applicant regarding the format of the evidence to be used in support of an interim application. They are: 20.33

(a) To provide sufficiently full factual information in support of the application in the body of the application notice itself (CPR, rr 22.1(3) and 32.6(2)(b)), and include a statement of truth in the notice. This is a signed statement that the applicant believes that any facts stated in the application are true (r 22.1(4) and (6); PD 22, para 2.1).
(b) To rely on the facts stated in a statement of case filed in the proceedings, provided it contains a statement of truth (CPR, r 32.6(2)(a)). This will usually have been previously served and filed, and if so there is no need to reserve or refile (r 23.7(5)).
(c) To rely on witness statements, each with statements of truth signed by the witnesses (rr 22.1(4) and 32.6(1)). The witness statements used may be ones drafted specifically for the interim application, or it may be possible to rely on the main witness statements that have been disclosed on the substantive issues in the case. The general rule is that any fact that needs to be proved at any hearing other than the trial should be proved by the evidence of witnesses in writing (r 32.2(1)), and it is further provided by r 32.6(1) that at hearings other than the trial evidence is to be by witness statement unless the court, a practice direction, or any other enactment requires otherwise. Consequently, evidence by witness statement is the primary means of adducing evidence at interim hearings. The format of witness statements is considered in Chapter 32.
(d) To rely on affidavit evidence. Rule 32.15(2) allows a witness to give evidence by affidavit at any hearing other than a trial if he or she chooses to do so. This also allows the use of affirmations (PD 32, para 1.7). However, using affidavits may result in the loss of the additional costs over and above the cost of using an ordinary witness statement. There are situations where affidavit evidence is required either by specific court order, or by virtue of a practice direction or other enactment. Affidavits are required, eg, in support of applications for search orders, freezing injunctions, orders to require an occupier to permit another to enter land, and applications for an order against a person for contempt of court. The format of affidavits is considered in Chapter 32.

The evidence in support must be filed at court, although the exhibits should not be filed unless the court otherwise directs (PD 23A, para 9.6). The evidence (including exhibits) in support must be served with the application (CPR, r 23.7(3)). If the evidence in support does not contain a statement of truth the usual order is to allow a limited period to refile the document duly verified. Setting aside an order based on unverified evidence was regarded as 20.34

disproportionate in *Colliers International Property Consultants v Colliers Jordan Sdn Bhd* [2008] 2 Lloyd's Rep 368.

20.35 Any evidence which a respondent wishes to rely upon must be served as soon as possible, and in any event in accordance with any directions the court may have given (PD 23A, para 9.4). The court will not take kindly to respondents who serve evidence in response at the last minute, particularly if this results in a wasted hearing and a need to adjourn.

20.36 In the Commercial Court, evidence in answer to an application must be filed and served within 14 days after service of the application notice and evidence in support (PD 58, para 13.1). Any evidence in reply must be filed and served seven days thereafter. If the hearing of the application is likely to last more than half a day, these periods are extended to 28 and 14 days respectively (para 13.2).

Bundles of documents

20.37 Sometimes it is appropriate to prepare bundles of documents for interim applications. Often it is sufficient to rely on the application notice, written evidence, and exhibits without the need to go to the expense of compiling formal bundles. Sometimes the statements of case and evidence on the substantive issues should be included, and sometimes previous orders and correspondence. Bundles should be prepared for applications whenever more than 25 pages are involved (*Chancery Guide*, para 7.9; *Queen's Bench Guide*, para 7.11.7) although it must be said that even in straightforward applications it is easy to exceed this. Copies of authorities should be included in the bundles (*Queen's Bench Guide*, para 7.11.9). In the Commercial Court, an application bundle must be filed by 1 p.m. one clear day before the hearing (two clear days for 'heavy' applications lasting more than half a day). The case management bundle must also be available at the hearing (*Commercial Court Guide*, paras F5.4, F6.4, F11).

20.38 All parties should cooperate in agreeing bundles, and should make clear whether they are simply agreeing which documents should be included in the bundles, or whether they are also agreeing that the included documents are to be treated as evidence of the facts stated in them and/or that the documents to be included are agreed to be authentic.

20.39 For Chancery applications, the applicant should ensure that one copy of the bundle is lodged at court at least three clear days before a hearing by order (those lasting more than two hours), or by 10 a.m. on the day before the hearing (shorter applications), whereas Queen's Bench masters are usually given their bundles at the hearing (*Chancery Guide*, para 7.15; *Queen's Bench Guide*, para 7.11.8). All parties and the court must be provided with identical bundles.

Skeleton arguments

20.40 Skeleton arguments are not often used on interim applications before district judges, masters, and registrars, but are usually required for hearings before High Court judges and are often used for interim hearings before county court judges. Even before High Court judges they are not insisted on if the application is likely to be short or if it is so urgent that preparation of a skeleton argument is impracticable. For substantial applications skeletons should be delivered to the court two clear days before the hearing. For shorter applications, or urgent applications, they may be delivered the day before the hearing or at the hearing.

In the Commercial Court, for ordinary applications lasting up to half a day, skeleton arguments must be filed by 1 p.m. on the day before the hearing. For heavy applications, the applicant must file and serve its skeleton argument and any *dramatis personae* two clear days before the hearing, and the respondent one clear day before the hearing (*Commercial Court Guide*, paras F5.5, F6.5). A chronology is often also useful. Copies of authorities must be provided with the skeleton arguments (para F13.1). Each party must provide the court with a reading list by 1 p.m. on the day before the hearing (para F8). **20.41**

A skeleton argument should provide a concise summary of the party's submissions on the issues raised by the application, and should be as brief as the nature of the case allows. There is a general ceiling of 20 pages of double-spaced A4 paper. It should cite the main authorities relied upon, be divided into numbered paragraphs, be paginated, make use of abbreviations (such as 'C' for claimant, 'A/345' for page 345 of bundle A) and give dates in the form '28.4.2010'. It should not go so far as to argue the case on paper. In more substantial applications it should have a reading list for the judge of the core documents. **20.42**

Skeleton arguments are often accompanied by chronologies. Good chronologies have short entries for the material events, phrased in a non-contentious way to promote agreement with the other parties. **20.43**

Draft orders

Paragraph 12 of PD 23A says that except in the most simple applications the applicant should bring to the hearing a draft of the order sought. The standard form N244 contains a question asking whether a draft of the order sought is attached. If the order is unusually long or complex, the draft should be supplied on disk as well as on hard copy (PD 23A, para 12.1). Preparing draft orders is particularly important in all types of interim injunction applications, and whenever the order is at all complicated or unusual. Draft orders are also useful if a detailed directions timetable needs to be laid down. For almost all other types of application the short particulars of the orders sought normally inserted in the N244 will be sufficient. **20.44**

Service

The normal rule is that the applicant will serve the application notice, any draft order and evidence in support, although the court may decide to deal with service (CPR, r 6.21(1)). There is no requirement to refile or reserve documents which have already been filed or served at an earlier stage (CPR, r 23.7(5)). **20.45**

Service must be effected as soon as possible after the application is issued, and in any event not less than three days before it is to be heard (r 23.7(1)). In accordance with the general rules on computing time in r 2.8, this means clear days (excluding the date of effective service and the date of the hearing), and, because the period is less than five days, also excluding weekends, bank holidays, Christmas, and Good Friday. Thus, take, eg, a hearing which is listed for Wednesday 6 October 2010. Assume the solicitor for the applicant decides to serve the application and evidence in support by document exchange. The three clear days before **20.46** the hearing are Friday 1, Monday 4, and Tuesday 5 October 2010. The documents must therefore be deemed to be served no later than Thursday 30 September. As this is a business day, and given the provision in r 6.26 that documents transmitted by DX are deemed to be served on the second day after being left at the document exchange, the latest the documents could be left at the document exchange would be Tuesday 28 September 2010.

20.47 Where it is not possible to serve within this time limit the circumstances may justify an application without notice (see 20.20), or an application may be made to abridge time under r 3.1(2)(a). Abridging time may be appropriate where a defendant is repeating behaviour previously adjudicated upon (*Secretary of State for the Environment, Food and Rural Affairs v Meier* [2009] 1 WLR 2780 at [82]).

Disposal without a hearing

20.48 Rule 23.8 of the CPR provides that the court may deal with an interim application without a hearing if either:

(a) the parties agree that the court should dispose of the application without a hearing (the applicant's view on whether there should be a hearing should be stated in the application notice); or

(b) the court does not consider that a hearing would be appropriate.

20.49 A party dissatisfied with any order or direction made without a hearing is able to apply to have it set aside, varied, or stayed (r 3.3(5)(a)). Such an application must be made within seven days after service of the order, and the right to make such an application must be stated in the order (r 3.3(5)(b) and (6)).

Hearings by telephone

20.50 Active case management in accordance with the overriding objective includes dealing with cases without the parties needing to attend court, and by making use of technology (CPR, r 1.4(2)(j) and (k)). Both may be achieved by dealing with some applications by telephone conference calls, which is specifically provided for by r 3.1(2)(d). The rule enables the court to hold a hearing by telephone or any other method of direct oral communication, so other means of electronic communication may be used as technology develops. A telephone hearing is most commonly used in a 'telephone conference-enabled court', and is most frequently used for case management hearings and interim hearings estimated to take no more than an hour.

20.51 If an application is to be heard by telephone, the application notice must be served at least five clear days before the hearing (PD 23A, para 4.1A). The 'designated legal representative', who is usually the solicitor for the applicant (para 6.1), is responsible for setting up the telephone hearing. In multi-track claims, and in other cases if the court so directs, the designated legal representative is required to file and serve a case summary and draft order by 4 p.m. at least two days before the hearing (paras 6.11 and 6.12). Any other documents relied upon must be filed and served by the party relying on them within the same time limit (para 6.13). The conference call for the hearing should be fully connected at least ten minutes before the time for the hearing (para 6.10(5)), with the call being set up with the designated legal representative (and counsel) being called first, then the other parties and their counsel, and finally the judge (para 6.10(4)). No party or representative may attend in person unless every other party agrees (para 6.9).

Orders made on the court's own initiative

Rule 3.3(1) of the CPR gives the court a power to make orders of its own initiative. This power is intended to be exercised for the purpose of managing the case and furthering the overriding objective (see r 3.1(2)(m)). Orders made in this way must, by virtue of r 3.3(5)(b) and (6), include a statement that parties who are affected may apply within seven days (or such other period as the court may specify) after service for the order to be set aside, varied, or stayed. Failing to make an application to vary or set aside is likely to result in the court assuming the orders or directions made were correct in the circumstances then existing (PD 28, para 4.2(2), for fast track cases; PD 29, para 6.2(2), for multi-track cases). **20.52**

There is a related power enabling the court to make orders on its own initiative after giving the parties an opportunity of making representations on the matter. Where the court proposes to make such an order it will specify a time within which the representations must be made (CPR, r 3.3(2)). **20.53**

Hearings convened on the court's own initiative

In addition, the court has a power to fix a hearing for the purpose of deciding whether to make any order it might propose to make of its own initiative. For example, in order to reduce the issues in a case it might convene a summary judgment hearing. Unless some other period is specified in the rules regarding notice, any application convened by the court must be notified to parties likely to be affected by the proposed order at least three clear days in advance (CPR, r 3.3(3)). **20.54**

G INTERIM HEARINGS

Procedure at hearings

The general rule is that interim hearings will be in public (CPR, r 39.2; European Convention on Human Rights, art 6(1)). In practice the public do not attend most hearings before masters and district judges, even if notionally they are heard in public, because most interim applications are conducted in chambers, with limited facilities for accommodating the public. If a large number of people wish to attend, the judge may adjourn to a larger room or court (PD 39A, para 1.10). **20.55**

In addition to dealing with the specific application that has been made, the court may wish to review the conduct of the case as a whole and give any necessary case management directions. The parties will therefore have to be prepared for this and be able to answer any questions the court may ask (PD 23A, para 2.9). The procedural judge will keep, by way either of **20.56** a note or a tape recording, brief details of all proceedings, including a short statement of the decision taken at each hearing (PD 23A, para 8).

20.57 In most courts applications are given specific hearing times, and are called in one at a time. The main exceptions are judge's applications in the Chancery Division. For these the judge sitting has a discretion as to the order in which applications are heard. However, urgent applications and applications affecting the liberty of the subject are given priority, followed by ineffective applications (those which are to be adjourned or have settled), then effective applications usually in order of their time estimates, with the shortest applications being heard earliest. Applications estimated for more than two hours are usually made applications by order.

Resolving disputes on the written evidence

20.58 The general rule is that at interim hearings the procedural judge has to accept the veracity of the written evidence filed by the parties. Where there is a conflict between the written evidence relied upon by opposing sides, there are four alternative approaches that may be adopted by the court:

(a) leave the resolution of the conflict until trial. As stated in *Shyam Jewellers Ltd v Cheesman* (2001) LTL 29/11/01, choosing between witnesses is the function of the trial judge. This means that the dispute is usually resolved in favour of the claim going to trial, or in favour of refusing relief that depends on disputed facts, or in favour of preserving the status quo;

(b) order the cross-examination of the disputed witnesses at the interim hearing under CPR, r 32.7. This power is rarely used because it involves delay and additional expense;

(c) go behind a disputed witness statement. This is done where there is some inherent improbability being asserted or where there is extraneous evidence contradicting it. It has also been held that it is permissible for the judge to disregard the contents of written evidence which lacks credibility (*National Westminster Bank plc v Daniel* [1993] 1 WLR 1); or

(d) determine the disputed issue (without rejecting the evidence as incredible) applying a 'good arguable case' standard of proof (*Re H Minors (Sexual Abuse): Standard of Proof* [1996] AC 563; *Bols Distilleries v Superior Yacht Services Ltd* [2007] 1 WLR 12). The good arguable case standard of proof is a lower test than the trial standard of proof, which is on the balance of probabilities. It is intended to reflect the limitations in deciding between competing versions inherent in an interim hearing with written evidence, and the need to avoid applications degenerating into mini-trials (*WPP Holdings Italy SRL v Benatti* [2007] 1 WLR 2316). While the good arguable case test is the general rule, there are in fact many different formulas used, with different meanings, throughout civil procedure. A higher standard of 'a much better argument on the material available' is insisted on where the matter is effectively determinative of a disputed issue as to whether the court has jurisdiction (*Canada Trust Co v Stolzenberg (No 2)* [1998] 1 WLR 547 at 555, approved by the House of Lords [2002] 1 AC 1; *Cherney v Deripaska* [2007] 2 All ER (Comm) 785 at [20]).

20.59 In choosing between these options the court will apply the overriding objective. In this context this includes avoiding interim applications becoming mini-trials, and finding the best way of resolving the dispute commensurate with its importance and not prejudicing either side.

Non-attendance

The court may proceed in the absence of any party to an application (CPR, r 23.11(1)). When this happens the court has a general discretion to relist the application, which is exercised by taking into account factors such as the reasons for the absence, the interests of justice, any undue delay since the missed hearing, whether either party has acted on the order, and whether there is a real prospect of the court changing the order (*Riverpath Properties Ltd v Brammall* (2002) *The Times*, 16 February 2002). **20.60**

H SUMMARY DETERMINATION OF INTERIM COSTS

Where an interim application is disposed of in less than a day (which will cover the vast majority of such applications), the court will normally make a summary assessment of the costs of the application immediately after making its order (PD Costs, para 13.2). In the absence of a specific order to the contrary, costs assessed summarily are payable within 14 days of the order (CPR, r 44.8). To assist the judge in assessing costs the parties are required by PD Costs, para 13.5, to file and serve not less than 24 hours before the interim hearing signed statements of their costs for the interim hearing in form N260 setting out: **20.61**

(a) the number of hours claimed;
(b) the hourly rate claimed;
(c) the grade of fee earner;
(d) the amount and nature of disbursements;
(e) the solicitor's costs for attending or appearing at the hearing;
(f) counsel's fees; and
(g) VAT on the above.

Any failure to file or serve a statement of costs, without reasonable excuse, will be taken into account in deciding the costs order to be made on the application. **20.62**

In cases where costs are awarded in any event, the court should make a summary assessment there and then, but may decide to give directions for a further hearing to deal with the costs (PD Costs, para 13.8). Summary assessment will be unnecessary in cases where the parties have agreed the amount of costs (para 13.4). The court must not make a summary assessment of the costs of a publicly funded party (para 13.9). Nor may it make a summary assessment of the costs of a party under a disability, unless that party's solicitor has waived the right to further costs (para 13.11(1)). These last two sentences do not prevent the court making a summary assessment of any interim costs which it decides are payable by an assisted party or a party under a disability (paras 13.10 and 13.11(2)), although the court should not make such costs payable immediately (in the case of an assisted paying party) unless it also makes a determination under the AJA 1999, s 11. **20.63**

KEY POINTS SUMMARY

20.64
- Interim applications without notice are exceptional, and are broadly restricted to urgent applications and applications made before a defendant has been served with the main proceedings.
- Applications are made by issuing an application notice (N244 or N244(CC)), and have to be supported by written evidence.
- If an application is made without notice, the applicant has a duty of full and frank disclosure.
- A respondent (or non-party) who is unhappy with an order made without notice can apply to the judge who made the order to set aside or vary the terms of the order.
- In the High Court, and particularly in the Chancery Division and Commercial Court, there are obligations to provide application bundles, skeleton arguments, chronologies, and reading lists.
- Summary assessment of costs is normally undertaken in interim applications lasting up to one day.

21

SUMMARY JUDGMENT

In cases where the defendant fails to defend it is usually possible to enter a default judgment (see Chapter 12). Where there is no real defence, a defendant may go through the motions of defending in order to delay the time when judgment may be entered. It is possible for defendants to put up the pretence of having a real defence to such an extent that some cases run all the way through to trial before judgment can be entered. The CPR provide several ways of preventing this happening. The court can use its power to strike out (see Chapter 22) to knock out hopeless defences, such as those that simply do not amount to a legal defence to a claim. Entering summary judgment is a related procedure, and is used where a purported defence can be shown to have no real prospect of success and there is no other reason why the case should be disposed of at trial. Indeed, PD 3A, para 1.7, recognizes that there will be cases where applications for summary judgment and striking out may be sought in the alternative. **21.01**

21.02 The procedure for entering summary judgment is not limited to use by claimants against defendants. Defendants may apply for summary judgment to attack weak claims brought by claimants. Further, summary judgment can be used by the court of its own initiative to perform the important function of stopping weak cases from proceeding. The procedure can also be used for the purpose of obtaining a summary determination of some of the issues in a case, thereby reducing the complexity of the trial.

A TIME FOR APPLYING FOR SUMMARY JUDGMENT

21.03 A claimant may apply for summary judgment only after the defendant has filed either an acknowledgment of service or a defence (CPR, r 24.4(1)). By analogy with r 25.2(2)(c), a defendant likewise can apply for summary judgment only after either filing an acknowledgment of service or a defence. Where the claimant has failed to comply with a relevant pre-action protocol, an application for summary judgment will only be entertained after the period for filing a defence has expired (PD 24, para 2(6)).

21.04 Applications for summary judgment should normally be made in the period between acknowledgment of service and filing of the applicant's allocation questionnaire (PD 26, para 5.3(1)). This is normally the appropriate time, because, if the other side has no realistic prospects of success, entering summary judgment early prevents unnecessary costs being incurred. Question D in the allocation questionnaire (see figure 14.1) specifically asks whether there is any intention of making an application for summary judgment. If for any reason the application is not made before allocation, there is still a general obligation to apply as soon as it becomes apparent that it is desirable to do so (PD 23A, para 2.7).

Summary judgment applications made before filing the defence

21.05 If the application is made after filing an acknowledgment of service, but before filing of the defence, there is no need to file a defence before the hearing (CPR, r 24.4(2)). At that stage the court will give directions, which will include providing a date for filing the defence.

Summary judgment applications made before allocation to a track

21.06 PD 26, para 5.3(2), provides that where a party makes an application for summary judgment before the claim has been allocated to a track the court will not allocate the claim before hearing the application. If a party files an allocation questionnaire stating an intention to apply for summary judgment but has not yet made an application, the judge will usually direct the listing of an allocation hearing (para 5.3(3) and (4)). The summary judgment application may be heard at the allocation hearing if the application notice has been issued and served in sufficient time.

Hearings fixed by the court of its own initiative

21.07 The rules specifically mention that the court may fix a summary judgment hearing of its own initiative (CPR, r 24.4(3)), and doing so may further the overriding objective, which includes deciding promptly which issues need full investigation and trial, and accordingly disposing summarily of the others (r 1.4(2)(c)). If the court is minded to make use of this power, it is most likely to do so on the initial scrutiny at the track allocation stage shortly after filing of the defence. If the court uses the power, it will not allocate the case to a track, but instead it will fix a hearing, giving the parties 14 days' notice and informing them of the issues it proposes to decide (PD 26, para 5.4).

B DEFENDANT'S APPLICATION: NO DEFAULT JUDGMENT

Where a defendant has applied for summary judgment against a claimant, the claimant cannot obtain a default judgment until the summary judgment application has been disposed of (CPR, r 12.3(3)(a)). **21.08**

C EXCLUDED PROCEEDINGS

Under CPR, r 24.3(2), an application for summary judgment cannot be brought against the defendant in: **21.09**

(a) residential possession proceedings against a mortgagor or a tenant or person holding over whose occupancy is protected by the Rent Act 1977 or the Housing Act 1988; or
(b) admiralty claims *in rem*.

In applications against claimants there are no excluded types of proceedings (CPR, r 24.3(1)).

D PROCEDURE

The general rules on making interim applications (see Chapter 20) apply on making an application for summary judgment, with certain refinements. The application is made by application notice (see figure 21.1), which must be supported by evidence (CPR, r 25.3(2)). The evidence in support is most likely to be contained either on page 2 of the application notice, or in a separate witness statement. It is a risky course to rely on facts set out in a statement of case without more detailed witness statement evidence, particularly in support of an alleged oral agreement (*Korea National Insurance Corporation v Allianz Global Corporate and Specialty AG* [2007] 2 CLC 748). The evidence in support of an application by a claimant will have to state a belief that there is no defence with a reasonable prospect of success and should give details of the background facts and exhibit relevant documentation. On an application by the defendant there may or may not be a filed defence. If not, clearly the evidence will have to explain why the claim is unlikely to succeed, and will probably have to go into the background in some detail. **21.10**

Figure 21.1 Application for Summary Judgment

Application Notice

- You must complete Parts A **and** B, **and** Part C if applicable
- Send any relevant fee and the completed application notice to the court with any draft order, witness statement or other evidence
- It is for you (and not the court) to serve this application notice

You should provide this information for listing the application

Time estimate 1 (hours) 30 (mins)

Is this agreed by all parties? Yes ☑ No ☐

Please always refer to the Commercial Court Guide for details of how applications should be prepared and will be heard, or in a small number of exceptional cases can be dealt with on paper.

In the	**High Court of Justice** **Queen's Bench Division** **Commercial Court** **Royal Courts of Justice**
Claim No.	2010 Folio 33884
Warrant no. (if applicable)	
Claimant(s) (including ref.)	Secure Bank Plc
Defendant(s) (including ref.)	Landmark Traders Grimstead Limited
Date	

Part A

1. Where there is more than one claimant or defendant, specify which claimant or defendant

(The claimant)(The defendant)[1]

Secure Bank Plc

2. State clearly what order you are seeking (if there is room) or otherwise refer to a draft order (which must be attached)

intend(s) to apply for an order (a draft of which is attached) that[2]

summary judgment be entered in favour of the Claimant under CPR, Part 24, for the total sum claimed, interest and costs

3. Briefly set out why you are seeking the order. Identify any rule or statutory provision

because[3]

the claimant believes that on the evidence the Defendant has no real prospect of successfully defending the claim and the claimant knows of no other compelling reason why the case should be disposed of at trial.

TAKE NOTICE that if the Defendant wishes to reply on written evidence at the hearing, it must file the written evidence at court and serve copies on the Claimant's solicitors at least 7 days before the summary judgment hearing.

The court office at the Admiralty & Commercial Registry, Royal Courts of Justice, Strand, London WC2A 2l1

is open from 10am to 4.30 pm Monday to Friday. When corresponding with the court please address forms or letters to the Clerk to the Commercial Court and quote the claim number.

N244 (CC) - w3 Application Notice (4.99) *Printed on behalf of The Court Service*

Figure 21.1 *continued*

Part B

(The claimant)(The defendant)[1] wishes to rely on: *tick one:*

the attached (witness statement)(affidavit) ☑ (the claimant)(the defendant)'s[1] statement of case ☐

evidence in Part C overleaf in support of this application ☐

Signed		**Position or office held** (if signing on behalf of firm, company or corporation)	
	(Applicant)('s litigation friend) ('s solicitor)		

4. If you are not already a party to the proceedings, you must provide an address for service of documents

Address to which documents about this claim should be sent (including reference if appropriate)[4]

			if applicable
Messrs Pamsoms 18 High Street, London		Tel. no.	0207 782 4647
		fax no.	
		DX no.	
Postcode	EC1A 6FB	e-mail	2010 Folio 33884

Part C

Claim No. 2010 Folio 33884

(Note: Part C should only be used where it is convenient to enter here the evidence in support of the application, rather than to use witness statements or affidavits)

(The claimant)(The defendant)[1] wishes to rely on the following evidence in support of this application:

Figure 21.1 *continued*

Statement of Truth

*(I believe)(The applicant believes) that the facts stated in this application notice are true

*I am duly authorised by the applicant to sign this statement

Full name..

Name of*(Applicant)('s litigation friend)('s solicitor)

....

Signed [ ]

*(Applicant)('s litigation friend)('s solicitor)

Position or office held (if signing on behalf of firm, company or corporation) [ ]

Date [ ]

**delete as appropriate*

21.11 Instead of the usual notice period of three clear days which applies to most types of interim application, the notice period in applications for summary judgment is 14 clear days (r 24.4(3)). The respondent must file and serve any evidence in reply at least seven clear days before the hearing (r 24.5(1)). The application notice must inform the respondent of this time limit (PD 24, para 2(5)). If the applicant wishes to respond to the respondent's evidence, the further evidence must be served and filed at least three clear days before the hearing of the application (r 24.5(2)). The 14-day period of notice may be varied by practice directions (r 24.4(4)) and has been shortened for specific-performance claims (see 21.55).

21.12 In cases where the hearing is fixed by the court on its own initiative, all parties must file and serve their evidence at least seven clear days before the return day, and if they want to respond to their opponents' evidence, that must be done at least three clear days before the return day (r 24.5(3)).

21.13 On an application by a claimant for summary judgment, the court cannot in effect reverse the tables on the claimant and dismiss the claim under PD 24, para 5.1, without the claimant being put on notice (usually through a cross-application) and being given an opportunity to address the court and place before it any relevant material (*P&O Nedlloyd BV v Arab Metals Co (No 2)* [2007] 1 WLR 2288).

E ORDERS AVAILABLE

Range of orders

Orders available on a summary judgment application include: 21.14

(a) giving judgment on the claim;
(b) striking-out or dismissal of the claim;
(c) dismissal of the application;
(d) making a conditional order; and
(e) granting summary judgment subject to a stay of execution.

Test for entering summary judgment

Rule 24.2 of the CPR provides: 21.15

The court may give summary judgment against a claimant or defendant on the whole of a claim or on a particular issue if—
(a) it considers that—
 (i) that claimant has no real prospect of succeeding on the claim or issue; or
 (ii) that defendant has no real prospect of successfully defending the claim or issue; and
(b) there is no other compelling reason why the case or issue should be disposed of at a trial.

Burden of proof

Although CPR, r 24.2 is not explicit about the burden of proof on an application for summary judgment, it appears to be settled by *ED and F Man Liquid Products Ltd v Patel* [2003] CPLR 384, that the burden rests on the applicant to prove that the respondent's case has no real prospects of success. 21.16

Standard for entering summary judgment

An application for summary judgment is decided applying the test of whether the respondent has a case with a real prospect of success, which is considered having regard to the overriding objective of dealing with the case justly. The question whether there is a real prospect of success is not approached by applying the balance of probabilities standard of proof required at trial (*Royal Brompton Hospital NHS Trust v Hammond* [2001] BLR 297). At the other end of the range, applying a test of whether the claim is arguable will also give grounds for appeal because this is too lax (*Sinclair v Chief Constable of West Yorkshire* (2000) LTL 12/12/00). In order to have a real prospect of success a case has to carry some degree of conviction, and has to be better than merely arguable (*Bee v Jenson* [2007] RTR 9). 21.17

In *Swain v Hillman* [2001] 1 All ER 91, Lord Woolf MR said that the words 'no real prospect of succeeding' did not need any amplification as they spoke for themselves. The word 'real' directed the court to the need to see whether there was a realistic, as opposed to a fanciful, prospect of success. The phrase does not mean 'real and substantial' prospect of success. 21.18

Nor does it mean that summary judgment will be granted only if the claim or defence is 'bound to be dismissed at trial'. If the defendant's evidence, taken at its highest, shows a distinctly improbable defence, it is right to enter summary judgment (*Akinleye v East Sussex Hospitals NHS Trust* [2008] LS Law Med 216). Lord Woolf MR went on to say in *Swain v Hillman* that summary judgment applications have to be kept within their proper role. They are not meant to dispense with the need for a trial where there are issues which should be considered at trial. If the respondent's case has some prospects of success, summary judgment should be refused (*Cotton v Rickard Metals Inc* [2008] EWHC 824 (QB)).

Defence on the merits

21.19 On an application for summary judgment by a claimant, the defendant may seek to show a defence with a real prospect of success by setting up one or more of the following:

(a) a substantive defence, eg, *volenti non fit injuria*, frustration, illegality, etc.;
(b) a point of law destroying the claimant's cause of action;
(c) a denial of the facts supporting the claimant's cause of action; or
(d) further facts answering the claimant's cause of action, eg, an exclusion clause, or that the defendant was an agent rather than a principal.

Weak defences

21.20 Most summary judgment applications are decided on the basis of the facts which are not disputed by the respondent, together with the respondent's version of the disputed facts (*HRH Prince of Wales v Associated Newspapers Ltd* [2008] Ch 57). This does not mean that filing a witness statement will prevent summary judgment being entered. This is because there are, as discussed at 20.58, cases where the court will go behind written evidence which is incredible, and the court will also disregard fanciful claims and defences. A claim or defence may be fanciful where it is entirely without substance, or where it is clear beyond question that the statement of case is contradicted by all the documents or other material on which it is based (*Three Rivers District Council v Bank of England (No 3)* [2003] 2 AC 1). There is no rule of practice that summary judgment cannot be given if a case is weak despite there being some documentary evidence in support (*Miller v Garton Shires* [2007] RTR 24). The judge should take into account the filed witness statements and also consider whether the case is capable of being supplemented by evidence at trial (*Royal Brompton Hospital NHS Trust v Hammond* [2001] BLR 297).

21.21 In *United Bank Ltd v Asif* (2000) LTL 11/2/00, CA, the court considered the defence put forward, and decided it was fanciful and no more than a sham, and so summary judgment was entered. This might be the case where there are no primary facts to support the alleged defence (*P & S Amusements Ltd v Valley House Leisure Ltd* [2006] EWHC 1510 (Ch)). There may be no real prospect of success if the defence consists entirely of admissions and bare denials (*Broderick v Centaur Tipping Services Ltd* (2006) LTL 22/8/06). In *Penningtons v Abedi* (1999) LTL 13/8/99 there had been ongoing litigation in which the defendant had advanced a series of defences which had each been shown to be false. An application was made for summary judgment, and it was held that the defendant's conduct of the litigation was such that there was no realistic prospect of her successfully defending the claim. In *ED and F Man Liquid Products*

Ltd v Patel [2003] CPLR 384, a defence which might have had a real prospect of success was destroyed by clear, written admissions made by the defendant.

In *Public Trustee v Williams* (2000) LTL 10/2/00 the claimant, as executor of a deceased's estate, sought to recover the sum of £74,000 which was received by one of the defendants and used by her to buy a house. The evidence of the recipient filed in response to an application for summary judgment was at its best unclear and at its worst confusing about where she thought the money had come from. However, there was no clear evidence that the money had come from the estate, and it was held that it was not a suitable case for summary judgment. A stronger case was *Architects of Wine Ltd v Barclays Bank plc* [2007] 2 Lloyd's Rep 471. In this case the key issue was a matter of banking practice, and the burden of proof as a matter of substantive law on that issue rested on the defendant bank. It was held that, where the only evidence on a summary judgment application on that issue was the bank's own evidence of its practices, it was impossible to say that the bank had no real prospect of success in its defence, so summary judgment was refused. 21.22

Mini-trials

Summary judgment hearings should not be allowed to degenerate into mini-trials of disputed facts (*Cotton v Rickard Metals Inc* [2008] EWHC 824 (QB)). They are simply summary hearings to dispose of cases where there is no prospect of success. Without allowing the application to become a mini-trial, there are occasions when the court has to consider fairly voluminous evidence before it can understand whether there is a real prospect of success (*Miles v ITV Networks Ltd* (2003) LTL 8/12/03), provided this will not require prolonged argument (*Three Rivers District Council v Bank of England (No 3)* [2003] 2 AC 1, see 21.27) 21.23

Negligence claims

Although there is nothing in principle preventing a claimant from applying for summary judgment in claims seeking damages for negligence, such cases invariably involve disputed factual issues, so it is rare for a court to find there is no real defence once liability is denied. An exception was *Dummer v Brown* [1953] 1 QB 710, where summary judgment was given against the defendant, a coach driver, who had previously pleaded guilty to dangerous driving in respect of the accident giving rise to the claim. Even if there is a conviction summary judgment may be refused if there are good reasons for believing that the conviction was erroneous (*McCauley v Vine* [1999] 1 WLR 1997). 21.24

Libel claims

Summary judgment will not be granted in a libel claim where there is a material issue of fact between the parties, because such issues must be decided by the jury (SCA 1981, s 69, and *Safeway plc v Tate* [2001] QB 1120). However, where the evidence, taken at its highest, was such that no properly directed jury could reach a verdict contended for by one of the parties, summary judgment is available (*Alexander v Arts Council of Wales* [2001] 1 WLR 1840). 21.25

Claims involving reprehensible conduct

21.26 Summary judgment will almost always be inappropriate where there are allegations of deceitful, dishonest, or unlawful conduct (*Espirit Telecoms UK Ltd v Fashion Gossip Ltd* (2000) LTL 27/7/00). The high standard of proof required at trial in fraud claims means that it will be difficult to succeed on a summary judgment application in such a case (*Allied Dunbar Assurance plc v Ireland* (2001) LTL 12/6/01).

Complex claims and points of law

21.27 Complex claims, cases relying on complex inferences of fact, and cases with issues involving mixed questions of law and fact where the law is complex, are likely to be inappropriate for summary judgment (*Three Rivers District Council v Bank of England (No 3)* [2003] 2 AC 1; *Arkin v Borchard Lines Ltd (No 2)* (2001) LTL 19/6/01). The simpler the case, the easier it is for the court to find the claim or defence to be fanciful or contradicted by the documentary evidence. Complex claims are unlikely to be capable of being resolved in this way. Summary disposal is also inappropriate if the case is in a developing field of law (*Brooks v Commissioner of Police of the Metropolis* [2005] 1 WLR 1495 at [3]).

21.28 Where a clear-cut issue of law is raised by way of defence in an application for summary judgment, the court should decide it immediately. This is so even if the question is, at first blush, of some complexity and therefore will take some time to argue fully (see Lord Greene MR in *Cow v Casey* [1949] 1 KB 474). Not deciding a case once full argument has been addressed to the court on the issue will result in the case going to trial where the argument will be rehearsed again, with consequent delay and unnecessary expense. Likewise, where the point at issue is one of the construction of contractual documents, the court will decide the point on the summary judgment application, provided it is relatively straightforward (*Coastal (Bermuda) Ltd v Esso Petroleum Co Ltd* [1984] 1 Lloyd's Rep 11). Although CPR, r 24.2, expressly says that the court can give summary judgment on particular issues, the court may consider that where there are connected issues, some of which should go to trial, summary judgment should be refused on the others as well (*Redevco Properties v Mount Cook Land Ltd* (2002) LTL 30/7/02).

Partial defence

21.29 Where the defendant has a defence to only part of the claim the most natural order is to grant judgment for the part of the claim against which there is no defence, and to dismiss the application as to the balance.

Cross-claims

21.30 Cross-claims fall into three categories. Where the only answer to the claim is a cross-claim, the nature and effect of the three types are as follows:

(a) Cross-claims unconnected with the claim. Here, summary judgment should be entered. An example is *Rotherham v Priest* (1879) 41 LT 558, where the claimant claimed arrears of rent, and the defendant counterclaimed in libel. It was held that the counterclaim was totally foreign to the claim, so summary judgment was given to the claimant. The result would be the same under the CPR.

(b) Counterclaims linked to the claim. The appropriate order is to enter judgment subject to a stay of execution pending trial of the counterclaim. In *Drake and Fletcher Ltd v Batchelor* (1986) 130 SJ 285, Sir Neil Lawson said that in considering whether to grant a stay of execution, 'the question is whether the two contracts are so closely linked that it would be fair and equitable to deprive the [claimant] of the fruits of its judgment until resolution of the counterclaim'. The judge said there were three matters which needed to be considered:
   (i) The degree of connection between the claim and the counterclaim.
   (ii) The strength of the counterclaim. The weaker it was, the weaker the case for granting a stay.
   (iii) The claimant's ability to satisfy any judgment on the counterclaim. Any doubt on this matter strengthened the case for granting a stay.

(c) Set-offs. Where a counterclaim amounts to a set-off it is a defence to the claim and any summary judgment application should be dismissed, provided the value of the set-off is at least equal to the value of the claim. Where a set-off is not worth as much as the claim, the appropriate order is for summary judgment for the undisputed balance. The nature of set-offs is considered below.

Set-offs

The following are established set-off situations: **21.31**

(a) Mutual debts. By virtue of the eighteenth-century Statutes of Set-off, mutual debts owed between the claimant and the defendant can be set off against each other. There is no need for the transactions giving rise to the debts to be connected other than through the parties. They need not be debts, strictly so called, but may sound in damages provided they are capable of being ascertained with precision at the time of the application (*Morley v Inglis* (1837) 4 Bing NC 58, applied in *Axel Johnson Petroleum AB v MG Mineral Group AG* [1992] 1 WLR 270).

(b) Sale of goods. By virtue of the Sale of Goods Act 1979, s 53(1), a buyer may set off counterclaims for breach of the statutory implied conditions about satisfactory quality, fitness for purpose, and correspondence to description against a claim by the seller for the price.

(c) On a claim for the price of services, eg, where a builder is suing for the price of building work done, the defendant can set off a counterclaim for damages for poor workmanship in respect of the contract the claimant is suing on (*Basten v Butler* (1806) 7 East 479).

(d) Arrears of rent. Where a landlord brings an action claiming arrears of rent, the tenant is allowed to set off a counterclaim for damages against the landlord for breach of a covenant in the lease in respect of which the landlord is claiming (*British Anzani (Felixstowe) Ltd v International Marine Management (UK) Ltd* [1980] QB 137, not following *Hart v Rogers* [1916] 1 KB 646, confirmed by *Agyeman v Boadi* (1996) 28 HLR 558).

(e) Equitable set-off. Although it is clear that an equitable set-off is a defence, and hence is a defence to a claim, it is difficult to be precise about the ambit of the doctrine. Nevertheless, 'one thing is clear—there must be some equity, some ground for equitable intervention, beyond the mere existence of a cross-claim' (*per* Lord Wilberforce in *Aries Tanker Corporation v Total Transport Ltd* [1977] 1 WLR 185). Perhaps the leading case is *Hanak v Green* [1958] 2 QB 9, where the claimant sued her builder for breach of contract for failing to complete certain building works at her home. The defendant sought to set off counterclaims for a *quantum meruit* for extra work done outside the original contract, for damages for loss sustained through the claimant's refusal to admit his workmen, and for damages for trespass to his tools. It was held that all three cross-claims were equitable set-offs, because the courts of equity before the Judicature Acts would have required the claimant to take the cross-claims into account before insisting on her own claim. Broadly, what is required is a sufficient degree of connection between the two transactions such that the one should not be enforced without taking the other into account (*Dole Dried Fruit and Nut Co v Trustin Kerwood Ltd* [1990] 2 Lloyd's Rep 309). It does not matter whether or not either or both claims are unliquidated (*Axel Johnson Petroleum AB v MG Mineral Group AG*). Over-payments of rent can be set off against claims for rent as an equitable set-off (*Fuller v Happy Shopper Markets Ltd* (2001) *The Times*, 6 March 2001). A former partner was held in *Hurst v Bennett* (2001) *The Times*, 15 March 2001 to be unable to set off claims for money allegedly owed to him on the taking of partnership accounts against the claim of certain of the former partners to be indemnified against expenses they had incurred on the ground of lack of mutuality.

21.32 Mutual debts amount to set-offs whether or not the relevant transactions are connected, but they must be liquidated. Set-offs in categories (b) to (d) above involve liquidated claims and unliquidated cross-claims arising from the same transaction. Equitable set-offs can arise where both the claim and the cross-claim are unliquidated, but there must be a sufficient connection between the two. Although set-offs usually arise between the immediate parties to a transaction, this is not always the case. A defendant who has guaranteed payment of a debt owed to the claimant by a principal debtor can rely on set-offs and cross-claims available to the debtor. This principle extends to certain types of bonds entered into in building contracts (whereby the party giving the bond promises to pay a specified sum to the claimant if one of the contractors fails to perform) provided the bond is construed as a guarantee: see *Trafalgar House Construction (Regions) Ltd v General Surety and Guarantee Co Ltd* [1996] AC 199.

21.33 It is open to the parties to a contract to exclude any right to set-off by an express term to that effect (*Hong Kong and Shanghai Banking Corporation v Kloeckner & Co AG* [1990] 2 QB 514), but it is possible that such a term may be unreasonable and rendered ineffective by virtue of the Unfair Contract Terms Act 1977, as happened in *Stewart Gill Ltd v Horatio Myer and Co Ltd* [1992] QB 600.

The cheque rule

21.34 Cheques are one form of bill of exchange. Where goods or services are paid for by cheque, two contracts are entered into by the parties. The first contract is the underlying contract for the sale of goods or for the provision of services. The second contract is contained in the cheque, whereby the drawer of the cheque undertakes to pay the payee the sum stated. If a cheque is dishonoured, the seller has the option of suing on the underlying contract or on the cheque. If the seller sues on the underlying contract, the buyer is entitled to rely on any set-off that may be available in respect of that contract by way of defence to an application for summary judgment. However, if the seller sues on the cheque, the buyer is permitted to raise only defences relating to the cheque itself. The reason probably stems from the unconditional nature of a bill of exchange, as provided by the Bills of Exchange Act 1882, s 3(1). As

Lord Wilberforce said in *Nova (Jersey) Knit Ltd v Kammgarn Spinnerei GmbH* [1977] 1 WLR 713, bills of exchange 'are taken as equivalent to deferred instalments of cash'. Therefore English law does not allow cross-claims or defences to be made. The rule is regarded as being of considerable importance to the business community, and the courts will not 'whittle away [the] rule of practice by introducing unnecessary exceptions to it under influence of sympathy-evoking stories' (*per* Sachs LJ in *Cebora SNC v SIP (Industrial Products) Ltd* [1976] 1 Lloyd's Rep 271). The cheque rule applies to:

(a) cheques and bills of exchange;
(b) direct debits (*Esso Petroleum Co Ltd v Milton* [1997] 1 WLR 938);
(c) letters of credit (*SAFA v Banque du Caïre* [2000] 2 All ER (Comm) 567); and
(d) performance bonds (*Solo Industries v Canara Bank* [2001] 2 All ER (Comm) 217).

The cheque rule does not apply in the context of statutory demands (*Hofer v Stawson* [1999] 2 BCLC 336, a case which turns on the wording of the Insolvency Rules 1986, r 6.5(4)). **21.35**

There are some exceptional cases where summary judgment will not be given in a claim on a bill of exchange (see 21.39–21.45). Before looking at these it is necessary to consider the nature of the claimant's title to the bill of exchange. **21.36**

Types of holder of a bill of exchange

Under the Bills of Exchange Act 1882 there are four types of holder of a bill of exchange. A mere holder is a person in possession of the bill. Although a mere holder can sue on the bill and give a valid discharge (s 38), any claim is prone to be defeated for want of consideration. A holder for value is a person in possession of a bill who has given consideration sufficient to support a simple contract, or who derives title directly or indirectly from a previous holder who gave value for the bill (s 27). A holder for value cannot be defeated on the ground of want of consideration. A holder in due course is broadly a holder of a complete and regular bill who gave value for it in good faith without notice of any defect in the title of the person who negotiated it (s 29). A holder in due course obtains title to the bill free from equities and defects in the title of the transferor. The fourth type of holder is one who derives title through a holder in due course, and who broadly has all the rights of a holder in due course (s 29(3)). **21.37**

An application for summary judgment by a mere holder will always be defeated by a plea of want of consideration, whereas an application by a holder in due course should always succeed as such a holder takes free of equities. If the claimant's title as a holder in due course is challenged by the defendant, judgment will be given for the claimant only if the claim to be a bona fide holder for value is supported by unchallenged or unchallengeable contemporary documents (*Bank für Gemeinwirtschaft AG v City of London Garages Ltd* [1971] 1 WLR 149). Holders for value are the most problematic category. They are also the most numerous, given that an immediate party to a bill cannot be a holder in due course (*R E Jones Ltd v Waring and Gillow Ltd* [1926] AC 670). **21.38**

Fraud, duress, and illegality

To amount to a defence against a holder for value, an allegation of fraud, duress, or illegality must be supported by evidence. A mere allegation in the defendant's written evidence is **21.39** insufficient (*Bank für Gemeinwirtschaft AG v City of London Garages Ltd* [1971] 1 WLR 149). Such a defence will not, however, avail against a holder in due course (see the Bills of Exchange Act 1882, s 30(2)).

No consideration

21.40 As explained above, there will be a defence where the claimant is a mere holder who has given no consideration for the bill sued on. A total failure of consideration arises where a buyer lawfully rejects goods sold, the buyer being entitled to recover the price from the seller. Again summary judgment should be refused. Likewise, a liquidated partial failure of consideration is a defence *pro tanto* (*Thoni GmbH & Co KG v RTP Equipment Ltd* [1979] 2 Lloyd's Rep 282).

Misrepresentation

21.41 A misrepresentation made to induce the defendant to give a cheque will be a defence to a claim on the cheque, but an allegation that the claimant made a misrepresentation about the quality of the subject matter of the underlying contract (such as the goods in a sale of goods) will not be a defence to a claim on a cheque. Following *SAFA v Banque du Caïre* [2000] 2 All ER (Comm) 567 and *Solo Industries v Canara Bank* [2001] 2 All ER (Comm) 217, a distinction needs to be drawn between:

(a) cases where there is a misrepresentation by a beneficiary which was made directly to induce the execution of the bill of exchange (or other payment obligation covered by the cheque rule). Provided there is a real prospect of establishing the misrepresentation, summary judgment on the cheque (or other payment obligation) should be refused; and
(b) cases where an allegation of misrepresentation is in reality an allegation relating to the underlying contract of services or sale on which the payment obligation is based. In these cases summary judgment should be entered on the cheque (or other payment obligation), with no stay of execution. The courts need to be particularly astute in ensuring the cheque rule is not diluted by treating cases in this category as ones affecting the cheque or other payment obligation covered by the cheque rule.

International trade

21.42 Irrevocable letters of credit are treated as cash and must be honoured. If the bank refuses to honour such a transaction, the court will grant summary judgment to the claimant (*Power Curber International Ltd v National Bank of Kuwait SAK* [1981] 1 WLR 1233). Summary judgment will also be given on a claim for freight even if there is a cross-claim relating to the cargo (*Aries Tanker Corporation v Total Transport Ltd* [1977] 1 WLR 185).

Performance bonds

21.43 A bank which gives a performance bond must honour that obligation according to its terms. The bank cannot rely on issues relating to the relations between the supplier and the customer, nor whether the supplier has performed its obligations, nor with any question of whether the supplier is in default. The bank must pay according to its guarantee, on demand if so stipulated, without proof or conditions. The only exception is where there is clear fraud of which the bank has notice at the date when payment was due (*Edward Owen Engineering Ltd v Barclays Bank International Ltd* [1978] QB 159 at 171).

21.44 The fraud exception applies where there is clear evidence both of the fraud and the bank's knowledge. There must be a real prospect on the material available that the only realistic inference is that the beneficiary could not have honestly believed in the validity of its demand on its performance bond (*United Trading Corp SA v Allied Arab Bank Ltd* [1985] 2 Lloyd's Rep 554n as interpreted by *Solo Industries UK Ltd v Canara Bank* [2001] EWCA Civ 1059; [2001] 1 WLR 1800 at [32]). In applying this test the court must be careful not to upset what is in effect a strong presumption in favour of fulfilment of the bank's obligation under a performance guarantee (*Czarnikow-Rionda Sugar Trading Inc v Standard Bank London Ltd* [1999] 1 All ER (Comm) 890 at 913). The effect is that there is a heightened test in relation to the fraud exception in an application for summary judgment against a bank (*Banque Saudi Fransi v Lear Siegler Services Inc* [2007] 1 All ER (Comm) 67 at [16]). Conversely, in an application for summary judgment by a bank which has honoured a performance bond against a person who has given the bank a counter-indemnity, the normal 'real prospect of success' test applies (*Banque Saudi Fransi v Lear Siegler Services Inc* at [18]).

Summary judgment on admissions

21.45 Admissions made by the other side may be relied upon in support of an application for summary judgment. Obviously, if a claim, or an important issue in a claim, is admitted there may be no real prospect of success in any filed defence. The nature of admissions, and the circumstances in which they may be retracted, are considered at 34.02–34.09.

Conditional orders

21.46 PD 24, para 4, provides that, where it appears to the court possible that a claim or defence may succeed but improbable that it will do so, the court may make a conditional order. Paragraph 5.2 provides that a conditional order is an order which requires a party:

(a) to pay a sum of money into court, or
(b) to take a specified step in relation to his claim or defence, as the case may be, and which provides that that party's claim will be dismissed or his statement of case will be struck out if he does not comply.

Where money is paid into court in compliance with a conditional order, the claimant is a secured creditor for that amount in the event of the defendant's bankruptcy (*Re Ford* [1900] 2 QB 211).

21.47 Conditional orders are appropriate for cases in the grey area between granting judgment and dismissing the application. For example, in *Homebase Ltd v LSS Services Ltd* (2004) LTL 28/6/04, the claimant made a claim against the defendant seeking five months' licence fees for occupying a site. The defendant filed a witness statement to the effect that the claimant had orally agreed that the defendant need pay nothing until the claimant had obtained consent from its landlord to assign the land to the defendant. The claimant denied there was any such agreement. A conditional order was made because, although the defendant's story was not incredible (which would have resulted in judgment for the claimant), its story was unlikely and was not supported by any contemporaneous documents.

21.48 If the court decides to make the respondent to the application pay money into court under a conditional order, it must decide how much should be paid in. The starting point has traditionally been the full amount of the claim. However, the court has a discretion, which it will exercise in accordance with the overriding objective. Obviously, the more uncertain the defence, the more likely it is that the court will order the full amount to be paid in. Another factor is the defendant's ability to pay. Lord Diplock in *M v Yorke Motors v Edwards* [1982] 1 WLR 444 endorsed the following principles:

(a) Defendants seeking to limit a financial condition must make full and frank disclosure of their finances. This is done on affidavit or witness statement. It is common for defendants who realize that a conditional order may be made to produce such written evidence in advance of the summary judgment hearing, and to disclose it to the claimant on the claimant undertaking not to refer to it unless a conditional order is made.
(b) Reliance on a public funding certificate as evidence of impecuniosity is not enough.
(c) The test is whether it will be impossible for the defendant to comply with the financial condition, as opposed to merely finding it difficult. An impossible condition is tantamount to entering judgment.

21.49 M V Yorke Motors were suing Mr Edwards for breach of warranty of title in relation to a contract for the sale of a car for £23,520. An order equivalent to a conditional order was made, because the court was sceptical about his defence that he was acting only as the agent for a foreign buyer. By the time of the hearing Mr Edwards was unemployed, living with his father, and in receipt of legal aid with a nil contribution. The House of Lords substituted a condition of bringing £3,000 into court.

21.50 The defendant should be given an opportunity to produce evidence as to means. A claimant may need to give advance notice that such an order is to be sought if summary judgment is not ordered, or an adjournment may be necessary (*Anglo-Eastern Trust Ltd v Kermanshahchi* [2002] EWCA Civ 198).

Summary judgment subject to a stay of execution

21.51 Summary judgment subject to a stay of execution has the effect that the claimant has won the case, but will not be paid until some other event, such as the trial of a counterclaim, when the stay will be lifted. It may be ordered where there is a counterclaim (not amounting to a set-off) which is linked to the claim (see 21.30(b) above). More generally, such an order may be appropriate where there is some unresolved matter which may mean it is unjust for payment to be required immediately. This may arise where the party required to make the payment may not be able to recover its money, for example, where there is a substantial risk of the claimant becoming insolvent (*Mead General Building Ltd v Dartmoor Properties Ltd* [2009] BCC 510).

F AMENDMENT AT HEARING

21.52 There are many cases where the defective nature of one side's statement of case becomes clear at the hearing of an application for summary judgment. If the defect is one of how the case is put rather than of substance, the court has a wide power to allow an amendment to correct the problem, which can be exercised at the hearing (*Stewart v Engel* [2000] 1 WLR 2268). A defendant seeking to avoid summary judgment being entered on an admission has to issue an application for permission to amend, otherwise the court is entitled to enter judgment on the unamended statement of case (*Loveridge v Healey* [2004] EWCA Civ 173).

G SOME OTHER COMPELLING REASON FOR A TRIAL

21.53 Summary judgment will be refused if there is some other compelling reason why the case should be disposed of at a trial (CPR, r 24.2(b)). Seeking an adjournment to negotiate with the claimant was not regarded as compelling in *Phonographic Performance Ltd v Planet Ice (Peterborough) Ltd* (2003) LTL 2/2/04. Reasons for going to trial include:

(a) The respondent is unable to contact a material witness who may provide material for a defence.
(b) The case is highly complicated such that judgment should be given only after mature consideration at trial.
(c) The facts are wholly within the applicant's hands. In such a case it may be unjust to enter judgment without giving the respondent an opportunity of establishing a defence in the light of disclosure or after serving a request for further information (*Harrison v Bottenheim* (1878) 26 WR 362). However, summary judgment will not necessarily be refused in cases where the evidence for any possible defence could only lie with the applicant if there is nothing devious or artificial in the claim (*State Trading Corporation of India v Doyle Carriers Inc* [1991] 2 Lloyd's Rep 55).
(d) The applicant has acted harshly or unconscionably, or the facts disclose a suspicion of dishonesty or deviousness on the part of the applicant, such that judgment should be obtained only in the light of publicity at trial. An example is *Miles v Bull* [1969] 1 QB 258, where possession proceedings had the appearance of a device to evict the defendant.

H DIRECTIONS ON SUMMARY JUDGMENT HEARING

21.54 If a summary judgment application is dismissed or otherwise fails finally to dispose of the claim, the court will give case management directions for the future conduct of the case (PD 24, para 10), which may include directions for filing and service of a defence (CPR, r 24.6), and may dispense with allocation questionnaires and allocate the case to a case management track.

I SPECIFIC PERFORMANCE, RESCISSION, AND FORFEITURE IN PROPERTY CASES

21.55 An even speedier process for obtaining summary judgment is available by virtue of PD 24, para 7, in claims for specific performance and similar claims arising out of mortgage and tenancy agreements. Summary judgment in these cases can be sought at any time after the claim is served, rather than having to wait until after acknowledgment or defence, and the application can be made even in the absence of particulars of claim. The application notice, evidence in support, and a draft order must be served no less than four clear days before the hearing.

J SUMMARY ORDERS FOR ACCOUNTS AND INQUIRIES

21.56 Under CPR, r 25.1(1)(o), the court may make an interim order directing accounts to be taken or inquiries to be made. The application notice seeking such an order should ask:

(a) for specified accounts to be taken or specified inquiries to be made;
(b) for directions for the taking of the account or for making the inquiries; and
(c) for payment of the amount found to be due on taking the accounts.

21.57 Written evidence is not always required in support, but if the matter is at all contentious such evidence should be filed and served with the application. The court may refuse to make the order if there is a preliminary question that ought to be tried, such as whether the defendant is under a duty to account.

21.58 The practice on taking accounts and conducting inquiries is dealt with by PD 40A. When making an order for accounts and inquiries the court may also at the same time or later give directions as to how the account is to be taken or the inquiry conducted (PD 40A, para 1.1). Among the directions that may be made are the following:

(a) that the relevant books of account shall be evidence of their contents, subject to the parties having the right to make objections (para 1.2);
(b) that an accounting party must make out his account and verify it by exhibiting it to an affidavit or witness statement (para 2.1); and
(c) that, if appropriate, and at any stage in the proceedings, the parties must serve points of claim and points of defence (para 5).

21.59 A party alleging that an account drawn by an accounting party is inaccurate (or making similar allegations) must give written notice of the objections to the accounting party (para 3.1). These objections must give full particulars, specify the grounds on which it is alleged that the account is inaccurate, and be verified by a statement of truth (or exhibited to an affidavit or witness statement). Directions may be given at any stage (para 5), and the court may direct that the matter be investigated in any manner (para 12).

K SUMMARY DETERMINATION OF CONSTRUCTION OF WILLS

The High Court may make an order authorizing trustees or personal representatives to act in reliance on an opinion of counsel of ten years' call on the construction of a will or trust (Administration of Justice Act 1985, s 48). Applications under s 48 are made in the Chancery Division without notice supported by written evidence stating the names of all persons who may be affected by the order sought; all admissible surrounding circumstances; counsel's call and experience; the value of the fund; and details of any known dispute. Instructions to counsel, counsel's opinion, and draft minutes of the order sought must be exhibited to the evidence in support. The papers are considered by a judge without hearing argument, who will make the order sought if that order is appropriate and if there appears to be no tenable argument contrary to counsel's opinion. **21.60**

L POSSESSION CLAIMS AGAINST TRESPASSERS

Machinery for obtaining possession orders without undue delay against trespassers and similar categories of unauthorized occupiers is provided by CPR, Part 55. Under these provisions there is no conventional trial. They are therefore appropriate only in cases where the defendants have no real defence. One of the main objects of these rules is to avoid the need for the claimant to investigate the identities of the people in unauthorized occupation, and to allow possession orders to be made even against 'persons unknown'. **21.61**

Conditions for granting possession orders against trespassers

By CPR, r 55.1(b), possession orders against trespassers may be sought: **21.62**

(a) by a person who claims possession of land;
(b) against a person or persons (not being tenants holding over after the termination of their tenancies) who entered into or remained on the land without the consent of a person entitled to possession of that land.

In addition to the obvious situation of the owner in fee simple in possession claiming against a squatter, the summary possession procedure may be used: **21.63**

(a) By a head landlord against unlawful subtenants (*Moore Properties (Ilford) Ltd v McKeon* [1976] 1 WLR 1278).
(b) By the owner of the premises against a person who had gone into possession as a licensee, but whose licence has expired (*Greater London Council v Jenkins* [1975] 1 WLR 155). This also applies where the occupant is a former employee whose right to remain was terminated on dismissal, even where the employee has applied to the employment tribunal for reinstatement if the employer has expressed an intention not to reinstate in any event (*Whitbread West Pennines Ltd v Reedy* [1988] ICR 807).

(c) By a tenant of premises against a person who, while the tenant was absent, was let into occupation with the consent of the landlord (*Borg v Rogers* (1981) 132 NLJ 134).

(d) By a licensee who was not in occupation of the land against a trespasser where possession was necessary to give effect to the licensee's contractual rights of occupation (*Dutton v Manchester Airport plc* [1999] 2 All ER 675). The land in this case was owned by the National Trust, and the airport was given a licence in order to fell some trees for purposes connected with the construction of a second runway. The trespassers were protesting against the construction. It was held that an order for possession would not interfere with the prior rights of the National Trust.

21.64 The procedure against trespassers cannot be used against a tenant or a tenant holding over at the end of the tenancy. In addition, the following situations have been considered by the courts:

(a) Where the defendant was allowed into the premises by a tenant, the landlord was held not to be entitled to use the procedure unless the tenancy had been determined or surrendered (*Auto Finance Ltd v Pugh* (10 June 1985, unreported)).

(b) Where the case involves a complicated issue as to title (*Cudworth v Masefield* (1984) *The Times*, 16 May 1984) or whether there has been a surrender of a tenancy by operation of law (*Cooper v Vardari* (1986) 18 HLR 299), or similar complexities, the procedure may be inappropriate.

County court or High Court

21.65 Possession claims must normally be started in the county court for the district in which the land is situated (CPR, r 55.3(1)). The High Court may be appropriate where there are complicated issues of fact, points of law of general importance, or the claim is against trespassers and there is a substantial risk of public disturbance or of serious harm to persons or property, which require immediate determination (PD 55A, para 1.3).

Claim form, particulars of claim, and evidence in support

21.66 There is a special claim form for the possession of property (form N5) which must be used in claims against trespassers. The claim form should name as defendants all the persons in occupation whose identities are known to the claimant. Where the claimant does not know the names of all the occupiers, the claim is brought against 'persons unknown' in addition to any named defendants.

21.67 The particulars of claim must be in the prescribed form, N121, which is specifically for claims against trespassers. This must identify the land, state whether it is residential property, state the claimant's interest in the property or the basis for claiming possession, the circumstances in which it has been occupied without his licence or consent, and give details of every person who, to the best of the claimant's knowledge, is in possession of the property (PD 55A, paras 2.1 and 2.6). Particulars of claim and witness statements in support must be filed when the claim is issued (rr 55.4 and 55.8(5)). When the claim is issued the court will fix a date for the hearing, which will usually be just a few days after issue.

Service

No acknowledgment of service form is required (CPR, r 55.7(1)), so the only documents that need to be served are the claim form, particulars of claim, any additional evidence in support, and any notice of the return day. Service copies of the claim form must be duly sealed. Individually named defendants must be served in accordance with the normal rules on service (see Chapter 8). **21.68**

Where the claim is against, or includes, persons unknown, in addition to serving any named defendants in the normal way, the documents must be served by: **21.69**

(a) attaching copies to the main door or some other part of the land so they are clearly visible, and, if practicable, by inserting another set of the documents through the letter box in a sealed transparent envelope addressed to 'the occupiers'; or
(b) attaching copies contained in sealed transparent envelopes addressed to 'the occupiers' to stakes placed in the land in places where they are clearly visible. This method is used where the trespassers are on open land. Where service is to be effected by the court the claimant must provide sufficient transparent envelopes and stakes (CPR, r 55.6; PD 55A, para 4.1).

Service must be effected not less than five days before the hearing in the case of residential property, and not less than two days before the hearing in respect of commercial property and open land (r 55.5(2)). Time is calculated from service on each of the various defendants. Time may be shortened under r 3.1(2)(a), (b), where the occupiers have threatened to assault the claimant or to cause serious damage to the property or other property in the locality (PD 55A, para 3.2). **21.70**

Defence

There is a prescribed form for the defence (form N11), which simply provides a space for giving the reasons for disputing the claim and a statement of truth. However, in possession claims against trespassers CPR, r 15.2, does not apply, and there is no need for a defendant to file a defence (r 55.7(2)). Default judgment does not apply (r 55.7(4)). **21.71**

Application by occupier to be made a party

By CPR, r 19.4, an occupier who is not named as a defendant and who wishes to be heard on the return day may apply at any stage to be joined as a defendant. An application notice should be filed and served in accordance with Part 23 (PD 19A, para 1.4). Such applications are often heard on the day of the hearing. All that need be shown is that the occupier wishes to be heard on whether an order for possession should be made, so permission to join is usually granted quite readily. **21.72**

Hearing in claims against trespassers

Summary possession hearings are generally heard by masters in the Royal Courts of Justice and by district judges in the county courts (PD 2B, para 11.1(b)). Unless the court orders otherwise, the facts are placed before the court at the hearing by relying on the evidence in the witness statements served with the claim form (CPR, r 55.8(3)). The fact of service is proved by producing a certificate of service (r 55.8(6) and form N215). **21.73**

21.74 If the defendants need an opportunity to file evidence in reply, the first hearing may be used for giving directions (particularly where there is not much time between service and the return date). If the necessary five or two clear days have not elapsed since service, the court should ordinarily adjourn the hearing to enable the proper time to elapse (*Westminster City Council v Monahan* [1981] 1 WLR 698). If the maker of a witness statement does not attend the hearing, and another party disputes material evidence contained in the statement, the court will normally adjourn the hearing so that oral evidence can be given (PD 55A, para 5.4). Adjournments are usually very short, as the whole point of the procedure is to provide an expeditious means of obtaining possession orders where there is no defence.

21.75 The summary procedure against trespassers is only appropriate where the defendants have no real defence. If the court takes the view that the case is not suitable for summary possession, it may dismiss the claim (particularly where it does not come within the scope of the procedure). If the defendants attend and adduce evidence showing a substantial defence the claim is usually converted into an ordinary possession claim.

Possession orders against trespassers

21.76 Normally, if the court is satisfied that there are grounds for granting possession of the land, the order will be for possession of the land occupied by the defendants forthwith. This may not provide sufficient protection for the claimant, because it is not unknown for defendants to relocate to other land owned by the claimant nearby. Added protection may be given by including the whole of the relevant parcel of land in the order. What the court cannot do is to include separate areas of land also owned by the claimant in the order (*Secretary of State for the Environment, Food and Rural Affairs v Meier* [2009] 1 WLR 2780, SC). The order may be supported by an injunction forbidding the defendants from re-entering the occupied site or from entering other sites.

Warrant of possession

21.77 A warrant of possession to enforce a possession order against a trespasser may be issued immediately after the order is made. However, permission to issue a warrant of possession is required if the warrant is not issued within the next three months (CCR, ord 24, r 6, in CPR, Sch 2). Orders for permission to enforce out of time are made on application to the Master or district judge without notice (unless the court otherwise directs). If permission is granted, the defendants may apply to vary or set it aside by making an application within seven days of service of the order granting permission (CPR, r 23.10).

M INTERIM POSSESSION ORDERS

21.78 An interim order for possession can be sought in a claim for possession against trespassers by following the procedure in CPR, rr 55.20 to 55.28. Such an order is available if the following conditions are satisfied:

(a) the only claim in the proceedings is for possession, so there can be no money claim;

(b) the claimant has throughout the period of alleged unlawful occupation had an immediate right to possession; and
(c) the application must be made within 28 days of the claimant knowing of the wrongful occupation.

The claim must be brought by issuing a claim form in N5, and an application for possession in form N130, supported by written evidence which is incorporated in form N130, and a notice of application for an interim possession order must also be issued (in form N131). Once the proceedings have been issued the court will fix a date for consideration of the application, which must be not less than three days after the proceedings were issued. Service must be effected by the applicant within 24 hours after issue. Service is effected by fixing one set of copies to the main door or other conspicuous part of the premises, and, if practicable, inserting a second set through the letter box in a transparent envelope addressed to 'the occupiers'. **21.79**

The respondents are permitted to file written evidence in reply, and a standard form for this must be used (form N133). At the hearing no oral evidence is adduced other than in response to questions from the court. One of the matters the court must consider before making an interim possession order is whether adequate undertakings have been given by the claimant (CPR, r 55.25(2)(b)). An interim possession order requires the respondents to vacate within 24 hours. A respondent who does not comply commits an offence contrary to the Criminal Justice and Public Order Act 1994, s 76. After an interim possession order is made there is a second return date when the court will consider whether to make a final order for possession or to dismiss the claim for possession. **21.80**

KEY POINTS SUMMARY

21.81

- Summary judgment applications can be made by either party or by the court.
- The test is whether the respondent has a case with a real prospect of success, or if there is some compelling reason for having a trial.
- Default judgment is for cases where the defendant does not respond. Summary judgment is for cases where the defendant does respond, and one side believes there is not much merit in the other side's case.
- Summary judgment applications are dealt with on the papers, and, if successful, result in judgment without a trial, which is why the test is so stringent.

22

STRIKING OUT, DISCONTINUANCE, AND STAYS

22.01 By CPR, r 3.4, the court has the power to order the whole or any part of a statement of case to be struck out. This power may be resorted to on an application by a party seeking to attack the statement of case drafted by the other side. It may also be used by the court of its own initiative, with (and sometimes without) the involvement of the 'innocent' party. This may be because of failure to comply with the requirement to give a concise statement of the facts on which the claimant relies (r 16.4(1)(a)) or the requirement to give the reasons for any denial in a defence (r 16.5(2)(a)). A related use of the power is where it is alleged that a statement of case, even if its contents are assumed to be true, does not amount to a sustainable claim or defence as a matter of law. Striking out is also used to prevent the misuse of the right to issue proceedings, on the ground that proceedings are an abuse of process. These facets of the jurisdiction to strike out will be considered in this chapter.

22.02 An alternative use of striking out is as a means of enforcing compliance with the general provisions of the CPR, practice directions, and court orders and directions as part of the court's case management functions. This aspect of striking out will be considered in Chapter 28 as part of the discussion on non-compliance and sanctions.

It is recognized in several places in the CPR and practice directions that striking out under r 3.4 is closely related to the jurisdiction to enter summary judgment under Part 24, discussed in Chapter 21. Both powers are used to achieve the active case management aim of summarily disposing of issues that do not need full investigation at trial (r 1.4(2)(c)). In *Three Rivers District Council v Bank of England (No 3)* [2003] 2 AC 1, Lord Hope at [91] said that, under r 3.4, the court generally is only concerned with the statement of case which it is alleged discloses no reasonable grounds for bringing or defending the claim. In *Monsanto v Tilly* (1999) *The Times*, 30 November 1999, Stuart Smith LJ said that Part 24 gives a wider scope for dismissing a claim or defence than striking out. The court should look to see what will happen at the trial and, if the case is so weak that it has no reasonable prospects of success, summary judgment should be entered. **22.03**

A THE MAIN RULE

Rule 3.4(2) of the CPR provides: **22.04**

> The court may strike out a statement of case if it appears to the court—
> (a) that the statement of case discloses no reasonable grounds for bringing or defending the claim;
> (b) that the statement of case is an abuse of the court's process or is otherwise likely to obstruct the just disposal of the proceedings; or
> (c) that there has been a failure to comply with a rule, practice direction or court order.

A striking-out order may apply to all or part of a statement of case (r 3.4(1)).

Endorsing the rule laid down in *Gardner v Southwark London Borough Council (No 2)* [1996] 1 WLR 561, r 3.4(4) provides that where a claim is struck out and the claimant is ordered to pay the defendant's costs, if the claimant commences a second claim (within the limitation period) arising out of substantially the same facts as those forming the basis of the struck-out claim, the defendant may apply for a stay of the second claim until the costs of the first claim have been paid. **22.05**

In addition, it is probable that the High Court retains its power to strike out under its inherent jurisdiction, as r 3.4(5) provides that r 3.4(2) does not limit any other power of the court to strike out a statement of case. **22.06**

B PROCEDURE ON APPLICATIONS MADE BY PARTIES

An application to strike out made by a party should be brought by issuing an application notice in accordance with the procedure in CPR, Part 23 (see Chapter 20). PD 3A, para 5.2, says that, while many applications to strike out can be made without evidence in support (the poor drafting of the statement of case may be self-evident, or the point may be one of law on which **22.07** no evidence would be required), the applicant should always consider whether facts need to be proved. If so, evidence in support should usually be filed and served, unless the facts relied upon have already been adequately evidenced in, say, a statement of case which included a statement of truth. The court has the power to treat an application to strike out as one for summary judgment in order to dispose of issues or claims that do not deserve full investigation at trial (*Three Rivers District Council v Bank of England (No 3)* [2003] 2 AC 1 at [88]).

22.08 In accordance with PD 23A, para 2.7, any application to strike out should be made as soon as it becomes apparent that it is desirable to make it. Applications to strike out should normally be made in the period between acknowledgment of service and filing of allocation questionnaires (PD 26, para 5.3(1), and see also PD 3A, para 5.1). A defendant who files a defence and defends on the merits will be taken to have acquiesced, and thereafter it is too late to apply to strike out as an abuse of process if the abuse is founded on the bringing of the claim (*Johnson v Gore Wood and Co* [2002] 2 AC 1). If a striking-out application is issued before the defence is filed, default judgment cannot be entered until the striking-out application has been disposed of (CPR, r 12.3(3)). If a striking-out application is dealt with before allocation and the claim survives, the court may be in a position to dispense with the need to file allocation questionnaires, and may allocate the case and make case management directions at the end of the striking-out hearing (PD 26, para 2.4). If a striking-out application is contemplated, but has not been dealt with by the time allocation questionnaires have to be returned, the intention to make the application should be included as extra information provided when the questionnaire is returned (PD 26, para 2.2(3)(a)).

22.09 PD 26, para 5.3(2), provides that where a party makes an application to strike out before the claim has been allocated to a track the court will not allocate the claim before hearing the application. By PD 26, para 5.3(3) and (4), where a party files an allocation questionnaire and states an intention to strike out but has not yet done so, the judge will usually direct that an allocation hearing is listed. The striking-out application may be heard at the allocation hearing if the application notice has been issued and served in sufficient time.

C REFERENCES BY COURT OFFICERS

22.10 A claim form that has been lodged for issuing may be referred by a court official to the judge (CPR, r 3.2), and this power may be exercised where it is felt that the claim form (which in context means the particulars of claim) is amenable to being struck out under r 3.4 (see PD 3A, para 2.1) or if it is totally devoid of merit. The court staff who receive a claim form, fee etc. for the purpose of issue are not performing any judicial function, and have no power to reject the documents (*Barnes v St Helens Metropolitan Borough Council (Practice Note)* [2007] 1 WLR 879 at [19]; PD 3A, para 2.1). If the claim form is very defective, such as through not naming any parties, or not including any details of the claim, it may be rejected on the basis that it is not a claim form at all (*per* Tuckey LJ). Where a claim form is referred to the judge, an order may be made which is designed to ensure the claim is disposed of, or proceeds, in a way that accords with the rules. The judge has a discretion whether to hear the claimant before making such an order (para 2.3). If an order is made without giving notice to the claimant, rr 23.9 and 23.10 of the CPR apply, so that the order has to include a statement that the claimant has the right within seven days after service of the order to apply to vary or set it aside.

One option available to the judge is to order a stay to allow the claimant an opportunity of putting the claim on a proper footing. This may take the form of a simple stay until further order, or an order that the claim form shall not be served until the stay is lifted, or an order that no application to lift the stay shall be made until the claimant files specified further documents, such as amended particulars of claim or a witness statement (PD 3, para 2.4). If the claimant does what the judge requires, and the stay is lifted, the judge may give directions regarding service etc. (para 2.5). The fact that the judge allows the claim to proceed does not preclude the defendant from making an application to strike out or for summary judgment once proceedings are served (para 2.6). **22.11**

Similar powers are available where a court official believes that a document purporting to be a defence is amenable to being struck out (para 3). A stay would be inappropriate in this situation, but the judge may strike out the defence on his or her own initiative, or allow the defendant an opportunity to file an amended defence, or may require the defendant to provide further information to clarify the defence within a stated time, failing which the judge may order the defence to be struck out. The fact that a judge does not strike out a defence under this power does not prejudice the claimant's right to apply for such an order or any other order. **22.12**

D GENERAL TEST

The jurisdiction to strike out is to be used sparingly, because striking out deprives a party of its right to a trial, and of its ability to strengthen its case through the process of disclosure and other court procedures such as requests for further information. Further, examination and cross-examination of witnesses often changes the complexion of a case. The result is that striking out is limited to plain and obvious cases where there is no point in having a trial. **22.13**

The principles from *W & H Trade Marks (Jersey) Ltd v W and H Trade Marks (Jersey) Ltd* [1986] AC 368, the leading case under the old rules, were approved in *Three Rivers District Council v Bank of England (No 3)* [2003] 2 AC 1 at [96]–[97]. The claimant's application to strike out the defence took seven days to argue before the judge, six days in the Court of Appeal, and four days in the House of Lords. The case reiterated the point that striking out was appropriate only in plain and obvious cases. Sometimes, a case would only become clear after protracted argument. Lord Templeman said that: **22.14**

> ...if an application to strike out involves a prolonged and serious argument the judge should, as a general rule, decline to proceed with the argument unless he not only harbours doubts about the soundness of the pleading but, in addition, is satisfied that striking out will obviate the necessity for a trial or will substantially reduce the burden of preparing for trial or the burden of the trial itself.

Where several of the grounds stated in CPR, r 3.4 are relied on in a single application, the court will often take a broad-brush approach and simply ask whether the case is a plain and obvious one for striking out, rather than considering each of the grounds in detail. The 'plain and obvious' test will not be adjusted where one of the parties is suffering from an inequality of arms (*Bank of Tokyo-Mitsubishi UFJ Ltd v Bashan Gida Sanayi ve Pazarlama AS* [2008] EWHC 659 (Ch)). **22.15**

E NO REASONABLE GROUNDS FOR BRINGING OR DEFENDING THE CLAIM

22.16 Applications under CPR, r 3.4(2)(a), may be made on the basis that the statement of case under attack fails on its face to disclose a claim or defence which is sustainable as a matter of law. On hearing such an application it will be assumed that the facts alleged are true (see *Morgan Crucible Co plc v Hill Samuel and Co Ltd* [1991] Ch 295 *per* Slade LJ). For purists it ought to be unnecessary to seek to undermine the claim or defence under r 3.4(2)(a) with evidence in support. The rules do not, however, contain any express ban on adducing evidence in support: see 22.07.

22.17 A number of examples of statements of case open to attack under CPR, r 3.4(2)(a), are given by PD 3A. A claim may be struck out if it sets out no facts indicating what the claim is about (such as a claim simply saying it is for 'Money owed £5,000'), or if it is incoherent and makes no sense, or if the facts it states, even if true, do not disclose a legally recognizable claim against the defendant. A defence may be struck out if it consists of a bare denial or otherwise fails to set out a coherent statement of facts, or if the facts it sets out, even if true, do not amount in law to a defence to the claim.

22.18 A cause of action that is unknown to the law will be struck out; as will, subject to the court giving permission to amend, a statement of case that omits some material element of the claim or defence. A statement of case ought also to be struck out if the facts set out do not constitute the cause of action or defence alleged, or if the relief sought would not be ordered by the court. A defence may be struck out if it does not answer the claim being made.

22.19 Striking out may be refused in developing areas of law (*Brooks v Commissioner of Police for the Metropolis* [2005] 1 WLR 1495), and will be refused if the application requires minute and protracted examination of documents (*Wenlock v Moloney* [1965] 1 WLR 1238; *Three Rivers District Council v Bank of England (No 3)* [2003] 2 AC 1). Judges often apply the test of whether the claim is bound to fail, so that even a case 'fraught with difficulty' will not be struck out (*Smith v Chief Constable of Sussex* [2008] PIQR P12). On the other hand, the documents may make it plain there is no case. In *Taylor v Inntrepreneur Estates (CPC) Ltd* (2001) LTL 31/1/01, the claimant brought a claim seeking a declaration that a lease agreement had come into force, damages for breach of the lease, and damages for misrepresentation resulting from having entered into the alleged lease. On the documents it was clear that throughout the parties had negotiated on a 'subject to contract' basis. It was held that as no written agreement had been signed, no lease had been entered into. It followed that there was no reasonable cause of action, and the claim was struck out.

22.20 The court may allow a party to amend rather than strike out, but the power to amend will be exercised in accordance with the overriding objective (see *Finley v Connell Associates* (1999) *The Times*, 23 June 1999, where permission to amend was granted, and *Christofi v Barclays Bank plc* [2000] 1 WLR 937, where permission was refused). An amendment should be permitted as an alternative to striking out only if there is a real prospect of establishing the amended case (*Charles Church Developments plc v Cronin* [1990] FSR 1).

F ABUSE OF PROCESS

The first half of CPR, r 3.4(2)(b), gives the court power to strike out a statement of case which is an abuse of the court's process. This is a power 'which any court of justice must possess to prevent misuse of its procedure in a way which, although not inconsistent with the literal application of its procedural rules, would nevertheless be manifestly unfair to a party to litigation before it, or would otherwise bring the administration of justice into disrepute among right-thinking people' (*per* Lord Diplock in *Hunter v Chief Constable of the West Midlands Police* [1982] AC 529 at 536). **22.21**

General examples of abuse of process

A claim that is issued after the expiry of limitation may be struck out as an abuse of process (alternatively, the limitation point may be determined as a preliminary issue, or at trial, or by way of an application for a direction under the LA 1980, s 33), but cannot be struck out on the ground of there being no reasonable cause of action. The reason is that limitation is a procedural defence, so does not prevent there being a cause of action. See *Ronex Properties Ltd v John Laing Construction Ltd* [1983] QB 398. **22.22**

Generally, it is an abuse of process for a claimant complaining about a public authority's infringement of the claimant's public law rights to seek redress by way of an ordinary claim rather than by way of judicial review (see *O'Reilly v Mackman* [1983] 2 AC 237). **22.23**

In *Barton Henderson Rasen v Merrett* [1993] 1 Lloyd's Rep 540 Saville J said that it is an abuse of the court's process to issue proceedings with no intention of taking the case any further. In contentious matters the courts exist for the purpose of determining claims. Therefore, starting a claim with no intention of pursuing it is not using the court's processes for the purposes for which they were designed. It is also an abuse of process to issue a claim form at a time when the claimant lacks knowledge of any basis for bringing the claim, even if by the time of the striking-out application the claimant has sufficient facts to plead a claim (*Nomura International plc v Granada Group Ltd* [2008] Bus LR 1). **22.24**

According to *McDonald's Corporation v Steel* [1995] 3 All ER 615, it is an abuse of process where the statement of case is incurably incapable of proof. The fact that a party's case may be incapable of proof may become apparent after disclosure of documents or after exchange of witness statements. However, in *McDonald's Corporation v Steel* it was said that striking out on this basis will be fairly unusual, as there are few cases which are sufficiently clearly and obviously hopeless that they deserve the draconian step of being struck out. **22.25**

Destruction of evidence before proceedings are commenced in an attempt to pervert the course of justice may result in a claim or defence being struck out. Destruction of evidence after proceedings are issued may be visited by striking out if a fair trial is no longer achievable (*Douglas v Hello! Ltd* [2003] 1 All ER 1087). A similar approach is taken where evidence has been forged or if a party or its witnesses engage in dishonest conduct relating to the proceedings. Such cases can result in striking out as an abuse of process if a fair trial is no longer possible (*Masood v Zahoor* [2010] 1 WLR 746). **22.26**

Relitigation amounting to an abuse of process

22.27 There have been several cases dealing with whether a claim which is inconsistent with an earlier claim or evidence given by the claimant in earlier proceedings (such as an affidavit used in an application to discharge a freezing injunction) should be struck out as an abuse of process.

22.28 Where the issues raised in an earlier claim are identical to the issues raised in a later claim, there is an absolute bar on the later proceedings unless fraud or collusion is alleged (*Arnold v National Westminster Bank plc* [1991] 2 AC 93). Issue estoppel applies where an order is made, and it does not matter whether the order was made by consent or after argument (*Lennon v Birmingham City Council* (2001) LTL 27/3/01). Where the parties in the two claims are not the same, issue estoppel does not apply (*Mulkerrins v PricewaterhouseCoopers* [2003] 1 WLR 1937).

22.29 Where issue estoppel does not apply, it is only an abuse of process to challenge the findings in the earlier claim if it would be manifestly unfair to a party in the later claim for the issues to be relitigated, or if relitigating will bring the administration of justice into disrepute (*Secretary of State for Trade and Industry v Bairstow* [2004] Ch 1). The underlying public interest is that there should be finality in litigation, and that a party should not be vexed twice in the same matter. In considering whether the second claim is an abuse it is necessary to decide not merely that the second claim could have been brought in the earlier claim, but whether it should have been brought in the first claim. The effect of the rule from the law of evidence in *Hollington v F Hewthorn & Co Ltd* [1943] 1 KB 587 is that previous findings from cases involving different parties are inadmissible as evidence of the facts on which those findings were based. What *Secretary of State for Trade and Industry v Bairstow* does is to provide a means of circumventing that rule on the theory that, if an abuse of process is established, the party against whom the previous finding was made is prevented from asserting facts contrary to the previous finding (*Conlon v Simms* [2008] 1 WLR 484 at [177], *per* Ward LJ).

22.30 In applying the *Secretary of State for Trade and Industry v Bairstow* principle, the court has to make a broad, merits-based judgment taking account of all the public and private interests involved, and all the facts. It is a decision which has only one answer, and is not an exercise of discretion (*Aldi Stores Ltd v WSP Group plc* [2008] BLR 1). The court must focus on the crucial question whether, in all the circumstances, the claimant is misusing or abusing the process of the court (*Johnson v Gore Wood & Co* [2002] 2 AC 1). In this case, Mr Johnson was a shareholder in a company which had sued the defendant solicitors. That first claim was settled, with the compromise agreement containing a clause seeking to limit the defendant's liability to Mr Johnson personally. Mr Johnson then sued the solicitors in his personal capacity, and the defendant applied to strike out his personal claim as an abuse. Certain heads of claim were struck out, as they merely reflected losses suffered by his company, but others were arguably recoverable in his own right, and it was held that, even though his personal claim could have been joined with the first claim by the company, it was not on the facts an abuse to have brought the personal claim by separate proceedings.

Settlement acting as a bar to later proceedings

Settling a claim can act as a bar to later proceedings. In *Jameson v Central Electricity Generating Board* [2000] 1 AC 455, in the original claim the deceased accepted £80,000 from his former employer in 'full and final settlement and satisfaction of all the causes of action' set out in his statement of claim against his employer in respect of asbestos-related disease. After his death his widow brought the present claim against the Board as the owner of premises where the deceased had been exposed to asbestos. The claim against the Board was struck out. The reasoning, as interpreted by the House of Lords in *Heaton v AXA Equity & Law Life Assurance Society plc* [2002] 2 AC 329, was that: **22.31**

(a) a claim for unliquidated damages, whether in contract or tort, is capable of being fixed in a specific sum of money either on judgment or by agreement;
(b) although a judgment invariably fixes the full measure of the claimant's loss, whether a compromise fixes the full measure depends on the proper construction of the compromise agreement. Lord Bingham in *Heaton v AXA Equity & Law Life Assurance Society plc* said that in construing a compromise agreement for this purpose one significant factor is whether the claimant has expressly reserved the right to sue other persons, although the absence of such a reservation is by no means conclusive in favour of an argument that other claims are extinguished; and
(c) if a compromise, on its proper construction, fixes the full measure of the claimant's loss, the compromise extinguishes the claim so that other claims for the same damage cannot be pursued against other persons, whether in contract or tort.

G OBSTRUCTING THE JUST DISPOSAL OF THE PROCEEDINGS

The second half of CPR, r 3.4(2)(b), allows the court to strike out a statement of case which obstructs the just disposal of the proceedings. This is expanded upon by PD 3A, para 1.5, which provides that a claim may come within r 3.4(2)(b) if it is vexatious, scurrilous, or obviously ill-founded. Poorly drafted statements of case may be struck out on this ground, such as where the pleading is unclear and not readily cured by amendment, or where it seeks to reverse the burden of proof (*Prince Radu of Hohenzollern v Houston* [2009] EWHC 398 (QB)). An overly pedantic approach to the niceties of pleading may, however, be contrary to the overriding objective (*Deutsche Morgan Grenfell Group plc v Commissioners of Inland Revenue* [2007] 1 AC 558). **22.32**

Whether a statement of case is vexatious depends 'on all the circumstances of the case: the categories are not closed and the considerations of public policy and the interests of justice may be very material' (*per* Stuart-Smith LJ in *Ashmore v British Coal Corporation* [1990] 2 QB 338). The applicant in *Ashmore v British Coal Corporation* was one of 1,500 women claiming they were employed on less favourable terms than certain male comparators. Fourteen cases were selected for determination, and the eventual finding was in favour of the employer. The applicant then sought to proceed with her claim. Although the previous determination was not strictly binding, the applicant's claim was struck out as being frivolous and vexatious. **22.33**

Pleadings under the old system have also been struck out on this ground where a party has been joined merely to obtain disclosure of documents or costs (*Burstall v Beyfus* (1884) 26 ChD 35) or where a claim is a disguised action for gaming debts (*Day v William Hill (Park Lane) Ltd* [1949] 1 KB 632).

22.34 *Rassam v Budge* [1893] 1 QB 571 concerned a claim for damages for slander. Instead of pleading to the words alleged by the claimant, the defence set out the defendant's rather different version of what he had said, and pleaded the words he alleged he had spoken were true. These allegations were struck out as tending to prejudice the fair trial of the claim, because they left it unclear whether the issue was whether the words complained of by the claimant were spoken and published, or whether those words were true.

22.35 In *Philipps v Philipps* (1878) 4 QBD 127 Cotton LJ said, at 139:

> ...in my opinion it is absolutely essential that the pleading, not to be embarrassing to the defendants, should state those facts which will put the defendants on their guard and tell them what they have to meet when the case comes on for trial.

22.36 A defence will be struck out if it does not make clear how much of the claim is admitted and how much is denied (*British and Colonial Land Association Ltd v Foster* (1887) 4 TLR 574). Mere prolixity or setting out of inconsistent claims or defences would be unlikely to result in striking out (see, eg, *Re Morgan* (1887) 35 ChD 492), although costs sanctions may be imposed if the case is protracted as a result.

H POWERS AFTER A STRIKING-OUT ORDER IS MADE

22.37 When a court strikes out a statement of case it may enter such judgment as the successful party appears entitled to (PD 3A, para 4.2) and make any consequential order it considers appropriate (CPR, r 3.4(3)). If a claim survives a striking-out application, the court may dispense with the need to file allocation questionnaires, allocate the claim to a track, and make case management directions (PD 26, para 2.4).

I DISCONTINUANCE

22.38 From time to time a claimant may think better of having commenced proceedings, and will want to pull out of them without incurring all the costs of litigating to trial. A claimant who wishes to discontinue proceedings must file a notice of discontinuance. The general rule is that once a claim is discontinued, the claimant has to pay the defendant's costs of the claim.

What may be discontinued

22.39 A claimant may discontinue:

(a) the whole claim (CPR, r 38.1(1)); or
(b) part of the claim (ie, some of the causes of action pleaded: r 38.1(1)); and

(c) against all of the defendants (r 38.2(3)); or
(d) against some of the defendants (r 38.2(3)).

Permission to discontinue

Generally, a claimant has the right to discontinue without seeking permission first (CPR, r 38.2(1)). However, in some circumstances permission is required. These are: **22.40**

(a) If an interim injunction has been granted in relation to the claim being discontinued, permission has to be sought from the court (r 38.2(2)(a)).
(b) If any party has given an undertaking to the court in relation to the claim being discontinued, permission has to be sought from the court (r 38.2(2)(a)).
(c) If the claimant has received an interim payment (whether by agreement or pursuant to a court order) in relation to the claim being discontinued, permission must be sought from the court or consent must be given in writing by the defendant (r 38.2(2)(b)).
(d) Where there is more than one claimant, the claimant wishing to discontinue must either obtain permission to discontinue from the court, or obtain consent in writing from all the other claimants (r 38.2(2)(c)).
(e) Where a claim is brought by a person under a disability, approval by the court is required if a discontinuance amounts to a settlement or compromise of the claim (*Sayers v SmithKline Beecham plc* [2005] PIQR P8).

If consent is required, the signed consent(s) must be obtained before the claimant files the notice of discontinuance. If the court's permission has to be sought, a separate application for permission must be issued, and the claimant is only allowed to file the notice of discontinuance after the order granting permission is made. **22.41**

Procedure for discontinuing

A claimant discontinues all or part of the claim by filing a notice of discontinuance (form N279) with the court, and serving a copy on all other parties. Regarding contents: **22.42**

(a) The notice of discontinuance that is filed at court must state that copies have been served on all other parties (CPR, r 38.3(2)).
(b) In cases where the consent of another party is required, all copies of the notice of discontinuance must have copies of the consent annexed (r 38.3(3)).
(c) In cases where there is more than one defendant, the notice of discontinuance must identify the defendants against whom the claim is being discontinued (r 38.3(4)).

Setting aside notice of discontinuance

A defendant may apply for an order setting aside a notice of discontinuance served without consent or permission, provided the application is made within 28 days of the notice (CPR, r 38.4). A notice of discontinuance was set aside in *Fakih Brothers v A P Møller (Copenhagen) Ltd* [1994] 1 Lloyd's Rep 103, where it was served to avoid the imposition of an onerous term in a consent order, and in *Ernst and Young v Butte Mining plc* [1996] 1 WLR 1605, where it was served in order to pre-empt the effective service of a counterclaim. **22.43**

Effect of discontinuance

22.44 Notice of discontinuance takes effect, and brings the proceedings to an end as against each defendant, on the date it is served upon that defendant. Unless the court orders otherwise, the claimant is liable for the defendant's costs up to the date of service of the notice of discontinuance (r 38.6(1)). However, there are no costs consequences regarding discontinued small claims track cases (r 38.6(3)). The court can reverse the usual costs rule on a discontinuance where the claimant has in effect obtained all the relief sought in the proceedings (*Amoco (UK) Exploration Co v British American Offshore Ltd* (2000) LTL 12/12/00), or where there has been a change of circumstances making it uneconomic to continue (*Walker v Walker* (2005) LTL 27/1/05).

22.45 If only part of the claim is discontinued, the claimant's liability is limited to the costs of the part of the claim that has been discontinued. Usually the claimant does not have to pay the defendant's costs following a partial discontinuance until the conclusion of the action. However, the court may in its discretion order these costs to be paid immediately, either after they have been agreed between the parties or after they have been assessed by the court (r 38.6(2)). Where the claimant is required to pay the costs of the discontinued part of the claim straight away, the liability to do so arises 14 days after the relevant costs are agreed or assessed by the court. Failure to pay gives grounds for the court imposing a stay on the remainder of the proceedings until the costs are paid (r 38.8).

Subsequent proceedings

22.46 A claimant who discontinues after a defence has been filed is not allowed to commence new proceedings against the same defendant arising out of the same or substantially the same facts as the original claim, unless the court first gives permission for the second claim to be issued (CPR, r 38.7). If permission is granted, the court will normally give directions regarding issuing the substantive second claim (r 25.2(3)).

J STAYS

22.47 By CPR, r 3.1(2)(f), the court has a general case management power to stay the whole or any part of any proceedings or judgment either generally or until a specified date or event. This rule derives from the SCA 1981, s 49(3), which provides that nothing in the Act affects the power of the High Court and Court of Appeal to stay proceedings where the court thinks fit to do so, either of its own motion or on the application of any person, whether or not a party to the proceedings. While a stay is in place the proceedings remain alive, but no further steps may be taken to progress the claim other than applying to lift the stay. A stay on a judgment prevents any steps being taken to enforce it, until the stay is lifted. Note that a stay may apply to only part of the proceedings, and where this applies obviously the remaining parts of the proceedings will continue. A stay may be lifted on proper grounds being shown (*Cooper v Williams* [1963] 2 QB 567).

Stay on settlement

Proceedings are stayed when a Part 36 offer is accepted (see Chapter 42). **22.48**

Ordinary consent orders following a compromise of a claim frequently provide for the stay of the proceedings (see *Rofa Sport Management AG v DHL International (UK) Ltd* [1989] 1 WLR 902). Similarly, a Tomlin order (see 41.19–41.21) provides for the stay of the proceedings on the terms set out in a schedule to the order, with liberty to apply. **22.49**

Stays in pending proceedings

There may be reasons relating to the efficient progress of the proceedings which make granting a stay desirable. Examples are: **22.50**

(a) Where there is no issue on liability in a personal injury case, but a clear prognosis will not be possible for some time. This possibility is referred to in PD 51A, para 19(3)(b), where the machinery referred to is an adjournment to determine prognosis.
(b) Where a personal injuries claim is issued without complying with the personal injuries, clinical disputes, or RTA pre-action protocols because the solicitor acting for the claimant is instructed shortly before the expiry of the limitation period. A stay may be granted in the early stages of the proceedings to enable the steps of the protocol to be completed.
(c) Where a personal injuries claim is issued close to the expiry of limitation without sufficient medical evidence substantiating the claimant's injuries because of difficulties in obtaining the necessary evidence. This arose in *Knight v Sage Group plc* (1999) LTL 28/4/99, where the court gave the claimant three months to obtain and disclose the necessary evidence.
(d) Where a claim is commenced, and subsequent events show that there is a possibility that the proceedings will not serve a useful purpose. For example, a claim may be brought in professional negligence seeking an indemnity in respect of the claimant's potential liability to a stranger to the proceedings. If it transpires that there is a possibility that the stranger to the litigation may never make a claim against the claimant, it may be appropriate to order a stay until the stranger's claim becomes time-barred.
(e) The court may order a stay at the allocation stage to allow for the possibility of settlement under CPR, r 26.4 (see 14.40–14.41).
(f) The usual stay ordered as part of an order making a reference to the European Court of Justice (see Chapter 40).
(g) Stays imposed pending the resolution of a test case (*Woods v Duncan* [1946] AC 401).

Stays to enforce compliance with orders

Sometimes the court imposes stays as a means of enforcing compliance with its orders. This is going to be effective only against a claimant or a party in the position of a claimant, such as a defendant making a counterclaim. Examples are: **22.51**

(a) Stays which are normally imposed pending the provision of security for costs (see Chapter 24).

(b) A stay imposed where the claimant in a personal injuries claim refuses a reasonable request for a medical examination (see *Edmeades v Thames Board Mills Ltd* [1969] 2 QB 67).
(c) A stay pending a satisfactory undertaking as to costs or otherwise connected with the way in which a claim is funded (*Grovewood Holdings plc v James Capel and Co Ltd* [1995] Ch 80).
(d) A second claim may be stayed pending payment of the costs of an earlier discontinued claim (see 22.45) or the costs of an earlier claim that was struck out (CPR, r 3.4(4), confirming *Gardner v Southwark London Borough Council (No 2)* [1996] 1 WLR 561).
(e) Where partners fail to comply with a demand for their names and addresses under PD 7A, paras 5B.1 to 5B.3.

Stays to protect concurrent claims

22.52 There is a general public interest in avoiding a multiplicity of claims. Sometimes it is simply an abuse of process to bring duplicate sets of proceedings, with the result that the later proceedings will be struck out (see *Buckland v Palmer* [1984] 1 WLR 1109). The following examples stop a little way short of being suitable for striking out, but stays may be imposed instead:

(a) Where the dispute should be dealt with by arbitration rather than by litigation. Costs after a stay (or anti-suit injunction) granted to prevent a breach of an arbitration clause are likely to be awarded on the indemnity basis (*Epping Electrical Co Ltd v Briggs and Forrester (Plumbing Services) Ltd, sub nom A v B (No 2)* [2007] 1 All ER (Comm) 633).
(b) Where the dispute should be dealt with in the administration of an insolvent person's estate.
(c) Stays on the ground of *forum non conveniens* (see 10.111–10.118).
(d) Stays under the Judgments Regulation (see arts 27 and 28 at 10.78–10.83).
(e) Stays until the resolution of connected pending criminal proceedings. Applications for such stays may be made by any party to the civil claim, or the prosecutor or any defendant to the criminal proceedings (PD 23A, para 11A.1). The evidence in support of the application must contain an estimate of the expected duration of the stay, and must identify the respects in which continuing the civil claim may prejudice the criminal trial (para 11A.3).

KEY POINTS SUMMARY

22.53
- Striking-out applications are often combined with applications for summary judgment.
- Striking out is aimed at the way in which a claim or defence is formulated in the statement of case, or if it is otherwise an abuse of process. Summary judgment is aimed at weakness on the merits.
- A party who realizes their case is doomed is often best advised to discontinue to prevent further costs building up, but usually has to pay the costs of the other parties to date.
- Stays are temporary halts in proceedings, and can be granted for a range of reasons. A stay is normally lifted once the reason no longer applies.

23

INTERIM PAYMENTS

An order for interim payment is defined in CPR, r 25.1(1)(k) as an order for payment of a sum of money by a defendant on account of any damages, debt, or other sum (except costs) which the court may hold the defendant liable to pay. Such orders are likely to be made in claims where it appears that the claimant will achieve at least some success, and where it would be unjust to delay, until after the trial, payment of the money to which the claimant appears to be entitled. The purpose behind this procedure is to alleviate the hardship that may otherwise be suffered by claimants who may have to wait substantial periods of time before they recover any damages in respect of wrongs they may have suffered. In addition to providing resources to the claimant, making an interim payment will sometimes enable the claimant to pay for treatment, or to save assets which would otherwise be lost, or to have an asset repaired earlier than might otherwise be the case, and may thereby reduce the amount of the claim. Further, making an early interim payment will reduce the defendant's liability to pay interest. **23.01**

Cases on the small claims track are unlikely to be large enough to justify the expense of applications for interim payments, and small claims and fast track cases, unless delayed, are likely to proceed to final hearing with such speed that there will be little point in making an application, unless the hearing results in a judgment for damages to be assessed. Most applications for interim payments are therefore likely to be made in multi-track cases (or cases likely to be allocated to the multi-track when track allocation is considered). **23.02**

There is nothing to prevent the parties agreeing to a voluntary interim payment, and these are quite common in cases where liability is not in dispute but where quantum is still being investigated. However, the permission of the court must be obtained if a voluntary interim payment is being considered where the claimant is a person under disability (PD 25B, para 1.2). **23.03**

A PROCEDURE

23.04 An application for an order for an interim payment cannot be made until the period for filing an acknowledgment of service has expired (CPR, r 25.6(1)). Applications are made on notice, and must be served at least 14 clear days before the hearing of the application. Applications must be supported by evidence which must be served with the application. PD 25B, para 2.1, provides that the evidence in support should set out all relevant matters including:

(a) the amount sought by way of interim payment;
(b) what the money will be used for;
(c) the likely amount of money that will be awarded;
(d) the reasons for believing the relevant ground (see 23.07ff) is satisfied;
(e) in a personal injuries claim, details of special damages and past and future loss; and
(f) in a claim under the Fatal Accidents Act 1976, details of the persons on whose behalf the claim is made and the nature of the claim.

23.05 All relevant documents in support should be exhibited. In personal injuries claims these will include the medical reports.

23.06 Respondents who wish to rely on witness statements in reply must file and serve their evidence at least seven clear days before the hearing. In personal injuries claims the respondent will need to obtain a certificate of recoverable benefits from the Secretary of State under the Social Security (Recovery of Benefits) Act 1997, which is needed for the purposes of framing the order. If the applicant wants to respond to the respondent's evidence, any further evidence must be filed and served at least three clear days before the return day (CPR, r 25.6(4) and (5)).

B GROUNDS

General conditions

23.07 The conditions which must be satisfied before an interim payment order can be made are set out in CPR, r 25.7. Under r 25.7(1), an interim payment may be ordered only if:

(a) the defendant has admitted liability to pay damages or some other sum of money to the claimant (r 25.7(1)(a)); or
(b) the claimant has obtained judgment against the defendant for damages or some other sum (other than costs) to be assessed (r 25.7(1)(b)); or
(c) the court is satisfied that, if the claim went to trial, the claimant would obtain judgment against the defendant from whom the interim payment is sought for a substantial amount of money (other than costs) (r 25.7(1)(c)); or
(d) the claimant is seeking possession of land, and the court is satisfied that if the case went to trial the defendant would be held liable to pay the claimant a sum of money for use and occupation of the land while the claim is pending (r 25.7(1)(d)); or
(e) the claim is brought against more than one defendant, and the further conditions set out in 23.08–23.10 are satisfied (r 25.7(1)(e)).

Multiple defendants

Applications for interim payments where there is more than one defendant, but it is clear the claimant has a very strong case against one identified defendant, are usually dealt with under r 25.7(1)(c). Provided there is a sufficiently strong case on the merits against an identified defendant, it does not matter under r 25.7(1)(c) that there are other defendants named in the proceedings. **23.08**

Rather more frequently, particularly where defendants are sued in the alternative, a claimant may be able to persuade a court on an application for an interim payment that a claim against multiple defendants will succeed, but cannot identify which of the defendants will lose. In such a case the claimant can rely on r 25.7(1)(e). This allows a court to make an interim payment order where: **23.09**

(a) there are two or more defendants;
(b) the court is satisfied that if the claim went to trial the claimant would obtain judgment for a substantial sum of money (other than costs) against at least one of the defendants;
(c) the court cannot determine under r 25.7(1)(c) which of the defendants will lose; and
(d) all the defendants are either insured, public bodies, or are defendants whose liability will be met by an insurer under the Road Traffic Act 1988, s 151, or an insurer acting under the Motor Insurers' Bureau Agreement or by the Motor Insurers' Bureau itself.

The requirement under r 25.7(1)(e) that all the defendants must be insured, etc., means that if it transpires that an interim payment has been ordered against a defendant who later avoids liability at trial, it should be possible to make effective adjustments (see 23.25) so that the defendants who are found liable (or their insurers) will reimburse those ordered to make the interim payment. **23.10**

Standard of proof

On an application under CPR, r 25.7(1)(c), (d), or (e) (see 23.07), the court has to be satisfied on the balance of probabilities that the claimant 'would' obtain judgment. This means that the court must be satisfied that the claimant will win on the balance of probabilities, but at the upper end of the scale, and the burden is a high one. Being likely to succeed at trial is not enough. See *British and Commonwealth Holdings plc v Quadrex Holdings Inc* [1989] QB 842 and *Heidelberg Graphic Equipment Ltd v Commissioners of HM Revenue and Customs* [2009] STC 2334. **23.11**

Relationship with summary judgment

It is quite common to combine applications for summary judgment with applications for interim payments. Summary judgment is available where the defence has no real prospect of success, and interim payments are available where the claimant can show that liability will be established. Obviously these are similar concepts. Further, on the summary judgment application the court may make a 'relevant order' (PD 26, para 12.1) entering judgment for damages to be assessed, which would itself provide grounds for making an order for an interim payment. Another possibility is that the court may make a conditional order on the summary judgment application, with the condition being compliance with an interim payment order. **23.12**

23.13 It is questionable whether it is possible to make an interim payment order if a summary judgment application is unsuccessful. As summary judgment will be given unless the defence has a real prospect of success, there can be no doubt that if summary judgment is refused it would be inconsistent for the court then to decide that the claimant 'would' succeed so as to give grounds for an interim payment. There is even a little doubt about whether making an interim payment order can be consistent with making a conditional order, because if the defence is on the border of having a real prospect of success (the situation where conditional orders are appropriate), it is difficult to see how the court can simultaneously find that the claimant will win for the purposes of making an interim payment order.

Effect of counterclaims and defences

23.14 When deciding on an order for interim payment the court 'must take into account' any relevant set-off or counterclaim and any contributory negligence (CPR, r 25.7(5)). From the context of this provision it clearly applies at the second stage of an interim payment application when the court is considering the amount to be ordered by way of an interim payment. Counterclaims and allegations of contributory negligence with reasonable prospects of success obviously affect the likely amount of the final judgment. Rule 25.7(5), however, has no express restriction to quantum. Unlike unconnected cross-claims, set-offs are also defences. Consequently, the existence of a set-off with a reasonable prospect of success should also be taken into account at the first stage when the court is considering the grounds for granting an interim payment, and may prevent the court being satisfied that the claimant will obtain judgment for the purposes of r 25.7(1)(c). See *Shanning International Ltd v George Wimpey International Ltd* [1989] 1 WLR 981.

23.15 Where there is a counterclaim worth less than the claim an interim payment may be appropriate. In *O2 (UK) Ltd v Dimension Data Network Services Ltd* (2007) LTL 8/11/2007 summary judgment on a claim for unpaid telephone services was refused as there was a real prospect that a defence of overcharging and a counterclaim might succeed. However, the court found that the defendant was bound to have to pay something for the services provided by the claimant, and an interim payment was made on that basis.

Discretion

23.16 Even if the claimant establishes a ground for making an interim payment, the court retains a discretion whether to make an order. In one of the old cases (*British and Commonwealth Holdings plc v Quadrex Holdings Inc* [1989] QB 842) it was said that the court may take into account the respondent's lack of means either in refusing to make an order or in fixing its amount.

C AMOUNT TO BE ORDERED

Reasonable proportion of total award

23.17 The court is not permitted to order an interim payment of more than a reasonable proportion of the likely amount of any final judgment, taking into account any contributory negligence and any relevant set-off or counterclaim (CPR, r 25.7(4) and (5)). The correct approach is to find the likely overall award, then apply a discount for any contributory negligence (or counterclaim), and then reduce the amount again to arrive at a suitable 'reasonable proportion'. The judge is obliged to make an actual assessment, and is not permitted to take shortcuts such as basing the interim payment on offers made by the defendant (*Eeles v Cobham Hire Services Ltd* [2010] 1 WLR 409). A reasonable proportion may well be a high proportion, provided the assessment of the likely final award is conservative. The objective is to avoid making an overpayment. In *Spillman v Bradfield Riding Centre* [2007] EWHC 89 (QB) the judge deducted 25 per cent as the 'reasonable proportion' from the overall likely award in order on the facts of the case.

The small claims limit may be a reasonable guide for what is meant by 'a substantial amount of money' in r 25.7(1)(c). This may lead to a threshold of £1,000 in personal injuries claims, and of £5,000 for most other claims. There is a standard interim payment of £1,000 under the RTA protocol (para 7.13), and of £50,000 in mesothelioma cases where the defendant fails to show cause on all issues (PD 3D, paras 2 and 6.7). **23.18**

Need for the interim payment

Paragraph 2.1(2) of PD 25B, which says the evidence in support of the application must deal with the items or matters in respect of which the interim payment is sought, could be misinterpreted as meaning that interim payments should be made only for purchases the claimant needs to make. This idea was rejected under the old rules for commercial claims (*Schott Kem Ltd v Bentley* [1991] 1 QB 61), personal injury claims (*Stringman v McArdle* [1994] 1 WLR 1653), and under the CPR by *Wade v Turfrey* (2007) LS Law Medical 352. Where the interim payment is limited to an advance payment out of the damages alleged to have been suffered to the date of the application the judge should not be influenced by how the claimant may intend to spend any interim payment (*Eeles v Cobham Hire Services Ltd* [2010] 1 WLR 409). **23.19**

Information on what the claimant intends to use the money for may assist the court on why the money is needed urgently, or in deciding how much to order. However, the court is not concerned with how a claimant of full capacity spends a final award in damages, and should not try to prescribe what an interim payment is spent on either. Despite the general principle, the rule in *Stringman v McArdle* must not be applied in a mechanistic way. There are cases where the intended use of the money may be relevant because the payment may prejudice the trial or the position of the defendant in the proceedings or prejudge an issue to be determined at the trial (*Tinsley v Sarker* (2004) LTL 23/7/04). Where the interim payment is sought in order to pay for future expenses, it is essential to establish a real need for the money, and an award will be made only if the judge can confidently predict that the trial judge will wish to award a capital sum greater than past special damages and damages for pain, suffering, and loss of amenity (*Eeles v Cobham Hire Services Ltd*). **23.20**

Certificate of State benefits

In personal injuries claims the defendant will need to obtain a certificate of recoverable benefits from the Secretary of State under the Social Security (Recovery of Benefits) Act 1997. A copy of the certificate should be filed at the hearing, and any order made must set out the amount by which the payment to be made to the claimant has been reduced in accordance **23.21** with the Act and the Social Security (Recovery of Benefits) Regulations 1997 (SI 1997/2205) (PD 25B, paras 4.1 to 4.4).

Payment by instalments

23.22 Rule 25.6(7) of the CPR allows an interim payment order to require payment by instalments. Where this happens, the order should set out the total amount of the interim payment, the amount of each instalment, the number of instalments and the date they are to be paid, and to whom the payments should be made (PD 25B, para 3).

D FURTHER APPLICATIONS

23.23 The claimant is permitted to make more than a single application for an interim payment (CPR, r 25.6(2)). In practice, a second or subsequent application will have to be justified by a change in circumstances or other cause being shown, such as an increase in the special damages claim through additional loss of income or expenses being incurred, or through unforeseen delays in determining the claim.

E NON-DISCLOSURE

23.24 The fact that a defendant has made an interim payment must not be disclosed to the trial judge until all questions of liability and quantum have been determined (CPR, r 25.9), unless the defendant agrees. This is important, as the trial judge may (unwittingly) be influenced by knowing that the court has previously decided that the claimant will win, and that the claim is worth more than the amount of the interim payment. In advance of trial a request should be made to the court office to remove all references to interim payments from the court file to avoid accidental disclosure to the trial judge. Where a claimant (usually through ignorance) does disclose this information prematurely, the judge may abort the trial and consider making a wasted costs order against the lawyer responsible.

F ADJUSTMENT

23.25 The court has powers to order all or part of an interim payment to be repaid, to vary or discharge an interim payment order, and to order a co-defendant to reimburse a defendant who has made an interim payment (provided the defendant who made the interim payment has claimed a contribution, indemnity, or other remedy against the co-defendant being ordered to reimburse) (CPR, r 25.8). Interest may be ordered in favour of the defendant on any overpaid interim payment. These powers are usually exercised, if at all, at trial. PD 25B, para 5, contains detailed rules on recording the effect of interim payments and any order for adjustment on the final award for damages.

KEY POINTS SUMMARY

- An interim payment provides the claimant with money on account of the likely award at trial. 23.26
- Different grounds for applying for interim payments are set out at 23.07.
- The amount ordered must not exceed a reasonable proportion of the likely final award taking into account any counterclaim and contributory negligence.

24

SECURITY FOR COSTS

24.01 Generally, the question of who pays for the costs of a claim is not determined until the claim is finally disposed of, whether by consent, interim process, or trial. This is because the usual rule is that the successful party recovers costs from the loser and the outcome on the merits is known only when judgment is obtained. It is for this reason that the parties are not generally allowed to anticipate the eventual costs order by asking for interim orders that their opponents provide funds as security to pay for the costs of the claim. Despite this, it is accepted that there have to be exceptions for cases where there is a significant risk of defendants suffering the injustice of having to defend proceedings with no real prospect of being able to recover costs if they are ultimately successful. An order for security for costs does not infringe art 6(1) of the European Convention on Human Rights, although the right of access to the courts has to be taken into account: *Nasser v United Bank of Kuwait* [2002] 1 WLR 1868.

24.02 An order for security for costs can be made only against a party in the position of a claimant. Once security is given it may be retained, subject to the court's discretion, pending an appeal. An order for security for costs usually requires the claimant to pay money into court as security for the payment of any costs order that may eventually be made in favour of the defendant, and staying the claim until the security is provided. On the application three matters arise:

(a) whether there are grounds for ordering security for costs;
(b) if so, whether the court's discretion should be exercised in favour of making the order; and
(c) if so, how much security should be provided.

24.03 Each of these three matters will be considered after first looking at the procedure for making the application and the capacity of the respondent to the application.

A PROCEDURE

The first application for security should normally be made at the first case management conference (see *Commercial Court Guide*, app 16, para 1). It is made using the usual Part 23 procedure of issuing an application notice (see figure 24.1) supported by written evidence. The written evidence should deal with the grounds on which security is sought, and with any factors relevant to the exercise of the court's discretion. These include the location of the claimant's assets, and any practical difficulties in enforcing any order for costs (see *Commercial Court Guide*, app 16, para 3). It also needs to include an estimate of the defendant's likely costs of defending the claim, which should usually be given in the same form of statement of costs as is used for summary assessments and exhibited to the written evidence. **24.04**

Invariably the application should be made on notice to the claimant, and should be served on the claimant at least three clear days before the day appointed for hearing the application (CPR, r 23.7(1)(b)). Applications for security for costs will be inappropriate in cases on the small claims track because of the restrictions on the recovery of costs in these claims. Applications for further security or to vary the terms on which security is given may be made as circumstances change during the course of a claim. **24.05**

B THE RESPONDENT

An order for security for costs can be made only against a party acting as a claimant (CPR, r 25.12(1)). This means that security for costs can be ordered against a defendant who counterclaims against a claimant. However, with regard to counterclaims, a distinction needs to be drawn between simple counterclaims, where it is possible to obtain orders for security against defendants (*Hutchison Telephone (UK) Ltd v Ultimate Response Ltd* [1993] BCLC 307), and set-offs, where it has been held that security will not usually be ordered: *Neck v Taylor* [1893] 1 QB 560. The reason for this distinction is that a set-off, if established, amounts to a defence to the claim, so a defendant raising a set-off is for this purpose regarded as simply defending and not as advancing a claim. **24.06**

A defendant who issues an additional claim form stands in the position of a claimant with regard to the third party, so may be ordered to provide security for the third party's costs. However, the original claimant does not stand in the position of a claimant with regard to a third party brought in by the original defendant, unless, as a result of directions given in the additional claim, the third party is ordered to defend jointly with the original defendant (see *Taly NDC International NV v Terra Nova Insurance Co Ltd* [1985] 1 WLR 1359 *per* Parker LJ). The question is one of capacity in the main action. There is therefore no jurisdiction to order a defendant to provide security for the costs of any interim application it may make: *Taly NDC International NV v Terra Nova Insurance Co Ltd*. **24.07**

Security for costs may be ordered against any party in the position of a claimant, even if not strictly a 'claimant'. An example is a petitioner on an unfair prejudice petition under the Companies Act 2006, s 994: *Re Unisoft Group Ltd (No 1)* [1993] BCLC 1292. **24.08**

Figure 24.1 Application for Security for Costs

Application notice

For help in completing this form please read the notes for guidance form N244Notes.

Name of court High Court of Justice Queen's Bench Division	
Claim no.	HQ10X21189
Warrant no. (if applicable)	
Claimant's name (including ref.)	CASPKEELER PRODUCTS LIMITED
Defendant's name (including ref.)	LOAMER TECHTRONICS LIMITED
Date	14.9.2010

1. What is your name or, if you are a solicitor, the name of your firm?

   Messrs Pamsoms

2. Are you a ☐ Claimant ☐ Defendant ☑ Solicitor

   ☐ Other *(please specify)*

   If you are a solicitor whom do you represent? Defendant

3. What order are you asking the court to make and why?

   (1) That the Claimant give security for the Defendant's costs of this claim in such amount as the Court may determine
   (2) That until such security is provided all further proceedings in this claim be stayed
   (3) That the Claimant do pay the Defendant's costs of this application.

   On the ground that the Claimant is a company and there is reason to believe it will be unable to pay the Defendant's costs if ordered to do so; alternatively that the Claimant has taken steps in relation to its assets which will make it difficult to enforce an order for costs against it.

4. Have you attached a draft of the order you are applying for? ☑ Yes ☐ No

5. How do you want to have this application dealt with? ☑ at a hearing ☐ without a hearing

   ☐ at a telephone hearing

6. How long do you think the hearing will last? 2 Hours 0 Minutes

   Is this time estimate agreed by all parties? ☑ Yes ☐ No

7. Give details of any fixed trial date or period: None

8. What level of Judge does your hearing need? Master

9. Who should be served with this application? Claimant

N244 Application notice (05.08) 1

Another example is an appellant to an appeal (or a respondent who cross-appeals): see CPR, r 25.15. By r 25.14, an order for security for costs may also be made against someone other than a claimant if the court is satisfied that the person against whom the order is sought either:

(a) assigned the claim to the claimant with a view to avoiding the possibility of being ordered to pay costs; or
(b) has contributed or agreed to contribute to the claimant's costs in return for a share of any money or property which the claimant may recover in the proceedings.

C CONDITIONS FOR GRANTING SECURITY FOR COSTS

Security for costs can be ordered only if one of the conditions set out in CPR, r 25.13(2), is satisfied. The conditions are: **24.09**

(a) the claimant is—
  (i) resident out of the jurisdiction; but
  (ii) not resident in a Brussels Contracting State, a Lugano Contracting State or a Regulation State, as defined in section 1(3) of the Civil Jurisdiction and Judgments Act 1982;
(c) the claimant is a company or other body (whether incorporated inside or outside Great Britain) and there is reason to believe that it will be unable to pay the defendant's costs if ordered to do so;
(d) the claimant has changed his address since the claim was commenced with a view to evading the consequences of the litigation;
(e) the claimant failed to give his address in the claim form, or gave an incorrect address in that form;
(f) the claimant is acting as a nominal claimant, other than as a representative claimant under Part 19, and there is reason to believe that he will be unable to pay the defendant's costs if ordered to do so;
(g) the claimant has taken steps in relation to his assets that would make it difficult to enforce an order for costs against him.

The court also has a power to make an order equivalent to providing security for costs as a sanction for breach of directions: *Olatawura v Abiloye* [2003] 1 WLR 275. However, apart from this, the court has no inherent jurisdiction to order security in other circumstances (see *Condliffe v Hislop* [1996] 1 WLR 753 where the claimant was bankrupt and his own costs were being paid by his mother). **24.10**

Resident outside the jurisdiction

Residence is determined by the claimant's habitual or normal residence, as opposed to any temporary or occasional residence (see *Lysaght v Commissioners of Inland Revenue* [1928] AC 234, a tax case, and *R v Barnet London Borough Council, ex p Shah* [1983] 2 AC 309, a case on entitlement to a grant for education, as applied in *Parkinson v Myer Wolff* (23 April 1985, **24.11** unreported), a case on security for costs). The question is one of fact and degree, and the burden of proof is on the defendant. An English merchant seaman should not be regarded as ordinarily resident abroad, nor should someone who intends to emigrate until he or she has left the country: *Appah v Monseu* [1967] 1 WLR 893. A foreign business person who makes regular visits to England would probably be regarded as resident abroad, but there will come a point, through the length of time spent in this country and other factors, such as owning a house here, when ordinary residence will be established.

24.12 Although most companies reside in the country where they are incorporated, strictly they reside where their central control and management are. This is a question of fact. In *Re Little Olympian Each Ways Ltd* [1995] 1 WLR 560 Lindsay J identified the following as matters to be considered: the contents of the company's objects clause, its place of incorporation, where its real trade or business is carried on, where its books are kept, where its administrative work is done, where its directors meet or reside, where it 'keeps house', where its chief office is situated, and where its secretary resides.

24.13 The wording of CPR, r 25.13(2)(a)(ii) was altered to take into account *De Beer v Kanaar & Co* [2003] 1 WLR 38 and it means that security for costs can be ordered where the claimant is resident in a jurisdiction outside the scope of the Judgments Regulation and the Lugano Convention, even if the claimant has assets within a Convention State.

24.14 Security for costs may be ordered where there are joint claimants, some of whom are resident outside the jurisdiction. According to Lord Donaldson of Lymington MR in *Corfu Navigation Co v Mobil Shipping Co Ltd* [1991] 2 Lloyd's Rep 52 the basic principle underlying CPR, r 25.13(2)(a), is that it is *prima facie* unjust for a foreign claimant, who is in practical terms almost immune from the enforcement of any costs order that may be made, to be allowed to proceed with a claim without making funds available within the jurisdiction against which such an order can be enforced. It would, however, be appropriate to refuse to order security where it is probable that each of the joint claimants will be held to be liable for all the defendant's costs if the action is unsuccessful, provided the English claimants are likely to be able to pay those costs (see *Winthorp v Royal Exchange Assurance Co* (1755) 1 Dick 282 as explained in *Slazengers Ltd v Seaspeed Ferries International Ltd* [1987] 1 WLR 1197 and in the light of *Corfu Navigation Co v Mobil Shipping Co Ltd*). Conversely, security may well be ordered where the English claimants are joined for the purpose of defeating an application for security (*Jones v Gurney* [1913] WN 72), or where it is impossible to predict the likely outcome on costs, or where each claimant is likely to be liable for only a portion of the defendant's costs: *Slazengers Ltd v Seaspeed Ferries International Ltd* [1987] 1 WLR 1197; [1988] 1 WLR 221.

Impecunious company

24.15 Impecuniosity is no ground for ordering security for costs against an individual claimant, the principle being that individuals should not be prevented from seeking justice through want of means. Companies, being artificial persons, need no such protection. Ground (c) applies to limited companies registered under the Companies Acts, and also unlimited companies, companies with a single member (*Jirehouse Capital v Beller* [2009] 1 WLR 751), and other corporations.

The defendant has the burden of proving that a claimant company will be unable to pay any costs that ultimately may be awarded in the defendant's favour. Proof that the company is in liquidation is *prima facie* evidence that it will be unable to pay any costs order: *Northampton Coal, Iron and Waggon Co v Midland Waggon Co* (1878) 7 ChD 500. Otherwise, what is now CPR, r 25.13(2)(c) requires credible testimony of the company's inability to pay. This obviously requires a comparison between the company's assets and the likely costs. Inability to pay may be inferred from evidence that the claimant has declared unusually large dividends after the dispute arose: *Frost Capital Europe Ltd v Gathering of Developers Inc Ltd* (2002) LTL 20/6/02. **24.16**

Taking steps to avoid enforcement

Under CPR, r 25.13(2)(g), security for costs may be ordered where the claimant has taken steps in relation to his assets to make it more difficult to enforce an order for costs. There is no need under this paragraph to show that steps were taken with a view to making enforcement more difficult. Thus, in *Aoun v Bahri* [2002] 3 All ER 182 security for costs was ordered because the claimant had sold his home in Australia, which made it objectively more difficult to enforce a costs order against him, even though there was no evidence that this was done with a view to avoiding paying costs. **24.17**

Security for costs of appeals

By virtue of CPR, r 25.15, the court may order security for costs against an appellant in respect of the costs of the appeal on the same grounds as security may be ordered against a claimant under r 25.13. Likewise, a respondent who cross-appeals may be ordered to provide security for the costs of the cross-appeal. **24.18**

D DISCRETION TO ORDER SECURITY FOR COSTS

Once it has been established that the case comes within one of the conditions set out in 24.09, the court has a general discretion whether to grant an order for security. In exercising this discretion the court will have regard to all the circumstances of the case, and consider whether it would be just to make the order (see CPR, rr 25.13(1)(a) and 25.14(1)(a)). **24.19**

Pre-CPR principles

There is a conflict in the Court of Appeal authorities on the extent to which it is appropriate to consider the pre-CPR cases on the exercise of the discretion to award security for costs. This reflects the wider conflict on whether the introduction of the CPR has achieved its objective of making a new start based on the fact it was a new procedural code (see 3.19 and 3.20). One view, exemplified by *Nasser v United Bank of Kuwait* [2002] 1 WLR 1868, is that the substantial body of pre-CPR case law is consigned to history. On this basis, the discretion has to be exercised applying the overriding objective, and by affording a proportionate protection **24.20** against the difficulty identified by the ground relied upon as justifying security for costs in the case in question.

24.21 Other cases, such as *Vedatech Corporation v Seagate Software Information* (2001) LTL 29/11/01, expressly apply pre-CPR principles, particularly those laid down in *Sir Lindsay Parkinson & Co v Triplan Ltd* [1973] QB 609. In that case Lord Denning MR said the following factors are relevant when the court is exercising its discretion whether to order security for costs:

(a) Whether the claim is bona fide and not a sham. Factors to be taken into account on this are:
   (i) whether the claimant has reasonably good prospects of success;
   (ii) whether the defendant has made any admissions in its statement of case or elsewhere; and
   (iii) whether there has been a substantial offer to settle (as opposed to a small offer to get rid of a nuisance claim).

(b) Whether the defendant is using the application for security oppressively so as to stifle a genuine claim.

(c) Delay in making the application.

Prospects of success

24.22 There is no doubt that the prospect of success at trial is one of the matters that may sometimes be taken into account on the application. If this is taken too far, an application for security may be blown up to an investigation similar to a trial. In a passage approved by the Court of Appeal in *Trident International Freight Services Ltd v Manchester Ship Canal Co* [1990] BCLC 263, Browne-Wilkinson V-C in *Porzelack KG v Porzelack (UK) Ltd* [1987] 1 WLR 420 said at 423:

> Undoubtedly, if it can clearly be demonstrated that the [claimant] is likely to succeed, in the sense that there is a very high probability of success, then that is a matter that can properly be weighed in the balance. Similarly, if it can be shown that there is a very high probability that the defendant will succeed, that is a matter that can be weighed. But for myself I deplore the attempt to go into the merits of the case, unless it can clearly be demonstrated one way or another that there is a high degree of probability of success or failure.

24.23 If there is no defence to the claim, it will almost certainly be unjust to order security. In such a case the defendant is highly unlikely to recover costs in any event, and ordering security often has the practical effect of preventing the claimant from proceeding with the claim.

Stifling a genuine claim

24.24 The question of stifling a genuine claim is a corollary to the question whether the claimant's claim is a sham. The essential policy is that the need to protect the defendant has to yield to the claimant's right of access to the courts to litigate the dispute if it is a genuine claim: *Hamilton v Al Fayed (No 2)* [2003] QB 1175, a case on costs orders against non-parties, where the importance of art 6(1) of the European Convention on Human Rights was stressed. Where the claimant's claim has a good chance of success (there being no need for anything higher), the court will hesitate before making an order which will have the practical effect of preventing the claimant from proceeding. If the case is one where the court feels that security should be ordered, it can fix the amount of the security at a level which will not stifle the claimant in proceeding further: *Innovare Displays plc v Corporate Broking Services Ltd* [1991] BCC 174. In deciding whether a claim is likely to be stifled by an order for security for costs, the court is entitled to take into account any ability the claimant may have of raising money from friends, relatives, or, if it is a company, its directors, shareholders, or other backers or interested persons. As this information is likely to be entirely within the claimant's knowledge, it is generally for the claimant to satisfy the court that it would be prevented from continuing the litigation by reason of the order (*Newman v Wenden Properties Ltd* (2007) 114 Con LR 95), though there are cases where the court will be prepared to infer that the company will be prevented from pursuing its claim if security is ordered (*Trident International Freight Services Ltd v Manchester Ship Canal Co* [1990] BCLC 263 as interpreted in *Keary Developments Ltd v Tarmac Construction Ltd* [1995] 3 All ER 534).

Delay in applying

Applications for security for costs should be made at an early stage in the proceedings. **24.25**
Lateness may of itself be a reason for refusing an order. There have been cases where security has been refused because the application was made just a few days or even a few hours before the trial. An example is *Innovare Displays plc v Corporate Broking Services Ltd* [1991] BCC 174 where a reduced order was made on account of delay.

Resident outside the jurisdiction

Where security is sought against a claimant outside the Brussels and Lugano Convention **24.26**
and Judgments Regulation States, the order should reflect the obstacles in the way of, or the costs of, enforcing an English judgment for costs against the particular claimant or in the particular country concerned: *Nasser v United Bank of Kuwait* [2002] 1 WLR 1868. It is the difficulty of enforcing in the place where the assets are likely to be, rather than enforcement in the country where the respondent happens to live, that has to be considered: *Aims Asset Management v Kazakhstan Investment Fund Ltd* (2002) LTL 22/5/02. Orders have been refused on account of the ease of enforcement in Monaco (*Somerset-Leeke v Kay Trustees* [2004] 3 All ER 406) and the British Virgin Islands (*Longstaff International Ltd v Baker and McKenzie* [2004] 1 WLR 2917). Having considered the evidence, according to *Texuna International Ltd v Cairn Energy Ltd* [2005] 1 BCLC 579, the court has to decide whether the claimant's country is:

(a) one where the obstacles to enforcement are so great that the claimant should be required to give security for the whole costs of the claim; or
(b) one where enforcement is simply more expensive than in England and Wales. In these cases the security should reflect the likely additional expense.

Since the effectiveness of enforcement is the most important consideration, the following **24.27**
factors need to be taken into account if present:

(a) Whether the claimant has substantial assets within the jurisdiction. If so this is a weighty factor against ordering security: *De Bry v Fitzgerald* [1990] 1 WLR 552. Assets within the jurisdiction include damages which the claimant hopes to recover in other proceedings: *Cripps v Heritage Distribution Corporation* (1999) *The Times*, 10 November 1999.

(b) The degree of permanence of those assets, and whether the claimant has a substantial connection with this country: *Leyvand v Barasch* (2000) *The Times*, 23 March 2000.

(c) The ability of the claimant to transfer assets around the world, as in *Berkeley Administration Inc v McClelland* [1990] 2 QB 407.

Impecunious company

24.28 The rationale behind ordering security against an impecunious company is to safeguard the defendant against the prospect of encountering real difficulty in enforcing any order for the costs of the claim. Megarry V-C in *Pearson v Naydler* [1977] 1 WLR 899 said, at 906:

> It is inherent in the whole concept of [CPR, r 25.13(2)(c)] that the court is to have power to order the company to do what it is likely to find difficulty in doing, namely to provide security for the costs which *ex hypothesi* it is likely to be unable to pay. At the same time, the court must not allow the [rule] to be used as an instrument of oppression, as by shutting out a small company from making a genuine claim against a large company.

24.29 The critical question is whether the company will be able to meet the costs order at the time when the order has to be paid (*Re Unisoft Group Ltd (No 2)* [1993] BCLC 532 at 534). The court must consider the nature and liquidity of the company's assets (*Longstaff International Ltd v Baker and McKenzie* [2004] 1 WLR 2917). It will also take into account whether the company's want of means has been brought about by any conduct by the defendant, such as, in a claim for breach of contract, delay in payment or the defendant's delay in performing its part of the contract (*Interoil Trading SA v Watford Petroleum Ltd* (2003) LTL 16/7/03).

E AMOUNT

24.30 *Procon (Great Britain) Ltd v Provincial Building Co Ltd* [1984] 1 WLR 557 establishes the principle that any security should be such as the court thinks just in all the circumstances. The amount should be neither illusory nor oppressive (*Hart Investments Ltd v Larchpark Ltd* [2008] 1 BCLC 589). The court needs assistance on the amount of costs the defendant is likely to incur in the claim, and for this reason it is usual to exhibit a summary statement of costs to the defendant's evidence in support. Security may be ordered for the entire costs of the claim, or up to a future point (such as a pre-trial review), and may include past as well as future costs. There is no rule of practice that the court will always reduce the defendant's estimate by a third (*Procon (Great Britain) Ltd v Provincial Building Co Ltd*), but it is usual to make a deduction from the defendant's costs estimate to take into account any likely reduction on assessment of costs, and also to make an arbitrary discount in respect of future costs to take account of the chances of settling. In suitable cases the court may sit with a costs officer as an informal assessor (see *Commercial Court Guide*, app 16, para 7).

24.31 As was mentioned at 24.24 and 24.25, relevant factors going to the court's discretion which are in the claimant's favour, but which are not strong enough to deprive the defendant of an order for security, may be taken into account when deciding the amount of security to order.

Thus, in *Innovare Displays plc v Corporate Broking Services Ltd* [1991] BCC 174, which was discussed at 24.24, the lateness of the application and the difficulty faced by the claimants in providing security were taken into account by ordering the claimants to provide security in the sum of £10,000 when the defendant's estimated costs were £147,000. In contrast, it is wrong in principle to order merely nominal security on the ground that the defendant has known all along that the claimant is a company of limited means (*Roburn Construction Ltd v Williams Irwin (South) and Co Ltd* [1991] BCC 726, where the judge's order for security in the sum of £5,000 out of estimated costs of £150,000 was increased to £40,000).

F ORDER

Orders for security for costs should follow form PF 44. It is usual to require security to be given by payment into court, although bonds and guarantees are alternatives, as are solicitors' undertakings. Until security is given the claim will be stayed. If the claimant fails to provide security in compliance with the order, the defendant can apply for the claim to be struck out: *Speed Up Holdings Ltd v Gough and Co (Handly) Ltd* [1986] FSR 330. If security is provided the claim continues. After trial, the defendant, if successful, will have a secured fund from which its costs can be paid. **24.32**

In the Commercial Court defendants are sometimes required to give undertakings in damages if security is ordered, and instead of ordering a stay it is more usual to give a time for providing the security with liberty to apply for dismissal of the claim in the event of default. **24.33**

G SUCCESS BY THE CLAIMANT

In cases where the claimant is successful, normally the trial judge will accede to an application on the claimant's behalf for the security money in court to be repaid to the claimant, or for the release of any other security. If the defendant wishes to appeal, however, the court has a discretion whether to impose a stay on the release of the security so as to provide continued security for the costs up to trial in the event that the defendant's appeal succeeds: *Stabilad Ltd v Stephens and Carter Ltd* [1999] 1 WLR 1201. In considering whether to impose such a stay, Auld LJ said that the fact that the claimant had succeeded at first instance was irrelevant. Factors to be considered were the risks of the claimant being unable to pay the costs to trial if the security was released, the claimant's need for the money provided as security for fighting the appeal, and the prospects of the appeal succeeding. **24.34**

KEY POINTS SUMMARY

- An order for security for costs requires a claimant to provide a fund which can be used by the defendant to pay its costs if it defeats the claim. **24.35**

- Security for costs is only available against claimants and parties in the position of claimants.
- The main grounds for seeking security for costs are that the claimant is resident outside the EU; that it is a company in financial difficulties; or that the claimant has taken steps to avoid enforcement.
- If a ground is made out, the court retains a discretion to refuse security for costs.
- The court also has a wide discretion on the amount of security to be provided.

25

SMALL CLAIMS TRACK

In accordance with the principles set out in the overriding objective that cases should be dealt with proportionately to the amount at stake and to the importance of the case, the CPR provide for the allocation of claims with a limited financial value to what is known as the small claims track. This is intended to provide a streamlined procedure with limited pre-trial preparation, with very restricted rules on the recovery of costs from the losing party, and without the strict rules of evidence. It is appropriate for the most straightforward types of cases, such as consumer disputes, accident claims where the injuries suffered are not very serious, disputes about the ownership of goods, and landlord and tenant cases other than claims for possession. As discussed at 14.22, broadly, claims allocated to this track will be those with a value not exceeding £5,000. **25.01**

Regulation (EC) 861/2007 of 11 July 2007 established a European Small Claims Procedure. The Regulation applies to cross-border cases in civil and commercial matters where the value of the claim does not exceed € 2,000. Procedural rules for European Small Claims can be found in CPR, Part 78. **25.02**

A PROVISIONS OF THE CPR THAT DO NOT APPLY

The idea behind having a small claims track is to provide a relatively inexpensive means of resolving disputes having a limited financial value. Some of the more sophisticated procedures available for larger claims are therefore inappropriate for cases on the small claims track, and do not apply (or do not apply in full) once a case has been allocated to the small claims track. These include: **25.03**

(a) most interim remedies, except interim injunctions;

(b) standard disclosure of documents (a more limited form of disclosure applies: see 25.04);
(c) most of the rules on experts, in particular, no expert may give evidence, whether orally or in writing, in a small claims track case without the permission of the court (CPR, r 27.5);
(d) requests for further information can only be made by the court (r 27.2(3)); and
(e) Part 36 offers (because this would interfere with the no costs rule: see 25.14–25.16).

B STANDARD DIRECTIONS

25.04 Once a case has been allocated to the small claims track the court will give directions, which are usually set out in the notice telling the parties that the case has been allocated to this track. A number of options are available to the court, but it is most likely that the court will give what are described as standard directions. Different forms of standard directions apply to different categories of small claims. However, the general form of standard directions provides for:

(a) the parties to serve on the other side copies of the documents they intend to rely upon no later than 14 days before the hearing;
(b) the original documents to be brought to the hearing;
(c) notice of the hearing date and the length of the hearing;
(d) the parties to contact each other with a view to settling the dispute or narrowing the issues, with an obligation to inform the court if the dispute is settled; and
(e) informing the parties that expert evidence is not allowed without the court's express permission.

C SPECIAL DIRECTIONS

25.05 A district judge allocating a claim to the small claims track may decide that standard directions will not ensure that the case is properly prepared, and may instead formulate special directions specifically for the case in hand. At the same time the district judge may fix the date for the final hearing, or may list the matter for further directions. Alternatively, if the district judge takes the view that it will be necessary to have a hearing with the parties present in court to ensure that they understand what they must do to prepare the case, or if the district judge is minded to consider whether the claim should be struck out or summarily disposed of, the case will be listed for a preliminary hearing where these matters can be dealt with.

25.06 Special directions may include the exchange of witness statements. Criteria for deciding whether to make such a direction are found in PD 27, para 2.5, which include the nature of the dispute, the amount claimed, and the policy of giving parties in small claims cases access to justice without undue formality.

25.07 The general rule in small claims track cases is that no expert evidence is allowed, whether oral or in the form of a report. In return, the court will not always insist on the production of expert evidence, whereas it might be required for a similar case on one of the other tracks

(*Bandegani v Norwich Union Fire Insurance Ltd* (1999) LTL 20/5/99, where the claimant did not produce expert evidence for the value of a car which had been damaged in an accident). If a party regards expert evidence as necessary, a special direction will be required, and this should be mentioned in the allocation questionnaire.

Where witness statements or expert reports are used in small claims cases, they do not have to comply with the strict rules on format discussed in Chapters 32 (witness statements) and 31 (experts), because the relevant provisions of the CPR are excluded from small claims cases by r 27.2(1). Expert evidence will be limited to the use of the expert's report unless calling the expert at the hearing is in the interests of justice (r 35.5(2)). **25.08**

D DETERMINATION WITHOUT A HEARING

If all the parties agree, a small claim can be determined by the district judge on the papers without a hearing (CPR, r 27.10). Consent is essential, because otherwise determination on the papers would infringe art 6(1) of the European Convention on Human Rights, which lays down a right to a public hearing. **25.09**

E FINAL HEARINGS

Final hearings in small claims track cases are usually dealt with by county court district judges. Hearings are generally conducted in the judge's room rather than in one of the courtrooms. **25.10**

The general intention is that parties should be able to represent themselves in small claims track cases. Corporate bodies may be represented by any of their officers or employees (PD 27, para 3.2(4)). There is nothing to stop a party being represented by a lawyer, and this is quite common in cases where one or both of the parties has the benefit of insurance. A party (including a company, see *Avinue Ltd v Sunrule Ltd* [2004] 1 WLR 634) may have a lay representative at the hearing, but generally only if the client also attends (Lay Representatives (Rights of Audience) Order 1999 (SI 1999/1225); PD 27, para 3.2(2)). **25.11**

Small claims hearings are informal, and the strict rules of evidence do not apply (CPR, r 27.8). The district judge may proceed in any way that is considered fair. The district judge may ask the witnesses questions before allowing the parties to do so, may refuse to allow cross-examination until all the witnesses have given evidence-in-chief, and may impose limits on the scope of cross-examination. Unless the district judge intervenes in one of these ways, the usual sequence of events is for the claimant's representative to make a short opening (just a few sentences) and then to call the claimant's evidence. Everyone will be sitting around the district judge's table, so no one leaves his or her seat when this is being done. Each witness is questioned first on behalf of the claimant, then on behalf of the defendant. The district judge makes a note of the evidence as it is given, and will ask questions as appropriate. There may be scope for some re-examination. Once all the claimant's evidence has been introduced, the claimant's representative says that is the case for the claimant. It is then the defendant's **25.12** opportunity to call evidence. Once the defendant's evidence has been introduced, the defendant's representative will make some closing remarks. The claimant's representative's closing submissions come last.

25.13 The district judge will usually give a short reasoned judgment there and then. The judgment is likely to be as short and simple as the nature of the case will allow. After giving judgment, the district judge will consider the form of the order to be made and costs are considered.

F COSTS

25.14 Claims allocated to the small claims track are subject to severe costs restrictions. The rule is that no costs will be ordered between the parties except:

(a) the fixed costs relating to issuing the claim;
(b) court fees. These are likely to include the issue fee, an allocation fee if the claim is worth more than £1,500, and a hearing fee;
(c) witnesses' expenses reasonably incurred for travel, subsistence;
(d) loss of earnings or leave up to £50 per day;
(e) experts' fees, up to £200 per expert;
(f) in cases involving a claim for an injunction or specific performance, the cost of legal advice and assistance up to £260; and
(g) Stage 1 and Stage 2 fixed costs under the RTA protocol (see Chapter 6 and RTA protocol, para 5.9) where the claimant reasonably believed the claim had a value exceeding the small claims limit and the defendant has not paid these fixed costs.

25.15 The above restrictions apply in the vast majority of small claims cases. There is, however, an exception if the court finds that one of the parties has behaved unreasonably (CPR, r 27.14(2)(g)). In a suitable case the court can treat a refusal of a Part 36 offer as 'unreasonable behaviour', and if so the offer would be taken into account on costs (r 27.14(3)). Where the court finds there has been unreasonable behaviour, the court may make a summary assessment of costs in favour of the innocent party.

25.16 Some cases are above the small claims financial limits, but are allocated to the small claims track by consent. In these cases costs are restricted to those allowed on the small claims track, unless the parties agree to the case being treated as on the fast track for costs (r 27.14(5), (6)).

G REHEARINGS

25.17 A party who did not attend the final hearing may apply to set aside the order made in his or her absence and for an order that the claim be reheard. An application for a rehearing must be made within 14 days of the absent party being notified of the judgment. A rehearing will be allowed only if there is a good reason for the absence and if the absent party has a reasonable prospect of success at a reconvened hearing (CPR, r 27.11(3)).

26

FAST TRACK

The fast track is intended to cover the majority of defended claims within the £5,000 to £25,000 monetary band. It will also deal with non-monetary claims such as injunctions, declarations, and claims for specific performance which are unsuitable for the small claims track and do not require the more complex treatment of the multi-track. The fast track provides a 'no-frills' procedure for medium-sized cases that do not justify the detailed and meticulous preparation appropriate for complex and important cases. Instead, a case allocated to this track will be progressed to trial within a short timescale after the filing of a defence. Rule 1.1(2)(c) of the CPR provides that part of the overriding objective is that cases should be dealt with proportionately, and it is this idea that underlies the whole concept of having a fast track. **26.01**

When claims are allocated to the fast track, directions will be given setting out the timetable to be followed, with a fixed trial date or trial period no more than 30 weeks later. It is intended that the timetable will be long enough for the parties to undertake the work necessary for preparing the case for trial, but sufficiently tight to discourage elaboration. The court will enforce the timetable it sets so as to ensure that fast track cases proceed to a speedy resolution by trial if they are not settled beforehand. It is for this reason that, as will be seen in this chapter, although some scope is given for the parties to alter some of the dates in the timetable set by the court, changing the date of the trial is only a matter of last resort. **26.02**

A ALLOCATION DIRECTIONS

26.03 When it allocates a case to the fast track, the court will at the same time give case management directions and set a timetable for the steps to be taken from that point through to trial (CPR, r 28.2(1)). The directions given will be designed to ensure that the issues are identified and the necessary evidence is prepared and disclosed (PD 28, para 3.3). Usually the court will give standard directions of its own initiative without a hearing, but will take into account the respective statements of case, the allocation questionnaires, and any further information provided by the parties. Occasionally it may hold a directions hearing, such as when it is proposing to make an unusual order, eg, to appoint an assessor (see PD 28, para 3.11). It is the duty of the parties to ask for all directions that might be needed on any hearing that may be fixed (para 2.5). If any direction or order is required that has not been provided for, it is the duty of the parties to make an application as soon as possible so as to avoid undue interference with the overall timetable (para 2.8). If a directions hearing becomes necessary because of the default of any of the parties, the court will usually impose a sanction (para 2.3).

26.04 Typically, by CPR, rr 28.2(2) and 28.3, the matters to be dealt with in directions given on allocation to the fast track will include:

(a) disclosure of documents;
(b) service of witness statements;
(c) expert evidence; and
(d) fixing a date for the trial, or a period in which the trial is to take place.

Disclosure

26.05 Disclosure is discussed fully in Chapter 29. In most cases, disclosure in some form should have taken place before proceedings were issued. Information about this should have been given with the allocation questionnaire. Based on the respective statements of case and these questionnaires, the procedural judge may direct the parties to give standard disclosure as one of the directions made at this stage, or may direct that no disclosure need take place, or may specify the documents or classes of documents which the parties must disclose (CPR, r 28.3(2); PD 28, para 3). The standard directions will provide for disclosure to be given by service of lists of documents, which must be delivered by a specified calendar date. It is also possible for disclosure to be given more informally without a list and with or without a disclosure statement. Disclosure is likely to be ordered for 28 days after service of the notice of allocation (PD 28, para 3.12).

Witness statements

26.06 The exchange of witness statements is considered further in Chapter 32. Standard directions will usually provide for simultaneous exchange by a specified calendar date of statements from all the factual witnesses on whose evidence each party intends to rely. Exchange is likely to be required between seven and ten weeks from the order for directions (PD 28, para 3.12).

Expert evidence

26.07 Under the CPR cases will not normally be on the fast track unless oral expert evidence at trial is limited to one expert per party in each expert field, and to two fields of expertise (CPR, r 26.6(5)). It is difficult to see how any more experts could give evidence within the time limit for a fast track hearing. In order to keep down costs and to reduce the length of fast track trials, it will be usual for the court to make directions for the instruction of a single joint expert unless there is good reason for doing something else (r 35.7 and PD 28, para 3.9(4)). In addition, in fast track cases the court will not direct an expert to attend at trial unless it is necessary to do so in the interests of justice (r 35.5(2)).

Normally expert evidence should be prepared and/or exchanged about 14 weeks after the order giving directions (PD 28, para 3.12). The standard fast track directions have several different options regarding expert evidence, as alternatives to the instruction of single joint experts. Options provided within the standard directions are: **26.08**

(a) Sequential service of experts' reports. Normally it will be the claimant who will serve first.
(b) Simultaneous exchange of reports on some issues, with sequential service on the others.
(c) Holding of a discussion between experts in cases where the other side's reports cannot be agreed within a short time (usually 14 days) after service. This form of direction provides for a specified calendar date by which the discussion must take place, and the filing of a joint statement of the agreed issues and those in dispute (with reasons for the lack of agreement) by another specified date (which will often be close to the date for filing pre-trial checklists).
(d) That expert evidence is not necessary and no party has permission to call or rely on expert evidence at the trial.
(e) That the parties may rely on experts' reports at trial, but cannot call oral expert evidence.
(f) That the parties may rely on experts' reports, and the court will reconsider whether there is any need for experts to be called when the claim is listed for trial.

Questions to experts

The standard directions also make provision pursuant to the power given by CPR, r 35.6, for written questions to be put to the other side's experts for the purpose of clarifying their reports. Questions can be sent direct to the expert, but copies should be sent to the other side's solicitors. **26.09**

Filing pre-trial checklists

Standard fast track directions will provide for all parties to file completed pre-trial checklists in form N170 no later than specific dates set out in the directions, unless the court considers the claim can be listed for trial without the need for these checklists. When they are used, pre-trial checklists must be returned within the time specified by the court, which will be no later than eight weeks before the trial date or the beginning of the trial period (CPR, r 28.5(2)). At the same time each party must file an estimate of costs in the standard statement of costs form (costs form H). The statement of costs must be divided into parts showing the costs already incurred and an estimate of the future costs to trial. Two fees are payable by the claimant whether or not pre-trial checklists are used (CPFO, fees 2.2 and 2.3). One is a listing fee of £100, which is not refundable. The other is a hearing fee of £500. If these fees are not paid the court will send a notice to pay in form N173, and failing payment within the time **26.10** stated in the notice, the claim will be struck out (r 3.7). As an incentive to settle, the hearing fee is refundable in whole or part (depending on the length of notice) if the court is notified at least seven days before trial that the case has settled or been discontinued.

Fixing the date for trial

26.11 When giving directions the court will fix the trial date or a period, not exceeding three weeks, in which the trial is to take place, and which will be specified in the notice of allocation (CPR, r 28.2(2) to (4)). Rule 28.2(4) provides that the 'standard' period between the giving of directions and the trial will be not more than 30 weeks. It is therefore open for procedural judges to lay down even tighter timetables, which may happen if the court decides that some or all of the usual steps can be omitted, or if it is informed that a pre-action protocol has been complied with or that the steps it was contemplating have already been taken (PD 28, para 3.13). There is also scope, if the procedural judge can be persuaded that it is necessary, for the timetable to be longer than the standard period.

B LISTING DIRECTIONS

26.12 The court may hold a listing hearing, after which it will confirm the trial date and may give further directions. However, in most cases it will not feel the need to have a listing hearing, and will simply confirm or alter the trial date as appropriate, and may make further directions.

C STANDARD FAST TRACK TIMETABLE

26.13 Table 26.1 charts the progress of a fast track case from issue, through allocation to the fast track, up to trial. The case illustrated takes 39 weeks, or about nine months, from issue to trial. The various stages will vary from case to case (such as where there is a stay for negotiation or if the claimant effects service rather than the court) and, as mentioned in 26.11, even the 30-week period between directions and trial may be considerably reduced in some cases. It will be obvious that the parties will have to be in a high state of preparedness before proceedings are issued in all but the very simplest of cases if they are to have any real prospect of adhering to such tight timetables without being forced on the mercy of the courts.

Table 26.1 Progress of fast track case to trial

Week	Step in the proceedings	Time limit
1	Issue of proceedings Service (takes effect on second day after posting)	Usual limitation period 4 months from issue (6 months if outside the jurisdiction)
3	Acknowledgment of service or filing of defence	14 days after deemed service of the particulars of claim
(Say) 5	Service of allocation questionnaires (may be dispensed with)	Not before all defendants have filed defences, or expiry of time for filing defences

Table 26.1 *continued*

Week	Step in the proceedings	Time limit
(Say) 5	Possible transfer to defendant's home court	On filing defence
7	Return of allocation questionnaires and cost estimates	Not less than 14 days after service of the questionnaire
(Say) 9	Allocation decision and directions given by the procedural judge	After return of questionnaires
13	Disclosure of documents	Usually 4 weeks after allocation
19	Exchange of witness statements	Usually 10 weeks after allocation
19	Service of hearsay notices	With exchanged witness statements
23	Experts' reports	Usually 14 weeks after allocation
29	Service of pre-trial checklists (may be dispensed with)	Usually 20 weeks after allocation
31	Return of pre-trial checklists with cost estimates	Usually 22 weeks after allocation
(Say) 33	Any directions arising out of the pre-trial checklists	Optional
(33)	Hearing if pre-trial checklists not returned	Only if parties in default
36	Confirmation of trial date	3 weeks before trial
36	Service of notice to admit	3 weeks before trial
38	Lodging trial bundle	3 to 7 days before trial
39	Service and filing of statements of costs	Not less than 2 days before the hearing
39	Trial	30 weeks after allocation

D AGREED DIRECTIONS

The parties are encouraged to seek to agree suitable directions to be submitted to the court with their allocation questionnaires. If this is done, the court will at least take them into account when giving directions, and if they are suitable, will simply approve them. To be approved the directions should essentially follow the above rules (see PD 28, para 3), which means they must deal with disclosure, witness statements, and expert evidence, lay down a timetable by calendar dates, and provide for a trial or trial period no more than 30 weeks after the start of the timetable. **26.14**

E VARYING THE DIRECTIONS TIMETABLE

A party that wishes to vary the date fixed for returning allocation questionnaires and pre-trial checklists or for the trial must apply to the court (CPR, rr 26.3(6A) and 28.4(1)). Any other date set by the court also cannot be varied by the parties if the variation would make it necessary to vary the dates for either filing pre-trial checklists or trial (r 28.4(2)). The effect of these rules is that it is quite permissible for the parties to agree to the variation of the other directions for service of lists of documents, witness statements, and experts' reports without troubling the **26.15** court, provided the three key dates (filing allocation questionnaires and pre-trial checklists and trial) are not affected by slippage elsewhere. If the parties agree to a variation which does not impinge on any of the key dates, they can act on their agreement without having to file anything at court (PD 28, para 4.5(1)). If a party falls behind on the timetable, the court can use its power to extend or abridge the time for compliance, even if the application is made after the time for compliance has elapsed (r 3.1(2)(a)).

26.16 It is made very clear by PD 28, para 5.4(6), that variations involving loss of the trial date on account of any failure to comply with case management directions will be considered matters of last resort. However, there will be cases where it will become necessary to vary the timetabled date for trial. Examples include cases where there are significant problems with the evidence, where there is a change of solicitor, where proceedings are issued at the very end of the limitation period, and in personal injuries cases where the prognosis is uncertain. If there is no option but to postpone the trial, the postponement will be for the shortest possible time, and the court will give directions for taking the necessary steps outstanding as rapidly as possible. In some of these cases the best course may be to have split trials of liability and quantum or to proceed only on those issues that are ready (PD 28, para 5.4(4)). Where this happens the court may disallow the costs of the remaining issues, or order them to be paid by the party in default in any event.

F LISTING FOR TRIAL

26.17 On receipt of the pre-trial checklists, under CPR, r 28.6(1), the court will:

(a) Fix the date for the trial (or, if it has already done so, confirm the date).
(b) Give any further directions for the trial as may seem necessary, including setting a trial timetable. Standard directions for this stage are set out in the appendix to PD 28.
(c) Specify any further steps that need to be taken before trial.

26.18 If none of the pre-trial checklists is returned within the stated time, the court will normally make an order that, if no pre-trial checklists are filed within seven days from service of the order, the claim and any counterclaim will be struck out. If only some of the parties are in default, the court will give listing directions based on the checklists that are returned (PD 28, para 6.5).

26.19 The parties should seek to agree directions at the pre-trial checklists stage, and they may submit a proposed order (PD 28, para 7.2(1)). Usually directions will be made by the court without a hearing, but it may decide to hold a listing hearing, giving the parties three clear days' notice (PD 28, para 6.3). Notice of a listing hearing will be in form N153.

Trial timetable

26.20 The court may, if it considers that it is appropriate to do so, set a timetable for the trial. Setting a timetable is discretionary (CPR, r 28.6(1)(b)). If it decides to set a timetable, the court must consult with the parties (r 39.4). A trial timetable defines how much time the court will allow at trial for the various stages of the trial itself. A simple direction may limit the time to be spent by each party in calling its evidence and in addressing the court in closing submissions.

More sophisticated timetables will define how much time will be allowed for each witness, or even for cross-examination and re-examination.

Trial bundles

Standard directions made after receipt of pre-trial checklists will provide that an indexed, paginated, bundle of documents contained in a ring binder must be lodged with the court not more than seven days or less than three days before the trial. The parties must seek to agree the contents of the trial bundle a reasonable time in advance, which in practical terms means no later than 14 days before the trial. All documents contained in agreed bundles are admissible at the hearing as evidence of their contents unless the court orders otherwise, or a party gives written notice objecting to the admissibility of particular documents (PD 32, para 27.2). The claimant is responsible for lodging the bundle. Bundles must be lodged at court so that the trial judge can read the case papers in advance of the trial. Identical bundles will be needed for each of the parties, with an additional bundle for the witness box. **26.21**

Case summary

Standard listing directions give the procedural judge the option of directing that a case summary should be included in the trial bundle. This document is intended to be non-partisan, and to be agreed if possible. It should be no more than 250 words long, and should outline the matters in issue, referring where appropriate to the relevant documents in the trial bundle. Again, responsibility for this rests with the claimant. **26.22**

G FAST TRACK TRIALS

The trial of a fast track claim will usually take place in the county court where it is proceeding, but may take place in a civil trial centre or any other court if it is appropriate because of listing difficulties, the needs of the parties, or for other reasons. The judge may be a district judge or a circuit judge. The trial judge will generally have read the trial bundle and will usually dispense with opening speeches. Unless the trial judge otherwise directs, the trial will be conducted in accordance with any order previously made (see 26.20), although the judge is free to set a fresh trial timetable (PD 28, para 8.3). Given the time constraints and the need for proportionality, the trial judge will almost invariably order witness statements to stand as the evidence-in-chief and otherwise control the evidence to be presented. If a trial is not concluded on the day it is listed, the judge will normally sit on the following day to complete it (PD 28, para 8.6). In such an event no further costs will be allowed to the parties. **26.23**

H COSTS IN FAST TRACK CASES

Costs in fast track cases are dealt with in a similar way to multi-track claims, with the exception of trial costs and the use of summary assessment. Trial costs are fixed with the amount allowed depending on the amount recovered, with a small uplift if counsel is attended by a solicitor (see 43.13–43.16). **26.24**

26.25 The general rule is that at the end of a fast track trial the court will make a summary assessment of the costs of the whole claim immediately after giving judgment (PD Costs, para 13.2). To assist the judge in assessing costs, the parties are required to file and serve, not less than two days before the trial, signed statements of their costs in form N260.

KEY POINTS SUMMARY

26.26

- Most cases on the fast track have a monetary value between £5,000 and £25,000.
- It is a 'fast' track because standard directions allow 30 weeks for completion of all the steps required to get the case ready for trial, and for the trial date or period.
- Fast track trials are proper trials, like multi-track trials (but unlike small claims track hearings).
- On the fast track the parties are usually required to use single joint experts, and directions usually permit expert evidence to be given simply by adducing the expert's report, rather than with the expert in attendance.
- Fast track trials usually last up to one day, and costs are usually dealt with on a summary assessment at the end of the trial.

27

MULTI-TRACK

The multi-track is intended for the most important cases. However, a vast range of cases are dealt with on this track, from simple contractual disputes involving little more than £25,000, to complex commercial cases involving difficult issues of fact and law with values of several million pounds, to cases where perhaps no money is at stake but which raise points of real public importance. Case management on the multi-track is intended to reflect this. Simpler cases are given standard directions without the need for hearings, and the parties are expected to comply with those directions without complicating or delaying matters. At the other end of the scale, the courts adopt a far more active approach, possibly with several directions hearings in the form of case management conferences and pre-trial reviews. The courts adopt a flexible approach to ensure that each case receives the right amount of case management input from the court (PD 29, para 3.2(2)). Straightforward multi-track cases may be given tight timetables from defence to trial that are similar to those on the fast track. **27.01**

Cases on the multi-track will generally be dealt with either in the Royal Courts of Justice or other civil trial centre (see PD 29, paras 2 and 3.1). The procedural judge may need to order a transfer on first consideration or at an allocation hearing: see 14.06–14.09. Case management will generally be dealt with by masters and district judges (see PD 2B). It is the duty of the parties at all hearings to consider whether any directions should be made, as this can avoid the need for additional case management hearings later on (PD 29, para 3.5). **27.02**

27.03 Once a case is allocated to the multi-track the court will give directions and hold such procedural hearings as may be appropriate in order to progress the case to trial or resolution by other means. Figure 27.1 illustrates the main stages in the progress of a multi-track case to trial.

Figure 27.1 The multi-track

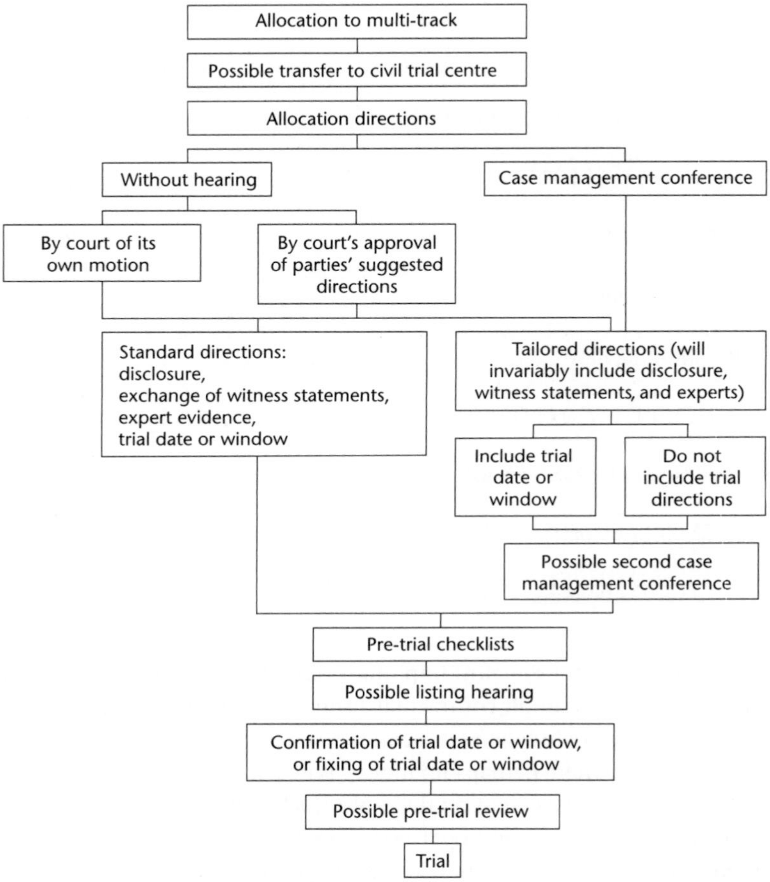

A AGREED DIRECTIONS

27.04 If the parties in a multi-track case agree proposals for the management of the case and the court considers that the proposals are suitable, the court may simply approve them without the need for a directions hearing (PD 29, paras 4.6 and 4.7). This is encouraged, as it obviously saves costs and court time. In order to obtain the court's approval the agreed directions must:

(a) if appropriate, include a direction regarding the filing of a reply;

(b) if appropriate, provide for amending any statement of case;
(c) include provision about the disclosure of documents;
(d) include provision about both factual and expert evidence (the provision about expert evidence may be to the effect that no expert evidence is required);
(e) if appropriate, include dates for service of requests for further information and/or questions to experts, and when they should be answered;
(f) include a date or a period when it is proposed the trial will take place; and
(g) if appropriate, a date for a case management conference.

It will be seen that only items (c), (d), and (f) are obligatory in all cases, although the others will frequently arise in practice. Proposed agreed directions must lay down a timetable by reference to calendar dates. The court will scrutinize the timetable carefully, with particular attention to the proposals for the trial and case management conference, and will be astute to ensure these are no later than is reasonably necessary. **27.05**

The court is free to reject directions that have been agreed between the parties, but will take them into account when making its own directions (either without a hearing or on a case management conference). The ultimate responsibility for case management remains at all times with the court, and parties will be unwise to assume that agreed directions will be automatically approved. **27.06**

B CASE MANAGEMENT CONFERENCES

Case management conferences are not simply directions hearings, but are intended to ensure that the real issues between the parties are identified. Side issues will be dispensed with either by agreement between the parties with due encouragement from the judge, or by means of summary judgment or striking-out determinations at an early stage. Case management conferences may be held immediately after a case is allocated to the multi-track or at any time thereafter through to the listing stage. They can be used as the vehicle for laying down directions at the allocation stage, or may be used later in order to assess how the case is progressing when the initial directions on allocation should have been completed. Normally the court has a discretion whether to call a case management conference. However, where it is contemplated that an order may be made either for the evidence on a particular issue to be given by a single expert, or that an assessor should be appointed, PD 29, para 4.13, provides that a case management conference must be held unless the parties have consented to the order in writing. **27.07**

Listing of case management conferences

There is a commitment towards having case management conferences listed as promptly as possible (PD 29, para 4.12(2)). The minimum period of notice the court will give to the parties of the date for the case management conference is three clear days (CPR, r 3.3(3); PD 29, para 3.7). **27.08**

Attendance at case management conferences

If a case management conference is to be attended by a legal representative on behalf of a party, the representative must be someone familiar with the case (CPR, r 29.3(2)). It is unacceptable to **27.09** send a trainee with a two-page briefing note on such a hearing. Instead it will have to be the fee-earner concerned, or someone (possibly counsel) who is fully familiar with the file, the issues, and the proposed evidence, who must attend. They must be able to field the questions that are likely to be covered at the hearing, and have the authority to agree and/or make representations on the matters reasonably to be expected to arise. Where the inadequacy of the person attending or his or her instructions leads to the adjournment of the hearing, it will be normal for a wasted costs order to be made (PD 29, para 5.2(3)), or even an order for indemnity-basis costs and interest on damages at a higher rate than usual (see *Baron v Lovell* [1999] CPLR 630).

Business at case management conferences

27.10 At a case management conference the court will, as stated by PD 29, para 5.1:

(a) make a thorough review of the steps the parties have taken to date in preparing the case for trial;
(b) consider the extent to which they have complied with any previous orders and directions;
(c) decide on the directions needed to progress the action in accordance with the overriding objective;
(d) ensure that reasonable agreements are made between the parties about the matters in issue and the future conduct of the action; and
(e) record all such agreements.

27.11 To assist the court the legal representatives for all parties should ensure that all documents (and in particular witness statements and expert reports) the court is likely to ask to see are brought to court. They should also consider whether the parties themselves should attend, and consider in advance what orders and directions may be appropriate (PD 29, para 5.6). If the witness statements and experts' reports have not been exchanged at the time of the case management conference, it should follow from *General Mediterranean Holdings SA v Patel* [2000] 1 WLR 272 that the only reports and statements that can legitimately be called for are those that have been disclosed or that may be voluntarily disclosed at the hearing.

Case summary

27.12 An additional matter the parties are required by PD 29, para 5.6, to consider is whether the court may be assisted by a written case summary. This should be a short document not exceeding 500 words which is designed to assist the court in understanding and dealing with the issues raised in the case (PD 29, para 5.7). It should give a brief chronology of the claim, and state the factual issues that are agreed and those in dispute, and the nature of the evidence needed to decide them. Responsibility for preparing the document rests with the claimant, and if possible it should be agreed by the other parties.

Usual directions

27.13 In all cases the court will set a timetable at the case management conference for the steps it decides are necessary for preparing the case for trial (PD 29, paras 5.3 and 5.4). Typically the court will consider giving directions on the following matters:

(a) Whether the claimant has made clear the claim that is being made and the amount being claimed, and whether the defence is no more than a bare denial or is otherwise unclear. Orders for amendment and/or for further information may be appropriate if the statements of case are insufficiently clear for the other side to understand the case that has to be met.

(b) The scope of disclosure of documents required.
(c) The nature of the expert evidence required, and how and when it should be obtained. The court will not give permission for the use of expert evidence unless it can identify each expert by name or field of expertise, and say whether each expert's evidence should be given orally or by use of a report. Further matters that may be considered are whether the evidence on a particular issue should be given by a single expert, or an assessor should be appointed, and whether there should be discussions between the experts.
(d) Disclosure of witness statements and summaries.
(e) Whether further information should be provided on matters other than statements of case, such as witness statements.
(f) Arrangements for questions that may be put to experts.
(g) Whether it would be just and save costs to have split trials on liability and quantum, or whether there should be the trial of one or more preliminary issues.
(h) Whether there should be another case management conference or a pre-trial review.
(i) Whether it is possible to fix a date for the trial, or to give a trial 'window'. The court will be anxious to comply with the rule that the trial should be fixed as soon as practicable (CPR, r 29.2(2)).
(j) Whether the trial should be dealt with by a High Court judge, or by a specialist judge. If so, the court will also consider transferring the case to the appropriate court (PD 29, para 5.9).

Unusual directions

It is the duty of the parties to ensure that all interim matters are dealt with at the case management conference. If they want an order dealing with a matter that is not normally dealt with at a case management conference, such as an order for an interim payment or for specific disclosure, and they know the application is likely to be opposed, they should issue and serve an application notice in time for it to be heard at the conference. If the time allowed for the conference is insufficient to deal with the contested application also, they must inform the court at once so that a fresh date can be fixed. Failure to take these steps may result in a costs sanction (PD 29, para 5.8). PD 23A, para 2.10, provides that where a party decides to make an application at a hearing that has already been fixed, but there is insufficient time to serve an application notice, it may be sufficient simply to give such written notice as is possible, and to make the application orally at the original hearing. **27.14**

Other directions from those provided for by CPR, r 3.1(2), that may be considered in appropriate cases include: **27.15**

(a) directing that part of the proceedings, such as a counterclaim, be dealt with as separate proceedings;
(b) staying the whole or part of the proceedings either generally or until a specified date or event;
(c) consolidating proceedings;
(d) trying two or more claims at the same time;

(e) deciding the order in which issues are to be tried; and
(f) excluding an issue from consideration.

Plans, photographs, and models

27.16 Where a party intends to use photographs, plans, models, and similar items as evidence at trial, then generally notice should be given to the other parties by the date for disclosing witness statements (CPR, r 33.6(4)).

Video evidence

27.17 Provided it is relevant, video evidence is generally admissible. A party may wish to use video evidence to illustrate a manufacturing process, or the scene of an accident (although photographs will usually be sufficient, and are far simpler to handle in court). Rather more striking are surveillance videos used from time to time in personal injuries claims to test whether the claimant is as badly injured as is claimed. As video recordings fall into the wide definition of 'documents' for the purposes of CPR, Part 31, the usual rules on disclosure and inspection apply (see Chapter 29). Furthermore, there is an obligation to inform the court at the first opportunity that such evidence will be relied upon, as arrangements need to be made to ensure video equipment is available at trial, and extra time will be required for the trial for showing the evidence (*Rall v Hume* [2001] 3 All ER 248).

Controlling evidence

27.18 Under CPR, r 32.1(1) the court has a general power to control evidence by making directions as to the issues on which it requires evidence, the nature of that evidence, and how it is to be placed before the court. This power may be exercised to exclude otherwise admissible evidence (r 32.1(2)), and may be used to limit cross-examination (r 32.1(3)). The power under r 32.1 could be used to exclude evidence obtained by unlawful means, but covert video evidence obtained in breach of art 8 of the European Convention on Human Rights and by trespassing inside the claimant's home was admitted in *Jones v University of Warwick* [2003] 1 WLR 954. The court was influenced by the fact that experts retained by both sides had already seen and commented on the video evidence, and by its power to impose other sanctions, such as in costs.

C FIXING THE DATE FOR TRIAL

27.19 The court will fix the trial date or the period in which the trial is to take place as soon as practicable (CPR, r 29.2(2)). This may be possible when it gives allocation directions, but in complex cases (and also, perhaps, badly prepared cases and cases where the facts are developing, such as many personal injuries claims) this may have to be delayed, perhaps for a considerable period of time. Where fixing the trial date is postponed, it may be revisited either at a later case management conference, or on the application of the parties, or after further scrutiny by the court.

When the court fixes the date for trial (or lays down a trial period or 'window'), it will give written notice to the parties, and will also specify a date by which the parties must file pre-trial checklists (r 29.2(3)). The court may alternatively make an order for an early trial on a fixed date and dispense with pre-trial checklists (PD 29, para 8.1(2)), or may simply list the case for trial (CPR, r 29.6(1)). **27.20**

In Queen's Bench Division cases proceeding in the Royal Courts of Justice in London, other than cases in the Admiralty and Commercial Courts and the Technology and Construction Court, a direction will be given as early as possible (often the first case management conference) with a view to fixing the trial or trial window (see *Queen's Bench Guide*, para 9.4.4). It will often direct that the trial is not to begin before a specified date, or that it will be held within a specified period. The claimant must then, within the next seven days, take out an appointment with the Clerk of the Lists and give notice of the appointment to the other parties. At the listing hearing the claimant must bring any case summary, the particulars of claim, and any orders relevant to listing, and all parties must have details of the dates of availability of their witnesses, experts, and counsel. The Clerk of the Lists will try to provide the earliest firm trial date or trial window consistent with the case management directions (para 9.4.8). **27.21**

In the Commercial Court most cases are given fixed trial dates after the pre-trial timetable has been set at the case management conference (*Commercial Court Guide*, para D16.1). Fixed dates are given on the understanding that, if other cases have been substantially underestimated, or if urgent matters need to be heard, the trial may be delayed. **27.22**

D PRE-TRIAL CHECKLISTS

Pre-trial checklists in form N170 will (unless dispensed with) be sent out to the parties by the court for completion and return by the date specified in the directions given when the court fixed the date or period for trial (CPR, r 29.6). The forms should be served by the court at least 14 days before they must be returned. PD Costs, para 6.4(1), says that costs estimates must be filed and served at the same time as pre-trial checklists are filed. Each party is under an obligation to return a completed checklist before the specified date, and the claimant is required to pay a listing fee of £100 and a hearing fee of £1,000 (CPFO, fees 2.2 and 2.3). If pre-trial checklists are dispensed with, these fees are payable within 14 days of dispatch of the notice of the trial date or period. In cases which are proceeding on a counterclaim alone the fees are payable by the defendant. The hearing fee is refundable (in whole or part depending on the amount of notice given) if the party who paid it gives written notice to the court at least seven days before the trial (or before the trial date has been fixed) that the claim has been settled or discontinued. There is a possible sanction of automatic striking out for non-payment after a reminder from the court (CPR, r 3.7). **27.23**

In the Commercial Court, pre-trial checklists must be in the form set out in the *Commercial Court Guide*, appendix 13. They must be returned to the court at least three weeks before the trial (para D14). **27.24**

Purpose of pre-trial checklists

27.25 Pre-trial checklists are used to check that earlier orders and directions have been complied with, and to provide up-to-date information to assist the court with deciding when to hold the trial and how long it will take, and in making trial timetable directions. Once all the checklists have been received, or the time limit has expired, the file will be placed before the procedural judge, who will make directions for trial along the same lines as those set out in 27.34, or direct that there should be a listing hearing or pre-trial review.

Failure to file pre-trial checklists

27.26 If no one returns a pre-trial checklist by the specified date, the court will usually make an order that the parties must do so within seven days of service of the order, failing which the claim and any counterclaim will be struck out (PD 29, para 8.3(1)). Where only some of the parties file pre-trial checklists, the court will fix a listing hearing. It will also fix a listing hearing if any of the checklists do not provide the necessary information, or if the court considers that such a hearing is necessary to decide what further directions should be given to complete the preparations for trial (CPR, r 29.6(3)).

E LISTING HEARINGS

27.27 Listing hearings (technically, these are called 'hearings under r 29.6(4)') serve a similar purpose to pre-trial reviews, but concentrate on making the decisions relevant to fixing the date of the trial. They are fixed for dates as early as possible, and the parties are given at least three clear days' notice of the date. Even if a listing hearing is fixed because some of the parties did not file their pre-trial checklists, the court will normally fix or confirm the trial date and make orders about the steps to prepare the case for trial (PD 29, para 8.3(2)).

F PRE-TRIAL REVIEW

27.28 If a pre-trial review is listed, it is likely to take place about eight to ten weeks before trial (four to eight weeks in the Commercial Court). Pre-trial reviews are not held in all cases, but only in those that merit the additional hearing. The intention is that they should be conducted by the eventual trial judge.

Before the pre-trial review

27.29 In some cases a pre-trial review may be required by directions made by the court at an earlier stage, such as on allocation or at a case management conference. In other cases the court may decide to hold a pre-trial review of its own initiative, such as when it considers the pre-trial checklists. In this event it will give the parties at least seven clear days' notice of the hearing of a pre-trial review (CPR, r 29.7).

In the Chancery Division the claimant should, seven days before the pre-trial review, circulate a list of matters to be considered at the pre-trial review, including suggestions for how the case should be tried. Other parties must respond at least two days before the hearing (*Chancery Guide*, para 3.23). The claimant's solicitors should deliver to the Listing Office (or master if the pre-trial review is to be conducted by a master) by 10 a.m. on the day before the hearing a bundle containing all the pre-trial checklists, the list of matters to be considered, the proposed trial timetable, and any other useful documents (para 3.24). **27.30**

In the Commercial Court, before the pre-trial review the parties must discuss and attempt to agree a draft trial timetable, which should be filed at least two days before the hearing (PD 58, paras 11.3 and 11.4). Any difference of view should be clearly identified. **27.31**

Attendance

The same rules about a fully informed representative being present apply to pre-trial reviews as apply to case management conferences (see 27.09) and in the specialist courts in particular they should be attended by the trial advocates. **27.32**

Pre-trial review directions

At a pre-trial review the court will not readily change earlier directions, and will assume the parties were content with the original directions if they failed to apply within 14 days for variation of case management directions (PD 29, paras 6 and 9.3). **27.33**

Perhaps the most important task on a pre-trial review is to determine the timetable for the trial itself. This can lay down time limits for examination and cross-examination of witnesses, and for speeches. Doing this is intended to force advocates to focus their preparation, and to produce well-managed trials. Other matters to be dealt with are: **27.34**

(a) Evidence, particularly expert evidence. At this stage there should have been full disclosure and perhaps also discussions between the experts. It may be possible to make more rigorous directions about which experts really do need to be called at the trial, and which experts (or which parts of the expert evidence) can be taken from the experts' reports.
(b) A time estimate for the trial.
(c) Preparation and organization of trial bundles.
(d) Fixing a trial date or week.
(e) Fixing the place of trial. This will normally be the court where the case is being managed, but it may be transferred depending on the convenience of the parties and the availability of court resources (PD 29, para 10.1).

Agreed pre-trial review directions

The parties are required to seek to agree the directions to be made on the pre-trial review, and may file an agreed order (PD 29, para 9.2). The court may then make an order in the terms agreed, or make some other order, or reject the proposals and continue with the pre-trial review. **27.35**

G DIRECTIONS GIVEN AT OTHER HEARINGS

27.36 The court is not restricted to making case management directions on the occasions described above, but can do so on any occasion on which the case comes before the court (PD 29, para 3.4). In fact, whenever there is a hearing it is the duty of the parties to consider whether any directions should be made, and to make any appropriate application on that occasion (PD 29, para 3.5). Further, the court may hold a directions hearing on its own initiative on three clear days' notice whenever it appears necessary to do so. This can include situations where progress is delayed because one or other of the parties is in default of directions previously made (PD 29, para 3.6). It can also occur because a party needs a direction not already in place, perhaps because a need to amend, or to ask for further information, has arisen since the last case management hearing. In such cases the application must be made as soon as possible so as to minimize the disruption to the original timetable (PD 29, para 3.8).

H VARIATION OF CASE MANAGEMENT TIMETABLE

27.37 Case management directions fall into two categories:

(a) Those that can be varied only by an order made by the court on an application by a party seeking a variation (CPR, r 29.5(1)). These 'key dates' are:
  (i) dates for returning allocation questionnaires;
  (ii) dates fixed for holding a case management conference;
  (iii) dates fixed for holding a pre-trial review;
  (iv) dates specified for the return of pre-trial checklists; and
  (v) dates fixed for trial (including a trial 'window').

(b) All other types of case management direction. These may be varied by the parties by consent, provided the variation does not affect any of the 'key dates' in category (a) above. There is no need to file anything with the court when a variation is agreed that does not affect any of the 'key dates' (PD 29, para 6.5(1)).

27.38 If there has been a real change in circumstances there is usually no objection to the court reviewing previous directions. Where there are no changed circumstances, any review of directions made on notice has to be made by way of appeal (*Umm Qarn Management Co Ltd v Bunting* [2001] CPLR 21).

I CASE MANAGEMENT IN THE COMMERCIAL COURT

27.39 Commercial list claims are treated as allocated to the multi-track (CPR, r 58.13(1)). Preparation for the first case management conference, including preparing the case memorandum and case management bundle, starts when a defence is filed (see 14.10ff). The case management conference should be attended by solicitors and at least one of the advocates retained by each side (*Commercial Guide*, para D8.2). If practicable the judge will use the case management conference to fix the entire pre-trial timetable (para D8.7). A standard set of directions is set out in the *Commercial Guide*, app 8. In addition to disclosure, witness statements, and experts, these usually include a progress monitoring date and a date for returning pre-trial checklists, and may include a date for a pre-trial review. A fixed trial date is usually given immediately after the pre-trial timetable has been set at the case management conference (para D16.1).

The court continues to take an active role in managing the case throughout its progress to trial (para D11). At least three clear days before the progress monitoring date the parties must file progress monitoring information sheets (in the form set out in app 12). These tell the court whether directions have been complied with, and whether the parties will be ready for trial (para D12.2). **27.40**

A pre-trial review will only be convened if this is appropriate, and if so, it will take place after the progress monitoring date, and usually about four to eight weeks before trial (para D18.2). Before the pre-trial review the parties must attempt to agree a timetable for the trial, which must be filed at least two clear days before the pre-trial review (PD 58, para 11.4). Advocates who are to represent the parties must attend (para 11.2). The purpose of the review is to ensure case management directions have been complied with (para 11.1) and set the trial timetable (or decide this is not necessary) (para 11.5). **27.41**

KEY POINTS SUMMARY

- The multi-track caters for cases over £25,000 and a wide range of specialist court claims. **27.42**
- Simple multi-track cases are dealt with in ways similar to cases proceeding on the fast track.
- More complex cases have case management which is tailored to the case in hand.
- Case management by the court can take place as 'box-work', based on allocation questionnaires and pre-trial checklists filed by the parties.
- Alternatively, the court may require the parties to attend case management conferences, listing hearings, and/or pre-trial reviews for the purpose of setting directions and agreeing trial timetables.
- Although the court may direct the joint instruction of experts in multi-track cases, the greater importance and complexity of these cases often means the court will permit the parties to instruct their own experts, who are often called as witnesses at trial.
- The Commercial Court has highly developed case management procedures, with its own forms, and with each case having a case memorandum and a case management bundle.

28

SANCTIONS

28.01 So that the court can ensure that its case management directions and orders are complied with, and to retain control over the conduct of litigation, it needs to be armed with suitable coercive powers. These are provided in the CPR in the form of sanctions. These range from adverse interim costs orders through to striking out the whole or part of the defaulting party's statement of case. In imposing a sanction the court will have two purposes in mind. It will primarily be concerned with ensuring its orders and directions are complied with, so that both parties can prepare properly for the trial, and that the trial can take place fairly and without undue delay. This is often achieved by making an 'unless' order giving the defaulting party a last chance to comply, failing which some draconian sanction will take effect. Its secondary purpose is to punish the defaulting party for the past default. The balance between these two concepts will vary from case to case.

A NON-COMPLIANCE WITH PRE-ACTION PROTOCOLS

If, in the opinion of the court, there has been non-compliance with a relevant pre-action protocol, various sanctions may be imposed: see 5.21–5.24. To ensure the parties are not taken by surprise by allegations of breach of the protocols, which may otherwise be raised as late as the trial, the parties have to set out whether there has been compliance in the claim form or particulars of claim (PD Pre-action conduct, para 9.7). This requirement implies that the defendant will need to plead a response to what the claimant says about compliance in the defence. **28.02**

B NON-COMPLIANCE WITH THE CPR

There are various provisions in the CPR and practice directions that impose sanctions in default of due compliance. For example, r 35.13 of the CPR provides that a party which fails to disclose an expert's report may not use the report at the trial or call the expert to give evidence orally unless the court gives permission. A more severe sanction is imposed by r 3.7, which provides for the striking-out of claims for non-payment of allocation and listing fees after the time set by a notice of non-payment. **28.03**

C NON-COMPLIANCE WITH DIRECTIONS

It is to be expected that from time to time one or other of the parties to proceedings will be unable to keep to the directions timetable imposed by the court. This will not generally be a problem provided the parties cooperate and can still keep to the directions relating to the key dates relating to filing allocation questionnaires, case management conferences, pre-trial reviews, filing pre-trial checklists, and trial (CPR, rr 26.3(6A), 28.4, and 29.5). If the non-compliance is through events outside the control of the defaulting party or is otherwise not deliberate, the parties should cooperate, in compliance with r 1.4(2)(a), and resolve the difficulty by agreeing a new timetable that preserves the key dates. The time specified by any provision of the CPR or by the court for doing any act may be varied by the written agreement of the parties, unless there is an express prohibition on variation in the rules (r 2.11). **28.04**

Both parties have obligations regarding compliance with court directions and the provisions of the CPR, and are required to cooperate with each other (see r 1.4(2)(a)). Where both sides are in breach, it is difficult to justify imposing a sanction purely on the claimant, provided it is reasonably possible to have a fair trial notwithstanding the breach (*Hateley v Morris* [2004] 1 BCLC 582). **28.05**

A party not in default faced with an opponent who has not complied with the court's directions is not entitled to try to make matters worse for the defaulting party by sitting back and allowing further time to go by. Nor is the party not in default entitled to jump the gun by making an immediate application for an order with sanctions. Instead, the correct procedure is for the innocent party to write to the defaulting party referring to the default, asking for it **28.06** to be rectified within a short reasonable period (usually seven or fourteen days), and giving warning of an intention to apply for an order if the default is not remedied. If there is continued default, the innocent party may apply for an order to enforce compliance or for a sanction to be imposed or both. Any application for such an order must be made without delay. If the innocent party does delay in making the application, the court may take the delay into account when it decides whether to make an order imposing a sanction or whether to grant relief from a sanction imposed by the rules or any practice direction.

D PRESERVATION OF TRIAL DATE

28.07 The general approach that will be adopted where there has been a breach of case management directions that may impinge on the date or window fixed for the trial of a claim is set out in PD 28, para 5.4 (fast track) and PD 29, para 7.4 (multi-track). These provisions apply on case management hearings, on applications to extend time (see 28.22) and applications for relief from sanctions (*Ethemi v Shiels* [2008] EWHC 291 (QB), see 28.24–28.32). According to PD 28 and PD 29:

(a) The court will not allow a failure to comply with directions to lead to the postponement of the trial unless the circumstances of the case are exceptional. The need to show exceptional circumstances only applies where the postponement of the trial is sought on account of a failure to comply with case management directions, not when the need to postpone arises through circumstances outside the control of the parties (*Collins v Gordon* [2008] EWCA Civ 110).
(b) If practicable to do so, the court will exercise its powers in a manner that enables the case to come on for trial on the date or within the period previously set.
(c) In particular the court will assess what steps each party should take to prepare the case for trial, direct that those steps are taken in the shortest possible time, and impose a sanction for non-compliance. Such a sanction may, eg, deprive a party of the right to raise or contest an issue or to rely on evidence to which the direction relates.
(d) Where it appears that one or more issues are or can be made ready for trial at the time fixed while others cannot, the court may direct that the trial will proceed on the issues that are or will then be ready, and order that no costs will be allowed for any later trial of the remaining issues or that those costs will be paid by the party in default.
(e) Where the court has no option but to postpone the trial it will do so for the shortest possible time and will give directions for the taking of the necessary steps in the meantime as rapidly as possible.
(f) Litigants and lawyers must be in no doubt that the court will regard the postponement of a trial as an order of last resort. The court may exercise its power to require a party as well as the party's legal representative to attend court at a hearing where such an order is to be sought.

E APPLICATION FOR SANCTIONS

28.08 Hearings where the court has to decide whether to impose a sanction can arise in a number of different ways. These include applications brought by the innocent party specifically for this purpose using the on-notice procedure described in Chapter 20, applications by the defaulting party to extend the time for complying with the relevant requirement, case management conferences and pre-trial reviews, and the trial itself.

Dependent on the nature of the default and its consequences both on the innocent party and the overall management of the case, the court may view the default on any of four different levels of seriousness: 28.09

(a) Minor breaches are usually dealt with by allowing the defaulting party a limited period of time to comply, together with an adverse costs order in respect of any interim application needed to bring the matter before the court (*Colliers International Property Consultants v Colliers Jordan Lee Jafaar Bhd* [2008] 2 Lloyd's Rep 368).
(b) If the matter is more serious the court will make it plain it requires compliance by stating a revised deadline is 'final', usually combined with an adverse costs order. Proportionality has to be kept in mind (*TIP Communications LLC v Motorola Ltd* [2009] EWHC 212 (Pat), where a hearing just to badge an order as 'final' was regarded as contrary to the overriding objective). Breach of a final order usually results in a sanction being imposed on a further application to the court (*Sports Network Ltd v Calzaghe* [2008] EWHC 2566 (QB)).
(c) More serious defaults will be met by enforcing compliance by making an 'unless' order with a stated sanction in default, again usually combined with an adverse costs order. Breach of an unless order results in the immediate imposition of the stated sanction (see 28.14). Unless orders should only be made if the court is satisfied that in all the circumstances such a sanction is appropriate (*Marcan Shipping (London) Ltd v Kefalas* [2007] 1 WLR 1864).
(d) Very serious defaults result in the immediate imposition of a sanction, which may restrict the evidence that may be adduced, or restrict the value of the claim, or even consist of striking out part or the whole of a party's statement of case with judgment for the innocent party.

Like all other orders, those containing final and unless orders must specify the time within which the step under consideration must be taken by reference to a calendar date and a specific time, typically 4 p.m. on a specific Friday (CPR, r 2.9: see 41.12). Also like all other orders, unless orders take effect on the day they are pronounced (immediately: see 41.01), and have to be complied with even if there is a delay in sealing the formal order (*Rahamim v Reich* (2009) LTL 10/2/09). 28.10

An applicant seeking the imposition of a sanction has the burden of proof, whereas on an application for relief from sanctions (see 28.24–28.32) after non-compliance with an unless order the onus is on the defaulting party (*Malekout v Medical Sickness Annuity and Life Assurance Society Ltd* (2003) LTL 20/10/03). 28.11

F UNLESS ORDERS

A court dealing with a procedural default, and particularly a persistent default, may make an order in the form of an unless provision. This is to the effect that, if the terms of the order are breached, the other party may file a request for judgment to be entered and costs (CPR, r 3.5). 28.12

PD 40B, para 8.2, lays down formulas for drafting unless orders. These are in the following forms (to be adapted as necessary):

(a) 'Unless the claimant serves his list of documents by 4.00 p.m. on Friday, 12 November 2010 his claim will be struck out and judgment entered for the defendant.' This is the preferred form.
(b) 'Unless the claimant serves his list of documents within 14 days of service of this order...' This should be used where the defaulting party did not attend the hearing where the order was made.

28.13 The test on expiry of an unless order is whether there has been complete compliance with the terms of the order, subject only to *de minimis* exceptions (*Jani-King (GB) Ltd v Prodger* (2007) LTL 10/4/07). There is a reluctance, however, to be drawn into disputes over what may appear to be a poor attempt at performance at the interim stage rather than leaving the matter to trial (*Rahamim v Reich* (2009) LTL 10/2/09).

G NON-COMPLIANCE WITH AN UNLESS ORDER

28.14 If a party fails to comply with a rule, practice direction, or court order imposing any sanction, the sanction will take effect unless the defaulting party applies for and obtains relief from the sanction (CPR, r 3.8). Therefore unless orders in the form that a claim 'shall' or 'will' be struck out or dismissed mean that on expiry of the time limit the claim is struck out or dismissed automatically, and no further order from the court is necessary (PD 3A, para 1.9). Rule 3.8(3) provides that extensions cannot be agreed between the parties.

28.15 Where the court has made an order providing that a statement of case shall be struck out if a party does not comply with the order, r 3.5 sets out the procedure for obtaining judgment on non-compliance with the order. A number of different situations are dealt with:

(a) Where the party in default is the claimant and the order provides for the striking-out of the whole of the particulars of claim, the defendant may enter judgment with costs by filing a request (there is no prescribed form) stating that the right to enter judgment has arisen because the court's order has not been complied with (r 3.5(2)(a) and (3)).
(b) Where the party in default is the defendant and the order provides for the striking-out of the whole of the defence, and the claim is limited to one of the following forms of relief, namely, a specified sum of money, damages, and/or delivery of goods with the alternative of paying their value, the claimant may enter judgment with costs by filing a request (again there is no prescribed form) stating that the right to enter judgment has arisen because the court's order has not been complied with (r 3.5(2)(b) and (3)).
(c) Where neither (a) nor (b) applies, such as where the order provided for striking out only part of a statement of case, or where the defendant is in default and the claimant has claimed equitable relief, the party seeking to enter judgment for non-compliance with the order must make an application in accordance with Part 23 (r 3.5(4)). This means that an application notice must be issued for a hearing on notice.

As mentioned at 28.14, the sanction embodied in an 'unless' order takes effect without the need for any further order if there is a material failure to comply (r 3.8). In *Marcan Shipping (London) Ltd v Kefalas* [2007] 1 WLR 1864 it was held that, if the innocent party applies for judgment under r 3.5, the court's function is limited to deciding what order should properly be made to reflect the sanction which has already taken effect. **28.16**

H STRIKING OUT

The most severe sanction that may be imposed is striking out. The CPR, r 3.4(2)(c) provides that the court may strike out a statement of case if it appears that there has been a failure to comply with a rule, practice direction, or court order. Striking out the whole of a party's statement of case ought to be reserved for the most serious, or repeated, breaches or defaults (see *UCB Corporate Services Ltd v Halifax (SW) Ltd* [1999] CPLR 691, where there was a total disregard of the court's orders). There are relatively few occasions where immediate striking out as opposed to some lesser sanction or the imposition of an unless order is appropriate (*Biguzzi v Rank Leisure plc* [1999] 1 WLR 1926). Striking out for failing to file a pre-trial checklist and being late for a case management hearing was regarded as disproportionate in *Lambeth London Borough Council v Onayomake* (2007) *The Times*, 2 November 2007. **28.17**

Courts considering striking out have to pay attention to the fact they may be depriving the claimant of access to the court, which has particular importance under art 6 of the European Convention on Human Rights (*Woodhouse v Consignia plc* [2002] 1 WLR 2558). In *Taylor v Anderson* [2003] RTR 305 it was said that a striking-out order based on delay should only be granted if there is a considerable risk that it will be impossible to have a fair trial. Where there has been delay, but a fair trial is still possible, the court has to consider imposing some lesser sanction. In *Powell v Boladz* (2003) LTL 22/9/03 the court was faced with competing arguments under art 6(1) of the European Convention on Human Rights. There were protracted delays, which infringed the defendant's right to a trial within a reasonable time, but despite the delays it was found that a fair trial was still possible. It was held it would be disproportionate to strike out the claim. **28.18**

Where there is prejudice to the innocent party, such as in *Purdy v Cambran* [1999] CPLR 843, where the defendant's expert died in the period of delay, the prejudice may offset an argument that striking out would be a disproportionate sanction. In the absence of prejudice it is usual to permit the defaulting party to rectify the matter (*Colliers International Property Consultants v Colliers Jordan Lee Jafaar Bhd* [2008] 2 Lloyd's Rep 368). **28.19**

I LESS SERIOUS IMMEDIATE SANCTIONS

In less serious cases of default or breach the court may be prepared to impose a sanction which 'fits the crime'. Rule 3.4 itself states that the power to strike out may be exercised over the whole or just a part of a statement of case. For example, a party may be in default of an order **28.20** to provide further information on a single issue in a case where several issues are raised. A suitable sanction in such circumstances may be striking out the part of the statement of case dealing with that issue (see *QPS Consultants Ltd v Kruger Tissue (Manufacturing) Ltd* (1999) LTL 10/9/99). Powers available to the court include ordering a party to pay certain costs forthwith or debarring a party in default from adducing evidence in a particular form or from particular witnesses. Alternatively, the court may impose sanctions that limit or deprive a party, if successful, of interest on any money claim, or which increase the amount of interest payable by the party in default. By a proper exercise of case management powers it should be possible for the courts to ensure parties do not disregard timetables, whilst producing a just result.

28.21 A striking-out order was set aside in *Grundy v Naqvi* (2001) LTL 1/2/01 on the ground that this was a disproportionate response to a failure to comply with an order to disclose witness statements. The defaulting party had some reason for not having complied (in that she wanted to amend her statement of case, which would have had an impact on the content of the witness statements), albeit she was also guilty of delay in seeking permission to amend. An order was made requiring the defaulting party to pay £50,000 into court.

J EXTENDING TIME AND CORRECTING ERRORS

28.22 The court has a general power to extend and abridge time (CPR, r 3.1(2)(a)). It can extend time on its own initiative under rr 3.1(2)(a) and 3.3, and can do so even where the extension relates to an unless order (*Keen Phillips v Field* [2007] 1 WLR 686). A party who will be unable to comply with an order or direction in time (or who is already in breach), and who has not been able to agree an extension with the other side, may make an application under this rule asking the court to extend time for compliance. There is a fundamental difference between applying for an extension of time before a time limit has expired, and seeking relief from a sanction after the event (*Robert v Momentum Services Ltd* [2003] 1 WLR 1577). In simple time applications under r 3.1 the court applies the overriding objective, with the principal consideration being whether there is any prejudice caused to the other side through the delay in taking the step in question. The court is not required to consider the checklist of factors set out in r 3.9, discussed at 28.24–28.32. In *Becker v Baileys Shaw and Gillet* (1999) LTL 4/11/99 a decision to refuse to extend time for complying with an unless order to supply particulars of loss was described as 'plainly wrong'. Part of the reasoning was that the particulars were complex and required the evidence of a forensic accountant experienced in Lloyd's claims.

28.23 On other occasions, a default may arise through defective performance. For example, it may be that the wrong form was used, or that it was sent to the wrong address (but still came to the attention of the other side), or that the document used was not completed correctly or fully. These are errors of procedure. By r 3.10 such errors do not invalidate the step purportedly taken, unless the court so orders. The court may make an order invalidating a step if it was so badly defective that the other side were misled, or where the defects are so great that it would not be right to regard the purported performance as performance at all. Further, by r 3.10(b) the court may make an order to remedy any error of procedure. In *Phillips v Symes (No 3)* [2008] 1 WLR 180, purported service in Switzerland was defective because the English language version of the claim form had been removed by the Swiss court from the package which was served. It was held that service had taken place, albeit irregularly. In the absence of any prejudice, it was said that the court could and should exercise its power to rectify the error of procedure using r 3.10(b). A defaulting party should consider seeking such an order where there is an objection made regarding defective performance.

K SETTING ASIDE AND RELIEF FROM SANCTIONS

There are two mechanisms for seeking to retrieve the position once a sanction comes into effect: **28.24**

(a) Where judgment has been entered under CPR, r 3.5 (see 28.15) following the striking out of a statement of case for breach of an unless order, the defaulting party may apply to set aside the judgment under r 3.6.
(b) A party in breach of any other rule, practice direction, or order imposing a sanction for non-compliance may apply for relief from the sanction (CPR, r 3.8(1)).

Both types of application are made by issuing an application notice, which must be supported by evidence. In both types of application the court applies the principles on seeking relief from sanctions in r 3.9 (rr 3.6(4) and 3.8(1)). Where a party has made an application to extend time (without an express application for relief from sanctions under r 3.9) for complying with an unless order, the court will also apply the criteria laid down under r 3.9 on the application (*Keith v CPM Field Marketing Ltd* (2000) *The Times*, 29 August 2000). Rule 3.9 provides that the court will consider all the circumstances, and then sets out nine factors which will be considered: **28.25**

(a) the interests of the administration of justice;
(b) whether the application for relief has been made promptly;
(c) whether the failure to comply was intentional;
(d) whether there is a good explanation for the failure;
(e) the extent to which the party in default has complied with other rules, practice directions, court orders, and any relevant pre-action protocol;
(f) whether the failure to comply was caused by the party or his legal representative;
(g) whether the trial date or the likely trial date can still be met if relief is granted;
(h) the effect which any failure to comply had on each party; and
(i) the effect which the granting of relief would have on each party.

The factors listed in r 3.9 are used generally when the court is exercising a discretion to relieve against provisions having an adverse effect, such as on applications to lift stays imposed for not taking steps and on applications for extending the time for appealing. **28.26**

The better view is that it is essential for the judge to consider each of the factors listed in r 3.9 systematically, and then to weigh the various factors in deciding whether granting relief would accord with the overriding objective. This is particularly necessary in complex cases: see *Woodhouse v Consignia plc* [2002] 1 WLR 2558 and *RC Residuals Ltd v Linton Fuel Oils Ltd* [2002] 1 WLR 2782. On the other hand, in *Jones v Williams* (2002) LTL 27/5/02, this was said to be unnecessary, provided the judge considered the relevant factors from the list and applied them to the case. **28.27**

28.28 In *RC Residuals Ltd v Linton Fuel Oils Ltd*, there had been previous defaults before breach of an unless order relating to expert evidence. It was held that the previous defaults, and an earlier adjournment of the trial date, were weighty factors. Nevertheless relief was given as these factors were offset by the fact that the present default was not intentional, did not affect the parties, the new trial date could still be met, and a full explanation had been given.

28.29 *Woodhouse v Consignia plc* is authority for saying it has to be kept in mind that refusing the order deprives the defaulting party of access to the court, which has particular importance, given art 6(1) of the European Convention on Human Rights. The possibility of having a fair trial is very important in applications for relief from sanctions, but not to the almost determinative extent it has in applications for the imposition of sanctions (*Hansom v E Rex Makin* (2003) LTL 18/12/03).

28.30 In *Woodward v Finch* [1999] CPLR 699, the claimant was three days late in complying with an unless order for service of witness statements. He explained his delay by pointing to a change in solicitors, and problems in transferring his legal aid certificate. He purported to serve his witness statements the day before his application was heard. The Court of Appeal refused to interfere with the judge's decision to grant relief, despite a history of non-compliance and the fact that the excuse put forward was not a good one. The main reasons were that relief had been applied for promptly; the default was more muddle-headedness than anything else; the trial date could still be met; there was not much effect on either party through the default; and refusing relief would have a devastating effect on the claimant.

No explanation for the delay

28.31 It is common in applications for relief from sanctions for the defaulting party to be unable to point to any adequate reason for the delay. This is sometimes because no reasons are advanced, and sometimes because the 'reasons' suggested on behalf of the defaulting party are regarded as unconvincing or inadequate by the court.

28.32 It appears from *Thorn plc v MacDonald* [1999] CPLR 660, that the court should consider all the circumstances in accordance with the overriding objective even if there is no explanation for the delay, but the fact that the delay is unexplained should be a weighty factor in the exercise of the discretion whether to grant relief from a sanction (or to extend time).

KEY POINTS SUMMARY

28.33
- Sanctions are imposed in order to ensure parties adhere to the directions timetable imposed by the court.
- In deciding what to do when faced with a breach of directions or the requirements of the CPR or practice directions, the court applies the overriding objective and also bears in mind the right to a fair trial under the European Convention on Human Rights, art 6(1).
- The court seeks to impose a proportionate sanction which fits the crime.

- Often the court will give a defaulting party a last chance to comply by imposing an 'unless order', which will result in some draconian sanction applying automatically if there is a further breach.
- A party who is likely to fall into default should apply for a 'time order' under CPR, r 3.1(2)(a) extending the time for compliance.
- After a sanction has come into effect, a defaulting party can apply for relief from the sanction under CPR, r 3.9.

29

DISCLOSURE

29.01 In almost all types of civil disputes there will be documentary evidence relating to the matters in issue. In a contractual claim, eg, there are likely to be documents evidencing or comprising the negotiations leading up to the contract being entered into, there are likely to be contractual documents, including things like quotations, orders, delivery notes, invoices, and standard terms of trading, documents recording any work done or materials bought for the purposes of the contract, and subsequent correspondence dealing with any complaints about performance. Even in claims which appear to be mainly concerned with oral evidence, such as accident claims, it is likely there will be accident report forms, accident book entries, documents made in compliance with the health and safety legislation, medical records about the treatment given, and financial documentation dealing with things like the claimant's salary (wages slips, P60s, and employers' salary records) and out-of-pocket expenses (for which there should be receipts). In commercial claims there may be vast amounts of documentation dealing with the issues raised.

29.02 The parties obviously need to retain and marshal the documentation in their own possession for the purposes of assisting their own cases. Beyond this, however, the CPR require the parties to give advance notice to their opponents of all the material documentation in their control, and this duty extends not only to favourable documentation, but also to documents that might assist the other side. This process of giving advance notice of documentation is known as 'disclosure'. Advance notice is given, generally in the early stages of litigation, shortly after the allocation stage, by serving a list of documents on the other side. The list is a formal document listing all the documents in a party's control that are material to the case. Disclosure is technically the first stage of a two-stage process. The second stage is 'inspection', which is the process by which the other side can either request copies of documents appearing in the list of documents, or attend at the disclosing party's offices and physically inspect the documents being disclosed.

A LAWYERS' RESPONSIBILITIES

Solicitors must inform their clients in the early stages after they are first retained of the obligations owed by the client in disclosing documentation, and must ensure (so far as possible) that all original documents are preserved and made available at the disclosure stage (*Rockwell Machine Tool Co Ltd v E P Barrus (Concessionaires) Ltd* [1968] 1 WLR 693). Counsel have similar duties, and must withdraw if a client refuses to accept counsel's advice to disclose material documents (Code of Conduct of the Bar of England and Wales, para 608(d)). **29.03**

B CLIENTS' RESPONSIBILITIES

The primary obligation to make full disclosure of material documents rests with the client. As will be seen, 'standard disclosure' in the course of fast track and multi-track claims involves the client conducting a reasonable search for disclosable documents, and then personally signing a 'disclosure statement' to the effect that the nature of the duty to disclose is understood and has been complied with. The obligation is a continuing one and includes documents that come into a party's possession at any stage until the proceedings are concluded (CPR, r 31.11(1)). If documents come to a party's notice after lists have been exchanged, the party is under an immediate obligation to notify every other party (r 31.11(2)). **29.04**

C STAGE WHEN DISCLOSURE TAKES PLACE

The main obligation to disclose documents arises in fast track and multi-track claims as a result of directions made at the allocation stage, or at the first case management conference. Generally, these directions will include provision for disclosure and inspection of documents. The direction will state whether lists of documents should be provided, and whether a disclosure statement is required (see below). It will also give a calendar date for the last day for compliance. Allocation takes place within a few weeks of the filing of defences and disclosure is normally ordered for a few weeks thereafter. The result is that disclosure is often required about two months after the defence is filed. As we saw in Chapter 25, the same does not apply in small claims track cases, where there is no obligation to serve lists of documents and disclosure is usually limited to disclosing the documents each party intends to rely upon. **29.05**

29.06 As discussed in Chapter 5, a wide range of documents that might be disclosed during proceedings will be disclosed beforehand in compliance with the pre-action protocols. If full disclosure has taken place in this way, the court should be informed with the allocation questionnaires so that the directions made on allocation reflect the correct position.

29.07 Important documents are also often disclosed when statements of case are served. Documents referred to in statements of case, particularly key documents such as a contract alleged to have been breached, are usually served with the relevant statement of case (see Chapter 13). Further, the other side is entitled to inspect documents (without waiting for standard disclosure) referred to in statements of case which are not served at the same time (CPR, r 31.14). In addition, if there is an interim application in the early stages of litigation, material documents will often be disclosed as exhibits to the written evidence in support of the application (see Chapter 32).

29.08 There are also a number of somewhat specialized disclosure procedures that are described in Chapters 30 and 37. Unlike disclosure by lists, which happens in most defended fast track and multi-track claims, these other procedures are resorted to only in cases where there is a real litigation reason for incurring the additional expense that they entail. These additional procedures are:

(a) *Norwich Pharmacal* orders (see 30.02–30.12), which are used to obtain information (which can include documentation) designed to assist in identifying a tortfeasor;
(b) pre-commencement disclosure orders under the SCA 1981, s 33(2): see 30.20;
(c) disclosure orders against persons who are not parties to the substantive litigation, under the SCA 1981, s 34(2): see 30.27;
(d) search orders, which allow a claimant, through a supervising solicitor, to take disclosable documents from the premises of a defendant who is likely to destroy the evidence rather than voluntarily providing it under an ordinary disclosure order: see Chapter 37.

D STANDARD DISCLOSURE

29.09 An order to give disclosure is an order to give standard disclosure unless the court directs otherwise (CPR, r 31.5). This involves each party making a reasonable search for material documents (see 29.19–29.20), and then making and serving on every other party a list of documents (see 29.22ff) identifying the documents being disclosed in a concise, convenient form (r 31.10(2) and (3)).

Documents to be disclosed under standard disclosure

29.10 The nature of the documents that must be disclosed under standard disclosure is described by CPR, r 31.6, which provides:

> Standard disclosure requires a party to disclose only—
> (a) the documents on which he relies; and
> (b) the documents which—
>   (i) adversely affect his own case;
>   (ii) adversely affect another party's case; or
>   (iii) support another party's case; and

(c) the documents which he is required to disclose by a relevant practice direction.

In addition to disclosing documents relied upon, it can be seen that adverse documents must also be disclosed. There is no relevant practice direction for the purposes of sub-para (c). **29.11**

Determining whether a document falls into any of these categories is to be judged against the statements of case, and is not enlarged by reference to matters raised elsewhere, even in exchanged witness statements (*Paddick v Associated Newspapers Ltd* (2003) LTL 10/12/03). In *Atos Consulting Ltd v Avis Europe plc* [2008] Bus LR Digest D20 redacted parts of certain board minutes were irrelevant as they did not relate to the project in issue or related matters, so no inspection was ordered for these documents. **29.12**

Standard disclosure will require an employer in a personal injuries claim to disclose documents relating to other accidents involving the same machinery; employers must also disclose the earnings of comparative employees (*Rowley v Liverpool City Council* (1989) *The Times*, 26 October 1989); and claimants must disclose their medical records, even back to birth, so the defendant's medical advisers can see whether the claimant had any medical history relevant to the extent or effect of the alleged injuries (*Dunn v British Coal Corporation* [1993] ICR 591; *OCS Group Ltd v Wells* [2009] 1 WLR 1895). In professional negligence claims against solicitors the entirety of the solicitor's original file is almost invariably covered by standard disclosure (*Martin v Triggs Turner Barton* (2008) *The Times*, 5 February 2008). In an unfair prejudice case under the Companies Act 2006, s 994, where it was alleged the directors were receiving excessive remuneration, standard disclosure included financial documents such as accounts and budgets (*Arrow Trading and Investments Est Ltd v Edwardian Group Ltd* [2005] 1 BCLC 696). Where there was a dispute as to whether a contractual document was sent by e-mail, disclosure was ordered of the relevant hard disks, backups, and server (*Marlton v Tektronix UK Holdings Ltd* (2003) LTL 10/2/03). However, the courts will not allow disclosure to be used to 'fish' for a case. A party which does not have the materials for even an arguable claim, but hopes to find evidence from the other side, is said to be fishing. Nor will disclosure be allowed on matters solely relevant to the credibility of witnesses (*Thorpe v Chief Constable of Greater Manchester Police* [1989] 1 WLR 665). **29.13**

A party's statement as to the relevance of documents for the purposes of standard disclosure is usually conclusive (*Loutchansky v Times Newspapers (No 1)* [2002] QB 321; *GE Capital Corporate Finance Group v Bankers Trust Co* [1995] 1 WLR 172) to avoid court time being wasted on satellite issues. Ultimately, the court may investigate the matter to avoid a party being the judge in his own cause (*West London Pipeline and Storage Ltd v Total UK Ltd* [2008] 2 CLC 258). **29.14**

Under the old, pre-1999, system, discovery (as disclosure was then called) extended beyond the CPR categories into 'train of inquiry' documents (*Compagnie Financière et Commerciale du Pacifique v Peruvian Guano Co* (1882) 11 QBD 55). These are documents which are not themselves relevant, but which could provide information that could lead to a train of inquiry resulting in finding relevant documents. Under the CPR orders for disclosure of train of inquiry documents are rare (albeit not unknown: see *Commissioners of Inland Revenue v Exeter City AFC Ltd* (2004) LTL 12/5/04), because they increase costs which are unlikely to be justified on proportionality grounds. **29.15**

'Document'

29.16 For the purposes of disclosure, the word 'document' means anything on which information of any description is recorded (CPR, r 31.4). It is not restricted to writing, nor to paper documents. It will cover e-mails, text messages on mobile telephones, and relevant information stored on a computer hard drive or floppy disk. The latter includes documents which have been 'deleted' and technical information known as 'metadata'. It also covers photographs, sound and video recordings.

'Control'

29.17 Disclosure must be made of documents which are, or have been, in a party's control (CPR, r 31.8(1)). 'Control' is defined as covering documents which are or have been in a party's physical possession, and also where a party had a right to possession or to inspect or take copies (r 31.8(2)).

29.18 For example, a bailee or agent has physical possession of documents entrusted to him or her on behalf of the owner. An employer or principal has a right to possession of documents in the hands of an employee in the course of the employee's employment or an agent in the course of the agency. A spouse does not have control over documents which he or she could call for in his or her capacity as a company director (*B v B (Matrimonial Proceedings: Discovery)* [1978] Fam 181). However, a company's documents may be under the control of a majority shareholder who has complete control over the company's affairs (*Re Tecnion Investments Ltd* [1985] BCLC 434), and it is possible for a subsidiary company's documents to be in the control of its parent company (*Lonrho Ltd v Shell Petroleum Co Ltd* [1980] QB 358, CA; [1980] 1 WLR 627, HL). Problems can arise where one subsidiary is sued and relevant documents are in the possession of another subsidiary in the group, especially if the other subsidiary is in another country (see *Unilever plc v Chefaro Proprietaries Ltd* [1994] FSR 135).

Duty to search

29.19 When giving standard disclosure, a party is required to make a reasonable search for documents falling within the meaning of standard disclosure (CPR, r 31.7). The rule sets out factors relevant in deciding on the reasonableness of a search, which include:

(a) the number of documents involved;
(b) the nature and complexity of the proceedings;
(c) the ease and expense of retrieval of any particular document; and
(d) the significance of any document which is likely to be located during the search.

29.20 The rule does not demand that no stone be left unturned (*Abela v Hammonds Suddards* (2008) LTL 9/12/08). It may be reasonable, eg, to decide not to search for documents coming into existence before some particular date, or to limit the search to certain specific places, or to documents falling into particular categories (PD 31, para 2). A more limited search would be appropriate for secondary as opposed to primary evidence (*Nichia Corporation v Argos Ltd* [2007] Bus LR 1753). Secondary evidence is merely an aid in assessing the primary evidence in a case.

Limiting standard disclosure

The court may dispense with or limit standard disclosure. Further, the parties may agree in writing to dispense with or to limit standard disclosure. The court may make directions requiring disclosure but dispensing with lists, or for disclosure to take place in stages, and the parties may agree to disclosure taking place in a similar informal, or staged, manner. For example, it is provided in CPR, r 31.10(8), that: **29.21**

> the parties may agree in writing—
> (a) to disclose documents without making a list; and
> (b) to disclose documents without the disclosing party making a disclosure statement.

E LIST OF DOCUMENTS

The list

Disclosure will usually be made by serving lists of documents (see the example in figure 29.1). As the name suggests, a list of documents simply lists the documents that a party has relating to the case. It must identify the documents in a convenient order and as concisely as possible. It must indicate which documents are said to be privileged (see 29.26), and which documents are no longer available and what has happened to them. Further, the list must contain a disclosure statement (see 29.23) unless this has been dispensed with (by the court or by agreement in writing between the parties). **29.22**

Figure 29.1 List of documents

List of Documents:

Standard Disclosure

In the High Court of Justice
Queen's Bench Division
Claim No HQ10X 96789
Claimant Chediston Wholesale Limited
Defendant Linstead Fruitgrowers Limited

Notes:

- The rules relating to standard disclosure are contained in Part 31 of the Civil Procedure Rules.
- Documents to be included under standard disclosure are contained in Rule 31.6.
- A document has or will have been in your control if you have or have had possession, or a right of possession, of it or a right to inspect or take copies of it.

Disclosure Statement

I, the above-named party (if the party making disclosure is a company, firm, or other organization identify here who the person making the disclosure statement is and why he is the

Figure 29.1 *continued*

appropriate person to make it) Graham McBride, the managing director of the Claimant Chediston Wholesale Limited. I negotiated the relevant contract on behalf of the Claimant with the Defendant and state that I have carried out a reasonable and proportionate search to locate all the documents which I am required to disclose under the order made by the court on 16 June 2010. I did not search for documents (pre-dating [ ]) [located elsewhere than the Claimant's offices and those of its solicitors] [in categories other than the contractual documents and correspondence] [for electronic documents].
[I carried out a search for electronic documents contained on or created by the following: the Claimant's computer system.]

[I did not search for the following:–

documents contained on or created by the [Claimant] [Defendant]

PCs	portable data storage media	databases
servers	back-up tapes	off-site storage
laptops	mobile phones	notebooks
PDA devices		handheld devices

documents contained on or created by the [Claimant] [Defendant]

mail files	document files	web-based applications
calendar files	spreadsheet files	graphic and presentation files

documents other than by reference to the following keyword(s)/concepts:

I certify that I understand the duty of disclosure and to the best of my knowledge I have carried out that duty. I further certify that the list of documents set out in or attached to this form, is a complete list of all documents which are or have been in my control and which I am obliged under the court order to disclose.

I understand that I must inform the court and the other parties immediately if any further document required to be disclosed by Rule 31.6 comes into my control at any time before the conclusion of the case.

(I have not permitted inspection of documents within the category or class of documents (as set out below) required to be disclosed under Rule 31.6(b) or (c) on the grounds that to do so would be disproportionate to the issues in the case.)

Signed: Date: 2 July 2010

Claimant

I have control of the documents numbered and listed here. I do not object to you inspecting them/producing copies.

1 Copy letters from Claimant to Defendant (42 items)	6.1.2008–2.7.2010
2 Letters from Defendant to Claimant	18.1.2008–2.7.2010
3 Sale contract	24.5.2008
4 Resale contract	15.6.2008

Figure 29.1 *continued*

5 Copy letters Claimant's solicitor to Defendant	various
6 Copy letters Claimant's solicitor to Defendant's solicitor	various
7 Letters Defendant's solicitor to Claimant's solicitor	various
8 Statements of case common to both parties	various

I have control of the documents numbered and listed here, but I object to you inspecting them:

1 Communications between the Claimant and its solicitors in their professional capacity for the purpose of giving and receiving legal advice	various
2 Instructions to, opinions of, and drafts settled by counsel	various
3 Communications between the Claimant's officers and employees when litigation was pending for the purpose of obtaining information or evidence for use in this claim	various

I object to you inspecting these documents because:

They are, as appears from their nature, protected from production by legal professional privilege being documents which came into being for and in contemplation of this claim.

I have had the documents numbered and listed below, but they are no longer in my control.

The originals of the copy documents numbered 1, 5, and 6 in the first part of this list, which are assumed to be in the control of their respective recipients.

Disclosure statement

A list of documents must contain a 'disclosure statement' setting out the extent of the search that has been made and certifying that the party understands the duty to disclose and that to the best of the disclosing party's knowledge the duty has been carried out. Where a party has not searched for a category or class of document on the ground that to do so would be unreasonable (see 29.20), this must be stated in the disclosure statement and the categories or classes of document not searched for must be identified (CPR, r 31.7(3)). Any such limitation on the search can be challenged by applying to the court (*Nichia Corporation v Argos Ltd* [2007] Bus LR 1753). The list of documents in figure 29.1 includes a disclosure statement. Making a false disclosure statement, without an honest belief in its truth, may be punished as a contempt of court (CPR, r 31.23). **29.23**

A disclosure statement is not a mere technicality. Its purpose is to impose a positive duty on each party to give full standard disclosure. It has to be signed by the party in person, not by their solicitor (r 31.10(6)). If there are several claimants or defendants in a case, each should sign a disclosure statement. Providing a single composite list of documents does not satisfy r 31.10 (*Arrow Trading and Investments Est Ltd v Edwardian Group Ltd* [2005] 1 BCLC 696). Where the party making the disclosure statement is a company, firm, or association, the statement must identify the person making the statement and explain why he or she is a suitable person to make it (CPR, r 31.10(7)). The statement will have to give that person's name **29.24** and address, as well as the office or position he or she holds within the organization (PD 31, para 4.3). An insurer is allowed to sign a disclosure statement on behalf of the insured (para 4.7), which is helpful because sometimes the insured has no real interest in the litigation, and leaves everything to the insurer under its right of subrogation.

Lost and destroyed documents

29.25 Documents that are no longer available, because they have been lost, destroyed, or sent to someone else, must still be 'disclosed' by identifying them in the list of documents (CPR, r 31.2). The third section of the list is specifically designed for documents in this category. All that is required is that such documents be identified, together with the reason why they are no longer available (r 31.10(4)(b)). Obviously, there is no requirement to give inspection.

F PRIVILEGE

29.26 Privileged documents must be disclosed, but need not be made available for inspection by the other side. This means they must be identified in the second section of the list of documents, and the party asserting the right or duty to withhold inspection must state in the list the grounds on which that assertion is based (CPR, r 31.19(3)). The three heads of privilege will be considered in this section (where there is a right to withhold disclosure), together with public interest immunity (where there is a duty to withhold disclosure). When considering these different heads of privilege, it is worth bearing in mind the comment made by Lord Edmund-Davies in *Waugh v British Railways Board* [1980] AC 521 at 543:

> ...we should start from the basis that the public interest is, on balance, best served by rigidly confining within narrow limits the cases where material relevant to litigation may be lawfully withheld. Justice is better served by candour than by suppression.

Privilege against self-incrimination

The common law rule

29.27 In *Blunt v Park Lane Hotel Ltd* [1942] 2 KB 253, Goddard LJ said:

> ...the rule is that no one is bound to answer any question [or produce any document] if the answer thereto would, in the opinion of the judge, have a tendency to expose [him or her] to any criminal charge, penalty, or forfeiture which the judge regards as reasonably likely to be preferred or sued for.

29.28 The claimant had objected to answering questions in a slander claim on the ground that her answers would tend to expose her to the risk of ecclesiastical penalties. It was held that it was purely fantastic to suppose that in 1942 she would be subject to any ecclesiastical penalty if she admitted adultery, and permission was granted to ask the questions. Exposure to the risk of a penalty under EU legislation forming part of the law of the UK by virtue of the European Communities Act 1972 is a penalty for these purposes.

In *Rank Film Distributors Ltd v Video Information Centre* [1982] AC 380, HL, it was held that the privilege could be relied on where a criminal charge was more than a contrived, fanciful, or remote possibility. The privilege may arise, not only when answering might increase the risk of being prosecuted, but also where the prosecution may make use of the answer in deciding whether to prosecute, and where the prosecution may seek to rely on the answer in establishing guilt (*Den Norske Bank ASA v Antonatos* [1998] QB 271, CA). Merely asserting there is a risk is not enough: the risk must be real and appreciable (*Rank Film Distributors Ltd v Video Information Centre*). **29.29**

In *C plc v P (Attorney-General intervening)* [2008] Ch 1 it was held that since the enactment of the Human Rights Act 1998 there has been no difference between civil and criminal cases, and that free-standing or 'independent' evidence is not protected by the privilege against self-incrimination. It is only 'compelled' evidence that may be protected by the privilege. Accordingly, no privilege attached to objectionable images found on a computer during the execution of a search order. **29.30**

The privilege extends to providing documents or answers that tend to expose the wife or husband of the person asserting the privilege to criminal proceedings or proceedings for the recovery of a penalty (Civil Evidence Act 1968, s 14(1)). As a corporation has legal personality it can claim the privilege (*Triplex Safety Glass Co Ltd v Lancegaye Safety Glass (1934) Ltd* [1939] 2 KB 395). In such cases it may be necessary to distinguish between the corporation and its officers and employees, and to consider whether all or only some of them may be at risk of criminal proceedings (*Sociedade Nacional de Combustiveis de Angola UEE v Lundqvist* [1991] 2 QB 310). **29.31**

The privilege may be lost by the turn of events. Once the party has been prosecuted, whether resulting in a conviction or an acquittal, he cannot be prosecuted again except in the limited circumstances provided by the Criminal Justice Act 2003, ss 75 to 97. In some cases the party may be given a pardon, which again eliminates the risk of prosecution (*R v Boyes* (1861) 1 B & S 311). If the Crown Prosecution Service indicates in writing that it will not make use of the information sought for the purposes of any criminal proceedings against the party or his wife, and if a clause stating that no disclosure made in compliance with the order will be used in evidence in the prosecution of any offence committed by the party or his wife is included in the order, the court may conclude there is no realistic risk of use by the prosecution, and hold the privilege does not apply (*AT & T Istel Ltd v Tully* [1993] AC 45). **29.32**

Statutory limitations on the rule

One of the strange consequences of these rules is that the risk of documents being used against the party for the purposes of criminal proceedings is obviously greater in cases where the defendant is alleged to have been particularly dishonest, and the worse the conduct alleged the greater the prospect of a successful claim to the privilege. After *Rank Film Distributors Ltd v Video Information Centre* [1982] AC 380 there were fears that the privilege would operate to frustrate the use of search orders in intellectual property piracy claims, and Parliament intervened by enacting the SCA 1981, s 72. This provides in part: **29.33**

> (1) In any proceedings to which this subsection applies a person shall not be excused, by reason that to do so would tend to expose that person, or his or her spouse, to proceedings for a related offence or for the recovery of a related penalty—

(a) from answering any question put to that person in the first-mentioned proceedings; or
(b) from complying with any order made in those proceedings.

(2) Subsection (1) applies to the following civil proceedings in the High Court, namely—
(a) proceedings for infringement of rights pertaining to any intellectual property or for passing off;
(b) proceedings brought to obtain disclosure of information relating to any infringement of such rights or to any passing off; and
(c) proceedings brought to prevent any apprehended infringement of such rights or any apprehended passing off.

(3) Subject to subsection (4), no statement or admission made by a person—
(a) in answering a question put to him in any such proceedings to which subsection (1) applies; or
(b) in complying with any order made in such proceedings, shall, in proceedings for any related offence or for the recovery of any related penalty, be admissible in evidence against that person or (unless they married after the making of the statement or admission) against the spouse of that person.

(4) Nothing in subsection (3) shall render any statement or admission made by a person as there mentioned inadmissible in evidence against that person in proceedings for perjury or contempt of court.

(5) In this section—
'intellectual property' means any patent, trade mark, copyright, design right, registered design, technical or commercial information or other intellectual property;
'related offence', in relation to any proceedings to which subsection (1) applies, means—
(a) in the case of proceedings within subsection (2)(a) or (b)—
(i) any offence committed by or in the course of the infringement or passing off to which those proceedings relate; or
(ii) any offence not within sub-paragraph (i) committed in connection with that infringement or passing off, being an offence involving fraud or dishonesty;
(b) in the case of proceedings within subsection (2)(c), any offence revealed by the facts on which the [claimant] relies in those proceedings.

29.34 It will be seen that the effect of the section is to remove the privilege against self-incrimination in relation to claims involving the infringement of intellectual property rights and passing off, but also to provide that the answers given shall not be used in any related criminal prosecution.

29.35 In addition to intellectual property claims covered by the SCA 1981, s 72, the privilege against self-incrimination has been removed:
(a) in civil proceedings for the recovery or administration of any property, for the execution of any trust or for an account of any property or dealings with property in relation to offences under the Theft Act 1968 (see Theft Act 1968, s 31);
(b) in civil proceedings for the recovery or administration of any property, for the execution of any trust or for an account of any property or dealings with property in relation to offences under the Fraud Act 2006 (see Fraud Act 2006, s 13). In *Kensington International Ltd v Congo* [2008] 1 WLR 1144, it was held that while certain corruption offences identified by the respondents were not offences under the Fraud Act 2006, they were 'related offences' for the purposes of s 13, as they involved 'fraudulent conduct or purpose'. Money laundering offences also come

within s 13 (*JSC BTA Bank v Ablyazov* [2010] 1 WLR 976). The result is that the Fraud Act exception to the privilege is fairly wide-ranging;

(c) in proceedings under Parts IV and V of the Children Act 1989 (see Children Act 1989, s 98); and

(d) certain proceedings under the Banking Act 1987 (this was held to be an implied result of the Banking Act 1987, s 42, by *Bank of England v Riley* [1992] Ch 465).

While there has been no universal removal of the privilege against self-incrimination in civil cases, the patchwork of removals covers most of the common situations.

Legal professional privilege

Legal professional privilege protects the right of a person to obtain skilled advice about the law without the fear that what is discussed may be used against them at a later stage. It is a fundamental human right long established at common law, buttressed by art 8 of the European Convention on Human Rights, and forms part of Community law (*R (Morgan Grenfell and Co Ltd) v Special Commissioner of Income Tax* [2003] 1 AC 563). There has been some debate in the House of Lords as to whether art 8 has resulted in the rule being elevated from a mere rule of procedure into a substantive right (*McE v Prison Service of Northern Ireland* [2009] 1 AC 908). It is clear from this case that it is not an absolute right. There is a long-established exception in the case of iniquity (see 29.45), and, with proper safeguards, there are statutory exceptions as well (for example, the Regulation of Investigatory Powers Act 2000, dealing with covert surveillance). **29.36**

There are two classes of legal professional privilege: that arising out of the relationship of solicitor and client even if no litigation is contemplated; and communications connected with contemplated or pending litigation. The privilege belongs to the client, not to the solicitor, though the solicitor is under a duty to the client to assert it unless it is waived by the client. There is an exception in relation to cases involving the welfare of a child, where the court has power to override claims of legal professional privilege (*Essex County Council v R* [1994] Fam 167). **29.37**

Solicitor and client

Confidential communications between a solicitor and client made for the giving or receiving of legal advice are protected by legal professional privilege. The principle is that a client should be able to get legal advice in confidence. In a decision that has generated a great deal of controversy within the legal profession, *Three Rivers District Council v Governor and Company of the Bank of England (No 5)* [2003] QB 1556 held that the 'client' for these purposes is the person who retained the solicitor. In the case of a company or corporation, this means that the privilege only covers communications between the lawyer and those personnel who have been authorized by the company or corporation to retain the services of the solicitor. On the facts the Bank had appointed three officials to deal with the Bank's communications with a private inquiry. It was held that those three officials were the client, so that communications between the solicitors and any other Bank official, even the Governor of the Bank, would not be protected. **29.38**

29.39 'Legal advice' covers telling a client the law, and also includes advice as to what should prudently and sensibly be done in the relevant legal context (*Balabel v Air India* [1988] Ch 317). To be protected the advice must be sought or given in a relevant legal context (*Three Rivers District Council v Governor and Company of the Bank of England (No 6)* [2005] 1 AC 610) and for a permissible (non-dishonest) purpose (*McE v Prison Service of Northern Ireland* [2009] 1 AC 908 at [117]). In doubtful cases, according to Lord Scott of Foscote in *Three Rivers* at [38] there are two questions. First, did the advice sought relate to the rights, liabilities, obligations, or remedies of the client under private law or under public law? Secondly, if so, did the occasion on which the communication took place and its purpose make it reasonable to expect that the privilege would apply? Putting it a different way, according to Lord Rodger of Earlsferry at [58], the important question is whether the lawyer is being asked in his capacity as a lawyer to provide legal advice. This means:

(a) Communications for the primary object of actual or contemplated civil or criminal proceedings will be privileged.
(b) Conclusions reached by a solicitor from such communications are also privileged (*Marsh v Sofaer* [2004] PNLR 24).
(c) Privilege attaches to advising on matters such as the conveyance of property or drawing up of a will (*Three Rivers District Council (No 6)* at [55]).
(d) Privilege does not apply to the actual conveyancing documents (*R v Inner London Crown Court, ex p Baines and Baines* [1988] QB 579) because they are not communications.
(e) Privilege applies to a solicitor advising on the best way to present evidence to a private, non-statutory inquiry, coroner's inquest, or statutory inquiry (*Three Rivers District Council (No 6)* at [44]).
(f) Privilege does not apply to client ledger accounts (*Nationwide Building Society v Various Solicitors* [1999] PNLR 53) because they are internal records, not communications dealing with advice.
(g) Privilege does not cover investment advice, nor advice as a patent or estate agent, nor when a solicitor is acting as a business adviser, because there is no relevant legal context.

Communications connected to litigation

29.40 Confidential communications between a solicitor or a client and a third party where the dominant purpose in creating the document is to use it or its contents in order to obtain legal advice or to help in the conduct of litigation which was at that time reasonably in prospect are privileged. This head of privilege is sometimes called litigation privilege. The rule is relatively straightforward in relation to solicitors' communications, and covers letters to and statements from witnesses, and letters to and reports from experts. In relation to clients' communications the rule has a more narrow effect.

29.41 In *Waugh v British Railways Board* [1980] AC 521 the claimants' representative sought disclosure of an internal inquiry report prepared by two of the Board's officers two days after the accident. The report was headed 'For the information of the Board's solicitor', but the written evidence on the application for disclosure made it clear that there were two purposes in providing the report, namely, to establish the cause of the accident so that safety measures could be introduced, and for legal advice in the event of any claim. The Board regarded both purposes as of equal importance. It was held that the report had to be disclosed. It would have been protected by legal professional privilege only if the legal advice aspect had been the dominant purpose. According to Lord Edmund-Davies, a dominant purpose is one with a 'clear paramountcy'.

Just because a report is compiled shortly after the relevant event does not mean that it cannot be privileged (*Re Highgrade Traders Ltd* [1984] BCLC 151, a fire investigation report in a suspected insurance arson case). This case is also authority for the proposition that the dominant purpose must be that of the person commissioning the report, not necessarily that of the author. **29.42**

Documents which came into existence otherwise than for the purposes of the present litigation, but which have been obtained for a party's solicitor for the purpose of use in the present litigation, are not privileged and must be produced to the other side for inspection (*Ventouris v Mountain* [1991] 1 WLR 607). **29.43**

Copies of documents

Copies and translations of privileged documents are themselves privileged. However, copies and translations of non-privileged documents are generally not protected by privilege. By way of exception, a compilation of copies or translations of documents obtained from third parties may be protected by legal professional privilege if disclosing them may betray the trend of advice given by the solicitor to the client. This exception does not apply, however, where the original documents came from the client (*Sumitomo Corpn v Crédit Lyonnais Rouse Ltd* [2002] 1 WLR 479). **29.44**

Crime and iniquity

The privilege does not apply where the purpose behind seeking legal advice is 'iniquitous', such as to devise a structure for a transaction to prejudice the interests of the client's creditors (see *Barclays Bank plc v Eustice* [1995] 1 WLR 1238). The privilege was lost on this ground in a case where a search order was obtained using information which had been gathered in breach of the Data Protection Act 1984 (*Dubai Aluminium Co Ltd v Al Alawi* [1999] 1 WLR 1964). Communications in furtherance of a fraud or crime are not protected by privilege (*Finers v Miro* [1991] 1 WLR 35). An affidavit setting out the details of an abusive telephone call (which was an offence contrary to the Telecommunications Act 1984, s 43(1)(a)), and a threat to rip someone's throat out (which was a threat to kill contrary to the Offences Against the Person Act 1861, s 16) was held not to be privileged in *C v C (Privilege: Criminal Communications)* [2002] Fam 42. It does not matter whether or not the solicitor was aware of the client's intent (*Gamlen Chemical Co (UK) Ltd v Rochem Ltd* [1979] CA Transcript 777). The principle applies whether or not the claim is founded on the particular fraud in question (*Kuwait Airways Corporation v Iraqi Airways Co (No. 6)* [2005] 1 WLR 2734). **29.45**

Other confidential relationships

In *Alfred Crompton Amusement Machines Ltd v Commissioners of Customs and Excise (No 2)* [1974] AC 405, the House of Lords held that legal professional privilege extends to in-house lawyers. The privilege also extends to communications with barristers, and to other persons authorized to provide advocacy, litigation, conveyancing, and probate services (Legal Services Act 2007, s 190). Communications with patent agents in pending or contemplated proceedings are also privileged by virtue of the Civil Evidence Act 1968, s 15. There is no duty of confidentiality between opposing lawyers in litigation (*British Sky Broadcasting Group plc v Virgin Media Communications Ltd* [2008] 1 WLR 2854). Privilege does not extend to doctors, **29.46** priests, or others entrusted with confidences (see *Wheeler v Le Marchant* (1881) 17 ChD 675). However, a third party, whether official or unofficial, who receives information in confidence with a view to conciliation between the parties will not be compelled by the courts to disclose what was said without the parties' agreement (*McTaggart v McTaggart* [1949] P 94; *D v National Society for the Prevention of Cruelty to Children* [1978] AC 171). This privilege, which is based on the sanctity of marriage, also extends to proceedings under the Children Act 1989 (*Re D (Minors) (Conciliation: Disclosure of Information)* [1993] Fam 231).

Without prejudice communications

29.47 'Without prejudice' communications, whether oral or in writing, which are made with the intention of seeking a settlement of litigation are privileged from disclosure (*Ofulue v Bossert* [2009] 1 AC 990). The policy is to encourage negotiations by removing the potential embarrassment of concessions made in the course of negotiations being used at trial against the party who made them. It has been said that the public policy rationale of the privilege is directed solely to protecting admissions, and if documents are to be used for a different purpose, such as to show the amount of compensation paid for an earlier injury, they are admissible (*Murrell v Healy* [2003] 4 All ER 345). This distinction was regarded as too subtle in *Ofulue v Bossert*, and is probably unsound.

29.48 The privilege applies even if the words 'without prejudice' are not used, provided the purpose was to seek a settlement (*Chocoladefabriken Lindt & Sprungli AG v Nestlé Co Ltd* [1978] RPC 287). Conversely, use of these words will not attach privilege to communications intended to prejudice the recipient or which are no more than an assertion of one party's rights (*Buckinghamshire County Council v Moran* [1990] Ch 623), nor to letters seeking time to pay an admitted liability (*Bradford and Bingley plc v Rashid* [2006] 1 WLR 2066). The important question is whether the communication was genuinely intended to be a negotiating document (*Schering Corporation v Cipla Ltd* (2004) *The Times*, 2 December 2004). The privilege applies to joint settlement meetings, except to the extent they are stated to be without prejudice save as to costs (*Jackson v Ministry of Defence* [2006] EWCA Civ 46). Where the parties enter into 'without prejudice' negotiations, ongoing negotiations will continue to be privileged until one party brings it home to the other party that the 'without prejudice' basis of the negotiations is at an end. Thus, in *Cheddar Valley Engineering Ltd v Chaddlewood Homes Ltd* [1992] 1 WLR 820 it was held that prefacing one telephone offer with the word 'open' was insufficient to bring home the change in basis when further telephone negotiations and a letter did not repeat the word 'open'.

29.49 Once a document is protected by 'without prejudice' privilege, it will always (subject to the following paragraph), be privileged. Thus an admission made in 'without prejudice' communications by one party will not be admissible in other proceedings against that party (*Rush and Tompkins Ltd v Greater London Council* [1989] AC 1280). Also, on an application for costs, it is not permissible to adduce without prejudice communications without the joint consent of the parties to establish whether a party had unreasonably refused a proposal for ADR (*Reed Executive plc v Reed Business Information Ltd* [2004] 1 WLR 3026).

29.50 'Without prejudice' negotiations which result in a settlement are, however, admissible to prove the terms of the settlement (*Walker v Wilsher* (1889) 23 QBD 335; *Oceanbulk Shipping and Trading SA v TMT Asia Ltd* (2010) *The Times*, 1 March 2010). Marking a letter 'without prejudice' will not protect the evidence of a threat as to what will happen if an offer is not accepted (*Kitcat v Sharp* (1882) 48 LT 64). Further, 'without prejudice' correspondence is often used in interim applications, particularly applications seeking sanctions for default or relief from sanctions (*Family Housing Association (Manchester) Ltd v Michael Hyde and Partners* [1993] 1 WLR 354). The privilege will not attach if it is being abused, but it will only be lost in truly exceptional circumstances. A mere inconsistency between an admission made on a without prejudice occasion and the pleaded case or the facts stated in a witness statement of the party making the admission will not result in the privilege being lost (*Savings and Investment Bank Ltd v Fincken* [2004] 1 WLR 667). This is so even if persistence in the inconsistent position might lead to perjury.

Not only are without prejudice documents privileged from use in the instant proceedings, they should not be used to found subsequent proceedings. If they are, the subsequent proceedings will be struck out as an abuse of process, unless the claimant in the subsequent proceedings can show that the statements relied upon were made improperly, or that there is some other public interest reason in favour of their subsequent use (*Unilever plc v Procter and Gamble Co* [2000] 1 WLR 2436). This exception applies only if there is a very clear abuse of a privileged occasion (*Berry Trade Ltd v Moussari* (2003) *The Times*, 3 June 2003). **29.51**

Waiver of privilege

Legal professional privilege belongs to, and can be waived by, the client. The privilege in 'without prejudice' communications belongs to both sides jointly, and can be waived only if both sides consent (*Rush and Tompkins Ltd v Greater London Council* [1989] AC 1280). Adverse inferences will not be drawn from a refusal to waive privilege (*Reed Executive plc v Reed Business Information Ltd* [2004] 1 WLR 3026). **29.52**

Waiver of privilege may be given expressly, or implicitly by disclosing a privileged document to the other side. Examples include disclosure by service of a hearsay notice; by inclusion as an exhibit to a witness statement; by using the document to refresh the memory of a witness while giving evidence; and use of documents in re-examination to rebut an allegation of recent fabrication. However, there is no waiver of privilege simply by referring to a document in a witness statement, despite r 31.14 (for which, see 29.75; *Rubin v Expandable Ltd* [2008] 1 WLR 1099). A party waives privilege for trial purposes by using materials in an interim application (*Derby and Co Ltd v Weldon (No 10)* [1991] 1 WLR 660). **29.53**

In *Great Atlantic Insurance Co v Home Insurance Co* [1981] 1 WLR 529 the Court of Appeal held that, where part of a document was used in counsel's opening, privilege was waived as to the whole of the document unless it was a clearly separable document with different parts dealing with completely different subjects. Once privilege on a subject has been waived, the waiver will be taken to extend to any associated material (*Derby and Co Ltd v Weldon (No 10)*), but the court will seek to define the subject matter of the waiver quite restrictively (*General Accident Fire and Life Assurance Corporation Ltd v Tanter* [1984] 1 WLR 100). The question in such cases is one of defining the 'transaction', because the waiver only extends to documents which are part of the transaction (*Fulham Leisure Holdings Ltd v Nicholson Graham and Jones* [2006] 2 All ER 599). **29.54**

A person who has been a client of a solicitor and who institutes legal proceedings against that solicitor impliedly waives privilege over all documents concerned with the claim to the extent **29.55** necessary to enable the court to adjudicate the dispute fully and fairly. In *Lillicrap v Nalder and Son* [1993] 1 WLR 94, property developers sued their solicitors for negligently failing to advise them about a right of way over some land they purchased. The claimants had used the solicitors on a number of other transactions, and the solicitors said their files on those other transactions showed the claimants habitually ignored their warnings, so would have bought the land even if they had been properly advised. The Court of Appeal held that the previous transactions were relevant to an issue in the present proceedings, so the implied waiver extended to them as well as to the transaction in question. However, there are limits on the implied waiver of privilege in solicitors' negligence claims. In *Paragon Finance plc v Freshfields* [1999] 1 WLR 1183 the first firm of solicitors had acted for the finance company in relation to a number of mortgage transactions. The finance company made a number of claims against insurance policies entered into in relation to the mortgages, which the insurer disputed. The finance company then retained a second firm of solicitors to pursue outstanding insurance claims, and later sued the first firm of solicitors for professional negligence. A question arose as to whether the finance company had, by suing the first firm of solicitors, impliedly waived its privilege in respect of the work done by the second firm in pursuing the insurance claims. It was held that by suing the first firm of solicitors the finance company had put only its relationship with that firm into the public domain, and had not done so in respect of the work done by the second firm, and so had not waived its privilege in respect of the work done by the second firm.

Secondary evidence

29.56 It was held in *Calcraft v Guest* [1898] 1 QB 759 that secondary evidence, such as a copy, of otherwise privileged material is admissible at trial. In *Goddard v Nationwide Building Society* [1987] QB 670, Nourse LJ said that it makes no difference how the privileged material was obtained. Even if confidential documents have been obtained by theft they will be admissible. However, the party who would otherwise be able to claim privilege may apply for an injunction to restrain use of such material if it has not yet been used in the litigation (*Goddard v Nationwide Building Society*). However, the manner in which the documents came into that party's possession is important, because the party claiming privilege may be held to have waived the privilege. Waiver may arise inadvertently (*Great Atlantic Insurance Co v Home Insurance Co* [1981] 1 WLR 529). In *Guinness Peat Properties Ltd v Fitzroy Robinson Partnership* [1987] 1 WLR 1027 a privileged letter was inadvertently disclosed. The defendant allowed the claimant to inspect certain files before serving a list of documents. By accident, the letter was left in one of the files, and the claimant took a copy of it. The document later appeared in the defendant's list of documents, without a claim for privilege, and the claimant was again allowed to inspect it at the defendant's solicitors' office, but was not given a copy. Slade LJ said at 1044:

> Care must be taken by parties to litigation in the preparation of their lists of documents and no less great care must be taken in offering inspection of the documents disclosed. Ordinarily, in my judgment, a party to litigation who sees a particular document referred to in the other side's list, without privilege being claimed, and is subsequently permitted inspection of that document, is fully entitled to assume that any privilege which might otherwise have been claimed for it has been waived.

29.57 As Slade LJ said, this is ordinarily the position. It is subject to two exceptions:

(a) where a party or its solicitor procures inspection of the relevant document by fraud; and

(b) where a party or its solicitor realizes on inspection that the document has been disclosed as a result of an obvious mistake.

Guinness Peat Properties Ltd v Fitzroy Robinson Partnership was an example of an obvious mistake, as, being a trained lawyer, the claimant's solicitor must have realized the privileged nature of the letter as soon as he read it. Another, more obvious, example is *English and American Insurance Co Ltd v Herbert Smith* [1988] FSR 232, where counsel's clerk allowed counsel's instructions and papers (including witness statements and counsel's written opinion) to be sent to the other side's solicitors. An injunction was granted restraining use being made of any of the information in the papers. Compare *Al Fayed v Commissioner of Police for the Metropolis* (2002) *The Times,* 17 June 2002, where the injunction was refused because the recipient solicitors genuinely thought the other side's counsel's opinions had been disclosed on purpose. **29.58**

Where either of these exceptions applies, Slade LJ in *Guinness Peat Properties Ltd v Fitzroy Robinson Partnership* said the court should ordinarily intervene, unless there is some equitable reason for not doing so, such as delay. **29.59**

Documents *publici juris*

Notes of proceedings in open court and counsel's endorsement on the brief of the order of the court are *publici juris* and are not privileged (*Nicholl v Jones* (1865) 2 Hem & M 588). Likewise, public records and documents are *publici juris*. However, a collection of extracts or copies from public documents may be protected from production by legal professional privilege where the collection is a product of the professional knowledge, research, and skill of a party's legal advisers: *Lyell v Kennedy* (1884) 27 ChD 1. **29.60**

Beneficiaries and shareholders

There is a general rule that in proceedings between trustee and *cestui que trust* (for which see *Tugwell v Hooper* (1847) 10 Beav 348) or company and shareholder (for which see *W Dennis and Sons Ltd v West Norfolk Farmers' Manure and Chemical Co-operative Co Ltd* [1943] Ch 220) privilege cannot be claimed for opinions from counsel and advice from solicitors paid for out of the fund or the assets of the company for the purpose of administering the fund or the company. The rule is subject to an exception where the legal advice was sought by the trustees or company in earlier hostile litigation against the beneficiary or shareholder in question. Where a company is merely a necessary but nominal party to proceedings which are essentially concerned with a dispute between its shareholders and directors there is no 'hostile' litigation for this purpose and the general rule applies: *Re Hydrosan Ltd* [1991] BCLC 418. **29.61**

Public interest immunity

General principles

Certain documents must be withheld from production on the ground that disclosure would be injurious to the public interest. Such documents fall into two categories: those which form part of a 'class' of documents which needs to be protected, and those which need to be **29.62** protected due to the sensitivity of their particular 'contents'. Contents immunity attaches, eg, to diplomatic dispatches and documents relating to national security. There is a wide variation in the 'classes' of documents protected, from Cabinet minutes to more routine documents like local authority social work records: *Re M (A Minor)* (1989) 88 LGR 841.

Ministerial certificates

29.63 The responsible minister may provide a certificate stating the grounds of the objection and identifying the class (if any) to which the document in question belongs. Such certificates are usually only issued on solid grounds, and are usually taken as determining the question whether the 'class' of documents specified is protected by public interest immunity. However, such certificates are not, as a matter of law, conclusive (see *Burmah Oil Co Ltd v Bank of England* [1980] AC 1090). If a strong case (there are in fact several formulations of the standard applicable: see *Burmah Oil Co Ltd v Bank of England*) is made out that the contents of the documents are material to the issues in the claim, and if there are grounds to doubt whether the balance of the public interest is against disclosure, the court has a discretion to review the claim to immunity. If these conditions are satisfied, the court will weigh (a) the public interest in the due administration of justice against (b) the public interest established by the claim to immunity. It is for the party seeking disclosure to establish clearly that the balance falls decisively in favour of (a) (*Air Canada v Secretary of State for Trade* [1983] 2 AC 394, HL). The weight on either side depends on the importance of the 'class' and the probable evidential value of the document—see Lord Fraser of Tullybelton in the *Air Canada* case—and the court may need to inspect the document.

Other confidential information

29.64 Privilege based on a confidential relationship is restricted to the legal profession, and does not extend to doctors, priests, social workers, etc. (*Wheeler v Le Marchant* (1881) 17 ChD 675). Interviews with medical advisers are nevertheless often treated as being in a similar position to legal advice. This is partly because they may be covered by litigation privilege, and partly because they are an aspect of the right to respect for private life which is protected by the European Convention on Human Rights, art 8 (*McE v Prison Service of Northern Ireland* [2009] 1 AC 908). Article 8 may also protect non-medical information, eg, some school records, on the basis that disclosure may interfere with the private lives of those discussed in the records (*Webster v Ridgeway Foundation School Governors* [2009] EWHC 1140(QB)).

G INSPECTION

Personal inspection

29.65 A party which has served a list of documents must allow the other parties to inspect the documents listed which are in its control, other than those for which a claim is made to withhold inspection on the grounds of privilege. A party wishing to inspect must send a written notice to that effect to the other side, and the other side must give its permission within the next seven days (CPR, r 31.15(a) and (b)).

Redacted copies

Normally the whole of a document can be inspected, but there is scope for blanking out irrelevant passages (*GE Capital Corporate Finance Group Ltd v Bankers Trust Co* [1995] 1 WLR 172) or passages with sensitive information (*Webster v Ridgeway Foundation School Governors* [2009] EWHC 1140(QB)). **29.66**

Provision of copies

Alternatively, the inspecting party can conduct the inspecting process at arm's length by sending a notice to the other party requiring the supply of copies of the documents in the first part of the list, and undertaking to pay reasonable copying charges. Such a request must be complied with within seven days (CPR, r 31.15(c)). **29.67**

H DISCLOSURE ORDERS

Failure to disclose or give inspection

Where a party fails to serve a list of documents in accordance with the court's directions, or fails to give inspection, an application can be made for an order compelling performance. Before issuing the application the innocent party should write to the defaulting party inviting them to remedy the default within a stated reasonable period. If the default has not been remedied by the time the application is heard, the court will usually make an 'unless order' requiring the matter to be put right within a stated period, and specifying some sanction in default. Sanctions can include striking out the defaulting party's statement of case. **29.68**

Documents that are not disclosed before trial can only be relied upon by the defaulting party with the court's permission (CPR, r 31.21). It is also open to the court to make adverse inferences against the defaulting party (*Infabrics Ltd v Jaytex Ltd (No 2)* [1985] FSR 75). **29.69**

Objections to disclosure or inspection

Procedures for determining disputed claims to withhold disclosure and inspection are provided in CPR, r 31.19. Claims for protection are usually made in the list of documents served by a party (r 31.19(4)). Alternatively, an order may be sought from the court for withholding disclosure (public interest immunity) or inspection (other claims to privilege or based on alleged irrelevance). The burden of proof rests on the party asserting privilege (*Akzo Nobel Chemicals Ltd v Commission of the European Communities* (cases T–125 and T–253/03) [2008] Bus LR 348). On a hearing under r 31.19, *Atos Consulting Ltd v Avis Europe plc* [2008] Bus LR Digest D20 said the court must: **29.70**

(a) consider the evidence produced on the application;

(b) uphold the right to withhold inspection if this is established on the evidence and no sufficient grounds are put forward for challenging that right;
(c) order inspection if the evidence does not establish a right to withhold the documents;
(d) order further evidence to be produced if insufficient grounds have been shown for challenging the alleged right to withhold, or for the court to inspect the documents if there is no other means of deciding the matter; and
(e) invite representations after any inspection.

29.71 In relation to claims to withhold disclosure on the ground of public interest immunity, r 31.19(2) provides that, unless the court otherwise orders, any order made under r 31.19 must not be served on any other person, and must not be open to inspection by any other person.

Specific disclosure

Jurisdiction

29.72 A party who believes the other side has material documents that have not been disclosed in the usual way under standard disclosure may make an application for specific disclosure. The procedure can also occasionally be used before service of the defence where the defendant needs to have disclosure to assist in drafting a full defence (*Dayman v Canyon Holdings Ltd* (2006) LTL 11/1/06). It is provided in CPR, r 31.12, that:

(1) The court may make an order for specific disclosure or specific inspection.
(2) An order for specific disclosure is an order that a party must do one or more of the following things—
  (a) disclose documents or classes of documents specified in the order;
  (b) carry out a search to the extent stated in the order;
  (c) disclose any documents located as a result of that search.
(3) An order for specific inspection is an order that a party permit inspection of a document referred to in r 31.3(2).

29.73 If it is established that the other side has not given standard disclosure, the order will usually be made (PD 31, para 5.4). This procedure may also be used before standard disclosure takes place or if a party wants disclosure of train-of-inquiry documents (see 29.15), but on such applications the court will be particularly astute to apply the overriding objective (PD 31, para 5.4).

Procedure

29.74 Applications for specific disclosure are made by application notice supported by written evidence, and are made on at least three clear days' notice to the other side. The application must specify the order asked for. It is usual to describe the various categories of documents sought in a schedule to the application. Descriptions must, however, be sufficiently precise for the other side to know what is required. An application for disclosure of 'all documents relating to [the other side's] financial and tax affairs which are necessary to prove quantum' was held to be too imprecise in *Morgans v Needham* (1999) *The Times*, 5 November 1999. The evidence in support must state a belief that the other side has or had certain specific documents relating to the claim in his or her control, and that each class of documents sought is disclosable under standard disclosure, or should otherwise be disclosed in accordance with the overriding objective.

I DOCUMENTS REFERRED TO IN STATEMENTS OF CASE, ETC.

By CPR, r 31.14(1), a party is entitled to inspect any documents mentioned in a statement of case, witness statement, witness summary, or affidavit. A document is 'mentioned' for the purposes of r 31.14 if there is a 'direct allusion' to it (*Rubin v Expandable Ltd* [2008] 1 WLR 1099). In this case a witness statement which said 'he wrote to me' made a direct allusion to the covering letter, even though the letter was not relied upon in the witness statement. The party wishing to inspect needs to serve a notice requiring documents to be made available for inspection. The other party then has seven days to permit inspection. Note that r 31.14 applies to documents 'mentioned'. The right to inspect can therefore arise through an incautious reference to documents in the narrative of (say) a witness statement. **29.75**

A party may also make an application for an order for inspection of a document mentioned in an expert's report (r 31.14(2)), but where the document mentioned is part of the expert's instructions, such an order will only be made if there are reasonable grounds for believing that the expert's report does not provide a complete and accurate statement of those instructions (r 35.10(4)). Provided the expert sets out the material parts of documents used in compiling the report, the court will not order the inspection of those documents (*Lucas v Barking, Havering and Redbridge Hospitals NHS Trust* [2004] 1 WLR 220). **29.76**

J ADMISSION OF AUTHENTICITY

By CPR, r 32.19(1), a party is deemed to admit the authenticity of documents disclosed by the other side under Part 31, unless the party serves a notice requiring the document to be proved at trial. Such a notice must be served by the latest date for serving witness statements (or seven days after disclosure if this is later) (r 32.19(2)). Notice to prove should be in form N268. **29.77**

K COLLATERAL USE

A party which receives documents disclosed under Part 31 may use those documents only for purposes connected with the proper conduct of the present litigation (CPR, r 31.22(1)). Any misuse of the documents may be restrained by injunction, or punished as a contempt of court, or by striking out subsequent proceedings based on documents disclosed in the course of earlier proceedings (see *Riddick v Thames Board Mills Ltd* [1977] QB 881). The protection against subsequent use of disclosed documents is not, however, absolute. Rule 31.22 provides: **29.78**

(1) A party to whom a document has been disclosed may use the document only for the purpose of the proceedings in which it is disclosed, except where—
- (a) the document has been read to or by the court, or referred to, at a hearing which has been held in public;
- (b) the court gives permission; or
- (c) the party who disclosed the document and the person to whom the document belongs agree.

(2) The court may make an order restricting or prohibiting the use of a document which has been disclosed, even where the document has been read to or by the court, or referred to, at a hearing which has been held in public.

(3) An application for such an order may be made—

(a) by a party; or

(b) by any person to whom the document belongs.

29.79 From *Barings plc v Coopers and Lybrand* [2000] 1 WLR 2353, it seems that documents read by the judge, whether in or out of court, should be regarded as in the public domain. Further, where documents have been put before the court for the purpose of being read in evidence, the onus is on the person contending that they were not read by the judge to prove that (which must be a difficult task, as the judge will not be called to be cross-examined about the matter). It will be noticed from r 31.22(2) that after use at trial, the court may reimpose the restrictions on subsequent use, and by r 31.22(3)(a) such an application may be made 'by a party'. That expression was interpreted in *Singh v Christie* (1993) *The Times*, 11 November 1993 as meaning a party to the original proceedings in which the documents were disclosed, and not the parties to any subsequent proceedings in which the documents may be used. Once documents have been used in open court, an order restricting or prohibiting subsequent use will be made only if there are very good reasons for departing from the usual rule of publicity (*Lilly Icos Ltd v Pfizer Ltd* [2002] 1 WLR 2253).

29.80 The prohibition against using material for collateral purposes does not apply to documents referred to in affidavits and witness statements, as these are regarded as having been voluntarily disclosed: *Cassidy v Hawcroft* [2000] CPLR 624.

KEY POINTS SUMMARY

29.81

- In fast track and multi-track claims the court typically makes a direction that the parties should give standard disclosure of documents about a month after the order for directions.
- Standard disclosure requires parties to disclose documents which support their own case, and also documents which adversely affect them, adversely affect another party, or which support another party's case.
- A document for this purpose is anything on which information is recorded, and extends to computer documents, metadata, sound and moving picture recordings.
- Parties give disclosure by serving lists of documents.
- Privileged documents appear in the second section of the list, and do not have to be made available for inspection.
- Inspection is the second stage of the disclosure process, and usually takes place by sending copies to the other side, although personal inspection is also possible.
- Orders for specific disclosure may be sought if it is felt that the other side have not complied with their disclosure obligations.

30

NORWICH PHARMACAL AND RELATED DISCLOSURE ORDERS

General disclosure of documents was considered in Chapter 29. Search orders, whereby the court makes mandatory orders requiring the defendant to give access to premises for the purpose of enabling the claimant to take documents which might otherwise be destroyed, will be discussed in Chapter 37. This chapter considers a number of other special forms of disclosure orders, the best known of which is the *Norwich Pharmacal* order. **30.01**

A *NORWICH PHARMACAL* ORDERS

Principles

There are situations where proceedings cannot be brought because the identity of the true defendant is unknown. By reviving the nineteenth-century Chancery procedure of the bill of discovery, the House of Lords in *Norwich Pharmacal Co v Customs and Excise* **30.02**

Commissioners [1974] AC 133 provided a possible means of discovering the identity of an unknown wrongdoer. Norwich Pharmacal owned the patent for a chemical used for immunizing poultry. It was aware that importers were infringing their patent, and knew that the Commissioners knew the identities of the importers. Proceedings were brought against the Commissioners to compel them to divulge the names of the importers. Lord Reid laid down the principle at 175:

> ...that if through no fault of his own a person gets mixed up in the tortious acts of others so as to facilitate their wrongdoing he may incur no personal liability but he comes under a duty to assist the person who has been wronged by giving him full information and disclosing the identity of the wrongdoers. I do not think that it matters whether he became so mixed up by voluntary action on his part or because it was his duty to do what he did. It may be that if this causes him expense the person seeking the information ought to reimburse him. But justice requires that he should co-operate in righting the wrong if he unwittingly facilitated its perpetration.

30.03 Although *Norwich Pharmacal* had no substantive cause of action against the Commissioners, the Commissioners had unwittingly facilitated the infringement by allowing the infringing goods into the country, so were ordered to disclose the identities of the importers. The *Norwich Pharmacal* jurisdiction is not restricted to claims in tort, but is of general application, and applies to claims in breach of confidence and breach of contract (*Ashworth Hospital Authority v MGN Ltd* [2002] 1 WLR 2033).

30.04 Provision of the documents or information must be necessary (*Ashworth Hospital Authority v MGN Ltd* at [57]). This is not intended to lay down a stringent test. Authorities such as *Mitsui and Co Ltd v Nexen Petroleum UK Ltd* [2005] 3 All ER 511, which said that *Norwich Pharmacal* orders are remedies of last resort, or that they can only be made if the evidence is the final piece in the jigsaw, were deprecated in *R (Mohamed) v Secretary of State for Foreign and Commonwealth Affairs (No 1)* [2009] 1 WLR 2579 (unaffected by the appeal, [2010] EWCA Civ 65). Rather, the court must consider all the circumstances, including the resources of the applicant, the urgency of the need for the information, and any public interest in satisfying the applicant's need for the information. There is no obligation to give standard disclosure of documents under a *Norwich Pharmacal* order (*Arab Monetary Fund v Hashim (No 5)* [1992] 2 All ER 911).

30.05 An order will not be made for the mere gratification of curiosity. Where the claimant genuinely intends to bring proceedings against the wrongdoer, this condition is clearly satisfied. In *British Steel Corporation v Granada Television Ltd* [1981] AC 1096 Lord Wilberforce said he would have been prepared to grant relief where the claimant intended to seek redress 'by court proceedings or otherwise'. Other forms of redress might include dismissal from employment and deprivation of pension rights (*Ashworth Hospital Authority v MGN Ltd* [2002] 1 WLR 2033).

30.06 A defendant who is a tortfeasor, and not simply a person who has innocently become 'mixed up' in some wrongdoing, is *a fortiori* under a *Norwich Pharmacal* duty to assist the claimant by disclosing the identities of other persons involved in the wrongdoing (*British Steel Corporation v Granada Television Ltd*). In *X Ltd v Morgan-Grampian (Publishers) Ltd* [1991] 1 AC 1 the House of Lords held that, where the claimant sought disclosure of the name of an unknown tortfeasor from a defendant against whom there existed a substantive cause of action related to that against the unknown party, the defendant was amenable to the full scope of the court's powers to order disclosure in the course of the proceedings. Such orders are commonly included in freezing injunctions and search orders.

Being part of the equitable jurisdiction of the court, *Norwich Pharmacal* relief is discretionary, and may be refused even if someone has got 'mixed up' in some wrongdoing so as to 'facilitate' its commission. Also, it will not override a respondent's right to assert privilege, public interest immunity, or state immunity (*Koo Golden East Mongolia v Bank of Nova Scotia* [2008] QB 717). **30.07**

Journalists' sources

The Contempt of Court Act 1981, s 10, gives a general protection to journalists' sources of information, and was enacted to give effect to the strong public interest in preserving the right to information. Section 10 provides: **30.08**

> No court may require a person to disclose, nor is any person guilty of contempt of court for refusing to disclose, the source of information contained in a publication for which he is responsible, unless it be established to the satisfaction of the court that disclosure is necessary in the interests of justice or national security or for the prevention of disorder or crime.

Section 10 applies despite any proprietary claim by the claimant for delivery-up of stolen documents if the documents could lead to identifying the 'source' (*Secretary of State for Defence v Guardian Newspapers Ltd* [1985] AC 339). It also applies despite non-publication of the information as long as the information was provided with a view to publication (*X Ltd v Morgan-Grampian (Publishers) Ltd* [1991] 1 AC 1). In *Totalise plc v Motley Fool Ltd* (2001) *The Times*, 15 March 2001, a website operator was ordered to disclose the identity of a website user who, it was alleged, had posted defamatory comments on the defendant's website. It was held that the Contempt of Court Act 1981, s 10, had no application to the facts because the defendant took no responsibility for items posted on their website, since the section applied to information 'contained in a publication for which he is responsible'. The interrelation between the Contempt of Court Act 1981, s 10, and the European Convention on Human Rights, art 10 (freedom of expression), was considered in *Ashworth Hospital Authority v MGN Ltd* [2002] 1 WLR 2033, where it was concluded that the section's aims coincided with those of art 10. **30.09**

The two exceptions to the section most likely to arise in *Norwich Pharmacal* applications are disclosure in the interests of justice and to prevent crime. The meaning of the phrase 'interests of justice' in the section is 'that persons should be enabled to exercise important legal rights and to protect themselves from serious legal wrongs whether or not resort to legal proceedings in a court of law will be necessary to attain these objectives' (*per* Lord Bridge of Harwich in *X Ltd v Morgan-Grampian (Publishers) Ltd*). Prevention of crime includes, according to Lord Oliver of Aylmerton in *Re an Inquiry under the Company Securities (Insider Dealing) Act 1985* [1988] AC 660, 'the detection and prosecution of crimes which are shown to have been committed and where detection and prosecution could sensibly be said to act as a practical deterrent to future criminal conduct of a similar type'. This may be the case where documents are stolen and later used as the basis of a journalistic article. **30.10**

Thus, where a *Norwich Pharmacal* order is sought against a journalist, the claimant must first satisfy the court that one of the exceptions applies. It is to be noted that the section requires such disclosure to be 'necessary'. The court must then weigh the importance of achieving justice or preventing crime in the circumstances of the case against the importance of protecting the source of the information. Factors to be taken into account include the degree of confidentiality **30.11** attaching to the information, the manner in which the information was obtained, the public interest in concealing journalists' sources, and whether the information brings to light iniquity on the part of the claimant. According to Lord Bridge in *X Ltd v Morgan-Grampian (Publishers) Ltd*, disclosure should be ordered only if the balance is clearly on the side of disclosure, since otherwise the courts would be undermining the clear policy stated in the section.

Procedure

30.12 A claim must first be commenced against the facilitator by issuing a claim form. An interim application is then made to a master in the QBD or to a judge in the ChD, supported by evidence by witness statement or affidavit. As previously mentioned, if the defendant is also a wrongdoer a *Norwich Pharmacal* order can be incorporated into freezing injunctions and search orders. In urgent cases where delay may result in substantial irreparable harm it is possible for the application to be made without notice, as happened in *Loose v Williamson* [1978] 1 WLR 639. If an order is made against an innocent party, the claimant is usually required to pay that person's costs, but may be able to recover them from the true defendant in either the same or a subsequent claim (*SmithKline and French Laboratories Ltd v R D Harbottle (Mercantile) Ltd* [1980] RPC 363).

B MERE WITNESS RULE

30.13 A person who has become mixed up in a tort in such a way as to facilitate its commission, against whom it is possible to obtain a *Norwich Pharmacal* order, must be distinguished from a mere witness. Although mere witnesses may be compelled by witness summons to give evidence at trial, they cannot generally be compelled to assist a party before then. The fact that a person knows the identity of a tortfeasor does not make that person a facilitator. Thus, in *Ricci v Chow* [1987] 1 WLR 1658 the claimant alleged that a journal published by the Seychellois National Movement defamed him. The defendant was the secretary of the Movement, knew the identities of the alleged tortfeasors, but had nothing to do with the publication of the journal. The *Norwich Pharmacal* order was refused. Also of interest is *Harrington v Polytechnic of North London* [1984] 1 WLR 1293. The claimant was a student who was prevented from attending the polytechnic by student pickets. Photographs were taken of the pickets, and the claimant sought an order compelling the lecturers to identify the pickets. It was held that the lecturers were mere witnesses when acting in their private capacity, but as employees of the polytechnic they could be compelled to provide the information as the polytechnic had become mixed up in and facilitated the wrongdoing.

C *BANKERS TRUST* ORDERS

30.14 By an extension of the *Norwich Pharmacal* principle, an order can be made for disclosure in aid of a tracing claim to find what has been done with the misapplied money. The purpose is to prevent equity being invoked in vain by the subject matter of an action disappearing by the time the case reaches trial. The order takes its name from *Bankers Trust Co v Shapira* [1980]

1 WLR 1274. It is an order requiring a third party, often a bank, to disclose information and documents relating to the financial affairs of the defendant.

Principles

Bankers Trust orders are granted only in urgent cases. If there is no urgency, the information should be sought under the Bankers' Books Evidence Act 1879. Otherwise, the preconditions to the granting of a *Bankers Trust* order are: 30.15

(a) there must be good reason to believe that the third party either holds or has held property belonging to the claimant; and
(b) the potential advantage to the claimant in obtaining the order has to be balanced against the detriment against the third party in terms of costs, invasion of privacy, and breach of obligations of confidentiality to others.

Although any documents produced by the third party in compliance with the order will be protected by an implied undertaking not to use them for any collateral purpose (see 29.78), it was held in *Omar v Omar* [1995] 1 WLR 1428 that documents obtained under such an order in a tracing claim could be used for the purpose of mounting personal claims against the individual responsible for the original breach of trust or theft. 30.16

Procedure

Bankers Trust orders are often included in freezing injunctions. Third parties subject to such orders are joined to the claim as additional defendants. The claimant is required to give an undertaking in damages, and must undertake to pay all expenses incurred by the third party in complying with the order. If granted, the third party is required to file and serve written evidence stating whether the property has ever been in its possession and what has become of it. 30.17

D DISCLOSURE BEFORE PROCEEDINGS START

Under the SCA 1981, ss 33 and 34, and the equivalent county courts provisions in CCA 1984, ss 52 and 53, the courts have a number of powers to order pre-action inspection of property and disclosure of documents, and also inspection and disclosure against non-parties. Without these provisions it is possible to require a party to allow inspection or to give disclosure only after proceedings are commenced, and a non-party can be required to do so only at trial. The purpose of these provisions is to bring forward the time when the parties can obtain full information, with the intention of promoting early settlement if possible, or proper preparation for trial if necessary. 30.18

The person against whom an order is made under any of these statutory provisions will usually be awarded his costs of the application and of complying with any order made against the applicant (CPR, r 48.1(2)). However, these costs are usually recoverable as damages against the defendant to the substantive claim. The usual rule on costs may be departed from, however, having regard to whether the respondent has acted reasonably and whether the respondent has complied with the terms of any relevant pre-action protocol (r 48.1(3)). As the starting 30.19

point is that the applicant must pay the respondent's costs, it is not usually unreasonable for a respondent to resist the application (*SES Contracting Ltd v UK Coal plc* (2007) 33 EG 90 (CS)). It might be right to depart from the normal rule if the application is resisted in an unreasonable way, such as by using written evidence not backed up by contemporaneous documents (*SES Contracting Ltd v UK Coal plc*).

Jurisdiction to order disclosure before proceedings

30.20 It is provided in SCA 1981, s 33(2), that:

> on the application, in accordance with rules of court, of a person who appears to the High Court to be likely to be a party to subsequent proceedings in that court the High Court shall, in such circumstances as may be specified in the rules, have power to order a person who appears to the court to be likely to be a party to the proceedings and to be likely to have or to have had in his possession, custody or power any documents which are relevant to an issue arising or likely to arise out of that claim—
>
> (a) to disclose whether those documents are in his possession, custody or power; and
> (b) to produce such of those documents as are in his possession, custody or power to the applicant or, on such conditions as may be specified in the order—
>   (i) to the applicant's legal advisers; or
>   (ii) to the applicant's legal advisers and any medical or other professional adviser of the applicant; or
>   (iii) if the applicant has no legal adviser, to any medical or other professional adviser of the applicant.

30.21 There are five conditions that must be satisfied before an order can be made under this section:

(a) The applicant must appear likely to be a party to future proceedings (CPR, r 31.16(3)(b)). *Black v Sumitomo Corporation* [2002] 1 WLR 1569 held there is no requirement that it be likely that proceedings will be issued, but merely that the persons involved are likely to be parties if proceedings are issued. It was also held that 'likely' means 'may well' rather than 'more probably than not'. Consequently, the court should not generally embark on an investigation into issues such as justiciability or the elements of the alleged cause of action (*Total E & P Soudan SA v Edmonds* [2007] EWCA Civ 50). These matters can be left until after proceedings are issued. It is different if the respondent can show beyond argument that a claim is hopeless or non-justiciable. It has also been said that if the case is weak or speculative that may be taken into account when the court exercises its discretion whether to make the order (*Snowstar Shipping Co Ltd v Graig Shipping plc* (2003) LTL 13/6/03). An applicant may be 'likely' to be a party to an additional claim even though permission may be required to issue the additional claim form (*Moresfield Ltd v Banners* (2003) LTL 3/7/03).

(b) The defendant must appear to be a likely party (r 31.16(3)(a)).

(c) It must appear likely that relevant documents are or have been in the defendant's possession, custody, or power (SCA 1981, s 33(2)).

(d) If proceedings had started, the respondent's duty by way of standard disclosure, set out in r 31.6, would extend to the documents or classes of documents of which the applicant seeks disclosure (r 31.16(3)(c)). In the case of a class of documents, the whole class has to be covered by standard disclosure (*Hutchison 3G UK Ltd v O_2 (UK) Ltd* [2008] EWHC 55 (Comm)).

(e) Disclosure before proceedings must be desirable (r 31.16(3)(d)) in order—
   (i) to dispose fairly of the anticipated proceedings;
   (ii) to assist the dispute to be resolved without proceedings; or
   (iii) to save costs.

It follows that the court has to be clear what the issues are likely to be in the anticipated proceedings, and must make sure that the documents being asked for are likely adversely to affect the case of one side or the other. The court has to undertake a balancing exercise to determine whether pre-action disclosure is 'desirable' in one of the three ways set out in r 31.16(3)(d): *Bermuda International Securities Ltd v KPMG* [2001] CPLR 252. Pre-action disclosure of medical records in non-clinical dispute cases is rarely 'desirable' as the issues will rarely be clear at this stage and there is the potential for disclosure of irrelevant but embarrassing information (*OCS Group Ltd v Wells* [2009] 1 WLR 1895). If the applicant already has sufficient material to plead a claim, it is unlikely to be 'desirable' to order pre-action disclosure (*First Gulf Bank v Wachovia Bank National Association* (2005) LTL 15/12/05). **30.22**

If the above conditions are satisfied, the court has a discretion to grant a pre-action disclosure order, which may be refused, applying the overriding objective. An order may be refused if the court is 'of the opinion that the order is . . . oppressive or would not be in the interests of justice or would be injurious to the public interest' (*per* Lord Mackay of Clashfern LC in *O'Sullivan v Herdmans Ltd* [1987] 1 WLR 1047). The court will also consider factors such as the strength of the substantive claim, the degree to which the documents sought are likely to support the proposed claim (or whether they are merely 'train-of-inquiry' documents), and the cost of complying (*Black v Sumitomo Corporation* [2002] 1 WLR 1569). **30.23**

Procedure

The procedure on applications for disclosure before proceedings start is laid down in CPR, r 31.16. Applications for pre-action disclosure are made by issuing an ordinary application notice supported by evidence in the anticipated substantive proceedings (but before the substantive proceedings are themselves issued). The written evidence in support must address the five requirements set out above. **30.24**

Orders for disclosure before proceedings start

It is provided in CPR, r 31.16(4) and (5), that: **30.25**

(1) An order under this rule must—
   (a) specify the documents or the classes of documents which the respondent must disclose; and
   (b) require him, when making disclosure, to specify any of those documents—
      (i) which are no longer in his control; or
      (ii) in respect of which he claims a right or duty to withhold inspection.

(2) Such an order may—
   (a) require the respondent to indicate what has happened to any documents which are no longer in his control; and
   (b) specify the time and place for disclosure and inspection.

Directions to commence substantive proceedings

30.26 Where the court grants an interim remedy before a claim has been commenced, it should give directions requiring a claim to be commenced (CPR, r 25.2(3)). A special rule, however, applies to applications for pre-action disclosure, with r 25.2(4) providing that the court need not direct that a claim be commenced where a pre-action disclosure order is made. The reason for the distinction is that pre-action disclosure orders may result in the claimant deciding not to bring substantive proceedings at all, as recognized in *Dunning v United Liverpool Hospitals, Board of Governors* [1973] 1 WLR 586, and it would not make sense to require the claimant to bring a substantive claim in such circumstances.

E DISCLOSURE BY NON-PARTIES

Jurisdiction

30.27 The court has, under SCA 1981, s 34(2) and CCA 1984, s 53(2):

> . . . power to order a person who is not a party to the proceedings and who appears to the court to be likely to have in his possession, custody or power any documents which are relevant to an issue arising out of the said claim—
>
> (a) to disclose whether those documents are in his possession, custody or power; and
> (b) to produce such of those documents . . . as may be specified in the order.

30.28 These provisions are similar to s 33(2), but under the present provisions the application is made after issue of proceedings and is made against a non-party, whereas under s 33(2) the application is made before issue in order to find out if proceedings are worth commencing and is made against the likely defendant.

30.29 There are three conditions which must be satisfied before the court can exercise its discretion whether to make the order:

(a) it must appear that there are likely to be relevant documents in the respondent's possession, custody, or power;
(b) the documents of which disclosure is sought are likely to support the case of the applicant or adversely affect the case of one of the other parties to the proceedings (CPR, r 31.17(3)(a)); and
(c) disclosure is necessary in order to dispose fairly of the claim or to save costs (r 31.17(3)(b)).

30.30 Disclosure against non-parties will therefore be granted only where the documents sought are likely to be relevant (as opposed to disclosable under standard disclosure): see *American Home Products Corporation v Novartis Pharmaceuticals UK Ltd* (2001) LTL 13/2/01. 'Likely' in this context means 'may well' as opposed to 'more probable than not': see *Three Rivers District Council v Governor and Company of the Bank of England (No 4)* [2003] 1 WLR 210, which is the same as in pre-action disclosure: see 30.20–30.23. The court should primarily consider relevance in the context of the statements of case, and should not embark on determining disputes of substance as to whether the documents are relevant: *Clark v Ardington Electrical Services* (2001) LTL 4/4/01.

Where the documents are likely to be relevant, it is then necessary to consider whether the court should refuse the order in its discretion, or impose some limit on disclosure, such as by ordering disclosure of documents only between stated dates. For example, it will require a very exceptional case to justify ordering the disclosure of a non-party's confidential medical documents (*A v X and B* (2004) LTL 6/4/04). Further, the court will not make an order if it is not satisfied that the documents sought in fact exist, so in *Re Howglen Ltd* [2001] 1 All ER 376 an application was made in general terms for documents against a non-party bank for bank records and interview notes. An order was made limited to the notes of three interviews identified in the evidence in support. **30.31**

Procedure

An application for disclosure against a non-party can be made at any time after substantive proceedings have been issued. It is made by application notice, and must be supported by written evidence (CPR, r 31.17(2)). **30.32**

The order

It is provided in CPR, r 31.17(4) and (5) that: **30.33**

> (4) An order under this rule must—
> (a) specify the documents or the classes of documents which the respondent must disclose; and
> (b) require the respondent, when making disclosure, to specify any of those documents—
> (i) which are no longer in his control; or
> (ii) in respect of which he claims a right or duty to withhold inspection.
>
> (5) Such an order may—
> (a) require the respondent to indicate what has happened to any documents which are no longer in his control; and
> (b) specify the time and place for disclosure and inspection.

F INSPECTION OF PROPERTY DURING PROCEEDINGS

It commonly happens in litigation that an expert instructed on behalf of one party will need to inspect property in the possession of another party. It may be that in a personal injury claim the claimant's engineering expert needs to inspect the machinery alleged to have caused the claimant's injuries, or that in a professional negligence claim against a surveyor the defendant's expert surveyor needs to inspect the claimant's house. Among the general interim remedies available to the court set out in CPR, r 25.1, are powers to make orders: **30.34**

(a) for the detention, custody, or preservation of relevant property;
(b) for the inspection of relevant property;
(c) for the taking of a sample of relevant property; and
(d) for the carrying out of an experiment on or with relevant property.

These orders can be combined with an order: **30.35**

(e) authorizing a person to enter any land or building in the possession of a party to the proceedings for the purposes of carrying out an order under (a) to (d).

30.36 For these purposes, 'relevant property' means property (including land) which is the subject of a claim or as to which any question may arise on a claim. Orders for inspection are commonly sought at the allocation stage. They can be asked for in a covering letter sent with the completed allocation questionnaire (the letter should be disclosed to the other parties at the same time), or in draft consent directions filed with the allocation questionnaire. Otherwise, such orders may be made on the case management conference or on an application issued for the purpose at any time after proceedings have been issued. No written evidence is required.

30.37 The main restriction on such application is that the rule is limited to physical things. It appears, therefore, that an order under the rule cannot extend to methods of manufacture or working (*Tudor Accumulator Co Ltd v China Mutual Steam Navigation Co Ltd* [1930] WN 200). However, in *Ash v Buxted Poultry Ltd* (1989) *The Times*, 29 November 1989 it was held that the court has inherent jurisdiction to make an order allowing the claimant to make a video film of the defendant's manufacturing process.

G INSPECTION OF PROPERTY IN THE POSSESSION OF NON-PARTIES

Jurisdiction

30.38 Under the SCA 1981, s 34(3) and CCA 1984, s 53(3), the court has:

> . . . power to make an order providing for any one or more of the following matters, that is to say—
>
> (a) the inspection, photographing, preservation, custody and detention of property which is not the property of, or in the possession of, any party to the proceedings but which is the subject-matter of the proceedings or as to which any question arises in the proceedings;
>
> (b) the taking of samples of any such property as is mentioned in paragraph (a) and the carrying out of any experiment on or with any such property.

The essential conditions are that:

(a) proceedings must already have been commenced; and

(b) the property must be the subject matter of the claim or a question must arise relating to the property in the claim.

Procedure

30.39 An order for inspection of property against a non-party is sought by issuing an application notice supported by evidence during the course of the substantive proceedings. It is provided in CPR, r 25.5 that:

> (2) The evidence in support of such an application must show, if practicable by reference to any statement of case prepared in relation to the proceedings . . . , that the property—
>
> (a) is . . . the subject matter of such proceedings; or
>
> (b) is relevant to the issues that will arise in relation to such proceedings.
>
> (3) A copy of the application notice and a copy of the evidence in support must be served on—
>
> (a) the person against whom the order is sought; and

(b) in relation to an application under section 34(3) of the Senior Courts Act 1981 or section 53(3) of the County Courts Act 1984, every party to the proceedings other than the applicant.

H INSPECTION OF PROPERTY BEFORE ISSUE OF PROCEEDINGS

Jurisdiction

The SCA 1981, s 33(1), and CCA 1984, s 52(1), have identical wording to s 34(3) (see 30.38), but without the reference to the property not being in the possession of a party to the proceedings. The effect is that on its face s 34(3) is wholly redundant, as any application under that subsection could also be made under s 33(1), and that s 33(1) applications can be made before proceedings are issued. The distinction between the two provisions lies in the exercise of the court's discretion, with orders under s 34(3) being more readily granted than orders under s 33(1). The interrelationship between s 33(1) and s 33(2) (see 30.20–30.23) was considered in *Huddleston v Control Risks Information Services Ltd* [1987] 1 WLR 701. The claimants sought an order for pre-action inspection of a prospectus prepared by the defendant on the ground that it might become the subject matter of subsequent proceedings or as to which a question might arise, namely, whether it was defamatory of the claimants. Hoffmann J held that whether a written instrument was 'property' within s 33(1) or was a 'document' within s 33(2) depended on whether the question arising on the instrument concerned the physical object itself or the message written on it. Thus if the issue is whether a signature on the instrument is a forgery, the application could be made under s 33(1). On the facts the claimants were concerned with the message in the prospectus, so their application was for disclosure. **30.40**

Procedure

Pre-action inspection orders are applied for by issuing an ordinary application notice in the anticipated proceedings supported by written evidence, but before those proceedings are issued. It is provided in CPR, r 25.5 that: **30.41**

> (2) The evidence in support of such an application must show, if practicable by reference to any statement of case prepared in relation to the proceedings or anticipated proceedings, that the property—
> (a) is or may become the subject matter of such proceedings; or
> (b) is relevant to the issues that will arise in relation to such proceedings.
> (3) A copy of the application notice and a copy of the evidence in support must be served on—
> (a) the person against whom the order is sought...

Like pre-action disclosure applications (see 30.26), the court will not usually give a direction for commencing the substantive proceedings as the decision to commence will usually turn on the nature of the evidence gathered from the inspection (see CPR, r 25.2(4)). **30.42**

I DATA PROTECTION

30.43 Under the Data Protection Act, 1998, s 7, on making a request in writing and paying a fee (if applicable), an individual is entitled to have communicated to him in an intelligible form any personal data relating to that individual and any information about the source of that data. For this purpose 'data' means information which is processed automatically (generally by computer), and also information recorded as part of a filing system, or which forms part of an accessible record (which by s 68 means health, education, and accessible public records). A manual filing system will only be covered if it is of sufficient sophistication to provide the same or similar ready accessibility as a computerized filing system. This means the files must be referenced or indexed in a way that makes it possible to identify with reasonable certainty and speed whether they contain personal data without having to leaf through the files themselves (*Durant v Financial Services Authority* [2004] FSR 28). The selection of data from various manual and electronic files is not 'processing' for this purpose (*Johnson v Medical Defence Union (No 2)* [2008] Bus LR 503).

30.44 Personal data is defined as meaning data relating to a living individual who can be identified from that data (or other information in the possession of the data controller), and includes expressions of opinion about the individual (s 1(1)). To come within this definition, according to *Durant v Financial Services Authority*:

(a) the information must be biographical in a significant sense, going beyond mere involvement in the events described in the file; and
(b) the data subject (the applicant) must be the focus of the information. Thus, a file dealing with a complaint made to the Financial Services Authority by the applicant about a bank was not personal data because its focus was the complaint, not biographical information about the applicant.

30.45 There are various exemptions and further detailed provisions, such as a restriction on revealing information that would identify other individuals without their consent (s 7(4)). The data controller is required to balance the interests of the other individuals with the interests of the data subject, and can redact the names of the other individuals if it is reasonable to do so.

30.46 The data controller is required to comply with a request promptly, and can be ordered to comply by the High Court or a county court (ss 7(9) and 15(1)). For the purpose of determining whether the applicant is entitled to the information under s 7, the court may require the information to be made available for inspection by the court (but not the applicant, who will not be allowed to inspect the information until after a determination in his favour (s 15(2)). The court has an untrammelled discretion whether to grant an order, but the main factor is that access under the Act is mainly for the purpose of correcting inaccuracy (*Durant v Financial Services Authority*).

30.47 Refusal of an order under s 7 does not act as a bar to a later application for specific disclosure (for which, see 29.72) of the same documents (*Johnson v Medical Defence Union* [2005] 1 WLR 750).

J INTERIM DELIVERY-UP OF GOODS

30.48 Under the Torts (Interference with Goods) Act 1977, s 4(2), the courts have power to make orders for the delivery-up of any goods which are, or may become, the subject matter of proceedings for wrongful interference, or as to which any question may arise in such proceedings. Applications under the 1977 Act are among the general interim remedies available under CPR, r 25.1, and are made by application notice, usually on notice, supported by written evidence. In urgent cases (for which, see 35.07–35.08) the application may be made without notice and even before the issue of process. A number of guidelines for the exercise of this jurisdiction were laid down by the Court of Appeal in *CBS United Kingdom Ltd v Lambert* [1983] Ch 37:

(a) there must be clear evidence that the defendant intends to dispose of the goods in order to prevent the claimant recovering them through an order of the court;
(b) there must be some evidence that the defendant acquired the goods wrongfully; and
(c) the order must not act oppressively on the defendant. Usually the court will need to balance the need to protect the claimant against the defendant's grounds for retaining the goods.

30.49 An order made under this section should clearly identify the goods to be delivered up, and may provide for delivery to the claimant or to a person appointed by the court. In *CBS United Kingdom Ltd v Lambert* it was said that the order should authorize the claimant to enter the defendant's land but only with the defendant's permission, and must make adequate provision for the safe custody of the goods. As an alternative to ordering delivery-up, the court may make orders for the preservation and detention of the goods.

Table 30.1 Comparison of various disclosure orders

Order	Type of case	Respondent	Stage	Procedure
Search, order	Real possibility of defendant destroying vital evidence	Defendant	On issue	Without notice to judge
Norwich Pharmacal identity of tortfeasor	Unknown defendant	Facilitator	Pre-action	Claim form and application
Bankers Trust whereabouts of stolen funds	Tracing claim	Recipient	Pre-action	Without notice
SCA 1981, s 33(2), pre-action disclosure	General application	Likely defendant	Pre-action	Application notice
SCA 1981, s 34(2), disclosure against non-party	General application	Non-party	After issue	Application notice
SCA 1981, s 33(1), inspection of property	General application	Party or non-party	Pre-action	Application notice
SCA 1981, s 34(3), inspection of property	General application	Non-party	After issue	Application notice
Torts (Interference with Goods) Act 1977, s 4, delivery up	Wrongful interference	Defendant	After issue (unless urgent)	Application notice

KEY POINTS SUMMARY

30.50
- *Norwich Pharmacal* orders are primarily used for finding the identity of an unknown potential defendant.
- They can only be sought against a person who facilitated and got 'mixed up' in the wrongdoing. *Norwich Pharmacal* orders therefore cannot be made against 'mere witnesses'.
- Pre-action disclosure orders bring forward the time when disclosure of documents takes place to the period before a claim is issued. The procedure can be useful where an intending claimant needs more information so they can plead an adequate claim.
- Pre-action disclosure is only ordered if exacting requirements are satisfied (see 30.20–30.23). These include the applicant being likely to be a party to a worthwhile claim, and pre-action disclosure being 'desirable' for fairly dealing with the claim or for saving costs.
- Disclosure against non-parties enables the court to order a witness to produce documents in advance of the trial, thereby avoiding adjournments when documents are produced at the last minute at trial.
- An overview of different disclosure and inspection procedures can be seen in table 30.1.

31

EXPERTS

At trial, questions of fact are decided by the tribunal of fact (in civil litigation usually the judge) based on the oral evidence of witnesses, documentary and real evidence, and any inferences which may fairly be drawn from that evidence. Increasingly, however, civil claims raise scientific and technical issues which a judge could not reasonably be expected to decide without the assistance of expert opinion from practitioners from the field in question. This chapter is concerned with the principles governing the use of expert evidence in civil claims. **31.01**

A ADMISSIBILITY OF EXPERT EVIDENCE

Issues of an artistic, scientific, or technical nature must be decided on the basis of expert evidence. Thus, the opinion of an eminent engineer was admitted in *Folkes v Chadd* (1782) 3 Doug KB 157 on the effect of an artificial bank on the silting of a harbour. In the absence of **31.02** expert evidence, such an issue must be decided against the party having the burden of proof. Expert evidence is subject to considerations of weight, and, even if uncontradicted, is not bound to be accepted by the court. As Lord President Cooper said in *Davie v Magistrates of Edinburgh* 1953 SC 34:

> Their duty is to furnish the judge . . . with the necessary scientific criteria for testing the accuracy of their conclusions, so as to enable the judge . . . to form [his or her] own independent judgment by the application of these criteria to the facts proved in evidence. The scientific opinion evidence, if intelligible, convincing and tested, becomes a factor (and often an important factor) for consideration along with the whole other evidence in the case, but the decision is for the judge.

31.03 There are four preconditions for the admission of expert evidence:

(a) the matter must call for expertise;
(b) the area must be an established field of expertise;
(c) the witness must be suitably qualified; and
(d) permission to adduce the expert evidence must be obtained from the court.

Matter requiring expertise

31.04 Experts, like other witnesses, may give evidence of primary facts within their own knowledge. Thus, an expert surveyor called to give evidence of comparable rents in rent review proceedings may give oral evidence of the dimensions of the premises in question if those facts are known to the witness. However, the real purpose in calling an expert is for the expert to express an opinion on a matter in issue. An expert is permitted to do this only if the matter calls for expertise. This means that the matter must be outside the knowledge and experience of the tribunal of fact. Typical examples are:

(a) medical evidence on the extent and prognosis of personal injuries;
(b) surveying evidence as to the state of an allegedly defective building;
(c) handwriting evidence as to the authorship of disputed writing; and
(d) accountancy evidence to establish an alleged loss of profits.

31.05 Conversely, if the matter is one within the experience of most members of the public, an expert's opinion on the matter is not admissible. For example, questions of credibility, even of children, are for the judge, and expert evidence on whether a child is to be believed is strictly inadmissible (*Re N (A Minor) (Sexual Abuse: Video Evidence)* [1997] 1 WLR 153). A more indulgent approach, however, was taken in *Re M and R (Minors) (Sexual Abuse: Expert Evidence)* [1996] 4 All ER 239, where Butler-Sloss LJ felt that expert evidence on children's credibility should be admitted, the proper control mechanism being in assessing its weight. Another example is *Larby v Thurgood* [1993] ICR 66 where it was held that the claimant's motivation to find better-paid employment was a matter within ordinary experience and that 'expert' evidence from an employment consultant on the matter was inadmissible. However, an employment consultant would be able to give expert opinion evidence concerning the employment situation in a particular area and the prospects for a person in the claimant's position of finding work.

31.06 In *Liddell v Middleton* [1996] PIQR P36 Stuart-Smith LJ gave guidance aimed at limiting the use of accident reconstruction experts in road traffic personal injuries claims. His Lordship accepted that such witnesses are necessary and useful in cases where there are no witnesses capable of describing what has happened, and where the expert is able scientifically to deduce pre-accident speeds and movements of vehicles from their positions after the accident, marks and debris on the road, and damage to the vehicles. What such an expert is not allowed to do is to analyse the witness statements and from them to draw conclusions about when the motorists should have seen each other, what avoiding action they should have taken, and whether any of the drivers should be criticized for what they did or did not do. Those are all matters for the judge, who does not require expert guidance on them.

It is also possible that an expert may be called to give factual evidence about facts known to the expert. In such a case the individual is called as a factual witness, not an expert (*Kirkman v EuroExide Corporation (CMP Batteries Ltd)* [2007] All ER (D) 209). **31.07**

Established field of expertise

In most cases this will be obvious, but in developing areas the court must be satisfied by the party seeking to call the evidence that there is a body of expertise governed by recognized standards or rules of conduct capable of influencing the court's decision on any of the issues which it has to decide, and that the witness has sufficient familiarity with and knowledge of the area of expertise to be of value to the court (*Barings plc v Coopers and Lybrand* [2001] PNLR 22). **31.08**

Qualifications

A person is an 'expert' if he or she is skilled in the field in question through qualifications or experience. A car mechanic may be an expert simply through experience in working with cars. A person with paper qualifications, but little experience, should be instructed as an expert with great caution, because even if accepted by the court as an expert, his or her opinion is unlikely to carry much weight. Furthermore, experts are permitted to express an opinion only within their field of expertise. So, a consultant orthopaedic surgeon would not be allowed to express an opinion on a psychiatric matter, nor would a surveyor be allowed to express an opinion on an architectural question. **31.09**

Ultimate issue rule

At common law an expert was not allowed to express an opinion directly on one of the issues in a case, on the ground that doing so would usurp the function of the tribunal of fact. Thus, a handwriting expert was said to be allowed to express views about the similarities between two pieces of writing, but could not express an opinion that they were written by the same person. This anachronistic rule was abolished for civil cases by the Civil Evidence Act 1972 ('CEA 1972'), s 3(3). However, it is not for experts to attempt to make findings of fact. Instead, they should express their opinions on the basis of assumed facts which should be clearly identified and stated in their reports (*JP Morgan Chase Bank v Springwell Navigation Corp* [2007] 1 All ER (Comm) 549 at [21]). **31.10**

Non-expert opinion evidence

Generally, witnesses who are not qualified as experts can only give evidence as to facts. The reason is that inferences to be drawn from the facts are matters for the tribunal of fact. Exceptionally, lay witnesses may express opinions about events within their personal **31.11** knowledge if describing those events in detail would be unduly difficult and artificial. For example, a lay witness is permitted to give an estimate of a person's age rather than describing the details of the person's appearance. Other examples include estimates of speed and distance, the state of the weather ('it was cold for that time of year'), and whether a person appeared to be drunk. Authority for the last of these propositions is *R v Davies* [1962] 1 WLR 1111. In this case three soldiers, who were witnesses to a road accident, were allowed to give evidence that they had formed the impression that the defendant had taken drink. Lord Parker CJ said the witness 'must describe of course the facts upon which he relies, but it seems to this court that he is perfectly entitled to give his impression as to whether drink had been taken or not'. Statutory confirmation of the general rule is given by the CEA 1972, s 3(2). However, a non-expert witness is not permitted to express an opinion on a matter calling for expertise.

B CONTROL OF EVIDENCE

31.12 It is provided in CPR, r 32.1, that the court may control the evidence to be adduced in the course of proceedings, which may involve excluding evidence that would otherwise be admissible, by giving directions as to:

(a) the issues on which it requires evidence;
(b) the nature of the evidence which it requires to decide those issues; and
(c) the way in which the evidence is to be placed before the court.

31.13 This power is exercised in accordance with the overriding objective. It has a particular relevance regarding expert evidence, which is often expensive and time-intensive. The power may be used to save expense, to ensure cases are dealt with proportionately, and to ensure that the real issues are addressed at trial.

C CHOICE OF EXPERT

31.14 The CPR place a lot of emphasis on the importance of experts remaining independent of the parties and state that the expert's primary duty is to the court rather than the party paying his or her fees. Rule 35.3 provides:

> (1) It is the duty of experts to help the court on the matters within their expertise.
> (2) This duty overrides any obligation to the person from whom experts have received instructions or by whom they are paid.

31.15 Despite *Liverpool Roman Catholic Archdiocese Trustees Incorporated v Goldberg (No 2)* [2001] 1 WLR 2337, which is regarded as wrongly decided (see *R (Factortame Ltd v Secretary of State for Transport, Local Government and the Regions (No 8)* [2003] QB 381), provided he has the necessary qualifications and understands his primary duty is to the court, an employee of a party can be called by that party as an expert witness (*Field v Leeds City Council* [2000] 1 EGLR 54). In *DN v Greenwich LBC* [2004] EWCA Civ 1659, an educational psychologist was held to be entitled to give expert evidence on his own behalf on why in his opinion his conduct did not fall below the relevant standard of care.

31.16 It is important that expert evidence should be, and should be seen to be, the independent product of the expert uninfluenced by the exigencies of the litigation (*Whitehouse v Jordan* [1981] 1 WLR 246 and PD 35, para 2.1). Where an expert adopts a biased or irrational approach, it may be appropriate for the judge to refer the witness's conduct to the relevant professional body, after giving the witness a suitable period of time to make representations: *Pearce v Ove Arup Partnership Ltd* (2001) LTL 2/11/01.

31.17 In *Stevens v Gullis* [2000] 1 All ER 527 an expert instructed by one of the parties demonstrated by his conduct that he had no conception of the requirements imposed on experts by the CPR. He failed to state in his report that he understood his duty to the court, failed to set out his instructions, and also failed to cooperate with the other experts in signing an agreed memorandum following a without prejudice meeting of experts. It was held that in the circumstances he should be debarred from giving evidence in the case.

D PRIVILEGED NATURE OF EXPERTS' REPORTS

31.18 An expert who is instructed to give an opinion in relation to proposed or actual proceedings will invariably do so initially in the form of a written report. Such a report is protected by legal professional privilege, and need not be disclosed to the other side. It has been held (subject to joint instruction, for which see 31.28), that an order compelling the exchange of experts' reports offends this privilege and will not be made (*Worrall v Reich* [1955] 1 QB 296).

31.19 Consequently, a party who does not like the opinion expressed by one expert is permitted to seek another opinion in the hope that it will be more favourable, and may rely at trial solely on the expert holding the most favourable view.

31.20 Privilege attaches to a report until it is disclosed, usually pursuant to directions (see 31.23). Disclosing the final version of an expert's report does not waive privilege in earlier drafts of the report (*Jackson v Marley Davenport Ltd* [2004] 1 WLR 2926). A directions order which provides that a party 'shall file and serve' a report must be read as subject to an implied 'if relied upon' clause, otherwise it would amount to a direction to waive privilege in the report (*Watts v Oakley* [2006] EWCA Civ 1905).

E DISCLOSURE OF EXPERTS' REPORTS

31.21 Rules of court have been made under the CEA 1972, s 2, providing for the disclosure of reports of experts intended to be called at trial. These rules do not abrogate legal professional privilege, and a party is still permitted to seek another expert if the first expert's advice is unpalatable. However, the rules do generally require prior disclosure as a condition precedent to the admissibility of expert evidence at trial. They do not alter the substantive rules on the admissibility of expert evidence. The rules are in keeping with the policy of open preparation for trial, with the object of avoiding trial by ambush and the promotion of early settlements.

Pre-action disclosure of reports

31.22 In several of the pre-action protocols it is contemplated that there should be pre-action disclosure of experts' reports. In some, eg, the personal injuries protocol, this is seen as inevitable for the purpose of assessing the extent of the claimant's injuries. In others, such as the construction and engineering disputes protocol (para 5.5) it is clear that seeking expert evidence is almost a last resort prior to commencing proceedings. The personal injuries protocol favours the joint selection of experts (see 31.28), whereas the professional negligence and the construction disputes protocols favour joint instruction.

Directions

31.23 Directions dealing with expert evidence will usually be made when the case is allocated to the fast track or multi-track, or on the case management conference. The primary rule is that no party may call an expert or put in evidence an expert's report without the court's permission (CPR, r 35.4(1)). In the absence of a direction, therefore, expert evidence is inadmissible. In deciding whether to grant permission, and if so to what extent, the court will seek to restrict expert evidence to that which is reasonably required to resolve the proceedings (r 35.1). The court also bears in mind the need to consider whether the benefits of taking a particular step, particularly instructing a number of experts, justify the costs involved (r 1.4(2)(h)). Where directions require an act to be done by an expert, or otherwise affect an expert, the party instructing the expert must serve a copy of the order on the expert (PD 35, para 8).

Limiting expert evidence

31.24 The court can use its power to control evidence to prevent the parties calling unnecessary expert evidence at trial. This is particularly important, because professional experts are entitled to charge fees at commercial rates for the time they are engaged on a case, and these are often well in excess of £1,000 per day. If the court decides that the parties may call expert evidence, it should generally give permission only for expert evidence from named experts in named fields (CPR, r 35.4(3)). It is wrong in principle to allow a party to call more than one expert in a particular field of expertise, without very good reasons (*JP Morgan Chase Bank v Springwell Navigation Corp* [2007] 1 All ER (Comm) 549). The court also has to decide whether to allow the expert evidence to be adduced simply by reference to experts' reports, or whether to allow the experts to be called to give oral evidence at the trial. Particularly in cases on the small claims and fast tracks, the court will allow an expert to give oral evidence only if it is necessary in the interests of justice to do so (r 35.5(2)), but even in multi-track claims oral expert evidence is regarded as a last resort: *Daniels v Walker* [2000] 1 WLR 1382. Although the court has power to limit the expert evidence the parties may call at trial, it does not have power to limit the experts a party can instruct. The court cannot impose a condition that a party must obtain the court's permission before instructing an expert (*Vasiliou v Hajigeorgiou* [2005] 1 WLR 2195).

31.25 It has been held that apparently one-sided expert directions are permissible if they accord with the overriding objective. Thus, in *Baron v Lovell* [1999] CPLR 630 the court felt there was not a great deal of difference between the two sides' medical reports, and directed that the medical evidence be limited to the claimant's medical reports. It is becoming increasingly common in fast track cases where the injuries are not too severe for directions to be made for the medical evidence to be restricted to the report served by the claimant with the particulars of claim.

Exchange of reports

If the court allows both parties to adduce expert evidence, it usually makes directions (usually at allocation or on a case management conference) for the mutual exchange of reports by a stated date. **31.26**

Sequential disclosure

In exceptional circumstances, directions may provide for sequential disclosure of reports. **31.27** Such a direction may be justified on costs grounds where it is likely that the claimant's report will be agreed. Another example is *Kirkup v British Rail Engineering Ltd* [1983] 1 WLR 1165, where a total of 8,661 claims were made by the defendants' employees for damages for industrial deafness. The statements of case in many of the cases were in very general terms. Mutual disclosure of experts' reports would have required the defendants to have compiled wide-ranging experts' reports on noise levels in all their engineering workshops. Sequential disclosure was ordered to enable the defendants to produce expert evidence relevant to each claim.

Single joint experts and joint selection of experts

Directions permitting each party to instruct its own expert often result in conflicting expert **31.28** evidence, which can lead to escalating costs. Whether this is worthwhile depends on the importance and complexity of the case, so such directions are more commonly met in multi-track cases. It is different in cases on the small claims and fast tracks, where the normal direction is for permission to be given for expert evidence from only one expert (CPR, r 35.4(3A)). A distinction has to be made between a single joint expert and a jointly selected expert. The former is instructed to prepare a report for the court on behalf of two or more parties (including the claimant), and as each side contributes to the expert's fees, each is entitled to a copy of the expert's report. The latter is instructed by one party, who is liable to pay the expert's fees, and who alone is entitled to see the report (*Carlson v Townsend* [2001] 1 WLR 2415). The joint selection of an expert under the Personal Injuries Pre-Action Protocol is of the latter type, with (in the usual case) the defendant's input being limited to objecting to certain of the experts proposed by the claimant, and with the report protected by legal professional privilege unless and until the claimant chooses to disclose it.

Letters of instruction

Detailed guidance on the information to be provided to experts when they are instructed is **31.29** given by the Experts Protocol in PD 35, para 8.1. The main obligation is to explain the purpose of the report, describe what needs to be investigated, and to explain the issues in the case. All the necessary background information should also be provided. Where there is a joint instruction of an expert, the parties should try to agree the joint instructions, and to agree on the documents to be provided to the expert (para 17.6). If the parties cannot agree, ultimately they can both send instructions to the expert, sending a copy to the other side (r 35.8). An example of a letter of instruction is shown in figure 5.3.

Directions for a single joint expert

31.30 Where two or more parties wish to submit expert evidence on a particular issue, the court may direct that the evidence on that issue is to be given by a single joint expert (CPR, r 35.7(1)). In deciding whether to make directions for separate experts or a single joint expert PD 35, para 7, provides that the court will take into account all the circumstances, and in particular whether:

(a) it is proportionate to have separate experts for each party on a particular issue with reference to:
  (i) the amount in dispute;
  (ii) the importance to the parties; and
  (iii) the complexity of the issue;
(b) the instruction of a single joint expert is likely to assist the parties and the court to resolve the issue more speedily and in a more cost-effective way than separately instructed experts;
(c) expert evidence is to be given on the issue of liability, causation or quantum;
(d) the expert evidence falls within a substantially established area of knowledge which is unlikely to be in dispute or there is likely to be a range of expert opinion;
(e) a party has already instructed an expert on the issue in question and whether or not that was done in compliance with any practice direction or relevant pre-action protocol;
(f) questions put to the expert (see 31.42) are likely to remove the need for the other party to instruct an expert if one party has already instructed an expert;
(g) questions put to a single joint expert may not conclusively deal with all issues that may require testing prior to trial;
(h) a conference may be required with the legal representatives, experts, and other witnesses which may make instruction of a single joint expert impractical; and
(i) a claim to privilege makes the instruction of any expert as a single joint expert inappropriate.

31.31 In substantial claims it may be wrong for the court to insist on a single joint expert. This is particularly so if there is more than one school of thought on the central issues (*Oxley v Penwarden* [2001] CPLR 1). In clinical disputes, it was suggested in *Peet v Mid-Kent Healthcare Trust* [2002] 1 WLR 210 that the balance between proportionality and expense could be achieved by allowing the parties to call their own experts on the medical issues, but to direct the instruction of a joint expert on the non-medical issues.

31.32 If the court makes such a direction, unless the parties agree on the expert to be instructed, the court may select an expert from a list submitted by the parties, or direct how the expert should be selected. Once selected, each instructing party may give instructions to the expert, sending a copy to the other instructing parties. The normal direction provides that the fees of the expert are to be met equally by the instructing parties.

31.33 A party will not be permitted to invite a jointly instructed expert to a conference without the written consent of the other parties: *Peet v Mid-Kent Healthcare Trust.*

Disagreement with joint report

31.34 According to Lord Woolf MR in *Daniels v Walker* [2000] 1 WLR 1382, obtaining a joint report should be regarded as a first step in obtaining expert evidence on the relevant issue.

Normally, it is hoped it will also be the last step. However, if on receipt of the joint report one of the parties, for reasons that are not fanciful, decides to challenge the expert's conclusions, that party may be allowed to obtain evidence from another expert to test the conclusions in the joint report. Factors to be taken into account in exercising the discretion to allow a second expert to report include the nature of the case, the amount at stake, the effect of allowing another expert to report, any delay, and any impact on keeping the trial date (*Cosgrove v Pattison* [2001] CPLR 177). Once a second report is available, the court should reconsider the matter, perhaps after directing questions to the experts and discussion between them (for which, see 31.42 and 31.43). If there are unresolved issues after this process, the court may give permission for both experts to give oral evidence at the trial.

Form of experts' reports

By virtue of CPR, r 35.10, and PD 35, para 3.2, an expert's report must: **31.35**

(a) give details of the expert's qualifications;
(b) give details of any literature or other materials the expert has relied on in making the report;
(c) contain a statement setting out the substance of all facts and instructions given to the expert that are material to the report. By CPR, r. 35.10(4) and PD 35, para 5, the instructions referred to will not be protected by privilege, but cross-examination of experts on the contents of their instructions will not be allowed without consent of the party who gave the instructions or unless the court permits it;
(d) make clear which facts stated in the report are within the expert's own knowledge;
(e) say who carried out any examination, measurement, test, or experiment which the expert has used in the report, give the qualifications of that person, and say whether the tests, etc., were carried out under the expert's supervision;
(f) where there is a range of opinion on the matters dealt with in the report, summarize the range of opinion and give reasons for the expert's own opinion;
(g) contain a summary of the conclusions reached;
(h) if the expert is unable to give an opinion without qualification, state the qualification;
(i) contain a statement that the expert understands their duty to the court, has complied with that duty, and is aware of the requirements of Part 35, PD 35 and the protocol annexed to PD 35.

An expert's report should be as concise as the nature of the case allows, and should avoid a convoluted approach such as by requiring a reader to track an argument from the main text and back and forth through various schedules. It must state clearly and prominently any key points of disagreement with the other side, and include reference to any facts known to the expert which may have a significant bearing on the issues in the case, even if unfavourable to his client (*Balmoral Group Ltd v Borealis (UK) Ltd* [2006] 2 Lloyd's Rep 629). **31.36**

An expert's report must be verified by a statement of truth in the following form: **31.37**

> I confirm that insofar as the facts stated in my report are within my own knowledge I have made clear which they are and I believe them to be true, and that the opinions I have expressed represent my true and complete professional opinion.

31.38 Can an expert's report be settled by counsel? In *Whitehouse v Jordan* [1981] 1 WLR 246, Lord Wilberforce commented at 256–7 that:

> while some degree of consultation between experts and legal advisers is entirely proper, it is necessary that expert evidence presented to the court should be, and should be seen to be, the independent product of the expert, uninfluenced as to form or content by the exigencies of litigation. To the extent that it is not, the evidence is likely to be not only incorrect but self-defeating.

31.39 If an expert changes his or her mind on a material matter after the exchange of reports, that change of view should be communicated to the other parties (and to the court if reports have been lodged at court): *National Justice Compania Naviera SA v Prudential Assurance Co Ltd* [1993] 2 Lloyd's Rep 68 and PD 35, para 2.5.

Supporting documents

31.40 Published and unpublished information forming part of the general corpus of knowledge in a particular field may be relied on by an expert in reaching an opinion: *Seyfang v G D Searle and Co* [1973] QB 148. Experts also often back up their opinions by referring to photographs, plans, survey reports, and other factual materials. Details of any material relied upon should be given in the report (PD 35, para 3.2(2)), and copies of factual documentation should be served on the other parties together with the report: *National Justice Compania Naviera SA v Prudential Assurance Co Ltd* [1993] 2 Lloyd's Rep 68. Important scientific papers relevant to the issues should be included in the report, and not simply produced at the trial (*Balmoral Group Ltd v Borealis (UK) Ltd* [2006] 2 Lloyd's Rep 629).

Failure to disclose report

31.41 By CPR, r 35.13, a party which fails to disclose an expert's report may not use the report at the trial or call the expert to give evidence orally unless the court gives permission. Similar principles apply on such an application as on any other application for relief from sanctions (see 28.24–28.32).

F WRITTEN QUESTIONS TO EXPERTS

31.42 A party may put to an expert instructed by another party, or to a single joint expert, written questions about the expert's report for the purpose of clarifying the report (CPR, r 35.6). This does not, of course, prevent a party putting written questions to his own expert (*Stallwood v David* [2007] 1 All ER 206 at [30]). Directions given allowing expert evidence to be introduced will usually provide a date by when questions should be put to the experts. The expert's answers to such questions are treated as part of the expert's report. Questions must be proportionate and purely for clarification if they are put to the expert without permission, but it is possible to ask about matters not in the expert's report (as long as they are within the expert's expertise) with the consent of the other side or the court's permission: *Mutch v Allen* [2001] CPLR 200.

G WITHOUT PREJUDICE DISCUSSION

There are occasions where wide divergences of view between the experts on the two sides are more apparent than real. An off-the-record discussion (either face to face or by telephone or other means of communication) can often narrow the areas of dispute. To assist this, the court has power, under CPR, r 35.12, at any stage to direct a discussion between experts, and the parties must consider with their experts, at an early stage, whether there is likely to be any useful purpose in holding an experts' discussion and if so when (PD 35, para 9.1). The purpose of discussions between experts is to agree and narrow issues, and is not for the purpose of the experts seeking to settle the case (para 9.2). A court direction for an experts' discussion will normally also provide that, following the discussion, the experts must prepare a statement within seven days of the discussion setting out: **31.43**

(a) the issues on which they agree; and
(b) the issues on which they disagree with a summary of their reasons for disagreeing.

In *Aird v Prime Meridian Ltd* [2007] BLR 105 directions were given for mediation, with a joint statement to be prepared by the parties' experts. A draft joint statement was headed 'without prejudice', but the final version had these words removed. The mediation failed to settle the case. It was held that the joint statement did not acquire without prejudice status by being used in the mediation, so was admissible in the proceedings. **31.44**

H EXAMINATIONS BY EXPERTS

It will be rare for an expert to be able to give a valuable opinion without first examining the subject matter relevant to that opinion. Where that subject matter is under the control of the party instructing the expert, there should be no problem. Where it is in the possession of the other side or of a non-party, it is necessary to seek either its consent or a court order for inspection by the expert. The powers available to the court were considered at 30.35–30.43. Some more specific issues will be considered here. **31.45**

Comparison of handwriting

A party seeking to prove or disprove the authenticity or authorship of a piece of writing may adduce evidence of the three following kinds: **31.46**

(a) Factual testimony from witnesses who saw the document being written, or who can say the alleged author did not write it. These witnesses may be the actual person concerned, or persons present at the time (such as attesting witnesses to a will).
(b) Opinion evidence from a person familiar with the handwriting of the alleged author. For example, a secretary may be an 'expert' on an employer's signature, having seen the employer regularly sign letters over a period of several years. Such a secretary would, of course, be allowed to give an opinion only on whether a disputed signature was that of the employer in question, and would not be an expert on signatures generally.

(c) Evidence from a handwriting expert comparing the disputed writing with a control sample from the alleged author. This method of proof will be considered in this section.

31.47 It is provided by the Criminal Procedure Act 1865, s 8 (which, despite the name of the statute, applies also to civil cases), that:

> comparison of a disputed writing with any writing proved to the satisfaction of the judge to be genuine shall be permitted to be made by witnesses; and such writings, and the evidence of witnesses respecting the same, may be submitted to the court and jury as evidence of the genuineness or otherwise of the writing in dispute.

31.48 Despite the use of the expression 'by witnesses' in s 8, it has always been held that a comparison of handwriting can be safely undertaken only by a witness who is an expert in the comparison of handwriting: *R v Rickard* (1918) 13 Cr App r 140; *R v Tilley* [1961] 1 WLR 1309. Although it was held that a solicitor who had made a study of handwriting as a hobby for ten years was an expert for this purpose in *R v Silverlock* [1894] 2 QB 766, a wasted costs order was made in *R v Secretary of State for the Home Department, ex p Abassi* (1992) *The Times*, 16 April 1992, where a barrister with no real experience in the matter was called to compare two pieces of handwriting.

31.49 In *Lockheed-Arabia v Owen* [1993] QB 780, the defendant did not admit an allegation in the particulars of claim that the defendant had signed and endorsed a cheque. The claimant's solicitors had photocopied both sides of the cheque, and placed the original in their safe. Before trial the safe was stolen. The question arose whether a handwriting expert should be permitted to make a comparison with the photocopies. It was held by the Court of Appeal that the fact that a photocopy would not reveal pressure marks, overwritten words, or pen lifts affected credibility and weight, not admissibility.

Medical examinations of the claimant

31.50 In personal injuries cases, unless the defendant is prepared to agree the claimant's expert's report, the defendant's medical experts will need to examine the claimant if they are to be able to give meaningful advice. However, any form of medical examination will infringe the fundamental human right to personal liberty, so it has always been held that there is no power to order a claimant to submit to a medical examination (given the sanction of committal to prison should the claimant fail to comply). As it is the sanction for non-compliance that is objectionable, the courts have been able to avoid the injustice of defendants being disadvantaged by the indirect method of ordering a stay of the claim if a claimant refuses a reasonable request for a medical examination on behalf of a defendant: *Edmeades v Thames Board Mills Ltd* [1969] 2 QB 67. In effect, the claimant is given a choice. Either the claimant consents to submit to the medical examination by the defendant's medical expert, or the claimant refuses and the action is stayed. A stayed action remains in being, but no further steps may be taken (with the effect of preventing the claimant going to trial).

31.51 In *Edmeades v Thames Board Mills Ltd* it was held that a stay would be granted if it was just and reasonable in the circumstances. As interpreted by Scarman LJ in *Starr v National Coal Board* [1977] 1 WLR 63, there are two elements:

(a) the defendant's request for the medical examination must be reasonable; and

(b) the claimant's refusal to consent to the examination, or agreement subject to conditions, must be such as to prevent the just determination of the claim.

In the usual run of cases, it will always be reasonable for the defendant to ask for at least one medical examination of the claimant to ensure that the defendant is not put at a disadvantage. If the claim takes a long time to get to trial, such that the claimant's condition may have materially altered since the defendant's initial medical examination, it will be reasonable for the defendant to be given a second examination. If the claimant's injuries cross the boundaries of several medical specializations, the claimant will be required to submit to examinations by several experts on behalf of the defendant. It may be that, having conducted a general examination of the claimant, an expert acting for the defendant comes to the view that the true extent of the claimant's injuries can only be discovered by some unusual procedure, or even by an exploratory operation. Whether the claim would be stayed if the claimant refused to undergo such a procedure depends on the balance between the need for the procedure for the proper preparation of the defendant's case and the reasonableness of the claimant's refusal on the grounds of pain, inconvenience, and risk to health (*Prescott v Bulldog Tools Ltd* [1981] 3 All ER 869). **31.52**

An objection to being medically examined by even a single named doctor is usually unreasonable. The reason for this is that the claimant can choose any expert, and the defendant should be given the same opportunity: *Starr v National Coal Board*. **31.53**

A claimant is entitled to insist on a number of minor conditions before consenting to a medical examination on the defendant's behalf, without risking the claim being stayed. These include: **31.54**

(a) that the defendant pays any loss of earnings incurred by the claimant in attending the examination;
(b) that the defendant pays any out-of-pocket expenses incurred by the claimant in attending;
(c) that the doctor will not discuss the accident with the claimant save in so far as this is necessary for the purpose of the examination; and
(d) that a friend, relative, or legal representative attends with the claimant for moral support unless the friend will interfere with the examination, such as where the expert is a psychiatrist: *Whitehead v Avon County Council* (1995) *The Times*, 3 May 1995.

It has been held that it is never reasonable to insist that the defendant must disclose the report compiled after the examination as a condition of consenting to an examination: *Megarity v D J Ryan and Sons Ltd* [1980] 1 WLR 1237. This is because the report is protected by legal professional privilege, and would give the claimant an advantage not enjoyed by the defendant. **31.55**

I ASSESSORS

Under the SCA 1981, s 70(1), and CCA 1984, s 63(1), the judge may call in aid one or more assessors when hearing a case. Assessors must be persons with suitable skill or experience in the area. They are frequently used, eg, in admiralty claims and in appeals concerning the **31.56** assessment of costs. Their role is to assist and advise the judge. It is permissible for the judge to put questions to an assessor after discussion with counsel. The answers should then be disclosed to counsel, either orally or in writing, who are then permitted to make submissions to the judge on whether the advice of the assessor should be followed (*Owners of the Ship Bow Spring v Owners of the Ship Manzanillo II* [2005] 1 WLR 144). Decisions on the law and the merits are for the judge alone: *The Aid* (1881) 6 PD 84.

J TRIAL

General position of experts

31.57 Directions for disclosure of experts' reports are merely procedural. Questions of admissibility remain in the province of the trial judge: *Sullivan v West Yorkshire Passenger Transport Executive* [1985] 2 All ER 134.

31.58 Experts often sit in court throughout proceedings to listen to the evidence and to advise counsel for the party instructing them. When they are called to give evidence, their reports are usually put in evidence at the commencement of their examination-in-chief. They will often explain any technical matters in their reports, and may comment on the evidence already given. They may seek to support their conclusions with published and unpublished materials. Although facts contained in such materials are not strictly proved, they are of some probative value and may be used by the court as supporting any inferences which can fairly be drawn from them: *H v Schering Chemicals Ltd* [1983] 1 WLR 143. An expert may be asked for an opinion on hypothetical facts (on the basis that those facts will be proved by subsequent evidence).

31.59 An expert should give the court independent assistance by way of objective, unbiased opinion regarding matters within the expertise of the expert: *Polivitte Ltd v Commercial Union Assurance Co plc* [1987] 1 Lloyd's Rep 379 *per* Garland J. Experts called to give evidence in both the High Court and the county courts should never assume the role of the advocate: *National Justice Compania Naviera SA v Prudential Assurance Co Ltd* [1993] 2 Lloyd's Rep 68.

31.60 By CPR, r 35.11, any party may put in evidence any report disclosed by the other side. This rule provides an absolute to rely on experts' reports disclosed by other parties, unrestricted by any discretion whether in rr 35.1 or 35.7 or otherwise (*Shepherd Neame Ltd v EDF Energy Networks (SPN) plc* [2008] Bus LR Digest D43).

Jointly instructed expert at trial

31.61 In the normal course of things, a jointly instructed expert's report should be the evidence in the case on the issues covered by that report. Normally there should be no need for such a report to be amplified or tested by cross-examination (*Peet v Mid-Kent Healthcare Trust* [2002] 1 WLR 210). It might be appropriate to order attendance for cross-examination where a single joint expert delivers his report shortly before the trial, or where the expert has not considered all the written questions put to him (*Coopers Payen Ltd v Southampton Container Terminal Ltd* [2004] 1 Lloyd's Rep 331). If, exceptionally, the expert is called at trial, any cross-examination should be restricted as far as possible: *Peet v Mid-Kent Healthcare Trust*. If there is no other direct evidence, the evidence given by a single joint expert is likely to be compelling (*Coopers Payen Ltd v Southampton Container Terminal Ltd*). A judge may depart from it only in exceptional circumstances and after fully explaining the reasons.

Conflicts between experts and other evidence

It is a common occurrence that the parties will adduce conflicting expert evidence. When this happens the duty of the judge is to make findings of fact and resolve the conflict: *Sewell v Electrolux Ltd* (1997) *The Times*, 7 November 1997. Where there is a conflict between an expert and lay witnesses, generally the judge should refuse to accept the lay evidence in preference to uncontradicted expert evidence: *Re B (A Minor)* [2000] 1 WLR 790. However, the judge is not obliged to accept expert evidence if there are sufficient grounds for rejecting it, such as where it does not speak to a relevant issue (see *R v Lanfear* [1968] 2 QB 77), or where the judge does not believe the expert or is otherwise unconvinced by it (*Dover District Council v Sherred* (1997) *The Times*, 11 February 1997). Also, there are cases where lay evidence may be preferred to expert evidence, such as where attesting witnesses are preferred to a handwriting expert over a contested will: *Fuller v Strum* [2002] 1 WLR 1097. **31.62**

Costs against an expert

An expert who has caused significant expense to be incurred through flagrant, reckless disregard of his duties to the court may be ordered to pay those costs (*Phillips v Symes (No 2)* [2005] 1 WLR 2043). **31.63**

K USE OF EXPERTS' REPORTS AFTER TRIAL

Unlike disclosed documents and exchanged witness statements, experts' reports disclosed to the other side are not subject to any implied undertaking not to use them for collateral purposes unconnected with the present litigation. See *Prudential Assurance Co Ltd v Fountain Page Ltd* [1991] 1 WLR 756. **31.64**

KEY POINTS SUMMARY

- Where a matter arising at trial is outside the reasonable experience of the judge, usually because it is a technical matter relating to art, science, or professional (non-legal) judgement: **31.65**
  - expert evidence on the matter is admissible; and
  - the judge is not competent to decide the matter without expert evidence.
- Expert evidence is not allowed except with the permission of the court. It is therefore essential both to obtain directions dealing with expert evidence and to comply with them.

- There is a vast range of possible directions that could be made relating to expert evidence. They include joint selection, joint instruction, separate instruction, disclosure of reports, putting written questions to experts, without prejudice discussions between experts, permission to rely on reports only at trial, and permission to call experts as witnesses at trial.
- An expert's primary duty is to the court, not to the party paying the fees.
- Experts are required to give their independent opinion on the issues within their area of expertise.
- There are detailed requirements on the format of experts' reports, which must include a statement of truth.

32

WITNESS STATEMENTS AND AFFIDAVITS

This chapter is concerned with the rules relating to the use of written evidence in civil proceedings. Traditionally, evidence given at trials has been by witnesses giving oral evidence from the witness box, and evidence given in support of interim applications has been in writing. Until the introduction of the CPR, written evidence was generally in the form of affidavits. Modern practice has seen some blurring of this distinction. Under the CPR evidence given in civil trials continues to be given primarily from the witness box, but with witness statements exchanged well before trial standing as the evidence-in-chief of the witnesses. The purpose behind requiring the parties to exchange their witnesses' statements is to save time and costs at trial, and to enable the parties to evaluate the merits of their dispute with a view to settlement. Written evidence in support of interim applications can be given by a variety of different methods, but the principal means is by way of signed witness statements. **32.01**

A TYPES OF WRITTEN EVIDENCE

There are six main types of written evidence used in civil proceedings: witness statements, witness summaries, affidavits, affirmations, statements of case, and the second page of an application notice. **32.02**

Witness statements

Witness statements are formal documents setting out in writing the facts that a witness is able to talk about. A witness statement must be signed by the witness, and must contain a statement of truth, which usually appears at the end. Witness statements are a means of adducing evidence on interim applications, and are also used for giving advance notice of the evidence that will be given by the lay witnesses at trial. The current practice is usually for exchanged witness statements to stand as the evidence-in-chief of the witnesses at trial. **32.03**

Witness summaries

32.04 Witness summaries are informal documents summarizing the evidence it is expected a witness will be able to give at trial. They are not used for interim applications. Permission must be obtained from the court if they are going to be used, and they are appropriate only if there has been some practical problem in arranging for a witness to sign a formal witness statement.

Affidavits

32.05 Affidavits take a form almost identical to that of witness statements, but have a 'commencement' at the beginning, and end with a 'jurat' rather than a statement of truth (see 32.31). An affidavit must be sworn by the deponent before a solicitor or someone else authorized to take oaths, and the fact they are sworn statements is the main difference between them and witness statements. Fees are payable when affidavits are sworn, which also marks them off from the more informal witness statements. There are a limited number of situations where affidavits must be used. These include applications for freezing injunctions and search orders, and on applications to commit for contempt of court. They can, generally, be used as an alternative to witness statements for other interim applications, but the additional cost of using this form of evidence may well be disallowed. Before the introduction of the CPR they were also widely used as a means of placing evidence before the court on final hearings, particularly Chancery matters, some landlord and tenant matters, and hearings to assess damages. (If there were any controversy, the deponent would often be called to be cross-examined on the contents of the affidavit.) This function has largely been replaced by the use of witness statements.

Affirmations

32.06 An affirmation is almost identical to an affidavit, but the maker of the affirmation will affirm to the truth of its contents, rather than swearing to its truth, as permitted by the Oaths Act 1978.

Statements of case

32.07 As seen in Chapter 13, statements of case have to be verified by a statement of truth. They can therefore be used as the evidence in support of interim applications (provided they cover the material relevant to the application). In practice the contents of a party's statement of case almost always have to be supplemented, even for the simplest forms of interim application.

Para 10 of an application notice

32.08 The prescribed form of application notice, form N244, contains a section (para 10 on the second page) where the applicant can set out the facts in support of the application. It is completed by a signed statement of truth. This is perhaps the least formal means of adducing evidence at an interim application, and also probably the most common. An example of an application notice is illustrated as figure 20.1.

B WITNESS STATEMENTS

Format

By CPR, r 32.4(1), a witness statement is a written statement signed by a person which contains the evidence which that person would be allowed to give orally. Detailed requirements are set out in PD 32. An example is illustrated in figure 32.1. **32.09**

Figure 32.1 Witness statement

Made on behalf of: Claimant
Witness: C. Holmes
Statement number: 1
Exhibits: CH 1–CH 3
Date made: 22.6.2010
Claim No 10BD 98858

IN THE BRADFORD COUNTY COURT
BETWEEN:—

COLIN HOLMES — Claimant
and
GILLIAN DUTTON — Defendant

WITNESS STATEMENT OF COLIN HOLMES

1 I am COLIN HOLMES, a Financial Services Adviser of 17 Conniston Road, Bradford BD8 3PR. I am the Claimant, and I make this witness statement in support of my application for an interim injunction against the Defendant.

2 17 Conniston Road is the house where my wife and I have made our home and raised our family since 1988. There is now shown to me marked **'CH 1'** a bundle containing true copies of relevant Land Registry office copy entries, and the entries, including Land Registry plan, for number 17 are at pages 1 to 3. It will be seen that I am the sole registered proprietor.

3 When we bought our house in 1988 we also bought a piece of land ('the garden'), formerly owned by the railway company, that lies at the rear of the gardens of the odd-numbered houses in Conniston Road. The garden is about 1/2 of an acre in area, and we use it as a garden to grow fruit and vegetables. True copies of the relevant Land Registry office copy entries are at pages 4 to 6 of exhibit **'CH 1'**. Again, I am the sole registered proprietor.

4 It will also be seen from page 4 of exhibit **'CH 1'** that the garden has the benefit of a right of way along the passage ('the drive') running between the houses at numbers 25 and 27 Conniston Road. The drive is located on land forming part of the title to number 27. It is about 30 metres long, about 3 metres wide, and its surface is of compacted gravel.

5 Number 27 is owned by the Defendant, and true copies of the Office Copy entries relating to this property can be found at pages 7 to 9 of exhibit **'CH 1'**. It will be seen on page 7 that the drive is subject to rights of way.

6 In March 2010 the Defendant fitted a gate across the drive together with a lock and bolt. This can be identified from my sketch drawing on page 1 of exhibit **'CH 2'**, which is now shown to me, which comprises two drawings that I have made which are relevant to this

Figure 32.1 *continued*

dispute. The Defendant stated that she had fixed the gate, lock and bolt in a letter to me and my wife dated 20 March 2010, which is at page 2 of exhibit '**CH 3**', which is a bundle containing true copies of relevant correspondence.

[*Continue with further narrative*]

Statement of truth

I believe that the facts stated in this witness statement are true.

Signed

COLIN HOLMES

Date 22 June 2010

32.10 It will contain a formal heading with the title of the proceedings. In the top right-hand corner it should state the party on whose behalf it is made; the initials and surname of the witness; whether it is the first, second, etc., statement of the witness; the references of the exhibits included; and the date it is made. The opening paragraph should give details of the witness's occupation or description, and if relevant state the position he holds and the name of his employer, and should also state if he is a party in the proceedings or employed by a party.

32.11 The text of the statement must, if practicable, be in the witness's own words. It should be expressed in the first person. It is usually convenient to follow the chronological sequence of events. Each paragraph should, so far as possible, be confined to a distinct portion of the subject. The statement should indicate sections of its content that are made only from knowledge and belief as opposed to matters within the witness's own knowledge, and should state the sources of any matters of information and belief. Documents referred to in the statement should be formally exhibited (*Tweed v Parades Commission for Northern Ireland* [2007] 1 AC 650). The statement must include a signed statement that the witness believes the facts it contains are true. False statements may be punished as contempt of court. The form of statement of truth is:

> I believe that the facts stated in this witness statement are true.

32.12 All numbers, including dates, should be expressed in figures. Witness statements must be produced on durable A4 paper with a 35 mm margin typed on one side of the paper only. Wherever possible they should be securely bound in a manner that will not hamper filing. If they are not securely bound, each page should bear the claim number and initials of the witness.

Disclosure of witness statements in interim applications

32.13 Witness statements for use in support of interim applications on notice should, where service is to be effected by the court, be filed and served when the application notice is issued (CPR, r 23.7(2)). The standard form of application notice (N244: see figure 20.1) contains at part B a section where the applicant has to indicate the nature of the written evidence relied upon, which should be attached to the notice. If the applicant is to effect service, the written evidence must be served with the application notice (r 23.7(3)). The court may well give directions as to when any further written evidence should be served and filed (PD 23A, para 9.2), this being particularly relevant for the evidence relied upon by the respondents. Respondents must comply with any such directions, and should, in any event, serve and file their written evidence as soon as possible (para 9.4). This is important, because if a respondent serves its evidence shortly before the hearing (or even at the door of the court), the probability is that the hearing will have to be adjourned, with the costs of the adjournment usually being paid by the party responsible for the late service of the evidence. The evidence (but not the exhibits) must be filed at court (para 9.6), but the copies served on the other parties should include the exhibits.

Interim applications without notice fall into two categories. First, there are those, such as **32.14** applications for freezing injunctions, where it is essential that no prior notification is given to the respondents in order to ensure the interim relief is effective. In this category, the evidence in support of the application is not served on the respondents until after the without notice application has been dealt with. In the second category it is simply a lack of time that makes it necessary to apply without giving the usual three clear days' notice. In these cases the applicant should take steps to give informal notice of the hearing to the respondents (PD 25A, para 4.3(3)), and this may include service of the written evidence in support.

Cross-examination of witnesses in interim applications

The usual position is that evidence in interim applications is placed before the court in **32.15** written form, and no 'live' evidence is called. However, there are occasions where the facts adduced in a witness statement (or affidavit) are seriously challenged, and the court may be persuaded to make an order granting permission to cross-examine the person who signed the witness statement or swore the affidavit (CPR, r 32.7(1)). These orders are made only if there are good reasons to justify the additional delay and expense. If such an order is made, the challenged evidence may be used only if the witness attends in compliance with the order, unless the court gives permission (r 32.7(2)).

Exchange of trial witness statements

The main rule relating to the use of witness statements is to be found in r 32.4(2) of the CPR, **32.16** which provides:

> The court will order a party to serve on the other parties any witness statement of the oral evidence which the party serving the statement intends to rely on in relation to any issues of fact to be decided at the trial.

Witness statements are not usually exchanged in small claims track cases, so the following **32.17** discussion is largely limited to fast track and multi-track cases. When directions are made on allocating a case to the fast track or multi-track, or at a case management conference, the court will make provision for the date by when witness statements must be exchanged. It is to be noted that the rule uses the word 'will', with the clear intention that disclosure directions are to be made in every fast track and multi-track case.

Normally mutual exchange is required, and it usually takes place a few weeks after disclosure **32.18** and inspection of documents. Part of the reason why witness statements are exchanged after disclosure of documents is that the witnesses may need to comment on some of the documentation in their statements. The court retains a discretion to order sequential disclosure of witness statements (r 32.4(3)(a)) and has a discretion whether to require the disclosed statements to be filed (r 32.4(3)(b)).

Privilege

32.19 Until a witness statement is disclosed, it is clearly protected by legal professional privilege. All that is required by r 32.4(2) of the CPR is for the statements of witnesses who are intended to be called to be disclosed. Therefore, any statements taken from harmful witnesses can be left on the solicitor's file, and need not be disclosed to the other side.

32.20 If, however, a witness is to be called at trial, his or her witness statement will have to be disclosed in accordance with the court's directions. Prior to the introduction of the CPR there were a number of conflicting reported cases dealing with whether a party disclosing a witness statement thereby waived its privilege. If so, the other side could rely on the witness statement at trial if the disclosing party decided, at some later stage, not to call that witness at trial. If the privilege still attached to the statement, this would not be possible. However, the correct answer was almost certainly that by serving a witness statement privilege was waived: see *Re Rex Williams Leisure plc* [1994] Ch 350. This is certainly the position under the CPR, as r 32.5(5) expressly provides that other parties may use a disclosed witness statement as hearsay evidence if they choose to do so.

Failure to comply with directions

32.21 If a witness statement is not served within the time specified in the directions, the witness may be called to give oral evidence only with permission (CPR, r 32.10). Non-compliance with directions is considered generally in Chapter 28.

Evidence-in-chief at trial

32.22 Exchanged witness statements stand as the witnesses' evidence-in-chief unless the court otherwise orders (CPR, r 32.5(2)). A witness may, however, and provided the court considers there is good reason not to confine the witness to the contents of the disclosed statement, amplify his or her witness statement and give evidence in relation to new matters that have arisen since the statement was served (r 32.5(3) and (4)).

Cross-examination at trial

32.23 Cross-examination in civil trials can range over any relevant matter that the witness can deal with, both as to the issues and as to credibility. It need not be confined to the matters addressed in the witness's statement. One of the tools of the cross-examiner is to pick out previous inconsistent statements made by the witness. In this connection, r 32.11 of the CPR provides:

> Where a witness is called to give evidence at trial, he may be cross-examined on his witness statement whether or not the statement or any part of it was referred to during the witness's evidence in chief.

Copies for the public

Where a direction is made that an exchanged statement shall stand as a witness's evidence-in-chief, members of the public present in court may not be able to follow the evidence, and the principle that justice should be administered in open court would be undermined. Members of the public are therefore, by CPR, r 32.13, able to request copies, although the court has a discretion to refuse permission. Normally inspection is allowed, although sometimes certain details will be edited out (*Cox v Jones* (2004) LTL 18/5/04). It seems from *GIO Personal Investment Services Ltd v Liverpool and London Steamship Protection and Indemnity Association Ltd* [1999] 1 WLR 984, that r 32.13 does not extend to documents exhibited to the statements. There is a reserve power vested in the court to refuse to make the statements available if there is a sufficient reason. This may be so if disclosure would be contrary to the interests of justice or national security, or if the statement included confidential medical evidence. **32.24**

Collateral use

After a statement has been exchanged, r 32.12 of the CPR provides that it may only be used for the purposes of the present proceedings, unless and to the extent that: **32.25**

(a) the witness gives consent in writing; or
(b) the court grants permission; or
(c) the statement has been put in evidence at a hearing in public.

The discussion on collateral use of disclosed documents (in 29.78–29.80) probably applies equally in relation to collateral use of witness statements. **32.26**

False witness statements

By CPR, r 32.14, proceedings for contempt of court may be brought against any person who makes a false statement in a document verified by a statement of truth without an honest belief in its truth. Such proceedings can be brought only by the Attorney-General or with the permission of the court. **32.27**

Striking out witness statements

There is no doubt that the court has a power to strike out written evidence which is scandalous, irrelevant, or oppressive, probably under CPR, r 32.1. Striking-out should be used sparingly, because the court's business would be seriously impeded if such applications were made as a matter of course whenever it is perceived that scandalous or irrelevant material is included in the other side's evidence (*Sandhurst Holdings Ltd v Grosvenor Assets Ltd* (2001) LTL 25/10/01). **32.28**

C WITNESS SUMMARIES

A party who is unable to obtain signed statements before the time prescribed for exchange may apply for permission to serve witness summaries instead of witness statements. The application is made without notice (CPR, r 32.9(1)). Such orders can be granted only if the **32.29** party is unable to obtain the relevant witness statement. Unless the court orders otherwise, a witness summary must be served within the period in which a witness statement would have had to be served.

32.30 Witness summaries are simply summaries of the evidence that would have been included in a witness statement. They could be unsigned draft statements, or even just an indication of the issues it is hoped the witness could deal with.

D AFFIDAVITS AND AFFIRMATIONS

Form of affidavits

32.31 Rule 32.16 of the CPR provides that affidavits must be in the form set out in PD 32, paras 2 to 16. The form of an affidavit is broadly similar to that of a witness statement, described at 32.09–32.12:

(a) An affidavit must be typed on one side only of consecutively numbered sheets of durable A4 paper with a 35 mm margin (PD 32, para 6.1(1), (2), and (4)).
(b) It must have the same corner markings as witness statements (PD 32, para 3.2).
(c) It must be headed in the same way as witness statements.
(d) After the heading and before the body of the affidavit there should appear a commencement (PD 32, para 4.1). This should read:

I [full name] of [address, which can be a business address if sworn in the deponent's professional, business, or occupational capacity] state on oath:

(e) Text and exhibits are dealt with in the same way as witness statements.
(f) Alterations need to be initialled by both the deponent and the person taking the affidavit (PD 32, para 8.1).
(g) Instead of a statement of truth, an affidavit ends with a jurat. The jurat must follow on from the body of the affidavit, and must not appear on a separate page. After giving the oath the affidavit has to be signed by all deponents (exceptionally an affidavit may be sworn by more than one person) and be completed by the person taking the affidavit. The person taking the affidavit must insert his or her full address, sign the jurat, and print his or her name and qualification under the signature (PD 32, para 5).

Qualification of person taking an affidavit

32.32 A person who takes an affidavit must be duly qualified (solicitors, commissioners for oaths, magistrates, certain court officials and judges, British consuls, and others authorized by statute, such as barristers), and independent of the parties and their representatives (PD 32, para 9).

Affirmations

32.33 Affirmations are similar to affidavits, but the deponent will affirm rather than swear when executing the document. They can be used whenever an affidavit may or must be used. All the provisions in PD 32 relating to affidavits apply also to affirmations (PD 32, para 16). For affirmations the commencement should read:

> I [full name] of [address] do solemnly and sincerely affirm:

In an affirmation, the word 'sworn' in the jurat is replaced by the word 'affirmed'.

Inability of deponent to read or sign an affidavit

Where an affidavit is sworn by a person who is unable to read or sign it, the person before **32.34** whom it is sworn must certify in the jurat that he or she has read the affidavit to the deponent and that the deponent appeared to understand it (PD 32, para 7.1(1) and (2)). The person who took the affidavit must also certify that, in his or her presence, the deponent signed it or made his or her mark (para 7.1(3)). Two versions of the form of the certificate appear in annex 1 to PD 32. If such a certificate is not included in the jurat, the affidavit may not be used unless the court is satisfied that it was read to the deponent and he or she appeared to understand it (para 7.2).

33

HEARSAY

33.01 This chapter considers the admissibility of and procedural matters relating to hearsay evidence in civil cases. Evidence is no longer excluded in civil cases solely on the ground that it is hearsay. Judicial suspicion of hearsay evidence continues, however, and a number of procedural requirements attach to the adduction of hearsay evidence. It therefore continues to be important to be able to identify hearsay evidence when it arises. Some general principles of evidence are dealt with in 33.02–33.08 before the main provisions of the Civil Evidence Act 1995 ('CEA 1995') are considered at 33.09ff. A party intending to rely on a hearsay statement must generally serve notice of that intention on the other parties, a matter considered at 33.16ff. Use of hearsay statements at trial is discussed at 33.26ff and 39.43–39.49.

A THE HEARSAY RULE

33.02 At common law, subject to a number of exceptions, hearsay evidence was inadmissible. The exact boundaries of the hearsay rule have never been easy to state. Broadly, a question of hearsay arises where a statement, whether of fact or opinion, no matter how it is made, is made otherwise than by a person while giving oral testimony in court and is relied on as evidence of the truth of its contents (see, for example, the speech of Lord Havers in *R v Sharp* [1988] 1 WLR 7, and the CEA 1995, ss 1(2)(a) and 13). There were two aspects of the hearsay rule, namely, the rule against narrative and the strict hearsay rule.

33.03 The rule against narrative arose when a witness who had sworn to the relevant facts in the witness box was asked whether he or she had told the same story on an earlier occasion. This was not allowed (subject to exceptions such as to rebut an allegation of recent fabrication) on the obvious basis that witnesses should not be allowed to manufacture corroboration for their evidence simply by repeating the story on several occasions before the trial.

The strict hearsay rule arose where an assertion on an earlier occasion was sought to be proved either by calling to give evidence a witness who heard the assertion being made or who saw some conduct which was alleged to convey a particular meaning (such as sign language), or by adducing a document containing the assertion. Hearsay also arose where a witness was called to prove conduct which impliedly contained an assertion, such as where a police officer gave evidence of telephone calls inquiring about drugs from unidentified members of the public to a particular address to prove that those premises were being used to supply drugs: *R v Kearley* [1992] 2 AC 228. **33.04**

It will be noted that the formulation of the hearsay rule in the first paragraph of this section extends the rule to cover expressions of opinion (including opinion expressed in experts' reports) as well as statements of fact by lay persons, to which the rule is traditionally applied. **33.05**

Conversely, a previous statement has never been hearsay when it is proved, not to establish the truth of its contents, but to prove that it was made. An example is where the claimant in a libel claim seeks to prove that the words complained of were published. In such a case the claimant does not assert the truth of the words (and in fact will contend that they are false), but needs to prove they were published to establish one of the elements of the cause of action. **33.06**

B REAL EVIDENCE

There is a distinction at common law between hearsay and real evidence. Unlike hearsay, real evidence is admissible at common law. Sometimes evidence which superficially resembles hearsay will in fact be regarded as real evidence. Generally, real evidence consists of physical objects that are produced for inspection by the court. For example, in an action for personal injuries against an employer, the machine which caused the injury may be produced to show how the accident happened, or in an action against a shop for breach of the statutory implied terms a radio may be produced to show it does not work. However, the distinction between hearsay and real evidence becomes rather fine when the court is asked to consider printouts and recordings made by various machines. In *The Statue of Liberty* [1968] 1 WLR 739 the disputed evidence consisted of a cinematograph film of the radar echoes, recorded mechanically without human intervention, of vessels involved in a collision at sea. Sir Jocelyn Simon P held the recording was admissible as real evidence, despite the fact that the purpose in adducing it was to prove that the recorded movements of the ships were true. This principle has been applied in criminal cases to a computer used to calculate the chemical composition of samples of metal (*R v Wood* (1982) 76 Cr App R 23); computer records showing details of access gained and attempts to gain access to certain web pages (*R (O'Shea) v Coventry Magistrates' Court* [2004] Crim LR 948); and photographs taken by a security camera in a building society office (*R v Dodson* (1984) 79 Cr App R 220). **33.07**

If information is produced by a machine in similar circumstances to those described above, it is probable that a civil court would also decide that it was not hearsay, but admissible as real **33.08** evidence. Some doubt must remain whether this is certainly so, because it is widely accepted that the above cases were decided before the position was liberated by statutory intervention (particularly the CEA 1968, the CEA 1995, and the Criminal Justice Act 2003), and were motivated by a desire to evade the hearsay rule in respect of otherwise highly persuasive evidence. Adducing mechanical recordings, computer printouts, and the like as real evidence may be seen as an evasion of the notice procedure under the CEA 1995.

C ADMISSIBILITY OF HEARSAY EVIDENCE

Under the CEA 1995

33.09 Hearsay, as an exclusionary rule, was abolished for all civil proceedings by the CEA 1995, s 1(1), which provides: 'in civil proceedings evidence shall not be excluded on the ground that it is hearsay'. By s 11 'civil proceedings' is defined as meaning civil proceedings before any civil tribunal in relation to which the strict rules of evidence apply, whether as a matter of law or by agreement of the parties.

33.10 Section 1(2)(b) extends the scope of admissible hearsay to include hearsay of whatever degree. This means that multiple hearsay (hearsay on hearsay) is generally admissible in civil proceedings. For example, Alan witnessed a road traffic accident, and saw one of the motor cars going through a red traffic light. If Alan told Bert, or wrote down his account of the accident in his notebook, proof either by calling Bert or by producing the notebook would amount to ordinary, first-hand, hearsay. Proof by calling Carol, who was told about the accident by Bert recounting what Alan had told him, or by calling Diane, who had read Alan's notebook, would amount to second-hand (multiple) hearsay. All of this is potentially admissible under s 1(1).

33.11 However, to prevent abuse by witnesses manufacturing supporting evidence along the lines of the old rule against narrative, CEA 1995, s 6(2), provides that a party which has called or intends to call a person as a witness in civil proceedings (Alan in the above example) in general may not also adduce previous statements made by that witness. There are three exceptions to this exclusion:

(a) Where the court grants permission for the adduction of the previous statement. Generally it is to be expected that permission will not be granted. It may be, however, that, due to the passage of time since witnessing the relevant events, the witness is, by the time of trial, unable to give a coherent account from the witness box. If this is simply through temporary forgetfulness, it can normally be remedied by the device of allowing the witness to see an earlier statement for the purpose of refreshing the memory. If the problem is more deep-rooted, however, such as where through the onset of some illness or the passage of a great deal of time, or because the only earlier statements were not made sufficiently contemporaneously with the events to be used as memory-refreshing documents, the court may well grant permission for the earlier statements to be adduced. Something rather similar occurred in the CEA 1968 case of *Morris v Stratford-on-Avon Rural District Council* [1973] 1 WLR 1059, where one of the drivers had made a written statement of the events at an accident to an insurance company about nine months after the accident. His evidence at trial was unexpectedly confused and inconsistent. The statement to the insurance company was too old to be used as a memory-refreshing document, but permission was granted for its admission under the CEA 1968. It is likely that permission would be granted in similar circumstances under the CEA 1995.

(b) Where it is sought to adduce the earlier statement to rebut a suggestion made in cross-examination that the witness's evidence has been fabricated. It is fairly unusual for suggestions to be made to witnesses to the effect 'When did you first make up this story?' However, when it does happen, the party calling the witness is entitled to adduce an earlier statement from the witness proving the witness has been telling a consistent story for some time.

(c) There is express provision in s 6(2) that the prohibition does not extend to precluding the practice of witnesses adopting their exchanged statements as their evidence-in-chief.

By s 14(1), nothing in the CEA 1995 affects the exclusion of evidence on grounds other than it being hearsay. The CEA 1995 therefore does not render admissible evidence which would otherwise be excluded by virtue of any other enactment, any rule of law, or for failure to comply with rules of court or an order of the court. Hearsay evidence may, therefore, be excluded eg, because it is irrelevant, non-expert opinion, or because the court refuses permission to call the witness who was to be called to prove it on a failure to exchange the witness's signed statement in accordance with the rules of court. Section 6(3) provides that the Act does not expand the circumstances in which previous inconsistent statements may be put in cross-examination, nor the degree to which a party may seek to cross-examine hostile witnesses (which remain governed by the Criminal Procedure Act 1865, ss 3, 4, and 5). Further, the CEA 1995, s 5(1), provides that hearsay evidence shall not be admitted in civil proceedings if and to the extent that either: **33.12**

(a) it consists of a statement of a person who would not be a competent witness; or
(b) it is to be proved by a person who is not a competent witness.

Incompetence of witnesses is based on an inability to understand the nature of the oath. It can extend to very young children (children who can give unsworn evidence under the provisions of the Children Act 1989, s 96, if they understand the duty to tell the truth and have sufficient understanding to justify their evidence being given, are not incompetent for this purpose) and adults suffering from certain mental or physical infirmities affecting their understanding. **33.13**

The effect of the CEA 1995 is in accordance with the present general policy that, particularly in cases tried by judges sitting alone, so far as possible all evidence should be admissible with the only question being one of weight. The general policy also dictates that the parties to litigation should prepare for trial in an open manner with as much prior disclosure as possible. Usually, notice of an intention to rely on hearsay evidence must be given at the same time as witness statements are exchanged (in accordance with directions from the court). Open preparation has the merit that it allows the parties to assess the merits of their respective cases with greater certainty. This should promote the prospects of an early settlement of an action, thereby avoiding the need for a trial. **33.14**

Former common law exceptions to the hearsay rule

33.15 Six former common law exceptions to the hearsay rule are preserved and converted into statutory exceptions by CEA 1995, s 7(2) and (3). The exceptions concerned are:

(a) published works on matters of a public nature;
(b) public documents, such as official registers;
(c) records of certain courts, treaties, pardons, etc.;
(d) reputation adduced to establish good or bad character;
(e) reputation or family tradition on a question of pedigree; and
(f) reputation or family tradition on the existence of a public or general right, or to identify a person or thing.

D NOTICE PROCEDURE

Advance notice

33.16 A party intending to rely on hearsay evidence at trial is required to serve notice of that intention on the other side in advance of the trial (CEA 1995, s 2). This section provides that rules of court may be made specifying the situations in which advance notice must be given where a party intends to rely on hearsay evidence. The CPR, r 33.2, provides:

> (1) Where a party intends to rely on hearsay evidence at trial and either—
> (a) that evidence is to be given by a witness giving oral evidence; or
> (b) that evidence is contained in a witness statement of a person who is not being called to give oral evidence;
>
> that party complies with section 2(1)(a) of the Civil Evidence Act 1995 by serving a witness statement on the other parties in accordance with the court's order.
>
> (2) Where paragraph (1)(b) applies, the party intending to rely on the hearsay evidence must, when he serves the witness statement—
> (a) inform the other parties that the witness is not being called to give oral evidence; and
> (b) give the reason why the witness will not be called.
>
> (3) In all other cases where a party intends to rely on hearsay evidence at trial, that party complies with section 2(1)(a) of the Civil Evidence Act 1995 by serving a [hearsay] notice on the other parties...

33.17 However, by r 33.3 there is no need to serve a hearsay notice in relation to:

(a) evidence at hearings other than trials;
(aa) an affidavit or witness statement which is to be used at trial but which does not contain hearsay evidence; or
(c) where the requirement is excluded by a practice direction.

33.18 Hearsay evidence is often given by witnesses who repeat what they were told on a previous occasion, and, as witness statements are supposed to set out the evidence each witness is expected to say in chief, hearsay evidence will usually be set out in the exchanged witness statements. The effect of rr 33.2 and 33.3 is that hearsay notices are not often required because any hearsay relied upon ought to be included in the exchanged witness statements.

Form of hearsay notices

By CPR, r 33.2(3), a hearsay notice must: 33.19

(a) identify the hearsay evidence;
(b) state that the party serving the notice proposes to rely on the hearsay evidence at trial; and
(c) give the reason why the witness will not be called.

By r 33.2(4), the party proposing to rely on the hearsay evidence must: 33.20

(a) serve the notice no later than the latest date for serving witness statements; and
(b) if the hearsay evidence is to be in a document, supply a copy to any party who requests one.

A single hearsay notice may deal with the hearsay evidence of more than one witness.

Failure to serve hearsay notice

By CEA 1995, s 2(4), failure to serve a hearsay notice whether in time or at all does not affect the admissibility of the hearsay evidence, but may be taken into account by the court: 33.21

(a) in exercising its discretionary powers, particularly on costs; and
(b) as adversely affecting the weight of the evidence.

Power to call witness for cross-examination on hearsay evidence

The CEA 1995, s 3, envisages parties in receipt of hearsay notices being able to summon the makers of hearsay statements for cross-examination. If this is to be done, an application for permission to call the maker of the statement must be issued no later than 14 days after the day on which a notice of intention to rely on the hearsay evidence was served on the applicant (CPR, r 33.4). The power in r 33.4 to order the maker of a hearsay statement to attend for cross-examination is usually exercised where the party who obtained the statement deploys it at trial. Rule 33.4 can also be used on the application of a party who obtained the statement if they serve it on the other side and then decide not to use the statement, but the other side later decide to use the statement as hearsay evidence at the trial (*Douglas v Hello! Ltd* (2003) LTL 4/3/03). 33.22

The application must be made by issuing an application notice. Consideration should be given to supporting the application with evidence in writing, although there is no strict requirement for this. 33.23

Credibility notices

By CPR, r 33.5, a party intending to adduce evidence (for which, see 33.27) to attack the credibility of the maker of the statement must serve a notice on the party intending to rely on the hearsay evidence of the intention of mounting such an attack within 14 days after service of the hearsay notice. 33.24

Business document certificates

33.25 By the CEA 1995, s 9(1), business (which is defined as including any activity regularly carried on over a period of time, whether for profit or not) and public authority (which includes any public or statutory undertaking or government department) records may be received in evidence without further proof. A document will, by s 9(2), be taken as being such a record if a certificate signed by an officer of the business or authority is produced to the court. A document purporting to be such a certificate is deemed by s 9(2)(a) to have been duly given by an appropriate officer and signed by him or her. These provisions are designed to facilitate the ease of proof of records without the need to call anyone from the records department of the business concerned. In practice, in addition to the certificate, a hearsay notice will also be required in order to satisfy the requirements of the rules of court.

E TRIAL

Adducing the evidence in court

33.26 (a) Where the hearsay statement is contained in a business record, it will be enough to adduce the record and a certificate complying with the CEA 1995, s 9.

(b) Where the hearsay statement is contained in a document, by the CEA 1995, s 8, it may be proved either:
- (i) by the production of that document; or
- (ii) by the production of a copy of that document (it being immaterial whether the original is still in existence or the number of removes between the original and the copy adduced in court),

authenticated in such manner as the court may approve. The words in parenthesis, which come from s 8(2), abolish the ancient best evidence rule in civil claims. The authentification needed is that the copy adduced is a true copy of the original. Normally it would be expected that a witness will be called to the witness box in order to testify to the authenticity of the document. As Staughton LJ said in *Ventouris v Mountain (No 2)* [1992] 1 WLR 887, a document is not produced to the court simply by counsel handing it to the court. Rather, it should be produced by a witness who is qualified to do so in accordance with the rules of evidence, and saying what the document is.

(c) Oral hearsay will need to be proved by calling a witness who heard the hearsay statement.

Credibility

33.27 By the CEA 1995, s 5(2), evidence is admissible to attack or support the credibility of hearsay statements adduced at trial, unless under the rules of evidence a denial by the witness would have been final. This means that evidence relevant to collateral issues cannot be adduced. What is allowed is evidence that the maker of the statement has been convicted of a crime, evidence of any bias of the maker of the statement in favour of the party adducing the statement, and evidence that the maker of the statement has made any previous statement inconsistent with the statement relied upon. As discussed above, prior notice of the intention to attack the hearsay statement in any of these ways must be given within 14 days of service of the hearsay notice.

Weight

In assessing the weight (if any) to be given to hearsay evidence the court is required, by the CEA 1995, s 4(1), to have regard to any circumstances from which inferences can reasonably be drawn as to the reliability or otherwise of the evidence. Section 4(2) lists a number of particular factors, namely: **33.28**

(a) whether it would have been reasonable and practicable for the party by whom the evidence was adduced to have produced the maker of the statement as a witness. It was stated by Finer J in *Rasool v West Midlands Passenger Transport Executive* [1974] 3 All ER 638 that if the whereabouts abroad of an important witness in a substantial case can be easily ascertained, but a party chooses to rely on hearsay evidence rather than calling the maker of the statement to give evidence, there is no doubt that little weight would be attached to the evidence;
(b) whether the original statement was made contemporaneously with the occurrence or existence of the matters stated;
(c) whether the evidence is multiple hearsay;
(d) whether any person involved had any motive to conceal or misrepresent the facts;
(e) whether the original statement was an edited account, or was made in collaboration with another or for a particular purpose;
(f) whether the circumstances in which the evidence is adduced as hearsay are such as to suggest an attempt to prevent proper evaluation of its weight; and
(g) any failure to give due notice of the adduction of the hearsay evidence.

KEY POINTS SUMMARY

- Hearsay evidence is where a witness gives evidence of facts they have not personally experienced for the purpose of proving the truth of those facts. **33.29**
- Hearsay may be written or oral, and may be first-hand, second-hand etc.
- In civil cases, evidence is not inadmissible purely on the ground that it is hearsay (CEA 1995, s 1(1)), even if it is multiple hearsay.
- Hearsay notices must be served at the same time as witness statements are exchanged when a party intends to rely on hearsay at trial.
- Hearsay notices are not required in respect of interim hearings. In most other situations service of a witness statement avoids the need for a hearsay notice.
- Where one party intends to rely on hearsay evidence, the other side can apply for an order that the maker of the statement attend trial for cross-examination.
- In practice, trial judges give limited weight to hearsay evidence.

34

ADMISSIONS AND DOCUMENTARY EVIDENCE

34.01 This chapter is concerned with the rules relating to the proof of admissions and documents at trial.

A NATURE OF ADMISSIONS

34.02 Admissions may be formal or informal. Formal admissions have the effect of establishing the facts admitted. As the matter will no longer be in issue, neither side is permitted to adduce evidence on it. Informal admissions, such as oral out-of-court statements made by a party against their own interests, are merely items of evidence. While an informal admission may be a compelling item of evidence (if it was not true, why say it?), being an item of evidence it can be disproved by other evidence in the case. Adverse statements made in the following situations are examples of formal admissions:

- admissions in acknowledgments of service;
- admissions made on filing admission forms from the response pack (forms N9A and N9C);
- admissions in statements of case, which include replies to requests for further information;
- admissions of the whole or part of another's case made by letter after proceedings have been commenced (CPR, r 14.1(2));
- admissions made and recorded at case management hearings;
- admissions made in reply to notices to admit (see 34.10–34.15);
- admissions made by counsel at trial.

Under the general law of evidence, binding admissions can sometimes be made by persons connected with a party. Typical examples are admissions made by partners (see the Partnership Act 1890, s 15), predecessors in title, and referees. **34.03**

An 'admission' made without knowledge of the facts said to have been admitted has little if any evidential value (see *Comptroller of Customs v Western Lectric Co Ltd* [1966] AC 367). Also, the 'admission' must be one of fact, not law. In *Ashmore v Corporation of Lloyd's* [1992] 1 WLR 446 the House of Lords held that statements made by members of the Committee of Lloyd's, said to be admissions that the defendants owed a duty of care to 'Names' (members of underwriting syndicates), concerned a question of law and so the statements were neither relevant nor admissible. **34.04**

B PRE-ACTION ADMISSIONS OF LIABILITY

One of the purposes of the pre-action protocols (Chapter 5) is to enable defendants to assess the strength of the claim they are facing, and to decide whether to admit liability at an early stage. Usually, defendants keep to such pre-action admissions, but sometimes defendants change their minds once proceedings are issued. At common law there is no restriction on a defendant withdrawing a pre-action admission (*Sowerby v Charlton* [2006] 1 WLR 568), as an admission made in correspondence is an informal admission. A withdrawn admission has still been made, so it remains an item of evidence, but has to be read together with the withdrawal when assessing its weight. For non-personal injuries claims, withdrawn pre-action admissions may be relied upon in a summary judgment application if, with the other facts in the case, any defence has no real prospects of success. It may also be possible to strike out the defence of a defendant who makes and then withdraws an admission if the withdrawal was made in bad faith (*Walley v Stoke-on-Trent City Council* [2007] 1 WLR 352). **34.05**

Personal injuries claims divide into those within and outside the RTA protocol (see Chapter 6). Admissions in cases within the RTA protocol can be withdrawn during the initial consideration period, but thereafter they can be withdrawn only with the consent of the claimant (and once proceedings have started, either with consent or court permission) (see CPR, r. 14.1B). In other personal injuries claims, provided the conditions set out below are satisfied, a pre-commencement admission may be withdrawn in the period before a claim is issued only with the consent of the claimant (r 14.1A(3)(a)). After proceedings are issued, a pre-action admission may only be withdrawn if all the parties consent or if the court gives permission (r 14.1A(3)(b)). **34.06**

The conditions are that the pre-action admission was made: **34.07**

(a) by a notice in writing (r 14.1A(1));
(b) in a claim governed by either the Pre-action Protocol for Personal Injury Claims; the Pre-action Protocol for the Resolution of Clinical Disputes; or the Pre-action Protocol for Disease and Illness Claims (PD 14, para 1.1(2)); and
(c) either after the defendant received a letter of claim written in accordance with the relevant pre-action protocol (r 14.1A(2)(a)) or if the admission is stated to be made under Part 14 (r 14.1A(2)(b)).

C PERMISSION TO WITHDRAW AN ADMISSION

34.08 Permission is required to amend or withdraw an admission if:

(a) it was a pre-action admission in a personal injury claim, proceedings have now started, and the other party will not consent to the admission being withdrawn (CPR, rr 14.1A(3)(b) and 14.1B(2)(b)); or
(b) it was made after proceedings were commenced (r 14.1(5)). It may also be necessary to amend the relevant statement of case or notice to admit.

34.09 In deciding whether to give permission, the court is required by PD 14, para 7.2, to have regard to all the circumstances of the case, including:

(a) the grounds upon which the applicant seeks to withdraw the admission, including whether or not new evidence has come to light which was not available at the time the admission was made. In *Les Laboratories Servier v Apotex Inc* [2007] EWHC 591 (Pat) the threshold was said to be whether there were plausible grounds for supposing that the admission made was in fact false;
(b) the conduct of the parties, including any conduct which led the applicant into making the admission;
(c) any prejudice that may be caused to any person if the admission is withdrawn. Permission to amend may be refused where, eg, the circumstances in which the admission was made give rise to an estoppel (*H Clark (Doncaster) Ltd v Wilkinson* [1965] Ch 694);
(d) the prejudice that may be caused to any person if the application is refused;
(e) the stage in the proceedings at which the application to withdraw is made, and in particular in relation to the trial date or window;
(f) the prospects of success (if the admission is withdrawn) of the claim or part of the claim in relation to which the admission was made; and
(g) the interests of the administration of justice.

D NOTICE TO ADMIT FACTS

34.10 In order to ensure that the court's time at trial is not wasted in having to determine facts and issues that could reasonably be admitted, a party may serve the other side with a notice to admit facts (CPR, r 32.18). A notice to admit facts must be served no later than 21 days before the trial. An example is shown in figure 34.1.

34.11 Notices to admit are looked on favourably by the courts, because they narrow the issues to be decided at trial and therefore tend to save costs and reduce delays. In *Baden v Société Générale pour Favoriser le Développement du Commerce et de l'Industrie en France SA* (27 February 1985, CA, unreported) Lawton LJ said that notices to admit were of the greatest importance in the administration of justice and ought to be more frequently used. In the same case at first instance, reported 11 years after the event at [1992] 4 All ER 161, Peter Gibson J at 277 said the commonly accepted basis for the proper use of the procedure is to procure admissions on matters not really in dispute as distinct from matters the subject of real controversy which the party served may reasonably refuse to admit.

Figure 34.1 Notice to admit facts

Notice to admit facts

In the High Court of Justice Queen's Bench Division	
Claim No.	HCQ 87105
Claimant (include Ref.)	Stephenson Hyperlink Plc
Defendant (include Ref.)	Lomax Fishing Equipment Limited

I (We) give notice that you are requested to admit the following facts or part of case in this claim:

1. Under cover of a letter dated 4th September 2006 the Claimant sent to the Defendant a copy of its price list dated 3rd June 2006.
2. On 23rd September 2006 Mrs Lisa Stephenson and Mr Vikesh Bharakhda attended the Defendant's premises for a full working day.
3. The purpose of the visit on the 23rd September 2006 was for the Defendant to give to the Claimant full information about its telephone sales operation so that the Claimant could commence work under the Contract.

I (We) confirm that any admission of fact(s) or part of case will only be used in this claim.

Signed

(Claimant)~~(Defendant)~~('s Solicitor)

Position or office held (If signing on behalf of firm or company): Solicitor

Date

Admission of facts

I (We) admit the facts or part of case (set out above)(in the attached schedule) for the purposes of this claim only and on the basis that the admission will not be used on any other occasion or by any other person.

1. Admitted.
2. Admitted, save that the visit lasted 6 hours.
3. It is admitted that the purpose of the visit was for the Defendant to give to the Claimant full information about its telephone sales operation, but it is denied that this was in order to enable the Claimant to commence work under the Contract. The Defendant repeats the denial in its Defence that there was a concluded contract.

Signed

~~(Claimant)~~(Defendant)('s Solicitor)

Position or office held (If signing on behalf of firm or company): Solicitor

Date

The court office at

is open between 10 am and 4 pm Monday to Friday. Address all communication to the Court Manager quoting the claim number

N266 - w3 Notice to admit facts (4.99) *Printed on behalf of The Court Service*

Use of admissions

34.12 Admissions made in response to a notice to admit are formal admissions as between the parties who served and were served with the notice, but only for the purposes of the case in hand. Other parties to the present action are not entitled to make use of such admissions, although they may be entitled to serve their own notice to admit (CPR, r 32.18(3)).

Costs consequences

34.13 Under the rules of court in force before the introduction of the CPR, a party which refused or neglected to make an admission after being served with a notice to admit facts would usually be ordered to pay the costs of proving those facts at trial, and the costs occasioned by and thrown away as a result (see RSC, ord 62, r 6(7)). There is no express equivalent of that rule in the CPR. However, the costs rules in Part 44, and in particular r 44.3(6), are wide enough to achieve the same result.

34.14 The effect is that if the party refusing to make the admissions wins at trial, instead of having an expectation of recovering the entire costs of the action under the principle that costs usually follow the event (for which, see 43.18ff), it will most likely have to pay the costs (including related costs) of proving the facts not admitted, and will only recover the balance of the costs of the claim.

34.15 The trial judge always has a discretion whether to impose this costs sanction. According to the Court of Appeal in *Lipkin Gorman v Karpnale Ltd* [1989] 1 WLR 1340, the judge should ask whether in the circumstances of the case the facts ought to have been admitted, and whether it would be just to require the winner at trial to pay the costs involved in proving the facts not admitted. It is open to the court to find that it was reasonable to contest some of the facts stated in a notice to admit, but not others, and to operate the costs rule over the facts which should reasonably have been admitted, as in *Baden v Société Générale pour Favoriser le Développement du Commerce et de l'Industrie en France SA* [1993] 1 WLR 501. The question whether the facts subject to a notice to admit are controversial in the context of the case is one of degree. Simply because the existence of a fact may not be capable of being finally established until it is found at trial does not mean that the court will refuse to penalize a party refusing to admit it (the *Baden* case).

E PROVING DOCUMENTS

Best evidence rule

34.16 At common law there was a general rule that a party relying on the contents of a document at trial had to prove those contents by producing the original. This was an aspect of the best evidence rule, but was abolished for civil cases by the CEA 1995, s 8(2) (see 33.26).

Exhibits to witness statements and affidavits

34.17 Exhibits in witness statements and affidavits are usually photocopies. The originals must be brought to court for inspection by the judge at the hearing (PD 32, para 13.1).

Documents in the possession of a witness

Where a document is in the possession of a non-party, that person is a witness and may be compelled under a witness summons to attend court at the trial with the document (see 39.03). Generally, if a witness fails to produce a document in answer to a witness summons the only remedy is to punish the witness for disobeying the summons and to claim damages. **34.18**

Authenticity of disclosed documents

Parties are deemed to admit the authenticity of documents disclosed to them under CPR, Part 31 (generally, the documents disclosed under a list of documents), unless they serve a notice to prove in form N268. This must specify the documents being challenged, and must be served by the latest date for serving witness statements, or within seven days of disclosure, whichever is the later (r 32.19). **34.19**

Trial bundles

Trial bundles are considered at 39.12. By PD 32, para 27.1, the court may give directions requiring the parties to use their best endeavours to agree the bundles of documents to be used at any hearing. Once this has been done, all the documents in the agreed bundles are admissible as evidence of their contents unless the court otherwise orders, or a party has given written notice of their objection to the admissibility of specified documents (para 27.2). The originals of the documents in the trial bundles should be made available at trial (PD 39A, para 3.3). **34.20**

35

INTERIM INJUNCTIONS

35.01 Interim injunctions are temporary orders made with the purpose of regulating the position between the parties to an action pending trial. Imposing an interim injunction is a serious matter, and should be restricted to appropriate cases. Such an order is particularly useful where there is evidence that the respondent's alleged wrongdoing will cause irreparable damage to the applicant's interests in the period between issue of process and trial.

35.02 Interim injunctions should be distinguished from perpetual injunctions, which are final orders, usually made at trial (but see 35.80–35.81), and which continue with no limitation of time. Further distinctions are:

(a) Injunctions made without notice. These are a form of interim injunction, usually made in circumstances of urgency, which are expressed to continue in force for a limited period, usually a few days, sufficient for the application to be renewed on a hearing with notice being given to the respondent.
(b) Mandatory injunctions require the other side to do specified acts (such as to deliver up documents or to demolish a wall), whereas prohibitory injunctions require the other side to refrain from doing specified acts (such as publishing a libel or breaching

a confidence). It is the substance of the order (rather than its wording) which makes it mandatory or prohibitory. Both types of injunction can be granted on an interim basis, but the courts are more wary of granting mandatory orders (see 35.85).

(c) Where the other side has not yet committed a civil wrong, but has threatened to do so in the future, it is possible to obtain an interim injunction on a *quia timet* basis.

Interim injunctions can be applied for even in claims allocated to the small claims track (CPR, r 27.2(1)). **35.03**

Any party to proceedings can apply for an interim injunction, and can do so whether or not a claim for the injunction was included in that party's originating process or statement of case (CPR, r 25.1(4)). **35.04**

A JUDGES ABLE TO GRANT INJUNCTIONS

Given the serious nature of injunctions and the consequences of breach, the general rule is that applications for interim injunctions must be made to a judge rather than a master or district judge. There are several exceptions and restrictions. The detailed rules are to be found in PD 25A, paras 1.1 to 1.4, together with PD 2B. For example, freezing injunctions and search orders should be sought from High Court judges, and at the other end of the scale, county court district judges can grant injunctions in cases where they have trial jurisdiction (small claims and fast track cases). **35.05**

B PRE-ACTION APPLICATIONS FOR INTERIM INJUNCTIONS

Rule 25.2(1) of the CPR empowers the court to grant an interim injunction before a claim form has been issued. By CPR, r 25.2(2), an interim injunction can be obtained prior to issue of proceedings provided: **35.06**

(a) no rule or practice direction prohibits the granting of the order;
(b) the matter is urgent or it is otherwise desirable to make the order in the interests of justice;
(c) in the less common circumstance in which the applicant is an intended defendant, the defendant has obtained the court's permission to make the application. The defendant cannot without this permission apply for an interim remedy prior to the filing of an acknowledgment of service or defence (which can only happen after issue).

Urgent cases

A case is 'urgent' where there is a true impossibility in giving the requisite three clear days' notice or in arranging for the issue of process. An 'impossibility' resulting from delay on the part of the claimant will not suffice: *Bates v Lord Hailsham of St Marylebone* [1972] 1 WLR 1373. There has to be a very good reason for departing from the general rule that notice must be given (*Moat Housing Group–South Ltd v Harris* [2006] QB 606), such as an element of threat or damage that requires the immediate intervention of the court (*Mayne Pharma (USA) Inc v* **35.07**

Teva UK Ltd (2004) LTL 3/12/04). The relief sought must be limited to that which is necessary and proportionate given the fact the application is made without notice (*Moat Housing Group–South Ltd v Harris*).

35.08 Where a case is urgent, the usual procedural requirements are relaxed in so far as is necessary to do justice between the parties. For example:

(a) The application may be made before issue of process.
(b) The application may be made without notice. However, it is still incumbent on the applicant to give the other side such notice as is possible, such as by telephone or by fax unless secrecy is essential (such as on applications for search orders and freezing injunctions). A defendant who is notified in this way may decide to attend the hearing, a situation which is known as an 'opposed hearing without notice'.
(c) Informal evidence may be relied on. This may be in the form of a draft witness statement, correspondence, or even simply facts related to the court by counsel on instructions. The applicant is usually required to undertake to put the oral facts and evidence into formal witness statements so there can be no confusion at any later stage (*Attorney-General v British Broadcasting Corporation* [2007] EWCA Civ 280).
(d) Although very much a last resort, the court may make an order without a draft having been prepared by counsel on behalf of the applicant.

Procedure on pre-action applications

35.09 There is a special form for applying for injunctions (form N16A) which must be used. It must include the title of the proposed action, the full name of the applicant, and, as the applicant is not yet a party, the applicant's address for service. It should contain a request for a hearing or ask that the application be dealt with without a hearing (PD 23A, para 2.1). PD 25A, para 2.1, provides that an application notice for an interim injunction should:

(a) state the order sought, and
(b) give the date, time, and place of the hearing.

35.10 Many pre-action applications for injunctions are made in cases of real urgency, and the court may in such cases exercise its power in CPR, r 23.3(2)(b), to dispense with the requirement for an application notice. If the court dispenses with the application notice, it will usually do so only for the purposes of the initial hearing. PD 25A, para 5.1(4), provides that in these circumstances the court will, unless it orders otherwise, require an undertaking from the applicant to file an application notice and pay the appropriate fee on the same or the next working day.

35.11 An application for an interim remedy must be supported by evidence, unless the court orders otherwise (CPR, r 25.3(2)). The evidence required is discussed further in 35.22–35.24.

35.12 The application should be made in the court in which the substantive proceedings are likely to be issued unless 'there is good reason to make the application to a different court' (CPR, r 23.2(4)).

35.13 Especially where the terms of the injunction sought are complex, it is good practice to attach a draft of the order (in form PF 39CH) to the application notice and to provide it on computer disk or digital storage device (PD 25A, para 2.4). Disks are not required in the Commercial Court, because orders there are drawn up by the parties (*Commercial Court Guide*, para F1.3).

Arrangements for pre-action injunction hearings

Pre-action interim injunction applications will almost always be considered at a hearing but without full (or any) notice to the respondent. If they arise during or shortly before the ordinary times when the court is sitting, the hearing will take place in court as soon as the circumstances permit. This means that generally such applications are heard before other matters that are listed, either as soon as the court sits in the morning or immediately after lunch. Sometimes urgent applications arise during the course of the morning or afternoon in circumstances where it is not possible to wait to the beginning of the next session. If the case is sufficiently urgent the court will invariably interrupt whatever it is doing at a convenient moment so that it can hear the urgent application. **35.14**

On other occasions the need for a pre-action interim injunction may arise at a time when it is not possible to wait until the next occasion when the court will be sitting. If the application is of extreme urgency it may be dealt with by telephone (PD 25A, para 4.2). If the problem has arisen outside office hours, the applicant should telephone either the High Court asking to be put in touch with the clerk to the appropriate duty judge (or the appropriate area circuit judge where known), or the urgent court business officer of the appropriate circuit, who will contact the local judge. **35.15**

If the facilities are available, a draft of the order sought will usually be required to be sent by fax to the duty judge who will be dealing with the application. Telephone hearings are available only if the applicant is acting by solicitors or counsel (PD 25A, para 4.5(5)). **35.16**

The pre-action order

If the order is granted, the court may give directions requiring a claim to be commenced (CPR, r 25.2(3)). As the application will invariably have been made without notice to the respondent, the order must, by PD 25A, para 5.1(2) and (3), include, unless the court orders otherwise: **35.17**

(a) an undertaking by the applicant to the court to serve the respondent with the application notice, evidence in support, and any order made, as soon as practicable; and
(b) a return date for a further hearing at which the other party can be present.

The order must contain a statement of the right to apply under r 23.10 to set aside or vary the order within seven days after it is served. Where possible the claim form should be served with the injunction order (PD 25A, para 4.4(2)). **35.18**

C APPLICATIONS DURING PROCEEDINGS

Procedure

Applications for interim injunctions after proceedings have been issued are made by issuing an application notice (in form N16A) supported by written evidence. The applicant will generally also need to provide a draft order (in form PF 40CH, and on a digital storage device) and a skeleton argument. **35.19**

Where the court is to serve the application, sufficient copies should be provided for the court and each respondent (PD 25A, para 2.3). Service should be effected as soon as possible, and in any event not less than three clear days before the hearing. **35.20**

35.21 Respondents to applications made on notice should disclose their evidence in reply in sufficient time in advance of the hearing to avoid an adjournment. If little more than the minimum three clear days' notice has been given by the applicant, the court may be prepared to give directions as to the service of evidence on the first hearing, but it may well impose sanctions if it considers the need to give directions was caused by the default of either party.

Evidence in support of an application for an interim injunction

35.22 An application for an interim injunction must be supported by evidence unless the court orders otherwise (CPR, r 25.3(2)). The evidence must cover the substantive issues and also, if the application is without notice, explain why notice has not been given (r 25.3(3); PD 25A, para 3.4). The evidence should also address the relevant principles for granting injunctive relief (see below).

35.23 PD 25A, para 3.2, states that unless the court or an Act requires evidence by affidavit, evidence is to be:

(a) by witness statement;
(b) set out in the application, provided it is verified by a statement of truth; or
(c) set out in a statement of case, provided it is verified by a statement of truth.

35.24 PD 25A, para 3.3, provides that 'the evidence must set out the facts on which the applicant relies for the claim being made against the respondent, including all material facts of which the court should be made aware'. This provision is not restricted to applications without notice. It appears to import at least some of the concepts of the duty of full and frank disclosure. The 'material facts of which the court should be made aware' are likely to be more wide-ranging in an application made without notice than in one made with the required three clear days' notice. Nevertheless, this paragraph of the practice direction may be intended to make parties address adverse facts in their evidence, even where the application is on notice and the respondent has a clear ability to file evidence and make representations at the hearing.

Hearing of interim injunction applications

35.25 Normally the hearing of an application for an interim injunction will be listed in the usual way for disposal in public (see CPR, r 39.2). There are exceptional circumstances in which the hearing will be in private, such as where the hearing involves confidential information, or the interests of children or protected parties.

D PRINCIPLES

Just and convenient

35.26 As with all forms of equitable relief, the granting of interim injunctions is a matter within the discretion of the court. The fundamental principle is contained in the SCA 1981, s 37(1), which provides:

> The High Court may by order (whether interlocutory or final) grant an injunction or appoint a receiver in all cases in which it appears to the court to be just and convenient to do so.

The same principle applies in the county courts (CCA 1984, s 38). With the introduction of the Human Rights Act 1998, the test to be applied may be whether granting relief is just and proportionate rather than just and convenient (*South Bucks District Council v Porter* [2003] 2 AC 558). **35.27**

Substantive cause of action

Injunctions are only remedies, so can usually be granted only if the applicant has a substantive cause of action. As stated by Lord Diplock in *The Siskina* [1979] AC 210: **35.28**

> A right to obtain an [interim] injunction is not a cause of action. It cannot stand on its own. It is dependent upon there being a pre-existing cause of action against the defendant arising out of an invasion, actual or threatened by him, of a legal or equitable right of the [claimant] for the enforcement of which the defendant is amenable to the jurisdiction of the court. The right to obtain an [interim] injunction is merely ancillary and incidental to the pre-existing cause of action.

In *The Siskina* the claimant had a cause of action against the defendant, but it was actionable only in a foreign country. It was therefore held that the English courts had no jurisdiction to grant an interim injunction to protect the applicant's position. The actual result in *The Siskina* has been reversed by the CJJA 1982, s 25 (see 10.84, 36.10, and 36.16). The underlying principle was restated by Lord Brandon of Oakbrook in *South Carolina Insurance Co v Assurantie Maatschappij 'De Zeven Provincien' NV* [1987] AC 24, where, in relation to domestic proceedings, he said the court has a discretion to grant injunctions in only two situations: **35.29**

(a) where a party has invaded or threatened to invade a legal or equitable right of another party; or
(b) where a party has behaved or threatened to behave in an unconscionable manner.

Injunctions in support of the criminal law

The High Court has jurisdiction to grant injunctions in support of the criminal law. In *Attorney-General v Chaudry* [1971] 1 WLR 1614 Lord Denning MR said: **35.30**

> There are many statutes which provide penalties for breach of them—penalties which are enforceable by means of a fine—or even imprisonment—but this has never stood in the way of the High Court granting an injunction. Many a time people have found it profitable to pay a fine and go on breaking the law. In all such cases the High Court has been ready to grant an injunction…
>
> Whenever Parliament has enacted a law and given a particular remedy for the breach of it, such remedy being in an inferior court, nevertheless the High Court always has reserve power to enforce the law so enacted by way of an injunction or declaration or other suitable remedy. The High Court has jurisdiction to ensure obedience to the law whenever it is just and convenient so to do.

In *Attorney-General v Blake* [1998] Ch 439 it was held that an injunction would be granted to prevent the defendant, a former secret service employee, from receiving any payment or other benefit from the exploitation of a book written in breach of the Official Secrets Act 1989. **35.31**

The American Cyanamid guidelines

35.32 In *American Cyanamid Co v Ethicon Ltd* [1975] AC 396 Lord Diplock laid down guidelines on how the court's discretion to grant interim injunctions should be exercised in the usual types of cases. Although these guidelines are of great authority, they must not be read as if they were statutory provisions, and in practice they are applied with some degree of flexibility. However, it is common for judges to give reasoned judgments in interim injunction cases following the sequence of steps set out by Lord Diplock (eg, *Rottenberg v Monjack* [1993] BCLC 374). The court must also be careful to apply the overriding objective, and to grant an injunction only if it is 'just and convenient'.

35.33 The underlying purpose of the guidelines is to enable the court to make an order that will do justice between the parties, whichever way the decision goes at trial, while interfering with the parties' freedom of action to the minimum extent necessary (see *Polaroid Corporation v Eastman Kodak Co* [1977] RPC 379 *per* Buckley LJ at 395).

Serious question to be tried

35.34 Before *American Cyanamid Co v Ethicon Ltd*, the courts would grant an interim injunction only if the applicant could establish a *prima facie* case on the merits. Consequently, the courts needed to consider the respective merits of the parties' cases in some detail. This encouraged the filing of detailed written evidence supported by voluminous exhibits, and resulted in lengthy interim hearings. As Lord Diplock said at 407:

> It is no part of the court's function at this stage of the litigation to try to resolve conflicts of evidence on affidavits as to facts on which the claims of either party may ultimately depend nor to decide difficult questions of law which call for detailed argument and mature consideration.

35.35 Therefore, the court needs to be satisfied only that there is a serious question to be tried on the merits. The result is that the court is required to investigate the merits to a limited extent only. All that needs to be shown is that the claimant's cause of action has substance and reality. Beyond that, it does not matter if the claimant's chance of winning is 90 per cent or 20 per cent: *Mothercare Ltd v Robson Books Ltd* [1979] FSR 466 *per* Megarry V-C at 474; *Alfred Dunhill Ltd v Sunoptic SA* [1979] FSR 337 *per* Megaw LJ at 373.

35.36 This is not a difficult hurdle to surmount. In *Porter v National Union of Journalists* [1980] IRLR 404, the issue was whether a strike instruction by the union affected a majority of its members. If it did, the union's rule book required a ballot. Neither party adduced accurate figures of the total numbers in the union, nor of the numbers affected by the strike instruction. It was held there was a serious question to be tried.

35.37 On the other hand, if there is no serious question to be tried on the substantive claim, for example if the claim is hopeless, the injunction must be refused (*National Commercial Bank Jamaica Ltd v Olint Corporation Ltd* [2009] 1 WLR 1405). *Morning Star Co-operative Society Ltd v Express Newspapers Ltd* [1979] FSR 113 should be regarded as not having passed this hurdle. At the time of the case, the *Daily Star* newspaper was about to be launched. The claimant alleged that it was going to be passed off as the established *Morning Star* newspaper. Apart from the fact that they were both newspapers and had the word 'Star' in their names, they were different in about every other respect. As Foster J commented, 'only a moron in a hurry would be misled' into thinking that the *Daily Star* was the *Morning Star*, so the claimant had failed to show a serious issue to be tried on the alleged cause of action.

Sometimes there are arguments about whether the claimant's allegations amount to a cause of action known to the law. An example was *Khorasandjian v Bush* [1993] QB 727, which decided before the current legislation on harassment was enacted. The Court of Appeal held by a majority that there was a tort of harassment, and on the facts the judge had been entitled to grant an interim injunction restraining the defendant from 'harassing, pestering or communicating' with the claimant. In a related case, it was held in *Burris v Azadani* [1995] 1 WLR 1372 that, when granting an interim injunction to restrain future assaults or harassment, the court has power to impose an exclusion zone at the same time. **35.38**

Adequacy of damages to the applicant

If there is a serious question to be tried on the merits of the substantive claim, the court should then consider whether the applicant will be adequately compensated by an award of damages at trial. The test was stated in the following way by Lord Diplock in *American Cyanamid Co v Ethicon Ltd* at 408: **35.39**

> If damages in the measure recoverable at common law would be an adequate remedy and the defendant would be in a financial position to pay them, no [interim] injunction should normally be granted.

Damages will often be an adequate remedy for the claimant in claims for breach of contract, including contracts of employment (see *Ali v Southwark London Borough Council* [1988] ICR 567, but the position regarding claims in respect of contracts of employment is not completely free from doubt: see *Powell v Brent London Borough Council* [1988] ICR 176). A claimant bringing an action for breach of copyright or confidence may also (depending on the facts) be refused injunctive relief on the ground that damages would be an adequate remedy: *Hubbard v Vosper* [1972] 2 QB 84. However, damages will be inadequate if: **35.40**

(a) The defendant is unlikely to be able to pay the sum likely to be awarded at trial.
(b) The wrong is irreparable, eg, loss of the right to vote.
(c) The damage is non-pecuniary, eg, libel, nuisance, trade secrets.
(d) There is no available market. In *Howard E Perry and Co Ltd v British Railways Board* [1980] 1 WLR 1375 the defendant refused to allow the claimant to remove a consignment of steel during a steelworkers' dispute. As steel was otherwise unobtainable at the time, damages were not an adequate remedy.
(e) Damages would be difficult to assess. Examples are loss of goodwill (*Foseco International Ltd v Fordath Ltd* [1975] FSR 507), disruption of business (*Evans Marshall and Co Ltd v Bertola SA* [1973] 1 WLR 349), and where the defendant's conduct has the effect of killing off a business before it is established (*Mitchelstown Co-operative Society Ltd v Société des Produits Nestlé SA* [1989] FSR 345).
(f) Liquidated damages provided by a term of a contract are lower than the probable actual loss suffered through a breach of contract (*Bath and North East Somerset District Council v Mowlem plc* [2004] BLR 153).

As where the claimant fails to show a serious question to be tried, if damages would be an adequate remedy that is the end of the matter and the injunction must be refused. **35.41**

Applicant's undertaking in damages being adequate protection

35.42 Subject to some limited exceptions, an undertaking in damages is always required when an interim injunction is granted. By the undertaking the claimant is required to compensate the defendant or any other person served with the order for any loss caused by the injunction if it later appears that the injunction was wrongly granted. The normal form of undertaking just gives protection to the defendant. There is an extended undertaking which also protects third parties, and the court should consider whether this extended version should be used (PD 25A, para 5.1A). Its purpose is to provide a safeguard for the defendant or other person who may be unjustifiably prevented from doing something it was entitled to do. As stated in *Wakefield v Duke of Buccleugh* (1865) 12 LT 628, this assists the court '. . . in doing that which was its great object, viz. abstaining from expressing any opinion on the merits of the case until the hearing'.

35.43 Undertakings in damages are not required where the Crown or a local authority is seeking an interim injunction to enforce the law (*Kirklees Metropolitan Borough Council v Wickes Building Supplies Ltd* [1993] AC 227; *United States Securities and Exchange Commission v Manterfield* [2010] 1 WLR 172), unless the defendant shows a strong *prima facie* case that its conduct is lawful (*F Hoffman–La Roche & Co AG v Secretary of State for Trade and Industry* [1975] AC 295). Where a quasi-governmental organization seeks an injunction having far-reaching consequences, but cannot offer an undertaking in damages, the court should (by way of an exception to *American Cyanamid*) only grant the injunction if there is a strong underlying cause of action (*Belize Alliance of Conservation Non-Governmental Organisations v Department of the Environment* [2003] 1 WLR 2839). The court has a discretion to order an interim injunction subject to a limited undertaking in damages: *RBG Resources plc v Rastogi* (2002) LTL 31/5/02. In *Customs and Excise Commissioners v Anchor Foods Ltd* [1999] 1 WLR 1139 the Commissioners applied to restrain the disposal of certain assets by the defendant. The purpose of the application was to protect funds which the Commissioners contended should be paid to them. Neuberger J said that in these circumstances the presence or absence of an undertaking in damages was a factor to be weighed when considering the balance of convenience, and was prepared to grant an injunction only if the Commissioners gave an undertaking in damages.

35.44 In *American Cyanamid Co v Ethicon Ltd* Lord Diplock said at 408:

> If damages in the measure recoverable under such an undertaking would be an adequate remedy and the [claimant] would be in a financial position to pay them, there would be no reason upon this ground to refuse an [interim] injunction. It is where there is doubt as to the adequacy of the respective remedies in damages available to either party or to both, that the question of balance of convenience arises.

35.45 The way it was put by Lord Hoffmann in *National Commercial Bank Jamaica Ltd v Olint Corporation Ltd* [2009] 1 WLR 1405 was that if there is a serious issue to be tried, and the claimant could be prejudiced by the acts or omissions of the defendant pending trial, and the claimant's undertaking in damages would provide the defendant with an adequate remedy if it transpires that his freedom of action should not have been restrained, an interim injunction should ordinarily be granted. If despite this the court goes on to consider the balance of convenience, the fact that the defendant is adequately protected will be a substantial factor in favour of granting the injunction: see *Bunn v British Broadcasting Corporation* [1998] 3 All ER 552. If the undertaking does not adequately protect the defendant, although that is a reason for refusing the injunction, normally the court will go on to consider the balance of convenience. Even a freezing injunction has been granted in favour of a legally aided claimant (who obviously could not give a valuable undertaking in damages) where otherwise it was a proper case for granting the injunction: *Allen v Jambo Holdings Ltd* [1980] 1 WLR 1252. In extreme cases, however, the court will refuse the injunction without considering the balance of convenience. *Morning Star Co-operative Society Ltd v Express Newspapers Ltd* was such a case, referred to at 35.37. In addition to the weak cause of action, the claimant had assets of £170,000 and liabilities of £260,000, so there was no realistic chance of it being able to honour the undertaking, especially as the defendants were likely to suffer appreciable, unquantifiable, damages.

Balance of convenience

Most injunction cases are determined on the balance of convenience. In *American Cyanamid Co v Ethicon Ltd* Lord Diplock said at 408: **35.46**

> . . . it would be unwise to attempt even to list all the various matters which may need to be taken into consideration in deciding where the balance lies, let alone to suggest the relative weight to be attached to them. These will vary from case to case.

This is often an exercise in seeking to determine whether granting or refusing the injunction will cause irremediable prejudice, and to what extent (*National Commercial Bank Jamaica Ltd v Olint Corporation Ltd* [2009] 1 WLR 1405). Among the matters the court may take into account are: **35.47**

(a) the prejudice the claimant may suffer if no injunction is granted or the defendant may suffer if it is;
(b) the likelihood of such prejudice actually occurring;
(c) the extent to which it may be compensated by an award of damages or enforcement of the undertaking in damages;
(d) the likelihood of either party being able to satisfy such an award; and
(e) the likelihood that the injunction will turn out to have been wrongly granted or withheld (see 37.53 to 37.55).

The claimants in *American Cyanamid Co v Ethicon Ltd* sought an interim injunction to prevent the defendants marketing a surgical suture alleged to be in breach of patent. The claimants' patented suture had recently been introduced, and the claimants were expanding their market. The defendants' product had not at that time been introduced. They asserted that their product did not infringe the claimants' patent, alternatively that the patent was invalid. If the injunction had been granted no factories would have closed, but if refused the claimants might have failed to increase their market and would effectively have lost the benefit of their patent. Therefore, the balance favoured the claimants. **35.48**

A claimant can reduce the potential injustice to the defendant by drafting the terms of the injunction as narrowly as is consistent with preserving the claimant's interests, or by offering undertakings to provide extra safeguards for the defendant. **35.49**

Each case turns on its own facts, but matters found to be important include: **35.50**

(a) being deprived of employment (*Fellowes and Son v Fisher* [1976] QB 122);
(b) damage to business through picketing (*Hubbard v Pitt* [1976] QB 142);
(c) damage to the goodwill of a business (*Associated Newspapers plc v Insert Media Ltd* [1991] 1 WLR 571);

(d) closing down a factory, which was described as being catastrophic in *Potters-Ballotini Ltd v Weston-Baker* [1977] RPC 202;
(e) although the fact that an injunction may result in a company being wound up is a weighty matter, in *Astor Chemicals Ltd v Synthetic Technology Ltd* [1990] BCLC 1 this was outweighed by other considerations, particularly the fact that the company wanted to continue trading on a very speculative venture while hopelessly insolvent;
(f) preserving confidential information (*X AG v A Bank* [1983] 2 All ER 464);
(g) the public interest in keeping a drug with life-saving qualities on the market (*Roussel Uclaf v G D Searle and Co Ltd* [1977] FSR 125);
(h) the length of time to trial (the shorter the stronger the argument for granting the injunction) (*Wake Forest University Health Sciences v Smith and Nephew plc* [2009] EWHC 45 (Pat)); and
(i) a failure by the claimant to respond to a letter from the defendant frankly stating its plans and enclosing sample containers, use of which is alleged by the claimant to amount to passing off (*Dalgety Spillers Foods Ltd v Food Brokers Ltd* [1994] FSR 504).

Status quo

35.51 In *American Cyanamid Co v Ethicon Ltd* [1975] AC 396 Lord Diplock said at 408 that, in considering the balance of convenience: 'Where other factors appear to be evenly balanced it is a counsel of prudence to take such measures as are calculated to preserve the status quo'. In *Garden Cottage Foods Ltd v Milk Marketing Board* [1984] AC 130, 140, Lord Diplock said the relevant status quo is the state of affairs existing in the period immediately preceding the issue of the claim form or, if there is unreasonable delay between issuing the claim and issuing the application for the interim injunction, the period immediately before the application. It is clear that excessive weight must not be placed on the word 'immediately'. Lord Diplock continued: 'The duration of that period since the state of affairs last changed must be more than minimal, having regard to the total length of the relationship between the parties in respect of which the injunction is granted; otherwise the state of affairs before the last change would be the relevant status quo'. A 10-day period between the defendant commencing activities infringing the claimant's intellectual property rights and issuing the claim was ignored as minimal in *Play It Ltd v Digital Bridges Ltd* [2005] EWHC 1001 (Ch) at [38], [39]. Nevertheless, it behoves the claimant to act quickly.

Special factors

35.52 As Lord Diplock said in *American Cyanamid Co v Ethicon Ltd* at 409, 'there may be many special factors to be taken into consideration [in the balance of convenience] in the particular circumstances of individual cases'. If American Cyanamid Co had been refused interim relief, but had established its claim at trial, it was probable that it would have been commercially impracticable for it to have insisted on Ethicon's sutures then being withdrawn, as doctors would have by then become used to using Ethicon's new sutures.

Merits of the claim

35.53 In *American Cyanamid Co v Ethicon Ltd* Lord Diplock said at 409 that, as a last resort:

> ...it may not be improper to take into account in tipping the balance the relative strength of each party's case as revealed by the affidavit evidence adduced on the hearing of the application.

> This, however, should be done only where it is apparent upon the facts disclosed by evidence as to which there is no credible dispute that the strength of one party's case is disproportionate to that of the other party. The court is not justified in embarking upon anything resembling a trial of the action upon conflicting affidavits in order to evaluate the strength of either party's case.

An example of a case where the merits were considered under this principle is *Cambridge Nutrition Ltd v British Broadcasting Corporation* [1990] 3 All ER 523. The merits were considered, because the incompensable damage to each party did not differ widely. **35.54**

There are some judges who, despite the principles set out above, in exceptional cases weigh the respective merits of the parties' cases as disclosed in the written evidence and exhibits in deciding whether or not to grant interim injunctive relief. This approach finds expression in the judgment of Laddie J in *Series 5 Software Ltd v Clarke* [1996] 1 All ER 853. In his judgment Laddie J said the following were the guidelines to be adopted on a proper analysis of the *American Cyanamid* decision: **35.55**

(a) that interim injunctions are discretionary and all the facts of the case must be considered;
(b) there are no fixed rules, and the relief must be kept flexible;
(c) the court should rarely attempt to resolve complex issues of disputed fact or law;
(d) important factors in exercising the jurisdiction to grant interim injunctions are:
    (i) the extent to which damages are likely to be an adequate remedy to either side, and the ability of the other party to pay;
    (ii) the balance of convenience;
    (iii) maintaining the status quo; and
    (iv) any clear view the court may reach about the relative strength of the parties' cases.

Exceptional cases

There are some well-settled categories of cases where the *American Cyanamid* guidelines are not applied. The usual difference is that in these cases the courts will investigate the merits of the cause of action. How these various cases can be reconciled with *American Cyanamid Co v Ethicon Ltd* [1975] AC 396 is a question of some theoretical controversy. Suggestions are that they are examples of the 'special factors' mentioned by Lord Diplock; that the *American Cyanamid* guidelines apply only where the facts are in dispute; that *American Cyanamid* applies only where a trial is likely; and that the existence of some or all of the categories were not directly considered by Lord Diplock. **35.56**

Final disposal of the claim

In *NWL Ltd v Woods* [1979] 1 WLR 1294 Lord Diplock said at 1306: **35.57**

> *American Cyanamid Co. v Ethicon Ltd* [1975] AC 396...was not dealing with a case in which the grant or refusal of an injunction at that stage would, in effect, dispose of the action finally in favour of whichever party was successful in the application, because there would be nothing left on which it was in the unsuccessful party's interest to proceed to trial.

Two questions arise (see *Cayne v Global Natural Resources plc* [1984] 1 All ER 225; *Channel Tunnel Group Ltd v Balfour Beatty Construction Ltd* [1993] AC 334): **35.58**

(a) on the assumption that the injunction is refused, and taking into account the likely length of time it will take to get to trial and the probable factual situation at that time, is there any realistic possibility that the claimant will wish to proceed to trial? Assertions by claimants that they will in any event proceed to trial to recover damages may be disregarded if in reality a trial would be a meaningless gesture: *Lansing Linde Ltd v Kerr* [1991] 1 WLR 251; and

(b) on the assumption that the injunction is granted, is there any realistic prospect of the defendant insisting on going to trial to vindicate its defence and having the injunction discharged?

Where neither party has a real interest in going to trial, the interim application will finally determine the claim.

35.59 Where the interim application will finally dispose of the claim, the court has to consider the underlying merits of the claim (Lord Diplock in *NWL Ltd v Woods,* at 1307). The degree to which the claimant must establish those merits varies with the circumstances. Thus, in *Cayne v Global Natural Resources plc*, the claimants, who were shareholders in the defendant company, sought injunctions, *inter alia*, to restrain the company from implementing a merger transaction without first obtaining the approval of the company in general meeting. There was no realistic prospect of a trial, because by the time the claim could be tried either the deal would have been implemented or the general meeting would have taken place. The claimants alleged that the purpose of the transaction was to maintain the directors in office. The defendants served evidence which, if true, completely destroyed the claimants' case. Instead of applying the *American Cyanamid* guidelines the court had to apply the broad principle of doing its best to avoid injustice. Eveleigh LJ said at 233:

> ...it would be wrong to run the risk of causing an injustice to a defendant who is being denied the right to trial where the defence put forward has been substantiated by affidavits and a number of exhibits.

35.60 Accordingly, an injunction would have been granted only if the claimants' case was overwhelming on its merits. It was not, so the injunction was refused. Conversely, the case of *Lansing Linde Ltd v Kerr* concerned an application for an injunction to enforce a covenant in restraint of trade. It was not possible for the claim to be tried before the expiry of the period of the restraint; the claimants were not realistically interested in pursuing their claim for damages; so there was no prospect of a trial. Staughton LJ said that in the circumstances justice simply required 'some assessment of the merits... more than merely a serious issue to be tried'. A case just on the other side of the line regarding final disposal was *Astor Chemicals Ltd v Synthetic Technology Ltd* [1990] BCLC 1. The main issue on this aspect of the case was whether the defendant had any real interest in taking the case to trial if the injunction was granted, given that the effect of the injunction was almost certainly to force it into liquidation. It was held that there was some prospect of the liquidator taking the claim to trial for the defendant, so *American Cyanamid Co v Ethicon Ltd* had to be applied.

Defamation claims

35.61 Since *Bonnard v Perryman* [1891] 2 Ch 269, it has been held that interim injunctions will not generally be granted in defamation cases if the defendant intends to plead justification. In *Bestobell Paints Ltd v Bigg* [1975] FSR 421 it was held that this principle is unaltered by *American Cyanamid Co v Ethicon Ltd* [1975] AC 396, because of the overriding public interest in protecting the right to free speech. In *Greene v Associated Newspapers Ltd* [2005] QB 972, it was held that the rule in *Bonnard v Perryman* is also unaltered by the Human Rights Act 1998, s 12(3) (see 35.63) or by the Human Rights Act 1998, s 6 (which requires public authorities to act in ways compatible with the Convention: see 3.34). There are two conditions:

(a) The defendant must state in the evidence in reply that it is intended to set up the defence of justification.
(b) The alleged libel must not be obviously untruthful. The claimant may accordingly adduce evidence to prove the falsity of the words published. However, the burden on the claimant is a heavy one: *Holley v Smyth* [1998] QB 726.

Similar principles apply where the defendant intends to plead fair comment on a matter **35.62** of public interest (*Fraser v Evans* [1969] 1 QB 349) and where the publication is privileged, unless, in the case of qualified privilege, there is overwhelming evidence of malice: *Harakas v Baltic Mercantile and Shipping Exchange Ltd* [1982] 1 WLR 958. There is even greater reluctance to restrain publication of an expression of opinion. The rule in *Bonnard v Perryman* cannot be evaded by pleading the claim in both libel and breach of confidence, where it is clear that the main claim is in libel: *Woodward v Hutchins* [1977] 1 WLR 760. However, the rule in *Bonnard v Perryman* is ousted where the publication amounts to a contempt of court as well as a libel: *Attorney-General v News Group Newspapers Ltd* [1987] QB 1. Further, the rule does not apply to trademark infringement cases, even where the trademark is used in comparative advertising (*Boehringer Ingelheim Ltd v Vetplus Ltd* [2007] FSR 29).

Freedom of expression

Article 10(1) of the European Convention on Human Rights provides that everyone has the **35.63** right to freedom of expression. This right is subject to safeguards in art 10(2), which include restrictions for the protection of the reputation or rights of others. The Human Rights Act 1998, s 12(3), provides that no relief to restrain publication before trial which might affect the art 10(1) right is to be allowed 'unless the court is satisfied that the applicant is likely to establish that the publication should not be allowed'. In *Cream Holdings Ltd v Banerjee* [2005] 1 AC 253 it was held that s 12(3) requires a flexible approach to be taken. In most cases the applicant must establish a case which will probably succeed (the usual standard of proof at trial). The court will then exercise its discretion, taking into account the jurisprudence on art 10 and any other relevant matters. In keeping with the flexible approach, there will be some exceptional cases where a lesser degree of likelihood will suffice to satisfy the test in s 12(3). Exceptional cases suggested by Lord Nicholls were where the potential adverse consequences of disclosure are particularly grave, and where a short-term injunction is needed to enable the court to give proper consideration to an application for an interim injunction. It was held in *Boehringer Ingelheim Ltd v Vetplus Ltd* [2007] FSR 29 that damage to reputation is not in itself sufficiently exceptional. Otherwise the exceptions would be so wide that s 12(3) would be rendered virtually meaningless.

Fair dealing and public interest defences

In *Hubbard v Vosper* [1972] 2 QB 84 Lord Denning MR said that in copyright actions defend- **35.64** ants with reasonable defences of fair dealing under what is now the Copyright, Designs and Patents Act 1988, s 30, should not be restrained by injunctions. Similarly, in claims for breach of confidence defendants should not be restrained if they have reasonable defences of public interest. The reason is that a defendant with such a defence 'is entitled to publish it: and the law will not intervene to suppress freedom of speech except when it is abused', a result now buttressed by art 10(1) of the European Convention on Human Rights.

Privacy and confidentiality

35.65 Related to defamation claims are proceedings to restrain newspapers from publishing articles that invade the claimant's privacy. Interim injunctions in these cases should normally be governed by *American Cyanamid*, as adapted by the Human Rights Act 1998, s 12(3) (see 35.63). The court has to balance the competing interests in protecting private and family life under art 8(1), and the freedom of expression in art 10(1) (*Campbell v Mirror Group Newspapers plc* [2004] 2 AC 457).

35.66 In *McKennitt v Ash* [2008] QB 73, Buxton LJ said there were two questions:

(a) whether the information is private in the sense that it is in principle protected by art 8. In most cases any duty of confidence arises out of a transaction or relationship between the parties. For example, an employee may have expressly agreed to maintain an employer's confidences, or sensitive information may have been communicated in a letter marked 'private and confidential' (see *Prince of Wales v Associated Newspapers Ltd* [2008] Ch 57). A duty of confidentiality expressly assumed under a contract should be given greater weight than an implied duty arising from the general principles of equity (*London Regional Transport v Mayor of London* [2003] EMLR 4). Activities such as family holidays and sporting activities are part of a person's private recreation time and are protected by art 8 (*Hannover v Germany* (Application No 59320/00) (2005) 40 EHRR 1). Photographs taken at a private wedding are therefore protected (*OBG Ltd v Allan* [2008] 1 AC 1). Photographs of a child taken in a public place, such as a street or on a shopping trip, may be protected, depending on the circumstances (*Murray v Express Newspapers plc* [2009] Ch 481). It was held in *McKennitt v Ash* that it is no defence to prove that the information to be published was untrue. If the information is not private, there is no case; and

(b) whether in all the circumstances the interest of the owner of the private information should yield to the right of freedom of expression conferred on the publisher by art 10. Much depends on whether there is a breach of confidence (*Prince of Wales v Associated Newspapers Ltd*). Where there is no breach of confidence, the balance between arts 8 and 10 usually involves weighing the nature and consequences of the breach of privacy against the public interest, if any, in the disclosure of the information. In cases where there is a breach of confidence, that is in itself a factor capable of justifying restrictions on freedom of expression under art 10(2). The court has to consider whether a fetter on the right of freedom of expression is in the particular circumstances necessary in a democratic society. This includes weighing the importance attached in a democratic society to upholding duties of confidence, as well as considering the nature of the information and the nature of the relationship giving rise to the duty of confidentiality.

Industrial disputes

35.67 After *American Cyanamid Co v Ethicon Ltd* [1975] AC 396, whenever an interim injunction was sought against a trade union that claimed it was acting in contemplation or furtherance of a trade dispute, the courts refused to investigate the respective merits of the case on each side, and tended to concentrate on the balance of convenience. Unions could rarely point to significant inconvenience if they were restrained from striking, whereas employers could readily identify their continuing financial losses. The result was that injunctions were invariably granted against unions involved in trade disputes despite the statutory defences. Legislation was accordingly passed to ensure the merits of the statutory defences are considered before injunctions are granted against trade unions. This legislation is now contained in the Trade Union and Labour Relations (Consolidation) Act 1992, s 221(2), which provides:

> Where—
>
> (a) an application for an interlocutory injunction is made to a court pending the trial of an action, and
>
> (b) the party against whom it is sought claims that he acted in contemplation or furtherance of a trade dispute,
>
> the court shall, in exercising its discretion whether or not to grant the injunction, have regard to the likelihood of that party's succeeding at the trial of the action in establishing any matter which would afford a defence to the action under section 219 (protection from certain tort liabilities) or section 220 (peaceful picketing).

Differing views have been expressed on the interpretation of this section. The approach **35.68** favoured by Lord Scarman in *NWL Ltd v Woods* [1979] 1 WLR 1294 was that the court must consider:

(a) whether the cause of action against the union discloses a serious action to be tried;
(b) the balance of convenience; and
(c) the likelihood of the union establishing the statutory defence.

Lord Fraser of Tullybelton in the same case pointed out that the word 'likelihood' is a word of **35.69** degree, and the weight to be given to establishing the trade dispute defence varies according to the degree of the likelihood.

Claims against public authorities

Smith v Inner London Education Authority [1978] 1 All ER 411 is authority for the propos- **35.70** ition that public authorities should not be restrained from exercising their statutory powers and duties unless the claimant has an extremely strong case on the merits. If the evidence indicates that the authority is exceeding the law, often upholding the rule of law will prevail over administrative inconvenience: *Bradbury v Enfield London Borough Council* [1967] 1 WLR 1311. Most cases of this nature should now be brought by proceedings for judicial review (Chapter 45). Where interim injunctions are sought in judicial review proceedings, the *American Cyanamid* principles will be applied (see *R v Ministry of Agriculture, Fisheries and Food, ex p Monsanto plc* [1999] QB 1161). The *Monsanto plc* case also considered how those principles ought to be applied in a public law case. An interim injunction may be granted to restrain the enforcement of a UK statute where there are strong grounds for finding that the statute contravenes EU law: *R v Secretary of State for Transport, ex p Factortame Ltd (No 2)* (Case C–213/89) [1991] 1 AC 603.

In considering an application to disapply national legislation by injunction pending a ref- **35.71** erence to the ECJ, the Court of Appeal in *R v HM Treasury, ex p British Telecommunications plc* [1994] 1 CMLR 621 said the following factors must be taken into account:

(a) The apparent strength of the Community right asserted. This is not to be considered in depth, as this is a matter for the ECJ. However, if the English court is almost persuaded that the applicant will succeed before the ECJ, albeit having enough doubt to refer the point to the ECJ, an injunction is far more likely to be granted than where the Community right is more speculative.

(b) The importance, in political terms, of the impugned legislation. An injunction is more likely to be granted where the legislation is obscure than where it is a major piece of legislation on which an election was fought.

(c) Other factors include whether the economic survival of the applicant depends on injunctive relief being granted, and the degree to which the applicant can be compensated in damages.

Negative covenants and covenants in restraint of trade

35.72 A perpetual injunction has been held to issue 'as of course' where it is established that the defendant is in breach of a valid express negative covenant: *Doherty v Allman* (1878) 3 App Cas 709. The same principle applies to applications for interim injunctions: *Attorney-General v Barker* [1990] 3 All ER 257.

35.73 Although covenants in restraint of trade are negative covenants, they will be valid only if reasonable in terms of the ambit of activities covered, geographical area, and period of time. In *Office Overload Ltd v Gunn* [1977] FSR 39, the defendant was the branch manager of the claimant's employment agency in Croydon. In his contract of employment he covenanted not to work for or set up a competing business in the Croydon area for one year after ceasing to work for the claimant. After giving notice the defendant immediately started competing. The claimant applied for an interim injunction. Given that to be valid a covenant has to be for a limited period of time, refusal of interim relief will usually deprive a claimant of the benefit of the covenant. Lord Denning MR accordingly said:

> Covenants in restraint of trade are in a special category . . . if they are *prima facie* valid and there is an infringement the courts will grant an injunction.

35.74 A covenant will be *prima facie* valid if:

(a) all the facts are before the court; and

(b) the covenant is reasonable in ambit, area, and duration.

35.75 Not all restraint of trade cases are exceptions to the *American Cyanamid* principles. *Office Overload Ltd v Gunn* applies to cases where there is no sustainable dispute concerning the claimant's cause of action. If there is real doubt about the claimant's case, *American Cyanamid* applies. Thus, in *Lawrence David Ltd v Ashton* [1991] 1 All ER 385, the claimant had dismissed the defendant from his employment, and there was a real issue as to whether that amounted to a repudiatory breach of the employment contract (and, if so, it could not insist on the covenant being observed). Further, the terms of the covenant were perhaps too wide. Given those two matters, the case was not an open-and-shut one in favour of the claimant, and the *American Cyanamid* guidelines were applied.

35.76 As the foundation of this exception is the effective deprivation of the employer of the benefit of the covenant due to the effluxion of time before trial, the exception does not apply if a trial can be arranged before the period of the covenant expires (eg, through ordering a speedy trial): *Dairy Crest Ltd v Pigott* [1989] ICR 92. An example of what can be done with cooperation from all sides is *Symphony Group plc v Hodgson* [1994] QB 179, where the action was tried six weeks after the employee gave his notice.

If a covenant in a contract of employment against working for competitors is too wide and therefore void, the employer may still be able to obtain some injunctive relief if the employee resigns and starts working for a competitor under the principle in *Evening Standard Co Ltd v Henderson* [1987] ICR 588. In this case the Court of Appeal found that a newspaper production manager, whose contract provided that he had to give a year's notice, was in clear breach of his contract of employment when he purported to give two months' notice, after which he intended to work for a competitor. The claimant refused to accept the defendant's repudiation of his contract, and undertook to pay the defendant his full normal salary during his period of notice. Applying *American Cyanamid*, an injunction was granted restraining the defendant from working for any competitor for his contractual period of notice, thereby giving the defendant a period of 'garden leave'. **35.77**

It is not always possible to obtain a 'garden leave' injunction even if the employee fails to give the contractual period of notice. The cases fall into two categories (see *Langston v Amalgamated Union of Engineering Workers (No 2)* [1974] ICR 510). In the first, the employment contract extends to an obligation to permit the employee to do the contractual work. Theatrical engagements usually fall into this category. In these cases the employer needs a provision in the employment contract entitling the employer to send the employee home on garden leave. There will be little scope for implying such a term into the contract. Without such a term, no injunction will be granted. In the second category the employment contract is confined to the employer agreeing to pay wages for the work done. In this category the employer is entitled to send the employee home on garden leave even in the absence of an express or implied term, because there is no contractual obligation to prevent this. Garden leave injunctions are therefore far more likely to be granted in this category. See *William Hill Organisation Ltd v Tucker* [1999] ICR 291. **35.78**

Other decisions have shown that forcing a period of idleness on the defendant is a factor to be taken into account in the balance of convenience against granting such an injunction (*Euro Brokers Ltd v Rabey* [1995] IRLR 206), and it may be appropriate to impose the injunction for a period shorter than the contractual period of notice where other 'defectors' are on shorter periods of notice than the defendant: *GFI Group Inc v Eaglestone* [1994] IRLR 119. **35.79**

No defence

In *Official Custodian for Charities v Mackey* [1985] Ch 168 Scott J said that the *American Cyanamid* principles: 'are not, in my view, applicable to a case where there is no arguable defence to the [claimant's] claim'. The court will not consider the balance of convenience, but will grant the relief claimed subject to the usual equitable considerations. Injunctions have been granted on this basis in cases of clear trespass (*Patel v W H Smith (Eziot) Ltd* [1987] 1 WLR 853) and of clear breach of contract (*Sheppard and Cooper Ltd v TSB Bank plc* [1996] 2 All ER 654). Similarly, if all that is at issue on the merits is a simple point of construction, the court will resolve it and dismiss or grant the application accordingly: *Associated British Ports v Transport and General Workers Union* [1989] 1 WLR 939 at 979. **35.80**

35.81 Alternatively, where there is no defence with real prospects of success the claimant may apply for summary judgment including a final order for an injunction, instead of applying for an interim order: *Viscount Chelsea v Muscatt* [1990] 2 EGLR 48.

Restraint of legal proceedings

35.82 *American Cyanamid* principles do not govern the exceptional jurisdiction of the courts to restrain the commencement of legal proceedings. An injunction to prevent the presentation of a petition to wind up a company will be granted if the petition would be an abuse of process, for example if the petition debt is disputed on substantial grounds. An injunction may also be sought to restrain foreign proceedings to prevent 'forum shopping', if it can be established that the foreign proceedings would be vexatious or oppressive: *Société Nationale Industrielle Aérospatiale v Lee Kui Jak* [1987] AC 871.

Worldwide injunctions

35.83 In exceptional cases the courts may make injunctive orders having a worldwide effect. Such orders have been made in a number of freezing injunction cases, and also in an application to enforce a covenant of confidentiality against a former employee of the Royal Household: *Attorney-General v Barker* [1990] 3 All ER 257.

Interim mandatory injunctions

35.84 In *Shepherd Homes Ltd v Sandham* [1971] Ch 340 Megarry J said that an interim mandatory injunction would only be granted if the court felt a 'high degree of assurance' about the merits of the claimant's cause of action. This formulation was approved in *Locabail International Finance Ltd v Agroexport* [1986] 1 WLR 657, where the Court of Appeal refused a mandatory injunction for the payment of money. Nevertheless, there are exceptions (see *Zockoll Group Ltd v Mercury Communications Ltd* [1998] FSR 354). In *Leisure Data v Bell* [1988] FSR 367, a dispute arose about the copyright in a computer program developed by the defendant for the claimant. The claimant was granted a mandatory injunction despite the merits being equally arguable either way. This was partly because the claimant was prepared to give wide-ranging undertakings to protect the defendant's position, and partly because the practical reality of the situation was that of the two parties only the claimant was in a position to make commercial use of the program. In *Incasep Ltd v Jones* (2001) LTL 26/1/01, the court considered an application for an interim mandatory injunction requiring a company to reinstate the claimant as an executive director pending the outcome of his unfair prejudice petition under the Companies Act 2006, s 994, applying the *American Cyanamid* guidelines, but having regard to the potential injustice that such an injunction could cause.

35.85 In *National Commercial Bank Jamaica Ltd v Olint Corporation Ltd* [2009] 1 WLR 1405, Lord Hoffmann said there is no underlying difference in principle between interim applications for prohibitory and mandatory injunctions. It is simply that it is more likely that there will be irremediable prejudice to the defendant if the injunction is mandatory in nature. If the injunction is likely to cause irremediable damage to the defendant, the court should be reluctant to grant the injunction unless it is satisfied that the chances that it will turn out to have been wrongly granted are low. It is for this reason that Megarry J in *Shepherd Homes Ltd v Sandham* [1971] Ch 340 said that such injunctions should be granted only if the court felt a 'high degree of assurance' that at trial it will turn out that the injunction was rightly granted.

E DEFENCES

Any of the following equitable defences and bars to relief may be raised on an application for an interim injunction: **35.86**

(a) Acquiescence (see 7.65).
(b) Delay or laches. Delay is a more significant factor in interim applications than at trial: *Johnson v Wyatt* (1863) De G J & S 18. To operate as a defence delay has to be combined with prejudice to the respondent. In *Bunn v British Broadcasting Corporation* [1998] 3 All ER 552 a delay of 20 days was held to bar relief, where an application to restrain the broadcast of confidential information was made just two working days before the intended date of the broadcast. More frequently, this defence only arises where the delay is measured in months. Delay interrelates with the status quo (for which, see 35.51).
(c) Hardship. This is taken into account in the balance of convenience.
(d) Clean hands. Inequitable conduct by the claimant may be a bar to equitable relief: *Hubbard v Vosper* [1972] 2 QB 84.
(e) Equity does not act in vain. In *Attorney-General v Guardian Newspapers Ltd (No 2)* [1990] 1 AC 109 an injunction to restrain breach of confidence was refused where there had already been widespread publication.
(f) 'The court will not and ought not to make an order performance or obedience to which it cannot enforce' (*per* Astbury J in *Amber Size and Chemical Co Ltd v Menzel* [1913] 2 Ch 239). Injunctions are rarely granted against children, because they cannot be committed to prison and can rarely pay a fine (*G v Harrow London Borough Council* (2004) LTL 20/1/04).
(g) Difficulty in compliance. An injunction was refused in *Unique Pub Properties Ltd v Licensed Wholesale Co Ltd* (2003) LTL 13/10/03 as it would have imposed on the defendant a serious obligation to check information given to it by its tenants, any error constituting a breach.
(h) An injunction will be refused if its effect is to enforce an agreement for personal services (eg, *Warren v Mendy* [1989] 1 WLR 853). This does not prevent the court granting an interim injunction prohibiting a ship owner from employing the vessel in a manner inconsistent with a non-demise charterparty (in which the owner provides a ship and crew) (*Lauritzencool AB v Lady Navigation Inc* [2005] 1 WLR 3686).

F THE ORDER

Interim injunction orders should be in the standard forms set out in PF 39CH (for urgent injunctions) and PF 40CH (for other interim injunctions, see figure 35.1). **35.87**

Figure 35.1 High Court interim injunction

IN THE HIGH COURT OF JUSTICE — Claim No HQ10X 21189

QUEEN'S BENCH DIVISION

BEFORE the Honourable Mr Justice Collier (judge in private)

Tuesday 23rd November 2010

BETWEEN

CASPKEELER PRODUCTS LIMITED — Claimants

—and—

LOAMER TECHTRONICS LIMITED — Defendants

ORDER FOR AN INJUNCTION

IMPORTANT

NOTICE TO THE DEFENDANTS

(1) This Order prohibits you from doing the acts set out in this Order. You should read it carefully. You are advised to consult a Solicitor as soon as possible. You have a right to ask the Court to vary or discharge this Order.
(2) If you disobey this Order you may be found guilty of Contempt of Court and any of your directors may be sent to prison or fined or your assets may be seized.
An Application was made on 23 November 2010 by Counsel for the Claimants to the Judge and was attended by Counsel for the Defendants. The Judge heard the Application and read the witness statements listed in Schedule 1 and accepted the undertakings in Schedule 2 of this Order.

IT IS ORDERED that

THE INJUNCTION

(1) Until after final judgment in this claim the Defendants must not:

(a) license the right to distribute the Loamer Techtron Capacitor anywhere in the world in the term of six years from 16 September 2008 granted to the Claimants Caspkeeler Products Limited under an agreement between the Claimants and the Defendants dated 16 September 2008;
(b) sell Loamer Techtron Capacitors otherwise than through the Claimants Caspkeeler Products Limited;
(c) assert or represent to customers that the Claimants Caspkeeler Products Limited are not the sole distributors of the Loamer Techtron Capacitor.

COSTS OF THE APPLICATION

(2) The costs of this application are to be the Claimants' costs in the case.

VARIATION OR DISCHARGE OF THIS ORDER
The Defendants may apply to the Court at any time to vary or discharge this Order, but if they wish to do so they must first inform the Claimants' Solicitors in writing at least 48 hours beforehand.

Figure 35.1 *continued*

NAME AND ADDRESS OF CLAIMANTS' SOLICITORS

The Claimants' Solicitors are:
Collins, Brown and Heath, of 7 Ingrave Road, Birmingham B5 8EP
Ref: JGB/4663, Telephone: 0121 215 8349.

INTERPRETATION OF THIS ORDER

(1) In this Order the words 'he' 'him' or 'his' include 'she' or 'her' and 'it' or 'its'.
(2) Where there are two or more Defendants then (unless the contrary appears):
  (a) references to 'the Defendant' mean both or all of them;
  (b) an Order requiring 'the Defendant' to do or not to do anything requires each Defendant to do or not to do it.

THE EFFECT OF THIS ORDER

(1) A Defendant who is an individual who is ordered not to do something must not do it himself or in any other way. He must not do it through others acting on his behalf or on his instructions or with his encouragement.
(2) A Defendant which is a corporation and which is ordered not to do something must not do it itself or by its directors, officers, employees or agents or in any other way.

SERVICE OF THIS ORDER
This Order shall be served by the Claimants on the Defendants.

SCHEDULE 1
Witness Statements

The Judge read the following witness statements before making this Order:

(1) Rachel Helen Radcliffe, made on 12 November 2010,
(2) Daniel Jordan Loamer, made on 17 November 2010.

SCHEDULE 2
Undertaking given to the Court by the Claimants

If the Court later finds that this Order has caused loss to the Defendants or any other party served with or notified of this Order, and decides that the Defendants or any other party should be compensated for that loss, the Claimants will comply with any Order the Court may make.
All communications to the Court about this Order should be sent to Room 307, Royal Courts of Justice, Strand, London WC2A 2LL quoting the case number. The office is open between 10 a.m. and 4.30 p.m. Monday to Friday. The telephone number is (020) 7936 6148.

A penal notice must be inserted on the front page of the order warning the defendant that breach may result in imprisonment or other penalties. The standard form of penal notice is in the following form: **35.88**

> If you disobey this Order you may be found guilty of Contempt of Court and [any of your directors] may be sent to prison or fined [and you may be fined] or your assets may be seized.

35.89 Undertakings given by the claimant, such as undertakings given in applications without notice (see 35.17), and the undertaking in damages (PD 25A, para 5.1(1)), are incorporated into the form of the order. An impecunious claimant may be required to fortify the undertaking in damages by providing security or paying money into court.

35.90 The operative part of the order should not be in terms wider than is necessary to do justice between the parties. It should be worded so that the defendant can know with certainty what is and what is not permitted (PD 25A, para 5.3). Thus, an order which restrained, among other things, the defendant 'from otherwise infringing' a patent lacked sufficient specificity: *Hepworth Plastics Ltd v Naylor Bros (Clayware) Ltd* [1979] FSR 521. In *EE and Brian Smith (1928) Ltd v Hodson* [2007] EWCA Civ 1210 the order was drawn too widely in that it prevented the company from fulfilling contracts already entered into, there was no sufficient definition of the information caught by the restrictions, and there was no exclusion of information in the public domain. It is usually best to avoid using legal terms of art, especially the names of torts, which often include matters of degree with the result that the defendant will often not know whether specific conduct will breach the order. Likewise, a proposed order restraining disclosure of 'confidential information' was regarded as oppressive, excessively general, and wide in *Raks Holdings AS v Tipcom Ltd* (2004) LTL 29/7/04. Instead, it should have been limited to defined confidential information. The judge will have regard to the draft prepared by the claimant, and may initial the draft without amendment. Ultimately, however, the choice of wording is a matter within the discretion of the judge: *Khorasandjian v Bush* [1993] QB 727. Where the order is made in the presence of all relevant parties (or at least at a hearing of which they had notice even if they did not attend), it may be expressed to last 'until trial or further order' (PD 25A, para 5.2).

G INQUIRY AS TO DAMAGES

35.91 Where it transpires that an interim injunction should not have been granted (for example, if the claimant loses at trial) the defendant or any other person served with the order may seek to enforce the undertaking in damages by applying for an order for an inquiry as to damages. Excessive, inexcusable delay may result in an application for an inquiry as to damages being dismissed: *Barratt Manchester Ltd v Bolton Metropolitan Borough Council* [1998] 1 WLR 1003. An order for an inquiry is not penal and does not depend on fault on the part of the claimant.

35.92 Where an interim injunction is discharged before trial, the court has a number of options on an application for an inquiry as to damages. These were identified in *Cheltenham and Gloucester Building Society v Ricketts* [1993] 1 WLR 1545, as being:

(a) To accede to the application and immediately proceed to determine the question of damages. This should be done only in the most straightforward cases. In *Fourie v Le Roux* [2007] 1 WLR 320 it was held to have been wrong in principle to order an immediate inquiry into damages on the discharge of a freezing injunction before trial. A second, replacement, injunction had been granted, and there was evidence that the frozen money was either itself, or the proceeds from, assets which had been fraudulently obtained by the defendant. The question of whether to order an inquiry was postponed to trial.

(b) To allow the application, and to order the inquiry by a master or district judge. The judge making the order will give directions for the inquiry.
(c) To stand the application over (that is, adjourn it) to a specified time. This is perhaps the usual order where an injunction is discharged during the interim stages of a claim. It is the most appropriate option where matters material to the question whether it is just to order an inquiry are still in issue and will only be determined at trial. The application is most frequently stood over to trial, when all the facts should be known.
(d) To order an inquiry and to direct that the question of liability on the undertaking be determined at the inquiry. This is unusual.
(e) To refuse the application. This is only done in straightforward cases where, eg, it is clear the defendant has suffered no loss as a result of the injunction.

An application for an inquiry made by a successful defendant at the end of the trial will **35.93** normally be refused only if it is unlikely that the defendant has suffered any provable loss: *McDonald's Hamburgers Ltd v Burgerking UK Ltd* [1987] FSR 112. Ordinary contractual principles are applied on causation and quantum, though it is possible for aggravated or exemplary damages to be awarded in cases where the claimant has acted oppressively. Inquiries are normally conducted by masters and district judges.

H UNDERTAKINGS

Instead of contesting an application for an interim injunction, a defendant may give under- **35.94** takings in similar terms to the injunction sought by the claimant. Such undertakings have the same force as an injunction ordered by the court, with the result that the defendant will be in contempt of court if the undertakings are broken. In some cases undertakings may be construed as having contractual effect between the parties (*Independiente Ltd v Music Trading On-Line (HK) Ltd* [2008] 1 WLR 608). In return, the claimant will be required to give a cross-undertaking in damages to safeguard the defendant. Undertakings given by a party may be released or modified if there are special or exceptional circumstances (*Warren v The Random House Group Ltd* [2009] QB 600).

I DISCHARGE

Applications to vary or discharge injunctions are made by application notice to a judge, often **35.95** the same judge who granted the initial injunction. Grounds for such applications include:

(a) material non-disclosure if the injunction was granted without notice;
(b) the particulars of claim being inconsistent with the written evidence on an application without notice;
(c) the facts not justifying relief without giving notice;
(d) the claimant's failure to comply with the undertakings incorporated into the order;

(e) the order having an oppressive effect;

(f) unreasonable interference with the rights of innocent third parties. Affected third parties are entitled to apply for a variation of the order. All the circumstances have to be considered, and it is sometimes within the court's powers to grant an injunction to restrain a defendant from fulfilling a contract already entered into with an innocent third party. An example is where this is necessary in order to protect the claimant's trade secrets (*PSM International plc v Whitehouse* [1992] IRLR 279);

(g) material change in the circumstances;

(h) a failure to prosecute the substantive claim with due speed;

(i) if the claim is stayed other than by agreement between the parties, any interim injunction will be set aside unless the court orders that it should continue in force (CPR, r 25.10);

(j) if the claim is struck out for non-payment of the fees payable at allocation or listing, the interim injunction will lapse 14 days after the claim is struck out. However, if within that 14-day period the claimant applies to reinstate the claim, the injunction will remain in force until the hearing of that application (unless the court otherwise orders) (r 25.11).

J BREACH

35.96 Breach of an injunction is a contempt of court punishable by imprisonment or sequestration. Contempt must be proved beyond reasonable doubt.

35.97 Clearly, the person against whom the order was made will be in contempt if he or she acts in breach of an injunction after having notice of it: *Z Ltd v A–Z and AA–LL* [1982] QB 558 *per* Eveleigh LJ. To establish a contempt by a non-party it must be demonstrated both that the non-party's acts defeated, in whole or in part, the court's purpose in granting the injunction, and that the non-party appreciated that this would be the effect: *Attorney-General v Punch Ltd* [2003] 1 AC 1046.

K EFFECT OF NOT APPLYING FOR INTERIM RELIEF

35.98 Delay in issuing proceedings after the claimant is aware of the defendant's breach, and deciding not to apply for an interim injunction to avoid giving an undertaking in damages, are matters to be taken into account in considering whether to grant a final injunction. They do not bar granting such an injunction where the claimant has made a clear objection to the defendant's conduct (*Mortimer v Bailey* (2004) LTL 29/10/04). Failing to apply for an interim injunction may also provide grounds for awarding damages in lieu of an injunction: *Jaggard v Sawyer* [1995] 1 WLR 269.

KEY POINTS SUMMARY

- Interim injunctions can be sought without notice if the case is urgent or if there is other sufficient reason. Otherwise, they are sought on notice to the respondents. **35.99**
- Injunctions are remedies, so applications for interim injunctions have to be founded on a substantive cause of action.
- In the past, parties in applications for interim injunctions in important cases were often tempted into deploying most or all their evidence on the merits of the claim on the interim application. The *American Cyanamid* guidelines are principally designed to prevent this being necessary.
- The *American Cyanamid* guidelines apply to the vast bulk of applications for interim prohibitory injunctions.
- Most of the exceptions to *American Cyanamid* are aimed at the first stage of the guidance (whether there is a serious issue to be tried), and impose a higher standard on the merits (eg, mandatory injunctions and interim injunctions which finally dispose of the case).
- Applicants are invariably required to undertake to compensate the defendant and sometimes any person served with the injunction if it later transpires that the injunction should not have been granted.

36

FREEZING INJUNCTIONS

36.01 A freezing injunction is an interim order restraining a party from removing assets located within the jurisdiction out of the country, or from dealing with assets whether they are located within the jurisdiction or not (CPR, r 25.1(1)(f)). Usually the order will be restricted to assets not exceeding the value of the claim. Until the CPR came into force on 26 April 1999 this form of order was known as a *Mareva* injunction, taking its name from *Mareva Compania Naviera SA v International Bulkcarriers SA* [1980] 1 All ER 213.

36.02 The purpose of a freezing injunction is to prevent the injustice of a defendant's assets being salted away so as to deprive the claimant of the fruits of any judgment that may be obtained. However, as Ackner LJ said in *A J Bekhor and Co Ltd v Bilton* [1981] QB 923, the jurisdiction to grant freezing injunctions has not rewritten the law of insolvency, and the imposition of such an order does not give the claimant any priority or security if the defendant becomes insolvent. It is a relief *in personam* which simply prohibits certain acts in relation to the assets frozen.

A PROCEDURE

36.03 County courts do not generally have jurisdiction to grant freezing injunctions, so applications must usually be made in the High Court (County Court Remedies Regulations 1991 (SI 1991/1222), reg 3(1)). Freezing injunctions may be granted by a county court where a High

Court or Court of Appeal judge sits, in Mercantile List and Patents County Court cases, certain family proceedings, and in aid of execution (reg 3(2) and (3)(a), (c), and (d)). Another exception where a freezing injunction can be ordered by a county court is where the proposed order seeks to preserve or detain property which is or may form the subject matter of the proceedings or proposed proceedings (reg 3(3)(b)). If, apart from the application for the freezing injunction the claim would or should proceed in a county court, it will be transferred down to a county court after the application for the freezing injunction has been disposed of.

Given that a freezing injunction can be ordered only against an unscrupulous defendant who is prepared to dissipate assets to prevent the claimant recovering on any judgment obtained, the application has to be made without informing the defendant if the injunction is to be effective. In *Oaktree Financial Services Ltd v Higham* (2004) LTL 11/5/04 one of the solicitors involved in the case wrote to the defendant unwittingly but in effect warning him of the possibility of a freezing injunction application being made. Laddie J was almost minded to refuse the injunction on this ground alone, as there was a strong prospect that any funds would have been dissipated once the defendant was put on notice. **36.04**

The application is made to a judge sitting in private. Invariably, the application is made before service of the claim form so as not to alert the defendant. A draft claim form, or its overseas equivalent, must be produced in order to identify the substantive claim against the defendant (see 36.10–36.11; *Fourie v Le Roux* [2007] 1 WLR 320). The application must be supported by an affidavit making full and frank disclosure of all material facts, including those going against the grant of the order. Applications for freezing injunctions are one of the exceptions where affidavits must be used (PD 25A, para 3.1). The affidavit must be clear and fair, and claimants should avoid the temptation to flood the court with voluminous exhibits, particularly where this will tend to obscure the real issues. In urgent cases informal evidence may be used, but in such cases the applicant will be required to confirm on affidavit all the evidence presented at the hearing (*Flightwise Travel Services Ltd v Gill* (2003) *The Times*, 5 December 2003). Counsel must produce a draft minute of the order sought. There is a standard form for the order, which is considered in 36.27ff. In urgent cases the application can be made before issue of the proceedings. **36.05**

The papers must, wherever possible, be delivered to the court at least two hours before the hearing to allow the judge to read them in advance (PD 25A, para 4.3(1)). Further, even on applications without notice and especially where 'worldwide' freezing injunctions (see 36.16) are sought, counsel should consider drafting a skeleton argument indicating how the requirements for granting the order are made out: see *ALG Inc v Uganda Airlines Corporation* (1992) *The Times*, 31 July 1992. As the application is made without notice, there is the usual duty of full and frank disclosure (see 20.25–20.28). There is a duty on counsel to ensure the court's attention is drawn to unusual features of the evidence adduced, to the applicable law, and to the formalities and procedure to be observed (*Memory Corporation plc v Sidhu (No 2)* [2000] 1 WLR 1443). A failure to formulate the substantive claim against the defendant is a reason in itself to refuse relief (*Fourie v Le Roux*). **36.06**

Paragraph 3 of the standard order provides for a return day for a further hearing on notice, which is normally a few days after the without-notice hearing. The respondent must be fully informed of the applicant's case well in advance of the hearing on notice, including being provided with the evidence and informed of the arguments advanced at the without-notice hearing (*Flightwise Travel Services Ltd v Gill*). **36.07**

B PRINCIPLES

36.08 The jurisdiction to grant freezing injunctions derives from the SCA 1981, s 37(1). This section enables the court to grant interim injunctions on such terms and conditions as the court thinks just where it appears 'just and convenient' to do so. The requirements laid down by the courts for granting freezing injunctions are:

(a) a cause of action justiciable in England and Wales;
(b) a good arguable case;
(c) the defendant having assets within the jurisdiction; and
(d) a real risk that the defendant may dissipate those assets before judgment can be enforced.

36.09 However, because injunctions are granted where it is just and convenient, the court retains a discretion to refuse relief, and, in rare, exceptional cases, has power to stretch the usual rules if that is in the interests of justice. Unless the case is truly exceptional, the above requirements must be established, and it is not sufficient to say that a freezing injunction should be granted because there is no immediate and obvious prejudice to the respondent (*Flightwise Travel Services Ltd v Gill* (2003) *The Times*, 5 December 2003).

Claim justiciable in England and Wales

36.10 The claimant must have a substantive cause of action, and there must be a basis for bringing the application in England and Wales. At one time, the focus under this heading was on the jurisdiction issue. Freezing injunctions, like all other types of injunction, are remedies, and depend for their existence on a substantive cause of action. It used to be the case that if there was no means of bringing a substantive claim in England and Wales, there was no basis for granting an injunction, freezing or otherwise (*The Siskina* [1979] AC 210). This was changed by the CJJA 1982, s 25, as extended by the Civil Jurisdiction and Judgments Act 1982 (Interim Relief) Order 1997 (SI 1997/302) (see 10.84). The CJJA 1982, s 25, enables the High Court to grant interim relief, including freezing injunctions, where proceedings have been or are to be commenced in an overseas jurisdiction. Two key restrictions in the original s 25 (that the overseas jurisdiction had to be a Brussels or Lugano Convention contracting state, and that the substantive proceedings had to come within the scope of what is now the Judgments Regulation, art 1) were removed by the 1997 Order. The only remaining limitation is under s 25(2), that the court may refuse relief if, in its opinion, the fact that the court has no jurisdiction apart from s 25 makes it inexpedient for it to grant the interim relief that is sought (see 36.16).

36.11 The result, as recognized by *Fourie v Le Roux* [2007] 1 WLR 320, is that jurisdiction, in the sense of whether the court has power to deal with the application, is no longer an issue. Instead, the focus in relation to the first requirement is whether the claimant can identify a cause of action against the defendant. To achieve this, the claimant is required to have formulated a claim for substantive relief against the defendant, whether that substantive claim is to be brought in England and Wales or an overseas jurisdiction (*Fourie v Le Roux* at [35]).

Good arguable case

Regarding the merits of the substantive claim, the minimum threshold for the exercise of the discretion is the establishment of a 'good arguable case'. This imposes a higher merits requirement than the 'serious issue to be tried' test used in applications for interim injunctions applying the *American Cyanamid* principles (*Fiona Trust Holding Corporation v Privalov* (2007) LTL 30/5/07). According to Kerr LJ in *Ninemia Maritime Corporation v Trave Schiffahrtsgesellschaft mbH & Co KG* [1983] 1 WLR 1412 (affirmed [1983] 2 Lloyd's Rep 660), the expression means 'a case which is more than barely capable of serious argument, and yet not necessarily one which the judge believes to have a better than 50 per cent chance of success'. This test will not be satisfied if the claimant does not have the evidence to substantiate the case relied upon, or if the case is likely to be struck out, and may not be satisfied if there is an arguable defence. **36.12**

The courts have on occasion been reluctant to find there is a good arguable case where fraud is alleged, as in *Cheltenham and Gloucester Building Society v Ricketts* [1993] 1 WLR 1545, given the difficulty of proving this particular allegation. In *Fiona Trust Holding Corporation v Privalov* matters pointing to a good arguable case included a lack of negotiations in allegedly fraudulent transactions, unconvincing evidence from the defendants to explain their conduct, a letter referring to 'the delicate nature of our exchanges', and attempts to prevent outsiders finding out. An arguable set-off may be taken as reducing or extinguishing the value of the claim. Anticipation that the defendant will be in breach of contract in the future has been held to be insufficient to satisfy this part of the test (*Veracruz Transportation Inc v VC Shipping Co Inc* [1992] 1 Lloyd's Rep 353). **36.13**

Assets

The requirement of proving that the defendant has assets within the jurisdiction stems from the principle that equity will not act in vain, so that if an injunction will not be effective it will not be granted. The claimant must show 'some grounds for believing' that the defendant has assets within the jurisdiction. 'Assets' includes money, shares, securities, insurance money, bills of exchange, motor vehicles, ships, aircraft, trade goods, office equipment, jewellery, and paintings. While ownership may be legal or beneficial, the defendant must own the assets in the same capacity as the defendant is or will be a party to the claim. **36.14**

The existence of an overdrawn bank account was held in one case, *Third Chandris Shipping Corporation v Unimarine SA* [1979] QB 645, to be some evidence of assets within the jurisdiction. This is so particularly where the court can infer that the account is likely to be secured in some way. Where an asset apparently belongs to a non-party, but the claimant claims it is beneficially owned by the defendant, it was said by Nicholls LJ in *Allied Arab Bank Ltd v Hajjar* [1988] QB 787 that the claimant must normally pass the *Ninemia Maritime Corporation v Trave Schiffahrtsgesellschaft mbH & Co KG* [1983] 1 WLR 1412 threshold (see 36.12) on the question of proving beneficial ownership. A slightly different situation arose in *TSB Private Bank International SA v Chabra* [1992] 1 WLR 231. It was clear that the claimant had a good cause of action against the first defendant, and equally clear there was no independent cause of action against the second defendant, a company owned by the first defendant and/or his wife. As there was credible evidence that the assets apparently owned by the second defendant in fact belonged to the first defendant, Mummery J granted a freezing injunction against **36.15** the second defendant on the ground that it was ancillary and incidental to the claim against the first defendant.

Worldwide freezing injunctions

36.16 Generally, freezing injunctions do not extend to assets outside the jurisdiction. A freezing injunction having extraterritorial effect can be granted only in an exceptional case. The power to grant worldwide freezing injunctions in support of domestic proceedings derives from the SCA 1981, s 37(1), not the CJJA 1982, s 25, or the Judgments Regulation, art 31 (*Masri v Consolidated Contractors International UK Ltd (No 2)* [2008] 1 All ER (Comm) 305 at [53]; [2009] QB 450 at [92]–[107]). Worldwide freezing injunctions are readily made against defendants within the jurisdiction where there is cogent evidence of international fraud (*Mediterranean Shipping Co v OMG International Ltd* [2008] EWHC 2150 (Comm)). A worldwide freezing injunction in aid of foreign proceedings affecting assets not located in the jurisdiction will only be granted where the respondent or the dispute has a sufficiently strong link with the jurisdiction, or if there is some other factor justifying the court's intervention despite the lack of such a link (*Mobil Cerro Negro Ltd v Petroleos de Venezuela SA* [2008] 1 Lloyd's Rep 684).

36.17 Under the CJJA 1982, s 25(2), an interim relief in aid of foreign proceedings must be refused if it is 'inexpedient'. According to *Motorola Credit Corporation v Uzan (No 2)* [2004] 1 WLR 113, the following factors should be considered under s 25(2):

(a) whether making the order will interfere with the management of the case in the primary court;
(b) whether it is the policy in the primary jurisdiction to refuse to make worldwide freezing orders;
(c) whether there is a danger that the order will give rise to disharmony or confusion, or the risk of conflicting, inconsistent, or overlapping orders in other jurisdictions; and
(d) whether the worldwide order can be enforced. Enforcement against each defendant has to be considered separately.

36.18 In *Banco Nacional de Comercio Exterior SNC v Empresa de Telecomunicationes de Cuba SA* [2007] 2 All ER (Comm) 1093 it was held to be inexpedient to grant a worldwide order because the judgment debtor was outside the jurisdiction, the original judgment was granted in Italy, any assets within the jurisdiction were covered by a domestic freezing injunction (which was granted), and granting a worldwide order would be likely to give rise to disharmony and confusion. A different view was taken in *Amedeo Hotels Ltd Partnership v Zaman* (2007) LTL 14/6/07, where the non-availability of worldwide freezing orders in New York was regarded as a reason in favour of granting an English worldwide order. It has been held that the court can make a worldwide order in cases where the defendant has no assets in England: *Derby and Co Ltd v Weldon (Nos 3 and 4)* [1990] Ch 65.

36.19 Worldwide freezing orders must include a *Babanaft* proviso that the order will not affect third parties outside the jurisdiction until, and to the extent that, it has been declared enforceable, or is enforced, by a foreign court. See *Babanaft International Co SA v Bassatne* [1990] Ch 13 and cl 19(2)(c) of the standard freezing injunction order. The claimant is further required to undertake not to enforce the order in a foreign court without first obtaining permission from the English court: (Sch B, para 10 of the standard freezing injunction order, and see *Dadourian Group International Inc v Simms (No 2)* [2007] 1 WLR 2967 for the principles on seeking permission).

Worldwide freezing injunctions must also include *Baltic* provisos to the effect that third parties served with the order may comply with what they reasonably believe to be their civil and criminal obligations in the country where the assets are located (*Bank of China v NBM LLC* [2002] 1 WLR 844 and cl 20 of the standard freezing injunction order). **36.20**

Risk of disposal

The claimant must provide 'solid evidence' that there is a real risk that the defendant will dissipate assets if unrestrained: *Ninemia Maritime Corporation v Trave Schiffahrtsgesellschaft mbH & Co KG* [1983] 1 WLR 1412; *Dean and Dean v Grinina* [2008] EWHC 927 (QB). In *Customs and Excise Commissioners v Anchor Foods Ltd* [1999] 1 WLR 1139 Neuberger J said that what is required is a good and arguable case for a risk of dissipation. This was found to be so where the defendant proposed to dispose of its entire business at a price which had been independently verified by a partner in a leading accountancy firm, because the purchaser was a company controlled by the same people who controlled the defendant and there was contrary valuation evidence (also from very eminent experts) indicating that the price was too low. **36.21**

At one time it was thought that freezing injunctions could be granted only against foreign defendants. The SCA 1981, s 37(3), now provides that the jurisdiction to grant these orders 'shall be exercisable in cases where [the defendant] is, as well as in cases where he is not, domiciled, resident or present within [the] jurisdiction'. Lord Denning MR in *Third Chandris Shipping Corporation v Unimarine SA* [1979] QB 645 said at 669: **36.22**

> The mere fact that the defendant is abroad is not by itself sufficient?... But there are some foreign companies whose structure invites comment. We often see in this court a corporation which is registered in a country where the company law is so loose that nothing is known about it—where it does no work and has no officers and no assets?... Judgment cannot be enforced against it. There is no reciprocal enforcement of judgments?... In such cases the very fact of incorporation there gives some ground for believing there is a risk that, if judgment or an award is obtained, it may go unsatisfied.

Reciprocal enforcement of judgments is considered in Chapter 44. Conversely, in *Barclay-Johnson v Yuill* [1980] 1 WLR 1259 Megarry V-C said: **36.23**

> A reputable foreign company, accustomed to paying its debts, ought not to be prevented from removing its assets from the jurisdiction, especially if it has substantial assets in countries in which English judgments can be enforced.

Factors relevant to the question of risk of dissipation include: **36.24**

(a) whether the defendant is domiciled or incorporated in a tax haven or country with tax company law;
(b) whether English judgments are enforceable in the country where the defendant's assets are situated: *Montecchi v Shimco (UK) Ltd* [1979] 1 WLR 1180. This is a particularly important factor where the assets are in an EU Member State due to the ease of enforcement under the Judgments Regulation;

(c) whether the evidence supporting the substantive cause of action discloses dishonesty or a suspicion of dishonesty on the part of the defendant. This is a weighty factor when it is present, and this is so whether or not it is pleaded as fraud: *Guinness plc v Saunders* (1987) *The Independent*, 15 April 1987;
(d) whether there is evidence that the defendant has been dishonest, outside the actual cause of action. This includes matters such as contrivances designed to generate an appearance of wealth;
(e) past incidents of debt default by the defendant, although it is not essential for the claimant to have such evidence: *Third Chandris Shipping Corporation v Unimarine SA;*
(f) evidence that the defendant has already taken steps to remove or dissipate its assets: *Aiglon Ltd v Gau Shan Co Ltd* [1993] 1 Lloyd's Rep 164.

Discretion

36.25 In its discretion, the court can refuse a freezing injunction even if the usual requirements are made out. In *Rasu Maritima SA v Perusahaan Pertambangan Minyak Dan Gas Bumi Negara* [1978] QB 644 the Court of Appeal refused to grant an order partly because the 'cleanliness' of the claimant's hands was open to question, and partly in the exercise of its discretion. The assets frozen were parts for a fertilizer plant, and were valued at $12 million in the hands of the defendants, but were worth only $0.35 million as scrap. This was regarded as only a 'drop in the ocean' in comparison with the size of the claim.

36.26 A freezing order covering 60 per cent of the assets of the defendant bank was discharged in the exercise of the court's discretion in *Polly Peck International plc v Nadir (No 2)* [1992] 4 All ER 769 as it would almost certainly have severely damaged its day-to-day banking business, and also was likely to result in a loss of confidence among investors with the possibility of a run on its deposits. In *Sions v Price* (1988) *The Independent*, 19 December 1988, an order was refused where the claim was £2,000. Freezing injunctions are only to be used in substantial cases.

C THE ORDER

Undertakings

36.27 The following undertakings by the claimant must be given to the court and incorporated into the order:

(a) as with other interim injunctions, to pay damages to the defendant if it transpires that the order should not have been granted. In appropriate cases this should be supported by a payment into court or the provision of a bond by an insurance company. The court should take into account factors similar to those on applications for security for costs (see Chapter 24), such as whether requiring the applicant to fortify the undertaking may stifle a genuine claim (*Sinclair Investment Holdings SA v Cushnie* (2004) LTL 23/3/04);
(b) to notify the defendant forthwith of the terms of the order, often by telex or fax, and to serve the defendant with the affidavit and exhibits in support. This is a consequence of applying without notice;

(c) to pay the reasonable costs and expenses incurred by third parties in complying with the order; and
(d) to indemnify third parties in respect of any liability incurred in complying with the order.

In urgent cases, the following further undertakings may be required: **36.28**

(e) to issue a claim form as soon as practicable in the terms of the draft used on the application; and
(f) to swear and file affidavits deposing to the facts relied on before the judge.

Under the SCA 1981, s 37(2), interim injunctions can be granted on such terms and conditions as the court thinks fit. A little latitude is permissible. So, in *Allen v Jambo Holdings Ltd* [1980] 1 WLR 1252 the Court of Appeal continued a freezing injunction in favour of a publicly funded claimant who could not give a valuable undertaking in damages. The case was unusual in that the defendants had sworn an affidavit blatantly exaggerating the effects of the order and had been less than forthcoming on a number of points. Also, in any event, the defendants could have obtained the release of their frozen aeroplane by providing security. **36.29**

Assets covered by the order

Considered in relation to the assets they cover, freezing injunctions can be divided into three types: **36.30**

(a) general orders, which cover all the defendant's assets;
(b) maximum-sum orders, which cover the defendant's assets up to the highest amount, together with interest and costs, for which there is a good arguable case. If the claim is unliquidated, the maximum sum is calculated by reference to the sum the claimant is likely to recover; and
(c) orders attaching to specific assets, such as a ship, a cargo, or an aeroplane.

Often, orders attaching to specific assets are combined with either general or maximum-sum orders. The choice between general and maximum-sum orders was considered in *Z Ltd v A–Z and AA–LL* [1982] QB 558. Maximum-sum orders are the norm. A general order is likely to provoke an application for a variation down to a maximum-sum order. One drawback with maximum-sum orders is that banks will not necessarily know whether they can honour transactions on the defendant's accounts as they will not know the total value of the defendant's assets covered by the order at any particular time. Where such practical difficulties result in a larger sum being 'frozen' than the sum stated in the order, the claimant may be held liable on its undertakings in damages. General orders may accordingly be used where the defendant's assets are not fully known by the claimant, and are also appropriate in fraud cases where the amount of the claim may be unknown. **36.31**

Where the claimant asks for a freezing injunction to cover assets which the defendant or some third party alleges belong to someone other than the defendant, the court has a wide power to do whatever is just and convenient, including ordering the question of ownership to be tried as an issue between the claimant and the third party: *SCF Finance Co Ltd v Masri* [1985] 1 WLR 876. The standard form of order does not cover assets held by a defendant on **36.32** trust, although an extended form of order may be made to cover such assets: *Federal Bank of the Middle East Ltd v Hadkinson* [2000] 1 WLR 1695.

Bank accounts

36.33 Bank accounts are one of the most common assets covered by freezing injunctions. The following points should be noted:

(a) A joint account will not be affected by a freezing injunction unless it is specifically covered by the wording of the order: *SCF Finance Co Ltd v Masri* [1985] 1 WLR 876.
(b) If the defendant has an account containing money over which the claimant asserts a proprietary interest, mixed with the defendant's own money and/or money held by the defendant on behalf of a third party, the court has jurisdiction to freeze the entire account: *Chief Constable of Kent v V* [1983] QB 34.
(c) The claimant must give the fullest possible details (bank, branch, account name, and number) in the affidavit in support. If it is necessary to ask the bank to search for an account, the number of branches involved should be as limited as possible. The claimant will be required to pay the costs of such searches immediately, which may or may not be recoverable from the defendant as costs of the action.
(d) The bank should honour transactions entered into before the order is made. The bank must also honour cheques backed by guarantee cards and irrevocable letters of credit: see, eg, *Cretanor Maritime Co Ltd v Irish Marine Management Ltd* [1978] 1 WLR 966, and *Lewis and Peat (Produce) Ltd v Almatu Properties Ltd* (1992) *The Times*, 14 May 1992. Cheque cards should be recalled once the order has been served on the bank.
(e) A freezing injunction can apply to the *proceeds* of a letter of credit when received: *Z Ltd v A–Z and AA–LL* [1982] QB 558.
(f) A provision must be incorporated into the order to allow any bank served with the order to exercise any right of set-off it may have in respect of facilities given to the defendant before the order: *Oceanica Castelana Armadora SA v Mineral-importexport* [1983] 1 WLR 1294 and cl 17 of the standard order.

36.34 A bank does not owe a duty of care in negligence to the claimant, even after receiving notice of a freezing injunction (*Customs and Excise Commissioners v Barclays Bank plc* [2007] 1 AC 181).

Port authorities

36.35 Where a freezing injunction affects a ship in harbour, the claimant will be required to undertake to reimburse the port authority for lost income, and a proviso will be incorporated into the order giving the port authority a discretion to move the ship for operational reasons: *Clipper Maritime Co Ltd v Mineralimportexport* [1981] 1 WLR 1262.

Land

36.36 Freezing injunctions can be granted over land, although it may be difficult to prove that there is a 'risk of disposal'. An order, if granted, would not be made for the purpose of enforcing a judgment, so would not be registrable as a land charge: *Stockler v Fourways Estates Ltd* [1984] 1 WLR 25.

Living expenses

A freezing injunction must allow an individual defendant to use a reasonable sum each week or month to pay his or her ordinary living expenses (cl 11 of the standard order). As decided in *PCW (Underwriting Agencies) Ltd v Dixon* [1983] 2 All ER 158, a defendant is not dissipating his assets by living as he has always lived. It is a misuse of the jurisdiction to grant freezing injunctions to seek to apply pressure on the defendant (perhaps with a view to obtaining a favourable settlement) by unreasonably limiting the money available for ordinary living expenses. Spending in excess of the living expenses clause is not a breach of the injunction if it is funded by borrowing from another source: *Cantor Index Ltd v Lister* (2001) LTL 22/1/01. Living expenses money must not, however, be spent on extraordinary items, such as expensive motor cars (see *TDK Tape Distributor (UK) Ltd v Videochoice Ltd* [1986] 1 WLR 141). **36.37**

Trade debts

A freezing injunction must allow a defendant who is engaged in trade to pay any legitimate trade debts as they would be paid in the ordinary course of the defendant's business (cl 11 of the standard order). The philosophy behind this is that a freezing injunction is not intended to confer priority over other trade creditors. A defendant should be allowed to pay a trade debt, if the defendant is acting in good faith and in the ordinary course of business, even if the debt is not strictly enforceable: *Iraqi Ministry of Defence v Arcepey Shipping Co SA* [1981] QB 65. Whether the defendant should use assets not covered by the order where such are available depends ultimately on the defendant's motive (*Campbell Mussels v Thompson* (1984) 81 LS Gaz 2140, interpreting *A v C (No 2)* [1981] QB 961). **36.38**

Costs of defending

A freezing injunction should normally also allow the defendant to pay the ordinary costs of the present claim if no other funds are available (cl 11 of the standard order). The permission to use money to pay reasonable legal costs (or living expenses or trade debts) does no more than to permit the expenditure without the defendant being in contempt of court. Thus, where the underlying cause of action asserts a proprietary claim against the defendant, the permission to use money to pay reasonable legal expenses is no guarantee that the recipients of that money will escape a later claim in constructive trust for knowing receipt should the claim be established: *United Mizrahi Bank Ltd v Doherty* [1998] 1 WLR 435. **36.39**

Ancillary orders

The court has power under CPR, r 25.1(1)(g), to make ancillary orders for disclosure and answers to requests for further information to ensure the effectiveness of the main freezing injunction. Orders requiring disclosure of the nature and whereabouts of all the defendant's assets within the jurisdiction are a standard requirement in freezing injunctions, and are generally required if the injunctions are to be effective: *Motorola Credit Corporation v Uzan* [2002] 2 All ER (Comm) 945 and cll 9 and 10 of the standard order. Disclosure orders are used more sparingly in injunctions in support of foreign proceedings (*Cinar Corporation v Panju* [2007] 1 All ER (Comm) 373). Defendants should be given a realistic time for compliance (*Oystertec plc v Davidson* (2004) LTL 7/4/04, where four working days was regarded as extremely short). **36.40**

In addition, the defendant's bank may be ordered, even if not a party, to give disclosure of documents relating to the defendant's bank account: *A v C* [1981] QB 956. There are two major limits on the jurisdiction to make ancillary disclosure orders. First, as with other forms of disclosure, such orders will not be granted if they are merely 'fishing' (see *Faith Panton Property Plan Ltd v Hodgetts* [1981] 1 WLR 927). Essentially, an application for disclosure will be 'fishing' if it is based on no more than suspicion as opposed to some evidence.

36.41 Secondly, problems can arise in relation to the privilege against self-incrimination (see 29.27).

36.42 It is only in exceptional circumstances that cross-examination will be ordered on an affidavit of assets sworn pursuant to a freezing order. However, where the claimant has justifiable concerns about whether the defendant has made a full disclosure as required by the order, the court may order the defendant to be cross-examined: *Den Norske Bank ASA v Antonatos* [1999] QB 271. The purpose of the cross-examination is solely to discover what assets the defendant has, with a view to freezing them, and so will be unnecessary if sufficient assets are known to meet the value of the claim: *Great Future International Ltd v Sealand Housing Corporation* [2001] CPLR 293. The examination will be conducted by a master or district judge unless the judge making the order otherwise directs (PD 2B, para 7).

Duration

36.43 A freezing order made without notice will remain in force for a limited period until the 'return date', which will be fixed by the judge when the order is granted. So far as practicable, any application to discharge or vary the order should be dealt with on the return date. Clause 13 of the standard form of freezing order in PD 25A enables the defendant or any third party notified of the order to apply to the court at any time (ie, less than the usual three clear days' notice), but must first notify the claimant's legal representatives. The standard form also says, at cl 5, that the order will continue 'until further order'. This is a reference to an order which expressly or impliedly discharges the freezing order. A freezing order does not therefore lapse when final judgment is entered against the defendant: *Cantor Index Ltd v Lister* (2001) LTL 22/11/01.

Standard form orders

36.44 The standard form freezing injunction order for domestic freezing injunctions and worldwide freezing injunctions can be found in the annex to PD 25A. This form should always be used, with only such modifications as are essential to fit the circumstances of the case. Any substantial variation should be brought to the attention of the judge at the hearing. Wherever possible, a draft of the order sought should be filed with the application notice, with a copy on a digital storage device (PD 25A, para 2.4).

D EFFECT OF THE ORDER

36.45 A defendant or anyone else with notice of a freezing injunction will be in contempt of court if they dispose or assist in the disposal or dissipation of enjoined assets: *Z Ltd v A–Z and AA–LL* [1982] QB 558 at 572 *per* Lord Denning MR. A non-party who hands an asset covered by a freezing injunction back to the defendant does not thereby dissipate or dispose of it (*Law Society v Shanks* [1988] 1 FLR 504), unless the non-party knows of a probability that after receiving it the defendant will dispose of it in breach of the order: *Bank Mellat v Kazmi* [1989] 1 QB 541.

A freezing injunction covering unspecified assets has an ambulatory effect (see *Cretanor Maritime Co Ltd v Irish Marine Management Ltd* [1978] 1 WLR 966 *per* Buckley LJ). Assets acquired by the defendant after the order is granted will be covered by it, up to the maximum sum (if any) stated in the order: *TDK Tape Distributor (UK) Ltd v Videochoice Ltd* [1986] 1 WLR 141. **36.46**

E VARIATION OR DISCHARGE OF A FREEZING INJUNCTION

Procedure on application to vary or discharge

Applications to vary or discharge freezing injunctions are made to a judge, either pursuant to the liberty to apply provision in the order itself, or on the claimant's application to renew the order on the return date. The application will be made in accordance with CPR, Part 23 (see Chapter 20). **36.47**

A non-party who is affected by the terms of a freezing injunction can apply to intervene in the action under CPR, r 19.2(2), and for the terms of the order to be varied. However, formal intervention may be unnecessary, as Buckley LJ in *Cretanor Maritime Co Ltd v Irish Marine Management Ltd* [1978] 1 WLR 966 said that a non-party may apply for a variation of a freezing order without intervening provided the non-party had a clear interest. Provided the intervention (whether formal or on the lines indicated by Buckley LJ) is justified, the non-party should be entitled to its costs on the indemnity basis (see *Project Development Co Ltd SA v KMK Securities Ltd* [1982] 1 WLR 1470). **36.48**

Where it is clear that the order should be varied or discharged, the parties may agree to this in the form of a consent order. **36.49**

Grounds for variation

Variations of freezing injunctions may be allowed where the original order is more onerous to the defendant than is necessary, or if it imposes unnecessary obligations on a non-party. Examples are failures to include necessary provisos, such as for ordinary living expenses, paying trade debts, allowing banks the usual set-off, or making a general order when a maximum-sum order is appropriate. Hardship to third parties may also give grounds for a variation. In *Camdex International Ltd v Bank of Zambia (No 2)* [1997] 1 WLR 632 a freezing injunction had caught a large quantity of banknotes for issue in Zambia. It was varied to allow the release of the banknotes, to prevent serious damage being inflicted on the general population of the country. **36.50**

Grounds for discharge

Case unsuitable for freezing injunction

A freezing injunction may be discharged on the ground that one of the usual requirements has not been made out. This may be on the basis, eg, that the claimant does not have a **36.51** good arguable case, as in *Cheltenham and Gloucester Building Society v Ricketts* [1993] 1 WLR 1545. Alternatively, what may have appeared to be a good arguable case on the application without notice may be wiped out by an arguable defence or set-off. It may be that evidence concerning the defendant's financial status, business history, or links with this country (or other countries where an English judgment would be enforceable) will persuade the court that there is no real risk of the defendant dissipating the enjoined assets in order to frustrate any judgment the claimant may obtain. Further, a change in the management of a company defendant may remove the risk of dissipation and merit a freezing injunction being discharged: *Capital Cameras Ltd v Harold Lines Ltd* [1991] 1 WLR 54.

Security

36.52 A freezing injunction should be discharged where the defendant provides sufficient security for the claim. Security can be provided by bond or guarantee, or by paying money into court. The standard security provision in a freezing injunction only gives 'security' against the risk of dissipation of assets. It does not provide security against the defendant's other creditors (*Technocrats International Inc v Fredic Ltd* [2005] 1 BCLC 467). Giving security can be to the advantage of the defendant, since it may be that the order has frozen an asset worth more to the defendant than the cost of the security being offered, and in any event it is often important for defendants for freezing injunctions to be discharged, as such orders carry a significant financial stigma and usually result in banking facilities being withdrawn.

Material non-disclosure

36.53 A consequence of freezing injunction applications being made without notice is that a claimant applying for a freezing injunction is under a duty to give full and frank disclosure of any defence or other facts going against the grant of the relief sought. This duty is discussed at 20.25–20.28.

Unfair conduct

36.54 In *Negocios Del Mar SA v Doric Shipping Corporation SA* [1979] 1 Lloyd's Rep 331 the claimants had agreed to buy a ship from the defendants. Before paying the agreed price, they discovered it was damaged. So they obtained a freezing injunction, which they served immediately on the exchange of the ship for the price. The effect was that the proceeds of the sale were immediately frozen in the hands of the sellers. This type of application is often called a 'trap application', and the circumstances are material facts which have to be disclosed under the duty of full and frank disclosure. On appeal, this was regarded as being unfair conduct on the part of the claimants, and the injunction was discharged.

Delay in the substantive proceedings

36.55 It was stated by Glidewell LJ in *Lloyds Bowmaker Ltd v Britannia Arrow Holdings plc* [1988] 1 WLR 1337 that:

> . . . a [claimant] who succeeds in obtaining a *Mareva* injunction is in my view under an obligation to press on with his action as rapidly as he can so that if he should fail to establish liability in the defendant the disadvantage which the injunction imposes upon the defendant will be lessened so far as possible.

A failure to press on with the substantive action will therefore provide grounds for discharging a freezing injunction. 36.56

F FREEZING INJUNCTIONS AFTER JUDGMENT

In *Orwell Steel (Erection and Fabrication) Ltd v Asphalt and Tarmac (UK) Ltd* [1984] 1 WLR 1097 it was held that a freezing injunction may be granted in aid of the execution of a judgment debt. Provided the judgment is enforceable in England and Wales, the requirements that the claimant must have a cause of action justiciable in England and Wales and a good arguable case are satisfied by the judgment itself. Consequently, the only requirements are that the defendant has assets within the jurisdiction and there is a real risk of those assets being dissipated before judgment can be enforced. Undertakings in damages are required in the same way as in freezing injunctions before trial (*Banco Nacional de Comercio Exterior SNC v Empresa de Telecommunicationes de Cuba SA* [2007] 2 All ER (Comm) 1093) unless one of the exceptions mentioned in 35.43 applies. 36.57

G PROPRIETARY CLAIMS

Unlike a claim for damages, an equitable tracing claim is a claim of a proprietary character. The only interim protection that can be sought in a damages claim is a freezing injunction. Freezing injunctions operate in person, and freeze assets which belong to the defendant in order to prevent dissipation of those assets with the aim of ensuring the effectiveness of any eventual judgment. On the other hand, the assets covered by a proprietary claim are alleged to belong to the claimant. Rather than seeking a freezing injunction under CPR, r 25.1(f), the claimant in a proprietary claim may seek an order for the detention, custody, or preservation of the property which is the subject of the claim under r 25.1(c)(i). This is not a freezing injunction at all (*Fourie v Le Roux* [2007] 1 WLR 320). The key questions on such an application are whether there is sufficient evidence to establish that the property belongs to the claimant, and whether it is just to make the order. A proprietary claim may also be protected by an ordinary interim injunction, which will be granted on the usual *American Cyanamid Co v Ethicon Ltd* [1975] AC 396 principles (for which, see Chapter 35): *Polly Peck International plc v Nadir (No 2)* [1992] 4 All ER 769. 36.58

H WRIT *NE EXEAT REGNO*

The writ *ne exeat regno* prevents a person from leaving the jurisdiction. It originated in the thirteenth century as a prerogative writ, but was subsequently adapted by equity as a means of coercing a defendant to give bail on pain of arrest in cases where the defendant owed a debt that was equitable (so that the defendant was not liable under the old procedure of arrest on mesne process). It may be granted where the defendant may leave the jurisdiction to the 36.59

damage of a claimant to whom the defendant is indebted until he or she gives security for the debt. A good deal of caution is applied before the writ will be issued: *Allied Arab Bank Ltd v Hajjar* [1988] QB 787.

KEY POINTS SUMMARY

36.60

- Freezing injunctions are prohibitory injunctions preventing dishonest defendants from dissipating their assets to frustrate any judgment that might be obtained.
- There are exacting requirements on the application (see 36.08ff).
- The order operates against the defendant personally, and does not give the claimant any advantages in any insolvency.
- It is recognized that freezing injunctions could have a draconian effect, and numerous safeguards for the defendant and persons holding the defendant's assets are built into the standard order.
- Alerting the defendant could well result in the defendant taking steps to hide its assets, so freezing injunctions are invariably sought without notice, and the applicant is under a duty of full and frank disclosure.

37

SEARCH ORDERS

37.01 A search order is a bundle of interim orders which require the respondent to admit another party to premises for the purpose of preserving evidence which might otherwise be destroyed or concealed by the respondent (see CPR, r 25.1(1)(h)). Statutory authority for the jurisdiction is given by the Civil Procedure Act 1997, s 7. Prior to the introduction of the CPR this form of order was commonly known as an *Anton Piller* order, taking its name from *Anton Piller KG v Manufacturing Processes Ltd* [1976] Ch 55.

37.02 A search order is both injunctive and mandatory in nature. It requires the intended defendant to allow a named supervising solicitor from an independent firm, a partner from the claimant's own solicitors, and a limited number of additional people to enter on to the defendant's premises, and any vehicles in the defendant's control in the vicinity of those premises, so that they can search for, inspect, take photocopies of, and remove specified items and documents. The specified items and documents are those likely to be probative in the proceedings. The order will also often require the intended defendant to deliver up relevant documents not located at the premises searched, and to verify information on affidavit. The potential oppression inherent in such an order is recognized by the courts, and a search order is regarded as at the extremity of the court's powers. Although the jurisdiction to make search orders may be invoked in any type of claim, it is most frequently encountered in claims for infringement of intellectual property rights in the entertainment industry.

A PROCEDURE

37.03 Search orders are, by virtue of the County Court Remedies Regulations 1991 (SI 1991/1222 as amended by SI 1995/206), available:

(a) in the High Court, which is the usual venue. Intellectual property claims, which form the bulk of the cases where this type of application is likely to be made, are assigned to the Chancery Division;
(b) in the patents county court; and
(c) in a county court, provided the judge dealing with the application is a High Court or Court of Appeal judge. Otherwise the application must be made in the High Court (*Schmidt v Wong* [2006] 1 WLR 561).

37.04 Search orders are obtainable only against defendants who are likely to destroy relevant evidence if an application on notice were to be made (see 37.12–37.14). Consequently, secrecy is essential, so the application will be made without notice and the court will sit in private. Many applications are also urgent, and many are made before proceedings are issued. The general procedure for applications for interim injunctions applies, for which see 35.06–35.25. Essentially, the claimant must:

(a) have issued a claim form in respect of the substantive cause of action, unless the application is too urgent to wait for this to be done;
(b) issue an application notice in form N16A;
(c) provide affidavit evidence in support (witness statements are not acceptable: PD 25A, para 3.1);
(d) provide a draft order, together with a copy on disk; and
(e) provide a skeleton argument in support.

37.05 As the application is made without notice, the claimant has the usual duty of full and frank disclosure. The courts have insisted that this is especially important in applications for search orders, and the claimant should err on the side of excessive disclosure. The affidavit must state the name and experience of the proposed supervising solicitor, and give the name and address of his or her firm. The proposed supervising solicitor must be someone experienced in the operation of search orders (PD 25A, para 7.2) and must not be a member or employee of the claimant's solicitors (para 7.6). The affidavit must disclose in very full terms the reason for seeking the order, including the probability that relevant material will disappear if the order is not made (para 7.3).

37.06 It is very common to combine applications for search orders with other forms of urgent interim relief. It is not unknown, to use the old terminology, to 'pile *Piller* upon *Mareva*' in fraud and pirating claims.

B PRINCIPLES

Ormrod LJ in *Anton Piller KG v Manufacturing Processes Ltd* [1976] Ch 55 laid down the following preconditions for granting search orders: **37.07**

(a) There must be an extremely strong *prima facie* case on the merits. It is worth contrasting this with the requirement to merely show a good arguable case in applications for freezing orders.
(b) The defendant's activities must be proved to result in very serious potential or actual harm to the claimant's interests.
(c) There must be clear evidence that incriminating documents or materials are in the defendant's possession.
(d) There must be a real possibility that such items may be destroyed before any applications on notice can be made. This is considered at 37.12–37.14.

In the early 1980s it was thought that these conditions had been relaxed by *Yousif v Salama* [1980] 1 WLR 1540 and *Dunlop Holdings Ltd v Staravia Ltd* [1982] Com LR 3. In the former it was inferred that there was a real risk of the defendant disobeying any orders made on applications on notice from evidence that he had forged a signature on a cheque. In the latter, Oliver LJ said: **37.08**

> ...it has certainly become customary to infer the probability of disappearance or destruction of evidence where it is clearly established on the evidence before the court that the defendant is engaged in a nefarious activity which renders it likely that he is an untrustworthy person. It is seldom that one can get cogent or actual evidence of a threat to destroy material or documents.

The claimant's solicitors in *Columbia Picture Industries Inc v Robinson* [1987] Ch 38 had applied for some 300 search orders between 1974 and 1985, and none of their applications had been refused. **37.09**

Since *Booker McConnell plc v Plascow* [1985] RPC 425 there has been a marked change in judicial attitude, and nowadays the courts insist on strict compliance with the principles enunciated by Ormrod LJ in *Anton Piller KG v Manufacturing Processes Ltd*. The order is regarded as a serious stigma on the defendant's commercial reputation, and will often result in banks refusing further credit or even calling in loans. The order itself often allows the claimant's representatives to remove the defendant's stock-in-trade, and the net result is often to drive the defendant out of business. Accordingly, the order is regarded as a remedy of last resort, and should be made only 'when there is no alternative' (*per* Ormrod LJ in *Anton Piller KG v Manufacturing Processes Ltd*). As Dillon LJ explained in *Booker McConnell plc v Plascow*: **37.10**

> ...the courts have always proceeded, justifiably, on the basis that the overwhelming majority of people in this country will comply with the court's order, and that defendants will therefore comply with orders to, eg, produce and deliver up documents without it being necessary to empower the [claimants'] solicitors to search the defendant's premises.

Putting the matter slightly differently, Hoffmann J in *Lock International plc v Beswick* [1989] 1 WLR 1268 said at 1281: 'there must be *proportionality* between the perceived threat to the [claimant's] rights and the remedy granted'. Before embarking on an application for a search order, it is therefore necessary to consider whether some less draconian measure, such as applying on notice for negative injunctions or for an order that the documents be deliv- **37.11** ered up to the defendant's solicitor, or even awaiting disclosure in the usual way, would adequately protect the claimant.

C REAL RISK OF DESTRUCTION

37.12 A search order will not be made unless there is a 'real possibility' that material evidence will be destroyed if the defendant is given notice of an application for disclosure (*Anton Piller KG v Manufacturing Processes Ltd* [1976] Ch 55). This formula has been adopted in numerous cases since 1976. It is possible that the CPR have made a slight alteration in this requirement. PD 25A, para 7.3(2), referring to the evidence needed in support of an application for a search order, says it must cover 'the probability' that relevant material would disappear if the order were not made. There is a slight difference between a 'real possibility' and a 'probability', in that the latter expression means that the risk of destruction has to be proved on the balance of probabilities, whereas the earlier expression can be satisfied by evidence coming a little distance short of establishing the risk on the balance of probabilities. However, it is doubtful that para 7.3(2), which is a provision dealing with the evidence required in support of an application, can have been intended to alter the established conditions for the remedy.

37.13 The requirement to show that there is a real risk that the defendant will destroy vital evidence lies at the heart of the jurisdiction to grant search orders. Sometimes it is possible to infer this risk from the nature of the defendant's alleged conduct, for instance, in video pirating claims and commercial fraud actions. Even in these cases, however, the claimant is still obliged to give full and frank disclosure of anything known about the defendant, including past responsible conduct or other matters which tend to show the defendant would obey the court's orders.

37.14 Outside the area of actions based directly on dishonesty, it will be rare for the claimant to have evidence of a real risk of destruction. An example is *Lock International plc v Beswick* [1989] 1 WLR 1268, where the claimant alleged that the defendants, who were former employees now competing with the claimant, were making use of its trade secrets and confidential information. A search order was executed, and the defendants successfully applied to discharge the order. Hoffmann J said the claimant's evidence:

> ...came nowhere near [establishing]...a 'grave danger' or 'real possibility' that the defendants might destroy evidence...these defendants were no fly-by-night video pirates. They were former long-service employees with families and mortgages, who had openly said that they were entering into competition and whom the [claimant] knew to be financed by highly respectable institutions.

D FORM OF THE ORDER

37.15 A model form of search order is provided in the annex to PD 25A. This form should always be used, with only such modifications as are essential to fit the circumstances of the case. Any substantial variation from the form should be brought to the attention of the judge at the hearing.

The main provision is cl 6, which provides that the defendant 'must permit [certain people] to enter' the defendant's premises. The rest of clauses 1 to 21 are designed to give effect to the basic purpose of the order, which is to allow the claimant to enter the defendant's premises and to take documents which might be disclosable in the proceedings or otherwise relevant, while providing suitable safeguards for the defendant. These include the appointment of an independent supervising solicitor to ensure that the order is not misused by the claimant. Clause 22 may be used to set out prohibitory injunctions ancillary to the main part of the order. Schedule B sets out the items that may be seized, and must extend no further than the minimum necessary to preserve the evidence which might otherwise be concealed or destroyed: *Columbia Picture Industries Inc v Robinson* [1987] Ch 38. **37.16**

E PRACTICE ON EXECUTION OF SEARCH ORDERS

Service of the order

Since *Universal Thermosensors Ltd v Hibben* [1992] 1 WLR 840, execution of search orders has been effected by supervising solicitors who are independent of the claimant's usual solicitors. Before this case there was mounting concern about the execution of search orders by enthusiastic but inexperienced persons. Execution by a solicitor related to the claimant or by one of the claimant's directors was deprecated in *Manor Electronics Ltd v Dickson* [1988] RPC 618. **37.17**

The order must be served personally by the supervising solicitor, unless the court otherwise orders. Together with the order there must be served an application notice for a hearing on notice in respect of the search order. The affidavits in support and any exhibits capable of being copied must be served at the same time as the order (PD 25A, para 7.4(1)). Confidential exhibits need not be served, but they must be made available for inspection by the defendant in the presence of the claimant's solicitors while the order is being executed. Copies of confidential exhibits may be retained by the defendant's solicitors on their undertaking not to permit the defendant to see them except in their presence, nor to allow the defendant to make or take away any note or record of them (para 7.4(2)). Unless the court otherwise orders, service may be effected only between 9.30 a.m. and 5.30 p.m. Monday to Friday (para 7.4(6)). The reason for this is that the defendant is entitled to seek legal advice, and this will be effective only if the order is executed during office hours. It is recognized that mistakes (on both sides) are less likely to occur if these orders are executed during office hours (for a recent example, see *Adam Phones Ltd v Goldschmidt* [1999] 4 All ER 486). **37.18**

Planning is essential for effective execution. If several addresses are included in the order, it is important that execution is simultaneous. To reduce its oppressive effect the order will limit the number of persons who can assist with its execution at each address specified. Further, if the defendant is a woman living alone, a woman must accompany those executing the order (para 7.4(5)). The police will be informed beforehand if there is any prospect of a breach of the peace. **37.19**

Gaining access

A search order is not a search warrant, and does not authorize the use of force to gain access. **37.20**
In cases where the defendant has committed both a civil wrong against the claimant and a

criminal offence, a search order must not be executed at the same time as a police search warrant. Clause 6 of the standard search order is a mandatory order that the defendant 'must permit' access to the supervising solicitor. Before entering the supervising solicitor must explain the terms and effect of the order in everyday language. The supervising solicitor must inform the defendant that legal advice may be sought before entry is permitted and of the defendant's right to apply to vary or discharge the order, and that the defendant may be entitled to avail himself of legal professional privilege and the privilege against self-incrimination. A solicitor who negligently failed to explain the effect of the order to the defendant in a fair and accurate manner was held to be in contempt of court in *VDU Installations Ltd v Integrated Computer Systems and Cybernetics Ltd* [1989] FSR 378. The right to seek legal advice means that the obligation to give permission for entry arises only after a reasonable period of time has elapsed for legal advice to be obtained: *Bhimji v Chatwani* [1991] 1 WLR 989. Thereafter, the defendant must give permission, or else will be in contempt of court. Even if there are grounds for seeking an order for the immediate discharge of the search order, while it subsists it is an order of the court and must be obeyed: *Wardle Fabrics Ltd v G Myristis Ltd* [1984] FSR 263. However, if entry is refused and the order is successfully discharged shortly thereafter, that will give the court grounds for imposing no penalty on an application to commit for contempt of court. Matters to be taken into account include whether an application to discharge is merely a device to delay the search, and whether the defendant has interfered with the evidence during the delay: *Bhimji v Chatwani*.

Search and removal

37.21 There is a heavy duty on the solicitors to comply strictly with the terms of the order as to the premises which can be searched and the items which can be removed. The defendant's premises must not be searched, and no items may be removed, except in the presence of the defendant or a person who appears to be a responsible employee of the defendant (PD 25A, para 7.5(2)). If any of the items covered by the order exist only in computer-readable form, the defendant must immediately give the claimant's solicitors effective access, including any necessary passwords, and arrange for the material to be printed out. The claimant must take all reasonable steps to ensure that no damage is done to the defendant's computer system, and must ensure that the person searching the defendant's system has sufficient expertise to avoid causing damage (para 7.5(8) to (10)). Items seized must be recorded by the supervising solicitor in a list, and must be retained by the claimant's solicitors for the minimum time necessary to take copies and in any case for no more than two days, after which they must be returned to their owner (para 7.5(3) and (6)). Nothing should be removed until the defendant has had a reasonable opportunity to check it against the list (para 7.5(7)). Where ownership of the material seized is in dispute, the claimant's solicitors should place it in the custody of the defendant's solicitors pending trial on the defendant's solicitors undertaking to retain it in safekeeping and to produce it to the court when required (para 7.5(4)). It may be appropriate for the order to require the claimant to insure the materials seized (para 7.5(5)).

37.22 Execution of a search order in an excessive or oppressive manner will render the claimant liable under the undertaking in damages. Seizing documents not specified in the order may be penalized by an award of aggravated damages. An award of £10,000 against the claimant was made on this ground in *Columbia Picture Industries Inc v Robinson* [1987] Ch 38.

It is important that neither the claimant nor the claimant's employees are allowed to conduct searches for documents belonging to a trade competitor. Safeguards must be built into the order to protect the confidentiality of the defendant's trade secrets. 37.23

Additional powers and duties of the supervising solicitor

It may become apparent that it is impracticable to comply fully with the requirement that the defendant be allowed to check the claimant's list of materials before anything is removed from the premises, or the conditions for accessing material stored on computer. If the supervising solicitor is satisfied that compliance is impracticable, he or she may permit the search to proceed and for items to be removed without full compliance (PD 25A, para 7.5(13)). 37.24

Once the search has been completed, the supervising solicitor must provide the claimant's solicitors with a report on the carrying out of the order. The claimant's solicitors must then serve a copy on the defendant and file a copy with the court (PD 25A, para 7.5(11) and (12)). 37.25

Non-compliance by the defendant

In *Alliance and Leicester Building Society v Ghahremani* (1992) 142 NLJ 313 a search order was executed at the premises of a firm of solicitors. The order required the defendant solicitor to disclose 'documents' of various categories. There was evidence that the defendant erased information stored on computer while the order was being executed. Hoffmann J held that the word 'document' in the order was, in the light of the earlier decision of *Derby and Co Ltd v Weldon (No 9)* [1991] 1 WLR 652, wide enough to include information stored on computer, and that the defendant was guilty of contempt of court. It is probable that if the defendant had not been a lawyer the court would have held that the wording was insufficiently clear to found an application for committal. It is for this reason that the standard search order contains specific provision in cl 17 for printing out information stored on computer. In addition to being a contempt of court, 'the refusal to comply may be the most damning evidence against the defendant at the subsequent trial' (*per* Ormrod LJ in *Anton Piller KG v Manufacturing Processes Ltd* [1976] Ch 55). 37.26

On the other hand, a petty breach of a search order in circumstances where the defendant had honestly tried to obey it should be ignored by the parties. Under the CPR, given the emphasis on proportionality, an application to commit for no more than a technicality is likely to be dismissed with costs: *Adam Phones Ltd v Goldschmidt* [1999] 4 All ER 486. 37.27

F PRIVILEGE

Legal professional privilege and the privilege against self-incrimination were discussed at 29.26ff. The operation of the privilege against self-incrimination threatened to destroy the utility of search orders in intellectual property piracy claims, but this was averted by the 37.28

passing of the SCA 1981, s 72, and the other statutory provisions discussed at 29.33ff. These statutory provisions are wide-ranging, but do not completely remove the privilege against self-incrimination.

37.29 In cases of disputed privilege, the usual procedure is for the defendant to ask the supervising solicitor to assess whether the materials are privileged. If they are, they will be excluded from the search. If the supervising solicitor feels they may be privileged, the supervising solicitor excludes them from the search, but retains them pending further order from the court (cl 11 of the standard order).

G DISCHARGE AND VARIATION OF SEARCH ORDERS

37.30 Applications to discharge or vary search orders are largely governed by the principles already discussed in relation to freezing injunctions at 36.47–36.57. However, if a search order has been executed, there is a strong argument that it is an unjustified waste of costs and of the court's time to seek its discharge before trial. Doing so was said by Browne-Wilkinson V-C in *Dormeuil Frères SA v Nicolian International (Textiles) Ltd* [1988] 1 WLR 1362 to be little more than an empty gesture, and that the right course was normally to adjourn an application to set aside the order to be dealt with at trial. In *Tate Access Floors Inc v Boswell* [1991] Ch 512 it was recognized there is a conflict between the public interest in ensuring that applications made without notice are made in good faith, and the public interest in ensuring that the courts are not clogged up with long interim hearings. The Vice-Chancellor suggested the solution may be that the circumstances in which an order without notice was obtained should be investigated at the pre-trial stage only if it is clear there has been a material non-disclosure or where the nature of the alleged non-disclosure is so serious as to demand immediate investigation. Where a search order has been executed at the defendant's home, the court should allow the defendant a hearing on an application to discharge the search order unless there is not even a *prima facie* case of abuse (*Indicil Salus Ltd v Chandrasekaran* (2006) LTL 16/2/06).

37.31 Further, it is sometimes argued that, even if the original order was granted on insufficient grounds, the fruits of the search may indicate that justice was done in the event. Such an argument was rejected in *Manor Electronics Ltd v Dickson* [1988] RPC 618 in the face of a clear material non-disclosure.

37.32 The court has a discretion to exclude documents seized under a search order which is subsequently discharged (CPR, r 32.1). The discretion is exercised in accordance with the overriding objective. Key factors are the importance of the documents, and the reasons why the search order was discharged.

37.33 One of the defendants in *Coca-Cola Co v Gilbey* [1995] 4 All ER 711 argued that he should not be required to disclose the identities of other persons involved with him in a highly organized passing-off operation, and other information, as required by a search order, on the ground that doing so might expose him and his family to physical violence from those other persons. It was held that, although violence or threats of violence would be legitimate grounds if put forward by innocent parties, when put forward by actual participants, public policy and the interests of the victim carried more weight, and disclosure was ordered forthwith.

H AFTER EXECUTION

After executing the order, the supervising solicitor is required to compile a report of what happened (see 37.24–37.25). The report is served on the defendant. Clause 3 of the standard search order provides that there will be a further hearing on notice to the defendants on a specified date (called the return date), which is usually a few days after the date of the original order. The applicant's solicitors are required (Sch D, para 1(iii)) to provide the supervising solicitor with an application notice for hearing on the return date, which is served with the search order. **37.34**

On the return date the court will consider the supervising solicitor's report and the defendant may apply to discharge the order. Once a search order has been executed, there is an enhanced duty on the claimant to prosecute the main claim without delay. In *Hytrac Conveyors Ltd v Conveyors International Ltd* [1983] 1 WLR 44, the claimant delayed for ten weeks after obtaining a search order without serving a statement of claim. The claim was dismissed, Lawton LJ saying that claimants 'must not use [search] orders as a means of finding out what sort of charges they could make'. **37.35**

If the application was made in the High Court, but is otherwise more suitable for the county court, after the application for the search order has been disposed of the claim will be transferred down to the county court (County Court Remedies Regulations 1991 (SI 1991/1222), reg 5). The application is not treated as disposed of until any application to set the order aside has been heard, or until the expiry of 28 days during which no such application is made. **37.36**

I COLLATERAL USE

As with other forms of disclosure (see 29.78–29.80), the claimant gives an undertaking not to use items seized under a search order for any collateral purposes (Sch C, para 4, to the standard search order). The court may sanction a relaxation of this undertaking in a proper case. The leading case is *Crest Homes plc v Marks* [1987] AC 829. In 1984 the claimant brought a claim against the defendant seeking injunctions to restrain breach of copyright in certain house designs. In the course of those proceedings a search order was obtained and executed. In 1985 the claimant commenced a second copyright claim against the defendant in relation to another house design, and obtained and executed a second search order. Some of the documents seized under the second search order were alleged by the claimant to show the defendant had not given full disclosure under the first search order. The claimant therefore sought to use those documents in contempt proceedings in relation to the first search order. The House of Lords held that, although there were technically two separate claims, in substance they were a single set of proceedings. As the defendant would suffer no injustice by **37.37** lifting the implied undertaking, permission was given to allow the claimant to use the documents in the contempt proceedings.

KEY POINTS SUMMARY

37.38
- Search orders are principally, but not exclusively, used in intellectual property claims against defendants who are likely to destroy incriminating evidence rather than disclose it voluntarily under standard disclosure.
- There are exacting requirements: see 37.07–37.14.
- A search order is a bundle of interim orders which require the defendant to permit entry to the claimant's solicitors for the purpose of searching for and taking away relevant evidence.
- It is recognized that these orders can be draconian, and various safeguards are built into the standard-form orders, including requirements that there should be an experienced supervising solicitor present during the search, and that the search should take place during office hours so that the defendant can obtain legal advice.

38

LISTING AND PRE-TRIAL REVIEWS

A LISTING FOR TRIAL

Claims that are not compromised and which do not end through striking out or summary or default judgment, have to be determined by the court at trial. Listing is the process whereby the court gives a date for the trial. Two main methods are used: **38.01**

(a) Giving a fixed trial date. This is often given many months before the date allocated.
(b) Giving a trial window of a defined period, usually between one and three weeks, during which the trial will start. If this method is used, the parties find out the actual date for the trial only shortly before it starts: it is not unknown for less than 24 hours' notice to be given, although the courts usually aim to give as much notice as possible.

Listing on the different tracks

In small claims track cases, a date for the hearing is usually fixed when the court gives standard directions at about the time the case is allocated to this track (see 25.04). **38.02**

In fast track claims there is a commitment to have trials heard within 30 weeks of allocation (see 26.11). Fixtures and trial windows are used as may be appropriate, and are usually given as part of the directions laid down on allocation. The detailed procedure on listing for trial in fast track claims was described at 26.17. **38.03**

In multi-track claims there is a requirement that the trial date or window must be set by the court as soon as practicable (CPR, r 29.2(2): see 27.19). This may be at the first case management conference, but will often be at some later stage. The detailed procedure was described at 27.23–27.27. **38.04**

38.05 In the Admiralty and Commercial Courts most cases are given fixed trial dates after the pre-trial timetable is set at the case management conference (*Commercial Court Guide*, para D16.1).

Pre-trial checklists

38.06 In fast track claims, about ten weeks before the expected trial date the court will send pre-trial checklists to the parties, which have to be returned within about two weeks. In multi-track claims the dates for dispatch and return of pre-trial checklists will be set by directions given by the court either of its own motion or at a case management hearing, and are normally set for the period shortly after the exchange of evidence has been completed. Pre-trial checklists in non-specialist claims are in form N170, and an example is given in figure 38.1. In Commercial Court cases parties must use the form in the *Commercial Court Guide*, app 13. These forms are used by the court to check:

(a) that directions have indeed been complied with;
(b) whether any complications have arisen;
(c) whether any further directions should be given; and
(d) whether the trial date or window can be kept.

Claimants are required to pay listing and hearing fees when returning the pre-trial checklist.

B PRE-TRIAL REVIEWS

38.07 Pre-trial reviews were discussed at 27.28–27.35 and 27.39–27.41, and are mainly used in multi-track cases. They tend to be conducted by the trial judge, and are usually held some weeks before the intended start of the trial. Their main purpose is to set a trial timetable (see 26.20) and to ensure that everything is prepared so the trial can proceed at the set date without any problems or delays.

C LISTING IN THE ROYAL COURTS OF JUSTICE

38.08 In non-specialist cases in the Queen's Bench and Chancery Divisions proceeding in the Royal Courts of Justice in London, a direction will be given as early as possible (often the first case management conference) with a view to fixing the trial or trial window. It will often direct that the trial is not to begin before a specified date, or that it will be held within a specified period. The claimant must then, within the next seven days, take out an appointment with the Listing Officer and give notice of the appointment to the other parties. At the listing hearing the claimant must bring any case summary, the particulars of claim, and any orders relevant to listing, and all parties must have details of the dates of availability of their witnesses, experts, and counsel. The Listing Officer will try to provide the earliest firm trial date or trial window consistent with the case management directions (*Queen's Bench Guide*, paras 9.4.5 to 9.4.8 and *Chancery Guide*, paras 6.7 to 6.9).

Figure 38.1 Form N170 Pre-trial checklist

Listing questionnaire (Pre-trial checklist)

In the	Northampton County Court
Claim No.	NN 982645
Last date for filing with court office	
Date(s) fixed for trial or trial period	

To be completed by, or on behalf of,

Phillippa May Myers

who is ~~[1st][2nd][3rd]~~[ ][Claimant]~~[Defendant]~~ ~~[Part 20 claimant][Part 20 defendant]~~ in this claim

This form must be **completed** and **returned** to the court no later than the date given above. If not, your statement of case may be struck out or some other sanction imposed.

If the claim has settled, or settles before the trial date, you must let the court know immediately.

Legal representatives only: You must **attach** estimates of costs incurred to date, and of your likely overall costs. In substantial cases, these should be provided in compliance with CPR Part 43.

For multi-track claims only, you must also **attach** a proposed timetable for the trial itself.

A Confirmation of compliance with directions

1. I confirm that I have complied with those directions already given which require action by me. ☑Yes ☐No

   If you are unable to give confirmation, state which directions you have still to comply with and the date by which this will be done.

Directions	Date

2. I believe that additional directions are necessary before the trial takes place. ☑Yes ☐No

   If Yes, you should attach an application and a draft order.

   Include in your application all directions needed to enable the claim ***to be tried on the date, or within the trial period, already fixed.*** *These should include any issues relating to experts and their evidence, and any orders needed in respect of directions still requiring action by any other party.*

3. Have you agreed the additional directions you are seeking with the other party(ies)? ☐Yes ☑No

B Witnesses

1. How many witnesses (including yourself) will be giving evidence on your behalf at the trial? *(Do not include experts - see Section C)* 2

Continued over

N170 Listing questionnaire (Pre-trial checklist) (12.02) *Printed on behalf of The Court Service* 1 of 3

Figure 38.1 *continued*

Witnesses continued

2. If the trial date is not yet fixed, are there any days within the trial period you or your witnesses would wish to avoid if possible? *(Do not include experts—see Section C)*

Please give details

Name of witness	Dates to be avoided, if possible	Reason
Mr. Alan Myers	See letter attached	

Please specify any special facilities or arrangements needed at court for the party or any witness (e.g. witness with a disability).

3. Will you be providing an interpreter for any of your witnesses? ☐ Yes ☐ No

C Experts

You are reminded that you may not use an expert's report or have your expert give oral evidence unless the court has given permission. If you do not have permission, you must make an application (see section A2 above)

1. Please give the information requested for your expert(s)

Name	Field of expertise	Joint expert?	Is report agreed?	Has permission been given for oral evidence?
Mr. S. Long	Orthopaedic	☑ Yes ☐ No	☑ Yes ☐ No	☐ Yes ☑ No
Miss J. Pearson	Neurology	☐ Yes ☑ No	☐ Yes ☑ No	☐ Yes ☑ No
		☐ Yes ☐ No	☐ Yes ☐ No	☐ Yes ☐ No

2. Has there been discussion between experts? ☐ Yes ☑ No

3. Have the experts signed a joint statement? ☐ Yes ☑ No

4. If your expert is giving oral evidence and the trial date is not yet fixed, is there any day within the trial period which the expert would wish to avoid, if possible? ☑ Yes ☐ No

If Yes, please give details

Name	Dates to be avoided, if possible	Reason
Miss J. Pearson	See attached list	Professional engagements

2 of 3

Figure 38.1 *continued*

D Legal representation

1. Who will be presenting your case at the trial? ☐ You ☐ Solicitor ☑ Counsel

2. If the trial date is not yet fixed, is there any day within the trial period that the person presenting your case would wish to avoid, if possible? ☑ Yes ☐ No

If Yes, please give details

Name	Dates to be avoided, if possible	Reason
Ms. L. Winter	See attached list	Professional engagements

E The trial

1. Has the estimate of the time needed for trial changed? ☑ Yes ☐ No

If Yes, say how long you estimate the whole trial will take, including both parties' cross-examination and closing arguments 2 days 0 hours 0 minutes

2. If different from original estimate have you agreed with the other party(ies) that this is now the **total** time needed? ☐ Yes ☑ No

3. Is the timetable for trial you have attached agreed with the other party(ies)? ☐ Yes ☑ No

Fast track cases only

The court will normally give you 3 weeks notice of the date fixed for a fast track trial unless, in exceptional circumstances, the court directs that shorter notice will be given.

Would you be prepared to accept shorter notice of the date fixed for trial? ☐ Yes ☐ No

F Document and fee checklist

Tick as appropriate

I attach to this questionnaire—

☑ An application and fee for additional directions

☑ A proposed timetable for trial

☑ A draft order

☑ An estimate of costs

☑ Listing fee

Signed

~~[Counsel]~~[Solicitor][for the]~~[1st][2nd][3rd]~~[ ]
[Claimant]~~[Defendant]~~
~~[Part 20 claimant][Part 20 defendant]~~

Date

Please enter your [firm's] name, reference number and full postal address including (if appropriate) details of DX, fax or e-mail

Smallwood & Co.,
4 Market Place,
Corby,
Northamptonshire
Postcode NN17 6AL

Tel. no.	01562 384110	DX no.	87456 Corby	E-mail	
Fax no.	01562 384572	Ref. no.	PMM		

3 of 3

D ADJOURNMENTS

38.09 There is a general power to adjourn hearings (CPR, r 3.1(2))(b)). Adjournments are usually granted where the need to adjourn arises through events outside the control of the parties, such as witnesses being unavailable or other practical impossibility in meeting a trial date. In *Bates v Croydon London Borough Council* (2001) LTL 23/1/01, an adjournment should have been given as the appellant was awaiting a determination of an application for legal aid, and she had been served with the respondents' witness statements and other documents very shortly before the hearing. However, where the need to adjourn is caused by a failure to prepare for the trial, usually the court will refuse to adjourn. This is emphasized by PD 28, para 5.4 (fast track) and PD 29, para 7.4 (multi-track), which require exceptional circumstances before the court will vacate a trial date on account of a failure to comply with directions. Not applying to adjourn until the day of the trial where a party has known for many weeks that it is in difficulties may be a sufficient reason to refuse an adjournment (*National Westminster Bank plc v Aaronson* (2004) LTL 9/3/04).

39

TRIAL

Trials are primarily intended finally to determine the dispute between the parties by a judgment of the court. Most of the procedures described in this book are designed to ensure that both sides are fully prepared in advance of the hearing so that justice can be done between both sides efficiently and without wasting costs. Nevertheless, only a tiny fraction of the claims commenced reach trial. Many of the procedures laid down by the CPR are also intended to encourage the parties to resolve their differences by settling. Further, the expense of the trial itself is a great incentive to settling, and a great many cases are compromised in the run-up to the trial, or even at the door of the court. **39.01**

39.02 A number of things must be done in the period leading up to a trial. These include warning the witnesses and ensuring that any reluctant witnesses are served with witness summonses. Trial bundles need to be prepared. Counsel may need to be briefed, and skeleton arguments, case summaries, and reading lists prepared. The rules give the courts a great deal of flexibility regarding how they will deal with trials. As discussed in Chapters 26 and 27, the court can lay down trial timetables prescribing how the time available for the trial will be used, and allocating specified, limited times for examination-in-chief, cross-examination, and so on. Another power available to the court is to direct that one or more issues should be dealt with before the others as preliminary issues. Most civil claims are heard by judges sitting alone, but libel and some other cases may be tried by juries.

A WITNESSES

Witness summonses

39.03 Reluctant witnesses may be compelled to attend trial by serving them with a witness summons. An example of such a summons is shown in figure 39.1. A witness summons may require the named witness simply to attend to give oral evidence, or to produce specified documents, or both. A witness summons to produce documents is not a form of disclosure in the sense of disclosure between parties, and is limited to the production of documents relevant to the substantive issues in the claim. Consequently, a witness cannot be summoned to produce train-of-inquiry documents: *Macmillan Inc v Bishopsgate Investment Trust plc* [1993] 1 WLR 1372. The documents to be produced must be sufficiently described, although classes of documents may be described compendiously: *Panayiotou v Sony Music Entertainment (UK) Ltd* [1994] Ch 142. A witness summons may require the witness to produce documents either at the trial or on such other date as the court may direct (CPR, r 34.2(4)(b)), which may be some time before the trial so as to enable the parties to take stock after receipt of the documents.

39.04 Issuing a witness summons is purely administrative. The form must be completed, a fee is paid, and the form is sealed by the court. Unless the court gives permission, a witness summons will be binding on the witness only if it is served at least seven days before the trial (r 34.5). A person served with a witness summons must also be offered a sum of money (known as conduct money) to cover travelling expenses to and from the court and compensation for loss of time (r 34.7).

39.05 The court may set aside or vary a witness summons (CPR, r 34.3(4)), and may do so if it appears that the person summoned is unable to give relevant evidence, or if there is some other strong reason for not requiring his or her attendance at the trial. A judge acting in his judicial capacity, even if able to give relevant evidence, is not a compellable witness: *Warren v Warren* [1997] QB 488.

Evidence by deposition

39.06 Where it appears to be necessary in the interests of justice to do so, the court may order a witness's evidence to be given by deposition (CPR, r 34.8). This power is usually exercised

Figure 39.1 Witness summons

Witness Summons

In the	Northampton County Court
Claim No.	NN 982645
Claimant (including ref)	Phillippa May Myers
Defendant (including ref)	Nigel James Staniforth
Issued on	

To

Jennifer Gilbert
48 Jesmond Road,
Northampton,
Northants,
NN5 9DH

You are summoned to attend at *(court address)* 85-87 Lady's Lane, Northampton, Northants, NN1 3HQ

on Monday 16 of January at 10.30 (am)(pm)

(and each following day of the hearing until the court tells you that you are no longer required.)

☑ to give evidence in respect of the above claim

☐ to produce the following document(s) *(give details)*

The sum of £ 63.75 is paid or offered to you with this summons. This is to cover your travelling expenses to and from court and includes an amount by way of compensation for loss of time.

This summons was issued on the application of the claimant (defendant) or the claimant's (defendant's) solicitor whose name, address and reference number is:

Smallwood & Co., 4 Market Place, Corby, Northants., NN17 6AL

Do not ignore this summons

If you were offered money for travel expenses and compensation for loss of time, at the time it was served on you, you must –

- attend court on the date and time shown and/or produce documents as required by the summons; and
- take an oath or affirm as required for the purposes of answering questions about your evidence or the documents you have been asked to produce.

If you do not comply with this summons you will be liable, in county court proceedings, to a fine. In the High Court, disobedience of a witness summons is a contempt of court and you may be fined or imprisoned for contempt. You may also be liable to pay any wasted costs that arise because of your non-compliance.

If you wish to set aside or vary this witness summons, you may make an application to the court that issued it.

The court office at 85-87 Lady's Lane, Northampton, Northants., NN1 3HQ

is open between 10 am and 4 pm Monday to Friday. When corresponding with the court, please address forms or letters to the Court Manager and quote the claim number.

where witnesses are over 70 years of age, or too infirm to give evidence, or intend to leave the country before trial. The order will provide for the witness's evidence to be taken before a judge, officer, or examiner of the court. It may provide for the examination to be taken at any place, including the witness's bedside, and may provide for the production of any documents that appear to be necessary for the examination. The witness is examined and cross-examined in the usual way, and the evidence is reduced into writing in the form of a deposition and signed by the witness. The examiner may write a report on events at the examination.

39.07 A party intending to use a deposition at trial must give other parties notice of that intention at least 21 days in advance of trial (CPR, r 34.11).

Letters of request

39.08 The evidence of witnesses already outside the jurisdiction may be obtained by the High Court on its own behalf or on behalf of a county court (see CPR, rr 34.13 to 34.24) by:

(a) the issue of letters of request to the judicial authorities of the country in question. The evidence may be given either orally or in answer to written questions. Where the witness is in an EU State (other than Denmark), the request must comply with the requirements of Council Regulation (EC) No 1206/2001; or
(b) examination before the British consular authority in the relevant country.

39.09 It was held in *Panayiotou v Sony Music Entertainment (UK) Ltd* [1994] Ch 142 that a letter of request may be confined to the production of documents in the possession of the witness outside the jurisdiction. The documents that may be required to be produced have to be identified, and must be restricted to documents which could have been the subject of a witness summons. In other words, this is not a procedure for obtaining disclosure of documents against the witness, but for obtaining admissible evidence on the issues in the claim.

Video links

39.10 The court has power under CPR, r 32.3, to allow a party to adduce the evidence of a witness by a live video link. This facility is regarded as being readily available to all litigants. In *Polanski v Condé Nast Publications Ltd* [2005] 1 WLR 637 a video-conferencing order was made to enable a fugitive to give evidence from outside the country without the risk of being extradited to the United States. Practical guidance is given by PD 32, Annex 3. A party obtaining permission to adduce evidence in this way will have to make the necessary practical arrangements.

Adjourning to bedside

39.11 The court has inherent power to adjourn trial to the bedside of an infirm witness: *St Edmundsbury and Ipswich Diocesan Board of Finance v Clark* [1973] Ch 323.

B TRIAL DOCUMENTATION

Trial bundles

All the documents likely to be referred to at fast track and multi-track trials should be placed into paginated files called trial bundles. Identical bundles should be made available for each of the parties, the judge, and a further set for use by the witnesses while giving evidence. This assists in ensuring that everyone is considering the same document at any one time, and avoids delays during the trial when documents are referred to. Poorly prepared bundles are perhaps the greatest source of complaint from judges. **39.12**

Trial bundles should be filed by the claimant not more than seven and not less than three days before the start of the trial (CPR, r 39.5(2)). The responsibility for preparation of the trial bundles rests with the legal representative of the claimant. PD 39A, para 3, lays down detailed rules for trial bundles. Unless the court otherwise orders, the trial bundle should include: **39.13**

(a) the claim form and all statements of case;
(b) a case summary and/or a chronology where appropriate;
(c) requests for further information and responses to the requests;
(d) all witness statements to be relied on as evidence;
(e) any witness summaries;
(f) any notices of intention to rely on hearsay evidence under r 33.2;
(g) any notices of intention to rely on evidence (such as a plan, photograph, etc.) under r 33.6 which is not:
    (i) contained in a witness statement, affidavit, or expert's report,
    (ii) being given orally at trial,
    (iii) hearsay evidence under r 33.2;
(h) any medical reports and responses to them;
(i) any experts' reports and responses to them;
(j) any order giving directions as to the conduct of the trial; and
(k) any other necessary documents.

The trial bundle should normally be contained in ring-binders or lever arch files. It should be paginated continuously throughout, and indexed with a description of each document and the page number. If any document is illegible a typed copy should be provided and given an 'A' number. The contents of the bundles should be agreed if possible. If there is any disagreement, a summary of the points in dispute should be included. Bundles exceeding 100 pages should have numbered dividers. Where a number of files are needed, each file should be numbered or distinguishable by different colours. If there is a lot of documentation a core bundle should also be prepared containing the most essential documents, and it should be cross-referenced to the supplementary documents in the other files. Identical bundles with the same colour-coded files have to be supplied to all the parties plus the bundle for the court and a further one for the use of the witnesses at the trial. See 34.20 on the admissibility of documents in agreed bundles. **39.14**

Reading lists

39.15 In all QBD and ChD claims where trial bundles must be lodged, the claimant or applicant must at the same time lodge:

(a) a reading list for the judge who will conduct the hearing;
(b) an estimated length of reading time; and
(c) an estimated length for the hearing.

39.16 This must be signed by all the advocates who will appear at the hearing. Each advocate's name, business address, and telephone number must appear below his or her signature. In the event of disagreement about any of these matters, separate reading lists and estimates must be signed by the appropriate advocates. See *Practice Direction (RCJ: Reading Lists and Time Estimates)* [2000] 1 WLR 208. In addition to the trial bundles the trial judge has a discretion about what other material to read by way of pre-trial preparation, and may read material containing inadmissible evidence: *Barings plc v Coopers and Lybrand* [2001] CPLR 451.

Case summaries

39.17 In a case of any size it is essential that a case summary should be prepared. This should be a short, non-contentious, summary of the issues in the case and of relevant procedural matters. If possible it should be agreed by all parties.

Skeleton arguments and authorities

39.18 Skeleton arguments are compulsory for High Court trials, and sometimes are required by directions in the county court. Trial skeletons are similar in concept to those used for interim applications (see 20.40–20.43), concisely summarizing the submissions to be made in relation to the issues raised and citing the authorities to be relied upon. They should be filed two days before the trial (QBD) or with the trial bundles (ChD). It is often useful to provide a short chronology of the important events.

39.19 In the Queen's Bench Division, lists of authorities must be provided to the court by 9 a.m. on the day of the hearing so the reports can be brought into court in advance of the hearing. In all cases lists of authorities should, as a matter of professional etiquette, be provided to the other side in good time before the hearing.

39.20 If an extract from *Hansard* is to be used in accordance with the principles in *Pepper v Hart* [1993] AC 593 as refined by *Wilson v First County Trust (No 2)* [2004] 1 AC 816, copies should be served on the other parties and the court, together with a brief summary of the argument based on the extract, five working days before the hearing: *Practice Direction (Hansard: Citations)* [1995] 1 WLR 192.

39.21 If it is necessary to rely on an authority referred to in the Human Rights Act 1998, s 2, the authority cited should be an authoritative and complete report, and copies must be served and filed not less than three days before the hearing (PD 39A, para 8.1).

C TRIAL LOCATION

Normally trials will take place at the court where the case has been proceeding, but it may be transferred to another court for trial if this is appropriate having regard to the convenience of the parties and the availability of court resources (PD 28, para 8.1, for the fast track; PD 29, para 10.1, for cases on the multi-track). Multi-track cases will generally have been transferred to Civil Trial Centres when allocated to the multi-track (if commenced in a feeder court), but they may be allowed to proceed elsewhere if that is appropriate given the needs of the parties and the availability of court resources. **39.22**

D ALLOCATION TO JUDICIARY

District judges can deal with all small claims and fast track cases, so effectively their trial jurisdiction is £25,000 (PD 2B, para 11.1). District judges may also hear most Part 8 claims automatically treated as allocated to the multi-track, certain landlord and tenant cases, assessments of damages, and cases allocated to a district judge with the permission of the Designated Civil Judge (para 11.1). Injunction and committal applications may be heard by a district judge only if the claim has been allocated to the fast or small claims tracks; or if the value is below £25,000 (in cases that have not been allocated at the time of the application); or if the terms have been agreed by the parties; or if the injunction is connected to a charging order or receivership order by way of equitable execution. **39.23**

Most multi-track cases will be tried by High Court judges and, in the county courts, by circuit judges and recorders. Cases (other than Part 8 claims) on the multi-track may be tried by a master or district judge only with the consent of the parties (PD 2B, para 4.1). Hearings to assess damages may be dealt with by masters and district judges without limit (para 4.2), although complex assessments should be dealt with by judges: *Sandry v Jones* (2000) *The Times*, 3 August 2000. **39.24**

E IMPARTIALITY OF JUDGE

It has long been established that a judge must not sit in his or her own cause. The rule laid down in *Dimes v Proprietors of Grand Junction Canal* (1852) 3 HL Cas 759 by Lord Campbell is now interpreted as not being confined to a claim in which the judge is a party, but applies also to a claim in which the outcome could, realistically, affect an interest of the judge. In *R v Bow Street Metropolitan Stipendiary Magistrate, ex p Pinochet Ugarte (No 2)* [2000] 1 AC 119 the House of Lords held that the principle that a judge is automatically disqualified from hearing a matter in his or her own cause is not limited to cases where the judge has a pecuniary interest in the outcome, but applies also to cases where the judge's decision would lead to the promotion of a cause in which the judge was involved together with one of the parties. The automatic disqualification rule is subject to the *de minimis* principle, in that some supposed financial interests are so small they can be ignored: *Locabail (UK) Ltd v Bayfield Properties Ltd* [2000] QB 451. **39.25**

39.26 Under art 6(1) of the European Convention on Human Rights, litigants are entitled to a fair hearing before an impartial tribunal, so a judge will also be unable to sit if there is an appearance of bias. According to *Porter v Magill* [2002] 2 AC 357 and *Taylor v Lawrence* [2003] QB 528, the court must first ascertain all the circumstances which have a bearing on the suggestion that the judge is biased. The court must then ask whether those circumstances would lead a fair-minded and informed observer to conclude that there was a real possibility that the judge was biased. Where the judge's explanation was not accepted by the party making the suggestion of bias (or apparent bias), that also had to be considered from the viewpoint of the fair-minded observer.

39.27 Guidance on situations where there may be a real danger of bias was given by the Court of Appeal in *Locabail (UK) Ltd v Bayfield Properties Ltd*, which is of particular relevance to cases dealt with by solicitor and barrister deputy judges. The Court of Appeal could not conceive of circumstances in which an objection could be soundly based on the religion, ethnic or national origin, gender, age, class, means, or sexual orientation of the judge. Nor, at least ordinarily, could there be a valid objection based on the judge's social, educational, service, or employment background, nor that of any member of his or her family. Nor could an objection be based on previous political associations, membership of social, sporting, or charitable bodies, or Masonic associations; previous judicial decisions; extra-curial utterances, whether in textbooks, lectures, speeches, articles, interviews, reports, or responses to consultation papers; previous receipt of instructions to act for or against any party, solicitor, or advocate engaged in the current case; or membership of the same Inn, circuit, local Law Society, or chambers.

39.28 By contrast, there might be a real danger of bias if there was personal friendship or animosity between the judge and anyone other than the lawyers involved in the present case; or if the judge was closely acquainted with a witness whose credibility was in issue; or if the judge had ruled against the credibility of a witness in a previous case in outspoken terms such as to cast doubt on whether the judge could deal with the witness in the current case with an open mind (but not if the judge had commented adversely on a party or witness in a previous case in temperate terms); or if the judge had expressed views on a matter also in issue in the present case in such extreme terms as to throw into doubt his or her ability to try the case objectively. If there is any doubt, it should be exercised in favour of refusing to sit. Judges are obliged to mention any possible conflict when they become aware of its existence. Wherever possible this is done in advance of the commencement of the trial, and any objection based on apparent bias must be made when it arises, rather than awaiting the result of the hearing (*Steadman-Byrne v Amjad* [2007] 1 WLR 2484).

39.29 Where proceedings are abandoned because of the appearance of bias on the part of a member of the court, the Lord Chancellor is not liable for any of the costs incurred at the wasted hearing: *Re Medicaments and Related Classes of Goods (No 4)* [2002] 1 WLR 269.

F PUBLIC OR PRIVATE HEARING

39.30 Under art 6(1) of the European Convention on Human Rights parties have a right to a public hearing. The general rule therefore is that trials will be conducted in public (CPR, r 39.2(1)). The general rule does not, however, impose an obligation to make special arrangements for accommodating members of the public. By way of exception to the general rule, r 39.2(3) provides that a hearing may be conducted in private if:

(a) publicity would defeat the object of the hearing;
(b) it involves matters relating to national security;
(c) it involves confidential information (including information relating to personal financial matters) and publicity would damage that confidentiality;
(d) a private hearing is necessary to protect the interests of any child or patient;
(e) it is a hearing of an application made without notice and it would be unjust to any respondent for there to be a public hearing;
(f) it involves uncontentious matters arising in the administration of trusts or in the administration of a deceased's estate; or
(g) the court considers a private hearing to be necessary, in the interests of justice.

Further, the court may order that the identity of any party or witness must not be disclosed if it considers non-disclosure necessary in order to protect the interests of that party or witness (r 39.2(4)). **39.31**

G RIGHTS OF AUDIENCE AND THE RIGHT TO CONDUCT LITIGATION

Rights of audience and the right to conduct litigation are reserved legal activities within the meaning of the Legal Services Act 2007 (s 12 and Sch 2). A person is only entitled to carry on these activities if they are a regulated person authorized to do so by an approved regulator or if they are exempt in relation to the relevant activity (ss 13 and 176). Approved regulators include the Law Society, the General Council of the Bar, the Institute of Legal Executives, the Council for Licensed Conveyancers, and the Association of Law Costs Draftsmen (Sch 4). These provisions ensure that persons with general rights of audience or to conduct litigation have to comply with the regulatory requirements of their approved regulator (s 176(1)). Any such person has a duty to the court to act with independence and in the interests of justice (s 188(2)). **39.32**

This means the following persons have rights of audience: **39.33**

(a) litigants in person (who are exempt, Sch 3, para 1(6));
(b) counsel (all courts);
(c) solicitors (all solicitors have rights of audience in the county courts. To exercise rights of audience in the High Court a solicitor needs a Law Society higher rights of audience qualification);
(d) members of the Institute of Legal Executives (county courts, for members with ILEX civil proceedings certificate);
(e) members of the Association of Law Costs Draftsmen (costs proceedings, with certification by the Association);
(f) persons given express permission by the court in relation to the relevant proceedings (who are exempt, Sch 3, para 1(2)); and

(g) persons given an express right of audience by statute (an example being the right given to local authority officers to present rent and possession claims on behalf of their employers under the County Courts Act 1984, s 60).

39.34 Rule 39.6 of the CPR provides that a company or corporation may appear at a hearing through a duly authorized employee provided the court gives permission. PD 39A, para 5.3, says that permission should usually be given unless there is some particular and sufficient reason why it should be withheld. Permission should generally be sought on an occasion prior to the hearing, but may be granted at the hearing itself.

H MCKENZIE FRIENDS

39.35 A McKenzie friend ('MF', from *McKenzie v McKenzie* [1971] P 33), is an unqualified person who assists a litigant who would otherwise be acting in person. The primary function of a MF is to provide moral support for a litigant at a hearing. A MF is not permitted to conduct litigation or act as an advocate without the court's permission.

39.36 *Practice Note (Family Courts: McKenzie Friends) (No 2)* [2008] 1 WLR 2757 sets out guidance based on the statutory provisions governing rights of audience (now in the Legal Services Act 2007), and various decisions of the courts (particularly *Re D (A Child)* [2005] EWCA Civ 347). This provides that a MF may:

(a) provide moral support for the litigant;
(b) take notes;
(c) help with case papers; and
(d) quietly give advice on points of law or procedure, issues the litigant may wish to raise in court, and questions the litigant may wish to ask witnesses. The litigant is permitted to communicate any information, including filed evidence, to the MF for these purposes.

39.37 Limitations on what MFs are permitted to do set out in the guidance are:

(a) a MF has no right to act on behalf of a litigant. It is the right of the litigant who wishes to do so to have the assistance of a MF;
(b) a MF has no right to address the court, or examine witnesses. Any person doing these is an advocate, and requires the grant of a right of audience. An application that a MF be permitted a right of audience must be made at the start of the hearing (*Clarkson v Gilbert* [2000] 2 FLR 839). An important factor is whether a right of audience is required to ensure the litigant receives a fair hearing (*Re N (A Child) (McKenzie Friend: Rights of Audience)* [2008] 1 WLR 2743); and
(c) a MF may not act as the litigant's agent in relation to the proceedings, nor manage the litigant's case outside court, such as by signing court documents.

I CONDUCT OF THE TRIAL

Before the hearing the court should be provided with a written statement of the name and professional address of each advocate, his or her qualification as an advocate, and the party he or she acts for (PD 39A, para 5). This is usually done by advocates completing a slip provided by the court immediately before the hearing. **39.38**

The rules give the courts a great deal of flexibility regarding how they will deal with trials. As previously discussed, the court can lay down trial timetables prescribing how the time available for the trial will be used, and allocating specified, limited times for examination-in-chief, cross-examination, and so on. The trial will then follow the timetable previously laid down, or laid down by the trial judge at the start, or will follow the traditional sequence of events. **39.39**

Generally it will be the claimant who begins. However, it will be the defendant if the defendant has admitted all the issues on which the burden of proof rests on the claimant, so that the only live issues have to be proved by the defendant. **39.40**

Opening speech

The trial judge will generally have read the papers in the trial bundle before the trial. It will often be the case that in those circumstances there is no need for an opening speech, which may be dispensed with (PD 28, para 8.2, for the fast track; PD 29, para 10.2, for cases on the multi-track). If an opening speech is allowed, counsel for the claimant will usually describe the nature of the claim, and will identify the issues to be tried by reference to the statements of case and/or the statement of issues. Some of the documentary evidence may be referred to. It sometimes happens that the judge will rise during the course of the opening to read some of the documents. **39.41**

Claimant's case

After the claimant's opening speech evidence will be called on behalf of the claimant. Broadly, evidence adduced at trial will be real evidence (ie, physical items), contemporaneous documentary evidence, views of the site, and the evidence of witnesses. **39.42**

The judge has a discretion to inspect the *locus in quo* if there are compelling reasons to do so, outweighing the time and expense of a view. Inspections should generally be conducted in the presence of the parties. **39.43**

There are occasions when evidence is adduced in a deposition, by affidavit, or in the form of hearsay statements. It is rather more usual for evidence from witnesses to be produced by calling the witnesses to give evidence from the witness box. Witnesses are sometimes asked to leave the court until they are called so they are not influenced by the evidence given by other witnesses, but they remain in court in the large majority of cases. Subject to any trial **39.44** directions they may be called in any order. When called they are sworn or affirm in a manner they consider binding (Oaths Act 1978). Traditionally they would give their evidence in answer to non-leading questions put to them by counsel for the party calling them. However, under the CPR witness statements of witnesses called at trial will stand as the evidence-in-chief unless the court otherwise orders (r 32.5(2)). Technically, it is possible to augment the evidence contained in the exchanged statements only if, by virtue of r 32.5(3) and (4), the court considers there is good reason not to confine the witness to the contents of his or her witness statement, and for the purpose of either:

(a) amplifying the witness statement; or
(b) giving evidence in relation to new matters which have arisen since the witness statement was served on the other parties.

39.45 The CPR, r 32.5(5), provides that where the party who has disclosed a witness statement does not use it at trial, 'any other party may put the witness statement in as hearsay'. In *McPhilemy v Times Newspapers Ltd* [2000] CPLR 335, the party who disclosed a witness statement decided against calling the witness. The opposite side then attempted to put the statement into evidence for the purpose of proving that its contents were untrue. Permission was refused, because of the general rule of evidence that a party is not allowed to adduce evidence that his own witnesses (in this case the witness who made the witness statement) are not to be believed on their oaths.

39.46 After being examined in chief, each witness may be cross-examined by counsel for the defendant. Where there is more than one defendant, they cross-examine in the order they appear on the court record. Cross-examination may be conducted using leading questions (ie, questions which suggest the required answer).

39.47 A witness who has been cross-examined may be re-examined by counsel for the claimant on matters covered in cross-examination. Leading questions are not allowed.

39.48 Exhibits which are handed in and proved during the course of the trial will be recorded in an exhibit list and kept in the custody of the court until the conclusion of the trial, unless the judge directs otherwise (PD 39A, para 7). At the conclusion of the trial the parties have the responsibility for taking away and preserving the exhibits pending any possible appeal.

Submissions of no case to answer

39.49 At the conclusion of the case for the claimant, the defendant may make a submission of no case to answer. This is made on the basis that on the evidence adduced by the claimant the claim cannot succeed. A submission of no case to answer should rarely, if ever, be entertained in cases tried by a judge sitting alone (*Benham Ltd v Kythira Investments Ltd* (2003) LTL 15/12/03). As the judge is the trier of both law and fact, it is embarrassing for the judge to be asked to rule on the merits of the claim while the evidence is still incomplete. Further, if the judge's ruling were to be reversed on appeal, there would be the added cost of having a retrial.

39.50 It is therefore the general rule that defendants seeking to make a submission of no case to answer will be put to an election as to whether they will call any evidence. It is only in exceptional cases that they will not be put to this election: *Boyce v Wyatt Engineering* (2001) LTL

1/5/01. If they are put to their election, and decide to call no evidence, they can make a submission of no case to answer, which will be decided on the basis of whether the claimant's case has been established by the evidence on the balance of probabilities, and judgment will be entered for whichever party succeeds on the submission. In cases where the defendant is not put to an election, the submission is considered on the basis of whether the claimant's case has no real prospect of success: *Miller v Cawley* (2002) *The Times*, 6 September 2002. In such a case, if the submission is unsuccessful the defendant is allowed to call its evidence and the trial continues in the normal way.

Defence case

Where the defence decides to call evidence, it may be allowed to make an opening speech (though this is now rather unusual). It then calls its evidence in the same way as the claimant. Where there is more than one defendant, they present their evidence in the order they appear on the record. **39.51**

Closing speeches

Where the defence has called evidence, the defence closing speech is made before that of the claimant. Speeches usually deal with how the evidence that has been adduced and the inferences that can be drawn from that evidence support the case for the party in question on the factual issues involved. Counsel also argue any legal points that arise, sometimes making use of skeleton arguments. The time limits imposed by trial timetables may have the practical effect of forcing advocates to make even greater use of skeleton arguments, so as to ensure they are able to cover the required ground within the time limited by the court. **39.52**

Role of the judge

During the course of the trial the judge may put questions to the witnesses, particularly if matters remain obscure after counsel's questions. Judges should be careful to avoid interrupting the flow of counsel's questions, particularly during cross-examination: *Jones v National Coal Board* [1957] 2 QB 55. The judge will have to rule on any applications and any objections to the admissibility of evidence or questions during the course of the trial. After hearing the evidence the judge must decide where the truth lies, decide any points of law, and give judgment. The claimant has the burden of proof on a balance of probabilities. If the party with the burden of proof fails to discharge that burden, the fact is treated as not having happened. If the burden of proof is discharged, the court treats the fact as having happened. There is no half-way house between the two (*Re B (Children) (Care Proceedings: Standard of Proof)* [2009] 1 AC 11). Inherent probabilities have to be taken into account as a factor 'to whatever extent is appropriate in the particular case' (Lord Nicholls of Birkenhead in *Re H (Minors) (Sexual Abuse: Standard of Proof)* [1996] AC 563 at 583), but do not alter the balance of probabilities test. **39.53**

Judgment is often given immediately, but in complicated cases may be reserved. The court will always record judgments given at trial, both in the High Court and county courts. Often the evidence will also have been recorded (PD 39A, para 6.1). Unofficial tape recording without permission (which will rarely be given) is a contempt of court. Transcripts can be obtained **39.54** on payment of authorized charges. After judgment is given the court will deal with the question of costs, the form of the judgment, and any application for permission to appeal.

J PRELIMINARY ISSUES

39.55 As a general rule, it is in the interests of the parties and the administration of justice that all issues arising in a dispute are tried at the same time. However, particularly in complex actions, costs and time can sometimes be saved if decisive, or potentially decisive, issues can be identified and ordered to be tried before or separately from the main trial.

39.56 There are three related types of order that can be made:

(a) for the trial of a preliminary issue on a point of law;
(b) for the separate trial of preliminary issues or questions of fact; and
(c) for separate trials of liability and quantum.

Procedure for trial of preliminary issues

39.57 Orders for the trial of preliminary issues are made either on the application of a party or by the court of its own initiative. It is rare for the court to make such an order without the concurrence of at least one of the parties. It is not possible to make such an order by consent. Normally the application is made at the allocation or listing stage, or on a case management hearing, although it is not unknown for an application to be made to the trial judge at the beginning of a trial.

39.58 Where an order for the preliminary trial of an issue of law or fact is made, the court must formulate the issue to be tried. It is important that the issue is defined with precision so as to avoid future difficulties of interpretation. If it is impossible to define the issue, no order should be made: *Allen v Gulf Oil Refining Ltd* [1981] AC 101. If the issue is one of law, the court must further order the issue to be tried either:

(a) on the statements of case;
(b) on a case stated; or
(c) on an agreed statement of facts.

39.59 In *Keays v Murdoch Magazines (UK) Ltd* [1991] 1 WLR 1184, an issue as to whether words were capable of a defamatory meaning was ordered to be tried on the pleadings in conjunction with the copy of the magazine in which the offending article appeared.

Practice

39.60 Factors to be taken into account when deciding whether to order the determination of a preliminary issue identified in *Steele v Steele* (2001) *The Times*, 5 June 2001, include:

(a) Whether the determination of the preliminary issue will dispose of the whole case or at least one aspect of the case.

(b) Whether the determination of the preliminary issue will significantly cut down the cost and the time involved in pre-trial preparation and in connection with the trial itself.
(c) If the preliminary issue is an issue of law, the amount of effort involved in identifying the relevant facts for the purposes of the preliminary issue.
(d) If the preliminary issue is an issue of law, whether it can be determined on agreed facts. If there are substantial disputes of fact it is unlikely to be safe to determine the legal issue until the facts are found.
(e) The risk that an order will increase the costs or delay the trial, and the prospects that such an order may assist in settling the dispute.

Issues raised in personal injuries cases as to the claimant's 'date of knowledge' under the Limitation Act 1980, s 14, may be suitable for trial as preliminary issues. In *Keays v Murdoch Magazines (UK) Ltd* [1991] 1 WLR 1184, the issue whether the words published were capable of bearing a defamatory meaning was determined as a preliminary issue. **39.61**

K TRIAL BY JURY

Jurisdiction

There is a right to trial by jury in actions involving claims in deceit, libel, slander, malicious prosecution, and false imprisonment. This right extends to claims in the county courts (CCA 1984, s 66) and the QBD of the High Court (SCA 1981, s 69), but not to claims in the ChD. The right to trial by jury is subject to the court otherwise being of the opinion that the trial requires prolonged examination of documents or accounts, or any scientific or local investigation which cannot conveniently be made by a jury. A request for trial by jury should be made within 28 days of service of the defence (CPR, r 26.11). **39.62**

There is a theoretical discretion to allow trial by jury in other cases, but the courts are extremely reluctant to exercise it: *Williams v Beesley* [1973] 1 WLR 1295. **39.63**

Jury procedure

Juries are eight strong in the county court and twelve strong in the High Court. Jurors are selected from the jury panel by ballot. They may be challenged and asked to stand down only for cause, such as proven bias. After inquiring, the trial judge should discharge any juror who will suffer inconvenience or hardship by having to serve for the estimated length of the trial (*Practice Direction (Juries: Length of Trial)* [1981] 1 WLR 1129). During the course of a High Court trial, a juror may be discharged on the ground of evident necessity. **39.64**

Questions of law are for the judge, and questions of fact are decided by the jury in the light of the judge's summing up. The jury should not deliberate until they are all together in the jury room. Verdicts should normally be unanimous, but if a jury cannot agree majority verdicts of 7:1 in the county court and 11:1, 10:2, 10:1, and 9:1 in the High Court may be accepted. **39.65**

L NON-ATTENDANCE AT TRIAL

39.66 A trial may proceed despite the non-attendance of any of the parties, and the court may simply strike out the claim or defence, and any counterclaim or defence to counterclaim (CPR, r 39.3(1)). The court has a power to restore the proceedings (or any part of the proceedings) that may have been struck out due to non-attendance (r 39.3(2)), and may set aside any judgment entered in such circumstances (r 39.3(3)). Applications to set aside or restore must be supported by evidence (r 39.3(4)). Orders to restore or set aside may, by r 39.3(5) be granted only if the applicant:

(a) acted promptly on finding out that the court had exercised its power to strike out or enter judgment or otherwise make an order against the applicant; and
(b) had a good excuse for not attending—claimants, in particular, are expected to keep in contact with their solicitors, and so have limited grounds for saying they were unaware of a hearing date: *Neufville v Papamichael* (1999) LTL 23/11/99; and
(c) has a reasonable prospect of success at a reconvened trial.

39.67 There is no residual discretion to reinstate if one of the factors is missing: *Barclays Bank plc v Ellis* (2000) LTL 9/8/00. One of the factors is making the application to reinstate promptly. This means 'with alacrity': *Regency Rolls Ltd v Carnall* (2000) LTL 16/10/00. The nine factors set out in r 3.9(1), which are to be taken into account on applications for relief from sanctions, will often be applied by analogy to applications to restore or set aside after non-attendance.

KEY POINTS SUMMARY

39.68 In the period leading up to trial, the following matters should be dealt with:

- Contacting witnesses to ensure they are available.
- Obtaining witness summonses where appropriate. This may be because a witness is reluctant to attend (although calling a reluctant witness is always very risky) or because the witness needs a witness summons to show to an employer.
- Briefing trial counsel.
- Considering whether there should be a pre-trial conference with counsel, the client, and any experts.
- Agreeing and compiling trial bundles (this is often a very onerous task).
- Counsel drafting skeleton arguments and reading lists for the judge.
- Drawing up chronologies and *dramatis personae*.
- Counsel preparing speeches, examination-in-chief, and cross-examination of witnesses. Depending on the nature of the case, this can be very time-intensive.
- In fast track trials, drawing up schedules of costs for the summary assessment.
- Lodging lists or bundles of authorities.

40

REFERENCES TO THE COURT OF JUSTICE OF THE EUROPEAN UNION

An English court faced with a question of European Community law may sometimes decide it itself, or may refer it to the Court of Justice of the European Union ('ECJ') in Luxembourg for a preliminary ruling. If a reference is made, the English proceedings will be stayed pending the ruling of the ECJ. Once it is made, the ruling is binding on the English court, but it is only a preliminary ruling, in that the English court is left to apply the ruling to the facts of the case and to give judgment. The general policy is that Community law should be applied consistently in all Member States. **40.01**

A QUESTIONS WHICH MAY BE REFERRED

References may be made: **40.02**

(a) under art 267 of the Treaty on the functioning of the European Union (the 'EU Treaty');
(b) under art 150 of the Treaty establishing the European Atomic Energy Community; or
(c) on the interpretation of any of the instruments referred to in the Civil Jurisdiction and Judgments Act 1982, s 1(1), or the Contracts (Applicable Law) Act 1990, s 1.

Article 267 of the EU Treaty is representative of the various treaties and enactments mentioned above. It provides in its first paragraph: **40.03**

> The Court of Justice of the European Union shall have jurisdiction to give preliminary rulings concerning:
>
> (a) the interpretation of the Treaties;

(b) the validity and interpretation of acts of the institutions, bodies, offices or agencies of the Union.

40.04 This includes questions on the amending Treaties and Treaties of Accession, and questions on Regulations, Directives, and Decisions of the Council or Commission. Although the ECJ can give rulings on the interpretation of the Judgments Regulation (see Chapter 10), it cannot do so on the modified version of the Brussels Convention which governs allocation of jurisdiction within the UK: *Kleinwort Benson Ltd v Glasgow City Council* (Case C–346/93) [1996] QB 57.

B MANDATORY REFERENCES

40.05 Article 267 of the EU Treaty provides:

> Where any such question is raised in a case pending before a court or tribunal of a Member State against whose decisions there is no judicial remedy under national law, that court or tribunal shall bring the matter before the Court.

40.06 Accordingly, references are mandatory in courts of last instance. In England, this is generally now the Supreme Court (formerly the House of Lords), unless by statute or rule some lower court is the final court of appeal. However, even in the Supreme Court there must be a 'question' that needs to be referred. If a point is covered by considerable and consistent authority from the ECJ, such that its answer is obvious, there is no 'question' within the meaning of art 267 (*per* Lord Diplock in *Garland v British Rail Engineering Ltd* [1983] 2 AC 751 at 771; *Srl Cilfit v Ministry of Health* (Case 283/81) [1982] ECR 3415). If it is not necessary to decide either whether Community law applied or the scope of its application to the present case, the reference procedure is not available even in the Supreme Court: *R v Secretary of State for Health, ex p Imperial Tobacco Ltd* [2001] 1 WLR 127.

C DISCRETIONARY REFERENCES

40.07 For courts below the Supreme Court, art 267 of the EU Treaty provides:

> Where such a question is raised before any court or tribunal of a Member State, that court or tribunal may, if it considers that a decision on the question is necessary to enable it to give judgment, request the Court to give a ruling thereon.

40.08 Two questions arise in such cases:

(a) whether a decision on a question of Community law is necessary to enable the court to give judgment; and
(b) if so, whether the court should in the exercise of its discretion order that a reference be made.

40.09 Guidelines on both questions were given by the Court of Appeal in *H P Bulmer Ltd v J Bollinger SA* [1974] Ch 401 by Lord Denning MR at 422–5.

Guidelines for discretionary references

In *H P Bulmer Ltd v J Bollinger SA* [1974] Ch 401 Lord Denning MR laid down four guidelines as to whether a decision from the ECJ is necessary. They are no more than guidelines, and cannot be considered as binding: *Lord Bethell v SABENA* [1983] 3 CMLR 1. **40.10**

Whether the point will be conclusive

Article 267 provides that the court must consider whether 'a decision on the question is necessary to enable it to give judgment'. Lord Denning's view was that the point must be such that, whichever way it is decided, it will be conclusive of the case. This is probably too onerous. Ormrod LJ in *Polydor Ltd v Harlequin Record Shops Ltd* [1982] CMLR 413 said it was sufficient if the point was 'reasonably necessary', and Bingham J in *Customs and Excise Commissioners v ApS Samex* [1983] 1 All ER 1042 said that the question must be substantially, if not quite totally, determinative of the litigation. **40.11**

Previous ruling

As Lord Denning said in *H P Bulmer Ltd v J Bollinger SA*: **40.12**

> In some cases... it may be found that the same point—or substantially the same point—has already been decided by the European Court in a previous case. In that event it is not necessary for the English court to decide it. It can follow the previous decision without troubling the European Court.

This is subject to the proviso that, with changing social and economic factors, the ECJ is not bound by its earlier decisions. **40.13**

Acte claire

Lord Denning MR went on to say in *H P Bulmer Ltd v J Bollinger SA*: **40.14**

> In other cases the English court may consider the point is reasonably clear and free from doubt. In that event there is no need to interpret the Treaty but only to apply it.

A point may be *acte claire* after considering the text, together with decisions of the ECJ and relevant *travaux préparatoires* (*Lucasfilm Ltd v Ainsworth* [2010] FSR 10 at [114], [129]).

This should be read in the light of Lord Diplock's comment in *R v Henn* [1981] AC 850 at 906 that the court should not be 'too ready to hold that because the meaning of the English text (which is one of [several official languages of the community each] of equal authority) seems plain no question of interpretation can be involved'. Where a point of EU law has been ruled upon by a domestic court whose decision binds the court in the instant case, a discretionary reference to the ECJ should only be made if there has been some development at the ECJ which indicates the domestic decision should be reviewed (*McCall v Poulton* [2009] PIQR P8). **40.15**

Deciding the facts first

In general, it is best to decide the facts before making a reference, because it should then be clear whether the question of Community law is necessary, and it enables the ECJ to take into account all the relevant facts when making its ruling. **40.16**

Factors relevant to the discretion

40.17 General guidance has been provided by the ECJ on when it is appropriate to refer matters, and the following factors were identified by Lord Denning MR in *H P Bulmer Ltd v J Bollinger SA* [1974] Ch 401 as being relevant in the exercise of the court's discretion:

(a) delay in obtaining a ruling from the ECJ. Delays have been reduced in recent years;
(b) the importance of not overloading the ECJ;
(c) expense to the parties;
(d) the wishes of the parties. Although clearly relevant, the court can nevertheless make a reference even if both parties object, and, also, there is no such thing as a reference by consent. Ultimately the decision is that of the judge;
(e) difficulty and importance. Simple points should be decided by the English court;
(f) questions involving the comparison of texts in the different languages of the Member States are best decided by the ECJ: *Customs and Excise Commissioners v ApS Samex* [1983] 1 All ER 1042;
(g) questions requiring a panoramic view of the Community and its institutions, the functioning of the Common Market, or a broad view of the orderly development of the EU should be decided by the ECJ: *Customs and Excise Commissioners v ApS Samex*; and
(h) whether the application for a reference is made in bad faith so as to delay judgment being given: *Customs and Excise Commissioners v ApS Samex*.

Questioning the validity of Community acts

40.18 Where a national court intends to question the validity of a Community act, it must refer the question to the ECJ: *Foto-Frost v Hauptzollamt Lübeck-Ost* (Case 314/85) [1987] ECR 4199. Where the national court has serious doubts about the validity of a Community act on which a national measure is based, the national court may, in an exceptional case, suspend or grant interim relief in respect of the national measure, but it must refer the question of validity to the ECJ: *Zuckerfabrik Süderdithmarschen AG v Hauptzollamt Itzehoe* (Joined Cases C–143/88 and C–92/89) [1991] ECR I–415.

D PROCEDURE IN ENGLAND

40.19 An order referring a question to the ECJ must be made by a judge, the Court of Appeal, or the Supreme Court. It cannot be made by consent, or by a master or district judge. It may be made by the court on its own initiative or on the application of any party. Although it can be made at any stage, it is usual for a reference to be made at trial after the facts have been found (CPR, r 68.2). There is also a streamlined procedure for urgent preliminary rulings (r 68.2A). Once final judgment has been given the court is *functus officio* and has no power at that stage to order a reference: *Chiron Corporation v Murex Diagnostics Ltd (No 8)* [1995] FSR 309.

40.20 Questions referred for preliminary rulings must concern only the interpretation or validity of a provision of Community law, since the European Court does not have jurisdiction to interpret national law or to assess its validity. The questions referred to the Court of Justice of the European Union must be drafted with care and simplicity as they will be translated into a number of European languages as part of the referral process (PD 68, para 1.2). The questions should be drafted in a general form, and not in a specific form tied to the facts of the case. Scheduled to the order should, by PD 68, para 1.3, be a document (which must not exceed 20 pages, para 1.5):

(a) giving the full name of the referring court;
(b) identifying the parties;
(c) summarizing the nature and history of the proceedings, including the salient facts, and indicating whether these are proved, admitted, or assumed;
(d) setting out the relevant rules of national law;
(e) summarizing the relevant contentions of the parties;
(f) explaining why a ruling of the ECJ is sought;
(g) identifying the provisions of Community law which it is being requested to interpret;
(h) stating the question on which the ECJ's ruling is sought; and
(i) stating any opinion on the matter that may have been expressed by the court in delivering judgment.

Often the applicant will prepare a draft, or the court may direct one of the parties to do so, **40.21** but the order will be settled finally by the court. An example of an order for reference to the ECJ is shown in figure 40.1. The senior master will send a copy of the order making the reference to the ECJ (r 68.3(1)) at the Registry of the Court of Justice of the European Union in Luxembourg. County court references are sent to the senior master by a court officer of the county court for onward transmission to the ECJ (r 68.3(2)) together with the court file (PD 68, para 2.2). Further guidance is given in the ECJ Information Note, PD 68, Annex.

Figure 40.1 Order for reference to the Court of Justice of the European Union

IN THE SUPREME COURT

ON APPEAL FROM HER MAJESTY'S COURT OF APPEAL (ENGLAND)

BETWEEN

EILEEN MARY GARLAND Petitioner

—and—

BRITISH RAIL ENGINEERING LIMITED Respondents

It is ordered that the questions set out in the schedule hereto concerning the interpretation of (a) article 141 of the Treaty establishing the European Community ('EC Treaty'), (b) article 1 of Council Directive 75/117/EEC, and (c) article 1 of Council Directive 76/207/EEC be referred to the Court of Justice of the European Communities for a preliminary ruling in accordance with article 267 of the EU Treaty.

And it is ordered that all further proceedings in the above-named cause be stayed until the said Court of Justice of the European Union has given its ruling on the said questions or until further order.

Figure 40.1 *continued*

SCHEDULE

REQUEST FOR PRELIMINARY RULING OF THE

COURT OF JUSTICE OF THE EUROPEAN UNION

1 The referring court is the Supreme Court of England and Wales.

2 The appellant in this appeal is Mrs Eileen Mary Garland of [address] and the respondents are British Rail Engineering Ltd, whose registered office is at [address].

3 Mrs Eileen Mary Garland is a married woman employed by the respondents, British Rail Engineering Limited ('B.R.E.L.'). The whole of the shareholding in B.R.E.L. is held by the British Railways Board which is a public authority charged by statute with the duty of providing railway services in Great Britain.

4 All employees of B.R.E.L. enjoy certain valuable concessionary travel facilities during the period of their employment. These facilities entitle each employee, regardless of sex, to travel free or at a reduced rate on British Rail and certain foreign railways. Such facilities are extended not only to the employee, but to his or her spouse and dependent children.

5 After employees of B.R.E.L. retire from their employment on reaching retiring age (which is earlier for women than for men) there is a difference in their treatment depending on their sex. In the case of former male employees, they continue to be granted (though on a reduced scale) travel facilities for themselves, their wives, and dependent children. In the case of former female employees, they receive (on a similarly reduced scale) travel facilities for themselves, but no such facilities are granted in respect of their husbands or dependent children. These facilities are not enjoyed by former employees as a matter of contractual right, but employees have a legitimate expectation that they will enjoy them after retirement and it would be difficult in practice for B.R.E.L. to withdraw them unilaterally without the agreement of the trade unions of which their employees are members.

6 On 25 November 1976, Mrs Garland complained to an employment tribunal that B.R.E.L. were discriminating against her contrary to the provisions of a United Kingdom Act of Parliament, the Sex Discrimination Act 1975. Her complaint after consideration also by two intermediate appellate courts, the Employment Appeal Tribunal [1978] ICR 495 and the Court of Appeal sub nom. *Roberts v Cleveland Area Health Authority* [1979] 1 WLR 754, has now reached the Supreme Court which is a court against whose decision there is no judicial remedy under United Kingdom law.

The preliminary ruling of the Court of Justice of the European Union is accordingly requested on the following questions:

1 Where an employer provides (though not bound to do so by contract) special travel facilities for former employees to enjoy after retirement which discriminate against former female employees in the manner described above, is it contrary to:

(a) Article 141 of the EC Treaty?
(b) Article 1 of Council Directive 75/117/EEC?

Figure 40.1 *continued*

(c) Article 1 of Council Directive 76/207/EEC?

2 If the answer to questions 1(a), 1(b), or 1(c) is affirmative, is article 141 or either of the Directives directly applicable in Member States so as to confer enforceable Community rights upon individuals in the above circumstances?

No opinion on these questions has been expressed by the referring court.

Dated the 9th day of November 2010.

Unless the court orders otherwise, the English proceedings will be stayed pending the ruling of the ECJ (CPR, r 68.4). If the reference is made by a court other than the Supreme Court, a domestic appeal against the decision to make the reference can be made (*R (Horvath) v Secretary of State for the Environment, Food and Rural Affairs* [2007] NPC 83). **40.22**

E PROCEDURE IN THE COURT OF JUSTICE OF THE EUROPEAN UNION

The EU Treaty, art 263, provides that the ECJ may review the legality of acts adopted by the European Union. Such proceedings may be brought by a Member State, the Council, or the Commission, but may also be brought by a natural or legal person if the Regulation or Decision under review is of direct and individual concern to them. This is usually interpreted as meaning that the applicant, if not a State or the Council or Commission, must be affected by the measure by reason of attributes peculiar to the applicant or a factual situation which differentiates the applicant from all other persons and distinguishes him individually (*Plaumann & Co v Commission of the European Economic Community* (Case 25/62) [1963] ECR 95). In *Union de Pequeños Agricultores v Council of the European Union* (Case C–50/00P) [2003] QB 893 it was held that the ECJ did not have jurisdiction to examine in an individual case whether national procedural rules permitted a challenge to the legality of Community measures. In *Jego-Quere et Cie SA v Commission of the European Communities* (Case T–177/01) [2003] QB 854 it was held that where there was no other satisfactory means of address, *Plaumann & Co v Commission of the European Economic Community* would not be followed, and that a person would be regarded as individually concerned if a Community measure affected his legal position in a definite and immediate manner by restricting his rights or imposing obligations on him. **40.23**

The registrar of the ECJ notifies the parties, Member States, and the Commission of any reference filed, and each has two months to submit written observations. There is then a hearing, where interested parties can present oral argument. The case is then adjourned, during which the Advocate-General delivers an opinion. The European Court Registry stays in contact with the national court until judgment of the ECJ is given, and sends various documents to the national court, including the written observations, the report of the hearing, the opinion of the Advocate-General, and the final judgment. **40.24**

The ruling binds the domestic court on the interpretation of the Community provision in question, but it is for the referring court to apply the relevant provision of Community law, **40.25** as interpreted by the ECJ, to the facts of the case (ECJ Information Note, PD 68, Annex, para 3). The ECJ will exceed its jurisdiction if it disagrees with the findings of fact of the referring court (*Arsenal Football Club plc v Reed* [2003] 3 All ER 865).

F COSTS

40.26 The costs of the parties in seeking a ruling from the ECJ are always reserved to the domestic court. No order for costs is made in respect of the involvement of Member States or the Commission.

41

JUDGMENTS AND ORDERS

Although there is likely to be a delay between judgment being pronounced and the judgment being sealed and served, r 40.7(1) of the CPR provides that judgment in fact takes effect from the day it was given. After a judgment or order has been pronounced by the court, the next step is to have it drawn up. In *Holtby v Hodgson* (1889) 24 QBD 103 Lord Esher MR said, at 107, 'pronouncing judgment is not entering judgment; something has to be done which will be a record'. The distinction between judgments and orders is that a judgment is the final decision which disposes of a claim (subject to appeal), whereas an order is an interim decision. However, there is no practical difference between the two, and both are enforceable in the same way. **41.01**

A SETTLEMENTS

It is very common for parties to agree terms of settlement rather than having their dispute determined by the court. In fact it is rare for actions to proceed all the way to trial for a final determination, given the delays inherent in litigation, the expense of trials, and the financial pressures often experienced by litigants. It is also very common for parties to agree interim orders and directions. This is usually done where the matters in question are uncontentious or where there is no real defence to the order sought being made. **41.02**

Where a settlement has been agreed, the parties must decide how to record it. An important consideration in this regard is how the agreement can be enforced in the event of either party failing to abide by its terms. **41.03**

41.04 The simplest form of judgment provides for immediate payment of the sum agreed together with costs (often on the standard basis, to be the subject of a detailed assessment if not agreed). Enforcement proceedings can be taken on such a judgment on the same day as it is entered. Agreements are not always this simple. Five further ways of recording agreed terms were discussed by Slade J in *Green v Rozen* [1955] 1 WLR 741 (in the context of an agreement reached at the door of the court):

(a) Where a claim is settled on terms as to the payment of money, judgment may be entered for the agreed sum, subject to a stay of execution pending payment of stated instalments. If the instalments fall into arrears, the stay will be lifted, and the judgment creditor can immediately take enforcement proceedings.
(b) A consent order may be drawn up embodying the undertakings of both parties in a series of numbered paragraphs. If any of the terms are not complied with, enforcement may be possible immediately or on application to the court depending on the nature of the term in question.
(c) The agreement may be recorded in a Tomlin order. A Tomlin order has the effect of staying the claim save for the purpose of carrying the terms set out in a schedule to the order into effect. See 41.19ff.
(d) A consent order may be drawn up staying all further proceedings upon the agreed terms. If the agreement is reached immediately before the hearing its terms will usually be endorsed on counsel's briefs and the court will be asked to make a consent order in those terms. Unlike with Tomlin orders, the courts are very unwilling to remove the stay imposed by such orders, so enforcement can usually be effected only by bringing fresh proceedings for breach of the contract embodied in the compromise (see *Rofa Sport Management AG v DHL International (UK) Ltd* [1989] 1 WLR 902).
(e) The court may be informed merely that the case has been settled upon terms endorsed on counsel's briefs. This is the most informal way of compromising a claim. Its effect is to supersede the existing claim with the compromise. Any breach can only be enforced by issuing fresh proceedings.

41.05 A sixth method was the subject of *Atkinson v Castan* (1991) *The Times*, 17 April 1991, where a consent order made 'no order' save as to costs, but set out the agreed terms in recitals. It was held that the claimants were entitled to enforce the terms stated in the recitals without the need to bring a fresh claim.

41.06 Where a case is settled in advance of a hearing, each party has a responsibility to inform the court so that the time set aside for the hearing can be reallocated to other litigants. Any order giving effect to the settlement should be filed with the listing officer (PD 39A, para 4.2). If the court is informed of a settlement at least 7 days before the trial, all or part of the hearing fee is refunded (CPFO, fee 2.3: there is a 100 per cent refund if more than 28 days' notice is given, 75 per cent if 15–28 days, and 50 per cent if 7–14 days). Often agreements to settle are not reduced into formal orders, although this is desirable, and will be essential if, for example, the parties agree that costs should be assessed by the court. The settlement is itself a contract, so is binding even if it is not made into a formal order of the court.

41.07 Settlements agreed after proceedings have been issued should deal with the costs of the parties and with the future status of the claim. Options on the latter include entering final judgment, dismissing the claim, granting a stay, or discontinuing or withdrawing it. Care should be taken to ensure that the wording used reflects the parties' intentions, especially as regards any previous interim costs orders. It should be kept in mind that if a claim is discontinued, the claimant is required to pay the defendant's costs unless specific provision is made to the contrary, and that the claimant is not necessarily barred from commencing fresh proceedings in respect of the same claim (see 22.44, 22.46).

B ORDERS MADE AT HEARINGS

Counsel are under a duty to take notes of the court's judgment, and must endorse a note of the court's decision on the backsheet of their briefs. Instructing solicitors may use this as the basis for drawing up the court's order, so accuracy in noting is of great importance. If the orders are at all complex, counsel for both sides will often consult each other immediately after the hearing to ensure that both sides are clear on what the court has ordered. Counsel's endorsement of the order is not protected by legal professional privilege. **41.08**

In addition, in interim applications the master, district judge, or judge will: **41.09**

(a) initial the relevant paragraphs of the application notice or draft minutes of the order; or
(b) initial together with making amendments; or
(c) endorse the order on the affidavit, witness statement, or application notice in abbreviated form or longhand.

Judgments in Queen's Bench Division trials are certified by the court associate. **41.10**

C FORM OF JUDGMENTS AND ORDERS

The heading of a judgment or order is the same as that for the claim, except that the name of the judge, master, or district judge, if any, is included above the names of the parties. Certain consent orders do not need to be approved by a judicial officer. There then follow any recitals. These are followed by the body of the order, which may be short or may be complex. Undertakings tend to be set out in schedules to orders. The terms of the orders must accurately reflect the pronouncement made by the court. Often it is necessary to amplify the court's words, or to put them in imperative form. To simplify this task and to ensure consistency, in both the High Court and the county courts there are many prescribed forms for judgments and orders. There are also model form orders contained in some of the practice directions, such as those for freezing injunctions and search orders in PD 25A. These must be used where applicable, with such variations as the circumstances of the case may require. Where a party has asked for permission to appeal (see 46.17ff), the order must state whether it is final, identify the appeal court, and state whether permission to appeal was granted (CPR, r 40.2(4)). **41.11**

Time limits

Where an order imposes a time limit for doing any act, the date for compliance must be expressed as a calendar date, and must include the time of day by which the act must be done **41.12**

(CPR, r 2.9(1)). Orders may be made subject to conditions, and may, at the court's discretion, specify the consequences of failing to comply (r 3.1(3)).

Injunction orders and penal notice

41.13 Injunction orders, whether prohibitory or mandatory, are intended to have penal consequences and non-compliance can be punished as a contempt of court. These orders need to be endorsed with a penal notice in the following form (PD 40B, para 9.1):

> If you the within-named [ ] do not comply with this order you may be held to be in contempt of court and imprisoned or fined, or [in the case of a company or corporation] your assets may be seized.

41.14 Undertakings given in lieu of injunctions are treated in the same way. A person giving an undertaking may also be required to sign a statement, which is endorsed on the court's copy of the order, to the effect that he or she understands the terms of the undertaking and the consequences of failure to comply with it (PD 40B, para 9.3).

Consent orders

41.15 Many orders are made 'by consent'. A true consent order is based on a contract between the parties. As such, the contract is arrived at by bargaining between the parties, perhaps in correspondence, and the consent order is simply evidence of that contract: *Wentworth v Bullen* (1840) 9 B & C 840. To be a true consent order there must be consideration passing from each side. If this is the case, then, unlike other orders, it will be set aside only on grounds, such as fraud or mistake, which would justify the setting-aside of a contract: *Purcell v F C Trigell Ltd* [1971] 1 QB 358.

41.16 However, there is a distinction between a real contract and a simple submission to an order. In *Siebe Gorman and Co Ltd v Pneupac Ltd* [1982] 1 WLR 185, Lord Denning MR said at 189:

> It should be clearly understood by the profession that, when an order is expressed to be made 'by consent', it is ambiguous...One meaning is this: the words 'by consent' may evidence a real contract between the parties. In such a case the court will only interfere with such an order on the same grounds as it would with any other contract. The other meaning is this: the words 'by consent' may mean 'the parties hereto not objecting'. In such a case there is no real contract between the parties. The order can be altered or varied by the court in the same circumstances as any other order that is made by the court without the consent of the parties.

41.17 A further distinction relates to family proceedings. In these the legal effect of a consent order derives from the order, not the agreement of the parties. Consequently, there is no jurisdiction to vary a matrimonial consent order: *Thwaite v Thwaite* [1982] Fam 1. Where such an order was obtained by fraud, misrepresentation, or mistake, the remedy is to appeal or bring fresh proceedings: *De Lasala v De Lasala* [1980] AC 546 *per* Lord Diplock.

41.18 Consent judgments and orders must be expressed as being 'by consent' (CPR, r 40.6(7)(b)) and must be signed by the legal representatives for each party (or by the litigants in person where this is allowed: see 41.42–41.44). Paragraph 3.4 of PD 40B provides that the signatures of the legal representatives may be those of the solicitors or counsel acting for the parties.

Tomlin orders

Tomlin orders are so named after Tomlin J who, in a *Practice Note* [1927] WN 290, said that, where terms of compromise are agreed and it is intended to stay the claim with the terms scheduled to the order, the order should be worded: **41.19**

> And, the [claimant] and the defendant having agreed to the terms set forth in the schedule hereto, it is ordered that all further proceedings in this claim be stayed, except for the purpose of carrying such terms into effect. Liberty to apply as to carrying such terms into effect.

Tomlin orders are used where complex terms are agreed, or where the terms of a compromise go beyond the boundaries of the claim (eg, *E F Phillips and Sons Ltd v Clarke* [1970] Ch 322), or where it is sought to avoid publicity of the agreement. In the event of the scheduled terms being breached, enforcement is a two-stage process. First, the claim must be restored under the 'liberty to apply' clause, and an order obtained to compel compliance with the term breached. Secondly, if that order is itself breached, enforcement can follow in the usual way. **41.20**

By PD 40B, para 3.5, where a consent order is in the form of a stay of proceedings on agreed terms recorded in a schedule (a Tomlin order), any direction for the payment of money out of court or for the payment and assessment of costs must be contained in the body of the order and not the schedule. The reason is that these two forms of direction require action on the part of the court, and must therefore be included in the public part of the order and not concealed in the schedule. If the amount of costs has been agreed this can be included in the schedule. **41.21**

Money judgments and payment by instalments

A judgment for the payment of money (including costs) must be complied with within 14 days of the judgment, unless the court specifies some other date for compliance (CPR, r 40.11). It may, eg, instead of requiring immediate payment, impose an order for payment by instalments. A judgment for payment by instalments must state the total amount of the judgment, the amount of each instalment, the number of instalments and the date on which each is to be paid, and to whom the instalments should be paid (PD 40B, para 12). **41.22**

Counterclaims

The court has power to give separate judgments when dealing with cases where there are claims and counterclaims. It also has power to order a set-off between the two claims, and simply enter judgment for the balance (CPR, r 40.13(2)). Where it does so, it retains power to make separate costs orders in respect of the claims and counterclaims (r 40.13(3)). **41.23**

State benefits recoupment

In personal injuries cases where some or all of the damages are subject to recovery under the Social Security (Recovery of Benefits) Act 1997, the judgment should include a preamble setting out the amounts awarded under each head of damage, and the amount by which it has been reduced in accordance with the Act (PD 40B, para 5.1). The judgment should **41.24** then provide for entry of judgment and payment of the balance. There are slightly different requirements under para 5.1A where there has been a deductible lump sum payment within s 1A.

Provisional damages

41.25 At common law an award of damages had to be by way of a single sum in compensation. This did not always produce a just result in personal injuries cases involving a risk of the claimant suffering some future deterioration related to the original injury. Although the court would increase the damages awarded to take into account the risk of the future deterioration, the uplift would be only a fraction of the true loss if it occurred, and the claimant would be overcompensated if it did not occur. To remedy this shortcoming, the courts have been given power to award provisional damages by the SCA 1981, s 32A, and the CCA 1984, s 51.

41.26 These sections provide that an award of provisional damages may be made in an:

> ...action for damages for personal injuries in which there is proved or admitted to be a chance that at some definite or indefinite time in the future the injured person will, as a result of the act or omission which gave rise to the cause of action, develop some serious disease or suffer some serious deterioration in his physical or mental condition.

41.27 A provisional damages award has two elements:

(a) immediate damages in respect of the existing injuries, calculated on the assumption that the claimant will not develop the future disease or that the future deterioration will not be suffered; and
(b) an entitlement to return to court to apply for further damages if the disease develops or the deterioration is suffered.

Conditions for awarding provisional damages

41.28 There are four conditions:

(a) The particulars of claim must include a claim for provisional damages (CPR, r 41.2(1)(a)).
(b) The future disease or deterioration must be to the claimant's physical or mental condition.
(c) The future disease or deterioration must be 'serious'. According to Scott Baker J in *Willson v Ministry of Defence* [1991] 1 All ER 638, this connotes something beyond the ordinary or commonly experienced consequences of the injury in question. It is relevant to consider the effect on the particular claimant, eg, a hand injury will be more serious to a concert pianist than to most other claimants. One matter particularly considered in *Willson v Ministry of Defence* was whether possible future osteoarthritis could be the subject of a provisional damages award. An increased risk of the onset of osteoarthritis is a common factor where an accident victim has suffered fractured bones. As such, it is not beyond the ordinary, and Scott Baker J took the view that even if the future risk of osteoarthritis involved a possible need for surgery or a change in employment it would not be 'serious'.
(d) There must be a 'chance' that the future deterioration 'will' be suffered. If this is not admitted by the defendant, it must be proved on the balance of probabilities. The

'chance' that must be proved is one that is measurable as opposed to being fanciful. In *Patterson v Ministry of Defence* [1987] CLY 1194, Simon Brown J found that the claimant had about a 5 per cent risk of developing further pleural thickening, and decided there was a 'plain' chance of that happening for the purposes of making a provisional damages award.

Discretion to award provisional damages

Once the above conditions have been established, the court has a discretion whether to make a provisional damages award as opposed to a conventional lump-sum award. The most important factors are usually the desirability of putting an end to litigation and the possibility of doing better justice by reserving the claimant's right to return to court for further damages. Provisional damages are more appropriate where the risk of the future deterioration is high and the nature of the possible future deterioration is very serious (eg, a future risk of severe epilepsy). Provisional damages are also more likely to be awarded if the claimant can point to some clear-cut future event that will trigger the entitlement to return to court for further damages. **41.29**

Provisional damages orders

A provisional damages order: **41.30**

(a) must specify the disease or type of deterioration in respect of which an application may be made for further damages at a future date;
(b) must specify the period within which that application may be made. The period for applying for further damages may be extended; and
(c) may be made in respect of more than one disease or type of deterioration, and may, in respect of each disease or type of deterioration, specify a different period for applying for further damages.

A model form of provisional damages judgment is set out in PD 41A. This includes a provision requiring a case file of documents to be filed and preserved until the expiry of the period (or any extension) during which the claimant is entitled to apply for further damages if the specified disease develops or the specified deterioration is suffered. The documents that will usually be included in the case file are the judgment, the statements of case, a transcript of the judge's oral judgment, all medical reports relied upon, and a transcript of the claimant's own evidence in so far as the judge regards it as necessary (PD 41A, para 3.2). The fact that there may be a few 'loose ends' where the parties cannot agree does not prevent the court making a provisional damages award: *Hurditch v Sheffield Health Authority* [1989] QB 562. **41.31**

Other matters dealt with in PD 41A are the entering of consent orders for provisional damages (para 4) and default judgments (which can only be entered with the court's permission, with the master or district judge having to decide whether the case is an appropriate one for a provisional damages award: para 5). **41.32**

Applying for further damages

If the deterioration occurs, an application for further damages should be made within the period specified in the order (as extended from time to time). Only one application for further damages can be made in respect of each disease or deterioration specified in the order. **41.33**

The claimant must give 28 days' notice of the intention to ask for further damages. Within 21 days of the expiry of the 28 days' notice the claimant has to apply to the court for directions. In other respects, the rules relating to applying for interim payments (described in Chapter 23) apply on the application for further damages (CPR, r 41.3(6)).

Periodic payments

41.34 By virtue of an agreement between the Inland Revenue and the Association of British Insurers in 1987, periodic payments made under certain settlements and orders are deemed to be instalments of antecedent debts. The result is that the payments are capital and not income and therefore are not taxable. This tax advantage is obtained by using the whole or a part of the lump sum which would otherwise be available to purchase an annuity. There are four types of annuity which qualify under the scheme:

(a) a basic-term annuity, which runs for a fixed number of years;
(b) an index-linked (ie, one which rises with inflation) fixed-term annuity;
(c) an annuity for life or for a minimum number of years (which survives for the claimant's beneficiaries); and
(d) an index-linked life or minimum-term annuity.

41.35 Annuities are bought from life offices. A life office will quote a price of an annuity if given certain details about the claimant (age, sex, medical reports, level of income required, etc.). A quotation will normally remain open for only a limited time. The basic idea is that the tax advantage should be shared between the parties, so that the claimant obtains a more favourable result which will provide more income than that obtainable under a lump-sum award, and the defendant will pay less for the annuity than the conventional award. An award in the form of periodic payments can be made where both parties agree, or may be ordered by the court if it awards damages for future pecuniary loss in respect of personal injuries (Damages Act 1996, s 2, as substituted by the Courts Act 2003, s 100). A periodic payments award can only be made if the court is satisfied the continuity of payments under the order is reasonably secure (s 2(3)). It is generally thought that structuring is viable only where damages run into six figures.

41.36 A periodic payments award must specify the annual amount of the award, how each payment is to be made and at what intervals, and the amounts of the main heads of loss (CPR, r 41.8(1)). There are further requirements where the court orders the award to continue after death for the benefit of the claimant's dependants, where the award is to increase or decrease, and where there is an award for substantial capital purchases (r 41.8(2)–(4), supplemented by PD 41B, para 2). Variations may be permitted pursuant to the Damages (Variation of Periodical Payments) Order 2005 (SI 2005/841).

41.37 Where a claim which includes damages for future pecuniary loss is settled on behalf of a claimant under a disability, court approval is required (see 17.16), and the rules in PD 21, paras 6.3 to 6.9 relating to periodic payments must be complied with.

41.38 Where an interim payment (Chapter 23) is awarded in a case where there is likely to be an award of periodic payments, the court has to consider the effect the interim payment might have on the ability of the court to do justice at trial (*Mealing v Chelsea and Westminster NHS*

Trust [2008] LS Law Med 236; *Braithwaite v Homerton University Hospitals NHS Foundation Trust* [2008] LS Law Med 261). Too large an interim payment may make it impossible to make an effective periodic payments order, or too little to provide for the necessary capital expenses for the claimant's care.

D GENERAL RULES RELATING TO DRAWING UP ORDERS AND JUDGMENTS

Rules 40.2(2) and 40.3(1) of the CPR provide that all judgments and orders have to be drawn up and sealed by the court, unless it dispenses with the need to do so. Normally the court will take responsibility for drawing up, but: **41.39**

(a) in the QBD, TCC, and Commercial Court, orders are drawn up by the parties; or
(b) the court may order a party to draw up an order; or
(c) a party may, with the permission of the court, agree to draw up an order; or
(d) the court may direct a party to draw up the order subject to checking by the court before it is sealed; or
(e) the court may direct the parties to file an agreed statement of the terms of the order before the court itself draws up the order; or
(f) the order may be entered administratively by consent, in which event the parties will submit a drawn-up version of their agreement for entry.

Every judgment or order (apart from judgments on admissions, default judgments, and consent judgments) must state the name and judicial title of the judge who made it (r 40.2(1)). **41.40**

A party who is required to draw up a judgment is allowed seven days to file the relevant document, together with sufficient copies for all relevant parties, failing which any other party may draw it up and file it for sealing (CPR, rr 40.3(3) and 40.4(1)). Once an order has been drawn up the court will serve sealed copies on the applicant and respondent, and also on any other person the court may order to be served (rr 6.21(2), 40.4(2)). The court is given a specific power by r 40.5 to order service on a litigant as well as the litigant's solicitor. **41.41**

Entering administrative consent orders

In order to save time and costs, r 40.6 of the CPR allows certain types of consent orders to be entered by a purely administrative process without the need for obtaining the approval of a judge. However, this process may not be used if any of the parties is a litigant in person (r 40.6(2)(b)). **41.42**

The types of orders covered are: **41.43**

(a) judgments or orders for the payment of money;
(b) judgments or orders for the delivery-up of goods (other than specific delivery);
(c) orders to dismiss the whole or part of the proceedings;
(d) orders for stays on agreed terms which dispose of the proceedings, including Tomlin orders;
(e) orders setting aside default judgments;

(f) orders for the discharge from liability of any party; and
(g) orders for the payment, waiver, or assessment of costs.

41.44 The consent order has to be drawn up in the agreed terms, has to bear the words 'By Consent', and has to be signed by the solicitors or counsel acting for each of the parties. In cases where terms are annexed in a schedule, provisions dealing with the payment of money out of court and for the payment and assessment of costs should be contained in the body of the order rather than in the schedule (PD 40B, para 3.5).

Consent orders approved by the court

41.45 If an order is agreed between the parties, but includes a provision going beyond the types of orders referred to in 41.43, or if one of the parties is a litigant in person, it will have to be approved by a judge (often a district judge or master). It will be drawn up as above. The name of the judge will not be known, so the draft will have to include a space for the judge's details to be inserted (PD 23A, para 10.3). If all the parties write to the court expressing their consent, the court will treat that as sufficient signing of the consent order (PD 23A, para 10.2). The court will not necessarily make the order in accordance with the agreement between the parties, as the court retains ultimate control, particularly over case management matters. However, it will always take the terms agreed between the parties into account in whatever order it decides to make (see, eg, PD 28, para 3.8).

41.46 In cases where the court's approval must be sought, either party may make the application for approval, and the application may be dealt with without a hearing (CPR, r 40.6(5), (6)).

Chancery Division orders

41.47 Most Chancery Division orders are drawn up by the court, although the court may direct or permit a party to draw them up, and in cases where the terms of an order are agreed between the parties, the agreed statement of the terms of the order will usually be adopted as the order of the court. The *Chancery Guide*, paras 9.13 to 9.15, also contains a number of detailed provisions relating to consent orders in the Chancery Division.

Redacted judgments

41.48 Judgments delivered giving reasons for the court's decision are usually given in open court and include all details relevant to the reasoning process used by the judge. There are cases where some of the details in the case are highly sensitive. If such details are protected by public interest immunity the relevant government minister may issue a certificate (see 29.63), which will usually result in the protected information being removed ('redacted') from the judgment that is made public. Cogent reasons are required before the court will go behind a ministerial certificate, a situation that arose in *R (Mohamed) v Secretary of State for Foreign and Commonwealth Affairs* [2010] EWCA Civ 65.

Reconsideration of judgments

41.49 The court may reconsider a judgment after it has been pronounced provided this is done before it is drawn up. During this period factual errors can be corrected: *Spice Girls Ltd v*

Aprilia World Service BV (No 3) (2000) *The Times*, 12 September 2000. Reconsideration should be sought only in exceptional circumstances (*Stewart v Engel* [2000] 1 WLR 2268). It would be a misuse of the jurisdiction to argue that a judge should reconsider an issue which was in dispute and already argued: that would be to subvert the appeal process: *Companie Noga d'Importation et d'Exportation SA v Abacha* [2001] 3 All ER 513.

Slip rule and appeals

Subject to the slip rule, once the judgment has been drawn up the judge is *functus officio*, which operates as a bar to further alterations by the judge (*Earl of Malmesbury v Strutt and Parker* (2007) 42 EG 294 (CS)). The slip rule (CPR, r 40.2(1)) gives the court power to correct any accidental slip or omission in any judgment. While the slip rule cannot be used to correct matters of substance, it can be used for the purpose of giving effect to the intention of the court (*Swindale v Forder* [2007] 1 FLR 1905). It cannot be used to enable the court to have second or additional thoughts (*Bristol-Myers Squibb Co v Baker Norton Pharmaceuticals Inc (No 2)* [2001] RPC 913), nor where the court and parties never had the point in mind (*Smithkline Beecham plc v Apotex Europe Ltd* [2006] 1 WLR 872). If the error is obvious the court may deal with the application without notice (PD 40B, para 4.3). Opposed applications will normally be listed before the judge who gave the judgment or made the order (para 4.4). Otherwise, a dissatisfied party is limited to its rights on appeal (see Chapter 46). **41.50**

E REGISTER OF JUDGMENTS

A register of High Court and county court money judgments is operated by Registry Trust Ltd under powers given by the Courts Act 2003, s 98. Courts provide periodic returns containing details of unsatisfied judgments to Registry Trust Ltd, a not-for-profit company, and the register kept by the company is open to inspection on payment of prescribed fees. The information is regularly used by financial institutions for credit scoring purposes. See <**http://www.registry-trust.org.uk**>. **41.51**

Tomlin orders are not regarded as money judgments (even if one of the terms provides for the payment of money) and so are not registrable, nor are exempt judgments. Judgments in family proceedings and judgments after contested hearings prior to enforcement are exempt from registration. When a registered judgment has been paid, there is provision for the court to send a certificate of satisfaction to Registry Trust Ltd, after which a note to that effect is entered on the register. Entries are cancelled after six years. **41.52**

KEY POINTS SUMMARY

- Drawing up judgments is a matter of producing an accurate record of the court's decision which can be enforced if not complied with by the relevant parties. **41.53**

- In the QBD, TCC, and Commercial Court drawing up is usually done by the parties. Elsewhere, it is generally done by the court.
- The general format of orders is discussed at 41.11ff.
- Orders with time limits (41.12), consent orders (41.15–41.18), Tomlin orders (41.19–41.21), and 'unless orders' (28.12) are particularly important in practice.

42

OFFERS TO SETTLE

A INTRODUCTION

Litigation is essentially about resolving disputes. Ultimately, this can be achieved by a judgment delivered at trial, but it has long been recognized that this has to be a last resort, and that there are better ways of bringing disputes to an end. There are various alternative dispute mechanisms that can assist in this process (for full details see Browne, Blake and Sime, *A Practical Approach to ADR* (Oxford, 2010). Part of this is direct negotiation between the **42.01** parties or their advisers. Negotiation can take place informally, eg, over the telephone, or at formal meetings, but probably most commonly through written correspondence. To ensure unfair advantage is not taken of comments made in negotiations if the case cannot be settled, communications between the parties for the purpose of seeking to settle a dispute are protected by without prejudice privilege (see 29.47–29.51). Most communications attempting to move towards settlement of a dispute are of this nature, and cannot be disclosed to the court (other than as evidence to prove that the claim has been settled, if one of the parties later resiles from the agreement). If this was the entire story, there would be no means available to a party who feels the other side have been unreasonably difficult in negotiations to bring that conduct to the court's attention for the purpose of having that conduct reflected in the order for costs.

42.02 What CPR Part 36 does is to provide a means for a party to make a formal offer in settlement of the claim which will be treated as without prejudice for the purposes of liability and remedies, but which can be disclosed to the court on the question of costs. This is done by making a written offer complying with certain formalities, which has an initial acceptance period of at least 21 days. Its function is to place the other side on risk as to costs if it is not accepted and the offeree then fails to achieve a result in the litigation which is more advantageous than the terms of the offer (*Matthews v Metal Improvements Co Inc* [2007] EWCA Civ 215). A party who receives a realistic formal offer is therefore best advised to accept it, thereby settling the claim.

42.03 The current version of Part 36 came into operation on 6 April 2007. The previous version used a combination of payments into court for money claims, and what used to be called '*Calderbank* offers' for non-money claims. Payments into court were abolished as from 6 April 2007, and the current system is based around making 'offers to settle'.

B OFFERS TO SETTLE BEFORE THE COMMENCEMENT OF PROCEEDINGS

42.04 An offer to settle within the meaning of CPR Part 36 (a 'Part 36 offer'), may be made at any time, including before the commencement of proceedings (r 36.3(2)(a)) or in appeal proceedings (r 36.3(2)(b)). Offers to settle before the commencement of proceedings were considered at 5.30–5.36. Offers to settle in claims governed by the RTA protocol are considered in Chapter 6. The rest of this chapter will consider the general rules applicable to all types of Part 36 offers.

C OFFERS TO SETTLE

42.05 Parties are not obliged to use the Part 36 format when making an offer to settle, but if they do not, the consequences in CPR, rr 36.10, 36.11, and 36.14, do not apply (r 36.1(2)).

Formalities

A Part 36 offer must: **42.06**

(a) be made in writing (CPR, r 36.2(2)(a)). Although a Part 36 offer may be made in a letter, it is better to use form N242A (see PD 36A, para 1.1);
(b) state on its face that it is intended to have the consequences of Part 36 (r 36.2(2)(b));
(c) if made at least 21 days before trial, specify a period of not less than 21 days within which the defendant will be liable for the claimant's costs in accordance with r 36.10 if the offer is accepted (rr 36.2(2)(c) and 36.2(3)). This 21-day period is called the 'relevant period' in Part 36. An offeree who needs more time to investigate should ask the offeror to consent to extend the relevant period, failing which a time application should be made under r 3.1(2)(a) (*Martin v Randall* [2007] EWCA Civ 1155). In cases where an offer is made less than 21 days before the start of the trial, the relevant period is the period up to the end of the trial or such other period as the court may determine (r 36.3(1)(c)(ii));
(d) state whether it relates to the whole of the claim, or part of it, or to an issue that arises in the claim, and if so, which part or issue (r 36.2(2)(d)). An offer may relate solely to liability (r 36.2(5)); and
(e) state whether it takes into account any counterclaim (r 36.2(2)(e)).

Terms of the offer

A Part 36 offer needs to state the terms of the proposed compromise, which should be sufficiently precise and certain for an effective contract to be formed if the offer is accepted. It is important to be clear on whether the offer is in full and final settlement of all matters in dispute between the parties, or defined matters between the parties, and whether the offer takes into account matters such as any cross-claim or previous interim payment. The terms of the offer must include the costs consequences of acceptance: see 42.06, para (c). **42.07**

Additional formalities for money claims

Part 36 offers made by defendants in claims for money must offer to pay a single sum of money (CPR, r 36.4(1)). An offer to pay all or part of a sum of money at a date later than 14 days following the date of any acceptance is not treated as a Part 36 offer unless the offeree accepts the offer (r 36.4(2)). The single sum offered is treated as inclusive of all interest to the end of the relevant period (r 36.3(3)). **42.08**

Deduction of benefits in personal injuries claims

When making a Part 36 offer in a claim for damages for personal injuries, the defendant should state (CPR, r 36.15(3)) either: **42.09**

(a) that the offer is made without regard to any liability for recoverable amounts under the Social Security (Recovery of Benefits) Act 1997; or
(b) that the offer is intended to include any deductible amounts under the 1997 Act. In such a case the defendant's offer should state the amount of gross compensation; the name

and amount of any deductible benefit or deductible lump sum; and the net amount after deduction of recoverable amounts (r 36.15(6)).

Figure 42.1 Notice of offer to settle—Part 36

Notice of offer to settle - Part 36

Name of court *(If proceedings have started)*	
Claim No. (or other ref)	
Claimant (including ref)	
Defendant (including ref)	

To the Offeree ('s Solicitor) *(Insert name and address)*

Take notice the (defendant)(claimant) offers to settle the claim. This offer is intended to have the consequences of Part 36. If the offer is accepted within ________ days (must be at least 21 days) of service of this notice the defendant will be liable for the claimant's costs in accordance with Rule 36.10 of the Civil Procedure Rules.

The offer is to settle:

(tick as appropriate)

- ☐ the whole of the claim
- ☐ part of the claim *(give details below)*
- ☐ a certain issue or issues in the claim *(give details below)*

The offer is:

(Insert details - expand box as necessary)

Note: Rule 36.5 specifies details that must be included in an offer including periodical payments of damages for future pecuniary loss.

Rule 36.11 requires that an offer by a defendant to pay a sum of money (other than periodical payments) must be paid within 14 days of acceptance.

☐ It (does)(does not) take into account all(part) of the following counterclaim:

(give details of the counterclaim)

N242A Notice of offer to settle - Part 36 (in settlement) (04.07)

Figure 42.1 *continued*

Include only if claim for provisional damages

☐ The offer is made in satisfaction of the claim on the assumption that the claimant will not [develop (state the disease)] **OR** [suffer (state type of deterioration)].

But if that does occur, the claimant will be entitled to claim further damages at any time before (insert date).

OR

☐ This offer does not include an offer in respect of the claim for provisional damages.

To be completed by defendants only

☐ This offer is made without regard to any liability for recoverable benefits under the Social Security (Recovery of Benefits Act) 1997.

OR

☐ This offer is intended to include any relevant deductible benefits for which I am liable under the Social Security (Recovery of Benefits Act) 1997.

The amount of [£] is offered by way of gross compensation.

[I have not yet received a certificate of recoverable benefits]

OR

[The following amounts in respect of the following benefits are to be deducted (insert details).

Type of benefit	**Amount**

The net amount offered is therefore [£]]

Signed ☐
Offeror('s solicitor)

Position held (If signing on behalf of a firm or company) ☐

Date ☐

Personal injuries claims for future pecuniary loss

42.10 Claims for future pecuniary loss in personal injury claims are governed by the Damages Act 1996, s 2(1): see 41.34–41.38. A number of additional formalities have to be included in a Part 36 offer in such a case (see CPR, r 36.5). The formalities include specifying whether the offer is for compensation in the form of either:

(a) a lump sum to cover the whole claim; or
(b) a mix of a lump sum and periodic payments in respect of the claim for future pecuniary losses; or
(c) periodic payments for the future pecuniary losses.

Offers in provisional damages claims

42.11 A Part 36 offer made in a claim which includes a claim for provisional damages must specify whether the offer includes an award of provisional damages (CPR, r 36.6(2)). The offer must by r 36.6(3) also state:

(a) that the sum offered is in satisfaction of the claim for damages on the assumption that the claimant will not develop the disease or suffer the deterioration specified in the offer; and
(b) that the offer is subject to the condition that the claimant must make any claim for further damages within a specified period.

Defence of tender before claim

42.12 A defendant who wishes to rely on a defence of tender before claim must make a payment into court of the amount said to have been tendered (CPR, r 37.2). This is a narrow exception to the abolition of payments into court. The payment in should be paid at the time of filing the defence (*Greening v Williams* (1999) *The Times*, 10 December 1999). Money paid into court in support of a defence of tender before claim may not be paid out without the court's permission, except where it is accepted without needing permission and the defendant agrees that the sum in court can be used to satisfy the offer (r 37.3). The rule (see 42.40ff) that Part 36 offers must not be communicated to the trial judge does not apply to tenders before claim (r 36.13(3)(a)).

Clarification

42.13 If the terms of a Part 36 offer are unclear, the offeree may ask the offeror to clarify the offer (CPR, r 36.8(1)). The request should be made within seven days of service of the offer, and the offeror should respond within seven days of receiving the request (r 36.8(2)). If the offeror fails to provide the requested clarification, the offeree is entitled to apply for an order that it be provided. Such an order will also specify the date when the Part 36 offer is to be treated as having been made (r 36.8(3)).

D MAKING A PART 36 OFFER

A Part 36 offer is made when it is served on the offeree (CPR, r 36.7(1)). One of the prescribed methods of service in r 6.20 should be used, see 8.16 and 8.41. Where the offeree is legally represented, the offer must be served on the legal representative (PD 36A, para 1.2). **42.14**

E ACCEPTANCE OF A PART 36 OFFER

Notice of acceptance

A Part 36 offer is accepted by serving written notice of acceptance (there is no prescribed form, so a letter will suffice) on the offeror (CPR, r 36.9(1)). It is also necessary to file the notice of acceptance with the court (PD 36A, para 3.1). In most cases the offeror should serve the notice of acceptance during the relevant period. When this happens the defendant must pay the claimant's standard-basis costs up to the date of notice of acceptance (see r 36.10(1), (3)). The claimant is entitled to 100 per cent of his assessed costs, and the court has no jurisdiction to order payment of only a proportion of those costs (*Lahey v Pirelli Tyres Ltd* [2007] 1 WLR 998). **42.15**

Late acceptance

Notice of acceptance may be served after the relevant period. If *Wakefield v Ford* [2009] EWHC 122 (QB) is correct, a Part 36 offer may be worded to provide that it is only open for a limited time. Late acceptance of a Part 36 offer in the usual form is effective only if the offer has not been withdrawn before service of the notice of acceptance (CPR, r 36.9(2)). In this situation the parties may agree the liability for costs, but if they do not, the court will make an order for costs (r 36.10(4)(b)). A costs order made by the court will usually provide that: **42.16**

(a) the claimant is entitled to costs up to the expiry of the relevant period; and
(b) the offeree will be liable for the offeror's costs for the period from the expiry of the relevant period to the date of acceptance.

Even where the late acceptance is of a claimant's offer to settle (rather than a defendant's offer), costs ordered under r 36.10(4) should be on the standard basis, although enhanced interest on costs after expiry of the relevant period may be appropriate (*Fitzpatrick Contractors Ltd v Tyco Fire and Integrated Solutions (UK) Ltd* [2009] BLR 144). **42.17**

It is permissible for the court to make some other order for costs (r 36.10(5)). Departure from the usual rule is only justified if the judge can identify some fact rendering it unjust for the claimant to pay the defendant's costs after the expiry of the relevant period (*Matthews v Metal Improvements Co Inc* [2007] EWCA Civ 215). It is not enough for the judge to say that it was reasonable for the claimant not to have accepted the Part 36 offer when it was made, and later to have accepted it. **42.18**

42.19 A notice of acceptance served after the trial has started will only be effective if the court's permission is given (r 36.9(3)(d)). A notice of acceptance served after the end of the trial but before judgment is handed down is only effective if the parties agree (r 36.9(5)).

42.20 Where the terms of the acceptance include the disposition of an interest in land, the court has the power to order the parties to sign a single document incorporating the terms of the settlement (*Orton v Collins* [2007] 1 WLR 2953).

Acceptance relating to part of the claim

42.21 An acceptance of a Part 36 offer relating to only part of the claim results in a settlement of the claim and the claimant's entitlement to costs only if the claimant abandons the balance of the claim (CPR, r 36.10(2)). If the balance is not abandoned, that part proceeds to trial, and the court has a discretion on the costs of the compromised part of the claim.

Permission to accept

42.22 The court's permission is required for an acceptance of a Part 36 offer where:

(a) the Part 36 offer is made by some, but not all, of a number of defendants and CPR, r 36.12(4), applies (r 36.9(3)(a));
(b) the claim is for damages for personal injuries, the offer is intended to include any deductible amounts, and further deductible benefits or a deductible lump sum have been paid to the claimant since the date of the offer (r 36.9(3)(b)). In this situation the application must state the net amount offered in the Part 36 offer, the deductible amounts accrued at the date of the offer, and those that have subsequently accrued. The application must be accompanied by a copy of the current certificate of recoverable amounts (PD 36A, para 3.3);
(c) an apportionment is required under r 41.3A (Fatal Accidents Act claims) (r 36.9(3)(c));
(d) the trial has started (r 36.9(3)(d)); or
(e) any of the parties is a child or protected party (r 21.10).

Stay on acceptance

42.23 If a Part 36 offer is accepted, the claim will be stayed (CPR, r 36.11(1)). The stay will be on the terms of the offer where the Part 36 offer relates to the whole claim (r 36.11(2)), but operates only in relation to the relevant part of the claim if the offer related to only part of the claim (r 36.11(3)). A stay under r 36.11(1) does not affect the power of the court to enforce the terms of the Part 36 offer, nor to deal with any question of costs or interest on costs relating to the proceedings (r 36.11(5)).

Time for payment

42.24 Unless the parties agree otherwise in writing, where a Part 36 offer to pay money is accepted, payment must be made within 14 days of the acceptance (CPR, r 36.11(6)(a)).

F REJECTION OF A PART 36 OFFER

There is no need for the offeree to give an express rejection of a Part 36 offer. An express rejection will operate in accordance with its terms. Making a counter-offer does not, contrary to the usual rules in the law of contract, operate as a rejection of a Part 36 offer (CPR, r 36.9(2)). Doing nothing (or only making a counter-offer) allows the offeree to serve a late notice of acceptance (see 42.16) if the offer has not been withdrawn (provided the Part 36 offer is not construed as time-limited). **42.25**

G WITHDRAWAL AND AMENDMENT OF PART 36 OFFERS

Before the expiry of the relevant period

Before the expiry of the relevant period, a Part 36 offer may be withdrawn or its terms changed in a way less advantageous to the offeree only with the court's permission (CPR, r 36.3(5)). Permission is sought by making an application in accordance with Part 23 (PD 36A, para 2.2(1)). **42.26**

After the expiry of the relevant period

After expiry of the relevant period and provided the offeree has not previously served notice of acceptance, the offeror may withdraw the offer or change its terms to be less advantageous to the offeree without the permission of the court (CPR, r 36.3(6)). This is done by serving written notice on the offeree (r 36.3(7)). A change in the terms of a Part 36 offer (whether it is an improved offer or one which is less advantageous to the offeree) takes effect when written notice of the change is served on the offeree (rr 36.2(2)(a), 36.7(2)). **42.27**

Effect of a withdrawn Part 36 offer

A withdrawn Part 36 offer ceases to have the effect on costs and interest of a subsisting Part 36 offer (CPR, r 36.14(6)(a)). However, r 44.3 requires the court to consider an offer to settle which does not have the costs consequences set out in Part 36 in deciding what order to make about costs. This gives the court a wide discretion, to be exercised applying the overriding objective. In a suitable case the court can even treat a withdrawn Part 36 offer as having the same costs consequences as if it had not been withdrawn (*Trustees of Stokes Pension Fund v Western Power Distribution (South West) plc* [2005] 1 WLR 3595). **42.28**

H FAILING TO OBTAIN JUDGMENT MORE ADVANTAGEOUS THAN A PART 36 OFFER

There are costs and interest consequences (see CPR, r 36.14(1)) where a Part 36 offer is not accepted and either: **42.29**

(a) the claimant fails to obtain a judgment more advantageous than the Part 36 offer if made by the defendant; or

(b) judgment is entered against the defendant which is at least as advantageous to the claimant as the proposals set out in the Part 36 offer if made by the claimant.

42.30 The consequences in r 36.14 do not apply where the Part 36 offer has been withdrawn, or changed to terms less advantageous to the offeree than the judgment, or if the Part 36 offer was made less than 21 days before the trial (unless the court abridges time).

42.31 In deciding whether a judgment is more advantageous than a Part 36 offer which includes interest, the court must recalculate the interest included in the judgment to find the sum in interest that would have been awarded on the relevant date (*Blackham v Entrepose UK* [2004] EWCA Civ 1109). Where there are deductible amounts the question is whether the claimant has failed to recover, after deduction of recoverable amounts, a sum greater than the net sum stated in the Part 36 offer in compliance with r 36.15(6)(c).

42.32 Obtaining judgment which is 'more advantageous' than the other side's Part 36 offer is a more open-textured issue than merely obtaining judgment for more than the amount offered. In *Carver v BAA plc* [2009] 1 WLR 113, CA, judgment was entered for just under £5,000 in a claim said to be worth about £20,000. The judgment was (after adjustment for interest) £51 more than the defendant's offer to settle. Nevertheless, the judgment was held not to be more advantageous than the offer, because no reasonable claimant would have embarked on litigation which cost the claimant £80,000, together with the stress and anxiety involved in taking the case to trial, for a gain of only £51.

Offers made by defendants

42.33 Where the judgment is not more advantageous than a Part 36 offer made by a defendant, unless the court considers it unjust to do so, the court will order:

(a) the defendant to pay the claimant's costs up to the expiry of the relevant period applying the usual principle that costs follow the event (CPR, r 44.3(2)(a)). This is an almost invariable rule, and an order running from the date of the offer rather than the expiry of the relevant period will be corrected on appeal (*Martin v Randall* [2007] EWCA Civ 1155);
(b) the claimant to pay the defendant's costs from the expiry of the relevant period (r 36.14(2)(a)); and
(c) the claimant to pay interest on the defendant's costs (r 36.14(2)(b)).

Offers made by claimants

42.34 Where the judgment is at least as advantageous as a Part 36 offer made by a claimant, unless the court considers it unjust to do so, the court will order:

(a) interest on the judgment (excluding interest) awarded at a rate not exceeding 10 per cent above base rate for some or all of the period since the expiry of the relevant period. Where interest is also awarded under the CCA 1984, s 69, or the SCA 1981, s 35A, the total rate of interest may not exceed 10 per cent above base rate (CPR, r 36.14(5));
(b) the defendant to pay the claimant's costs after the expiry of the relevant period on the indemnity basis; and
(c) interest on those indemnity-basis costs at a rate not exceeding 10 per cent above base rate.

Unjust to make usual costs and interest orders

It is far from easy to persuade a judge that it would be unjust (see 42.34) to apply the usual rule that the claimant must pay the defendant's costs from the expiry of the relevant period. The fact the claimant may have made its own Part 36 offer which was higher than the award at trial was regarded as irrelevant in *Quorum AS v Scramm* [2002] CLC 77 (which may be decided differently today given the decision in *Carver v BAA plc* [2009] 1 WLR 113). Even where the defendant loses on an important issue at trial, if the claimant fails to obtain judgment more advantageous than a Part 36 offer the usual rule should be applied (*Burgess v British Steel* (2000) *The Times*, 29 February 2000). **42.35**

In considering whether it would be unjust to make an order under CPR, r 36.14(2), or (3) on costs or interest, the court will, by r 36.14(4), take into account all the circumstances of the case, including: **42.36**

(a) the terms of the Part 36 offer;
(b) the stage in the proceedings when the Part 36 offer was made, and in particular the period between the offer and the start of the trial;
(c) the information available to the parties at the time when the Part 36 offer was made; and
(d) the conduct of the parties with regard to giving or refusing to give information for the purposes of enabling the offer to be made or evaluated.

It may be unjust to apply the usual rule where: **42.37**

- a party was late in disclosing important video surveillance evidence (*Ford v GKR Construction Ltd* [2000] 1 WLR 1397);
- a party was unwilling to participate in proposed mediation (*Re Midland Linen Services Ltd, Chaudry v Yap* (2004) LTL 28/10/04); or
- a claimant deliberately exaggerated the claim (*Painting v University of Oxford* [2005] PIQR Q5).

I EFFECT OF NON-COMPLIANCE WITH PART 36

A Part 36 offer should be interpreted as it would be read by a reasonable solicitor (*Onay v Brown* [2009] EWCA Civ 775). Minor defects in Part 36 offers are likely to be corrected under CPR, r 3.10, which gives the court a discretion to correct errors in procedure. In *Hertsmere Primary Care Trust v Administrators of Balasubramanium's Estate* [2005] 3 All ER 274 the offeree noticed a minor drafting defect in a Part 36 offer, but refused to tell the offeror what it was. The court held that this was a failure to cooperate, and ignored the defect. In *Trustees of Stokes Pension Fund v Western Power Distribution (South West) plc* [2005] 1 WLR 3595 the defendant made an offer which did not comply with Part 36, and at a later stage withdrew the offer. At trial the claimant was awarded slightly less than the offer. Despite the non-compliance with Part 36, the court took the offer into account on costs. Withdrawal of the offer was held to be irrelevant, because the claim was for over 30 times more than the amount recovered, and the claimant was not realistically going to accept any offer near the judgment sum. **42.38**

J ADVISING ON PART 36 OFFERS

42.39 There is a heavy responsibility on legal representatives advising their clients on whether offers should be made or accepted. Clients must be fully informed of the costs implications of an offer. This will include the amount that will be deducted by the adviser's firm in respect of costs, how that sum is calculated, and the client's right to the assessment of the firm's costs (Solicitors' Code of Conduct 2007, Guidance to r 2, para 37). Frequently, lawyers find themselves advising clients on these matters at the door of the court. When this happens they should concentrate on giving clear advice that can be readily understood by the client. They are not required to catalogue every factor that may have a bearing on whether an offer should be made or accepted (*Moy v Pettman Smith* [2005] 1 WLR 581).

K NON-DISCLOSURE TO JUDGE

42.40 The fact there has been a Part 36 offer (except in the case of a tender before claim) must not be disclosed to the court at trial until all questions of liability and remedies have been decided (CPR, r 36.13(2)). This embargo applies to trials, not interim applications. In advance of trial a request should be made to the court office to remove all references to any offers to settle from the court file to avoid accidental disclosure to the trial judge. If all the parties agree in writing, this embargo can be lifted (r 36.13(3)(c)).

42.41 If the fact there has been a Part 36 offer is disclosed in error to the judge, the judge has a discretion whether to continue with the trial or to withdraw. The judge is entitled to continue if satisfied there will be no prejudice to either side: *Garratt v Saxby* [2004] 1 WLR 2152. A judge should not be too ready to withdraw, and if satisfied that no injustice will be done, may continue with the trial. Matters to consider include the overriding objective, saving expense, and dealing with claims justly and proportionately.

42.42 The embargo on disclosing Part 36 offers to the judge applies to all questions relating to liability and remedies. A Part 36 offer cannot be referred to for the purpose of assessing damages or the amount of interest payable on a money claim (*Johnson v Gore Wood (No 2)* (2004) *The Times*, 17 February 2004).

L PART 36 OFFERS IN APPEALS

42.43 A Part 36 offer which is made before trial has effect in relation to the costs of the proceedings up to the final disposal of the proceedings at first instance (CPR, r 36.3(4)). Costs protection for appeal proceedings may be obtained by making a separate Part 36 offer in the appeal proceedings (rr 36.3(2)(b), 36.3(4)).

KEY POINTS SUMMARY

- Part 36 offers are formal offers to settle having costs consequences if they are not accepted. **42.44**
- If they are accepted, the case is settled, usually on terms that the defendant will also pay the claimant's costs (because in effect the claimant has won).
- If they are not accepted, the important question on costs is whether the eventual judgment is more advantageous than the offer, rather than the usual question of which party has won.
- Part 36 offers are made without prejudice save as to costs, and must not be mentioned to the trial judge until all questions on liability and quantum are finally determined.

43

COSTS

Legal costs will be incurred on behalf of a litigant from the time a solicitor is first consulted until the solicitor's retainer is terminated, perhaps after enforcement of any judgment that is obtained. The client (or the Community Legal Service Fund if the client is publicly funded) bears the primary responsibility for paying its own solicitor's bill. The bill comprises the solicitor's remuneration for the work done on the case, together with counsel's and any experts' fees, court fees, and any other charges, expenses, and disbursements. Solicitors' costs are divided into contentious and non-contentious costs, the distinction being that contentious costs relate to cases where proceedings have been begun before a court (see the Solicitors Act 1974, s 87(1)). Preliminary work prior to proceedings and work in proceedings before tribunals and inquiries are regarded as being non-contentious. This chapter is mainly concerned with the rules relating to contentious costs. **43.01**

Although each client is primarily responsible for its own solicitor's costs, it is usual for the successful party in a claim to be awarded an order for costs against the unsuccessful party. Orders for costs are invariably made after each interim hearing (for the costs of the interim application), the trial (for the costs of the whole proceedings other than any interim costs orders), and any appeal or enforcement proceedings. There are different bases for assessing, on the one hand, the costs payable by a client to its own solicitor, and, on the other hand, the costs recoverable by a successful litigant from an unsuccessful litigant. The result is that even a successful litigant usually has to pay something to its own solicitor, and an unsuccessful litigant has to pay both its own solicitor's costs and a substantial proportion of the other side's costs. **43.02**

This chapter describes the current system of costs. Sir Rupert Jackson has conducted a thorough *Review of Civil Litigation Costs* (December 2009), containing 109 recommendations which will have far-reaching effects not only on costs but also many other aspects of civil procedure. Key recommendations include a revised definition of proportionality (43.04 below), the abolition of the indemnity principle (43.31 below), the abolition of the recovery of success fees in CFAs, the legalization of contingency fees, and a 10 per cent increase in damages in a range of tort-based claims. **43.03**

A PROPORTIONALITY

One of the main aims of the CPR is to provide a system of civil justice which is reasonably affordable. Allied to this is the goal of making the costs of litigation more predictable, so that clients will have a fairly clear idea of the likely cost of proceedings they might become involved in at as early a stage as possible. A combination of measures seeks to achieve these objectives. These are: **43.04**

(a) Solicitors are under a duty to give their clients the best information possible about the overall costs of a matter both at the outset and as the case develops (Solicitors' Code of Conduct 2007, r 2.03).
(b) Encouraging use of conditional fee agreements (see Chapter 4). Litigants who take advantage of CFAs will know that, provided they keep to the agreement they reach with

their solicitors, they will not have to pay anything towards their own lawyers' costs. By taking out ATE insurance they may also be able to obtain protection against having to pay the costs of the other side.

(c) There is a system of fixed costs for road traffic accident claims up to £10,000 and fixed CFA success fees for certain personal injury claims in CPR Part 47.

(d) Judicial case management of cases, with the aim of focusing case preparation on the real issues in the case, and ensuring litigation progresses to trial without undue delay.

(e) Requiring the parties' solicitors to provide the court with costs estimates at the allocation and pre-trial checklist stages (see figure 14.1).

(f) Costs recoverable from the losing party in small claims track cases are limited to the court fees paid by the successful party, a nominal fixed sum to cover the claimant's solicitor's costs of issuing the claim, and limited witness expenses and experts' fees (CPR, r 27.14). Costs in small claims track cases are dealt with in Chapter 25.

(g) At the end of any fast track trial the usual position will be that the trial judge will simply make a summary assessment of the winner's costs of the claim there and then. Further, on the fast track there is a system of limited fixed trial costs, which depend on the value of the claim (see 43.13).

(h) A limit on recoverable costs may be imposed by making a costs capping order. An application for a costs capping order may be made at any stage of the proceedings (r 44.18(5)), although it should be made as soon as possible and preferably before the first case management hearing (PD Costs, para 23A.2).

B SUMMARY ASSESSMENT

43.05 Summary assessment of costs involves the court determining the amount payable by way of costs immediately at the end of a hearing, usually on a relatively rough-and-ready basis. The starting point will be the statement of costs, which should have been served 24 hours before the hearing. A failure to serve a statement of costs 24 hours in advance of the hearing should be met with a proportionate response: *Macdonald v Taree Holdings Ltd* [2001] CPLR 439. Options include:

(a) adjourning for a detailed assessment;

(b) adjourning to a later date for a summary assessment before the same judge, or for the summary assessment to be dealt with in writing; and

(c) adjourning for a short period to allow the unsuccessful party a chance to consider a late statement of costs, with the judge then considering the summary assessment, but with added leniency towards the paying party.

43.06 Courts sometimes develop conventional figures for specified costs for certain types of proceeding, such as the costs awarded for straightforward landlord and tenant possession proceedings. Although this may be acceptable in straightforward possession claims, it is contrary to principle in the majority of claims. On a summary assessment of costs the court must focus on the detailed breakdown of costs actually incurred by the party in question as shown on its statement of costs. The court is entitled to draw on its general experience of costs in comparable cases, and it may be helpful to draw on that experience in deciding whether the sum provisionally assessed by the court based on the figures in the schedule of costs is reasonable and proportionate. The court can call for whatever evidence is available at the time in deciding on the figure to be specified, such as looking at counsel's brief to see the brief fee, as well as hearing the advocates on the work involved in the matter.

Summarily assessed costs are generally payable within 14 days of the date of the order (CPR, r 44.8). The court retains a discretion to decide when such costs are to be paid (r 44.3), but any application for an extension of time in which to pay such costs should be supported by evidence: *Pepin v Watts* [2001] CPLR 9. **43.07**

C DETAILED ASSESSMENT

A detailed assessment of costs involves leaving the quantification of costs to a costs officer, who will consider the amount to be allowed at an assessment hearing at some stage in the future after the parties have been given the opportunity of setting out the amount claimed and points of dispute in writing. Detailed assessments are carried out mainly by district judges in the county courts, and there is a special office, called the Senior Courts Costs Office, for the High Court. Generally the court has a discretion to decide whether to make a summary assessment or to order a detailed assessment if the costs cannot be agreed. However, where money is claimed by, or ordered or agreed to be paid to, or for the benefit of a child or protected party, the court in general must order a detailed assessment of the costs payable by the claimant to his solicitor (CPR, r 48.5). **43.08**

D BASIS OF QUANTIFICATION

There are two bases of assessment of costs: the standard basis and the indemnity basis. As its name suggests, the standard basis is the one usually applied in costs orders between the parties in litigation. The indemnity basis is used when a client is paying its own solicitor, and also when a trustee's costs are payable out of the trust fund. It can also be used between competing parties in litigation as a penalty for misconduct, or as a result of a claimant recovering more at trial than the amount offered in a Part 36 offer. Costs orders should identify the intended basis of quantification. On both bases the court will not allow costs which have been unreasonably incurred or which are unreasonable in amount. **43.09**

On an assessment on the standard basis, which is the least generous basis, r 44.4(2) of the CPR provides that the court will: **43.10**

(a) only allow costs which are proportionate to the matters in issue; and
(b) resolve any doubt which it may have about whether costs were reasonably incurred or reasonable and proportionate in amount in favour of the paying party.

On an assessment on the indemnity basis there is no reference to proportionality, and any doubt whether costs were reasonably incurred or were reasonable in amount is resolved in favour of the receiving party (r 44.4(3)). **43.11**

E PROCEDURE ON DETAILED ASSESSMENT OF COSTS

43.12 Assessment proceedings must be commenced within three months of the judgment, order, award, or other determination giving rise to the right to costs (CPR, r 47.7). This is done by serving on the paying party a notice of commencement in form N252 together with a copy of the bill of costs (r 47.6(1)). The paying party may dispute any item in the bill by serving the receiving party with points of dispute. These must be served within 21 days after service of the notice of commencement (r 47.9). If the paying party fails to serve points of dispute within the permitted time, the receiving party may, on filing a request, obtain a default costs certificate (rr 47.9(4) and 47.11). The receiving party has the right, but is not obliged, to serve a reply to any points of dispute. Any reply should be served on the party who served the points of dispute within 21 days after service (r 47.13). Hearings are relatively informal, with the points in dispute being taken in turn and both sides making submissions and the costs officer making rulings on each point in turn.

F FAST TRACK TRIAL COSTS

43.13 Rule 46.2 of the CPR provides that advocates' trial fees in fast track cases will be:

Value of claim no more than £3,000	£485
Value of claim between £3,000 and £10,000	£690
Claims for non-money remedies	£690
Value of claim over £10,000 up to £15,000	£1,035
Value of claim over £15,000	£1,650
Additional fee for solicitor attending trial with counsel	£345

43.14 For a successful claimant the value of the claim is the amount of the judgment excluding interest, costs, and any reduction for contributory negligence, whereas for a successful defendant it is the amount of the claim specified on the claim form (or the maximum amount that could have been recovered on the pleaded case) (r 46.2(3)). If there is a counterclaim and both parties succeed, the relevant amount is the difference between the value of the two claims (r 46.3(6)). If there is a counterclaim with a greater value than the claim, and the claimant succeeds on the claim and defeats the counterclaim, the relevant amount is the value of the counterclaim (r 46.2(6)). There are detailed rules dealing with cases where there are several claimants or several defendants, including whether more than one party can be awarded fast track trial costs, which are set out in r 46.4. For claims for non-monetary remedies the court has a discretion to make some other order: see r 46.2(4).

43.15 The solicitor's attendance fee will be payable only if the court awards fast track trial costs and if the court considers that it was necessary for a legal representative to attend to assist counsel (r 46.3(2)).

43.16 A successful party may, by r 46.3(7), be awarded less than the above fixed fast track trial costs for unreasonable or improper behaviour during the trial, and the losing party may be ordered to pay an additional amount if it is guilty of behaving improperly during the trial (r 46.3(8)).

G FIXED AND PREDICTABLE COSTS IN PERSONAL INJURIES CLAIMS

There is a system of fixed and predictable costs and CFA success fees in various types of personal injury claims. For some types of claim there are fixed amounts of costs payable, regardless of the costs actually incurred. In others there are set success fee uplifts for CFAs. Full details can be found in BCP, Chapter 67. **43.17**

H GENERAL PRINCIPLES

The two main principles when it comes to deciding which party should pay the costs of an application or of the whole proceedings are: **43.18**

(a) the costs payable by one party to another are in the discretion of the court (SCA 1981, s 51; CPR, r 44.3(1)); and
(b) the general rule, as now stated in r 44.3(2), is that the unsuccessful party will be ordered to pay the costs of the successful party ('costs follow the event' in the old terminology). It is incumbent on a judge to give reasons for departing from the usual rule that costs follow the event: *Aspin v Metric Group Ltd* (2007) LTL 25/9/07.

The starting point on final costs orders is that the winner should be awarded the whole of his costs of the proceedings, even if there are issues on which he had been unsuccessful (*Actavis Ltd v Merck and Co Inc* (2007) LTL 7/8/07). This is a strong principle, and despite the fact that costs orders are discretionary (SCA 1981, s 51; CPR, r 44.3(1)), an appeal court will intervene where a judge fails to give the principle sufficient weight (*Adamson v Halifax plc* [2003] 1 WLR 60). A claimant who wins on primary liability should normally recover the whole of its costs even if there is a finding of contributory negligence (*Krysia Maritime Inc v Intership Ltd* [2009] 1 All ER (Comm) 292). In a suitable case it will give way to other considerations, such as partial success, or past failure to comply with protocols or directions. Merely failing to recover as much as had been claimed does not give grounds for reducing the winner's costs (*Hall v Stone* (2007) *The Times*, 1 February 2008). However, depriving the winner of a percentage of his costs does not rest on a need to find unreasonable or improper conduct. **43.19**

The discretion granted by the SCA 1981, s 51(1), is very wide, and the courts are opposed to limitations being imposed on it by implication or rigid rules of practice (see *Bankamerica Finance Ltd v Nock* [1988] AC 1002). However, like any other discretion, it must of course be exercised judicially and on reasons connected with the case (see *Donald Campbell and Co Ltd v Pollock* [1927] AC 732, and the speech of Viscount Cave LC). **43.20**

In exercising its discretion on costs the court is required to have regard to all the circumstances, and in particular to the following matters (CPR, r 44.3(4) and (5)): **43.21**

(a) the extent to which the parties followed any applicable pre-action protocol;
(b) the extent to which it was reasonable for the parties to raise, pursue, or contest each of the allegations or issues;

(c) the manner in which the parties pursued or defended the claim or particular allegations or issues;
(d) whether the successful party exaggerated the value of the claim;
(e) whether a party was only partly successful; and
(f) any admissible offer to settle.

43.22 The first of these factors is one of the methods by which pre-action protocols will be enforced, albeit indirectly (see 5.23). Factors (b) and (e) require the court to take into account the extent to which the overall winner was in fact successful on the various issues, heads of claim, etc., raised in the case, when dealing with costs. This is intended to support the aspects of the overriding objective relating to identifying the real issues in the case, and only pursuing those issues to trial (see CPR, r 1.4(2)(b) and (c)). Generally, when a party is partially successful, the trial judge should award one party a percentage of its costs rather than awarding costs on different issues to different parties, because a percentage order avoids a great deal of complication on assessment of costs (*English v Emery Reimbold and Strick Ltd* [2002] 1 WLR 2409).

43.23 The third factor, which covers unreasonable conduct, has always been relevant on costs, but could also be used against parties who fail to conduct litigation in accordance with the new ethos, such as those who are unreasonably uncooperative (see r 1.4(2)(a)). Exaggeration of the value of a claim (factor (d)) will obviously be relevant where the claim is inflated for the purpose of bringing it in the High Court or to have the case allocated to a higher track than it deserves. It could also be used in cases where exaggeration of the claim makes it difficult for the defendant to assess its true value for the purposes of making an offer to settle or a payment into court.

Nominal damages

43.24 A claimant who has claimed substantial damages but has recovered only nominal damages will normally be ordered to pay the defendant's costs: *Texaco Ltd v Arco Technology Inc* (1989) *The Times*, 13 October 1989. Where a claimant recovers more than nominal damages but only a small proportion of the amount claimed, costs should follow the event unless this conflicts with some other established principle: *Gupta v Klito* (1989) *The Times*, 23 November 1989.

Misconduct by the successful party

43.25 Misconduct by the successful party may result in costs not following the event (CPR, r 44.3(4)(a)). The court can take into account conduct before, as well as during, the proceedings, and in particular the extent to which the parties followed any relevant pre-action protocol. It can also take into account the manner in which a party pursued or defended the claim or a particular issue or allegation, and whether the claim was exaggerated by the claimant (r 44.3(5)).

Failure to consider or participate in ADR

43.26 In *Dunnett v Railtrack plc* [2002] 1 WLR 2434 the successful respondent in an appeal to the Court of Appeal had refused to submit to ADR on the ground that doing so would necessarily involve paying sums over and above those previously offered to the appellant. This was regarded as a misunderstanding of the purpose of ADR. To reflect this, instead of the respondent being awarded costs of the appeal, no order was made as to costs. Taking an unreasonable stance in a mediation is treated in the same way as unreasonably refusing to mediate at all (*Earl of Malmesbury v Strutt and Parker* [2008] 118 Con LR 68). In *Leicester Circuits Ltd v Coates Industries plc* [2003] EWCA Civ 333 a successful appellant was deprived of costs on the ground that it had unreasonably withdrawn from mediation shortly before the trial. On the other hand, a 10–15 per cent reduction in the costs order was regarded as a proportionate response to failing to consider negotiating in *Straker v Tudor Rose* [2007] EWCA Civ 368.

The burden is on the unsuccessful party in an application to disallow a successful party's costs for unreasonably refusing to use ADR procedures (*Halsey v Milton Keynes General NHS Trust* [2004] 1 WLR 3002). Factors relevant to the question of whether a refusal to agree to ADR was unreasonable include: **43.27**

(a) the nature of the dispute and circumstances of the case;
(b) the merits of the case (it may not be reasonable for a party with a weak case to insist on the use of ADR);
(c) the extent to which other settlement methods had been attempted; and
(d) the costs and delays involved in using ADR.

There is no presumption that costs will be awarded against a party who does not use ADR. Each case depends on its own facts. There are no special rules relating to different categories of parties, and public authorities are under no enhanced obligation to mediate compared to other parties. A defendant who refused to negotiate after receiving a Part 36 offer from a claimant was held not to have acted unreasonably in *Daniels v Commissioner of Police for the Metropolis* [2005] EWCA Civ 1312. The result at trial in this case (dismissal of the claim) rather established the reasonableness of the defendant's stance. Otherwise, defendants with meritorious defences would in effect be compelled to negotiate or else be penalized in costs. **43.28**

Costs consequences of misconduct

Much depends on the nature of the misconduct and its consequences. Misconduct which might justify depriving the successful party of its costs would not necessarily be sufficient to justify an order requiring the successful party to pay the unsuccessful party's costs (see *Scherer v Counting Instruments Ltd* [1986] 1 WLR 615 at 622). A successful defendant was deprived of half the costs of the hearing in *Cable v Dallaturca* (1977) 121 SJ 795 for failing to serve an expert's report in accordance with the rules of court. In *Hobbs v Marlowe* [1978] AC 16, the successful claimant was deprived of all of his costs apart from the issue fee because he had exaggerated his claim to avoid the action being referred to small claims arbitration. In *Smiths Ltd v Middleton (No 2)* [1986] 1 WLR 598 the defendant had made a payment into court exceeding the amount recovered by the claimants, but the judge made no order as to costs after the payment in, because the defendant had brought the action on himself through keeping incomplete accounting records. A claimant who would have lost on the original statements of case, but who won on the basis of an amendment made at a very late stage, was ordered to pay the defendant's costs of the action in *Anglo-Cyprian Trade Agencies Ltd v Paphos Wine Industries Ltd* [1951] 1 All ER 873. In *Liverpool City Council v Rosemary Chavasse Ltd* (1999) **43.29**

LTL 19/8/99 the successful council had acted in flagrant disregard for the approach embodied in the CPR, and left matters to the last minute. This resulted in a costs order being reduced from 75 per cent to 50 per cent.

43.30 As well as disallowing costs, the court has various other powers that may be exercised to reflect a finding of misconduct against either party. These powers include:

(a) Ordering costs to be paid on the indemnity basis rather than the standard basis. The discretion to award indemnity-basis costs has to be exercised judicially, taking into account the circumstances of the case, and having regard to the matters set out in r 44.3: *Reid Minty v Taylor* [2002] 1 WLR 2800. In most cases of adversarial litigation indemnity-basis costs will not be justified unless there are reasons to disapprove of the way the case has been conducted, but indemnity costs may be justified if the litigation has been conducted in an unreasonable manner even if that falls short of conduct which lacks moral probity or conduct deserving moral condemnation. Such conduct would have to be unreasonable to a high degree to justify an order for indemnity-basis costs: *Kiam v MGN Ltd (No 2)* [2002] 1 WLR 2810.

(b) Ordering payment of interim costs forthwith, rather than requiring the party obtaining the costs order to wait until after trial for payment (CPR, r 44.3(1)(c)). Note that an order stating the amount payable in respect of costs (such as a summary assessment) must be complied with within 14 days (r 44.8).

(c) Ordering payment of interest on costs from or until a certain date, including a date before judgment (r 44.3(6)(g)). The normal rule is that Judgments Act 1838 rate interest (currently 8 per cent a year simple interest) is payable on costs arising from court orders and judgments from the date of the judgment on liability.

(d) Ordering interest on costs at a rate different from the Judgments Act 1838 rate (eg, PD Pre-action conduct, para 4.6(5), which allows the court to impose interest on costs at a rate up to 10 per cent above base rate in cases where a protocol has been breached leading to proceedings being commenced which might otherwise have been avoided).

Claims wrongly commenced in the High Court

43.31 Where a claim has been commenced in the High Court which should have been commenced in a county court in accordance with the Courts and Legal Services Act 1990, s 1, or any other enactment, the court must take that error into account when quantifying costs (SCA 1981, s 51(8)). Usually this will result in a reduction in the costs which would otherwise be allowed, but such reduction must not be in excess of 25 per cent.

I INFORMING THE CLIENT

43.32 Where a costs order is made against a legally represented client who is not present in court when the order is made, the solicitor representing the client is under a duty to inform the client of the costs liability within seven days of the order being made (CPR, r 44.2). The 'client' may be an insurer, or trade union, or other body which has instructed the solicitor (PD Costs, para 7.1). At the same time as informing the client about the order, the solicitor should explain why it was made. The court has the power to order the solicitor to produce evidence that reasonable steps were taken to comply with the duty to notify the client (PD Costs, para 7.3).

J INDEMNITY PRINCIPLE

The 'indemnity principle' is that a party cannot be liable to pay more to the other side in costs than the winner is liable to pay its own lawyers. Thus, if the lawyers representing the successful party have intimated that their client need 'not worry' about paying their fees, there is a prospect that the court will hold the loser has no liability in costs: *British Waterways Board v Norman* (1993) 26 HLR 232. **43.33**

If the arrangement between the solicitor and the client amounts to an unlawful agreement to conduct litigation on a contingency basis (see 4.13), the client will not be entitled to seek an order for costs even if successful (*Hughes v Kingston upon Hull City Council* [1999] QB 1193; *Awwad v Geraghty and Co* [2000] 1 All ER 608). In *Bailey v IBC Vehicles Ltd* [1998] 3 All ER 570 it was held that the court has the power to order disclosure of documents and the provision of information to check whether the indemnity principle has been infringed, but went on to say that the jurisdiction to do so should not be over-enthusiastically deployed. **43.34**

Solicitors are under a duty to provide the best information possible about the cost of a matter, which must include the charging arrangements between them and their client, how the client should pay, and likely payments and liabilities to others. This is usually done in a client care letter (see Solicitors' Code of Conduct 2007, rr 2.02 and 2.03). Where there is a dispute as to the receiving party's liability to pay its own solicitors, that letter, or any other written arrangement affecting the costs payable between solicitor and client, must be filed with the court as part of any detailed assessment (PD Costs, para 40.2(i)). Further, the bill of costs used in any detailed assessment must set out a short but adequate explanation of any agreement or arrangement between the solicitor and client which affects the costs claimed against the paying party. **43.35**

K RANGE OF POSSIBLE COSTS ORDERS

Under CPR, r 44.3(6), there are seven possible variations from the main rule that the unsuccessful party should pay the whole of the successful party's costs. These variations are that a party must pay: **43.36**

(a) only a proportion of another party's costs;
(b) a specified amount in respect of the other side's costs;
(c) costs from or until a certain day only;
(d) costs incurred before proceedings have begun;
(e) costs relating only to certain steps taken in the proceedings;

(f) costs relating only to a certain distinct part of the proceedings, although an order of this type can only be made if an order in either of the forms set out at (a) or (c) would not be practicable (r 44.3(7)); or
(g) interest on costs from or until a certain date, including a date before judgment.

43.37 All these variations restrict the amount of costs that a winning party may recover from the loser. They are appropriate, therefore, to mark the court's displeasure at some conduct on the part of the winning party, or to reflect a partial rather than a full win. However, they are all given a positive wording, which seems to point to a need, in particular, to get a specific order for pre-commencement costs to make sure that these are included in the costs recoverable from the losing party.

L INTERIM COSTS ORDERS

43.38 At the end of almost every interim application, and when almost any interim application is disposed of by consent, an order will be made or agreed declaring which party should pay the costs of that application. Costs of interim applications are in the discretion of the court, but the discretion is usually (but not always) exercised in favour of the party who was successful in the application. Success may be established either by winning a contested application, or by showing that the need to make the application arose through the default of the other party. Other types of application are essentially of a case management nature, so there is no 'winner', and in these applications the costs are usually treated as part of the general costs of the claim. To cater for these various possibilities (and situations where neither party is entirely successful) the courts can resort to a wide selection of different interim costs orders.

43.39 If an order makes no reference to costs, the general rule is that none are payable in respect of the proceedings to which the order relates (CPR, r 44.13(1); PD 23A, para 13.2). There are exceptions for:

(a) trustees and personal representatives, who are entitled to their costs from the relevant fund;
(b) landlords and mortgagees, who may be able to recover their costs under the terms of the relevant agreement; and
(c) orders which are silent on costs made on applications without notice, which mean 'applicant's costs in the case' (r 44.13(1A)).

43.40 Detailed provisions dealing with interim costs orders are made in PD Costs. Paragraph 8.3 provides that the court may make an order about costs at any stage in a case, and in particular it may make interim costs orders when it deals with interim applications. Paragraph 8.5 sets out in tabular form the meanings of commonly used interim costs orders: see table 43.1.

Summary assessment of interim costs

43.41 The costs of interim hearings likely to last less than a day will often be dealt with by way of summary assessment there and then. This was considered at 20.61, where it was pointed out that the parties are required to file and serve statements of their costs not less than 24 hours before the hearing. Summary assessment is not possible of the costs incurred by any of the parties who is publicly funded, or generally of a party who is under a disability (see PD Costs, paras 13.9 and 13.11(1)). However, the court may make a summary assessment of costs payable by an assisted person (PD Costs, para 13.10) or by a person under a disability (para 13.11(2)).

Table 43.1 The meanings of common interim costs orders

Term	Effect
Costs/costs in any event	The party in whose favour the order is made is entitled to the costs in respect of the part of the proceedings to which the order relates whatever other costs orders are made in the proceedings.
Costs in the case/costs in the application	The party in whose favour the court makes an order for costs at the end of the proceedings is entitled to his costs of the part of the proceedings to which the order relates.
Costs reserved	The decision about costs is deferred to a later occasion, but if no later order is made the costs will be costs in the case. Costs reserved may be appropriate for interim applications without notice, and after a split trial on liability (where the judge has a wide discretion on whether to reserve costs to the remedies hearing: see *Shepherds Investments Ltd v Walters* [2007] EWCA Civ 292).
Claimant's/ defendant's costs in the case/ application	If the party in whose favour the costs order is made is awarded costs at the end of the proceedings, that party is entitled to his costs of the part of the proceedings to which the order relates. If any other party is awarded costs at the end of the proceedings, the party in whose favour the costs order is made is not liable to pay the costs of any other party in respect of the part of the proceedings to which the order relates.
Costs thrown away	Where, eg, a judgment or order is set aside, the party in whose favour the costs order is made is entitled to the costs which have been incurred as a consequence. This includes the costs of— (a) preparing for and attending any hearing at which the judgment or order which has been set aside was made; (b) preparing for and attending any hearing to set aside the judgment or order in question; (c) preparing for and attending any hearing at which the court orders the proceedings or the part in question to be adjourned; and (d) any steps taken to enforce a judgment or order which has subsequently been set aside.
Costs of and caused by	Where, eg, the court makes this order on an application to amend a statement of case, the party in whose favour the costs order is made is entitled to the costs of preparing for and attending the application and the costs of any consequential amendment to his own statement of case.
Costs here and below	The party in whose favour the costs order is made is entitled not only to his costs of the proceedings in which the court makes the order but also to his costs of the proceedings in any lower court. In the case of an appeal from a Divisional Court the party is not entitled to any costs incurred in any court below the Divisional Court.
No order as to costs/each party to pay his own costs	Each party is to bear his own costs of the application, subject to the exceptions referred to at 43.39.

Detailed assessment of interim costs

Orders for costs will be treated as requiring detailed assessment unless the order specifies the sum to be paid or states that fixed costs are to be paid (PD Costs, para 12.2). Detailed assessments generally take place after the proceedings are concluded. 43.42

Representation by counsel

43.43 PD Costs, para 8.7(3) provides that the court should consider recording whether the hearing was fit for counsel where the paying party asks for the court to express a view, where more than one counsel attended for a party, and where the judge thinks the hearing was not fit for counsel.

Set-off of interim costs orders

43.44 In *Arkin v Borchard Lines Ltd* (2001) LTL 19/6/01, interim costs orders had been made in favour of the claimant and the defendant respectively on different interim applications. The claimant had entered into a CFA, and wished to set off the two sets of interim costs. Colman J held that the terms of the CFA in question, which said the lawyers were successful if they 'recover[ed] costs . . . or interim awards during the litigation', meant that the costs award in favour of the claimant did not infringe the indemnity principle (for which, see 43.33). The two costs orders could therefore be set off against each other. Further, where one costs order is summarily assessed, and the competing costs order is directed to be subject to a detailed assessment, the court could legitimately preserve the set-off by varying the time for payment of the summarily assessed costs.

Amendment

43.45 The costs of and arising from any amendment to a statement of case are, unless the court orders otherwise, borne by the party making the amendment (see notes to PD 19A).

43.46 An order for payment of the costs of an amendment will also require payment of the costs of making consequential amendments to other documents. It is possible to ask for a less onerous costs order where, eg, the need to amend cannot be characterized as being the fault of the party seeking permission. Another point is that if permission is sought at a very late stage to make amendments having a fundamental effect on the way the case is set out, particularly where the other side are prejudiced, such as by being unable to make an effective Part 36 offer, the court may impose very stringent costs terms when granting permission to amend. Thus in *Beoco Ltd v Alfa Laval Co Ltd* [1995] QB 137 permission to amend was granted on terms that the claimant paid the defendant's costs up to the date of the amendment, and 85 per cent of the defendant's costs thereafter.

M TRACK ALLOCATION AND APPEALS

Costs and track allocation

43.47 Once a claim is allocated to either of the small claims or fast tracks the costs rules relating to that track will apply to work done before as well as after allocation, with the exception that any costs orders made before a claim is allocated to one of these two tracks are not affected by any subsequent allocation (CPR, r 44.9(2); PD Costs, para 15.1(2)).

This means, eg, that where default judgment is entered on a small-value claim, the costs restrictions in Part 27 do not apply (although the fixed costs rules in Part 45 will be applied instead).

A claim that exceeds the small claims limit which is allocated to the small claims track under r 26.7(3) is governed by the small claims costs rules unless the parties agree to use the fast track costs rules (r 27.14(5), (6)). Where a small claims case is reallocated to another track, the fast track or multi-track costs rules apply only from the date of reallocation (r 27.15). **43.48**

Costs after an appeal

A court dealing with a case on appeal can make orders relating to the costs of the proceedings giving rise to the appeal as well as the appeal itself (CPR, r 44.13(2)). If an appeal is successful, the appeal court may order the losing party to pay the costs 'here and below', or may make different orders relating to the proceedings at the two levels, or may leave the costs order of the court below undisturbed while making whatever order may be appropriate for the costs of the appeal. It may be appropriate to deprive a party of its costs if the decision on the appeal turned on points not raised below, or on points not raised in the notice of appeal, or where the appeal is only partly successful, or where the court's time has been wasted. **43.49**

N COSTS FOLLOW THE EVENT

The main rule was considered at 43.18ff. There now follows a discussion of how this principle is applied in a number of different situations. **43.50**

Situations in which costs do not follow the event

The following are situations where costs orders usually do not follow the event. **43.51**

(a) The costs of any application to extend time are borne by the party making the application.
(b) A party failing to make admissions of facts or in relation to documents after service of a notice to admit facts or documents, or after service of a list of documents, is usually responsible for paying the costs of proving those matters.
(c) In claims under the Slander of Women Act 1891, costs must not exceed the damages awarded, unless the court is satisfied that there were reasonable grounds for bringing the claim.
(d) If successive claims are brought against persons jointly or otherwise liable for the same damage, costs will be ordered in favour of the claimant in the first action only unless there were reasonable grounds for bringing the later actions (Civil Liability (Contribution) Act 1978, s 4).

Multiple parties

Multiple defendants

43.52 Where a claimant succeeds against joint tortfeasors, costs will be ordered against each defendant, and the claimant can then recover costs against any one (or more) of the defendants. Any defendant paying such costs can then seek a contribution from the others under the Civil Liability (Contribution) Act 1978. If successful defendants are separately represented, the claimant should be liable for any additional costs only if the separate representation was reasonable. An example of what can happen where joint defendants are successful is *Korner v H Korner and Co Ltd* [1951] Ch 10. Eight defendants were jointly represented, and seven of them were successful in the action. It was held that generally the defence costs should be regarded as incurred by each defendant equally, which would in this case have resulted in the claimant paying seven-eighths of the total defence costs. However, as different defences had been delivered for each defendant, each successful defendant was awarded one-eighth of the general costs of the proceedings, together with such costs and counsel's fees as were attributable to their own defence.

Bullock and *Sanderson* orders

43.53 Where a claimant claims against two defendants in the alternative in circumstances where it was reasonable to join both defendants, and succeeds against one only, the court has a discretion to make a *Bullock* or *Sanderson* order (*Bankamerica Finance Ltd v Nock* [1988] AC 1002). These orders take their names from *Bullock v London General Omnibus Co* [1907] 1 KB 264 and *Sanderson v Blyth Theatre Co* [1903] 2 KB 533. In deciding whether to make one of these orders, the court must look at all the facts the claimant knew or could reasonably have discovered as at the date the defendants were joined and consider whether the joinder was reasonable. If it was not reasonable to join the two defendants, costs should follow the event.

43.54 For the purposes of exposition, assume that the claim of the claimant ('C') against the first defendant ('D1') is dismissed, but that C obtains judgment against the second defendant ('D2'). In a *Bullock* order, C is ordered to pay D1's costs, and D2 is ordered to pay C's costs and is also ordered to reimburse (for the costs paid to D1). The difference between a *Bullock* order and the usual rule that costs follow the event is that if costs followed the event C would not be reimbursed by D2 for the costs C had to pay D1. In a *Sanderson* order, D2 has to pay C's costs, and D2 also has to pay D1's costs direct. C has no liability to pay D1's costs. Provided all parties are solvent, the eventual effect of *Bullock* and *Sanderson* orders is the same. However, the *Bullock* form is more usual because it most closely follows the rule that costs follow the event. Traditionally, the *Sanderson* form has been said to be appropriate where C is either publicly funded or insolvent, because in those circumstances only a *Sanderson* order adequately protects the successful D1. Despite the traditional view, a *Sanderson* order was upheld by the House of Lords in *Bankamerica Finance Ltd v Nock* where D2, not C, was insolvent, the judge having decided to make a *Sanderson* order because it tended to spread the hardship caused by irrecoverable costs most fairly between C and D1, the successful defendant.

Multiple claimants

Problems are not so likely to be caused through having different judgments in respect of different claimants because actions with joint claimants are allowed to proceed only if the claimants are jointly represented. It is implicit in this that there must be a large degree of identity of interest between the joint claimants, so split judgments must be very rare. **43.55**

Multiple issues

Partial success

Where both parties are successful on some, but not all, of the issues in a case, the court may, instead of awarding the whole costs of the action to the ultimately successful party, award the costs of proving some of the issues to the unsuccessful party. In deciding whether there has been partial success the judge needs to consider the underlying realities of the litigation, and should not be too hasty in finding some reverse in the winner's overall case. For example, a finding of 25 per cent contributory negligence did not justify any reduction in costs in *Onay v Brown* [2009] EWCA Civ 775. **43.56**

In *Stocznia Gdanska SA v Latvian Shipping Co* (2001) *The Times*, 25 May 2001, Thomas J said that the reasonableness of raising an issue which was lost by the party who was the overall winner is not necessarily relevant to the question of depriving the successful party of part of its costs under r 44.3(4)(b). In *Carver v Hammersmith & Queen Charlotte's Health Authority* (2000) LTL 31/7/00, Nelson J held that the appropriate way on the facts for dealing with a claimant who won, but had to abandon a number of issues, and who had been guilty of delay, was to deprive her of 15 per cent of her costs. In *Winter v Winter* (2000) LTL 10/11/00, the claimant had litigated over two issues, abandoned one a few days before trial, and won at trial on the remaining issue. It was held that the trial judge was plainly wrong to award the claimant the entire costs of the claim, as that failed to reflect the fact that one of the main issues had been abandoned. In *Williams Corporate Finance plc v Holland* (2001) LTL 22/11/01, the claim consisted of seven heads, totalling £40,000. Most of the heads of claim were defeated, and the defendant succeeded on his counterclaim, but there was a net finding in favour of the claimant of about £2,500. The Court of Appeal substituted no order as to costs. **43.57**

Counterclaims

Where a claimant succeeds on a claim and defeats a counterclaim, or a defendant defeats a claim and succeeds on a counterclaim, the principle that costs follow the event simply means that the successful party is entitled to the costs of the proceedings. Where one party succeeds on the claim, but the other party succeeds on the counterclaim, the court may award one party the costs of the claim, and the other party the costs of the counterclaim. In *Medway Oil and Storage Co Ltd v Continental Contractors Ltd* [1929] AC 88 the House of Lords decided that this form of judgment entitled the party who won on the claim to all its costs of the proceedings save those costs exclusively referable to the counterclaim. Under this principle there is no apportionment of costs, but items of costs common to both the claim and counterclaim, such as counsel's brief fee, may be divided between the claim and counterclaim. This approach is nowadays regarded as too technical, and it is more common to make a simple percentage costs order (*English v Emery Reimbold and Strick Ltd* [2002] 1 WLR 2409). **43.58**

Additional claims under Part 20

43.59 Where a claimant succeeds in an action against a defendant, and the defendant successfully claims an indemnity from a third party, the third party should be ordered to pay all the defendant's costs, including the costs the defendant will have been ordered to pay the claimant: *Jablochkoff Co v McMurdo* [1884] WN 84. In such a case, if the defendant proves to be insolvent, the claimant will be unable to recover its costs from the third party, because it has no direct order against the third party. Therefore, it may, in a proper case, be appropriate to make an order akin to a *Sanderson* order requiring the third party to pay the claimant's costs directly: *Edginton v Clark* [1964] 1 QB 367. If a claimant succeeds against a defendant who succeeds against a third party, but the court considers that the defendant has defended the claim for reasons which provided no benefit to the third party, the third party will be ordered to pay the costs of the additional claim only: *Blore v Ashby* (1889) 42 ChD 682.

43.60 Where a claimant loses to a defendant who therefore loses against a third party, the claimant should be ordered to pay the defendant's costs of the whole action, including the additional claim, but only if it was reasonable for the defendant to have brought the additional claim.

Litigants under a disability

43.61 An order for costs can be made against the litigation friend acting for a claimant who is a person under disability by virtue of the undertaking to pay the costs that may be ordered against the person under disability required by CPR, r 21.4(3)(c). A successful party seeking such an order must apply promptly after judgment. The litigant normally indemnifies the litigation friend, but will not be required to do so where the litigation friend has acted for his or her own personal benefit (*Huxley v Wooton* (1912) 29 TLR 132) or if the litigation friend is guilty of some misconduct in relation to the proceedings.

Trustees and personal representatives

43.62 Trustees and personal representatives are, in so far as costs are not recovered from another party, entitled to recover their costs on the indemnity basis out of the fund (*Grender v Dresden* [2009] EWHC 500 (Ch)). The court may, however, order otherwise and may do so where the party otherwise entitled to the costs has acted unreasonably. A trustee or personal representative who has acted substantially for his or her own benefit is likely to be treated like any other party. This may be the case where the proceedings are adversarial in nature (see *Holding and Management Ltd v Property Holding and Investment Trust plc* [1989] 1 WLR 1313).

Mortgagees

43.63 It is an established principle that a mortgagee is entitled to add any properly incurred costs, charges, or expenses to the secured debt. Many mortgages make express provision for this, but even if they do not such a term will be implied: *Cottrell v Stratton* (1872) LR 8 Ch App 295. A court may disallow any costs, charges, or expenses which were not 'properly incurred', unless the mortgage makes express provision to alter this (although a mortgage deed that purported to entitle the mortgagee to add improperly incurred costs might be open to question on public policy grounds: *Gomba Holdings (UK) Ltd v Minories Finance Ltd (No 2)* [1993] Ch 171).

Principles were laid down in *Gomba Holdings (UK) Ltd v Minories Finance Ltd (No 2)* which are reflected by PD Costs, paras 50.2 to 50.4, which are to the effect that generally the court will not assess a mortgagee's costs, because the mortgagee can simply add its indemnity basis costs to the security. If the mortgagor wishes to object to the amount added to the security in this way, the mortgagor must apply for the taking of an account and inquiries as to whether items added to the security were unreasonably incurred or were of an unreasonable amount. If the order is made, the accounts will be conducted before a costs officer. **43.64**

Beddoe orders

By what is known as a *Beddoe* application, trustees and similar persons may apply to the court in the early stages of litigation for orders that they be indemnified against the costs of and incidental to the action to be paid out of the trust or other fund. Such an application takes its name from *Re Beddoe* [1893] 1 Ch 547. Such a pre-emptive costs order, made well in advance of the trial, is, of course, of great benefit to trustees who have nothing to gain personally from an action but are under a duty to preserve the funds under their care. Such orders have traditionally been made mainly in favour of trustees and executors, but the discretion is not necessarily restricted to those categories, and orders have been made in favour of a receiver in a company liquidation (*Re Wedstock Realizations Ltd* [1988] BCLC 354) and a minority shareholder complaining about the conduct of a company's directors (*Wallersteiner v Moir (No 2)* [1975] QB 373). Such orders will not be made where the litigation is really a hostile claim by one beneficiary against another: *The Trustee Corporation Ltd v Nadir* [2001] BPIR 541. Nor will they be made where the litigation can be of no benefit to the trust: *Weth v HM Attorney-General* (2001) LTL 23/2/01. **43.65**

Practice Statement (Trust Proceedings: Prospective Costs Orders) [2001] 1 WLR 1082 sets out a model form of prospective costs order, and provides that in the absence of a dispute whether such an order is appropriate most such applications will be dealt with on the papers. **43.66**

O PUBLICLY FUNDED LITIGANTS

Successful publicly funded party

If a publicly funded party succeeds, the court will make an order for costs on exactly the same principles as apply in unassisted cases. The assisted party has no beneficial interest in the costs, which must be paid to the assisted party's solicitor to obtain a valid discharge (Community Legal Service (Costs) Regulations 2000 (SI 2000/441), reg 18). The recovered costs are used to pay the publicly funded costs. Any damages or property recovered or preserved in the proceedings will be subject to the first charge under the Legal Aid Act 1988, s 16(6), or the Access to Justice Act 1999, s 10(7), in respect of any shortfall between the solicitor's charges and costs recovered from the other side and contributions paid by the assisted person. **43.67**

Costs against a publicly funded party

43.68 An unsuccessful assisted person is protected from the usual costs consequences by the Access to Justice Act 1999, s 11(1), but costs protection does not extend to clients receiving legal help, help at court, general family help, help with mediation in family proceedings, or legal representation in family proceedings (Community Legal Service (Cost Protection) Regulations 2000 (SI 2000/824), reg 3). Nor does costs protection apply in favour of a claimant who obtains public funding to pursue a fraudulent claim (*Jones v Congregational and General Insurance plc* [2003] 1 WLR 3001). Section 11(1) provides:

> Except in prescribed circumstances, costs ordered against an individual in relation to any proceedings or part of proceedings funded for him shall not exceed the amount (if any) which is a reasonable one for him to pay having regard to all the circumstances including—
>
> (a) the financial resources of all the parties to the proceedings, and
>
> (b) their conduct in connection with the dispute to which the proceedings relate;
>
> and for this purpose proceedings, or a part of proceedings, are funded for an individual if services relating to the proceedings are funded for him by the Commission as part of the Community Legal Service.

43.69 Under the Community Legal Service (Costs) Regulations 2000, the court is required to consider whether, but for costs protection, it would have made a costs order against the funded party, and, if so, whether it would have specified the amount payable (reg 9(1)). If so (or if the court decides to make a reasonably modest order), and if the court considers it has enough information to do so, the court can immediately make an order under s 11(1) specifying the amount the funded party shall pay (reg 9(2) and (3)). If the court does not make an immediate order under s 11(1), but decides that it would have ordered costs against the funded party but for the costs protection rule, the non-funded party has three months to request a hearing to determine the costs payable by the funded party (reg 10(2)).

43.70 An unsuccessful party who has been publicly funded for part of the time during which litigation has been pending, and who privately funded the litigation for the rest of the time, obtains the benefit of costs protection only for the period the public funding was in place: *Dugon v Williamson* [1964] Ch 59. Costs protection is lost on the date of giving notice of acting in person: *Burridge v Stafford* (1999) *The Times*, 14 September 1999. The same result applies where, as in *Turner v Plasplugs Ltd* [1996] 2 All ER 939, proceedings continue beyond a limitation in a certificate without the certificate being amended to cover the further stages in the action.

Costs against the Legal Services Commission

43.71 Under the Access to Justice Act 1999, s 11(4)(d), and Community Legal Service (Cost Protection) Regulations 2000 (SI 2000/824) the court deciding a claim in favour of an unassisted party may make an order requiring the Legal Services Commission to pay the unassisted party's costs.

Procedure

43.72 A non-funded party may make an application for costs to be payable by the Legal Services Commission at any time within three months of a s 11(1) costs order being made (Community Legal Service (Costs) Regulations 2000, reg 10(2)). The application must usually be accompanied by the receiving party's bill of costs, a statement of resources, and a notice to the effect that a costs order is being sought against the Commission (reg 10(3)), and all these documents must be served on the funded party and the Commission (reg 10(4)). After being served with the application, the publicly funded litigant must file and serve a statement of resources within 21 days (for the purpose of determining his personal liability under the Access to Justice Act 1999, s 11(1)), and may serve written points of dispute concerning the bill of costs (PD Costs, para 23.5). If the publicly funded litigant does not provide a statement of resources, the court may make a s 11(1) determination without a hearing (PD Costs, para 23.6). Determination hearings are listed giving at least 14 days' notice (para 23.7), and may be heard by a costs judge or district judge (para 23.8). The decision whether to make an order against the Commission is expressly assigned to the costs judge or district judge under the Community Legal Service (Costs) Regulations 2000 (SI 2000/441), reg 10(10), and should not be exercised by the trial judge: *R (Gunn) v Secretary of State for the Home Department* [2001] 1 WLR 1634. The Regional Director may appear at the hearing, or may instead rely on a written statement, which should be served and filed seven days before the hearing (para 23.10).

Conditions for costs against the Commission

The following conditions must be satisfied before a costs order can be made against the Legal Services Commission: **43.73**

(a) the proceedings must be finally decided in favour of the non-publicly funded litigant. Where an appeal may be brought, any order against the Commission will not take effect until the time limit for seeking permission to appeal has elapsed without permission being granted, or, if no permission is required, no appeal is brought within the time limit for bringing an appeal (PD Costs, para 21.20). Where an appeal is brought, any order against the Commission never takes effect, but a fresh application may be brought in the appeal court;
(b) the non-publicly funded litigant must make the application for a costs order against the Commission within three months of the making of a costs order under the AJA 1999, s 11(1), unless there is a good reason for the delay (Community Legal Service (Costs Protection) Regulations 2000 (SI 2000/824), reg 5(3), as amended by SI 2001/3812); and
(c) the court must be satisfied that it is just and equitable in the circumstances that provision for the costs should be made out of public funds. It will normally be just and equitable that the Commission should stand behind the client unless the costs judge is aware of facts rendering that result unjust or inequitable (*R (Gunn) v Secretary of State for the Home Department* [2001] 1 WLR 1634).

Further, in respect of costs incurred in proceedings at first instance, the following additional conditions must be satisfied: **43.74**

(d) the proceedings must have been instituted by the publicly funded litigant; and
(e) the non-publicly funded litigant is an individual who will suffer financial hardship if the order is not made.

Finally decided in favour of publicly funded client

43.75 Proceedings are finally decided in favour of a publicly funded client (condition (a)) when no appeal lies, or the time for appealing has expired (see PD Costs, para 21.20). In *Kelly v London Transport Executive* [1982] 1 WLR 1055 the unassisted defendants had made a payment into court exceeding the damages awarded to the claimant. It was held that for this reason the defendants had been substantially successful, and the claim had been finally decided in their favour for this purpose.

Proceedings at first instance

43.76 Conditions (d) and (e) apply only where the proceedings were at first instance, and so do not apply to costs of appeals. The Divisional Court is not a court of first instance when reviewing the decision of a court or tribunal (*R v Leeds County Court, ex p Morris* [1990] 1 QB 523), but is a court of first instance when reviewing the decision of a person or body other than a court or tribunal (*R v Greenwich London Borough Council, ex p Lovelace (No 2)* [1992] QB 155).

Financial hardship

43.77 The applicant must be an individual rather than a company or government body. Until an amendment to the regulations that came into force on 3 December 2001 (SI 2001/3812, reg 4), condition (e) was that the applicant must suffer 'severe' financial hardship. Removal of the word 'severe' was intended to ensure that orders are made in deserving cases.

Both parties publicly funded

43.78 An order cannot be made against the Commission where both parties are publicly funded. This can produce rather harsh results, as in *Almond v Miles* (1992) *The Times*, 4 February 1992. In this case an assisted defendant successfully resisted a claim by the legally assisted claimant to a share in the equity of the defendant's flat. Under what is now AJA 1999, s 10(7), the defendant's costs of £18,000 were a first charge on her flat, which had been 'preserved' in the proceedings. The claimant, being legally assisted herself, was required to pay certain instalments towards the defendant's costs, but was largely protected in this respect by what is now AJA 1999, s 11(1). Although the defendant had been financially prejudiced by the proceedings, the court could not make an order against the Commission, because the defendant was herself an assisted party.

P PRO BONO COSTS ORDERS

43.79 The Legal Services Act 2007, s 194, allows the court to order any person to make a payment to the charity prescribed under the Act in respect of legal representation of a party which was provided free of charge. By CPR, r 44.3C(2)(a), such an order will be for fixed costs under Part 45 where Part 45 would otherwise apply. Where Part 45 does not apply, PD Costs, paras 10A.1 and 13.2, says the general rule is that the court will make a summary assessment of the pro bono costs unless there is good reason to order a detailed assessment.

Q COSTS AGAINST NON-PARTIES

In *Aiden Shipping Co Ltd v Interbulk Ltd* [1986] AC 965 the House of Lords decided that the SCA 1981, s 51, confers a sufficiently wide discretion on the court on the question of costs to allow it to award costs against non-parties. Such orders are always exceptional (*Re Land and Property Trust Co plc* [1991] 1 WLR 601). The essential policy is that the need to protect the successful party by granting an effective costs order has to yield to the right of access to the courts to litigate the dispute in the first place (*Hamilton v Al Fayed (No 2)* [2003] QB 1175 and art 6(1) of the European Convention on Human Rights). It is in the public interest that funding for litigation should be available, provided the essential motivation is to enable a party to litigate what the funders perceive to be a genuine case. Consequently, a pure funder of litigation should not ordinarily be liable to a non-party costs order, and it is only if there is something exceptional in the circumstances that such an order can be justified. Even if there is some exceptional feature present, an order will also be refused if there is no causation (*Hamilton v Al Fayed*). **43.80**

Such orders may possibly be made against an outsider who was funding the litigation on behalf of the unsuccessful party (*Singh v Observer Ltd* [1989] 2 All ER 751, doubted in *Symphony Group plc v Hodgson* [1994] QB 179); against directors of a company who improperly cause the other side to incur costs in a winding-up petition (*Re a Company (No 004055 of 1991)* [1991] 1 WLR 1003); and where the non-party has been found, under the law concerning maintenance and champerty, to have maintained the action (*McFarlane v E E Caledonia Ltd (No 2)* [1995] 1 WLR 366). Such an order may also be made in the case of wanton and officious intermeddling with litigation falling short of champerty in the strict sense: *Nordstern Allgemeine Versicherungs AG v Internav Ltd* [1999] 2 Lloyd's Rep 139. Costs orders against non-parties are, however, unlikely to be made against a liquidator funding litigation in the name of the company: *Eastglen Ltd v Grafton* [1996] 2 BCLC 279. By extension of the jurisdiction, a costs order can be made in favour of a non-party who has funded litigation (*J v Oyston* [2002] CPLR 563, where an order was made in favour of the Solicitors Indemnity Fund Ltd). **43.81**

R WASTED COSTS ORDERS

Under the SCA 1981, s 51(6), legal representatives may be made personally liable for any wasted costs. Wasted costs orders can be made against the legal representatives for the other side or against the legal representatives acting for the applicant: *Medcalf v Mardell* [2003] 1 AC 120. Applications can be made against legal or other representatives exercising rights of audience and rights to conduct litigation (s 51(13)). Applications against counsel are not restricted to their conduct in court, but extend to counsel's involvement in advising, drafting, and settling documents in relation to proceedings: *Brown v Bennett* [2002] 2 All ER 273. However, in *Byrne v Sefton Health Authority* (2001) *The Times*, 28 November 2001, it was held that a wasted costs order cannot be made against a party's former solicitors who had ceased acting for the party before proceedings were issued. Wasted costs may simply be disallowed or an order may be made that the legal representative responsible must pay the whole or a part of them. **43.82**

43.83 This provision is intended to arm the courts with an effective remedy where loss and expense have been caused by the unjustifiable conduct of litigation by either side's lawyers.

Nature of wasted costs

43.84 The wasted costs powers against lawyers and other parties are compensatory in nature. Therefore, in *Ridehalgh v Horsefield* [1994] Ch 205 the Court of Appeal held that a wasted costs order can be made only if three conditions are satisfied:

(a) The applicant must satisfy the court that the lawyer has acted improperly, unreasonably, or negligently (SCA 1981, s 51(7)). 'Improper' conduct covers any substantial breach of the relevant codes of professional conduct for solicitors and barristers such as making unsupported allegations of fraud contrary to para 606 of the Code of Conduct of the Bar of England and Wales (*Medcalf v Mardell* [2003] 1 AC 120). It also includes conduct which would be regarded as improper according to the consensus of professional opinion. 'Unreasonable' conduct includes anything that is designed to harass the other side or is otherwise vexatious. The acid test is whether there is a reasonable explanation for the conduct. 'Negligence' in this context does not have the same meaning as in the well-known tort, but simply means a failure to act with the competence reasonably expected from ordinary members of the profession.

(b) The conduct complained of caused the applicant to incur unnecessary costs.

(c) In all the circumstances of the case it must be just to order the lawyer to compensate the applicant for the whole or part of the wasted costs.

43.85 Conduct justifying a wasted costs order may include failing to attend an appointment, failing to comply with the court's orders, negligent mispleading of the case, inefficient presentation of the case at trial through being ill-prepared, and pressing on with an action after it has become hopeless (for example, through failing to read the materials disclosed by the other side on disclosure). A solicitor is not entitled to abdicate all responsibility for a case by instructing counsel, but the more specialist the area the more reasonable it is to follow counsel's advice. Thus in *R v Horsham District Council, ex p Wenman* [1995] 1 WLR 680 a solicitor was absolved from liability when acting on counsel's advice in judicial review proceedings. In *Ridehalgh v Horsefield* the Court of Appeal expressed the view that, largely because of the 'cab rank rule' whereby barristers (and to some extent solicitors) are not entitled to pick and choose their clients, it is not improper for a lawyer to represent a client who is bound to lose. However, pursuing a case which amounts to an abuse of process would be 'improper'. The distinction is largely one of degree. The Court of Appeal also made a point of deprecating the practice of making threats to apply for wasted costs orders as a means of unacceptable intimidation, although there is a distinction between that and giving proper notice that an application will be made if improper, unreasonable, or negligent conduct is persisted in.

43.86 Where legal professional privilege is not waived by the client, the court should be slow to draw adverse inferences on the quality of advice given, and where there is room for doubt, assumptions and inferences should be made in favour of the legal representatives: *Brown v Bennett* [2002] 2 All ER 273. Consequently, a wasted costs order in such cases should not be made unless, proceeding with extreme care, the court is satisfied that there is nothing the practitioner could say, if unconstrained, to resist the order, and provided also that it is fair in all the circumstances to make the order: *Medcalf v Mardell*.

Procedure on wasted costs applications

Applications for wasted costs orders should generally be made after trial, as interim applications would deprive the other side of the advisers of their choice (*Filmlab Systems International Ltd v Pennington* [1995] 1 WLR 673; PD Costs, para 53.1). Wasted costs orders can be made on an application by a party made under Part 23, or by the court on its own initiative (PD Costs, para 53.2). On an application by a party, the legal representative against whom the order is sought must be given written notice, at least three days before the hearing, of what he or she is alleged to have done or failed to do and of the costs sought (PD Costs, para 53.8). The court is required to give the legal representative a reasonable opportunity to attend a hearing to give reasons why the order should not be made. The court will give directions to ensure that the issues are dealt with in a way that is fair and as simple and summary as the circumstances permit (PD Costs, para 53.5). The court may also direct that notice be given to the legal representative's client. **43.87**

Wasted costs applications will generally be considered in two stages (PD Costs, para 53.6): **43.88**

(a) At the first stage the applicant has to adduce evidence which, if unanswered, would be likely to lead to a wasted costs order, and the court must be satisfied that the wasted costs application appears to be justified having regard to the likely costs involved.

(b) At the second stage the court will give the legal representative an opportunity of putting forward his or her case, and will make a wasted costs order only if (PD Costs, para 53.4):
   (i) the legal representative has acted improperly, unreasonably, or negligently;
   (ii) the legal representative's conduct has caused another party to incur unnecessary costs; and
   (iii) it is just in all the circumstances to order the legal representative to compensate that party for the whole or part of those costs.

If the court makes an order, it must specify the amount to be paid or disallowed.

KEY POINTS SUMMARY

- Costs orders are always discretionary. **43.89**
- Costs usually follow the event, in that the winner usually is awarded costs against the loser.
- These principles apply to interim costs orders as well as costs orders made at trial.
- The different formulae used in interim costs orders described in table 43.1 are designed to give effect to the principle that costs follow the event.
- Likewise, the detailed rules on *Bullock* orders, counterclaims, additional claims, etc. at 43.50ff are designed to give effect to the principle that costs follow the event when the court is faced by situations at trial where there is no clear-cut winner.
- A court may depart from the costs follow the event principle where (broadly) there has been unreasonable conduct by the winner (see CPR, r 44.3, described at 43.23).
- Different types of untoward conduct may result in costs orders being made against non-parties (43.80) or wasted costs orders being made against the lawyers (43.82).
- Special provision is made for litigants who are publicly funded (43.67ff), in particular protecting them against the usual effects of costs following the event.

44

ENFORCEMENT

44.01 Entering judgment does not provide a litigant with the remedy sought in the proceedings. Parties occasionally refuse to comply with the judgments and orders of the court. Public confidence in the legal system would be eroded if the court were without powers to enforce compliance. In fact, a range of enforcement procedures is available, each being designed to deal with different situations. Where a number of procedures are available, a judgment creditor can choose whichever one seems likely to be the most effective. Largely, the procedures are similar in both the High Court and the county courts. The major exception is that attachment of earnings orders (see 44.24) are generally available only in the county courts. One practical difference is that High Court enforcement is carried out by enforcement officers authorized under the Courts Act 2003, who are independent of the courts, whereas county court enforcement is carried out by bailiffs, who are employed by the Ministry of Justice. It is often suggested that enforcement officers, who are remunerated by fees and poundage on money they recover, have a greater incentive than bailiffs and hence have a reputation for being more successful.

44.02 The Tribunals, Courts and Enforcement Act 2007 will make a number of far-reaching revisions to the law relating to enforcement of money judgments. At the time of writing commencement dates have only been set for debt relief orders. When the other provisions dealing with enforcement are brought into force there will be substantial changes to the rules of court. Many of these are preserved provisions of the RSC and CCR, which are currently found in the schedules to the CPR. This chapter will deal with the existing law. The new provisions will deal with:

(a) information requests and orders (see 44.05): Tribunals, Courts and Enforcement Act 2007, ss 95 to 105;
(b) enforcement by taking control of goods (see 44.08): Tribunals, Courts and Enforcement Act 2007, ss 62 to 70 and Sch 12;
(c) administration orders (see 44.15): Tribunals, Courts and Enforcement Act 2007, s 106, and new enforcement restriction orders (s 107);
(d) attachment of earnings (see 44.24): Tribunals, Courts and Enforcement Act 2007, ss 91 to 92 and Sch 15;
(e) charging orders (see 44.31): Tribunals, Courts and Enforcement Act 2007, ss 93 to 94;
(f) debt relief orders came into force on 6 April 2009, and are really an insolvency procedure (see, eg, Chapter 19): Tribunals, Courts and Enforcement Act 2007, s 108 and Schs 18 and 19, as are the new debt management schemes (ss 109 to 123).

A ENFORCEMENT OF MONEY JUDGMENTS

General provisions

Transfers

A case may need to be transferred before enforcement proceedings are taken: **44.03**

(a) A county court claim will have to be transferred to the High Court if:
  (i) (other than judgments arising from regulated agreements under the Consumer Credit Act 1974) execution against goods is sought of a judgment exceeding £5,000 (High Court and County Courts Jurisdiction Order 1991 (SI 1991/724), art 8(1)(a)); or
  (ii) enforcement of a charging order by sale is sought where the amount owing exceeds £30,000 (CCA 1984, s 23(c)).
(b) A High Court claim will have to be transferred to a county court if:
  (i) execution against goods is sought of a judgment for under £600 (High Court and County Courts Jurisdiction Order 1991, art 8(1)(b));
  (ii) a charging order is sought where the judgment debt is under £5,000 (Charging Orders Act 1979, s 1(2)); or
  (iii) an attachment of earnings order is sought (Attachment of Earnings Act 1971, s 1).
(c) A county court claim will have to be transferred, under CCR, ord 25, r 2, to the county court serving the district where the judgment debtor resides or carries on business where the judgment creditor wishes to apply for:
  (i) information from a debtor;
  (ii) a charging order;
  (iii) an attachment of earnings order; or
  (iv) a judgment summons.

Stay of execution

A judgment debtor who is unable to pay or who alleges that it is otherwise inexpedient to enforce an order may apply for a stay of execution (RSC, ord 47, r 1; CCR, ord 25, r 8). Such an **44.04** application must be supported by written evidence substantiating the grounds relied on, and usually has to include a full statement of the debtor's means. Often the result of a successful application will be a stay of execution pending payment of the judgment by instalments.

Obtaining information from debtors

44.05 Where little is known about a judgment debtor's finances, an application can be made to obtain information from the judgment debtor. This requires the debtor to attend court to be questioned to establish the debtor's financial status, including amounts, names, addresses, account numbers, and policy numbers. A 'debtor' for these purposes includes a director of a debtor company *(Masri v Consolidated Contractors International (UK) Ltd (No 4)* [2009] Bus LR 246 but it is not possible to use Part 71 against an officer who is outside the jurisdiction (*Masri v Consolidated Contractors International Co SAL* [2010] 1 AC 90). There is a prescribed form for the application notice (form N316), which must state the debtor's name and address, identify the judgment, and state the amount presently owing under the judgment (PD 71, para 1.2). If the creditor wishes the debtor to be questioned before a judge (which will be allowed only if there are compelling reasons: para 2.2) or to produce specific documents (such as bank statements and other financial material), these matters must be stated in the application notice (para 1.2).

44.06 If the application complies with the above requirements it will be dealt with by a court officer without a hearing (CPR, r 71.2), who will make an order requiring the debtor to attend court, produce documents, and answer questions. That order has to be served personally not less than 14 days before the hearing (r 71.3), with service usually being effected by the creditor rather than the court (PD 71, para 3). Once served, the debtor has seven days to ask the judgment creditor for a reasonable sum to cover the debtor's travelling expenses to court, which must be paid (r 71.4). The judgment creditor must swear an affidavit (a witness statement being insufficient) giving details of service of the order, any request for and payment of travelling expenses, and how much of the judgment remains unpaid. This affidavit must be filed two days before the hearing or produced at the hearing (r 71.5). At the hearing the court officer will ask a set of standard questions as set out in the appendices to PD 71. The judgment creditor may ask questions, or may request the court officer to ask additional, written questions (PD 71, para 4.2). If the hearing takes place before a judge, the questioning is conducted by the creditor or the creditor's legal representative (para 5.1).

44.07 If the debtor fails to attend or otherwise fails to comply, the court usually makes a suspended committal order, which gives the debtor a second chance to comply (PD 71, para 7.1). If the debtor again fails to comply, a committal order can be made by the judge (CPR, r 71.8).

Execution against goods

44.08 Execution against goods is the most common method of enforcement. In the High Court it is effected through the writ of *fieri facias*, often abbreviated to '*fi. fa.*', and in the county courts by warrants of execution.

Issue of writ or warrant of execution

44.09 Issue is usually purely a matter of producing the correct documents and paying a fee. In the High Court the judgment creditor produces a draft writ of *fieri facias*, a *praecipe*, and the judgment. The writ is issued by being sealed (RSC, ord 46, r 6). It is then served on the enforcement officers for the county where the debtor resides. In the county court the judgment creditor simply sends a request for the issue of a warrant of execution to the court, and the court informs its bailiffs.

In some cases, such as where six years have elapsed since the date of the judgment or order, permission to enforce is required (RSC, ord 46, r 2; CCR, ord 26, r 5). **44.10**

Seizing goods

The enforcement officers or bailiffs must first gain lawful entry to the debtor's premises. Outer doors must not be broken open, nor is it lawful to place a foot in an open door and push it open against the debtor's attempts to close it. Once inside, sufficient goods will be seized to satisfy the judgment and the costs of enforcement. 'Goods' includes motor vehicles, money, promissory notes and securities, furniture, etc., but excludes, by the CCA 1984, s 89(1) and the Courts Act 2003, Sch 7, para 9(3): **44.11**

(i) such tools, books, vehicles and other items of equipment as are necessary to [the debtor] for use personally by him in his employment, business or vocation;

(ii) such clothing, bedding, furniture, household equipment and provisions as are necessary for satisfying the basic domestic needs of [the debtor] and his family.

The dividing line is whether such goods are 'necessary'. A debtor claiming the protection of this provision must give notice to the sheriff within five days of the seizure identifying the goods and the grounds for the claim in respect of each item. Further, the goods seized must belong to the debtor. Goods belonging to other members of the debtor's family, a limited company (even if itself owned by the debtor), or a hire-purchase company must not be seized. If there is doubt about the ownership of goods seized, the enforcement officer or bailiff can gain protection by interpleading: see 17.65ff. **44.12**

Once goods have been seized, it is usual for the enforcement officer or bailiff to enter into an agreement with some responsible person in the house to take 'walking possession' of the goods. The goods can then remain where they are until payment or sale, the responsible person promising not to remove or damage them without the enforcement officer's or bailiff's permission, and authorizing the enforcement officer or bailiff to re-enter the premises at any time to complete the process of enforcement: *National Commercial Bank of Scotland v Arcam Demolition and Construction Ltd* [1966] 2 QB 593. Once walking possession has been taken, the enforcement officer or bailiff can use force to retake possession: *McLeod v Butterwick* [1996] 1 WLR 995. **44.13**

Removal and sale

Often, the threat of sale is sufficient incentive to persuade the debtor to pay. On payment the execution is superseded and the goods are released: see, eg, CCA 1984, s 87(2). Otherwise, unless an order is obtained under the Courts Act 2003, Sch 7, para 10, for sale by some other means, the goods will be removed and sold by public auction. On removal the debtor must be provided with an inventory, and must be given advance notice of the auction. The auction must be publicly advertised and must be conducted by an appointed broker or appraiser. After the sale the debtor is given a detailed account in writing of the sale and the application **44.14** of the proceeds. Purchasers of goods sold after execution acquire good title (see, eg, CCA 1984, s 98(1)).

Administration orders

44.15 By virtue of the CCA 1984, s 112, a county court has power, of its own motion or on the application of either the debtor or the creditor, in respect of a debtor who is unable to pay his or her debts, to make an administration order in respect of the debtor's estate. Such an order has the immediate effect of restricting creditors named in the order from joining in bankruptcy petitions against the debtor. The order will usually provide for the debtor to make specified payments by instalments, with periodic dividends being paid to the named creditors.

Third-party debt orders

44.16 A third-party debt order has the effect of transforming a debt payable by a third party to the debtor into an obligation to pay the debt to the judgment creditor. This is a particularly effective method of enforcement where the third party is a responsible body, such as a bank or building society. For this purpose, evidence that the judgment debtor had an account which in the past was in credit is sufficient, at least for the purposes of obtaining an interim order (*Alawiye v Mahmood* [2007] 1 WLR 79). It is not restricted to such bodies. Enforcement by this method is a two-stage process. First, the creditor makes an application without notice for an interim third-party debt order. Secondly, there is a hearing on notice for a final order.

Procedure

44.17 The first stage is commenced by a without-notice application (CPR, r 72.3) verified by a statement of truth in form N349 containing the information prescribed by PD 72, para 1.2. The required information includes details of the judgment debtor, the judgment, and the third party debt. Speculative applications will be rejected, and orders will be made only if there is evidence substantiating the belief that the debtor has (say) an account with a specific bank or building society (PD 72, para 1.3). The application is considered without a hearing by a judge (r 72.4(1)), who may make an interim third-party debt order directing the third party not to make any payment which reduces the amount he owes the judgment debtor to less than the amount specified in the order. The judge will also fix a hearing to consider making the order final.

44.18 An interim order must be served on the third party who owes money to the judgment debtor not less than 21 days before the date fixed for the hearing to consider making the order final (r 72.5(1)(a)), and is binding on the third party when it is served on him (r 72.4(4)). If the third party is a bank or building society it must carry out a search to identify all accounts held by the judgment debtor, and must disclose to the court and the judgment creditor the account numbers, whether they are in credit, and, if so, whether the balance is sufficient to cover the amount specified in the interim order or the amount in the account if insufficient (r 72.6(1), (2)). Unless the court orders otherwise, an interim third-party debt order only affects bank or building society accounts in the sole name of the judgment debtor (PD 72, para 3.1), and the bank or building society is not required by r 72.6 to retain money in, or disclose information relating to, joint accounts (para 3.2). Any third party who is not a bank or building society has seven days after service to notify the court and the judgment creditor in writing if he claims not to owe any money to the judgment debtor or to owe less than the amount specified in the interim order (r 72.6(4)).

The interim order must also be served on the judgment debtor. This needs to be done not less than seven days after service on the third party, and not less than seven days before the date fixed for the hearing (r 72.5(1)(b)). Where service is effected by the judgment creditor a certificate of service must be filed not less than two days before the hearing, or must be produced at the hearing (r 72.5(2)). A judgment debtor who is an individual and who is suffering hardship in meeting ordinary living expenses as a result of the interim order may apply for a hardship payment order permitting one or more payments out of the account (r 72.7). **44.19**

The second stage is when the court considers whether to make a final third-party debt order on the date fixed when the interim order was made. A judgment debtor or third party objecting to the final order, or who knows or believes someone else has a claim to the money, must file and serve written evidence stating the grounds of any objection or details of the other claim not less than three days before the hearing (r 72.8). If the court is notified that another person has a claim to the money it will serve notice of the application and the hearing on that person (r 72.8(5)). At the hearing the court may make a final third-party debt order, discharge the interim order, decide any issues, or direct a trial of any issues (r 72.8(6)). **44.20**

Attachable money

It is possible to obtain a third-party debt order only over a 'debt due or accruing due' to the judgment debtor. Examples are money in a bank account, trade debts, judgment debts, and rent due to a landlord. Conversely, actions for damages, matrimonial maintenance orders, and salary not presently payable are not attachable. **44.21**

Effect of the orders

Once served, an interim order binds the third party to freeze any debts due to the judgment debtor up to the amount of the judgment debt and fixed costs (r 72.4(3)). A final third-party debt order is enforceable as an order to pay money. By r 72.9(2) the third party is discharged as against the judgment debtor to the extent of the amount paid under the order. **44.22**

Discretion

A third-party debt order may be refused if it would be inequitable to grant it. This may be so if there is a possibility of the third party having to pay twice over, such as where the third party would remain liable before a foreign court: *Deutsche Schachtbau- und Tiefbohr-Gesellschaft mbH v Shell International Petroleum Co Ltd* [1990] 1 AC 295; *Société Eram Shipping Co Ltd v Compagnie Internationale de Navigation* [2004] 1 AC 260. The insolvency of the judgment debtor is a sufficient reason for refusing to make an order, because its effect may be to prefer the judgment creditor over the general body of creditors: *Roberts Petroleum Ltd v Bernard Kenny Ltd* [1983] 2 AC 192. **44.23**

Attachment of earnings

44.24 Where a judgment debtor is employed, but has no other substantial assets, the most effective method of enforcement is by obtaining an attachment of earnings order. Such an order can be made, unless the application is by the debtor, only if the debtor has failed to make one or more payments as required by the relevant adjudication (Attachment of Earnings Act 1971, s 3(3)). The Attachment of Earnings Act 1971, s 6(1), provides:

> An attachment of earnings order shall be an order directed to a person who appears to the court to have the debtor in his employment and shall operate as an instruction to that person—
>
> (a) to make periodical deductions from the debtor's earnings . . . and
>
> (b) at such times as the order may require, or as the court may allow, to pay the amounts deducted to the collecting officer of the court, as specified in the order.

44.25 As mentioned at 44.03, the High Court has no jurisdiction to make attachment of earnings orders, and High Court claims need to be transferred to a county court for enforcement in this manner. Magistrates' courts have some jurisdiction to make these orders, such as to enforce payment of arrears of council tax.

Earnings attachable

44.26 An attachment of earnings order may be made in respect of wages, salaries, fees, bonuses, commission, and overtime payable under a contract of service, including occupational pensions and statutory sick pay. An order cannot be made in respect of self-employed income, nor State pensions, benefits, or allowances (Attachment of Earnings Act 1971, s 24).

Procedure

44.27 An application for an attachment of earnings order is made by filing a request in a standard form certifying the amount of money remaining due under the judgment, and paying the fee. The court then notifies the debtor of a hearing date at least 21 days in advance, enclosing a questionnaire concerning the debtor's means. The questionnaire should be completed by the debtor and filed at court within eight days after service. A copy of the questionnaire is sent to the judgment creditor. The questionnaire is considered by an administrative officer of the court, who may make an attachment of earnings order if there is sufficient information to do so (CCR, ord 27, r 7(1)). If either party objects, or if the court officer decides not to make an order, the application is referred to the district judge.

44.28 At the hearing the district judge confirms that the debtor is not unemployed or self-employed. Provided the debtor is employed, the district judge will consider the debtor's income and regular outgoings, and will fix:

(a) The debtor's protected earnings rate. This is the amount the debtor is considered to need to maintain his or her family, each week or month, and any deductions made under the order will not reduce the debtor's income below this level.

(b) The debtor's normal deduction rate. This is the amount, subject to the protected earnings rate, which is deducted from the debtor's earnings each week or month.

44.29 Normally, the order will then be served on the debtor's employer, who will make the deductions specified and pay the money deducted to the court. Alternatively, the court may make a suspended attachment of earnings order, which will be served on the employer only if the debtor fails to pay agreed instalments promptly. A debtor with several creditors may be ordered to file a list of creditors with a view to making an administration order (see 44.15) or a consolidated attachment of earnings order.

Supplementary points

While an attachment of earnings order is in force, permission of the court is required before a warrant of execution will be issued for the judgment debt (Attachment of Earnings Act 1971, s 8(2)(b)). Also, during the currency of the order the debtor is under a duty (enforceable by imprisonment or a fine: s 23) to notify the court of any change in his or her employment (s 15). **44.30**

Charging orders

A charging order is defined by the Charging Orders Act 1979, s 1(1), as an order 'imposing on any such property as may be specified in the order a charge for securing the payment of any money due or to become due under [a] judgment or order'. A charging order therefore *secures* a judgment debt: it does not of itself produce any money. By s 3(4) a charge imposed by a charging order has the same effect, and is enforceable in the same way, 'as an equitable charge created by the debtor by writing under his hand'. Once obtained and registered at the Land Registry, a charging order can give a measure of long-term security, which is necessary if there is no immediate prospect of recovery by other methods. It was held in *Ezekiel v Orakpo* (1994) *The Times*, 8 November 1994 that a charging order extends to cover the judgment debt, interest, and costs even if it does not expressly say so. Exceptionally, it may be possible to enforce the charge by bringing sale proceedings (see 44.37), or the charge may result in the judgment being paid if the charged property is sold by the judgment debtor and the purchaser wishes (as is usual) to purchase it clear of encumbrances. **44.31**

Chargeable property

The Charging Orders Act 1979, s 2, specifies the property which may be charged: **44.32**

(1) Subject to subsection (3) below, a charge may be imposed by a charging order only on—
  (a) any interest held by the debtor beneficially—
    (i) in any asset of a kind mentioned in subsection (2) below, or
    (ii) under any trust; or
  (b) any interest held by a person as trustee of a trust ('the trust'), if the interest is in such an asset or is an interest under another trust and—
    (i) the judgment or order in respect of which a charge is to be imposed was made against that person as trustee of the trust, or
    (ii) the whole beneficial interest under the trust is held by the debtor unencumbered and for his own benefit, or
    (iii) in a case where there are two or more debtors all of whom are liable to the creditor for the same debt, they together hold the whole beneficial interest under the trust unencumbered and for their own benefit.

(2) The assets referred to in subsection (1) above are—
  (a) land,
  (b) securities of any of the following kinds—
    (i) government stock,
    (ii) stock of any body (other than a building society) incorporated within England and Wales,

(iii) stock of any body incorporated outside England and Wales or of any State or territory outside the United Kingdom, being stock registered in a register kept at any place within England and Wales,

(iv) units of any unit trust in respect of which a register of the unit holders is kept at any place within England and Wales, or

(c) funds in court.

(3) In any case where a charge is imposed by a charging order on any interest in an asset of a kind mentioned in paragraph (b) or (c) of subsection (2) above, the court making the order may provide for the charge to extend to any interest or dividend payable in respect of the asset.

Procedure

44.33 Like third-party debt orders (see 44.16), applications for charging orders follow a two-stage procedure. The first stage is to apply for an interim charging order by issuing an application notice in form N379 verified by a statement of truth (CPR, r 73.3(4)) containing the information prescribed by PD 73, para 1.2. The required information includes details of the judgment debtor, the judgment, and details of the property which it is intended to charge. The application is dealt with by a judge without a hearing, who will consider making an interim order and fixing a hearing to consider making a final charging order (r 73.4). If the interim order relates to registered land, it is usual to protect it by entering a unilateral or agreed notice under the Land Registration Act 2002, ss 32 and 34.

44.34 At least 21 days before the final hearing (which is the second stage) the judgment debtor, such other creditors as the court may direct, and certain other specified persons must be served with the interim charging order, application notice, and any supporting documents (r 73.5(1)). Service of an interim charging order effectively prevents dealings with the assets charged pending the final hearing (r 73.6). If service is effected by the judgment creditor, a certificate of service must be filed at least two days before the final hearing or produced at the hearing (r 73.5(2)). Any person objecting to the order being made final must file and serve written evidence setting out the grounds of the objection not less than seven days before the hearing (r 73.8). At the hearing the court may make a final charging order, discharge the interim order, decide any issues, or direct a trial of any issues (r 73.8(2)).

44.35 Particular matters laid down in the Charging Orders Act 1979, s 1(5), that the court must consider in deciding whether to make a charging order, are:

(a) the personal circumstances of the debtor; and

(b) whether any other creditor of the debtor would be likely to be unduly prejudiced by the making of the order.

44.36 If a final charging order is made it is usual to register it under the Land Registration Act 2002. This is probably not strictly necessary if the interim order was registered, because there is only one charging order, which is continued by the final order.

Sale proceedings

44.37 Proceedings for the sale of charged property are commenced by issuing separate proceedings under CPR, Part 8, supported by written evidence (CPR, r 73.10). The written evidence gives details of the charging order, the property charged, verifies the debtor's title to the property charged, identifies prior encumbrances, certifies the amount outstanding on the judgment, and estimates the price which would be obtained on sale (PD 73, para 4.3). It is usual to apply for an order that the debtor vacate the premises as well, so that a sale can be made with vacant possession. Such an order can be enforced by writ or warrant of possession: see 44.43ff.

Where the charged property is owned by more than one person, instead of using r 73.10, any application for an order for sale has to be made under the Trusts of Land and Appointment of Trustees Act 1996, s 14 (PD 73, para 4.5). **44.38**

Insolvency

Often a failure to pay a judgment debt is evidence that the judgment debtor is insolvent. Consequently, it may be more apt to bring bankruptcy or winding-up proceedings than to apply for enforcement. A brief guide to the procedure on winding-up petitions can be found at 19.15ff. **44.39**

Judgment summonses

A judgment summons is a procedure for punishing a defaulting judgment debtor who could pay, but has chosen not to, with a period in prison (Debtors Act 1869, s 5). The punitive nature of the provision was stressed in *Woodley v Woodley* (1993) *The Times*, 15 March 1993. Since the Administration of Justice Act 1970, s 11, came into force, judgment summonses have been available only for enforcing matrimonial maintenance orders and arrears of some taxes. **44.40**

B ENFORCEMENT OF JUDGMENTS FOR THE DELIVERY OF GOODS

Enforcement of judgments for the delivery of goods is by means of warrants (or, in the High Court, writs) of delivery. There are two types, corresponding with the forms of relief stated in the Torts (Interference with Goods) Act 1977, s 3. The first is known as a warrant (or writ) of specific delivery. It requires the bailiff (or enforcement officer) to seize the goods specified in the judgment with no alternative of seizing other goods up to the assessed value of the goods forming the subject matter of the judgment. The second is known as a warrant (or writ) of delivery. It requires the bailiff (or enforcement officer) to seize either the goods specified in the judgment or other goods up to the value (specified in the judgment) of the goods forming the subject matter of the judgment. **44.41**

Like execution against goods (see 44.08), issue is simply a matter of the creditor filing a request (county court) or *praecipe*, draft writ of delivery, and judgment (High Court), and paying the court fee. **44.42**

C ENFORCEMENT OF JUDGMENTS FOR THE POSSESSION OF LAND

Common law

At common law, a claimant who has obtained judgment for the possession of land may enter the land after the judgment has been obtained and take it back, provided no force is used. This right does not apply to land within the scope of the Rent Act 1977, Housing Act 1988, **44.43**

Landlord and Tenant Act 1954, Part I, etc., and see the Protection from Eviction Act 1977. The invariable practice in present times is for enforcement to be effected under warrants (county court) or writs (High Court) of possession.

Procedure

44.44 Again, as with execution against goods (see 44.09), issue is simply a matter of filing a request (county court) or a *praecipe*, draft writ of possession, and judgment (High Court) and paying a fee. It is of the utmost importance that the land is adequately described. The police are often informed of the time when possession will be enforced, as entry may be gained by force if necessary. The claimant will also usually need to attend to change the locks and make the premises secure after possession is obtained.

44.45 When enforcing the warrant or writ, the bailiff or enforcement officer is required to turn out everyone on the premises, even if they are not parties: *R v Wandsworth County Court, ex p Wandsworth London Borough Council* [1975] 1 WLR 1314. However, there is a divergence of practice regarding goods in the premises. In the High Court, these too must be removed by the enforcement officer, but in the county courts this is unnecessary (CCA 1984, s 111(1)).

Warrants and writs of restitution

44.46 It sometimes happens that persons ejected when a warrant or writ of possession is enforced regain entry at some later date. Such persons may be removed a second time under a warrant (county court) or writ (High Court) of restitution. These are a species of warrant (or writ) in aid of a primary warrant (or writ). Permission is required for the issue of such warrants or writs (RSC, ord 46, r 3; CCR, ord 26, r 17(4)). The application is made without notice by application notice supported by written evidence giving details of the wrongful re-entry. The court looks for a plain and sufficient nexus between the original recovery of possession and the need to effect further recovery of the same land: *Wiltshire County Council v Frazer (No 2)* [1986] 1 WLR 109.

D RECEIVERS BY WAY OF EQUITABLE EXECUTION

Nature of receivership

44.47 A receivership order has the effect of appointing some responsible person to receive rents, profits, and moneys receivable in respect of the judgment debtor's interest in certain property, and to apply that income in specified ways, including payment of a judgment debt. According to *Maclaine Watson and Co Ltd v International Tin Council* [1988] Ch 1, such an order can only be made where:

(a) it is impossible to enforce using any of the other methods of enforcement; and
(b) the appointment of a receiver will be effective.

44.48 On the question whether the appointment of a receiver will be effective, the SCA 1981, s 37(1), provides that an appointment can be made only if it is just and convenient. Under

PD 69, para 5, the court must have regard to the amount claimed by the judgment creditor, the amount likely to be obtained by the receiver, and the probable costs of the appointment. It may be appropriate to appoint a receiver where the judgment debtor has some valuable right not in the nature of a debt (and hence not amenable to a third-party debt order). A receiver might also be appointed to receive rents from a number of tenants who are suing their landlord for failing to maintain the premises, and to apply the money in effecting necessary repairs: *Hart v Emelkirk Ltd* [1983] 1 WLR 1289.

Procedure

An application for the appointment of a receiver may be made without notice, but is made by issuing an application notice supported by written evidence (CPR, r 69.3). The evidence needs to address the circumstances making the appointment of a receiver desirable, and must also address the suitability of the person nominated to act as the receiver. There are further detailed requirements in PD 69, para 4. If an order is made it is usually served on the receiver and all the parties to the proceedings, and the court may direct that it be served on other interested persons (r 69.4). The receiver may be required to provide security to cover his liability for any acts and omissions as a receiver (r 69.5 and PD 69, para 7). Once appointed a receiver will be remunerated (often out of the income of the property managed by the receiver), and the receiver will be required to provide accounts for his dealings with the property (r 69.8 and PD 69, para 10). Once the receiver's duties are completed the receiver or any party may apply for the receiver to be discharged (r 69.10). **44.49**

E CONTEMPT OF COURT

Contempt of court consists of interfering with the administration of the law: see *Attorney-General v Leveller Magazine Ltd* [1979] AC 440 *per* Lord Edmund-Davies at 459. It can take many forms, but the most common are: **44.50**

(a) disobedience by the contemner of an order requiring him or her to take or refrain from taking specified action;
(b) assisting another to breach such an order; and
(c) taking action which impedes or interferes with the course of justice.

Proceedings for contempt are essentially punitive in character, although they also have the purpose of securing compliance with the court's orders. The main punishments for contempt are imprisonment (for up to two years: Contempt of Court Act 1981, s 14(1)), fines, and sequestration, although the court can order the taking of security, award damages, or deliver a strong reprimand. Given the nature of the punishments for contempt, the courts have insisted on the establishment of *mens rea* and proof beyond reasonable doubt. **44.51**

Committal for breach of an order

Formalities

Committal for breach of a court order normally arises in relation to injunctions, although it is possible for other orders and judgments to be couched in a form rendering breach a contempt **44.52** of court. The order must contain a warning prominently displayed on its front that disobedience will be a contempt of court punishable by imprisonment (or sequestration if a body corporate). Also, the original injunction must have been served personally on the defendant (RSC, ord 45, r 7; CCR, ord 29, r 1).

Procedure on application

44.53 Applications to commit a contemner to prison are made by Part 8 claim form or, if made in existing proceedings, by application notice (PD RSC, ord 52, paras 2.1, 2.2). In either case the notice sets out the provisions in the injunction or undertaking which have been broken, and lists the ways in which it is alleged that the injunction or undertaking has been broken. The notice must be supported by an affidavit (not a witness statement) stating the grounds on which the application is made.

44.54 The respondent must be served with the claim form or application notice and affidavit by personal service at least 14 clear days before the return day, unless the court orders otherwise (RSC, ord 52, r 3(1)). The hearing has to be before a judge.

44.55 A respondent may give oral evidence at the hearing despite not filing any written evidence (PD RSC, ord 52, para 3.3).

Purging contempt

44.56 A contemner does not necessarily serve the entire term of imprisonment imposed by the judge. An application for discharge may be made on the ground that the contempt has been purged or that the contemner desires to purge the contempt. The main consideration is whether the contemner has been sufficiently punished for the contempt, although the court will also be concerned with whether the contemner is likely to obey the court's order in the future, and whether the contemner has shown suitable remorse: *Enfield London Borough Council v Mahoney* [1983] 1 WLR 749.

Sequestration

44.57 Applications for permission to issue writs of sequestration are made by issuing an application notice supported by written evidence, and are heard by a judge. If the contempt is proved and sequestration is ordered, four sequestrators are appointed to enter the contemner's lands, and to seize the contemner's personal property, and to hold the same until the contempt is purged. Third parties are under a duty not knowingly to take any action which will obstruct compliance by the sequestrators with the terms of the writ of sequestration: see the judgment of Donaldson P in *Eckman v Midland Bank Ltd* [1973] QB 519. Sequestration was used in a number of well-publicized trade union cases in the 1980s to enforce compliance with injunctions.

F ENFORCEMENT OF FOREIGN JUDGMENTS

44.58 At common law a foreign judgment can be enforced in this country by bringing an English action claiming the amount of the judgment as a debt. In theory, the foreign judgment gives rise to an implied contract to pay, which can be enforced in England: *Grant v Easton* (1883) 13

QBD 302. However, English proceedings can be commenced only if the English courts have jurisdiction (see Chapter 10), and although it may be possible to obtain summary judgment on such a claim, a number of defences can be raised (eg, that the foreign court lacked jurisdiction, fraud, that the judgment is contrary to public policy, that the foreign proceedings were in breach of an agreement as to the settling of the dispute, or that the judgment is for the enforcement of a foreign penal law).

The United Kingdom is party to international conventions providing for the direct enforcement of foreign judgments which have been incorporated into English law by the following provisions: **44.59**

(a) The Administration of Justice Act 1920, by which an application can be made by issuing a Part 8 claim form for the registration of a judgment of a superior court of a Commonwealth country in the High Court within 12 months of the date of the judgment in question. The court has a discretion whether to register the judgment, and the defendant can make use of most of the defences available at common law.
(b) The Foreign Judgments (Reciprocal Enforcement) Act 1933, by which an application can be made by issuing a Part 8 claim form for the registration of judgments of recognized courts and tribunals of States with which this country has entered into reciprocal enforcement arrangements, provided the application is made within six years of the judgment. This Act considerably increased the circumstances in which foreign judgments can be registered, but enforcement is subject to a wide range of defences similar to those available at common law.
(c) The Judgments Regulation, by which a judgment of a court of another EU Member State may be registered in the courts of this country. When registered, such a judgment has the same force and effect as if the judgment had been given in this country. Applications for registration are made without notice supported by an affidavit or witness statement stating whether the judgment provides for payment of money or interest, the grounds on which the applicant has a right to enforce the judgment, and the amount unsatisfied on the judgment, and giving an address for service within the jurisdiction. The written evidence must exhibit the judgment or a certified copy, evidence of service, legal aid documents from the State in which the judgment was given, and translations. Articles 34 and 35 of the Judgments Regulation set out a number of defences to registration, such as recognition being contrary to public policy, the defendant not having been duly served with the document instituting the foreign proceedings, and the judgment being irreconcilable with another judgment. Recognition of a Dutch judgment which had been obtained in manifest contravention of art 6(1) of the European Convention on Human Rights was refused as being contrary to public policy under what is now art 34(1) in *Maronier v Larmer* [2003] QB 620. However, art 36 provides that there cannot, under any circumstances, be a review of the substance of such a judgment.
(d) European Enforcement Orders. Certification and enforcement of European Enforcement Orders is governed by Council Regulation (EC) No 805/2004 (the 'EEO Regulation'). The EEO Regulation is annexed to PD 74B, and the procedure for enforcement under the EEO Regulation is dealt with by CPR, rr 74.27–74.33.

Detailed provisions dealing with the registration in the Queen's Bench Division of foreign judgments can be found in CPR, Part 74. **44.60**

KEY POINTS SUMMARY

44.61
- A judgment creditor can ask for the court's assistance in discovering the assets available for enforcement by applying to obtain information from the judgment debtor.
- A money judgment can be enforced by writ or warrant of execution against the judgment debtor's goods, by third-party debt order against a bank (etc.) account, by attachment of earnings against the judgment debtor's salary, or can be secured by obtaining a charging order.
- Each type of non-money judgment has its own enforcement procedure (land, goods, injunctions).
- Most enforcement procedures are dealt with administratively by the court.
- Exceptions are third-party debt orders, charging orders, and committal, which all require court orders.
- Third-party debt orders and charging orders have a two-stage process. Interim orders are sought without notice, and final orders are sought at a final hearing.
- Personal service is required for an application to commit for contempt, at least 14 clear days before the hearing.

45

JUDICIAL REVIEW

'Judicial review, as the words imply, is not an appeal from a decision, but a review of the manner in which the decision was made.' So said Lord Brightman in *Chief Constable of the North Wales Police v Evans* [1982] 1 WLR 1155. In the same case, Lord Hailsham of St Marylebone LC said that the purpose of judicial review is to ensure that an individual is given fair treatment by a wide range of authorities, whether judicial, quasi-judicial, or administrative, to which the individual has been subject. It is no part of that purpose to substitute the opinion of the judiciary or of individual judges for that of the authority constituted by law to decide the matters in question. **45.01**

Applications for judicial review must be brought in the High Court (CCA 1984, s 38(3)), and in fact are brought in the Administrative Court Office of the QBD. The law governing when judicial review will lie is a subject in its own right, and reference should be made to specialist books on the subject, such as H W R Wade and C F Forsyth, *Administrative Law* (10th edn, Oxford: OUP, 2009). This chapter will deal with judicial review in civil matters. For commentary on judicial review in criminal cases, see J Sprack, *A Practical Approach to Criminal Procedure* (13th edn, Oxford: OUP, 2009). A brief summary of the salient principles is given in 45.03–45.45, and the rest of the chapter will consider the procedural aspects. **45.02**

A PRINCIPLES

Parties

45.03 Judicial review proceedings are not brought by or at the instigation of the Crown, whose only involvement is as a nominal party: *R (Ben-Abdelaziz) v Haringey London Borough Council* [2001] 1 WLR 1485. They are therefore not brought by or at the instigation of a public authority within the meaning of the Human Rights Act 1998, s 22(4), and consequently do not give rise to a right to claim damages against a public authority under s 7(1)(b) of the Act.

45.04 In general, judicial review will lie against any body charged with the performance of a public duty. In *R v Criminal Injuries Compensation Board, ex p Lain* [1967] 2 QB 864, Lord Parker CJ said:

> The only constant limits throughout [on what is now known as judicial review] were that [the body concerned] was performing a public duty. Private or domestic tribunals have always been outside the scope of [judicial review] since their authority is derived solely from contract, that is, from the agreement of the parties concerned...
>
> We have as it seems to me reached the position when the ambit of [judicial review] can be said to cover every case in which a body of persons of a public as opposed to a purely private or domestic character has to determine matters affecting subjects provided always that it has a duty to act judicially.

45.05 The ambit of judicial review has developed apace since 1967, and the requirement that the body being reviewed should have a duty to act judicially was removed by the House of Lords in *O'Reilly v Mackman* [1983] 2 AC 237. In *Council of Civil Service Unions v Minister for the Civil Service* [1985] AC 374 the House of Lords extended the possibility of judicial review to a person exercising a purely prerogative power, and in *Gillick v West Norfolk and Wisbech Area Health Authority* [1986] AC 112 the view was expressed *obiter* that judicial review would extend to guidance circulars issued by a government department without any statutory authority.

45.06 Judicial review lies against any inferior court or tribunal. Inferior courts include magistrates' courts, county courts, election courts, coroners' courts, and (on matters unconnected to trial on indictment) the Crown Court. It is only in rare situations that judicial review will lie against a decision of a county court, because the proper remedy is to seek to appeal rather than to seek a judicial review (*R (Sivasubramaniam) v Wandsworth County Court* [2003] 1 WLR 475). A distinction is drawn between cases where the judge has simply got it wrong, or even extremely wrong, on the law, or the facts, or both (where judicial review is not available) and cases where the judicial process itself had been frustrated or corrupted (where it is) (*Strickson v Preston County Court* [2007] EWCA Civ 1132). The superior courts (the Crown Court, in matters connected with trials on indictment, the High Court, Court of Appeal, and House of Lords) are not subject to judicial review.

45.07 Bodies other than courts which have been held to be subject to judicial review include:

(a) government ministers (see *Pyx Granite Co Ltd v Ministry of Housing and Local Government* [1960] AC 260);
(b) the Inland Revenue Commissioners (see *R v Commissioners of Inland Revenue, ex p Preston* [1985] AC 835);

(c) immigration officers (see *R v Secretary of State for the Home Department, ex p Khawaja* [1984] AC 74);
(d) local authorities (see *Secretary of State for Education and Science v Tameside Metropolitan Borough Council* [1977] AC 1014);
(e) a limited liability company set up by a local authority pursuant to its statutory powers to manage farmers' markets in its area (*R (Beer) v Hampshire Farmers Market Ltd* (2003) 31 EGCS 67);
(f) police authorities (see *Ridge v Baldwin* [1964] AC 40);
(g) prison governors (see *Leech v Deputy Governor of Parkhurst Prison* [1988] AC 533); and
(h) disciplinary bodies exercising statutory powers (see, eg, *R v General Medical Council, ex p Gee* [1986] 1 WLR 226, confirmed by the House of Lords [1987] 1 WLR 564).

Regarding non-statutory bodies, the Criminal Injuries Compensation Board in its pre-statutory days was held to be subject to judicial review in *R v Criminal Injuries Compensation Board, ex p Lain* [1967] 2 QB 864. Although the Takeover Panel, an extra-statutory body which is part of the self-regulatory system of the City, was held to be subject to judicial review by the Court of Appeal in *R v Panel on Takeovers and Mergers, ex p Datafin plc* [1987] QB 815, the ruling committee of Lloyd's is not so subject: see *R v Lloyd's of London, ex p Briggs* [1993] 1 Lloyd's Rep 176. **45.08**

The position of what used to be university visitors was considered in *R v Hull University Visitor, ex p Page* [1993] AC 682. As a university is an eleemosynary charitable foundation, the visitor had exclusive jurisdiction to decide disputes arising under its domestic law. Judicial review therefore did not lie to impeach decisions made by visitors within their jurisdiction (in the sense of having power under the internal laws of the institution to adjudicate upon the dispute) on the ground of error of fact or law. This meant that judicial review could be available where visitors purported to hear disputes outside their jurisdiction, or declined to exercise their jurisdiction: *R v Visitors to the Inns of Court, ex p Calder* [1994] QB 1. **45.09**

As stated by Lord Parker CJ in the quotation at the beginning of this section, judicial review does not lie against a purely domestic tribunal. Examples include the stewards of the National Greyhound Racing Club (*Law v National Greyhound Racing Club Ltd* [1983] 1 WLR 1302), the Jockey Club (*R v Disciplinary Committee of the Jockey Club, ex p Aga Khan* [1993] 1 WLR 909), the Football Association (*R v Football Association Ltd, ex p Football League Ltd* [1993] 2 All ER 833), and an employer's disciplinary tribunal (*R v British Broadcasting Corporation, ex p Lavelle* [1983] 1 WLR 23). **45.10**

Locus standi

A claimant seeking judicial review must have 'a sufficient interest in the matter to which the application relates' (see SCA 1981, s 31(3)). The essential idea is to exclude busybodies. A direct or personal interest in the decision should suffice. Whether a general interest is sufficient is a mixed question of law and fact. It depends on the relationship between the claimant and the complaint, with the court needing to consider the relevant duties of the authority concerned, the complaint made, and the relief sought (*Inland Revenue Commissioners v National Federation of Self-Employed and Small Businesses Ltd* [1982] AC 617). In that case it was held that a group of taxpayers did not have standing to impugn **45.11** the Inland Revenue Commissioners' dealings with other taxpayers. In *R v Inspectorate of Pollution, ex p Greenpeace Ltd* [1994] 1 WLR 570, Otton J said that the court had to take into account the nature of the claimant, the extent of the claimant's interest in the issues raised, and the nature of the relief sought. On the latter point, if a mandatory order is sought the court is more likely to hold that the applicant has no standing than if the primary relief is a quashing order. In this decision Greenpeace Ltd, an environmental interest group of international standing, was held to have *locus standi* in relation to an issue involving the discharge of radioactive waste. In *R v Secretary of State for Employment, ex p Equal Opportunities Commission* [1995] 1 AC 1 the EOC was held to have *locus standi* in judicial review proceedings relating to sex discrimination.

45.12 Where there is a justiciable issue which cannot be aired in any other way, and if the application seeks a remedy which can be granted and which will be effective if granted, the courts adopt a generous approach to the question of *locus standi*. Thus, in *Gillick v West Norfolk and Wisbech Area Health Authority* [1986] AC 112 the House of Lords held that a mother had *locus standi* to challenge contraceptive advice issued by the Department of Health and Social Security to doctors on the ground that it was wrong in law.

Grounds

45.13 As mentioned at the beginning of this chapter, judicial review is not a means of appeal but of review. Judicial review does not issue merely because a decision maker makes a mistake (*R v Independent Television Commission, ex p TSW Broadcasting Ltd* (1992) *The Times*, 30 March 1992, HL). What must be shown is some ground for vitiating the decision-making process. These are, broadly, illegality, procedural impropriety, and irrationality, and are described in the following sections. The court's approach to an issue of proportionality under the European Convention on Human Rights has to go beyond that traditionally adopted in domestic judicial review cases. The modern approach was described by Lord Steyn in *R (Daly) v Secretary of State for the Home Department* [2001] 2 AC 532, at [25]–[28]. Lord Bingham of Cornhill in *R (SB) v Governors of Denbigh High School* [2007] 1 AC 100, at [30] said, 'There is no shift to a merits review, but the intensity of review is greater than was previously appropriate, and greater than the heightened scrutiny test' previously used in *R v Ministry of Defence, ex p Smith* [1996] QB 517.

Jurisdictional error

45.14 Judicial review will lie where an inferior court or tribunal or public body has acted without or in excess of its jurisdiction. Such bodies must not act outside their powers, or *ultra vires*. They must abide by any jurisdictional conditions, must follow prescribed procedures, and cannot delegate except as expressly laid down. In making its decision such a body must not ask itself the wrong questions, and it must not take into account matters which it has not been directed to take into account. To provide a basis for judicial review, such a mistake must form a material part in the reasons for the decision (*E v Secretary of State for the Home Department* [2004] QB 1044). Any order made must be one which the relevant body has jurisdiction to make.

45.15 The landmark case in this area is *Anisminic Ltd v Foreign Compensation Commission* [1969] 2 AC 147. The Foreign Compensation Commission rejected a claim for compensation on the erroneous ground that as the claimant's successor in title was not of British nationality the claim did not comply with the terms of the relevant delegated legislation. This was an error of law. The House of Lords held that the courts could interfere with the Commission's decision because, as a result of that error of law, the Commission had based its decision on a matter which they had no right to take into account. The decision was accordingly *ultra vires* and a nullity.

The principle in *Anisminic Ltd v Foreign Compensation Commission* that errors of law as such are automatically reviewable almost certainly only applies to decisions of administrative tribunals and other administrative authorities, and does not apply to decisions of inferior courts. This is because there is a presumption that administrative tribunals and authorities are confined, in the absence of clear words, to deciding the questions defined by Parliament, and that questions of law are for the court. There is no similar presumption in relation to the inferior courts. See *Re Racal Communications Ltd* [1981] AC 374. **45.16**

Error on the face of the record

Where there is an error on the face of the record judicial review will lie even if the body being reviewed has kept within its jurisdiction. In *R v Northumberland Compensation Appeal Tribunal, ex p Shaw* [1952] 1 KB 338, a former employee claimed compensation on the termination of his employment. Under the relevant regulations, the tribunal was required to assess the compensation payable by aggregating two periods of employment. In its decision the tribunal stated there had been the two periods of employment, but that in its view only the second period should be taken into account. As the error appeared on the face of the order, the decision was quashed. **45.17**

The 'record' includes the document which initiates the proceedings, the statements of case, and the adjudication (*R v Northumberland Compensation Appeal Tribunal, ex p Shaw*). It also includes any reasoned decision (see *R v Knightsbridge Crown Court, ex p International Sporting Club (London) Ltd* [1982] QB 304). Tribunal rules made under the Tribunals, Courts and Enforcement Act 2007, s 22 (see **<http://www.tribunals.gov.uk>** for the wide range of procedural rules governing various First-tier tribunals and the Upper Tribunal) typically either require written reasons for decisions, or allow the parties to make a request for written reasons within a short period (such as a month) of the decision. The reasons given need only be intelligible and adequate. Provided they refer to the main issues there is no need to discuss every material consideration (*South Bucks District Council v Porter (No 2)* [2004] 1 WLR 1953). **45.18**

The main remedy where there is an error on the face of a record is a quashing order. The reason is that, unlike the other grounds, a decision containing an error on its face is valid until it is quashed. It is therefore useless to apply for a declaration, and injunctions and damages have no place while the order remains valid. However, it is possible to obtain a prohibiting order to prevent execution of an order containing an error on its face. **45.19**

Natural justice

Grounds for an application for judicial review will be made out where there has been a breach of the rules of natural justice. The leading case is *Ridge v Baldwin* [1964] AC 40. The Chief Constable of Brighton had been tried and acquitted of conspiracy to obstruct the course of justice. The Watch Committee then dismissed him from office without giving him any **45.20** notice and without giving him an opportunity of being heard. The Committee later convened another meeting, and heard representations from the Chief Constable's solicitor, but no notice of any specific charge was given. The Committee confirmed its earlier decision. The initial and reconvened decisions of the Watch Committee were quashed as being contrary to the rules of natural justice.

45.21 Whether, and the extent to which, the rules of natural justice apply depends on the extent to which the decision under scrutiny affects the applicant's pecuniary interests or livelihood. The procedure adopted should reflect the facts of the case, and the importance of what is at stake for the individual and for society (*R (West) v Parole Board* [2005] 1 WLR 350). In a non-exhaustive analysis, Lord Diplock in *Council of Civil Service Unions v Minister for the Civil Service* [1985] AC 374 said that the rules apply where a decision affects some other person either:

(a) by altering rights or obligations which are enforceable by or against that other person in private law; or
(b) by depriving that other person of some benefit or advantage which either:
   (i) he had in the past been permitted by the decision maker to enjoy and which he can legitimately expect to continue until rational grounds for withdrawing it have been communicated on which he is to be given an opportunity to comment; or
   (ii) he has received assurance from the decision maker will not be withdrawn without first giving him an opportunity of advancing reasons for not withdrawing it.

45.22 The rules have been held to apply in compulsory purchase decisions, disciplinary procedures, and licence applications. A 'legitimate expectation' to some benefit may arise from a published circular (*R v Secretary of State for the Home Department, ex p Asif Mahmood Khan* [1984] 1 WLR 1337) or from an established practice, as in the *Council of Civil Service Unions* case. There may be a legitimate expectation even if the claimant is unaware of the policy (*R (Rashid) v Secretary of State for the Home Department* [2005] Imm AR 608). It is clear from *R v East Sussex County Council, ex p Reprotech (Pebsham) Ltd* [2002] 4 All ER 58 that private law estoppel principles have no place in public law, and that the public law legitimate expectation concept is an established independent principle. However, where the decision-making body is required to act urgently to protect the public (as in *R v Birmingham City Council, ex p Ferrero Ltd* [1993] 1 All ER 530) or to protect investors (as in *R v Life Assurance and Unit Trust Regulatory Organisation Ltd, ex p Ross* [1993] QB 17) the rules of natural justice do not apply to the initial decision which can be made without giving any person affected by it prior warning. This is so even if such persons are likely to suffer serious financial consequences by virtue of the decision.

45.23 The rules of natural justice include a right to be heard, a right to be informed of any adverse allegations made, and that the tribunal must not be a judge in its own cause. The latter may arise if a member of the tribunal has an interest in the matter being decided, or if a member of the tribunal is biased against the applicant (for which, see 39.25ff).

Wednesbury unreasonableness

45.24 A decision will be quashed where it is so unreasonable that no reasonable person or body properly directing itself on the law could ever make it. This is often known as *Wednesbury* unreasonableness, from Lord Greene MR's judgment in *Associated Provincial Picture Houses Ltd v Wednesbury Corporation* [1948] 1 KB 223. The principle applies to exceptional cases where the unreasonableness of a decision verges on an absurdity (see the speech of Lord

Scarman in *Nottinghamshire County Council v Secretary of State for the Environment* [1986] AC 240). As mentioned earlier in this chapter, the courts do not wish to be seen as interfering in the legitimate exercise of administrative discretions given by Parliament. On the other hand, the courts do not accept that administrative discretions are completely unfettered, and insist that they must be exercised in accordance with the general policy and objects of the Act or other statutory source of the power in question (see *Padfield v Minister of Agriculture, Fisheries and Food* [1968] AC 997).

The following cases are no more than examples. In *R v Ealing London Borough Council, ex p Times Newspapers Ltd* (1986) 85 LGR 316 the council was held to be unreasonable in refusing to provide certain newspapers in their libraries because they did not agree with the newspapers' proprietors on political grounds. In *R v Hackney London Borough Council, ex p Evenbray* (1987) 86 LGR 210 the council temporarily placed a number of homeless persons in the applicant's hotel. The council then served notice under the Housing Act 1961, s 19, on the applicant imposing the standards applicable to houses in multiple occupation on the hotel rather than those applicable to hotels. The notice was held to be plainly unreasonable. The section was intended to deal with defective premises, and the building was not defective as a hotel. In *Roberts v Hopwood* [1925] AC 578 the House of Lords held that a council policy of paying its employees a minimum weekly wage of £4 was unreasonable because the wages paid were substantially above the prevailing rates of pay and amounted, in effect, to gifts from ratepayers' money. A surprising decision, coupled with a failure to give reasons, may be held to be irrational: *R v Civil Service Appeal Board, ex p Cunningham* [1991] 4 All ER 310. **45.25**

Conspicuous unfairness amounting to abuse of power linked to legitimate expectations has been seen as emerging as a ground for judicial review (*R (Rashid) v Secretary of State for the Home Department)* [2005] Imm AR 608). Caution against such a development was expressed in *R (S) v Secretary of State for the Home Department* [2007] ACD 94, although the Court of Appeal said that an administrative decision could be subject to such obvious unfairness and the remedy could be so plain that there would be only one way that the discretion could be exercised. **45.26**

Sometimes local authorities rely on the limited extent of their financial resources to justify restrictions on the services they provide. Whether this is legitimate depends on the nature of the duty to provide the services in question. Thus lack of resources could be taken into account in assessing the needs of the disabled (*R v Gloucestershire County Council, ex p Barry* [1997] AC 584) and in the level of policing given (*R v Chief Constable of Sussex, ex p International Trader's Ferry Ltd* [1999] 2 AC 418), but not in relation to the type of education that is suitable for a child of compulsory school age (*R v East Sussex County Council, ex p Tandy* [1998] AC 714) or when deciding to defer the implementation of the authority's duties under the National Assistance Act 1948 once a need had been established (*R v Sefton Metropolitan Borough Council, ex p Help the Aged* [1997] 4 All ER 532). **45.27**

Proportionality

Public law cases involving European Community law or rights under the European Convention on Human Rights are decided applying the principle of proportionality rather than the traditional *Wednesbury* principles. Although most cases will be decided in the same way whichever approach is taken, the proportionality approach involves a more intense **45.28** scrutiny of the administrative decision. In *de Freitas v Permanent Secretary of Ministry of Agriculture, Fisheries, Lands and Housing* [1999] 1 AC 69, Lord Clyde said proportionality requires a three-stage test. The court must ask itself whether:

(a) the legislative objective is sufficiently important to justify limiting a fundamental right;
(b) the measures designed to meet the legislative objective are rationally connected to it; and
(c) the means used to impair the right or freedom are no more than is necessary to accomplish the objective.

45.29 Commenting on the difference between this approach and *Wednesbury*, Lord Steyn in *R (Daly) v Secretary of State for the Home Department* [2001] 2 AC 532 said that the doctrine of proportionality:

(a) may require the reviewing court to assess the balance which the decision maker has struck, not merely whether it is within the range of reasonable or rational decisions;
(b) may require attention to the relative weight accorded to various interests and considerations; and
(c) demands a more intense scrutiny because of the requirement that limitations on Convention rights have to be necessary in the sense of meeting a pressing social need.

45.30 It is probable that at some stage the *Wednesbury* principles will be replaced by proportionality in judicial review cases which do not involve Community law or human rights. Such a change will require a decision of the House of Lords, and until then the *Wednesbury* principles will continue to apply (*R (Association of British Civilian Internees: Far East Region) v Secretary of State for Defence* [2003] QB 1397).

Alternative remedy

45.31 Where an applicant has the alternative of appealing from the decision in question or applying for a case to be stated, judicial review will normally be refused. As Sir John Donaldson MR said in *R v Epping and Harlow General Commissioners, ex p Goldstraw* [1983] 3 All ER 257 at 262, 'it is a cardinal principle that, save in the most exceptional circumstances, [the jurisdiction to grant judicial review] will not be exercised where other remedies were available and have not been used'. Whether there are 'exceptional circumstances' justifying the application for judicial review depends on the suitability of the alternative remedy in the context of the particular case. Factors include whether the alternative remedy will resolve the question at issue fully and directly, whether the alternative procedure will be quicker or slower than judicial review, and whether the matter depends on some particular or technical knowledge more readily available to the alternative body (see *R v Birmingham City Council, ex p Ferrero Ltd* [1993] 1 All ER 530).

Decision susceptible to judicial review

45.32 The subject matter of an application for judicial review is either a decision or a refusal by the respondent to make a decision. According to Lord Diplock in *Council of Civil Service Unions v Minister for the Civil Service* [1985] AC 374 (referred to at 45.21) a decision must affect some other person either by altering rights which are enforceable in private law or by depriving that other person of some benefit or advantage. A government department's circular dealing with contraception advice was held to be a 'decision' in *Gillick v West Norfolk and Wisbech Area Health Authority* [1986] AC 112. However, an applicant wishing to apply for judicial review of government policy or of a statutory provision cannot manufacture a decision by engaging in correspondence with the appropriate government department, and then relying on the department's reply as a 'decision' (*R v Secretary of State for Employment, ex p Equal Opportunities Commission* [1995] 1 AC 1).

Issues of public law

Generally, an applicant complaining of an infringement of public law rights must proceed by way of judicial review rather than by ordinary claim. In *O'Reilly v Mackman* [1983] 2 AC 237 Lord Diplock said at 285: **45.33**

> ...it would in my view as a general rule be contrary to public policy, and as such an abuse of the process of the court, to permit a person seeking to establish that a decision of a public authority infringed rights to which he was entitled to protection under public law to proceed by way of an ordinary action and by this means to evade the provisions [governing judicial review] for the protection of such authorities.

Lord Bridge of Harwich in *Cocks v Thanet District Council* [1983] 2 AC 286, HL, identified the various protections given by the rules governing judicial review as: **45.34**

> ...the need to obtain [permission] to apply on the basis of sworn evidence which makes frank disclosure of all relevant facts known to the applicant; the court's discretionary control of both [disclosure of documents] and cross-examination; the capacity of the court to act with the utmost speed when necessary; and the avoidance of the temptation for the court to substitute its own decision of fact for that of the [authority].

As recognized in *Mercury Communications Ltd v Director General of Telecommunications* [1996] 1 WLR 48, the precise limits of what is known as 'public law' and 'private law' have not been fully worked out, so there is often scope for argument whether the *O'Reilly v Mackman* principle applies to any individual case. In *O'Reilly v Mackman* the claimants were prison inmates who commenced common law claims complaining of a loss of remission. These claims were struck out, because the claimants had no right to remission in private law. Their claims raised questions of public law, so should have been brought by way of judicial review. Whether a claim should be struck out on this basis depends on a consideration of all the relevant circumstances (*Phonographic Performance Ltd v Department of Trade and Industry* [2004] 1 WLR 2893). In *Cocks v Thanet District Council* the claimant brought a county court claim against a housing authority claiming he was homeless and in priority need, and that the authority owed him temporary and full housing duty. Under housing law, the authority had public law functions in determining whether the circumstances gave rise to a housing duty. Once the authority had decided there was a housing duty, the applicant immediately acquired private law rights which could be enforced by injunctions and awards of damages. As the public law decision was a condition precedent to the private law right, Mr Cocks should have challenged the authority by way of judicial review, and his private law claim was struck out as an abuse of process. **45.35**

45.36 There are exceptions to the above general rule. In *O'Reilly v Mackman*, Lord Diplock expressly referred to two of them:

(a) where the invalidity of the decision arises as a collateral issue in a claim for the infringement of the claimant's rights under private law, eg, where the validity of a planning authority's enforcement notice is an issue in a claim by the claimant against its solicitors for professional negligence;
(b) where none of the parties objects to the matter being brought by a common law claim.

45.37 Later decisions of the House of Lords provide further exceptions to the general rule:

(c) where the claim has been framed in tort without raising any issue of public law as a live issue (*Davy v Spelthorne Borough Council* [1984] AC 262);
(d) where the validity of an authority's decision is raised by way of defence (*Wandsworth London Borough Council v Winder* [1985] AC 461);
(e) where a claim, although involving a challenge to a public law decision, is dominated by a consideration of the claimant's private law rights (*Roy v Kensington and Chelsea and Westminster Family Practitioner Committee* [1992] 1 AC 624).

Remedies

45.38 There are six remedies available on applications for judicial review. The first three (see 45.39 to 45.41) are the old prerogative remedies. Generally, the various forms of relief may be claimed either in the alternative or in addition to each other, provided they arise out of, or relate to, or are connected with, the same matter.

Quashing order

45.39 Quashing orders used to be known as orders of *certiorari*. A quashing order is an order quashing the decision of an inferior court, tribunal, or public authority. It will often also remit the matter with a direction for the lower court, tribunal, or authority to reach a decision consistent with the findings of the High Court (SCA 1981, s 31(5)). When it is brought into force, the Tribunals, Courts and Enforcement Act 2007, s 141, will enable the High Court to substitute its own decision if it quashes a decision of a lower court or tribunal for an error of law. A quashing order is the general remedy available where a decision is made in circumstances giving rise to any of the grounds discussed at 45.13ff. Where permission is sought to apply for a quashing order in respect of a judgment or order which is subject to appeal, the QBD may adjourn the application for permission until the appeal is determined or the time for appealing has expired. If permission to apply is granted, the judge may, under CPR, r 54.10(2), impose a stay of the impugned proceedings.

Mandatory orders

45.40 Mandatory orders used to be known as *mandamus*. A mandatory order is an order requiring an inferior court, tribunal, or public authority to carry out its duties. It is the appropriate order where the body in question is guilty of wrongful inaction, which includes a refusal to exercise a discretion. Disobedience is a contempt of court (*R v Poplar Borough Council, ex p London County Council (No 2)* [1922] 1 KB 95). The remedy does not lie against the Crown (*R v Powell* (1841) 1 QB 352).

Prohibitory order

Prohibitory orders used to be known as prohibitions. A prohibitory order is an order restraining an inferior court, tribunal, or public authority from acting outside its jurisdiction. In *R v Electricity Commissioners, ex p London Electricity Joint Committee Co (1920) Ltd* [1924] 1 KB 171, Atkin LJ said: **45.41**

> I can see no difference in principle between [a quashing order] and [a prohibitory order], except that the latter may be invoked at an earlier stage. If the proceedings establish that the body complained of is exceeding its jurisdiction by entertaining matters which would result in its final decision being subject to being brought up and [a quashing order made], I think that [a prohibitory order may be made] to restrain it from so exceeding its jurisdiction.

Declaration

A declaration is a decision of the court on a question of law or rights. It is a discretionary remedy. The question involved must be a real rather than a theoretical question, and it must be raised between parties with a true interest in having it resolved (*Russian Commercial and Industrial Bank v British Bank for Foreign Trade Ltd* [1921] 2 AC 438). The declaration is a particularly useful remedy in administrative law as it can be granted against the Crown (*Dyson v Attorney-General* [1912] 1 Ch 158). **45.42**

Injunction

An injunction is a mandatory or prohibitory order designed to regulate the future relationship between the parties. This remedy cannot be ordered against the Crown under English law (Crown Proceedings Act 1947, s 21(2)), but may be granted against the Crown or an officer of the Crown if it is necessary to protect rights deriving from European Community law (*R v Secretary of State for Transport, ex p Factortame Ltd (No 2)* (Case C–213/89) [1991] 1 AC 603, ECJ and HL). **45.43**

Injunctions and declarations are granted only where the court considers it just and convenient to do so. An interim injunction can be granted in pending judicial review proceedings, the court applying much the same rules as apply in other cases (see Chapter 35; *R v Advertising Standards Authority Ltd, ex p Vernons Organisation Ltd* [1992] 1 WLR 1289). **45.44**

Money awards

An award of damages, restitution, or the recovery of a sum due may be made on an application for judicial review, but only in conjunction with the other remedies available in judicial review claims (CPR, r 54.3(2)). Money may be awarded if the court is satisfied that, if the claim had been made in ordinary proceedings, the applicant could have been awarded such a remedy. **45.45**

B JUDICIAL REVIEW PRE-ACTION PROTOCOL

Persons intending to apply for judicial review should generally comply with the judicial review pre-action protocol before issuing proceedings. Compliance with the protocol will not be appropriate where the defendant has no legal power to change the decision being **45.46** challenged, or if the application is urgent, such as the failure of a local housing authority to secure interim accommodation for a homeless claimant. It does not affect the time limit in CPR, r 54.5 (see 45.49). Under the protocol the intending claimant should send a letter of claim to the defendant seeking to establish whether litigation can be avoided and identifying the issues. A template for this letter is set out at Annex A to the protocol. Defendants should normally reply within 14 days, and a template for the letter of response is set out in Annex B. Where it is not possible to reply within this time, an interim reply should be sent proposing a reasonable extension. The response should say in clear and unambiguous terms whether the claim is conceded in full, in part, or is disputed. Where appropriate it should contain a new decision, fuller reasons for the decision, or address any points of dispute. It should also enclose any documents requested by the claimant or explain why they are not being provided.

C APPLYING FOR PERMISSION TO PROCEED

45.47 There are two stages in an application for judicial review. These are, first, an application for permission to proceed with the application for judicial review, and if permission is granted, secondly, the substantive hearing. The purpose of the requirement of obtaining permission is to filter out frivolous and hopeless applications with the minimum waste of court time.

45.48 If it becomes clear that the paperwork is incorrect, the court may be prepared to allow it to be amended. In *R (Burkett) v Hammersmith and Fulham London Borough Council* [2002] 1 WLR 1593 the House of Lords allowed an application to be amended from a review of a planning resolution to a review of a planning permission. In public law the emphasis should be on substance rather than form.

Time limit for filing the claim form

45.49 The claim form initiating an application for judicial review must be filed promptly, and in any event not later than three months after the grounds to make the claim arose (CPR, r 54.5(1)). This time period may not be extended by agreement between the parties (r 54.5(2)).

45.50 It follows from this wording that an application may be refused for delay even if it is made within three months if it has not been made promptly: *R v Independent Television Commission, ex p TV NI Ltd* (1991) *The Times*, 30 December 1991. An extension beyond three months can only be granted by the court, applying the overriding objective. The court has a discretion to refuse an application for permission if there has been delay, where it considers that granting the relief sought would be likely to cause substantial hardship to, or substantially prejudice the rights of, any person (including the general public), or if it would be detrimental to good administration (SCA 1981, s 31(6); *R v Stratford-on-Avon District Council, ex p Jackson* [1985] 1 WLR 1319). In considering whether the application is likely to be detrimental to good administration, the court may take into account the effect of the application in relation to other potential applicants: *R v Dairy Produce Quota Tribunal for England and Wales, ex p Caswell* [1989] 1 WLR 1089. There is no requirement for a causal connection between prejudice and the delay. What is required is a connection between prejudice and the grant of the relief sought: *R v Secretary of State for Health, ex p Furneaux* [1994] 2 All ER 652.

Issuing the claim form

A claim for judicial review is made using a Part 8 claim form (which is described at 19.05ff), which, in addition to the usual requirements, must, by virtue of CPR, r 54.6, PD 16, para 15, and PD 54A state: **45.51**

(a) the name and address of any person the claimant considers to be an interested person. Where the claim for judicial review relates to proceedings in a court or tribunal, all other parties to those proceedings must be named as interested persons (PD 54A, para 5.1);
(b) that the claimant is requesting permission to proceed with a claim for judicial review;
(c) any remedy (including any interim remedy) that is being claimed, and any relief sought under the Human Rights Act 1998 (see PD 16, para 15.1(2));
(d) where the claimant is seeking to raise any issue under the Human Rights Act 1998, or seeks a remedy available under that Act, precise details of the Convention right alleged to have been infringed and details of the infringement;
(e) where the relief sought includes a declaration of incompatibility under the Human Rights Act 1998, s 4, precise details of the legislative provision and the alleged incompatibility;
(f) where a claim under the Human Rights Act 1998 is founded on a finding of unlawfulness by another court or tribunal, details of the finding; and
(g) where a claim under the Human Rights Act 1998 is founded on a judicial act which is alleged to have infringed a Convention right as provided by the Human Rights Act 1998, s 9, details of the judicial act and of the lower court or tribunal.

PD 54A, para 5.6 provides that the claim form must include, or be accompanied by, the following: **45.52**

(a) a detailed statement of the claimant's grounds for bringing the claim for judicial review;
(b) a statement of the facts relied upon;
(c) any application to extend the time limit for filing the claim form; and
(d) any application for directions.

PD 54A, para 5.7 provides that the claim form must be accompanied by: **45.53**

(a) any written evidence in support of the claim or any application to extend time;
(b) a copy of any order that the claimant seeks to have quashed;
(c) where the claim relates to the decision of a lower court or tribunal, an approved copy of the reasons for that decision;
(d) copies of any documents relied upon by the claimant;
(e) copies of any relevant statutory material; and
(f) a list of the essential documents for advance reading by the court, with page references for the passages relied upon.

45.54 Two copies of a paginated and indexed bundle containing all the documents required under PD 54A, paras 5.6 and 5.7 must be filed when the claim is issued (para 5.9 and CPR, r 54.6(2)).

Service of the claim form

45.55 The claim form and the other documentation described at 45.53–45.54 (see CPR, r 54.6(2)) must be served on the defendant and the other interested parties within seven days after the date of issue (r 54.7). The usual rules on service apply; see Chapter 8.

Acknowledgment of service

45.56 Any person served with the claim form who wishes to take part in the judicial review proceedings must file an acknowledgment of service within 21 days after service (CPR, r 54.8(2)(a)). The acknowledgment must also be served on the claimant and any other interested parties within seven days after it is filed (r 54.8(2)(b)). Acknowledgments used in judicial review proceedings must set out a summary of the grounds on which the claim is contested, and give the names and addresses of any other persons whom the person filing it considers to be interested persons (r 54.8(4)). A person who fails to file an acknowledgment of service is not allowed to take part in any hearing to decide whether permission should be granted, unless the court allows him to do so (r 54.9(1)).

Considering whether to grant permission

45.57 Generally, the papers are considered by a judge without a hearing. Permission should be granted if, on the material available and without going into the matter in depth, there is an arguable case for granting the relief claimed (*Inland Revenue Commissioners v National Federation of Self-Employed and Small Businesses Ltd* [1982] AC 617 *per* Lord Diplock). The judge's order, and the reasons for the decision, are then served on the claimant, defendant, and any other person who filed an acknowledgment of service (CPR, r 54.11). This is the most convenient and least costly way of proceeding. Alternatively, if so requested in the notice, the applicant can ask for the question of permission to be considered at a hearing with the applicant being able to make representations through counsel.

Reconsideration

45.58 Where an application for permission to proceed is refused on the papers, the claimant may file a request for the decision to be reconsidered at a hearing (CPR, r 54.12(3)). The application must be made within seven days of service of the refusal of permission. The claimant, defendant, and any other person who filed an acknowledgment will be given at least two days' notice of the hearing date. Neither the defendant nor any other interested person is expected to attend the hearing, unless the court otherwise directs (PD 54A, para 8.5), and if they do attend, the court will not generally make an order for costs against the claimant.

D THE SUBSTANTIVE HEARING

Permission

Where permission is granted, the court will give reasons, and may also give case management directions (CPR, r 54.10). These may include provisions about serving the claim form and evidence on other persons. Where a claim is made under the Human Rights Act 1998, a direction may be made for giving notice to the Crown or for joining the Crown as a party (see 3.59–3.60 and PD 54A, para 8.2). Once permission is granted, other parties are not allowed to apply to have the permission set aside (CPR, r 54.13). **45.59**

Contesting the claim

Assuming that permission to proceed is granted, a defendant or any other person served with the claim form who wishes to contest the claim (or support it on additional grounds) must file and serve detailed grounds and any written evidence relied upon within 35 days after service of the order giving permission (CPR, r 54.14). A party relying on any documents not already filed must file a paginated bundle of those additional documents with his detailed grounds (PD 54A, para 10.1). Claimants and their legal advisers are under an obligation to reconsider the merits of their claim in the light of the written evidence served by the other parties. **45.60**

Joinder

Any person may apply for permission to file evidence or to be able to make representations at the hearing (CPR, r 54.17). Under the old rules, a person was regarded as sufficiently affected to justify being joined only if they were affected without the intervention of any intermediate agency: *R v Liverpool City Council, ex p Muldoon* [1996] 1 WLR 1103. Any such application should be made promptly. If permission is granted, it may be given subject to conditions, and the court may make case management directions (PD 54A, para 13.2). **45.61**

Interim orders

The usual position in judicial review claims is that there will be no oral evidence, and any disputes of fact are resolved in favour of the defendant (*R v Board of Visitors of Hull Prison, ex p St Germain (No 2)* [1979] 1 WLR 1401). Nevertheless, it is possible to apply for orders for disclosure of documents, further information under Part 18, and for permission to cross-examine any person who has given written evidence as well as for interim injunctions to restrain the body under review. Disclosure is not required except under an express court order (PD 54A, para 12.1). Disclosure is more likely to be ordered in cases where proportionality issues arise, but even in these cases will be carefully limited: *Tweed v Parades Commission* [2007] 1 AC 650. Disclosure, further information, and cross-examination will not be allowed where the applicant is seeking to fish for the existence of some mistake by the decision maker: *R v Independent Television Commission, ex p TSW Broadcasting Ltd* (1992) *The Times*, 30 March 1992. Indeed, cross-examination of deponents will be granted only where the interests of justice so require: *O'Reilly v Mackman* [1983] 2 AC 237 *per* Lord Diplock. **45.62**

Additional grounds

45.63 Where a claimant seeks to rely on additional grounds beyond those for which permission has been granted, notice must be given to the court and to the other persons who have been served with the claim form no later than seven clear days before the substantive hearing (or the warned date for the hearing) (PD 54A, para 11.1). Permission must be sought for the additional grounds (CPR, r 54.15).

Skeleton arguments

45.64 The claimant must file and serve a skeleton argument not less than 21 working days before the hearing date (or warned date) (PD 54A, para 15.1). Other parties must file and serve their skeleton arguments not less than 14 working days before the hearing or warned date (para 15.2). The claimant's skeleton argument must be accompanied by a paginated and indexed bundle of all relevant documentation (para 16.1). Skeleton arguments must contain:

(a) a time estimate for the complete hearing, including delivery of judgment;
(b) a list of issues;
(c) a list of the legal points to be taken (together with relevant authorities and page references for passages relied upon);
(d) a chronology (with page references to the bundle of documents);
(e) a list of the essential documents for advance reading by the judge; and
(f) a list of the persons referred to.

The hearing

45.65 Hearings are conducted in public, subject to the usual principles justifying a hearing in private (see 39.30). Proceedings under the Prevention of Terrorism Act 2005 are often held in private (CPR, r 76.22). As there will often be 'closed material' (see r 76.28) in cases under this Act, the Attorney General may appoint a 'special advocate' to represent the interests of the relevant party (r 76.23). *Secretary of State for the Home Department v AHK* [2009] 1 WLR 2049 deals with the discretion to appoint a special advocate in these cases.

45.66 Normal judicial review hearings are conducted on the basis of written material and legal submissions to the court. There are rare cases where the court will order witnesses to attend for cross-examination (*R (Wilkinson) v Responsible Medical Officer Broadmoor Hospital* [2002] 1 WLR 419). In addition to the materials before the decision maker, it was held in *R v Secretary of State for the Environment, ex p Powis* [1981] 1 WLR 584 that the court will consider the following categories of fresh evidence:

(a) evidence bearing on any question of fact as to whether the decision maker had jurisdiction;
(b) evidence on whether any procedural requirements were observed; and
(c) evidence to prove misconduct—examples are bias on the part of the decision maker, and fraud or perjury by a party.

45.67 The court is not bound by the decision to grant permission, and considers whether the applicant has standing, whether the grounds for seeking review are made out, and whether, in its discretion, it ought to grant relief.

The position where the decision-making authority has expressed more than one reason for a decision and the applicant successfully impugns one or some of them was considered in *R v Broadcasting Complaints Commission, ex p Owen* [1985] QB 1153. May LJ said that where the reasons can be disentangled, and the court is satisfied that, despite one reason being bad in law, the same decision would have been reached for the valid reasons, then, as a matter of discretion, the High Court would not intervene by way of judicial review. **45.68**

E CONVERSION TO A COMMON LAW CLAIM

The court has power (under CPR, r 54.20) to order judicial review proceedings to continue as proceedings brought under CPR, Part 7. This power may be exercised where the relief claimed is a declaration, an injunction, or damages, and the court considers that such relief should not be granted on an application for judicial review, but might be granted in an ordinary claim. **45.69**

F CONSENT ORDERS

Where the parties to an application for judicial review agree terms for disposing of the application, it is possible to obtain an order from the court to put that agreement into effect without the need for attending at a hearing. The procedure is laid down in PD 54A, para 17 and *Practice Direction (Administrative Court: Uncontested Proceedings)* [2008] 1 WLR 1377. A document setting out the terms of the proposed order and containing a short statement of the matters relied on as justifying the making of the order, quoting the authorities and statutory provisions relied on, should be signed by all of the parties. The original of this document, together with two copies, should be handed in to the Administrative Court Office, which will submit the document to a judge. If the judge is satisfied that an order can be made, the proceedings will be listed for hearing and the order will be pronounced in a public hearing without the parties needing to attend. If the judge is not satisfied that it would be proper to make the proposed order, the proceedings will be listed for hearing in the usual way. **45.70**

KEY POINTS SUMMARY

- Judicial review lies against public bodies, and must be brought by a person with a sufficient interest. **45.71**
- The various grounds for seeking judicial review are described at 45.13ff.
- The six public law remedies are described at 45.38ff.
- Before commencing judicial review proceedings, a claimant should comply with the judicial review pre-action protocol.
- Judicial review proceedings must be started promptly, and in any event not later than three months from the events complained of.
- Permission must be sought to proceed with a claim for judicial review.
- The procedure leading to the substantive hearing is described at 45.59ff.

46

APPEALS

46.01 From time to time decisions are made in error, and the system of appeals is designed to ensure that these are corrected. Of course, a decision is not necessarily 'wrong' just because it is not the result hoped for by the client. There is a strong public interest in regarding judicial decisions as final and binding, and an open-ended appeals system would undermine this by encouraging unsuccessful litigants to have 'another bite at the cherry'. Striking a balance between encouraging finality and correcting mistakes is not easy, and explains some of the complications that arise in the area of appeals.

Lawyers appearing at a hearing, whether it is an interim matter or a trial, will invariably hold a formal or informal conference with their clients immediately afterwards. Whatever the result, most clients ask, or are concerned about, whether the decision can be appealed. The lawyer must be able to give sound advice on this topic. Indeed, the question of an appeal will often have to be addressed by the lawyer before the judge rises at the end of the hearing, because permission to appeal must often be sought from the court appealed from. In these cases the lawyer asks for permission to appeal at the end of the hearing after the question of costs has been decided. **46.02**

Careful thought must be given before embarking on an appeal. Lord Donaldson of Lymington MR once said: **46.03**

> The question which the adviser may ask himself is whether, looking at the matter objectively, there are sufficient grounds for believing not only that the case should have been decided differently, but that in all the circumstances it can be demonstrated to the satisfaction of the Court of Appeal that there are grounds for reversing the judge's findings. In considering this question the adviser must never forget the financial risk which an appellant undertakes of having not only to pay his own costs of the appeal, but those of his opponent and, for this purpose, the adviser has two clients if the litigant is [publicly funded]. Nor must he underrate the effect upon his client of the emotional and other consequences of a continued state of uncertainty pending an appeal. In a word, one of the most important duties of a professional legal adviser is to save his clients from themselves and always to remember that, whilst it may well be reasonable to institute or to defend particular proceedings at first instance, a wholly new and different situation arises once the claim has been fully investigated by the court and a decision given.

There are a number of salient points that need to be addressed: **46.04**

(a) The court to which any appeal will lie. This is considered at 46.06ff.
(b) The period within which the appeal must be commenced. This is usually 21 days from the decision of the lower court; see 46.30ff.
(c) The grounds on which appeals may be allowed. Generally, it is necessary to show that the decision in the lower court was wrong, or that it was unjust because of a serious procedural or other irregularity. This is considered further at 46.76 to 46.84.

This chapter considers the structure of non-family civil appeals. For family appeals, see specialist works on family law, such as J Black, J Bridge, T Bond, and L Griffin, *A Practical Approach to Family Law* (8th edn, Oxford: OUP, 2007). **46.05**

A ROUTES OF APPEAL

The basic civil appeals structure

The basic civil appeals structure is, by the Access to Justice Act 1999 (Destination of Appeals) Order 2000 (SI 2000/1071) (the 'Destination of Appeals Order') and PD 52, para 2A.1, as follows: **46.06**

(a) county court district judges may be appealed to the county court circuit judge;
(b) High Court masters and district judges may be appealed to a High Court judge;

(c) county court circuit judges may be appealed to a High Court judge;
(d) High Court judges may be appealed to the Court of Appeal; and
(e) the Court of Appeal may be appealed to the Supreme Court. The Supreme Court replaced the House of Lords in September 2009 when the Constitutional Reform Act 2005, ss 23–60, came into force.

46.07 These basic routes of appeal also apply in relation to deputy judges and their equivalents, such as recorders sitting as county court circuit judges.

46.08 However, appeals from county court circuit judges ((c) above) are made to the Court of Appeal rather than to a High Court judge if the county court matter was either:

(f) a final decision made in a multi-track claim or in specialist proceedings (Destination of Appeals Order, art 4); or
(g) itself an appeal from a county court district judge (in other words, the current appeal is a second appeal: see Destination of Appeals Order, art 5).

Final decisions

46.09 One of the exceptions referred to in the previous paragraph where county court appeals are taken to the Court of Appeal concerns 'final decisions' in multi-track and specialist proceedings. For this purpose a decision is final if it would determine (subject to any possible appeal or detailed assessment of costs) the entire proceedings whichever way the court decided the issues before it (Destination of Appeals Order, art 1(2)(c)). Further, a decision is treated as final where it is made at the conclusion of part of a hearing or trial which has been split into parts, and would, if made at the conclusion of that hearing or trial, be a final decision because it determines the entirety of that part of the claim (art 1(3)).

46.10 This means that if a judge makes a final decision on any aspect of a claim, such as limitation, or on part of a claim which has been directed to be tried separately, this is a final decision within the meaning of the provision. On the other hand, orders striking out the proceedings or a statement of case, and orders giving summary judgment, are not final decisions because they are not decisions that would finally determine the entire proceedings whichever way the court decided the issues before it: *Tanfern Ltd v Cameron-MacDonald* [2000] 1 WLR 1311. Orders on summary and detailed assessments of costs, and on applications to enforce final decisions, are not themselves 'final' (PD 52, para 2A.4).

46.11 If a non-specialist claim has never been allocated to a track, an appeal will not be to the Court of Appeal even if the judge would have allocated it to the multi-track if he or she had thought about it: *Clark (Inspector of Taxes) v Perks* [2000] 4 All ER 1. This can arise, eg, if a claim is dealt with as an assessment of damages.

Destination of second appeals

46.12 Appeals will come within the Destination of Appeals Order, art 5 (see sub-para (g) at 46.08) where they are second appeals. Thus, where an interim application is first dealt with by a master or district judge, a first appeal will be to the circuit judge (for county court claims) or High Court judge (for High Court claims). A second appeal based on the same application, which will be an appeal either from the circuit judge or High Court judge, is, by virtue of the exception, always to the Court of Appeal.

In *Southern & District Finance plc v Turner* (2003) LTL 7/11/03 a county court district judge dismissed an application to set aside a possession order. Eight months later the defendant brought an appeal against that decision, but omitted to seek permission to appeal out of time (see 46.32). The circuit judge dismissed the appeal on the ground that no permission to extend time for appealing had been included in the appellant's notice. An appeal from the circuit judge's refusal to consider extending time (whether this was on the basis of the judge deciding he had no jurisdiction to extend time, or a decision not to extend time) was held to be a first appeal, not a second appeal coming within art 5, so should have been taken to a High Court judge in accordance with the general routes of appeal. **46.13**

Appeals in Part 8 claims

Although Part 8 claims are automatically allocated to the multi-track by CPR, r 8.9(c), the exception laid down in the Destination of Appeals Order, art 4, does not apply to this category of claim. Therefore appeals in these claims, even from final orders, follow the general routes of appeal. Where the normal appeal court is not the Court of Appeal, a court granting permission to appeal in such a case from a final order should consider whether to order the appeal to be transferred to the Court of Appeal under r 52.14 (see 46.16). **46.14**

Appeal centres in High Court appeals

County court and District Registry appeals to a High Court judge must be brought in the District Registry for an appeal centre on the Circuit in which the lower court is situated (PD 52, para 8.4). A list of appeal centres for each of the six Circuits can be seen in para 8.2. **46.15**

Diversion from the normal route to the Court of Appeal

If the normal route for a first appeal from a decision of a district judge or master would be to a circuit judge or to a High Court judge: either the lower court or the appeal court may order the appeal to be transferred to the Court of Appeal. This may be done if it is considered that the appeal will raise an important point of principle or practice or there is some other compelling reason for the Court of Appeal to hear it (CPR, r 52.14(1)). This power is not available to the judge in the lower court if permission to appeal (see 46.17) is refused, because if permission is refused there is no appeal (*7E Communications Ltd v Vertex Antennentechnik GmbH* [2007] 1 WLR 2175). The Master of the Rolls has a similar power to divert appeals to the Court of Appeal (Access to Justice Act 1999, s 57(1)). **46.16**

B PERMISSION TO APPEAL

The general need for permission to appeal

46.17 Rule 52.3(1) of the CPR provides that an appellant or respondent requires permission to appeal:

(a) where the appeal is from a decision of a judge in a county court or the High Court, except where the appeal is against:
   (i) a committal order (but only if the appellant is the contemnor: *Poole Borough Council v Hambridge* [2007] EWCA Civ 990);
   (ii) a refusal to grant habeas corpus; or
   (iii) a secure accommodation order made under the Children Act 1989, s 25; or

(b) as provided by PD 52.

Exceptions

46.18 The exceptions set out in CPR, r 52.3(1)(a) are cases where the liberty of the subject is in issue, and in these three cases appeals may be brought as of right. Nor is permission required for appeals from decisions of authorized officers in detailed assessment proceedings to a costs judge or district judge (rr 47.21 and 52.1(2)).

Seeking permission

46.19 Generally, permission to appeal may be sought either from the lower court at the hearing at which the decision to be appealed was made or from the appeal court (CPR, r 52.3(2)). However, r 52.13(1) provides that permission is required from the Court of Appeal for all appeals to that court from a decision of a county court or the High Court which was itself made on appeal. Where the lower court refuses an application for permission to appeal, a further application for permission to appeal may be made to the appeal court (r 52.3(3)).

46.20 Applications for permission to appeal sought from the lower court are made orally at the end of the hearing, usually as the last item of business after costs have been determined. Permission that is sought from the appeal court is asked for initially by seeking permission in writing in the appeal notice (r 52.3(2)(b)) and is normally considered without a hearing (PD 52, para 4.11). If permission is granted, the parties are notified in writing (para 4.12). If permission is refused, the appellant can request the matter to be reconsidered at an oral hearing (see 46.25).

46.21 There is some reluctance in giving permission to appeal against case management decisions, such as disclosure orders and orders dealing with the timetable of the claim. In these cases the court will also consider whether the issue is of sufficient significance to justify the costs of an appeal; the procedural consequences of an appeal (such as losing a trial date); and whether it would be more convenient to determine the point at or after trial (PD 52, para 4.5).

Test for granting permission

Rule 52.3(6) of the CPR provides that permission to appeal may be given only where either: **46.22**

(a) the court considers that the appeal would have a real prospect of success; or
(b) there is some other compelling reason why the appeal should be heard.

Permission to appeal should be granted if there is an arguable case that the decision of the lower court was plainly wrong or unjust through a serious irregularity (*Re W (Children) (Permission to Appeal)* [2007] Fam Law 897). Lord Woolf MR said in *Swain v Hillman* [2001] 1 All ER 91, that a 'real' prospect of success means that the prospects of success must be realistic rather than fanciful. **46.23**

Second appeals to the Court of Appeal

As discussed at 46.19–46.21, generally permission to appeal may be sought from either the lower court or the appeal court. Second appeals are in a different category. Rule 52.13(1) of the CPR provides that permission is required from the Court of Appeal (and cannot be given by the lower court) for any appeal to that court from a decision of a county court or the High Court which was itself made on appeal. By r 52.13(2) the Court of Appeal will not give permission unless it considers that either: **46.24**

(a) the appeal would raise an important point of principle or practice; or
(b) there is some other compelling reason for the Court of Appeal to hear it.

Reconsideration of whether to grant permission

There is no appeal from a decision of the appeal court, made at an oral hearing, to allow or refuse permission to appeal to that court (Access to Justice Act 1999, s 54(4)). However, where the appeal court, without a hearing, refuses permission to appeal, the person seeking permission may request the decision to be reconsidered at a hearing (CPR, r 52.3(4)). If the court considers a paper application for permission to appeal is totally without merit, it may make an order that the person seeking to appeal may not request a reconsideration at a hearing (r 52.3(4A)). A request for reconsideration of whether to grant permission to appeal must be filed within seven days after service of the notice that permission has been refused (r 52.3(5)), and the request must be served on the respondent (PD 52, para 4.14). The appellant's advocate must file and serve on the respondent at least four days before the hearing a brief written statement (para 4.14A): **46.25**

(a) setting out the points he intends to raise at the hearing; and
(b) setting out his reasons why permission should be granted.

The court will give notice of the permission hearing to the respondent, but the respondent is not required to attend unless the court requests him to do so (para 4.15). **46.26**

Limiting the issues on granting permission

By CPR, r 52.3(7), an order giving permission to appeal may limit the issues to be heard and be made subject to conditions. If a court confines its permission to some issues only, it should **46.27** expressly refuse permission on any remaining issues. Those other issues may then be raised at the hearing of the appeal if limited permission was granted on the papers, and then only with the appeal court's permission. The appeal court and the respondent should be informed of any intention to raise such an issue as soon as practicable after notification of the court's order granting permission to appeal (PD 52, para 4.18 to 4.21).

Practice in refusing permission

46.28 Short reasons are usually all that is given on a refusal of permission. Just because they are short does not mean they infringe the requirement for a reasoned decision in art 6 of the European Convention on Human Rights: *Hyams v Plender* [2001] 1 WLR 32 at [17].

46.29 A judge faced with an application for permission to appeal made out of time may come to the conclusion both that the appeal is weak on the merits and that time should not be extended. By reason of the AJA 1999, s 54(4), refusing permission to appeal will result in an end to the appeal process. Taking the easier course of refusing permission to extend time will not, as the appellant can apply for permission to appeal the refusal of the extension, which can be renewed to the Court of Appeal. This difference should be kept in mind when deciding which course to take: *Foenander v Bond Lewis & Co* [2002] 1 WLR 525. The ban in s 54(4) prevents the Court of Appeal from reviewing a High Court judge's refusal of permission to appeal from the decision of a costs judge, and there is no residual inherent jurisdiction to hear such an appeal: *Riniker v University College London* [2001] 1 WLR 13.

C TIME FOR APPEALING

General rule

46.30 An appellant must normally initiate an appeal or seek permission to appeal no later than 21 days from the date of the decision of the lower court (CPR, r 52.4(2)(b)). However, the lower court may direct some other period for filing a notice of appeal (r 52.4(2)(a)), but this should not normally be longer than 35 days (PD 52, para 5.19). Judgments and orders take effect from the date on which they are given or made, or such other date as the court may specify (r 40.7(1)). Delays in formally drawing up the order do not, therefore, delay time running for the purposes of appeals.

46.31 Where the lower court judge announces a decision and reserves the reasons for the judgment until a later date, the judge should exercise the power under r 52.4(2)(a) in fixing the period for filing a notice of appeal to take account of the fact that reasons will not be given immediately (PD 52, para 5.20).

Extending time for appealing

46.32 Rule 3.1(2)(a) of the CPR provides that the court may extend or shorten the time for compliance with any rule, practice direction, or court order (even if an application for extension is made after the time for compliance has expired). This includes the time for bringing an appeal. By r 52.6(1), an application to vary the time limit for filing an appellant's notice must be made to the appeal court. The parties may not (by r 52.6(2)) agree between themselves to extend any date or time limit for the purposes of appealing.

Permission to extend time for appealing is sought by including an application for more time in the appellant's notice (PD 52, para 5.2). The notice should state the reason for the delay and the steps taken prior to the application being made. Failing to seek permission in the appellant's notice is an irregularity, which the court has jurisdiction to cure under CPR, r 3.10 (*Southern & District Finance plc v Turner* (2003) LTL 7/11/03), applying the criteria laid down in r 3.9 for granting relief from sanctions (see 28.25). **46.33**

Where an extension is sought and permission to appeal is given (as will be seen, usually the respondent is not given an opportunity to make representations on whether permission to appeal should be granted), the respondent has the right to be heard on the question whether an extension of time should be allowed. However, a respondent who unreasonably opposes an extension of time runs the risk of being ordered to pay the appellant's costs of the application to extend time (para 5.3). **46.34**

Principles for granting extensions of time

In *Sayers v Clarke Walker* [2002] 1 WLR 3095, it was held that when considering an application to extend the time for appealing of any complexity the court should have regard to the checklist of factors contained in r 3.9 (see 28.25), and avoid judge-made checklists. On the facts, where the delay was less than two months, refusing the extension was held to be a disproportionate response. **46.35**

D PROCEDURE ON APPEALING

Appellant's notice

An appellant must file the appellant's notice at the appeal court within such period as may be directed by the lower court or, where the court makes no such direction, 21 days after the date of the decision of the lower court that the appellant wishes to appeal (CPR, r 52.4(2)). Filing can be done electronically (PD 52, para 15.1B). **46.36**

An appellant's notice must be in form N161. It must set out the grounds of the appeal (PD 52, para 3.2). These must identify specific incidents, directions, or findings made by the court below which are alleged to be wrong or unjust through serious procedural or other irregularity, and say why the decision was wrong or unjust (*Perotti v Collyer-Bristow* [2004] 4 All ER 53 at [37] and [40]). Each ground must be stated as an appeal on a point of law or against a finding of fact (para 3.2(2)). An appellant seeking, for the first time, to rely on any issue or to seek any remedy under the Human Rights Act 1998 must include information complying with PD 16, para 15.1 in the appeal notice (PD 52, para 5.1A). The notice may also need to include an application for permission to appeal (para 5.1), for permission to appeal out of time (para 5.2), and may include applications for interim remedies in the course of the appeal (para 5.5). **46.37**

46.38 By CPR, r 52.11(5), a party may not rely at the hearing of the appeal on a matter not contained in its appeal notice unless the appeal court gives permission.

Appeal bundle

46.39 An appeal bundle must be lodged with the appellant's notice (PD52, para 5.6(2)). The appeal bundle must contain the documents listed in para 5.6A(1). This sets out a list of 13 categories of document, including a sealed copy of the appellant's notice, a copy of the appellant's skeleton argument, relevant statements of case, and other documents which the appellant reasonably considers necessary to enable the appeal court to reach its decision. Appeal bundles must be confined to the documents that are relevant to the issues in the appeal (para 5.6A(2)). No more than a single copy of each document should be included unless there is a good reason for doing so (para 15.4(2)). Where the appellant is represented, the appeal bundle must contain a certificate signed by his solicitor or counsel to the effect he has read and understood para 5.6A(2), and that the bundle complies with it. If permission to appeal is granted, the appellant must add a number of documents, including the respondent's notice and the respondent's skeleton argument, to the appeal bundle.

46.40 Appeal bundles are primarily for use by the judges in the appeal court, particularly to assist them with pre-reading. To further assist pre-reading in complex Court of Appeal cases (ie, where the bundle exceeds 500 pages), core bundles not exceeding 150 pages must also be prepared containing the documents which are central to the appeal.

Skeleton argument

46.41 Form N163 should be used (or used as a cover sheet) for the skeleton arguments. The appellant's skeleton argument should include a time estimate, and must be lodged with the appellant's notice or within the next 14 days (PD 52, para 5.9). It should contain a numbered list of points stated in no more than a few sentences, which should both define and confine the areas of controversy. Each point should be followed by references to any documentation on which the appellant proposes to rely (para 5.10(2)). Points of law should be backed by authorities which should be cited with references to the particular pages where the relevant principles are set out (para 5.10(3)). In the case of questions of fact, the skeleton should state briefly the basis on which it is contended that the Court of Appeal can interfere with the finding of fact concerned, with cross-references to the passages in the transcript or notes of evidence which bear on the point (see *Practice Direction (Court of Appeal: Procedure)* [1995] 1 WLR 1191).

46.42 Lists of relevant persons, chronologies, and glossaries of technical terms are often usefully included with skeleton arguments.

Record of the judgment of the lower court

46.43 If the judgment of the lower court was recorded, an approved transcript should accompany the appellant's notice (PD 52, para 5.12). Photocopies are not acceptable. If there is no official transcript, the next best is the lower court judge's written judgment duly signed by the judge. If the lower court's judgment was oral and not recorded, the advocates should confer and submit, if possible, an agreed note of the judgment to the judge for signature. If the note cannot be agreed, both versions should be submitted with a covering letter explaining the situation. These points are important, because appeals, even from district judges and masters, can succeed only by attacking the decision-making process in some way, and injustice may result if no reliable record is available of what was said in the lower court.

Transcripts or notes of the evidence (as opposed to the judgment) are not generally needed on applications for permission to appeal, but may become necessary if permission is granted for the purposes of the substantive appeal (PD 52, para 5.15). If so, the transcript must be obtained if the evidence was recorded, otherwise a typed version of the judge's notes must be obtained (para 5.16). **46.44**

Documents in small claims appeals

There are simplified rules on the documents to be filed in small claims track appeals in PD 52, para 5.8. This requires only the filing of an appellant's notice, a sealed copy of the order under appeal, and any order granting or refusing permission to appeal. An appellant may file additional documents, and may be ordered to file the reasons for the judgment of the lower court. **46.45**

Service on the respondent

By CPR, r 52.4(3), unless the appeal court orders otherwise, an appellant's notice must be served on each respondent as soon as practicable, and in any event not later than seven days after it is filed. A copy of the appellant's skeleton argument should also be served (PD 52, para 5.21). **46.46**

A respondent need not take any action when served with an appellant's notice until notified that permission to appeal has been given (PD 52, para 5.22), and there is also generally no requirement at this stage for appeal bundles to be served on the respondent (para 5.24). **46.47**

Respondents are served merely to keep them informed of the landmarks in the appeal process. Where the court does not request submissions or attendance by the respondent, costs will not normally be allowed to a respondent who makes submissions or attends (para 4.23). **46.48**

After the permission stage

In cases where permission to appeal has to be obtained from the appeal court, it will send the parties copies of the order granting permission and any other directions (PD 52, para 6.3(2) and (3)). The appeal bundle has to be served by the appellant on the respondents within seven days of receiving the order granting permission (para 6.2). **46.49**

In all cases, other than those in the Court of Appeal, which are to proceed to a full hearing, the appeal court will send the parties notification of the hearing or the period during which the appeal is likely to be heard ('the listing window'). Appeals in the Court of Appeal are given 'hear-by dates', which are the dates by which the appeal will be heard. **46.50**

Court of Appeal questionnaires

46.51 At the same time as giving the parties a hear-by date, the Court of Appeal will send the appellant an appeal questionnaire. This must be returned within 14 days, and must include the appellant's advocate's time estimate for the hearing, confirmation that the transcript for the lower court's hearing has been requested, confirmation that appeal bundles are being prepared, and confirmation that copies of the questionnaire and appeal bundle have been served on the respondents (PD 52, para 6.5). A respondent who disagrees with the time estimate must inform the court within seven days of receipt of the questionnaire.

Court of Appeal listing

46.52 Appeals to the Court of Appeal are divided into several categories, or lists (PD 52, para 15.8); for which see BCP, para 71.35.

Authorities

46.53 In the High Court lists of authorities should be provided to the head usher by 5.30 p.m. on the working day before the appeal hearing. In the county courts it is usually necessary to have photocopies of reports available at the hearing.

46.54 For Court of Appeal hearings (only), once the parties have been notified of the date fixed for hearing, the appellant's advocate must file a bundle containing photocopies of the principal authorities each side will be relying upon (PD 52, para 15.11). Obviously, this can be done only after conferring with the advocate for the respondent. There is no need to provide authorities for propositions not in dispute. Normally, the bundle should contain no more than ten authorities. The bundle should be lodged at least 28 days before the hearing. If any party intends to refer to other authorities, they may be included in a second agreed bundle to be filed at least 48 hours before the hearing.

46.55 The *Law Reports* published by the Incorporated Council of Law Reporting for England and Wales should be cited in preference to other reports, as they contain counsel's arguments and are readily available. Next best are the *Weekly Law Reports*, then the *All England Law Reports* if a case is not, or not yet, reported in the official *Law Reports*. Other reports, even obscure reports, may be used for sufficient reason, but advocates should provide photocopies (of the title page and relevant pages only). Occasionally it is useful to refer to more than one source if there are discrepancies between reports. If unreported decisions are relied upon, the official transcript should be produced rather than the handed-down text of the judgment (*Practice Direction (Court of Appeal: Citation of Authority)* [1995] 1 WLR 1096), and they should be used only if they contain statements of principle not found in reported authorities (*Practice Statement (Court of Appeal: Authorities)* [1996] 1 WLR 854). Excessive citation of authorities and reliance on summaries of cases which may not have been summarized by a professional lawyer, will not be tolerated: *Hamblin v Field* (2000) *The Times*, 26 April 2000.

Dismissal list

Where the rules on lodging documents, skeleton arguments, etc., are broken, an appeal to the Court of Appeal may be listed on the 'dismissal list'. These cases are often listed before the Master of the Rolls's court. The court sees it as its duty to protect the interests of respondents, who already have a decision of a competent authority in their favour, by insisting on all reasonable expedition and strict compliance with the timetable laid down. **46.56**

Final deadline

For appeals to the Court of Appeal, all the papers needed for the appeal must be filed at least seven days before the hearing (PD 52, para 15.11B(1)). Any party who fails to comply may be required to attend before the presiding lord justice to seek permission to proceed with or to oppose the appeal (para 15.11B(2)). The Court of Appeal expects strict compliance with this final deadline, because it is essential for effective pre-reading by the judges. Any party summoned under this provision is advised to ensure that all their documents have been filed before their attendance before the presiding lord justice (*Scribes West Ltd v Anstalt (No 1)* (2004) *The Times*, 8 July 2004). **46.57**

E RESPONDENT'S NOTICE

Need for a respondent's notice

In any appeal a respondent *may* file and serve a respondent's notice (CPR, r 52.5(1)). A respondent's notice *must* be filed by a respondent who: **46.58**

(a) is asking the appeal court for permission to appeal; or
(b) wishes to ask the appeal court to uphold the order of the lower court for reasons different from or additional to those given by the lower court (r 52.5(2)).

Respondents accordingly fall into three broad categories: **46.59**

(a) Those who simply wish to uphold the decision of the court below for the same reasons as given by the judge below. Such a respondent need not serve a respondent's notice.
(b) Those who wish to uphold the decision of the court below for reasons different from or additional to those given by the lower court. Such a respondent is not appealing as such, so there is no question of seeking permission to cross-appeal. However, a respondent's notice is required for the purpose of setting out the different or additional reasons (PD 52, para 7.3).
(c) Those who wish to ask the appeal court to vary the order of the lower court are cross-appealing, and permission to appeal must be sought on the same basis as for an appellant (PD 52, para 7.1). A respondent's notice is required for setting out the grounds on which it is to be argued that the order of the court below should be varied.

Form of respondent's notice

46.60 A respondent's notice is similar to an appellant's notice (see 46.36–46.38) and must be in form N162. Together with appellants' notices they are called 'appeal notices' in the CPR (r 52.1(3)(f)). Where the respondent seeks permission from the appeal court it must be requested in the respondent's notice (CPR, r 52.5(3)).

Filing and serving a respondent's notice

46.61 A respondent's notice must be filed within such period as may be directed by the lower court or, where the court makes no such direction, 14 days, after the date in CPR, r 52.5(5) (see r 52.5(4)). Rule 52.5(5) provides:

> The date referred to in paragraph (4) is—
> (a) the date the respondent is served with the appellant's notice where—
>   (i) permission to appeal was given by the lower court; or
>   (ii) permission to appeal is not required;
> (c) the date the respondent is served with notification that the appeal court has given the appellant permission to appeal; or
> (d) the date the respondent is served with notification that the application for permission to appeal and the appeal itself are to be heard together.

46.62 Unless the appeal court orders otherwise a respondent's notice must be served on the appellant and any other respondent as soon as practicable, and in any event not later than seven days, after it is filed (r 52.5(6)).

Respondent's skeleton argument

46.63 A respondent who proposes to address arguments to the court must provide it with a skeleton argument. It should conform to the principles applicable to the appellant's skeletons, but should also seek to answer the arguments in the appellant's skeleton. It may be included in the respondent's notice, or may be lodged and served within 14 days of filing the notice (PD 52, para 7.7).

F APPLICATIONS WITHIN APPEALS

General

46.64 Notice of an application made to the appeal court for a remedy incidental to the appeal (such as an application for security for costs) may be included in the appeal notice or by an ordinary application notice under CPR, Part 23 (PD 52, para 5.5).

46.65 The applicant must file the following documents with the application (see PD 52, para 11.2):

(a) one additional copy of the application notice for the appeal court and one copy for each of the respondents;

(b) where applicable, a sealed copy of the order which is the subject of the main appeal; and
(c) a bundle of documents, which should include the application notice and any written evidence in support of the application.

Amendment of an appeal notice

An appeal notice may be amended with permission (CPR, r 52.8). Such an application will normally be dealt with at the hearing of the appeal, unless that course would cause unnecessary expense or delay, in which case a request should be made for the application to amend to be heard in advance (PD 52, para 5.25). **46.66**

G STAY

By CPR, r 52.7, an appeal shall not operate as a stay of any order or decision of the lower court unless: **46.67**

(a) the appeal court or the lower court orders otherwise; or
(b) the appeal is from the Immigration Appeal Tribunal.

For many years the courts have acted on the principle stated in *Atkins v Great Western Railway Co* (1886) 2 TLR 400 that a stay may be granted where the appellant produces written evidence showing that, if the judgment were to be paid, there would be no reasonable prospect of getting it back if the appeal were to succeed. This was regarded as too stringent a test in *Linotype-Hell Finance Ltd v Baker* [1993] 1 WLR 321 by Staughton LJ, who said a stay could be granted if the appellant would face ruin without a stay provided the appeal had some prospect of success. **46.68**

H STRIKING OUT APPEAL NOTICES AND SETTING ASIDE OR IMPOSING CONDITIONS

An appeal court may strike out the whole or part of an appeal notice, set aside permission to appeal in whole or in part, or impose or vary conditions upon which an appeal may be brought (CPR, r 52.9(1)). It is recognized that the power to strike out an appeal notice 'is one that is just as capable of abuse as is the power to put in hopeless notices of appeal': *Burgess v Stafford Hotel Ltd* [1990] 1 WLR 1215, *per* Glidewell LJ. Rule 52.9(2) therefore provides that the court will exercise its powers under r 52.9(1) only where there is a compelling reason for doing so. There may be a compelling reason where the appeal is being brought to secure some collateral advantage, or where the application will achieve a substantial saving of time. A party who was present at the hearing at which permission was given may not subsequently apply for an order that the court exercise its powers to set aside permission or to impose conditions (r 52.9(3)). **46.69**

46.70 A condition requiring an appellant to pay the costs whether he won or lost was held to be excessive in *King v Daltray* [2003] EWCA Civ 808, substituting an order that there be no order as to costs. A condition requiring a payment into court may be varied on the ground that the appellant cannot afford to make the payment, but evidence will be required that the amount is such as to prevent the appellant funding the appeal (*Branch Empire Ltd v Coote* (2003) LTL 16/6/03).

I HEARING OF APPEALS

Composition of the court

46.71 Substantive appeals to the Court of Appeal from interim orders, the county courts, and masters' and district judges' final orders are generally heard by two-judge courts; otherwise appeals to the Court of Appeal are heard by three-judge courts (SCA 1981, s 54). Where a two-judge court is equally divided, either party may apply for a rehearing before a three-judge court.

46.72 For other appeals from first-instance decisions, the appeal court will generally consist of the judge sitting alone. Occasionally a judge will sit with assessors, such as some appeals on costs issues. The Supreme Court generally sits in five-member courts.

Last-minute settlements

46.73 Solicitors and counsel have a duty to inform the court as soon as it is known that an appeal which has been listed for hearing will not proceed, so that judges can avoid unnecessary preparation. Even if a case settles very late in the day steps must taken through the Royal Courts of Justice switchboard to notify the appeal court judges' clerks (*Tasyurdu v Immigration Appeal Tribunal* [2003] CPLR 343).

The hearing

46.74 Normally it is unnecessary for the advocate for the appellant to open the appeal, as the judges normally do fairly extensive pre-reading. In most cases the judges will have pre-read the appeal bundle and skeleton arguments, and usually will have read the core authorities bundle (if there is one). The judge (or presiding judge in a multi-member court) usually indicates the extent of the pre-reading that has been done. In appeals to the Court of Appeal, if it is felt that it would be helpful for the appellant's advocate to open the appeal, the presiding judge will notify the advocates in advance. The intention is that court time is spent dealing with the substance of the arguments, and time should not be wasted in extensive reading from documents.

Rehearing or review

46.75 By CPR, r 52.11(1), every appeal is, with limited exceptions, heard by way of a review of the decision below. An appeal from an interim application will generally involve consideration of all the material before the court below. It is nevertheless technically a review (*McFaddens Solicitors v Chandrasekaran* [2007] EWCA Civ 220). The exceptional nature of holding a rehearing rather than a review on an appeal was stressed in *Secretary of State for Trade and Industry v Lewis* (2001) *The Times*, 16 August 2001. The power to conduct an appeal by way of rehearing is to be exercised in rare cases where that is necessary in order for justice to be done. The fair trial requirements of the European Convention on Human Rights, art 6, do not compel the court to conduct rehearings in appeals from without-notice decisions (*Dyson Ltd v Registrar of Trademarks* (2003) *The Times*, 23 May 2003).

Grounds for allowing an appeal

Appeals dealt with by way of reviewing the decision below will be successful (see CPR, r 52.11(3)) only if the decision below was either: **46.76**

(a) wrong (which means 'unsustainable': see *Abrahams v Lenton* [2003] EWHC 1104 (QB)); or

(b) unjust because of a serious procedural or other irregularity in the proceedings in the lower court.

An insubstantial point, even if a technical error, does not render a decision wrong (*Orford v Rasmi Electronics Ltd* (2004) LTL 4/8/04). The strength of the other evidence at trial may mean that, despite an error, the decision below was not wrong (*Daly v Sheikh* (2004) LTL 13/2/04). A party can appeal against a decision of a lower court, but not against the reasons for a decision given in his favour (*Compagnie Noga d'Importation et d'Exportation SA v Australia and New Zealand Banking Group Ltd* [2003] 1 WLR 307). **46.77**

Questions of fact

The trial judge sees the demeanour of witnesses, and can assess their intelligence and credibility in a way that an appeal court cannot, even with the benefit of a transcript. Nevertheless the parties are entitled to a decision of the appeal court on questions of fact. As Lindley MR said in *Coghlan v Cumberland* [1898] 1 Ch 704: **46.78**

> ...the court must reconsider the materials before the judge with such other materials as it may have decided to admit. The court must then make up its own mind, not disregarding the judgment appealed from, but carefully weighing and considering it; and not shrinking from overruling it if on full consideration the court comes to the conclusion that the judgment is wrong.

Discretion

The most important statement on the role of an appellate court in a discretionary matter is that of Lord Diplock in *Hadmor Productions Ltd v Hamilton* [1983] 1 AC 191. This was an appeal in respect of an interim injunction, but his Lordship's comments are equally applicable in other types of interim appeals. His Lordship said: **46.79**

> Upon an appeal from the judge's grant or refusal of an [interim] injunction the function of an appellate court, whether it be the Court of Appeal or your Lordships' House, is not to exercise

> an independent discretion of its own. It must defer to the judge's exercise of his discretion and must not interfere with it merely upon the ground that the members of the appellate court would have exercised the discretion differently. The function of the appellate court is initially one of review only. It may set aside the judge's exercise of his discretion on the ground that it is based upon a misunderstanding of the law or of the evidence before him or upon an inference that particular facts existed or did not exist, which, although it was one that might legitimately have been drawn upon the evidence that was before the judge, can be demonstrated to be wrong by further evidence that has become available by the time of the appeal; or upon the ground that there has been a change of circumstances after the judge made his order that would have justified his acceding to an application to vary it. Since reasons given by judges for granting or refusing [interim] injunctions may sometimes be sketchy, there may also be occasional cases where even though no erroneous assumption of law or fact can be identified the judge's decision to grant or refuse the injunction is so aberrant that it must be set aside upon the ground that no reasonable judge regardful of his duty to act judicially could have reached it. It is only if and after the appellate court has reached the conclusion that the judge's exercise of his discretion must be set aside for one or other of these reasons, that it becomes entitled to exercise an original discretion of its own.

46.80 The way it was put by Lord Fraser of Tullybelton in *G v G (Minors: Custody Appeal)* [1985] 1 WLR 647 is that the appeal court:

> ...should only interfere when it considers that the judge of first instance has not merely preferred an imperfect solution which is different from an alternative imperfect solution which the Court of Appeal might or would have adopted, but has exceeded the generous ambit within which a reasonable disagreement is possible.

Inferences

46.81 Rule 52.11(4) of the CPR provides that the appeal court may draw any inference of fact which it considers justified on the evidence. This includes inferences to be drawn from the facts found by the judge in the lower court and inferences to be drawn from the documents: *The Mouna* [1991] 2 Lloyd's Rep 221.

Errors of law and principle

46.82 Pure errors of law and applying the wrong principles do not require any explanation.

Substantial procedural irregularities

46.83 Procedural irregularities include misdirections to the jury (in jury trials), and the improper admission or non-admission of evidence. Frequent or intemperate interventions may give grounds for an appeal. An appeal may be based on excessive delay in delivering judgment. A lapse of 12 months in delivering judgment after trial would be excessive (*Cobham v Frett* [2001] 1 WLR 1775), as would a delay of three or four weeks in relation to an interim injunction (*EE and Brian Smith (1928) Ltd v Hodson* [2007] EWCA Civ 1210). In appeals based on delay, the appellate court should consider the quality of the judge's notes, and carefully scrutinize the findings of fact and the reasons given by the judge. It is only if there are errors possibly attributable to the delay that an appeal should be allowed on this ground: *Cobham v*

Frett. By CPR, r 52.11(3), this is a valid ground for appeal only if the irregularity was a serious one, and the irregularity caused an unjust decision in the lower court: *Tanfern Ltd v Cameron-MacDonald* [2000] 1 WLR 1311.

Inadequate reasons

The definition of issues, marshalling of evidence, and giving of reasons are the building blocks of the reasoned judicial process. A failure to make findings on the secondary issues on which counsel had relied justified setting aside a judgment in *Glicksman v Redbridge Healthcare NHS Trust* (2001) LTL 12/7/01, although *Clifford v Grimley* (2001) LTL 23/10/01 shows that an appeal on this ground is rarely going to be successful. Whether reasons are inadequate has to be considered by looking at the judgment in the light of the evidence and submissions at the hearing (*English v Emery Reimbold and Strick Ltd* [2002] 1 WLR 2409). Advocates advancing an appeal on this ground have to raise the matter with the judge in the lower court, who is permitted to provide supplementary reasons (which may remove the ground of complaint). An appeal court dealing with such an appeal may remit the case back to the lower court for additional reasons, which again may result in the point disappearing. **46.84**

J APPEAL COURT'S POWERS

General powers vested in the appeal court

By CPR, r 52.10(1), in relation to an appeal the appeal court has all the powers of the lower court. In particular, by r 52.10(2), the appeal court has power: **46.85**

(a) to affirm, set aside, or vary any order or judgment made or given by the lower court;
(b) to refer any claim or issue for determination by the lower court;
(c) to order a new trial or hearing, although this is a matter of last resort: *White v White* (2001) LTL 21/6/01. When making such an order the appeal court must make it clear on the face of its order whether the rehearing should be at appeal court level, or remitted back to the lower court (*Fowler de Pledge v Smith* (2003) *The Times*, 27 May 2003);
(d) to make orders for the payment of interest; and
(e) to make a costs order.

By r 52.10(3), in an appeal from a claim tried with a jury the Court of Appeal may, instead of ordering a new trial, make an order for damages or vary the award made by the jury. **46.86**

Fresh evidence

By CPR, r 52.11(2), unless it orders otherwise, the appeal court will not receive oral evidence or any evidence which was not before the lower court. Under the old rules a restrictive approach was taken to the introduction of fresh evidence on appeals, the guiding principles being laid down in *Ladd v Marshall* [1954] 1 WLR 1489. The rule in *Ladd v Marshall* applied to appeals from trials and final determinations, and reflected the policy of requiring parties to **46.87** advance their entire case at trial, and not deliberately leaving over points for the purpose of appeals (and thereby obtaining a 'second bite at the cherry'). Since the introduction of the CPR, the discretion to admit fresh evidence has to be exercised in accordance with the overriding objective, but the *Ladd v Marshall* principles remain relevant as matters which must necessarily be considered, rather than as strict rules: *Banks v Cox* (17 July 2000, CA, unreported). Strong grounds have to be shown before fresh evidence will be admitted, and the *Ladd v Marshall* principles will be looked at with considerable care: *Hertfordshire Investments Ltd v Bubb* [2000] 1 WLR 2318. Under *Ladd v Marshall* fresh evidence would only be allowed on an appeal if the evidence:

(a) could not have been obtained with reasonable diligence for use at the hearing in the lower court;
(b) would probably have an important influence on the result; and
(c) was apparently credible.

46.88 Applications for permission to adduce fresh evidence can be made to the master of the Court of Appeal, but they are often directed to be listed for hearing at the same time as the appeal (*Practice Direction (Court of Appeal: Procedure)* [1995] 1 WLR 1191). A separate bundle should be prepared for the further evidence application, so it can be kept separate from the main appeal bundles.

Handed-down judgments

46.89 Below the Court of Appeal, it is usual for the court to give judgment immediately after the arguments, although occasionally judgment will be reserved. Reserving judgment is rather more common in the Court of Appeal, where written judgments are sent out to the advocates two working days before being pronounced in court (PD 52, para 15.13 and PD 40E). This is to enable the parties' legal advisers to consider the judgment and any consequential orders they should seek. It is an abuse of process for advocates to lodge detailed commentaries on draft judgments (*R (Edwards) v Environment Agency* [2008] 1 WLR 1587). Judgments are released in this way on the condition that they are to be kept confidential until they are pronounced in court.

Reopening appeals

46.90 Confirming the decision in *Taylor v Lawrence* [2003] QB 528, CPR, r 52.17 enables the Court of Appeal and the High Court to reopen an appeal (or application for permission to appeal, PD 52, para 25.2) in exceptional circumstances. The jurisdiction is based on the court's inherent jurisdiction, so there is no such power to reopen an appeal to a circuit judge in the county court (r 52.17(3)). An appeal may be reopened (see r 52.17(1)) if:

(a) it is necessary to do so to avoid real injustice (such as where new facts come to light after the court makes its decision, as in *Taylor v Lawrence*);
(b) the circumstances are exceptional and make it appropriate to reopen the appeal; and
(c) there is no alternative effective remedy (so if the injustice could be remedied by a readily available further appeal, the court will not reopen the present appeal).

Costs

Under CPR, r 52.10(2)(e), the appeal court has power to make costs orders in relation to the appeal hearing and for the proceedings in the lower court. 46.91

Costs of appeals are likely to be summarily assessed (see PD 52, para 14.1) at the following types of hearings: 46.92

(a) contested directions hearings;
(b) applications for permission to appeal at which the respondent is present;
(c) dismissal list hearings in the Court of Appeal at which the respondent is present;
(d) appeals from case management decisions; and
(e) appeals listed for one day or less.

Non-disclosure of Part 36 offers

The fact that a Part 36 offer has been made must not be disclosed to any judge of the appeal court who is to hear and finally determine an appeal or application for permission to appeal until all questions (other than costs) have been determined, unless the Part 36 offer is relevant to the substance of the appeal (CPR, r 52.12). 46.93

K APPEALS BY WAY OF CASE STATED

Appeals to the High Court by way of case stated may be brought on questions of law or jurisdiction. Such appeals may be brought from any of the inferior courts, so can be brought from the county courts as well as the magistrates' courts, and from certain tribunals and under certain statutes (see PD 52, paras 22 and 23). This section will only consider such appeals from the magistrates' courts. 46.94

The appellant must apply in writing to the justices within 21 days after the relevant decision to state a case for the opinion of the High Court (Magistrates' Courts Act 1980, s 111). If the justices are of the opinion that an application to state a case is frivolous, they may refuse to do so (s 111(5)). Such a refusal may be reviewed and a mandatory order may be granted. The procedure for drafting the case is governed by the Magistrates' Courts Rules 1981, rr 76 to 81. Within 21 days after receiving a request, the magistrates' clerk must send a draft case to the parties for comments. After receiving comments, the case may be amended, and is then signed by two justices or their clerk. The case stated must state the facts found by the magistrates and the question or questions of law or jurisdiction on which the opinion of the High Court is sought. Unless one of the questions is whether there was evidence on which the magistrates could have come to their decision, the case must not contain a statement of the evidence: see *Bracegirdle v Oxley* [1947] KB 349. 46.95

The appellant must file an appellant's notice at the appeal court within 10 days of receiving the case, together with the following documents: 46.96

(a) the stated case;

(b) a copy of the judgment, order, or decision in respect of which the case has been stated; and
(c) where the lower court's decision was itself a decision on an appeal, a copy of the judgment, order, or decision of the original court (PD 52, paras 18.4 and 18.5).

46.97 The appellant's notice and the accompanying documents must be served on all respondents within four days after they are filed at the appeal court (para 18.6). Thereafter the procedure follows the usual scheme under Part 52 (para 18.2).

L APPEALS TO THE SUPREME COURT

Leapfrog appeals

46.98 Very exceptionally, a direct appeal from the decision of a High Court judge to the Supreme Court is possible under the Administration of Justice Act 1969, ss 12, 13, and 15 (which continue in force after the commencement of the Constitutional Reform Act 2005). There are five conditions:

(a) the appeal must involve a point of law of general public importance;
(b) the point of law must either relate to the construction of an Act of Parliament or statutory instrument, or else be a point on which the judge at first instance is bound by a decision of the Court of Appeal, or of the House of Lords or Supreme Court;
(c) all parties must consent;
(d) the trial judge must certify, either immediately at the end of the trial or within the next 14 days, that the case is a suitable one for a direct appeal to the Supreme Court; and
(e) the Supreme Court must grant permission to bring the appeal direct on an application made by any of the parties within one month of the date of the judge's certificate.

Appeals from the Court of Appeal

46.99 An appeal from the Court of Appeal generally lies to the Supreme Court. Permission must be obtained either from the Court of Appeal or from the Supreme Court. The Court of Appeal can deal with an application for permission to appeal by written submissions (PD 52, para 15.19), and will apply the same criteria as those applied by the Supreme Court (*Henry Boot Construction Ltd v Alstom Combined Cycles Ltd* [2005] 1 WLR 3850). If permission is refused by the Court of Appeal, an application for permission to appeal may be made to the Supreme Court on form SC001, which is a combined notice of appeal and application for permission to appeal (Supreme Court Rules 2009 (SI 2009/1603) 'SCR', r 10(1); PD Supreme Court 3, para 3.1.2). The application must be served on every respondent and any intervener in the court below before it is filed (SCR, r 12). Filing in the Registry of the Supreme Court must be in accordance with r 7, and effected within 28 days of the date of the order of the court below (r 11(1)). This period runs from the date of the substantive order appealed from, not from the date on which the order is sealed or the date of any subsequent procedural order (eg, an order refusing permission to appeal) (see PD 2 Supreme Court, para 2.1.12(a)).

Applications for permission to appeal are considered on paper without a hearing by a panel of justices (SCR, r 16(1)). Permission to appeal is granted for applications that, in the opinion of the appeal panel, raise an arguable point of law of general public importance which ought to be considered by the Supreme Court at that time, bearing in mind that the matter will already have been the subject of judicial decision and may have already been reviewed on appeal (PD 3 Supreme Court, para 3.3.3). **46.100**

Where permission to appeal is granted by the Supreme Court, the application for permission to appeal will stand as the notice of appeal and the grounds of appeal are limited to those on which permission has been granted (SCR, r 18(1)). The appellant must, within 14 days of the grant of permission to appeal, file notice under r 18(1)(c) that he intends to proceed with the appeal. When the notice is filed, the application for permission to appeal will be resealed and the appellant must then serve a copy on each respondent, and on any intervener. After service, the appellant must file the original notice of appeal and three copies (r 18(2); PD 4 Supreme Court, para 4.1.1), together with a certificate of service. **46.101**

There are detailed rules on the documents that have to be filed. They include the orders of the courts below, all the documents relevant to the arguments on the appeal, and bundles of authorities. The Supreme Court has a president, deputy president, and ten justices of the Supreme Court. It sits with at least three justices, but always with an uneven number of justices. Judgment is usually delivered in open court, but may be promulgated by the Registrar (SCR, r 28). **46.102**

KEY POINTS SUMMARY

46.103

- Appeals are always exceptional.
- With limited exceptions (mostly related to the liberty of the person), permission is always required for civil appeals.
- Permission should be granted if the appeal has a real prospect of success.
- An appellant's notice must be filed within 21 days of the decision under appeal.
- There are strict routes of appeal, and special rules for second appeals.
- The basic test at the appeal hearing is whether the decision of the court below is wrong. A wide ambit is given to discretionary decisions, which is why many interim orders and costs orders are very difficult to appeal.
- Fresh evidence is rarely allowed on appeals, and applications to adduce fresh evidence are guided by the *Ladd v Marshall* principles.

INDEX

Black Holes

Les Astres Occlus

Université Scientifique et Médicale et
Institut National Polytechnique de Grenoble
Ecole d'été de Physique théorique Les Houches

1951 Mécanique quantique. Théorie quantique des champs. (Polycopié) Epuisé

1952 Quantum mechanics. Mécanique statistique. Chapitres de physique nucléaire. (Polycopié) Epuisé

1953 Quantum mechanics. Etat solide. Mécanique Statistique. Elementary particles. (Polycopié) Epuisé

1954 Mécanique quantique. Théorie des collisions; two-nucleon interaction. Electrodynamique quantique. (Polycopié) Epuisé

1955 Quantum mechanics. Non-equilibrium phenomena. Réactions nucléaires. Interaction of a nucleus with atomic and molecular fields. (Polycopié) Epuisé

1956 Quantum perturbation theory. Low temperature physics. Quantum theory of solids; dislocations and plastic properties. Magnetism; ferromagnetisme. (Polycopié) Epuisé

1957 Théorie de la diffusion; recent developments in field theory. Interaction nucléaire; interactions fortes. Electrons de haute énergie. Experiments in high energy nuclear physics. (Polycopié) Epuisé

1958 Le problème à *N* corps. Dunod, Wiley, Methuen

1959 La théorie des gaz neutres et ionisés. Hermann, Wiley

1960 Relations de dispersion et particules élémentaires. Hermann, Wiley

1961 La physique des basses températures. Low Temperature Physics. Gordon and Breach, Presses Universitaires

1962 Géophysique extérieure. Geophysics: The Earth's Environment. Gordon and Breach

1963 Relativité, groupes et topologie. Relativity, Groups and Topology. Gordon and Breach

1964 Optique et électronique quantiques. Quantum Optics and Electronics. Gordon and Breach

1965 Physique des hautes énergies. High Energy Physics. Gordon and Breach

1966 Hautes énergies en astrophysique. High Energy Astrophysics. Gordon and Breach

1967 Problème à *N* corps. Many-Body Physics. Gordon and Breach

1968 Physique Nucléaire. Nuclear Physics. Gordon and Breach

1969 Aspects physiques de quelques problèmes biologiques. Physical Problems in Biology. Gordon and Breach

1970 Mécanique statistique et théorie quantique des champs. Statistical Mechanics and Quantum Field Theory. Gordon and Breach

1971 Physique des Particules. Particle Physics. Gordon and Breach

1972 Physique des Plasmas. Plasma Physics. Gordon and Breach

1972 Les Astres Occlus. Black Holes. Gordon and Breach

En préparation

1973 Hydrodynamique

1973 Liquides

1974 Physique Atomique et Moléculaire et Matière Interstellaire